THE ELOQUENT OBOE

A HISTORY OF THE HAUTBOY
1640–1760

BRUCE HAYNES

UNIVERSITY PRESS

OXFORD

UNIVERSITY PRESS

Great Clarendon Street, Oxford OX2 6DP

Oxford University Press is a department of the University of Oxford.
It furthers the University's objective of excellence in research, scholarship,
and education by publishing worldwide in

Oxford New York

Athens Auckland Bangkok Bogotá Buenos Aires Cape Town
Chennai Dar es Salaam Delhi Florence Hong Kong Istanbul Karachi
Kolkata Kuala Lumpur Madrid Melbourne Mexico City Mumbai Nairobi
Paris São Paulo Shanghai Singapore Taipei Tokyo Toronto Warsaw

with associated companies in Berlin Ibadan

Oxford is a registered trade mark of Oxford University Press
in the UK and certain other countries

Published in the United States
by Oxford University Press Inc., New York

British Library Cataloguing in Publication Data

Data available

Library of Congress Cataloging in Publication Data

Haynes, Bruce, 1942–
The eloquent oboe: a history of the hautboy from 1640 to 1760/Bruce Haynes.
p. cm.—(Oxford early music series)
Includes bibliographical references (p.) and index.
1. Oboe. I. Title. II. Oxford early music series (Unnumbered)
ML940.H39 2001   788.5'2'09—dc21   00–050419

ISBN 0–19–816646–X

1 3 5 7 9 10 8 6 4 2

Typeset by Graphicraft Ltd, Hong Kong
Printed in Great Britain by
Bookcraft Ltd, Midsomer Norton, Somerset

OXFORD EARLY MUSIC SERIES

THE ELOQUENT OBOE

'Diana with hautboy' (detail from *Juno and Attendants*). Tapestry, 3.26 × 5.13 m, Brussels, *c.*1700. Stuttgart: Württembergisches Landesmuseum. Photo: Marie-France Richard

This book is dedicated with humility and affection
to my two hautboy teachers

Frans Brüggen
and
Gustav Leonhardt

'Wie het zelfde anders zegt, zegt iets anders'

FOREWORD

Being an orchestra conductor, I am constantly aware how important that perfect triangle: first violin, first oboe, and basso continuo—the core of Lully's orchestra—really is. Any hesitation there, any loss of contact, and all the surrounding army will feel uncomfortable, even in much later music. Mr Haynes's scrutiny throughout this book teaches us that truth at the beginning may guarantee the most forceful speech at the end.

Frans Brüggen

Amsterdam
December 1998

PREFACE

It has been almost a half-century since the appearance of Philip Bate's *The Oboe*, a book that (supplemented by Anthony Baines's *Woodwind Instruments and their History*) has served us well for two generations. For reasons that are as yet too obscure to understand or explain, our age has seen a growing interest in early music, and with it has come the revival of oboes played in the Renaissance, Baroque, and Classical periods. The result has been an exponential increase in information about the history of the oboe.

While researchers have been compiling historical 'paper' data, performers and makers (using more empirical techniques) have been rediscovering the possibilities of the early oboe as a tool for making music. Musicians and instrument makers are actually the 'front line' historical researchers: the cooks with their fingers in the dough. The kind of work they do is rarely begun with the goal of discovering historical 'facts'; it is rather to make an instrument, or a technique, or a piece of music make sense and function musically. But this is often exactly what a historian tries to do with the paper records of past actions, by trying to understand the motivations behind them. Musicians performing early music often go through a process directly comparable to the historian's attempt to know the past by re-enacting its thought processes. As Collingwood put it (1946: 213–14), when the historian 'knows what happened, he already knows why it happened'. The act of performing music written down on paper, playing an old instrument, copying one, or reconstructing its reed, implies an attempt to understand the mental processes of a composer or player of the past. If they are inspired by historical interest, the discoveries of early-music performers can be at least as valid in producing historical information as the interpretations of paper historians. But we do not need to choose between them. Both activities are enlightening; they are in fact two sides of the same coin.

The time seems ripe to try to bring all this information together. Fortune (in the form of a grant from the Canadian government) has given me time to make the attempt. This book has taken me nearly five years of full-time writing (plus twenty-five-odd years of active—albeit irregular—research).

I bought my own first 'Baroque oboe' in 1965, and started seriously playing it in 1968. What I needed then was a book that dealt with the practical history of the early oboe and how it was played, a 'vade mecum' like David Boyden's *History of Violin Playing*. That book was not yet there, and it gradually became clear that if I wanted it, I would have to write it myself. Over the years I have collected the bits that would go into it, though (fortunately) a number of my colleagues have been working on the material too. I found the actual writing of this book a great pleasure because the history of the oboe, being a relatively new field, is full of discoveries that make studying it something like doing a series of jigsaw puzzles. After years of collecting the puzzle 'pieces', it has been a delight to put them together at last and watch the pictures that emerge, often unexpectedly. I have learned much about the hautboy since I began writing this.

The history of a musical instrument involves many disparate elements: morphology and mutation, players, repertoire and composers, where it was played and who listened to it (and why), technique, makers. The subtitle of Boyden's book shows how he struggled to define his subject: *and its Relationship to the Violin and Violin Music*. I sympathize with his struggle for clarity. In like manner, Don Smithers called his book *The Music and History of the Baroque Trumpet*. What I ended by writing is the story of the oboe during the last sixty years of the seventeenth century and the first sixty of the eighteenth: a tale of past events, and therefore, simply, a history.

Since all these different categories of information are mutually dependent and interactive, finding a method of mixing them into a coherent narrative strategy was not immediately apparent. I gradually developed an approach centred on the players, who after all developed the techniques, ordered the instruments, inspired the music that has come down to us, and were the first to play these dusty 'old' instruments and 'early' music; items that were for them state-of-the-art equipment and avant-garde compositions.

Histories of 'Heroes'—the lives of famous politicians and soldiers—are no longer in style. But the pages of this book are peopled with heroes of a special kind. Although the hautboy players of the seventeenth and eighteenth centuries were generally more peaceable and less obsessed with power than politicians and soldiers, it doubtless took a certain foolhardy courage to play the oboe—any kind of oboe— in public (as it still does). If they are heroes anywhere, it is in a book like this that the great hautboy players of past centuries can be acknowledged and celebrated —both those we are already able to make out through the glass darkly and those as yet in obscurity. I admire their talent and industry, and am grateful to them for the heritage they have given my instrument through their playing, which by all evidence must often have been very fine indeed.

The window in time this book looks through may at first appear small. But for the oboe, it was a glorious period of 120 years in which the instrument went through dramatic changes in both function and physical form, in which the majority of its solo and chamber literature was composed, and in which (to judge from the salaries and titles of some of its players) it was among the most highly valued instruments in use. In many ways, these were the oboe's vintage years, the like of which it has never seen since.

In the Baroque period, oboe players generally played other wind instruments, and in that sense, a study limited specifically to the oboe might seem anachronistic. But in order to be good at an instrument, most musicians need to specialize. While a certain amount of crossover is possible, to play an instrument well requires regular practice, and there is only so much time in the day. As Mattheson wrote (1739: XXV §3), an instrumentalist has to play a single main instrument if he wants to master it. The oboe demands time for reed-making, and it challenges players for a good part of their working careers. Most oboe players who played other instruments still probably played oboe *more* than those instruments; or else they moved over to the other instrument altogether (like many traverso players of the early eighteenth century, and later, clarinettists). So a study based on the viewpoint of the early oboe player, if it keeps in mind the unspecialized spirit of eighteenth-century players, has its logic and uses.

Personally, I see no point in going to the trouble to learn to play an ancient instrument whose technique has been lost if one proceeds to play it in a modern performing style. There is a reward for the effort, and it is the discovery of something new. But this is not a 'how to' book (or rather, that is not its first purpose). It is meant to be a report on the hautboy in the past. But if you happen to believe (as I do myself) that the history of a 'historical instrument' is a guidebook to how to play it, then it might possibly give you ideas about not only how the hautboy *was* played, but how it *should be* played. That, however, is a decision each player and listener makes alone. 'That was then, this is now', and it is not the humble mandate of this book to establish the relation between the two.

Be that as it may, no book of history can ever pretend complete objectivity. My choice of subjects reflects current concerns, and I freely indulge my own judgements on the qualities of the music I discuss; I believe there is, in the end, no other way to discuss it. (Apropos, I have not mentioned mediocre pieces in the repertoire merely for the sake of balance and completeness.)

Having lived closely with the instrument for more than thirty years, I have long been struck by Mattheson's characterization of it (1713: 268) as 'der gleichsam *redende* Hautbois': the *eloquent* Hautbois. This word captures the eighteenth-century oboe's mellowness and lack of tension, its ability to start and stop instantly, its remarkable capacity to convey and impart meaning, to declaim and discourse, to express forcibly and appropriately, to charm, and to provoke. For me as a player, Mattheson's phrase has always served as a kind of motto; hence the title of this book.

B.H.

Montréal
April 2000

ACKNOWLEDGEMENTS

This book owes much to the contributions of the people listed below, and I should like to thank each of them for their contribution.

Bruce Phillips convinced me that the time had come to put a book like this together, and arranged to have it published.

Two of the five years this book took to write were sponsored by a Postdoctoral Fellowship from the Social Sciences and Humanities Research Council of Canada. During the period of the Fellowship, William Waterhouse, despite his many research projects, graciously consented to be my Fellowship adviser. The book has benefited from his perspective and his penetrating comments.

Ton Koopman made an important contribution by sharing with me the contents of his extraordinary library, each book of which he has personally indexed. Those indexes have located brief references to the hautboy in books on other subjects that would not otherwise have been found.

As the basis of this study I used the more than 700 works listed in the bibliography, as well as the private communications recorded in footnotes. For historical framework, I often relied on articles in the excellent anthologies of the Music and Society series directed by Stanley Sadie, supplemented with articles from *Grove* and the new *MGG*, as well as musical monographs on individual towns and cities.

Some of the basic approaches to the origins of the earliest hautboys and the nature of the instrument's fingering were developed together with Marc Écochard, with whom I have had many pleasant discussions over a number of years.

Jeremy Montagu, Geoffrey Burgess, Tony Bingham, and Peter Holman all took time to read the entire draft and offer useful advice and comments.

The following people read sections and commented on them, provided information or ideas, and/or allowed the reproduction of illustrations: Rob van Acht, Cecil Adkins; Katharina Arfken; Masahiro Arita; Alfredo Bernardini; Joseba Endika Berrocal Cebrian; Tony Bingham; Jan Bouterse; Clare Brown (Victoria and Albert Museum); Willi Burger; Gregory G. Butler; Giovanni Caviglia; Aaron Cohen; Georg Corall; Olivier Cottet; Jill Croft-Murray; Reiner Dahlqvist; Sand Dalton; Piet Dhont; Thomas van Essen; Michael Finkelman; Fred Fox; Alain Girard; Abigail Graham; Paul Hailperin; Peter Hedrick; Jean-Pierre van Hees; Peter Holman; Masashi Honma; Friedrich von Huene; Herman Keahey; Martin Kirnbauer; Hans-Otto Korth; Barthold Kuÿken; David Lasocki; Eva Legêne; Herbert W. Myers; Graham Nicholson; Peter Noy and Courtney Westcott; Samantha Owens; Jérémie Papasergio and Elsa Franc; Hugo Reyne; Joshua Rifkin; Christian

Schneider; David Schulenberg; Han de Vries; William Waterhouse; Bruce Wetmore; Henk de Wit; Bruce Wood.

I should also like to thank a number of museums included in the List of Illustrations which granted permission to reproduce illustrations free of charge.

I should like to take this opportunity to thank the staff of Oxford University Press for their expert treatment of all aspects of this book, and especially Bonnie J. Blackburn for her perceptive editing.

CONTENTS

LIST OF ILLUSTRATIONS

LIST OF FIGURES

LIST OF TABLES

LIST OF MUSICAL EXAMPLES

MECHANICS

The recent publication of three source books has allowed me to reduce the number of references. These are the following:

Repertoire: Bruce Haynes (1992a), *Music for Oboe: A Bibliography* (2nd edn.)
Hautboy makers and instruments: William Waterhouse (1993), *The New Langwill Index*
Instruments: Phillip T. Young (1993), *4900 Historical Woodwind Instruments*

In addition, I hope in the near future to publish a biographical dictionary of over 1,000 early oboe players, including bibliographic citations.

I use first names of writers, players, and composers sparingly; full names can be found in the index or the bibliography.

The letter 'a' before a date stands for 'ante' (before); 'p' stands for 'post' (after).

Fingerings are designated 123 456 78, counting from the top of the hautboy. '7' is the Small-key, '8' the Great-key (see Ch. 1, §C.4). The numbers indicate holes that are closed. 123 4 7 means, for instance, that the top four holes are closed and the Small-key is pressed. A line through a number indicates that the hole is half closed, and an underlined number shows which finger is to be moved in a trill.

Note names are given as C1 co c1 c2 c3, where c1 equals middle C on the piano. The hautboy's range is normally c1–d3.

Pitch frequencies are given in semitones from A-440. A semitone below A-440 is A–1, for example; a whole step lower is A–2; a semitone above is A+1, etc.; A-440 itself is A+0. Because it was so common and widespread, I also use 'A–1½', which is A≈403. By identifying pitch standards by semitones, I am assuming a tolerance half that size (that is, one-quarter tone, or 50 cents). Approximate pitch levels are therefore identified throughout this study as follows:

Pitch name	Hz value for A	Frequency range
A+3	523 Hz	509–31
A+2	495	480–508
A+1	466	454–79
A+0	440	428–53
A–1	415	410–27
A–1½	403	398–409
A–2	392	381–97
A–3	370	360–80

Instrument 'Y' numbers, such as 'Y2', refer to the numbering found in Young (1993). Libraries are sometimes identified by their RISM sigla; see Abbreviations.

Many historical terms were not standardized in spelling, and for the sake of consistency I have chosen one form which was the most common.

A player of the hautboy was sometimes called an 'hautboist' (cf. Verschuere-Reynvaan 1795: 370). But the term *Hautboist* (capitalized and in italics) had a more specific meaning in Germany: that of a member of a small band (of lower status than chamber groups) that played winds and often strings as well. We will examine *Hautboisten* in Chapter 3, §F. The distinction is worth keeping in mind.

'Flute' does not necessarily mean 'traverso'. It is used that way by some modern musicians because the recorder was non-existent in the minds of most musicians until a generation ago. In the language and thought of the time, however, 'flute' could generally mean either recorder or traverso, and sometimes both. 'Flûte' is the modern French word for both transverse flute and recorder (one 'à bec', the other 'traversière'). When a distinction between the instruments is appropriate or necessary, I use the specific terms.

The word 'bass', sometimes abbreviated as 'B', usually means 'continuo'.

ABBREVIATIONS

Library sigla

A-Wn	Vienna, Öesterreichische Nationalbibliothek
B-Bc	Brussels, Conservatoire Royal de Musique
CS-K	Český Krumlov, Pracoviště Státního Archívu Třeboň, Hudební Sbírka
D-Bs	Berlin, Berliner Stadtbibliothek
D-Bsb	Berlin, Staatsbibliothek Preußischer Kulturbesitz
D-Dlb	Dresden, Sächische Landesbibliothek
D-DS	Darmstadt, Hessische Landes- und Hochschulbibliothek
D-F	Frankfurt am Main, Stadt- und Universitätsbibliothek
D-HRD	Herdringen, Bibliothek des Freiherrn von Fürstenberg, private collection administered by the Deutsches Musikgeschichtliches Archiv, Kassel
D-Kl	Kassel, Murdhardsche Bibliothek der Stadt und Landesbibliothek
D-ROu	Rostock, Universitätsbibliothek
D-SWl	Schwerin, Mecklenburgische Landesbibliothek, Musikabteilung
D-WD	Wiesentheid, Musiksammlung des Grafen von Schönborn-Wiesentheid, private collection
DK-Kk	Copenhagen, Det Kongelige Bibliotek
F-Pc	Paris, Conservatoire National de Musique
F-Pn	Paris, Bibliothèque Nationale de France
GB-Lbl	London, British Library
I-Bc	Bologna, Civico Museo Bibliografico Musicale
NL-DHgm	The Hague, Gemeentemuseum
P-GD	Gdańsk, Biblioteka Polskiej Akademii Nauk
S-L	Lund, Universitetsbiblioteket
S-SK	Skara, Stifts- och Landsbiblioteket
S-Uu	Uppsala, Universitetsbiblioteket
US-DW	Private Collection of David Whitwell, Los Angeles, Calif.
US-NYp	New York, Public Library at Lincoln Center, Library and Museum of the Performing Arts
US-R	Rochester, Eastman School of Music, Sibley Music Library

Other abbreviations

AfMw	*Archiv für Musikwissenschaft*
AL	acoustic length
BC	Hans-Joachim Schulze and Christoph Wolff, *Bach Compendium: analytisch-bibliographisches Repertorium der Werke Johann Sebastian Bachs*, 5 vols. (Frankfurt am Main, 1986–)
BG	Bach Gesellschaft
BWV	Bach Werke-Verzeichnis
EM	*Early Music*
FoMRHIQ	*Fellowship of Makers and Researchers of Historical Instruments Quarterly*
FWV	work register for Johann Friedrich Fasch
Grove 5	*Grove's Dictionary of Music and Musicians*, 5th edn., ed. Eric Blom (London, 1953)
GSJ	*Galpin Society Journal*
HBSJ	*Historic Brass Society Journal*
HG	Händel Gesellschaft edition (Chrysander)
HHA	Hallische Händel-Ausgabe
HWV	work register for George Frideric Handel
JAMIS	*Journal of the American Musical Instrument Society*
JAMS	*Journal of the American Musicological Society*
JIDRS	*Journal of the International Double Reed Society*
LH	left hand
LWV	work register for Jean-Baptiste Lully
MGG	*Die Musik in Geschichte und Gegenwart* ed. Friedrich Blume, 16 vols. (Kassel, 1949–79)
MGG²	*Die Musik in Geschichte und Gegenwart*, 2nd edn., ed. Ludwig Finscher (Kassel, 1994–)
ML	*Music and Letters*
MMR	*Monthly Musical Record*
NBA	*Neue Bach Ausgabe*
New Grove	*The New Grove Dictionary of Music and Musicians*, ed. Stanley Sadie, 20 vols. (London, 1980)
New Grove II	*The New Grove Dictionary of Music and Musicians*, ed. Stanley Sadie and John Tyrrell, 29 vols. (London, 2001)
PRMA	*Proceedings of the Royal Musical Association*
PSE	Purcell Society Edition
Recherches	*Recherches sur la musique française classique*
RH	right hand

RV	work register for Antonio Vivaldi
SIMG	*Sammelbände der Internationalen Musikgesellschaft*
TWV	work register for Georg Philipp Telemann
Utrecht 1993	*The Recorder in the 17th Century: Proceedings of the International Recorder Symposium, Utrecht 1993*, ed. David Lasocki (Utrecht, 1995)
Utrecht 1994	*A Time of Questioning: Proceedings of the International Early Double-Reed Symposium, Utrecht 1994*, ed. David Lasocki (Utrecht, 1997)
ZWV	work register for Jan Dismas Zelenka

Introduction

The Oboe's Evolution

It has been argued that modern woodwind design has now reached its natural evolutionary end and is essentially beyond further refinement. I prefer to look at the situation from a different angle. The oboe of the modern symphony orchestra has changed very little since the period when the music it normally plays was written: so-called 'classical' concert music (classical in the sense of repertoire that has become canonical, starting with Beethoven). If we continue to play this same repertoire, some of which is now almost two hundred years old, why would we need to change the instrument?

If, on the other hand, concert programmes start to change, the oboe will face a situation precisely like that of the shawm at about the beginning of the seventeenth century. The shawm had by then achieved a stability of design that attested to its perfect adaptation to the music it had been playing. But (as often seems to happen) the music it played best went out of style. The result was a stop-gap experiment, a provisional adaptation to a different task: the type of oboe developed to play the new music of the mid-seventeenth century. Being experimental, this instrument did not reach a steady, defined form for some time—not, in fact, until the latter part of the seventeenth century. Even then, however, it remained 'transitional' in design, because its repertoire (not just part of it, all of it) continued to change.

It was rare in the seventeenth and eighteenth centuries for a piece of music to survive the generation in which it was composed. Even genres and forms of music changed rapidly: the opera and cantata were invented, the orchestra was a new idea, whole classes of instruments were adopted or discarded. It is a sign of the times that London's 'Concert of Ancient Music', founded in 1776, performed no work less than twenty years old: a piece of that age, in other words, was already considered 'ancient'. After meeting Quantz in 1772, Burney commented: 'His taste is that of forty years ago; but though this may have been an excellent period for composition, yet I cannot entirely subscribe to the opinion of those who think musicians have discovered no refinements worth adopting, since that time'.[1]

---

[1] Burney (1773), ii. 157.

In 1778 Leopold Mozart wrote that the music of the great hautboist Carlo Besozzi (who was born nineteen years after him) 'ein wenig in den ältern Styl fällt' (smacks a little of the older style).[2] The spirit of the age encouraged progress, and there was little sympathy with past practices, even recent ones. This spirit still permeates our culture in areas where no pantheon of immortals is allowed to exist, like styles of clothing, for instance, and popular music, where the passage of a single year seriously changes the scene.

In the 1770s Burney articulated the typical assumption of artistic progress: a continuing advance towards a perfection that, in his view, had reached its zenith in the music of his own day. Burney shared this assumption with most of his contemporaries, including his fellow music historians Hawkins and Forkel. For him, 'contemporary music' was by definition superior to the music of the past. He wrote: 'To say that music was never in such high estimation, or so well understood as it is at present, all over Europe, would be only advancing a fact as evident, as that its inhabitants are now more generally civilized and refined, than they were in any other period to be found in the history of mankind.'[3] This view is in marked contrast to our own. It is revealing to observe Burney's view of Sebastian Bach, who, though dead less than a generation when he wrote, seemed by his description to be a figure from the distant past, from 'the Gothic period of the grey contrapuntists'.[4] Burney held Bach's son Emanuel in high esteem, and commented:

How he formed his style, where he acquired all his taste and refinement, would be difficult to trace; he certainly neither inherited nor adopted them from his father, who was his only master; for that venerable musician, though unequalled in learning and contrivance, thought it so necessary to crowd into both hands all the harmony he could grasp, that he must inevitably have sacrificed melody and expression.[5]

A revival of earlier methods of performing music would have made little sense to Burney:

There are classics in poetry, sculpture, and architecture, which every modern strives to imitate; and he is thought most to excel, who comes nearest to those models.

But who will venture to say, that the musician who should compose or perform like Orpheus, or Amphion, would be deservedly most applauded now? Or who will be bold enough to say, *how* these immortal bards *did* play or sing, when not a single vestige of their music, at least that is intelligible to us, remains? As far as we are able to judge, by a comparative view of the most ancient music with the modern, we should gain nothing by imitation. To copy the *canto fermo* of the Greek church, or that of the Roman ritual, the most

[2] Leopold Mozart, 28 May 1778.   [3] Burney (1771a), 3.
[4] This phrase was used by Gerber (*Lexikon*, 1790) and cited in *New Grove* iv. 450.
[5] Burney (1773), ii. 263. See also ii. 80–3.

ancient music now subsisting, would be to retreat, not to advance in the science of sound, or arts of taste and expression. It would afford but small amusement to ears acquainted with modern harmony, joined to modern melody. In short, to stop the world in its motion is no easy task; on we *must* go, and he that lags behind is but losing time, which it will cost him much labour to recover.[6]

In such a climate, new pieces of music were obviously in constant demand, and if a performer or composer ever got a reputation for being old-fashioned or passé, it was disastrous for his career. Burney wrote further: 'Musical compositions are so short-lived in Italy, such is the rage for novelty, that for the few copies wanted, it is not worth while to be at the expence of engraving, and of the rolling-press.'[7]

With repertoire mutating so quickly, no instrument design could have been expected to serve for long. Throughout the eighteenth century models of oboe were changing at something like the same speed as models of personal computer today, mutating rapidly to meet new or specialized demands. Laborde (1780: 265) spoke of 'Le Hautbois dont on se sert maintenant' (the oboe in use nowadays). Each of the periods covered in this book saw major developments: the mutation from shawm to protomorphic hautboy around the time Louis XIV took power; the crystallization and consolidation of the late seventeenth century; the adoption of shorter, higher-pitched instruments in the early eighteenth; the appearance of new designs and a narrower bore after 1730; and more radical changes waiting to come in the classical period.

A measure of the speed at which things changed are the few commentaries that survive on earlier instruments and styles of playing. Reflecting a common assumption of cultural progress, they are invariably condescending, in the manner of Burney. Parke wrote in 1804 of Thomas Vincent and Redmond Simpson, well-respected players who had been active scarcely two generations before his own: '[Fischer] arrived in [England] under very favourable circumstances, the oboe not being in a high state of cultivation, the two principal oboe players, Vincent and Simpson, using the old English oboe, an instrument which in shape and tone bore some resemblance to that yclept a *post-horn*.'[8]

A portrait like Zoffany's (Pl. Int.1) shows an hautboist, obviously at the height of his powers, holding an absolutely up-to-date instrument in his hand. But this man is no longer young. When he began playing the oboe, probably in his teens (and thus probably in the 1730s), he had played a very different instrument. The instrument he is holding must have been brand new, as such instruments (as far as we know) were not made before 1770. Players probably changed instrument designs regularly to keep up with the latest developments. Changes, once discovered or invented in one place, would quickly become known elsewhere.

---

[6] Burney (1771), 34–5.   [7] Ibid. 197.   [8] Parke (1830), i. 334–5.

PL. Int.1. Johann Joseph Zoffany [?], *The Oboe Player*, *c.*1770. Oil painting.
Smith College Museum of Art, Northampton, Mass.

The Name 'Hautboy'

When modern historians first began considering the instruments of the seventeenth and eighteenth centuries, it was natural to regard them as earlier analogues of the ones they were used to. Since no one knew at first how, and to what degree, the oboe of the Baroque period differed from the A6-model Conservatoire system oboe used in modern symphony orchestras across the world, it was given the same name, 'oboe', but qualified as 'Baroque'.

Just thirty years ago, the 'Baroque oboe' was still generally regarded as a museum curiosity. But those days are gone: in the space of a generation, it has become commonplace in musical ensembles, an instrument as modern as what we used to call the 'modern oboe'; the days when it had to be explained to an audience are now themselves history.

In fact, the names of the two instruments can actually be turned on their heads: the revival of the 'early' oboe is very much a modern phenomenon, whereas the so-called 'modern' oboe, bound to traditional concert repertoire, has changed so little precisely because it is a 'historical oboe', an instrument that reached its present form in the 1860s and 1870s.[9]

What about the subject of this book, then? What should we call it if we want to distinguish it from the Romantic oboe? 'Historical oboe', 'Baroque oboe', and 'early oboe' are no longer terms that accurately describe it.

---

[9] Cf. a parallel idea in Taruskin (1989), 152 ff.

As they have developed clear identities in modern times, many 'historical' instruments have been given their own names, usually based on how they were originally known. The harpsichord is clearly distinguished from the piano, the recorder from the Boehm-flute, and the viola da gamba from the cello. (The harpsichord was spared the name 'Baroque piano', even if its literature was played on the piano.) Two more recent examples of names that bestow identities are 'traverso', which has proven useful in distinguishing the early cross-flute from both the recorder and the Boehm-flute,[10] and 'sackbut', commonly used to distinguish (somewhat arbitrarily) pre-Romantic trombones from later models.[11]

In the Baroque period, the standard English name for the oboe was the 'Hautboy' (pronounced 'O-Boy', or in the international phonetic alphabet, [*oboi*]).[12] This word was a mispronunciation of the French name 'Hautbois', which in France until the nineteenth century was pronounced 'O-bway' (or [*obwe*]) rather than, as it is now, [*obwa*]. The same kind of mispronounced transliteration existed in the same period in other languages (*hobooij* and *Hoboy* in Dutch, *Oboè* in Italian, and *obué* in Spanish, for instance). 'Hautboy' seems an appropriate term for our time, especially because (as can be seen from the dates and titles of the various 'Fischer' tutors) it was a name that began to go out of fashion at about the same time the instrument began adding keys and rejecting cross-fingerings:[13]

> *c.*1770 *The Compleat Tutor for the Hautboy*
> *c.*1780 *New and Complete Instructions for the Hautboy*
> *c.*1780 *New and Complete Instructions for the Oboe or Hoboy*
> *c.*1790 *The Compleat Tutor for the Hautboy*
> *c.*1790 *New and Complete Instructions for the Oboe or Hoboy*

Hoyle wrote in his *Dictionarium musica* of 1770 that 'Oboe, or Oboy, is the same as Hauboy, or Hoboy; but the proper way of spelling it is Hautboy.'[14] By 1792 Wragg was calling his treatise (which was relatively advanced for its day) *The Oboe Preceptor or the Art of Playing the Oboe*.

The word 'hautboy' is admittedly not perfect for our need. Historically, it was used both before 1640 and after 1760. 'Hautboy' (or variants) was used in English

---

[10] It was Verschuere-Reynvaan (1795, under 'Dwarsfluit') who proposed the name *traverso* to distinguish the one-keyed flute from flutes with more keys.

[11] As McGowan notes (1994: 441): 'The English term "sackbut" is used currently as much as anything as a statement of intent.' The violin is by definition Baroque, despite the way it is generally set up and bowed nowadays.

[12] There was disagreement about whether to pronounce the 'H'. Hoyle's wording (see below) implies it was silent, and according to Unverricht (1980: 456), military hautboy players were called both *Hautboisten* and *Oboisten* in Germany, suggesting that the H was dropped there as well. But Burney (1773, i. 328), Busby (*c.*1783–6), Hawkins (1776; see below, Ch. 2, §D.3), and Simpson used the phrase 'a Hautboy'. North, and perhaps others, used 'Haut-boys' as the singular form: 'the Haut-boys sounds'.

[13] Although the name did not entirely cease to be used until the mid-19th c. As Geoffrey Burgess points out (pers. comm.), Barret's *Method* of 1850 still used it.

[14] Fischer (*c.*1800: 1) began 'The Hoboy, Hautboy or Oboe . . .'. The 4th edn. of Busby (1813; originally published in *c.*1783–6) had the following entry: 'OBOE. (Ital.) A Hautboy. See that word.'

from as early as 1575. And as we shall see, 'Oboe' was already being used in Germany by the 1710s.

Defining the Hautboy

The name for the shawm in French is *Hautbois*; the name for the early oboe in French is *Hautbois*; and finally, the name for the keyed, 'modern' oboe in French is *Hautbois*. While the physical form altered, the function (and thus the name) remained. The *Hautbois* was (and still is) the double-reed instrument that played the treble line in art music. As the music changed, the 'Hautbois' adapted to new demands by evolving. This process was not only continuous but without conspicuous breaks. By using different words (shawm, oboe, etc.) to denote stages of the instrument's development, we are merely identifying sets of general attributes. And in fact the physical characteristics that distinguish a shawm from an hautboy are of the same order as those that distinguish the hautboy from the keyed oboe; these instruments are all part of a historical continuum (as reflected in the French language). Thus, either the shawm is a kind of oboe (like the hautboy and the keyed oboe) or else—and this seems to me an absurdity—all three are different kinds of instruments.[15]

The identifiable trait that oboes had in common before the Romantic period was the regular use of half-holing and cross-fingering.[16] These fingerings were the answer to obtaining accidentals on woodwind instruments without using keys. Although some instruments like the larger shawms and the musette had used keys to extend the reach of the fingers before the hautboy appeared, most Baroque woodwinds, including the hautboy, used half-holing and cross-fingering as the basis of their fingering technique.

Half-holing lowered a fingered note a semitone by half closing the next lowest hole. The note A, for example, produced by closing holes 1 and 2, was lowered to A♭ by half closing hole 3. Half-holing was most effective on holes of relatively large diameter, which meant that it worked poorly on instruments with small tone-holes like the hautboy. Cross-fingering, on the other hand, worked well.

Cross-fingering involved lowering a simple fingering by closing one or more holes immediately below the first open hole. The B produced by closing the first hole could be lowered to a B♭, for instance, by also closing hole 3. In direct contrast

---

[15] There are other types of oboe as well, of course: the Schalmey, the cromorne, the hautbois de Poitou, the chalumeau simple of the musette, the classical hautboy (still without a key system), and the various larger sizes like hautbois d'amour, tenor hautboy, etc. Going a step further, the bassoon might also be categorized as a type of oboe; it was often called a 'bass hautboy' in the 17th and 18th cc., and players moved back and forth between it and the smaller instruments.

[16] Borjon (1672: 11) called cross-fingerings 'les croisées des doigts'. Some cross-fingerings are also called forked fingerings (those that involve 1 and 3 of each hand).

to half-holing, cross-fingering was more effective with smaller tone-holes, since the first open hole had to be of small diameter in relation to the bore in order to alter the pitch enough to be usable.[17]

Cross-fingerings were an essential part of the hautboy's sound quality and technique. They sounded different, demanded complex finger combinations, and produced notes more compatible with meantone tuning than equal temperament. They added colour, variety, and character to the various tonalities. Compared with the natural fingerings, the cross-fingerings felt stuffy to the player, and they produced a more covered or veiled timbre;[18] the result was the characteristically uneven scales of eighteenth-century woodwinds, which gave the effect of singing a scale using different vowels for each note.[19] Each key had its own particular sound and character, because cross-fingerings fell on different degrees of the scale.

The hautboy's music usually stayed within the bounds of four sharps and flats. By the early nineteenth century, when more distant tonalities that required many accidentals started to be used, cross-fingerings came to be seen as a hindrance, and the idea of adding keys became a subject of discussion—and dispute. In 1800 the well-known woodwind maker Heinrich Grenser, speaking of the traverso, expressed the sentiment that

Nicht in der Anzahl der Klappen, nein, in der möglichsten Einfachheit der Flöte, ohne deren Eleganz etwas aufzuopfern, muß die wahre Vervollkommnung dieses schönen Instruments gesucht werden. Zu Verbesserung dieses oder jenes Tones aber eine Klappe anzubringen, ist weder Schwierigkeit noch Kunst. Auch sind die Klappen ganz nichts neues . . . Die Hauptkunst . . . besteht, Flöten zu bauen, auf denen man alles, ohne Klappen, leisten kann, so ist erforderlich, die in solchen Flöten noch herrschenden Mängel auf eine Art zu heben, welche eben so entsprechend, als eine Klappe ist.[20]

Not in the number of its keys; no, it is in striving for utter simplicity, with no sacrifice to elegance, that the true perfection of this beautiful instrument lies. To improve this or any note by adding a key is neither difficult nor clever. The keys are after all nothing new . . . The real art . . . consists in making flutes on which everything can be achieved without keys. We must remove the deficiencies that still afflict such flutes in a way that is just as effective as a key.

---

[17] Cf. Écochard, article 'Fingering' in *New Grove II*.

[18] The nearest equivalent I know on the keyed oboe is the use of the forked f1 with the automatic opening of the E♭ key disabled, as can be heard on recordings by Marcel Tabuteau. Benade (1976: 452–3) points out that the proportional size between tone-holes and bores on bass instruments is more suitable for cross-fingerings than that of treble instruments. This is supported by William Waterhouse's observation (pers. comm.) that cross-fingerings often sound quite clear on the bassoon. For a discussion of the acoustic properties of woodwind cross-fingerings, see Myers (1981), 23–4.

[19] As discussed in Ch. 4, §G.4, cross-fingerings were not used in making woodwind ornaments, except as initial appoggiaturas.   [20] Grenser (1800), 44.

By the 1820s the issue had been decided. Louis-Auguste Vény wrote in *c.*1828 (p. 30) of the 'hautbois ordinaire' (by which he meant the traditional two-keyed hautboy):

Le Hautbois ordinaire est un instrument à vent défectueux puisqu'il présente des doigtés bizarres, des sons inégaux et l'impossibilité de jouer dans tous les tons.

The traditional hautboy is a defective wind instrument; it uses irrational fingerings, uneven tones, and cannot be played in all the tonalities.

This marked the end of the hautboy's career of some 180 years. The distinguishing characteristic of the new Romantic oboe advocated by Vény, Brod, and Sellner in the 1820s was its use of separate tone-holes for every chromatic note. Since there were not enough fingers to close all the holes, the accidentals were controlled by close-standing keys using the same principle as the Small-key on the hautboy. This was followed within a generation by the application of a key system: a complex interactive mechanism that used metal rings and plates that not only closed tone-holes, but were connected to pivoting axles that controlled the simultaneous opening and closing of further holes. The principal purpose of the new keys was to eliminate half-holing and cross-fingering, and when it was applied to the oboe, it marked a clear break with earlier instruments, changing both tone quality and playing technique. The oboe from about 1820 can therefore be characterized as a *keyed oboe*, and from the mid-nineteenth century onwards as a *key-system oboe*.

Long before 1820, however, the hautboy had undergone another fundamental shift. Between the extremes of the keyed oboe of the 1820s and the Baroque hautboy were several models that eventually coalesced into the so-called 'classical' hautboy, which appeared at about the time the steam engine was invented in 1765. Although cross-fingerings remained, the classical hautboy was designed for different functions than its Baroque cousin. The beginnings of this shift are discussed in the introduction to Chapter 7.

Thus, although they happened gradually, the phases of the oboe's career are distinctly marked: shawm, Baroque hautboy, classical hautboy, and keyed oboe. These distinctions explain the time period covered by this book, which is the era of the Baroque hautboy used from approximately 1640 to 1760. There is another reason for stopping at 1760: it is from this date that original reeds survive (in fact, quite a few). Considering the basic importance of the reed, this makes the classical hautboy and later oboe models historically accessible in a way the Baroque and Rococo models of oboe will never be, and removes from them some of the mystery and creative imagination that surround the playing of earlier models.

The International Character of the Hautboy

There are two obvious ways to organize a body of historical information that extends from the first half of the seventeenth century to the second half of the eighteenth and that covers all of Europe: by time or by space, that is, by period or by country. In the case of the hautboy, time is the significant driver, since neither its construction nor its technique was particularly dependent on location.

National distinctions (like the differences between Flemish and Italian harpsichords) are of little consequence on small, portable, and relatively inexpensive instruments like woodwinds. An English hautboy player might easily have access to a German hautboy, and vice versa. It would not have been difficult for players to replace earlier models, since woodwinds were not costly compared with strings and keyboard instruments; considering how quickly tastes changed, professional players were thus likely to have the latest 'state of the art' equipment.[21]

In the mid-twentieth century, national schools of oboe playing were distinct enough that on hearing a recording, an oboist could instantly recognize the country from which the orchestra came by the sound of its oboes. It is natural to assume that the same separations were to be found in the eighteenth century. After all, there were certainly national composing styles (Italian and French, at least). But the historical evidence indicates just the reverse; like nationalism in general, the crystallization into national schools was a nineteenth-century phenomenon.

The hautboy was (and to a certain extent, still is) associated with France. Everybody in the eighteenth century called it by its French name (literal or transliterated). A tradition that revered the techniques developed in France tended to make French performing style dominant everywhere among woodwind players. In most cases, the first players outside France were either themselves French, or had been trained by Frenchmen. As all the French words peppered through Telemann's dedication of the *Kleine Cammer-Music* suggest,[22] to speak of woodwinds was to think in French. And in this period, the French produced an unusual number of theory and instruction books on music that were read all over Europe.

Besides the 'French' way of playing, which was simply the normal way to play the hautboy, there was no particular style of playing that could be associated with a particular country. Thus it gradually came to seen as the international standard. Players frequently travelled or moved to other countries, bringing with them techniques of playing and instruments of the latest design.

An obvious example of an international hautboy player is Giuseppe Sammartini, trained in Milan by his French father, and culminating his career in London. To

---

[21] Modern woodwind players frequently replace their instruments, even though models change much less radically or quickly now than they did in the 18th c.   [22] For the text, see Ch. 5, §D.14.

take a few other cases at random, Jacob Lebrun (solo hautboist at Mannheim, 1747–71) came from Brussels; Claude Aubry was attached to the Comédie in Paris in 1718, in 1728 was at Dresden, and in 1736 moved to Versailles. Most of the hautboy soloists at the Concert Spirituel in Paris were Italian and German, and the hautboys in Handel's orchestra in London were Dutch, Flemish, German, or French. Albinoni's Opus 9 was written by an Italian, dedicated to a German, premièred by a Fleming, and published in Holland (the soloist, Jacob Loeillet, later went on to play at Versailles).

There is considerable evidence that not only players but hautboys commonly crossed borders. To judge from surviving instruments, for instance, the Dutch, with a relatively small population, produced more hautboys in the early eighteenth century than any country except Germany (see Ch. 2, §A). Many of those instruments must have been played abroad.

Historical Periods

Since there is no particular reason to study this history by country, it is more to the point to watch the progress of the hautboy's gradual and constant mutation through short units of time. This book thus divides the 120 years it covers into four thirty-year periods. These periods happen to correspond quite logically to changes in the instrument's structure, roles, and repertoire.

As the hautboy maker Paul Hailperin has said, 'Instruments are very rarely created to fit into slots; it is the other way around . . .'. Like all divisions, there is something arbitrary about dates; Couperin's *Nations*, for instance, appeared in the same year (1726) and city (Paris) as Boismortier's trios. Still, the periods used here generally reflect changes in musical styles and methods of instrument-making. They are also long enough to reconcile our sometimes patchy knowledge of the working dates of instrument makers. Most of all, they provide a common context for comparing and relating various aspects of the hautboy's history (its music, instructional materials, texts on its role and character, descriptions of players or playing, and surviving instruments), all of which may be more or less difficult to date when studied separately, but, when taken together, can produce plausible estimates.

An indication that the history of the hautboy is coming of age is that it is now possible to follow a thread connecting many great oboe players of the present right back to the instrument's origins. Most modern oboists can trace their backgrounds directly or indirectly to the Paris Conservatoire (which, at the very least, has provided them with the design of instrument they play, the French keyed oboe). The Conservatoire was an institution of immense influence throughout Europe in the nineteenth century, and all over the world in the twentieth century. The founder of the oboe school there was Auguste Vogt, Professeur at the Conservatoire from 1816 to 1853. Vogt had been a student of the first Professeur of hautboy at the new Conservatoire, Antoine Sallantin (1755–*c*.1830), who had had a very successful career in Paris from 1768. In the years just after the Revolution, Sallantin went to London to study with Johann Christian Fischer. Fischer had studied with Antonio Besozzi at Dresden in the 1750s. Some of Besozzi's ideas no doubt filtered through Fischer to Sallentin, who in turn probably passed them on to his pupils, including Vogt. But the thread continues backward: Besozzi had probably studied with his father Giuseppe, who was taught by his father Cristoforo, who in turn had learned his art from Aléxis Saint-Martin, a Frenchman by birth, who had been in Milan since about 1690, and was the father of Giuseppe Sammartini. Thus the circle is closed: a direct line can be traced from a Frenchman living in Italy (Saint-Martin, 1690s) to Italians in the early eighteenth century (the Besozzis), to a German (Fischer, *c*.1790), to a Frenchman (Sallantin, *c*.1795), to the French Conservatoire school, and thus to many modern players.

I

1640–1670: The Transition from Shawm to Hautboy in France

A. The Renaissance Shawm and the Protomorphic Hautboy

The hautboy was a response by shawm players to new demands in the music of the middle of the seventeenth century. The process through which it was conceived was gradual, and it crystallized out of elements of several different double-reed instruments of the time, probably including the hautbois de Poitou, the musette de cour, the cromorne, possibly the bassanello, and of course the grand Haut-bois, or shawm. The origins of this evolution are traceable back to the 1580s, and the definitive hautboy (the instrument that was to retain its approximate form and proportions up to the present day) appeared in the late 1660s.

It is ironic that at this critical and interesting period of development, chance has left us so little documentation.[1] As late as 1620, Praetorius was still describing a traditional 'Discant Schalmeye', or treble shawm, of the type that had been perfected and maintained without basic change all over Europe for centuries (see Pl. 1.1).[2] But just fifteen years later, evidence of an evolution towards the hautboy began appearing. In his *Harmonicorum instrumentum* (1635; Pl. 1.2), Mersenne shows a picture of a treble shawm whose reed is without the usual pirouette.[3]

The pirouette was a piece of turned wood that projected beyond the end of the shawm and surrounded the lower part of the reed. Its upper surface was used to support the lips. (The shawm reed did not vibrate freely in the mouth cavity, how-

---

[1] As Halfpenny wrote (1949c: 149): 'Contemporary documentation of this transition is scanty, and the investigator who would complete the picture must be prepared to read between the lines. Sometimes the evidence has been staring us in the face for many years, and is only illuminated by fresh information from other sources, or by a re-reading from, so to speak, a new focal angle.'

[2] For a definition of the shawm, see Masel (1995), 1351.

[3] See ibid. 1352 and 1394–5. Mersenne's other picture of a treble shawm, included with the whole family, does include a pirouette (1635: 88). Herbert W. Myers (pers. comm.) points out that the text that accompanies his other drawing actually mentions the parallel nature of the pirouettes found on the *taille* and the *dessus*. This reed may therefore have been experimental. There are other 17th-c. pictures of shawms with reeds but without pirouettes:

Tapestry 'Herminie chez les paysans', series *Tancrède et Clorinde*, after Michel Corneille I (2nd h. 17th c.), Château de Châteaudun

Jan Steen, *De Dansles,* oil painting, [? *c.*1660], Amsterdam, Rijksmuseum

[? François] Guérard, *Le noble joüeur d'instrument,* etching, [? 1690s], F-Pn.

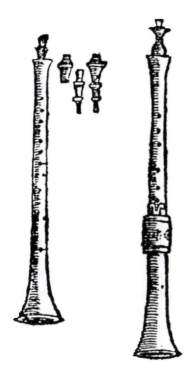

Pl. 1.1. Praetorius (1620), shawms in
plate XI

Pl. 1.2. Mersenne (1635: 84 and 1636:
295), treble shawm showing reed without
the usual pirouette. Detail (not to scale)

ever, like those of oriental oboes that use a disk and whose reeds, made of rush or
straw, are too delicate to vibrate when in direct contact with the lips.) The reed
without pirouette shown in Mersenne is significant because it implies a change in
the contact between the player and the reed. With the pirouette, it was not necessary to control the reed completely with the teeth and lips; without it, the player's
embouchure took full responsibility.[4] This in turn affected the way the reed itself
was made (as we will discuss below).

At about the same time Mersenne's book appeared, Trichet mentioned that the
hautbois de Poitou (see below, §B.2) was sometimes played 'en mettant l'anche dans

---

[4] Despite the lack of a thumb-hole, the shawm was sometimes able to overblow to the second register, an indication that some lip control was involved. The presence or absence of a pirouette is thus a question of degree, not
kind. For a good summary of the historical evidence on pirouettes and shawm reeds, see Myers (1981), 104–14.
Myers is less convinced of the significance of Mersenne's picture, suggesting it may be a schematic view, since the
pirouette is present in Mersenne's other illustration of a treble shawm; cf. Myers (1997b), 84.

la bouche' (by putting the reed in the mouth).[5] Also, where Praetorius normally gave his shawm a range of an octave and a sixth, Mersenne's and Trichet's had two octaves, like the first hautboys; this extension upward implied a certain degree of embouchure control, pirouette or no.

The instrument Mersenne attached to this free-blown reed did not yet show the physical attributes we now associate with the hautboy. Those attributes first appear in an engraving by Blanchet that serves as the frontispiece to Borjon's musette book of 1672 (Pl. 1.3).[6] The new hautboy must therefore have taken definition at some point between the appearance of Mersenne's and Borjon's books, in the period from about 1640 to 1670.

German and English sources tell us the hautboy originated in France.[7] This is confirmed by its name in all European languages, which was either taken over directly or transliterated from the French 'Hautbois' (pronounced [*oḃwe*]). The hautboy's rise is associated with the composers Cambert and Lully, who combined it with strings to accompany their ballets and operas. But finding a date for the definitive emergence of the hautboy is complicated by the fact that in France shawms and hautboys had the same name. Unlike in other countries, the hautboy developed gradually in France and was not suddenly introduced as a foreign import. A new name was not therefore necessary. As late as 1751, under the term *hautbois*, Diderot still described both instruments: 'Nous distinguerons le hautbois en ancien & en moderne' (We make a distinction between the early hautbois and the modern one). Terminology therefore gives no clue as to exactly what instrument Lully knew and used. Shawms were still played at Louis XIV's coronation in 1654 (not that that was the kind of occasion on which to look for innovative instruments designed to blend with violins and voices).

La Barre wrote of Lully, who became *Surintendant de la Musique* in France in 1661:

Son Elevation fit la chute totalle de tous ces entiens istrumens [la musette, le hauboïs, la cornemuse, le cornet, le cromorne, et le cacbouc[8]] a l'exception du haubois, grace aux Filidor et Hautteterre lesquels on tant gâté de bois et soutenus de la musique, qu'ils sont enfin parvenus a le rendre propre pour les Conçerts. Des ce tems la on laissa la musette aux bergers, les violons, les flutes douces, les théorbes et les violes, prirent leur place, car la flute traverssiere n'est venue qu'apres.[9]

His promotion meant the downfall of all the old instruments [the musette, the hauboïs, the bagpipe, the cornett, the cromorne, and the sackbut] except the haubois, thanks to the Filidors and Hautteterres, who spoiled so much wood and [? played so much music] that they finally succeeded in rendering it usable in ensembles. From that time on, musettes were left to shepherds, and violins, recorders, theorbos, and viols took their place, for the traverso did not arrive until later.

[5] Lesure (1955), 374.
[6] Cf. the discussion of the portrait by David Teniers of the painter and his family in Ch. 3, §A.
[7] See Ch. 3, §C. As late as 1827, an anonymous English writer attributed the hautboy to the French (Anon. 1827: 464).
[8] Probably 'saqueboute'.   [9] La Barre (? *c.*1740).

PL. 1.3. [Thomas] Blanchet, shepherd playing hautboy, opposite title-page to Borjon's
Traité de la musette [N. Auroux fec.]. By 1672

Information that La Barre supplies on traverso players allows us to situate this date more precisely:

C'est Philbert qui en a joué le premier en France, et puis presque dans le même temps Descoteaux. Le roi aussi bien que toute la cour à qui cette instrument plut infiniment, adjouta 2 charges aux 4 musettes du Poitou et les donna à Philbert et à Descoteaux . . .

Philbert was the first to play it in France, and almost immediately afterwards, Descoteaux. The instrument was a great success with the King, and indeed everyone at court, and His Majesty caused two new positions to be created in the *Musettes de Poitou* and conferred them on Philbert and Descoteaux . . .

Court documents record that Philippe Rebillé dit Philbert and René Pignon dit Descoteaux were both part of the *Hautbois et Musettes de Poitou* by 1667.[10] If La Barre's information is accurate, the traverso would have appeared in the mid-1660s.[11] Since La Barre wrote that 'the traverso did not arrive until later' than the hautboy, some kind of usable hautboy must have predated the mid-1660s. It has long been thought that such an instrument was first heard in Lully's ballet *L'Amour malade* of 1657 (this theory is discussed below).

La Barre wrote that the Philidors and Hotteterres eventually succeeded in rendering the haubois 'propre pour les Conçerts', suitable for ensembles. What kind of ensemble did he mean? Shawms had traditionally been consort instruments, played as an independent family. Strings, like the *Grande Bande*, also played as a closed consort. It is now generally agreed that an important element in the creation of the 'orchestra' was when the two families, the shawms and the strings, began to be played in combination instead of in discrete groups.

In France, the idea of combining shawms and strings was already in the air in the 1620s. In 1626 violins and hautbois performed together in a *grand bal*.[12] A piece in the Philidor Collection is entitled *Concert à Louis XIII par les 24 Viollons et les 12 Grand hautbois . . . 1627*.[13] In these performances, however, the violins and shawms probably played in alternation rather than together.[14]

---

[10] Benoit (1971b), 18. René's father François was appointed in 1658, but that is probably too early for the new traverso, and he was known as a recorder player. A note beside François's name in 1667 says 'Demeure a Laval; son filz joue a sa place avecq les musettes.' A *carton* designed by Charles Le Brun for the baptism of the Dauphin, Louis de France, which took place on 24 Mar. 1668 at Saint-Germain-en-Laye, shows a one-keyed, three-piece traverso. This design is reproduced in Benoit 1971a, pl. XX.

[11] Semmens (1975: 134) suggested that a remodelled traverso took part in Lully's *Ballet des muses* in 1666. Blanchet's frontispiece (1672) shows a straight-sided transverse flute, but it may be a fifre.

[12] Buch (1993), 32. Buch writes that 'other general references to the combination of winds and strings can be found as well'.

[13] F-Pn Rés. F. 494, pp. 1–24. This piece is published in Buch (1993). The *hautbois* have two pieces alone in the keys of F and G major (one piece requires an e♭1), with a range of c1 to f2.

[14] Jérémie Papasergio (pers. comm.) points out that there are two consistently distinct types of pieces, distinguished by clef usage as well as density and complexity of part-writing, suggesting a different treatment for the two groups of instruments. Between these two types, however, pieces are in the same keys; if the two groups played

La Barre mentioned 'les Filidor'. There is a tradition recounted by Ernest Thoinan (1867: 398), perhaps fictitious, that may give a clue to the Philidors' involvement in the process leading from the shawm to the hautboy:

Michel Danican, né dans le Dauphiné, avait acquis une grande habileté sur le hautbois, et réussit, en arrivant à Paris, à se faire entendre et applaudir de Louis XIII.	Michel Danican, born in the Dauphiné, had become very skilful on the shawm, and on his arrival in Paris, succeeded in being heard and appreciated by Louis XIII.

(Since Danican was probably born about 1600, and Louis XIII was crowned in 1613, Danican might have caught Louis's attention in about 1620.)

Ce prince, grand amateur de musique et musicien lui-même, fut enchanté de l'artiste dauphinois, dont le jeu, disait-il, lui rappelait celui d'un célèbre hautboïste italien nommé Filidori, venu de Sienne quelques années avant, et dont le talent avait produit une certaine sensation à la cour de France. Le roi dilettante s'écria même dans son enthousiasme, en écoutant Michel: 'J'ai trouvé un second Filidori'. Il n'en fallut pas davantage, et les courtisans, toujours disposés à renchérir encore sur les éloges du maître, n'appelèrent plus Danican que Philidor.	This monarch, a lover of music and a musician himself, was enchanted by the artist from the Dauphiné, remarking that his playing reminded him of a famous 'oboe' player named Filidori, who had come from Siena a few years previously, and whose talent had caused rather a sensation at the French court. The music-loving King even exclaimed in his enthusiasm at hearing Michel, 'I have found a second Filidori!' It took no more than that for the courtiers, who were quite ready to exaggerate their praises of the maestro, to call him no longer Danican, but rather Philidor.

(Filidori would thus probably have played for the King some time before 1620. What kind of instrument was he playing? We will return to this question below.)

Cette anecdote ne se trouve pas dans les mémoires du temps; cependant, comme elle est très-vraisemblable et que la tradition s'en est conservée dans la famille Danican, il faut en accepter la sincérité.	This anecdote is not to be found in documents of the period, but as it appears highly probable and has been safeguarded in the Danican family, we should accept its veracity.

The most significant part of this story, if it is true, is Louis XIII's evident interest in the use of a treble double-reed instrument in a solo capacity, a role that had not been part of the shawm's tradition. It would have occurred between about 1620 and 1643 (the year of Louis XIII's demise). Trichet (*c*.1630–44) also mentioned the idea of playing the shawm 'in solos', as well as Louis XIII's interest in the 'haubois':

separately, they were evidently at the same pitch. Peter Holman (pers. comm.) also suggests that the word 'Concert' in this context implies the mixture of instruments of different families—as in the contemporary English word 'consort'.

[Si les haubois] sont maniés d'une scavante main et sonnés soit séparément soit conjoinctement, ils sont si charmants et ravissants que j'ai oui dire à plusieurs personnes, le roi Louis 13 estant a Bourdeaux l'an 1622, qu'ils prisoint plus cet instrument entre les mains du maistre de musique des galeres qu'aucune autre sorte d'instrument.[15]

[If shawms] are handled by a skilled hand and played either in solos or in consorts, they are so charming and delightful that I have heard it said by several persons that when he was in Bordeaux in 1622, King Louis XIII prized this instrument above all others in the hands of the leader of the navy band.

1. *Reasons for 'improving' the shawm*

The idea that the hautboy was an 'improved' shawm was a seventeenth-century one. Partially confirming La Barre's description, Talbot wrote in *c.*1692–5: 'The present Hautbois not 40 years old & an improvement of the great French hautbois [i.e, the *grand Haut-bois*, or shawm of Mersenne's time] which is like our Weights.' Talbot got his information on the French hautbois from two French hautboy players active in England, Jacques Paisible and François La Riche. Paisible had arrived in England in 1673, La Riche in the 1680s (see below, Ch. 3, §D). What did these players consider 'improvements' to the shawm?

The shawm had reached a steady form probably by the fifteenth century, and the bugs had long since been worked out of it (as much as they can be on a woodwind) by the end of the sixteenth century. As David Smith wrote, 'Among all the early woodwinds, the family of shawms employs perhaps the most ingenious and sophisticated method for improving stability through the acoustics of its bell design.'[16] The shawm in itself had no need of 'improvement'. What changed was the context in which it functioned, so that what it could do well was marginalized in the music of the seventeenth century. By the beginning of that century, the shawm had lost considerable status to other instruments, and was being used less and less frequently. It was this situation, along with new musical necessities, that led mid-seventeenth-century makers to replace the quite satisfactory design of the shawm with an experiment that eventually stabilized in the form of the hautboy.

One of the great achievements of the shawm was that it was the prototypical consort instrument; as Peter Holman (pers. comm.) points out, 'it was almost certainly the first instrument to be made in more than one matched size'. But what was demanded of the shawm by the mid-seventeenth century—and what it could not do without changing its form—was to express *affections*. Rather than lay down a broad swath of sound through a group of similar instruments like a shawm band, it was

---

[15] Lesure (1955), 351.   [16] Smith (1992), 29.

asked to play alone in imitation of a solo singer, to express the emotional force of texts (real or imagined), to 'speak' by bringing out the meaning of words, and to move listeners.

This new 'eloquent' music of the seventeenth century frequently used classical rhetoric as a metaphor to explain how it was conceived and assembled. Music and rhetoric shared a common objective: to convince the listener. In music, the case being pleaded was a particular affect (a mood or emotion). The idea was to arouse that affect in the performer in order to communicate it to the listener.[17]

Comparing music to rhetoric revealed the fundamental premiss of the Baroque period: that music not only accompanied and commented on speech (as it had done previously), but was itself a kind of speech.[18] Mattheson defined music as 'Klang-Rede' (speaking in notes),[19] and it was therefore of unusual significance that he singled out the hautboy as an instrument that was 'gleichsam redende' (eloquent).[20] La Barre, writing of the invention of Baroque woodwinds, considered that the break-through to 'perfection' in music had been realized by

Le Camus, Boisset, Dembris, et Lambert[21] [, qui] ont estez les premiers a faire des airs qui exprimassent les parolles, mais sur tout le celebre Luly . . .	Le Camus, Boësset, D'Ambruys, and Lambert [, who] were the first to write airs that expressed their texts, and above all the famous Lully . . .

'Expressing texts' is a very effective way of saying that what they achieved that was new, as he saw it, was to 'speak' with their music. These composers were working at just the period when the new hautboy appeared,[22] and in La Barre's mind these developments were linked.

The solo voice was the primary tool used for expressing emotions and, by singing, intensifying the meanings of words. As the epitome of the musical instrument, it served as a model for other single instruments playing alone, 'speaking' as individuals. Diderot remarked that, since the voice was without question the best 'instrument' for transforming affects into sound, he considered those instruments best that were most appropriate

. . . à accompagner & à imiter le chant de la voix humaine dans toutes les modifications des ses tons. C'est ce qui fait que le hautbois tient un des premiers rangs.[23]	at accompanying and imitating the infinite abilities of the singer. It is for this reason that the hautboy ranks among the first.

---

[17] For more thoughts on this subject, see Harnoncourt (1988), 120.   [18] Dahlhaus (1985), 56.
[19] Mattheson (1739), 82 (cf. also 127).   [20] Mattheson (1713), 268. Cf. Ch. 3, §C.
[21] These are (respectively) Sebastien Le Camus, Antoine Boësset, Honoré D'Ambruys, and Michel Lambert.
[22] Le Camus published works in 1678, Boësset in 1617–42, D'Ambruys in 1685, 1696, and 1702, and Lambert in 1660 and 1689.   [23] Diderot 1751–72 (this quoted from the edition of 1782, xviii. 846–7).

Discussing good diction in his treatise on singing of 1723, Tosi implied that an hautboy was like a voice without words. He wrote: 'For if the words [of the singer] are not heard so as to be understood, there will be no great Difference between a human voice and a Hautbois.'[24]

It was thus no accident that the first solos for the hautboy were obbligatos with solo voice in opera arias. For this new expressive role, the instrument needed enhanced abilities to make contrasts of tone, dynamics, and fine shades of articulation by the direct and complete control of the reed with the player's embouchure. Direct control of such a reed produced an instrument whose special ability was to express short intense musical gestures, to make quick and extreme changes of dynamics, frequent starts and stops, and striking tonal contrast between notes and within notes—an 'eloquent' oboe: the hautboy.

The new hautboy was developed specifically for use in Lully's productions, so it was expected to be a kind of wind parallel to the violin, able to blend with other instruments and use a two-octave range centred on the usual notes of the violin, with easy scales in C and D major. As North wrote of Lully's orchestra at the end of the seventeenth century, 'Here were many instruments, all waiters upon the violin, which was predominant, and lowdness a great ingredient, together with a strong snatching way of playing, to make the musick brisk and good.'[25] To have the needed range, the ideal bottom note of this 'improved' instrument was c_1. Banister wrote in 1695:

And whereas most other single *Wind-Instruments* (especially the *Flute*) go so very high, for want of the lower Notes, that it is impossible to play upon them in Consort with the *Violin*, &c. The *Hautboy* is free from this defect, and may be play'd upon in Consort, without transposing or advancing the Key.[26]

Talbot (*c.*1692–5: 14) also commented: 'Its compass [c_1–c_3 with all intermediate tones and semitones] more proper for Consort [that is, playing with other instruments] than most Wind Instruments.' Thus range was an important issue, and when we consider range, we must also consider absolute pitch.

The shawm was considered a loud instrument, and was pitched quite high (the name *Haut-bois* was thus doubly appropriate, as 'haut' means both loud and high in French). Mersenne (1636–7: 243) implied a difference in pitch between wind ensembles and 'concerts', comparing the fife and the flute (the latter evidently used in mixed consorts) in the following:

---

[24] 1723; from Galliard's translation (1742), 15.   [25] North (1959), 221.

[26] The recorder and traverso may have been pitched higher in order to be better heard, as they were softer than the hautboy.

Mais l'on ne fait pas ordinairement toutes les parties de Musique avec les Fifres, comme avec les Flustes d'Allemande, que l'on met au ton de chapelle pour faire des concerts.

But it is not usual to put fifes on all the parts of an ensemble, as is done for German flutes (which are made at *Ton de chapelle* so they can be played with other instruments).

Since singers were involved early on in Lully's productions, it is likely his earliest *ballets de cour* were already being performed at A−2 (Mersenne's 'ton de chapelle', which later came to be called *Ton d'Opéra*, about A-390); this was a 'singer's pitch'.

This was considerably lower than the shawm of the period. Mersenne's *grand Haut-bois* was probably pitched at the standard known in France as *Ton d'Écurie*, or A+1 (like shawms everywhere else in Europe);[27] the acoustic length or AL (the distance from the top of the instrument to the middle of hole 6) he gave for the treble shawm was 276.7 mm, in the same range as surviving hautboys probably at A+1 (see Ch. 2, §D.2.a). Its six-fingered note would presumably have sounded at about modern f1.[28] Thus the new hautboy probably ended up sounding a fourth lower than the treble shawm, and (as we will see) was softer in sound (a 'Bas-bois', as it were).[29] This may be why Quantz (1752, ch. XVII/vii/7), speaking of the woodwinds, observed

Dem tiefen Tone haben sie eigentlich ihren Ursprung zu danken.

Indeed, their very origin is due to the low pitch.

Douwes (1699: 115) also wrote

De *Haubois* sijn niet anders als groote Schalmeijen.[30]

Hautboys are nothing else but large treble shawms.

A change of that magnitude would have implied a new design.

---

[27] Cf. Haynes (1995), §4–2.

[28] This is based on the fact that Mersenne's shawm sizes are closely equivalent to Praetorius' and thus presumably sounded at about the same absolute pitch. Myers (1989: 3) wrote: 'Certainly Mersenne's dimensions for woodwinds of Renaissance type do not differ significantly from those of surviving examples from elsewhere.' In 1997a: 13 n. 30, Myers determined that the total length of the treble shawm Praetorius depicts is 653 mm, 'the same length as trebles I have measured in Brussels [at 653 and 654 mm]'. Mersenne gives a length for the treble shawm of 2 pieds = 648 mm. Praetorius called the 7-fingered note d1, which at A+1 sounded about modern d♯1 (cf. Haynes 1995, §5–1). The six-fingered note a tone above this would thus have sounded at about f1.

[29] Myers points out (1997b: 82) that in the third volume of the *Syntagma musicum*, Praetorius (1618b, iii. 66–8) had recommended that the 'screaming' treble shawm (*discant Schalmey*) be eliminated from the shawm choir and that only pommers be used. In terms of pitch, the new design represented just such a change.

[30] He also added that the Haubois had twin third and fourth holes.

2. How the hautboy differed from the shawm

In order to achieve a softer sound that blended with the violin and matched its range, the makers who developed the new hautboy seem to have retained the treble shawm's approximate bore shape but shortened the bell, repositioned and reduced the size of the tone-holes, and narrowed the reed. If by 'shawm' we assume the traditional instrument described by Praetorius (before it began to mutate), and by 'hautboy', any example from about 1690 onwards, a comparison of the two instruments shows the following differences:

1. The hautboy's reed had much less of a fan or fish-tail shape than the shawm's, and it dispensed with the pirouette.

2. About half the length of a treble shawm was below the finger-holes, whereas the bell was relatively foreshortened on the hautboy.

3. The hautboy had only one pair of resonance-holes below the tone-holes; the treble shawm had three sets, a total of five resonance-holes.

4. The tone-holes were placed much lower along the hautboy's length.

5. The tone-holes were drilled smaller on the hautboy.

6. The walls of the treble shawm were about 1 cm thick; the walls of the hautboy were a third to half as thick.

7. The hautboy's tone-holes were undercut; shawms generally had cylindrical or even overcut holes (that tapered slightly outwards).

8. The tone-holes of treble shawms were usually drilled straight;[31] on the hautboy, holes 1, 2, 3, and 6 were often drilled at a slant.

9. The hautboy was divided into three joints linked by tenons; the shawm was normally in one piece.[32]

10. The hautboy bore had a broken profile, or steps at the changes of joint, especially noticeable at the beginning of the bell.

11. The hautboy had a complex outer profile with ornamental thickenings at specific places along its length, corresponding to the divisions between the joints (the shawm had a simple smooth exterior).

12. The hautboy bell had a lip (that is, a thick interior contraction rim at the bottom) which was not present on the shawm.

13. Besides the articulated open-standing Great-key for C, the hautboy had a closed Small-key (sometimes duplicated) for the note E♭.

---

[31] Herbert W. Myers (pers. comm.): 'The usual exception being the (often doubled) hole 7, which slants downwards in some, but not all, surviving examples.' Trichet (*c.*1630–44: 351) may thus have been describing a mutant when he wrote: 'les trous des haubois [i.e. shawms] sont percés de biais et qu'ils ne respondent pas par dedans directement à l'ouverture de dehors'. Diderot, describing the shawm, said something similar, and indicated that the direction of the slant was 'vers l'anche, c'est-à-dire en montant'.

[32] Hailperin (1970: 28) points out several precedents for woodwinds divided into joints.

14. The shawm's fontanelle, a detachable barrel perforated with small holes that protected the key mechanism, was absent on the hautboy.[33]

It is difficult to isolate which of these elements came first. The lip control implied by the absence of the pirouette allowed for more nuance of tone and dynamics than had been needed on the shawm. And the rejection of the pirouette implied the use of a different reed shape. According to Smith (1992: 26), the ideal shape for a shawm reed is squat and fan-shaped, with a relatively narrow throat (which allows overblowing) but a wide tip (cf. his fig. 1.9a). The wide tip stabilized the low notes and cross-fingered notes, and produced a loud sound and bright timbre. Some modern players are able to control reeds of this type without a pirouette,[34] but it is not easy. Smith writes:

A reed with a rapidly flaring shape is extremely sensitive to the amount of lip damping by the player. This becomes very apparent when one tries to play a treble shawm without a pirouette, using a fan-shaped reed. It is actually difficult for the embouchure to remain in one place on the reed, and pitch becomes erratic . . . When the pirouette is added to the setup, it actually becomes part of the embouchure and positions the lips in their normal playing position on the reed, making the instrument feel comfortable and easily manageable.

Thus, if the pirouette did in fact begin to be abandoned (as indicated by Mersenne and Trichet), it suggests that the reeds being used on shawms in the latter part of Louis XIII's reign had less flare towards the tip, being consequently softer and duller in sound. These were characteristics that were advantageous to the new hautboy.

As far as changes to the bore, Hailperin reported in a comparative study of sample instruments that

It is clear that the oboe bores fall neatly within the range of the descant shawm bores, and that the conicity of the main bore of both types of instruments is remarkably similar . . . In fact if one considers the bell as being acoustically a separate part of the instrument, it is hard to nail down any difference in the bore of shawms and oboes.[35]

Thus radical changes to the bore were probably not part of this evolution.[36] The long bell of the treble shawm had acted as a very effective stabilizer of the notes of the lower register through cooperative resonances with the vent-holes. But the hautboy represented a categorical rejection of this lower bore extension. Had the treble shawm simply been expanded to play a fourth lower, with the same long

---

[33] Although modern copies of shawms often use a cylindrical reed well with a step, original shawms were made with a tapered counterbore (which was taken over by the hautboy).

[34] Georg Corall (pers. comm.).   [35] Hailperin (1970), 15.

[36] Marc Écochard (pers. comm.) has also noticed the similarity of the bores of French treble shawms to early hautboys.

resonating bell, it would have roughly resembled the Catalan tenora in proportions and length.[37] But the hautboy's bell was less than a quarter of the instrument's total length. In this way, it was closer to the Pommer, which was rather an exception among the shawms in this respect,[38] with a bell only roughly two-fifths of the instrument's total length, and with only two resonance-holes.

It is curious that the treble and tenor shawm were of almost equal lengths (cf. Pl. 1.1). Praetorius wrote:

Der Altpommer, welcher fast einer grösse mit der Schalmeyen ist, ohne daß er ein Schlussel hat, und eine *Quint* tieffer ist, wird *Bombardo Piccolo* genennet.[39]	The tenor Pommer, which is almost the same size as the [treble] Schalmeye, but has a key, and sounds a fifth lower, is called Bombardo Piccolo.

Like Praetorius', Mersenne's treble and tenor shawms were nearly the same length (Pls. 1.1 and 1.4). Herbert W. Myers (pers. comm.) points out that

the reason the two instruments are so close in length despite the difference of a 5th in pitch between them is the proportionately longer resonating 'bell' of the treble shawm. The highest of the five resonance holes of the latter is usually right at the midpoint of the length of the instrument, or at the most a couple of mm lower. The resonance holes of the . . . tenor shawm [or Pommer] . . . are situated much further down, closer proportionately to their position on the oboe.

The hautboy had other superficial resemblances to the Pommer: it took over the Great-key, and sounded only a tone higher in pitch.[40]

Short-belled shawms with a reed bound on a staple and no pirouette, probably derived originally from bagpipes, existed in many cultures as folk instruments. The new hautboy also incorporated elements of this 'bagpipe' shawm (see 'Hautbois de Poitou' below, §B.2) as opposed to the 'band shawm' with a pirouette and a long resonating bell.[41] By 1664, the two models of protomorphic oboe (the transitional design shown in the Gobelins tapestry 'L'Air' described below) both had shorter bell lengths than the shawm.[42]

Giving up subtleties of design that had been worked out over centuries was not the kind of thing musicians would have done without a purpose. Nor would developing this new design have been easy. Two radical changes probably intended to lower pitch were repositioning the tone-hole centre further from the reed (i.e.

---

[37] The tenora is about 835 mm long, while the average hautboy is about 572.

[38] Cf. Smith (1992), 146 n. 39.   [39] Praetorius (1618a), 37.

[40] The six-fingered note on the tenor shawm was about modern a♭0, which would have been a whole step below the new hautboy at A−2.   [41] See Baines (1957), 230 and Smith (1992), 91.

[42] Bell length in proportion to total length was evidently an experimental factor: the longer protomorphic hautboy had a bell ratio similar to later hautboys at about 3:20; that of the shorter one was about twice as long at 3:10.

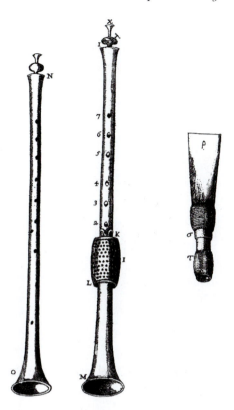

PL. 1.4. Mersenne (1636: 320), illustration of treble and alto shawms
plus reed (not to scale). Detail

lowering the holes on the bore; see Ch. 2, §B) and reducing the diameter of the
tone-holes. Placing a tone-hole of the same diameter lower on the bore will produce
a lower-pitched note. And of course making it smaller has the same effect.

Lowering the tone-hole centre also apparently affected the fingering 123 4 (f♯1
on the hautboy). This note had been flat on the treble shawm (as it is on many bagpipes and folk oboes), and closer to a semitone above 123 45 (e1 on the hautboy).
It was also flat on the hautboy, but whereas shawmists were able to use 123 57 as
an alternative,[43] that fingering was ineffective on the hautboy with its shorter bell.
It was probably for this reason that on certain examples of both types of protomorphic hautboy shown in the Gobelins tapestry 'L'Air' of 1664 (see below, §A.3),
hole 4 was twinned.[44] A half-closed 4th hole would have raised the pitch of the

---

[43] Herbert W. Myers (pers. comm.).   [44] Cf. panels D, F, and G (Pls. 1.5–7).

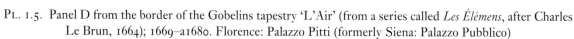

PL. 1.5. Panel D from the border of the Gobelins tapestry 'L'Air' (from a series called *Les Élémens*, after Charles Le Brun, 1664); 1669–a1680. Florence: Palazzo Pitti (formerly Siena: Palazzo Pubblico)

PL. 1.6. Gobelins 'L'Air', Panel F

PL. 1.7. Gobelins 'L'Air', Panel G

fingering 123 4. This fingering was a problem that remained with the hautboy (and the traverso as well) throughout its career, as it was flat. It was only partially solved by opening the Small-key when it appeared (see Ch. 4, §G.3).

As a tone-hole chimney becomes longer, either through a thicker side wall or by being drilled slanted, it produces a tone that is both stuffier and lower in pitch. These effects can be balanced by making its diameter larger. The tone-holes of the hautboy, however, were made smaller. To avoid producing stuffy notes, smaller tone-holes must have shorter chimneys, and thus the side walls have to be thinner. That is what happened to the hautboy: compared with the shawm, the side walls were considerably reduced in thickness.

Diminishing the size of the tone-holes caused the tone to be less stable,[45] softer, and darker, all changes that were advantageous for the new hautboy. A gentler sound blended rather than stood out.

The reduction in stability also helped with register shifts, which on the hautboy were produced without 'speakers' like the thumb-hole on the recorder or octave keys on woodwinds with key-systems (register shifts were made by the action of the breath and lips).[46]

As mentioned above, another advantage of smaller tone-holes was that the cross-fingerings were more effective. On a woodwind, there are three different methods of getting reliable notes that are not part of the natural six-hole scale: (1) opening holes halfway (half-holing), (2) adding keys, or, (3) systematically using cross-fingerings. In redesigning the instrument, the makers had to choose between these options.

Half-holing worked on certain notes. Hole 4 was twinned on at least one example of both types of protomorphic hautboy of the 1660s,[47] and hole 6 was twinned on the larger shorter-belled model. Twinning was eventually applied to hole 4 on the definitive hautboy as well, and also to hole 3. The cross-fingering 12 4 that raised the note 123 a semitone had worked well on the treble shawm in both registers, but was uncooperative in the fundamental register of the new hautboy. A half-hole on 3 was the eventual solution; it was a mixed blessing (it allowed for very sensitive tuning when time allowed, but quick passages that involved A♭/G♯ were always more difficult).[48]

Twinning hole 6 also evidently had its limitations. A partial covering of hole 6 (single, not twinned) had worked well on the treble shawm because of the long bell.[49] But for the sake of a comfortable finger reach, hole 6 on most late seventeenth-century

---

[45] Myers (1981), 16.
[46] 'Irregularities in the bore profile (steps, bell lip, counterbore, etc.) also enhanced this octave instability.' Giovanni Caviglia (pers. comm.).   [47] Cf. panels D, F, and G (Pls. 1.5–7).
[48] Twinned third holes were still being used on 'military system' oboes in the 20th c.
[49] See Smith (1992), 30.

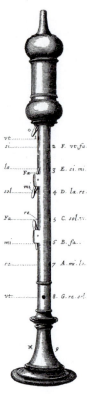

PL. 1.8. Borjon de Scellery, illustration of capped musette chanter,
page 22 of his *Traité de la musette* (1672)

woodwinds was raised longitudinally from its ideal position, and had therefore to
be smaller than holes 4 and 5, making it somewhat stuffier than the other notes.
Twinning it increased the stuffiness. The purpose of half-opening hole 6 would
have been to obtain E♭/D♯, and since this note was indispensable, a key was eventually adopted.[50]

   The technology for keys was already in place. Shawms had used articulated open-
standing keys to extend the natural reach of the fingers, and the Pommer's Great-
key was taken over on the hautboy. The hautboy's Small-key for E♭, when it came,
resembled the simple close-standing side keys of the bellows-blown musette de cour
(see Pl. 1.8), an instrument that by Borjon's time (1672) sometimes had eleven
keys.[51]

   [50] The analogous key was later applied to the traverso and sometimes the bassoon.
   [51] On the musette, keys were used relatively early because its 'closed' finger technique did not allow cross-
fingerings.

PL. 1.9. Gobelins tapestry: Danse des Nymphes, de la gauche; 5e pièce du série *Sujets de la Fable*, 1684–1795 (model by 1684). Detail. Paris: Louvre

For the remaining notes that were not in the hautboy's natural scale (f1, bb1, c2, f2, ab2/g♯2, and bb2) the third option, cross-fingering, was carried over from the shawm.[52] As MacGillivray observed (1961: 251), the musette makers who developed the hautboy for Lully's orchestra were used to making instruments with many keys, so choosing to use cross-fingerings and half-holing was apparently 'a matter of deliberate choice'. One of the earliest pictures of the hautboy is another Gobelins tapestry (model by 1684, Pl. 1.9), that shows a player using a fictitious fingering obviously inspired by a cross-fingering.

Cross-fingerings had long been required in shawm music. Myers writes (pers. comm.):

The treble shawm was thought of originally (and through the 1st half of the 16th century) as in neither c′ nor d′ but seven-fingers g. Just to play a scale of naturals in the fundamental octave involves cross-fingerings for written c′, f′, and g′ (they are, in fact, exactly the fingerings for f′, b′b, and c′ on the hautboy, and they work just as well) . . . [In addition,] written Bbs—absolutely required by music in the Casanatense MS, for instance, that was definitely played on shawms—correspond to Ebs on the hautboy . . . And this is before we take [*musica*] *ficta* into account.

The smaller tone-holes of the hautboy made cross-fingering effective, and it became an indispensable part of the instrument's technique and sound. As more and more

---

[52] Cross-fingering is defined in the Introduction.

tonalities came into use, cross-fingerings were regularly called for. On the hautboy, there was more difference in timbre between natural and cross-fingered notes than on the shawm because the tone-holes were smaller and because the hautboy lacked the shawm's long bell.[53]

3. The protomorphic hautboys

The 'Hautbois' that Lully began using in about 1657 incorporated some of the changes described above, but their outward appearance was not yet that of the hautboy in Blanchet's engraving of 1672 (Pl. 1.3). These transitional shawm/oboes were depicted by Charles Le Brun, painter to Louis XIV and director of the royal Academy of Painting and Sculpture. Le Brun designed two tapestries for the royal Gobelins workshops in 1664, 'L'Air' from the series *Les Élémens* and 'Le Printemps ou Versailles' from the series *Les Saisons*. The King may have seen these designs, as they were executed during the time he was regularly visiting Le Brun's studio.

Le Brun used the same border for the two tapestries, which consisted of trophies of many kinds of contemporary wind instruments, including nine Hautbois, presumably of the type current as of 1664.[54] The clearest surviving version of these borders is a tapestry known as the Gobelins 'L'Air', the first of several duplicates (*tentures*) of 'L'Air' (Pls. 1.5–7, 1.10–11). Some of the instruments in the borders are familiar, like the trumpets, drums, musettes, and recorders. The depictions are detailed and (to judge from the instruments already known) entirely accurate.[55]

There are two distinct forms of Hautbois in this border. One is black, with a long bell; the other is of a light-coloured wood—probably box—with a short bell. They correspond to the two types of Haut-bois that were in standard use in France by at least the 1630s,[56] as described by Mersenne in his chapter on the 'grands Haut-bois' (shawms):

Il faut remarquer qu'il y a deux sortes de Haut-bois qui sont en vsage en France, à sçavoir ceux de Poitou . . . et ceux que l'on appelle simplement Haut-bois . . .[57]	I should say that there are two types of Haut-bois in use in France, namely those of Poitou [the Haut-bois de Poitou] . . . and those that are called simply Haut-bois . . .

[53] Herbert W. Myers (pers. comm.). For a discussion of lower-bore resonances, see Smith (1992), 29 ff.

[54] Le Brun's original designs (cartoons) are now lost, but copies of them survive in several different media. Besides the Gobelins tapestries (six surviving *tentures* of 'L'Air' and three of 'Le Printemps'), watercolours on vellum exist (by Bailly, 1672), as well as engravings (by LeClerc, 1670 and 1679). The Gobelins 'L'Air' (made by the Lefebvre atelier in 1666–9; see Fenaille (1903), ii. 51–66) is at Florence in the Palazzo Pitti (formerly Siena: Palazzo Pubblico), and is called there *Allegoria dell'Aria*.

[55] It is noteworthy that both this border and the other tapestry that shows a protomorphic hautboy (Pl. 1.14) have Versailles, the royal residence, as their subject.   [56] I owe this insight to Marc Écochard.

[57] Mersenne (1636–7), 295.

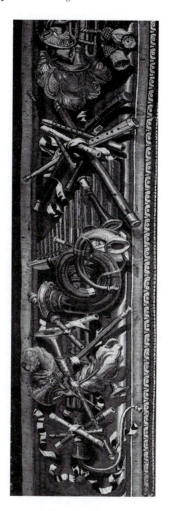

PL. 1.10. Gobelins 'L'Air', Panel H PL. 1.11. Gobelins 'L'Air', Panel A

The long-belled instruments resemble Mersenne's shawms (called simply Hautbois) and the short-belled ones look very much like his Haut-bois de Poitou
(see below, §B.2 and Pl. 1.12). We will call these new instruments *protomorphic
hautboys*.

The two types of protomorphic hautboy differ in acoustic length (AL), being
in a regular ratio of about 1:1.329, not very different from the length ratio of later
treble and tenor hautboys. We can assume, therefore, that the instruments with
short bells are pitched a fifth lower than those with long bells, and we will call the

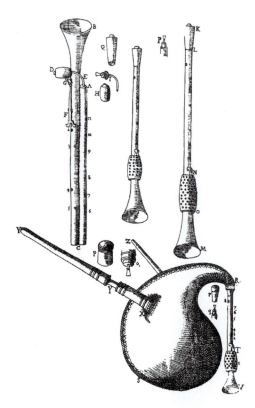

PL. 1.12. Mersenne (1635: 90) and (1636: 306), hautbois de Poitou

two types 'treble' and 'tenor'. Theoretically, absolute lengths might be deduced by comparing control instruments (cornetts and musettes), but the lengths of all these types of instrument are so inconsistent in the borders that no firm conclusions on their lengths can be drawn (if anything, they indicate that the treble hautboys were at A+1).

Both types of protomorphic hautboy represent a mixture of elements of shawm and hautboy as defined above (cf. Pl. 1.13). Traditional shawmlike elements are the fontanelle, the relatively long bell of the treble, and the largish tone-holes. Hautboy characteristics include:

- thinner side-walls
- complex turning on the upper part of the top joint (finial on the treble, finial and baluster on the tenor)
- separation to a new joint between the hands (the treble)
- a bell lip (apparently the treble only)

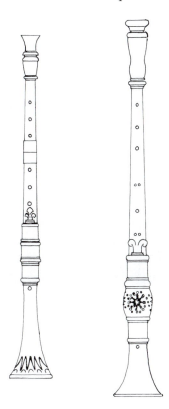

PL. 1.13. Schematic drawing by Marc Écochard of long-belled and short-belled protomorphic hautboys, based on the borders of the Gobelins tapestry 'L'Air' and Le Brun's cartoon
for the Gobelins tapestry *Les mois: avril ou le Château de Versailles* (Pl. 1.14)

- a Great-key on the treble (absent on the treble shawm)
- a bell shorter than the shawm
- a reed without pirouette (the tenor; no reeds—or pirouettes—are visible on the
  treble)
- twin holes for 4 (both types) and 6 (the tenor)

On both types, the tone-hole centre has been lowered; i.e. the six finger-holes have
descended longitudinally along the bore. Only a single pair of resonance-holes
appears to be present. Neither instrument yet has the Small-key, although the twin
sixth holes on the tenor would have produced the same note (Pls. 1.6–7, 1.10).

Somewhat later (1668–p1680), Le Brun designed another tapestry, *Les mois: avril
ou le Château de Versailles*, that portrays another protomorphic hautboy of the treble
type (Pl. 1.14). The instrument is leaning on a balustrade together with a cromorne.

PL. 1.14. Charles Le Brun, detail from cartoon (preparatory painting) for the Gobelins tapestry *Les mois: avril ou le Château de Versailles*, 1668–p1680. Musée National du Château de Versailles

It is interesting that it looks long enough to be a tenor. (The shawm player in Lairesse's painting on the shutter of the organ at the Westerkerk in Amsterdam (1685) is also holding a remarkably large instrument that could be a tenor (see Pl. 1.15).)

These two types of protomorphic hautboy can be seen in other pictures made in the decades between 1660 and 1680.[58] A clearly recognizable tenor-type short-belled model appears in a painting by Slingeland dated 1677 (Pl. 1.16).

4. *Surviving protomorphic hautboys from the 1650s and 1660s*

It would be surprising if many (indeed, any) of these protomorphic hautboys survived. Not only were they made relatively early, but they were used for less than a

---

[58] Both are shown in another Gobelins tapestry produced by Le Blond between 1701 and Jan. 1703 called 'L'air ou Junon', which may have borrowed its borders from the earlier examples. The tenor type is also shown in:

F. Cheveau, title-page to Lully's *Alceste* (engraving), 1674. Reproduced in *Concerto*, 120 (Feb. 1997), 15.

Etienne Gantrel (after Louis Le Roux), *Sainte Cécile concertant avec cinq anges*. Engraving. [2nd h. 17th c.]. F-Pn, Cabinet des Estampes. Reproduced in Mirimonde (1974), 117.

Title-page to Chambonnières's *Pièces de Clavessin*, pub. Jollain, Paris, 1670.

Anthony Leemans, *Stilleben mit Musikinstrumenten*, [? oil] painting, 1664. Nuremberg: Germ. Nationalmuseum (Gm 1215).

Cornelis Vermeulen, 'Allégorie de la musique', after Mignard (engraving), original Mignard *c.*1665. F-Pn, Cabinet des Estampes. Reproduced in Mirimonde (1975), i, fig. 19.

PL. 1.15. Gerard de Lairesse, player of shawm-hautboy hybrid,
on organ doors at the Westerkerk, Amsterdam, 1685. Oil painting on wood

PL. 1.16. Pieter Cornelisz van Slingeland, detail from *Violin
Player*, 1677. Oil, 23.5 × 19 cm. Schwerin: Staatliches Museum

generation, and were then superseded. It is unlikely that more than a few of them
were ever made (fewer than a dozen would have served the *Douze Grands Hautbois*).
One or both of the '2 hautboys, one old and the other in a different pitch'[59] that
Jacques Philidor left when he died in 1708 may have been relics from these days.

---

[59] '2 hautbois, dont l'un vieux et l'autre de ton différent'. Dufourcq and Benoit (1963), 195; Benoit and
Dufourcq (1966), 206.

Even if instruments currently survive from before 1670, our limited understanding of their physical attributes has as yet prevented us from recognizing them.[60]

Similarities between the treble protomorphic hautboy and the Schalmey, a form of shawm (the so-called 'deutsche Schalmey') suggest they are closely related if not identical.[61] More will probably be learned about these mid-century Hautbois by studying Schalmeys (over thirty of which survive).

5. *The makers of protomorphic hautboys*

At least five woodwind makers are known to have been at work in Paris in the mid-seventeenth century, all members of the Hotteterre family. Jean (Jehan) (3) Hotteterre ('père'; *c.*1605–90/2)[62] was a master turner at the time of his marriage in 1628, and was a 'Maître faiseur d'instr.' (that is, he probably ran his own workshop) by 1646. He was an active player, and a member of the *Hautbois et Musettes de Poitou* from 1650 and the twelve *Violons, Hautbois, Saqueboutes et Cornets* (also called the *Douze Grands Hautbois*) from 1664. Jean (3) Hotteterre's career spans the critical period between the appearance of Mersenne's books and the first documentation of the definitive hautboy. He was credited by his grandson Jacques (le Romain) as having improved the *bourdons* of the musette. By the 1670s he was highly regarded as an instrument maker. Borjon (1672: 38) wrote that he was

un homme unique pour la construction de toutes sortes d'instrumens de bois, d'yvoire et d'ebeine, comme sont les Musettes, flûtes, flageolets, haubois, cromornes; & mesme pour faire des accords parfaits de tous ces mêmes Instrumens.	unique as a maker of all kinds of wooden, ivory, and ebony instruments, such as musettes, flutes, flageolets, hautboys, and cromornes. He is also known for making such instruments perfectly in tune.

As the senior craftsman of the Hotteterre family at the time, Jean (3) Hotteterre was probably the principal maker responsible for the development of the hautboy. But according to Borjon, he had two sons who were also makers:

Ses fils ne luy cèdent en rien pour la pratique de cet art.	His sons are in no way inferior to him in the practice of this art.

Hotteterre's elder son Jean (8) died in 1667. The younger, Martin (*c.*1640–1712, later a celebrated player), was living and working with his father in 1658.

---

[60] Early surviving instruments are the Dupuis (Berlin 2933) and an instrument that was formerly at the Paris Conservatoire, depicted in Dufourcq (1946: 41), that resembles a treble protomorphic hautboy.

[61] See Ch. 3, §H and Haynes (2000).

[62] There were numerous members of the Hotteterre family with the same names (there are five 'Jean Hotteterres', for example). In ambiguous cases, I use the genealogical numbers in Waterhouse (1993), 182.

Jean's brother Nicolas (4; d. 1693) and his son Nicolas (10; b. about 1636, d. 1694) were also active makers. They opened their workshop about 1660 and by 1682 were settled in Versailles. An inventory at the death of the younger Nicolas (10) listed tools for making wind instruments such as recorders, flageolets, and bassoons.[63]

La Barre wrote that it was the 'Filidors' and 'Hautteterres' who had redesigned the hautbois. Of members of the Danican Philidor family, two could have been involved: Michel (the 'second Filidori') and (? his son) Jean (c.1620–79). No instruments with either name appear to survive.[64] It is of course possible that they worked with the Hotteterres as consultants rather than makers.

B. Related Instruments

Before discussing players and repertoire for the new hautboy, it will be useful to consider several other instrument types: the cromorne, the hautbois de Poitou, and the chalumeau simple. From our present historical vantage point, these now appear as separate instruments, but they were probably regarded in their own day as sub-divisions of the concept 'Hautbois'. Each of them seems to have contributed to the genesis of the instrument that eventually became the hautboy.

1. The cromorne

In the late seventeenth century, sources suggest that the instrument known in France as the 'cromorne' was of some importance.[65] Borjon wrote (1672: 33)

Les representations pastorales & champestres ne s'en sçauroient passer, & nous en voyons presque tous les ans dans les balets du Roy . . . Les haubois & les cromornes font aussi vn agreable effet avec les Musettes assemblées.

The pastoral and rustic entertainments cannot be performed without them, and we see them almost every year in the King's ballets . . . Hautboys and cromornes also provide a pleasant impression, together with the group of musettes.

In 1682, Menestrier said something similar:

On peut mêler aux violons les flageolets, les flutes, les musettes, les hautbois & les cromornes, pour fortifier certaines parties

To the violins, one can add flageolets, flutes, musettes, hautboys, and cromornes, in order to strengthen parts of dance

---

[63] Waterhouse (1993), 183.

[64] A 'Filidor' is listed in Du Pradel (1692) as 'Maître pour le Jeu et pour la Fabrique des Instruments à Vent' (cited in Waterhouse 1993: 301). This could have been Jacques Philidor, who left at his death in 1708 'outils servans à faire des instruments de simphonie' (Dufourcq and Benoit 1963: 195).

[65] This section is similar to Haynes (1997d) but adds several new elements discovered since then.

que l'on veut qui marquent davantage dans les mouvemens de la danse. On peut les interrompre & les mêler pour plus de varieté.[66]

movements that need to be more clearly emphasized. For variety, they can play intermittently, or mixed together.

The phrase 'les haubois & les cromornes' suggests a logical connection between these instruments, as if they might have played regularly together. Borjon (1672: 38) noted that Jean (3) Hotteterre also made cromornes. It would be worthwhile, therefore, to try to determine just what a cromorne was, what kind of music 'haubois & cromornes' would have played together, and what their respective functions would have been. For the moment this discussion remains speculative, awaiting the discovery of further evidence.

The cromorne's identity has been obscured because its name resembles that of the Renaissance instrument known in German as 'Krummhorn' and in English as 'crumhorn', a windcap instrument with a range of a ninth. As Boydell explains in his book on the crumhorn (1982: 193), it is clear that the cromorne was something else; Mersenne and Trichet called the crumhorn the 'tournebout', an instrument evidently never much used in France. It was just about the time that the tournebout became extinct that the French court ensemble known as the _Cromornes et Trompettes Marines_ was first established.[67]

Besides references to this ensemble, there were other regular allusions to the cromorne in France in the second half of the seventeenth century and throughout the eighteenth. Menestrier listed it, with the hautboy, in 1669: 169. Charpentier's _Messe pour plusieurs instruments au lieu des orgues_ (H513), written in 1674,[68] included a cromorne as well as two hautboys. The libretto of 1675 for Lully's opera _Thésée_ (IV, 7) mentioned two cromornes, which appeared on stage.[69] The _a 4_ episode in the 'Entrée des Zephirs' in Lully's _Atys_ (1676) was originally for five hautboys and three cromornes (range g0–g2).[70] The cromorne appeared briefly in Collasse's _Énée et Lavinie_ (1690: 115) in a march introducing Bacchus (III, 4), where it had its own line in the score.[71] In the only known complete listing of wind instrumentation for a Lully production (_Le Triomphe de l'amour_ of 1681), there are thirteen flutes, ten hautboys, two cromornes, one musette, and one bassoon (some individual players played as many as three of these instruments).[72] Cromornes may have played the

---

[66] Menestrier (1682), 205.

[67] Eppelsheim (1986), 71 n. 12 points out that for Diderot in 1780 and 1785 [_sic_] the terms 'Tournebout' and 'cromorne' were identical. But Diderot was writing well after the period of main use of either instrument, and was not aware of the continued existence of the _cromorne_ in his own day (Boydell 1982: 191).

[68] Thomas van Essen (pers. comm.).

[69] Eppelsheim (1961), 119 and Anhang 13; La Gorce (1989), table 2.

[70] 'Jouänts [_sic_] dans la Gloire', according to the original libretto, which Geoffrey Burgess (pers. comm.) informs me means they were in a stage machine. Eppelsheim (1961), 119; Anthony (1973), 95; Lemaître (1988–90), 101. There are other pieces with a two-octave range.   [71] In C1 clef with a range from bb0 to a1.

[72] La Gorce (1989), 109.

bass line, since there is only a single bassoon. Talbot (*c*.1692–5) listed a Bass Cromhorne but did not describe it.[73]

One of the cromorne players in *Le Triomphe de l'amour* was André Philidor (Philidor *l'aîné*, eldest son of Jean and intimate of Louis XIV), who seems to have had a particular association with the instrument. He was a member of the *Cromornes et Trompettes Marines* from *c*.1659 to 1680. Philidor was employed for a time as an *hautbois de la chapelle*, and in 1692 the Chapelle had an orchestra that included two bassoons and a basse de cromorne.[74] He also played basse de cromorne (in F4 clef) in his own *Mascarade du Roy de la Chine* produced in 1700, which included four tailles de hautbois and two bassoons.[75] Curiously, two dessus de hautbois ou cromorne (one of them being Philidor) and two bassoons were attached to the *Petits Violons*, or *Violons du Cabinet*, from 1690.[76]

The first illustration of an instrument categorically identified as a cromorne did not appear until relatively late, in Garsault 1761 (Pl. 1.17). Garsault's cromorne had a number of keys, mostly extensions to the reach of the hand (he wrote on p. 658 that the cromorne had previously been used as 'la contre-basse du Hautbois', and was 'six pieds de haut').[77]

The information given by Garsault makes it possible to go backwards chronologically and locate similar instruments. One is in Blanchet's engraving in Borjon 1672 (Pl. 1.3; cf. the large horizontal instrument at the player's feet);[78] Borjon mentioned the cromorne at least three times in his text.[79] With these two pictures as coordinates, it becomes possible to recognize two other relatively clear cromornes in Gobelins tapestries made in the 1660s. What is probably a bass appeared in the border of the Gobelins 'L'Air' (Pl. 1.5, designed in 1664; see above, §A.3).[80] The other is in Pl. 1.14 (1668–p1680), together with a protomorphic hautboy (that the two instruments are together confirms an association between them).

Less clear, but worthy of consideration as depictions of a set of cromornes being played, is Le Pautre's engraving of *La Pompeuse et Magnifique Cérémonie du sacre de Louis XIV* (1655, Pl. 1.18), which shows a band of twelve wind players, five of whom are holding vertical woodwinds with bocals; details are indistinct and no

---

[73] Boydell (1982), 185.

[74] Pierre (1899), 5–6. The cromorne was no longer present in 1718.

[75] Philidor's *Marche de Roy de la Chine* (25 in the Philidor Manuscript), which is for tailles de hautbois, may come from this work.   [76] Harris-Warrick and Marsh (1994), 7, 16, 16 n. 8, 72 n. 15, 73.

[77] Garsault also mentions the cromorne's bocal on p. 627.

[78] This one not the 'six pieds de haut' size. Blanchet's 'cromorne' has a length ratio of about 1.84 to his treble hautboy. The usual length ratio of a Taille to a treble is about 1.30 to 1.48.

[79] The connection between the pictures of Garsault and Blanchet, which is an important link in this deduction, was first noticed by Vincent Robin (1995).

[80] It is possible that a cromorne and a chalumeau simple are depicted in the lower right corner of Weigel's engraving of a woodwind maker (? Christoph Denner) in the *Abbildungen der gemein-nützlichen Haupt-Stände* (1698).

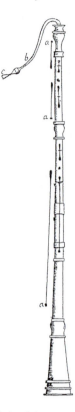

PL. 1.17. Garsault (1761), cromorne, pl. XXXVI, p. 660

keys are visible.[81] This *cérémonie* (coronation) took place at Rheims in 1654. A suite 'faitte . . . par M.r Degrignis pour les Cromornes l an [*sic*] 1660' (written by Mr Degrignis for cromornes in the year 1660), with a range of two octaves for the bass part, C to c1, is included in a volume copied by Philidor entitled *Recueil de plusieurs vieux Airs faits aux Sacres, Couronnements . . .* (Collection of several old airs written for coronations and crownings).[82] Members of the de Grigny family were well-known organists at Rheims in the seventeenth century. It is conceivable that this suite was copied as a souvenir of the coronation, at which it was played on the cromornes depicted in Le Pautre's engraving.

Since La Barre included the cromorne among the 'entiens istrumens' (see above), it was evidently in existence prior to the development of the new hautboy. It is not

[81] The band is discussed in Oldham (1961), 237. Jérémie Papasergio (pers. comm.) suggests that this group consists of the traditional formation of cornetts, shawms, sackbuts, and curtals; still, the bocals on some instruments (misplaced as they are) are an intriguing element.   [82] Boydell (1982), 183 and Eppelsheim (1986), 73 n. 35.

PL. 1.18. Jean Le Pautre, 'Les Trompettes, Tambours, Hautbois & Fifres', detail from *La Pompeuse et Magnifique Cérémonie du sacre de Louis XIV* (1654). 73.5 × 48.5 cm. F-Pn

mentioned by Mersenne or Praetorius, but Trichet wrote (*c*.1630–44) that organs imitated the sound of the cromorne.[83]

In Blanchet's picture, there is little to distinguish the hautboy from the cromorne beyond the reed crook, the extension keys, and the integral mounting rings these keys require (the keys were necessary to an instrument of this size). The cromorne is longer, and lacks a bell baluster. Its crook and extra keys suggest a deepish pitch, and cromornes may usually (although not always) have been considered low-sounding instruments.

As a working hypothesis, it is possible to imagine that various sizes of cromorne served as the original complements of the treble hautboy in double-reed ensembles until the larger hautboys and bassoon were developed. This idea is supported by the

---

[83] Boydell (1982), 190. One illustration in Virgiliano's manuscript *Il dolcimelo* (*c*.1600) shows two instruments ('Tonante' and 'Armilla') that resemble cromornes.

fact that neither the two Gobelins (1664 and a1668) nor Blanchet (1672) shows any bassoons together with hautboys, but all three include the apparent cromorne (see Pls. 1.5, 1.14, and 1.3). The royal *Cromornes et Trompettes Marines* had posts for *dessus*, *taille*, *quinte*, and *basse*,[84] which could have left, in five-part band music (which was the norm before 1670), a top part for the hautboy.[85]

The 1689 edition of *Atys* replaces at least one of the original cromornes of 1676 with a 'Taille de hautbois'.[86] We could conclude from this that the tenor hautboy was not yet developed by 1676, but had appeared by 1689, derived as a larger form of the treble hautboy.[87] In 1685 Richard Haka made up a bill for a 'franse tenor Haubois' along with four 'franse discant Haubois'.[88] Development of the tenor might have been delayed by the problem of finger-reach (which had been solved on the cromorne by the use of extension keys). Extension keys were a particularly useful solution for larger instruments, and in the 1680s the smaller sizes of cromorne may have atrophied as their functions were taken over by larger hautboys. But there is evidence suggesting that the basse de cromorne continued to flourish into the eighteenth century.[89]

It is unclear when the four-jointed, three-keyed bassoon with low B♭ extension first appeared.[90] Considering the change in pitch represented by the new hautboy, a criterion for determining a new model of bassoon would be its ability to play with the hautboy (that is, to play at its pitch, which it could only have done, presumably, by having been fundamentally redesigned in a manner analogous to the hautboy). Already in 1672, Borjon (33) writes of 'avoir des Musettes à l'octave l'une de l'autre, & d'y mesler quelques cromornes, flûtes & bassons' (having musettes an octave apart, and combining them with some cromornes, flutes, and bassons), indicating that the bassoon was capable of playing with these other instruments. Since bassoons played with cromornes and musettes, and hautboys did as well, hautboys and bassoons were probably able to play together by 1672, and thus the 'new model' bassoon would have been in existence by that date.

---

[84] An *haute-contre de cromorne* is never listed in court documents.

[85] This would have been a parallel combination to that of Praetorius' treble shawm and Pommers; he wrote (1618a: 37) that 'Allein der oberste Diskant, welcher keinen Missings Schlüissel hat/wird Schalmeye . . . genennet.'   [86] La Gorce (1989), 107.

[87] The title 'taille de hautbois' existed in the *Joueurs de violons, haultbois, sacquebouttes et cornets* long before this, in the days when shawms were still used. The name cannot therefore be used to determine when the newer type of Taille de hautbois began to be used. Cf. Ch. 6, §C.2.a.

[88] Haka (1685), kindly communicated by Jan Bouterse.

[89] Michael Finkelman (pers. comm.) draws a parallel here to the history of the sarrusophone, originally made in six sizes. 'These were in use for a single generation only, as band instruments, and then faded out, never to be seen again, with the exception of the contrabass, which survived another two full generations, both as a band and orchestral instrument.'

[90] There is clearly a problem with the attribution of the painting in the Museum of Art at Aachen (Harmen Hals, 1669 or before; see Kopp (1991), 109). It is not signed.

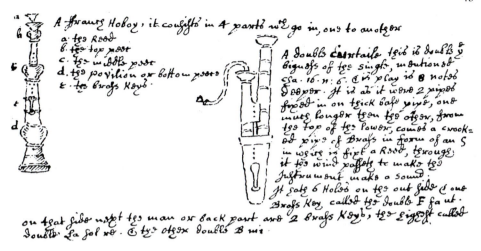

PL. 1.19. Randle Holme III, drawing in *Academy of Armory*, *c*.1688. GB-Lbl Harl. 2034f,
fo. 207b

In the 1680s, there are several references to bassoons that seem to have been of
the new type. The basson was mentioned by name in Lully's *Proserpine* (Prologue)
in 1680,[91] and regularly in his works thereafter. The bill that Haka wrote in 1685
included a four-piece 'franse dulsian Basson' along with the 'discant Haubois' and
'tenor Haubois'.[92] A French bassoonist, Maillard, was appointed at the Darmstadt
court in October 1686.[93] Holme in *c*.1688 (Pl. 1.19) shows the new model, though
without a separate bell. Talbot indicated that the French 'basson' was being played
in England by the early 1680s.

A marginal note on the manuscript score of an *Offerte pour l'orgue et pour les
violons, flûtes, et hautbois* by Charpentier (H514, ? early 1670s) instructs that the
bass line was to be reinforced by 'serpent, cromorne, and bassoon'.[94] Cromorne and
bassoon were thus separate entities, and apparently existed side by side, at least for
a time.[95]

All this suggests the possibility that early on it was the basse de cromorne that
served as a bass line for the hautboy rather than the bassoon. That is what Laborde
said, though he was writing a century later, in 1780:

[91] Eppelsheim (1961), 111–12. In the same work (II, 8) there are parts in F4 clef together with two upper
parts in G1 clef that are all labelled 'Hautbois'. Sandman (1974), 245 cites evidence that *Psyche* (1678) included
bassoon.   [92] Haka (1685).
[93] Noack (1967), 157. On Maillard, see Hodges (1980), 438 and Seifert (1987), 15, 23.
[94] Lewis (1964), 486.   [95] Garsault (1761), 658 also distinguished the cromorne from the bassoon.

[Le Basson] est denommé dans
l'Encyclopédie, *Basson de Hautbois*; c'est
vraisemblablement parce que cet
instrument aura été formé pour faire la
basse du Hautbois, lorsqu'on a cessé de
faire usage du Cromorne, qui était
l'ancienne basse du Hautbois.[96]

In the *Encyclopédie*, [the basson] is termed
Basson de Hautbois, probably because this
instrument was developed to act as the bass
for the hautboy, when the cromorne, which
had formerly been the hautboy's bass,
ceased to be played.

By 1705 when it was completed, the *Partition de plusieurs marches* or Philidor
Manuscript, a collection of music for hautboy band (see §C.3), nowhere calls for
cromornes. And in preparations for the coronation of Louis XV in 1722, cromornes
were not mentioned among the instruments to be used.[97] La Barre (? *c*.1740)
thought the cromorne had vanished long before. But François Philidor had a title
as player of bass cromorne in the Chapelle from 1708, and the inventory of the
Naust/Delerablée workshop made in 1734 lists 'un vieil model de Cromorne de six
pieds de haut'.[98] In 1731, the *Cromornes et Trompettes Marines* were called the 'Cinq
Cromornes'; by 1755 it appears that titles in that ensemble had become empty
sinecures owned by non-players.[99] If in 1761 the cromorne was considered a contrabass hautboy, as Garsault says, it may have continued to serve this specialist
function into the eighteenth century. That, and the possibility that the basse de
cromorne had provided the hautboy's bass until the development of the bassoon,
could explain why Brossard (1703) thought the cromorne and bassoon were the
same.[100]

A surviving 8-keyed 'Kontrabaß-Oboe' by Conrad Heise of Kassel, built early
in the eighteenth century to judge from the style of its keys,[101] uses the same principle of keywork as Blanchet's cromorne, with extensions to holes 1, 3, 4, and 6; to
half-close the third hole, Heise added another close-standing key. This particular
instrument shows signs of having been extensively used.[102] Although Bollioud de
Mermet mentioned it in 1746 (p. 35), Garsault classified the cromorne as 'hors
d'usage' in 1761, and Diderot (1751–72) thought it was no longer in existence.[103]
Despite this, Delusse made one in 1781 (called by then a 'Contre-Basse de
Hautbois') which closely resembles those of Heise and Garsault.[104] The differences
between these eighteenth-century examples and the cromornes shown in the
seventeenth-century sources are minor; the earlier instruments show full key rings,

---

[96] Laborde (1780), 323.   [97] Boydell (1982), 187.
[98] Giannini (1993b), 11.   [99] Boydell (1982), 189.
[100] This notion was repeated by Mattheson (1713), Majer (1732), Walther (1732), and Adlung (1758), each
writer probably quoting his predecessors.   [101] Heise was born in 1703 (cf. Waterhouse (1993), 170).
[102] Schmid (1994), 111.   [103] Boydell (1982), 191.
[104] Paris 459/E.150, illustrated in Young (1982), pl. XIII and Fleurot (1984), pl. XIIb. The close connection between Garsault and the Delusse instrument was detailed by Eppelsheim (1986: 64). See Schmid (1994),
105–7 and Robin (1995), 9–11. A further uncompleted contrabass oboe is preserved at Paris (Schmid 1994: 109).

which are reduced to bosses on the later ones, giving the instrument a more stream-lined look.

What may represent a late eighteenth-century holdover of the French cromorne are some twenty-five specimens of the trompette d'église (also called in modern times the 'basse de musette') that survive in the Protestant western part of Switzerland.[105] Trompettes d'église resemble the cromorne in the Blanchet plate in the long bocal projecting from the top, the pirouette at the upper end, and the use of keys to close holes 1, 3, 4, 6, and 8 (only two examples of a smaller size lack the upper keys).[106] These instruments were used to accompany village church congregations in psalm-singing; they were probably made and used by Huguenots who had left France after the revocation of the Edict of Nantes, and their descendants. Many Huguenots had lived in Poitou, which in the early seventeenth century had been a centre of woodwind making.[107]

The trompette d'église may in any case offer clues as to the nature of cromornes; compared with the hautboy, the instrument is relatively conical and has thin walls. A description of its sound survives from 1781, which qualifies it as 'très aigu . . . insupportable' (very sharp . . . unbearable).[108] Its name also implies that it was comparatively loud. This may have been true of the cromorne as well, which evidently used a pirouette.[109] The possibility that it produced a strong and direct sound could explain why the cromorne was eventually replaced by the tenor hautboy and bassoon.

2. Detached bagpipe chanters: the hautbois de Poitou and the chalumeau simple

When they practise, bagpipers often play the chanter separated from the bag. When a player detached the chanter (the chalumeau) from the musette de Poitou, he created the hautbois de Poitou (or common mouth-blown bagpipe;[110] see Pl. 1.12). Mersenne described and depicted three sizes of hautbois de Poitou. The hautbois de Poitou had a straight-sided cap that tapered inward towards its base, a Great-key, and a fontanelle. In folk music, there is a long tradition of combining a shawmlike

---

[105] See Staehelin (1970) and Waterhouse (1993), 193. Alain Girard (pers. comm.) has located further instruments with the 'I · IR' mark.

[106] Staehelin (1970), Abb. 8 and Tabelle 3. An extant instrument in Brussels (depicted in Gétreau 1984: 542) that might be a small *trompette d'église* resembles very convincingly Watteau's oil *L'amour au théâtre françois* (c.1712, reproduced in Grasselli and Rosenberg (1984), 337). Alain Girard (pers. comm.) points out that instruments with the 'I · IR' mark now in Basle and Berne are also very similar. An hautboy by Lutringer (Private coll., Vancouver [ex Kraus]) resembles in its turning a small *trompette d'église*, and the Rouge (DCM 423) also shows similarities.   [107] Pierre (1893), 414.

[108] Staehelin (1970), 111.

[109] But with a range of two octaves, the embouchure must have partially controlled the reed.

[110] The words 'musette' and 'cornemuse' are used interchangeably in French. In the 18th c., the term 'musette' always referred to an instrument with a bag (the late 19th-c. term 'musette' was an aberration). For advice on this and other questions about these instruments, my thanks to the Belgian musette player Jean-Pierre van Hees.

PL. 1.20. Mersenne (1636: 289), 'chalumeau simple'

instrument with a bagpipe,[111] and this is indeed how the musette de Poitou and the hautbois de Poitou were played, the musette de Poitou doubling the treble line and giving support with its drones.[112]

The hautbois de Poitou had a conical bore like the shawm and hautboy. As I shall discuss below, the windcap was not always used, and when it was not, this instrument was (as Mersenne wrote) essentially a small hautboy.[113]

The chanter of another kind of bagpipe, the bellows-blown musette de cour, was also played without its bag, as can be seen, for example, in a plate in Borjon's book (1672: 22; Pl. 1.8). The plate is labelled 'Chalumeau simple'. This detached *chalumeau simple* is also included among the instruments in the frontispiece by Blanchet (Pl. 1.3), and Mersenne shows one in his chapter on the musette (Pl. 1.20).[114] A painting by Pater called *La Danse* (Pl. 1.21) shows the top of an

---

[111] Cf. the Breton traditional ensemble of 'bombarde' and 'biniou', still heard today.

[112] In 1661 there were two players of *dessus de haulbois de Poictou* (François Descoteaux and Jean [3] Hotteterre) at court, and two others of *dessus de muzette de Poictou* (the two Brunets). Benoit (1971b), 4.

[113] Furetière (1690), s.v. 'Hautbois', probably paraphrasing from a copy of Mersenne, wrote: 'Les *hautsbois* [*sic*] de Poitou sont de même figure [que les Hautbois], & ne different des grands *hautsbois* qu'en longueur, & en la disposition de leurs trous & de leurs boëtes.'

[114] Mersenne's description of the hautbois de Poitou is more thorough in 1636 than 1635, whereas his description of the chalumeau simple of the musette is better in 1635: 94 than in 1636 (Book 5, Proposition XXVIII).

PL. 1.21. Jean-Baptiste-François Pater, detail from *La Danse*, oil, by 1736. Reproduced by permission of the Trustees of the Wallace Collection, London

hautboy that strongly resembles a chalumeau simple, but it is clearly being played with a reed that projects out of the top of the 'cap'. Played separately, the chanter of the musette differed in several ways from the hautbois de Poitou. Its bore was cylindrical rather than conical, its cap had a characteristic turning consisting of two bulbs joined by a column, it had a key for the left thumb that entered the cap, and it had no fontanelle.

An instrument in the Gobelins 'L'Air' border with its top facing left (Pl. 1.10) looks like a composite of the hautbois de Poitou and the chalumeau simple, since it has a key for the right little finger with a fontanelle, typical of the hautbois de Poitou (and which is not otherwise seen on the chalumeau simple).[115] On the other hand, this instrument also shows the cap with bulbs that is characteristic of the chalumeau simple, and a key is visible for the left thumb. A possible hautbois de Poitou is seen crossing this one, and has its top facing right. It has a fontanelle as well as a formation at the top that could be a tapered cap.

Mersenne stated (1636: 307) that the ranges of the three sizes of hautbois de Poitou were identical to those of the shawm family, which he gave as two octaves. As Écochard noticed,[116] there is a discrepancy here, since capped reeds overblow

---

[115] Cf. Borjon (1672), Hotteterre (1737).   [116] Écochard (1997).

less than two octaves.[117] The only way the hautbois de Poitou could have matched the range of the shawm was with direct lip control by pinching and blowing harder; it is possible that this is what Mersenne had in mind. Trichet had documented the use of direct lip control on the chalumeau simple of the musette as early as the 1630s. He wrote:

Si l'on veut sonner séparément le chalumeau on le peut faire en deux façons, l'une en mettant l'anche dans la bouche, l'autre en la mettant dans une boëte faicte expressément en queue de lampe et percée au bout pour insinuer le vent par cet endroit.[118]	If a player wishes to use the chanter separately, there are two ways it can be done. One is to put the reed in one's mouth, the other is to put it in a windcap made for it, in the form of a lamp base, with a hole in the top to blow through.

Mersenne wrote that bagpipe chanters played 'embouchez' (that is, with the reed in the mouth)

ont beaucoup plus de grace & de vigueur . . . que quand ils tiennent à la peau, parce que l'on articule leurs sons par le moyen de la langue, . . . ce qui ne peut se faire auec le vent du soufflet, ou de la peau . . .[119]	are more graceful and full of life . . . compared with when they are attached to the bag. This is because their notes are articulated with the tongue, . . . which is not possible when they are played with air from the bellows, or the bag . . .

Mersenne compared the effect of the bagpipe chalumeau played directly with the mouth to 'speaking':

. . . c'est à dire en remuant la langue comme si l'on parloit . . . ce qui rend le son de cet instrument beaucoup plus agréable, plus esveillé et plus vigoureux.[120]	. . . that is, by moving the tongue as if speaking . . . which makes the sound of this instrument much more pleasant, more alive, and more energetic.

Mersenne implied here that professional players would actually have preferred playing on the separate chanter for its musical advantages. In 1635 he noted that to play the capped chanter of the musette was 'frequentantur', or common.[121] He also mentioned 'the royal wind player Destouches', who preferred the detached chalumeau simple 'above all other wind instruments'.[122] The player in question was probably Jean Herbinot dit Destouches, who played in the *Hautbois et Musettes de*

---

[117] With a conical bore and the right reed, a Renaissance-type cornemuse can overblow an octave and a fourth (Jean-Pierre van Hees, pers. comm.).   [118] Lesure (1955), 374.
[119] Mersenne (1636), 289.   [120] Ibid. 285, cited in Écochard (1997).
[121] 1635, Proposition XIII, p. 94.
[122] 'Tibicine Regio *des Touches* inflatum reliquis instrumentis . . .'. Original Latin text and translation in Boydell (1982), 352.

Poitou from at least 1629 to 1661.[123] Mersenne said of him in 1636 that he played the musette 'à la perfection'.

How much the hautbois de Poitou and the chalumeau simple were played is difficult to determine. Considering the generic meaning of the word 'hautbois', it is quite possible that it was sometimes used in the seventeenth century to mean one of these two bagpipe chanters. A capped instrument with its protected reed would lend itself particularly to the regular appearances of woodwind players on stage.[124] And since it was also sometimes played uncapped, the compass of 'hautbois' parts in Lully's early works would not tell us which instrument was employed. In any case, in the experimental atmosphere of the time, it seems clear that (like skateboards and rollerblades today) the abilities of these instruments had a mutual influence on each other, borrowing and lending techniques back and forth. As they developed in new ways, they helped focus the concept of an instrument that eventually crystallized into the hautboy.

C. Hautboy Players at the French Court *and the* Grande Écurie

Music at the French court was divided into three sections: the *Chambre*, the *Chapelle*, and the *Grande et la Petite Écurie*. Most court hautboy players were employed by the *Écurie* (or royal Equerry) and were lent to the *Chambre* and *Chapelle* when needed. The *Écurie* was responsible for the music for all solemnities and occasions at the court that were not religious or private. The *Écurie* itself was further subdivided into categories, and the four groups that employed hautboy players were the *Violons, Hautbois, Saqueboutes et Cornets*, the *Hautbois et Musettes de Poitou*, the *Fifres et Tambours*, and the *Cromornes et Trompettes Marines*.

Of these groups, the only ones whose activities were documented in Louis XIII's period (1613–43) were the *Violons, Hautbois, Saqueboutes et Cornets* and the *Hautbois et Musettes de Poitou*. It seems therefore possible that as a shawm band, the *Violons, Hautbois, Saqueboutes et Cornets* was originally more active than it later became, providing all the loud ceremonial music, and that the *Hautbois et Musettes de Poitou* was already considered a chamber group by this time.

At any given moment from the mid-seventeenth to the late eighteenth century, the French court had thirty-five posts for woodwind players. If, as seems likely, they played principally hautboy and bassoon, this number is higher than any other

---

[123] His title was 'taille de haulbois et basseconte de muzette de Poictou' in 1661. This player could also have been Jehan Destouches (fl. a1620, d. 1645).

[124] See Harris-Warrick and Marsh (1994), 8.

establishment in Europe—many courts managed with two or three hautboy players and one or two bassoonists. In addition, four woodwind players were attached to the *Petits Violons*, or *Violons du Cabinet*, from 1690.[125] Some of these positions did not pay enough to live on, however, even with the many payments 'in kind' in the form of food, clothing, etc.;[126] making a living depended on how active at court a musician was. But the court title provided prestige that allowed musicians to perform, teach, and/or publish in Paris, activities which gave many of them their main source of income.[127] Some players held more than one title at a time, and some titles did not require regular presence at court. Still, it is unlikely that any other court, city, or abbey, even those with hautboy bands, employed so many hautboy players on a regular basis.

There are records of at least 198 players officially employed by the French court from the 1640s to the 1760s. The remarkable quantity of woodwind playing there makes it easier to understand why woodwind technique and the making of woodwind instruments have been associated with France for centuries, and continue to be so now.

The major problem in studying the musical activities of the royal *Écurie* is to determine what instruments were being played by which musicians. There are several issues. First, the players were normally doublers, switching from drum to bassoon to violin according to need, and the French attitude towards instrumentation was purposely ambiguous (as epitomized by the concept 'en symphonie'— see Ch. 3, §G.1). Secondly, the fanciful appellations of groups like the *Joueurs de Violons, Haultbois, Sacquebouttes et Cornets* and *Cromornes et Trompettes Marines* may after about 1660 have become official titles without literal meaning; in some cases we know the titles were fictive (see below). On the face of it, an independent ensemble made up of various sizes of cromornes together with one-string marine trumpets is an absurdity, for example, and there is obviously some element we have yet to discover.

The individual royal musicians were of two types: *officiers* (those with a *charge*, or official post), and *ordinaires* (the others).[128] In a reflection of the fact that kings occupied their positions by virtue of inheritance, it was usual for a son to inherit his father's *charge* at court, in music as well as other callings within the royal service.[129] It was this custom that encouraged the virtual dynasties of court musicians. Players (or others) could accumulate *charges* as a kind of investment, and they could be sold to the highest bidder.[130] The procedure by which *charges* were transferred was known as *survivance* (or reversion). The successor to a *charge* who was not already a member of an established family had to purchase it (at a very high price) from his

---

[125] Cf. above, §B.1.   [126] Cf. Benoit (1971a), 174.   [127] House (1991), 27.
[128] Morby (1971), 85 ff.   [129] Cf. House (1991), 27.   [130] Cf. Benoit (1971b), 372.

predecessor, or *titulaire*. *Survivanciers*, or heirs (often underage sons of *titulaires*) were frequently designated years in advance of an actual change of players, and from payment records it is sometimes unclear which specific musician was actually performing. Nor were the musical abilities of a *survivancier* guaranteed; many were well trained by family members, but others may have had to hire substitutes to execute their official functions. This seems often to have been the case after the passing of Louis XIV in 1715, when official titles were no longer necessarily related to actual functions. A striking example of this was the exchange in 1733 between Antoine Forqueray and Jean Louis de Bury: Forqueray took Bury's place as 'singer' in the Chamber, while Bury took Forqueray's place as 'flutist'. In fact Bury was a harpsichordist and Forqueray a gambist.[131] The *État de la France* in 1722 stated that Chapel singers were listed according to posts they had bought or were given, which might be quite different from their real functions. Some singers in the Chapel held two different voice posts simultaneously.

The system of *charges* was officially abolished as part of the reforms of 1761 (which also amalgamated the *Chapelle* and *Chambre*).[132] But things had altered long before this. On the basis of the documents he studied, Écorcheville wrote:

En 1690, la musique-écurie du roi est un organisme déja vieux qui devient caduque à partir de la régence. De 43 musiciens, il n'y en a guère que 6 ou 8 qui servent effectivement; les autres font de rares apparitions à la cour . . .[133]	The *Écurie* was already an old institution in the 1690s, and by the start of the Regency [1715], it was obsolete. Of its forty-three musicians, scarcely six to eight actually played regularly, the others making only rare appearances at court . . .

Documentation for the *Chambre* is sketchy compared with that for the *Écurie*. In the Baroque period 'chamber music' did not normally mean smaller ensembles, as it does now, but rather instrumental music. And indeed, the *Chambre* was large: it included both the *Petits Violons* and the *Grande Bande*. Wind players attached to the *Chambre* may have played primarily orchestral music as well as (or instead of) solos, trios, and quartets. From 1690 the *Petits Violons* included André Philidor and Philippe Desjardins as 'Dessus de hautbois ou cromorne'.[134] Later Colin Hotteterre, Pierre Philidor, and Jean-François Coutant all had posts in the *Chambre*.[135] Ford suggests that hautboys were part of the *Chambre* in the 1680s as well, deducing their presence through the titles of pieces in Dieupart's MS of 1680 (described in Ch. 3, §A) that call for winds.

---

[131] Benoit (1971a), 130; Morby (1971), 98.
[132] Morby (1971), 92, 98, 90.   [133] Écorcheville (1903), 641.
[134] Ford (1981), 60 citing *l'Etat de la France* (1692), i. 227.
[135] Benoit (1971b), 394; Benoit (1971a), 221; Machard (1971), 46.

There was regular intermixing among the various court groups. The *Vingt-quatre Violons de la Chambre*

se rencontrent essentiellement aux bals du roi, où ils se mêlent à la famille des hautbois; mais ils participent aussi aux ballets, divertissements, et viennent grossir les rangs des symphonistes de l'Opéra, lors de certains spectacles montés pour la Cour.[136]

met principally for the king's balls, where they were combined with the hautboy family; but they also took part in ballets, divertissements, and augmented the ranks of the *Opéra* orchestra for certain productions organized for the court.

Cette participation aux fêtes de la Cour les mêle constamment à leurs collègues de la Chambre et de la Chapelle, en des offices religieux ou des spectacles profanes, de théâtre, de plein air.[137]

This participation in courtly festivities constantly combined [the musicians of the *Écurie*] with their colleagues in the *Chambre* and *Chapelle*, in religious services and secular presentations in the theatre and out of doors.

Considering the vagueness of terminology at the time and the kind of evidence available, it is clear that some of the 'hautboy players' listed in court documents were bassoonists, drummers, or players of the recorder, traverso, or musette. But (with the possible exception of the traverso and musette players) it is likely that most or all of them played all these instruments, since the concept of a specialist who played only the hautboy did not exist.

1. The Violons, Hautbois, Saqueboutes et Cornets *(also called the* Douze Grands Hautbois*)*

By Louis XIV's day, the *Violons, Hautbois, Saqueboutes et Cornets* (from the 1730s, officially called the *Douze Grands Hautbois*) probably limited themselves to double reeds. In 1727 a document noted that the *Violons, Hautbois, Saqueboutes et Cornets* 'ne jouaient plus que du hautbois et du basson' (no longer played anything but hautboy and bassoon).[138] L'Etat of 1736 noted that formerly they played violin 'when it was requested, or shawm, sackbut, and cornett', but 'now they no longer play anything but hautboy and bassoon'.[139] This group appears to have had the highest status among the hautboys at court, although it had only three fixed duties per year plus extraordinary events.[140] The players were thus seldom present at court, unless they played in other royal ensembles. There were two dozen players who had appointments in the period 1640–70; they (like the other members of the *Écurie*) are listed in Appendix 1.

---

[136] Benoit (1971a), 207.   [137] Ibid. 222.
[138] Ibid. 221.   [139] Quoted in Machard (1971), 18.
[140] A contemporary description of the job of 'Grand Hautbois' is reproduced in Benoit (1971b), 453–4.

2. *The* Hautbois et Musettes de Poitou

In his *Paralèle des italiens et des françois* (1702), Raguenet singled out Philbert, Philidor, Descoteaux, and the Hotteterres as special virtuosos on woodwinds. With the exception of Philidor, these were members of the *Hautbois et Musettes de Poitou*, an ensemble that dated back to the beginning of the seventeenth century.[141] Everything indicates that this group was an exceptional one among those of the *Écurie*, using special instruments and performing a different kind of music. Benoit suggests that in the eighteenth century at least, its members played hautboys and musettes, despite their titles. From 1661, however, certain players were associated with the recorder (the Brunets, the Pièches, the Descoteaux,[142] Hotteterre) and traverso (Philbert, René Descoteaux, Hotteterre le Romain[143]), and it is probable that the group regularly performed on these instruments.[144] In 1708, a document called it the 'Six Hautbois, Musettes et Flutes de la Chambre et grande Escurie'.[145] Of a total of thirty-eight players in the ensemble's history, only seven are known to have been hautboy players, while five were associated with the 'flute' and four with the musette. These instruments, and the small size of the ensemble, suggest its main purpose was to perform indoor music; members are survived by a considerable body of chamber music, at least part of which probably formed its repertoire. It may be significant that whereas there was a certain permeability between the various ensembles of the *Écurie* that involved hautboys, several well-known members of the *Hautbois et Musettes de Poitou* played in no other groups, and that no Philidors or Desjardins were ever members of the ensemble. Its musicians were also employed in 'grands divertissemens', in the Chapelle, and in smaller locales like the *Appartemens* and *Cabinet du roi*. Some of them performed in operas produced at court, especially in the 1650s and 1660s, suggesting the ensemble played at the lower pitch appropriate for singers.[146]

These players organized concerts outside the court as well. In 1658 six of the then seven members of the 'haultbois et musettes du roy', Jean (3) Hotteterre, Jean Brunet, François Descoteaux, Pierre Pièche, Martin Hotteterre, and Michel Destouches, formed an ensemble to perform in Paris.[147]

3. *The* Fifres et Tambours

In Louis XIV's time, the *Fifres et Tambours* consisted of four 'fifres' and four 'tambours;' in 1731 there were still eight members. But as early as 1667 a note made

---

[141] Benoit (1971a), 223, citing Thoinan and Mauger (1894).
[142] Both François and René Descoteaux had the separate title of 'Joueur de flûte et de hautbois'.
[143] He had the added title 'Joueur de flûte'.
[144] Écorcheville (1903: 640) noticed 'Les musettes de l'écurie avaient une préférence pour la flûte'.
[145] Benoit (1971a), 224–5.   [146] Haynes (1995), §§4-4 to 4-6.   [147] Lesure (1955), 83.

PL. 1.22. Nicolas Henri Tardieu, detail from 'Le festin Royal'; fifth Tableau in the series *Le Sacre de Louis XV*, soon after 25 Oct. 1722. Paris: Louvre, Cabinet des Dessins (26.324)

against Danican's name indicates that the musicians whose titles were 'fifre' actually played hautboy: 'Jean Danican, fifre (Il joue du dessus de haultbois . . .)'. In 1697 the *Fifres et Tambours* was described as 'Les 4 fifres présentement hautbois', and in 1712, 'Les 4 fifres ou plutôt hautbois de la chambre'.[148] It is likely these musicians played all kinds of woodwinds, although principally hautboy. The *Fifres et Tambours* were the King's most active hautboy ensemble; they were the group responsible for the daily secular ceremonies at court.[149]

At least part of the repertoire of the *Fifres et Tambours* is preserved in the Philidor Manuscript (*Partition de plusieurs marches*, F-Pn Rés. F.671), an important source of French hautboy band music.[150] The manuscript contains ninety-one short marches, airs, solo drum marches, trumpet fanfares, sets of hunting calls, and a *Carousel*. It is mostly in four parts with accompanying 'Batterie de tambour' or drum-beat. Although the Philidor Manuscript was finished in 1705, it is a compilation of pieces used for military and court ceremonies that were composed from 1670 or even earlier, and includes many compositions by Lully and André Philidor, as well as (among others) Martin Hotteterre, Lalande, and Philippe Hannès Desjardins.[151]

---

[148] Écorcheville (1903), 617 n. 1. The Philidor Manuscript sometimes distinguishes fifres and hautbois (Sandman 1974: 215 ff.), however, suggesting that fifres were still in use.   [149] Benoit (1971a), 226.

[150] The manuscript is tabulated, transcribed, and studied in Sandman (1974).

[151] The Hannès Desjardins family included ten hautboy players who served the court from *c.*1669 to 1781. The family was generally associated with the more military court ensembles: the *Mousquetaires*, the *Fifres et Tambours*, and the *Grands Hautbois*.

It was copied under the supervision of André Philidor. Philidor, mentioned above as a cromorne player, was the compiler of the famous multi-volume 'Philidor Collection'. This collection contains most of the surviving music of 'l'école classique française'.[152] In his position as Garde de la Bibliothèque de la Musique, Philidor employed numerous copyists in the 'ateliers Philidor', and was responsible for supplying all the musical material used at court.[153]

According to Sandman (1974: 71), Rés. F.671 was the main repertory of the *Fifres et Tambours*, but it also includes pieces for the *Mousquetaires*, the *Garde Marine*, the *Régiment du Roy*, the *Dragons du Roy*, the *Fussilliers*, and other military formations.[154]

The *Fifres et Tambours* had many duties, including escorting flags, accompanying the King on voyages, playing for large festivities, court readings and proclamations, religious ceremonies, and indoor concerts and stage works.[155] The group was officially 'de la chambre et Grande Écurie', which explains why it was occasionally classified as part of the *Chambre*.[156]

4. *The* Cromornes et Trompettes Marines

As we have seen, the *cromorne* was a kind of hautboy, and among the members of the *Cromornes et Trompettes Marines* were well-known hautboy players.[157] There is no record of members prior to 1661, although Boydell (1982: 184) claims the group existed by 1651. Officially, it was given court title on 17 May 1668.[158] When the other ensembles of the royal *Écurie* are mentioned, this group is occasionally left out, and the budget for their livery was less than other musicians, suggesting it was the least important group. It functioned at balls, ballets, plays, and chamber music as needed.

5. *The* Mousquetaires, *or* Plaisirs du roi

Another hautboy ensemble that was not part of the *Écurie*, though it served the court, was the *Mousquetaires*, also called the *Plaisirs du roi*. Originally military, it had participated in battle campaigns until 1683, when by royal edict hautboys were no longer used in military engagements. There is no record of members prior to 1679, but the regiment was created in 1657.[159] Lully's 'Premiere Marche des Mousquetaires' (Sandman 6/M1, LWV 10) was written for them in 1658; it is the

---

[152] For a portrait of Philidor, see *New Grove* xiv. 626.

[153] Philidor retired from this post in 1729, which reverted to his son-in-law, the hautboy player Schwartzenberg 'dit Le Noble'.   [154] Cf. table 1 in Sandman (1974), 10 ff.

[155] Ibid. 93 ff.   [156] Their duties are reported in detail in Écorcheville (1903), 617.

[157] Plumet, Aubry, Ballois, Bernier, François Desjardins, Dieupart, André Philidor, Jacques Philidor, Jean Philidor, and Royer.   [158] Boydell (1982), 184, 187.

[159] Sandman (1974), 86.

first of a set of marches for four hautboys and drum in the Philidor Manuscript.[160]
The *Mousquetaires* were divided into two groups, each with six drums and four
hautboys; occasionally the two groups would play together. They evidently had a
favoured position; they had adopted the (protomorphic) hautboy by 1663 (using
it even in battle situations). Lully wrote his '9 Trios' for the ensemble in 1667.
This company was the only military one that did not have trumpets or military
drums (the drums they used were smaller and 'beaucoup plus gaïe').[161] They were
frequently heard: they played at 'divertissements, comédies, fêtes sur le canal,
bals . . .', the latter being their principal function. The *Mousquetaires* doubled on
violins, and sometimes substituted for the *Violons du Roy* when the latter were
busy elsewhere.[162]

D. *The Development of the New Hautboy, 1664–1670*

The makers discussed above (Jean (3), Martin, Nicolas (4), and Nicolas (10)
Hotteterre, and possibly Jean Philidor) were closely involved with about two dozen
hautbois players active at court and in the city of Paris in the critical decades of the
1650s and 1660s when the instrument was undergoing major changes. Some or all
of these players would have been involved in the experiments, acting as consultants
(or guinea pigs). There are indications that there was one year that was critical in
this process: 1664. In this year, exactly half (6) of the veteran players of the *Violons,
Hautbois, Saqueboutes et Cornets* left the group; the same year also saw five members
of the *Cromornes et Trompettes Marines* leave service. It is the year Le Brun produced the design for the borders of the Gobelins tapestries showing the two types
of protomorphic hautboy. It was in this year that the earliest of Lully's *Trios de
la chambre* (LWV 35) was written. It was also the year Jean (3) Hotteterre began
service in the *Violons, Hautbois, Saqueboutes et Cornets*.

The year 1664 is remarkable for two other reasons. After the production of *Les
Plaisirs de l'isle enchantée* in May, Lully seems to have stopped using hautboys in his
dramatic productions for several years. Between 1664 and 1670 he produced fourteen large-scale ballets and comédie-ballets. Some of these productions called for
'flûtes', but none seems to have involved the hautboy.[163] We do not in fact hear of
the instrument again until the production of *Le Bourgeois Gentilhomme* (1670). The

---

[160] Sandman (1974), 87. Kastner (1848: 4) cites this Air as an early version of the 'fameuse marche des
Mousquetaires du Roi de France, appelée aussi Marche du Roi, dont Rousseau a parlé dans son Dictionnaire de
Musique sans paraître soupçonner quel en était l'auteur'. Kastner reports various minor changes over time, and
gives two other versions. It was cited also in Brenet (1917), 349.   [161] Benoit (1971a), 236.

[162] The last known position in the *Mousquetaires* was closed in 1736 (François-Sappey 1988–90: 158).

[163] Hitchcock (1990) does not list any works by Charpentier that include the hautboy written before the 1670s.

fragmentary state of surviving Lully sources makes it difficult to draw definite conclusions on this basis alone, but the regular mention of 'hautbois' again after 1670 (now in four rather than five parts) suggests that the instrument had been purposely omitted from court performances for these six years.

Whether a new model, the definitive hautboy first shown in Blanchet's engraving of 1672, had appeared by 1664 and players were learning to use it, or whether it was being developed in the years following the performance of *Les Plaisirs de l'isle enchantée*, Lully seems deliberately to have allowed his wind players a grace period, in which they were given a chance to work on the design of the new instrument and the technique of playing it.

1664 was also the year Lully first began working with the *Grande Bande* (the *Vingt-quatre Violons*) and was thus able to mount large productions that used all the King's musicians together.[164] It is possible that it was this development that precipitated the process of redesigning the hautboy, because it is fairly certain that the *Vingt-quatre* were already at A−2, whereas the *Petits Violons* (Lully's ensemble up to that point) were apparently still at the old traditional A+1 indicated by Mersenne's illustrations of instruments.[165] Thus the protomorphic hautboy at A+1 had at this point to be lowered to A−2, so that all those changes described above in §A.2 (not already consolidated on the treble protomorphic hautboy) followed naturally.

During this period Lully wrote the first of his *Trios de la chambre* (LWV 35), an anthology of fifty-four movements.[166] Some (perhaps all) of this music was written for hautboys; the first nine pieces, the '9 Trios' (single movements), were written for the *Mousquetaires* in 1667 for performance out of doors at Fontainebleau,[167] and may have been demonstration pieces for the new design of hautboy.[168] The other pieces are for the most part simple dances in which the two *dessus* parts play the same rhythms, frequently crossing each other's lines. They may have been among the first repertoire of the new instrument. There are also a number of excerpts from vocal works with titles like 'Où êtes vous allé?' and 'La jeune Iris'[169] that were probably well known at the time. Some of them are fairly good, particularly those at the end, and suites could have been assembled by selecting movements. The movements are in no particular order, and in various keys. They are intermixed with movements from Marais's *Pièces en trio* and *Pièces de violes* (which are of noticeably

---

[164] See Anthony (1973), 285.

[165] This is based on the keys of the music to Cavalli's opera *Ercole amante* and the instrumental ballets or *entr'actes* by Lully interspersed in the opera (see Haynes forthcoming, 2–5d).

[166] F-Pn Rés. 1397, copied out after Lully's death by André Philidor. It is published by Heugel as *Trios pour le Coucher du Roy*, ed. Herbert Schneider. Cf. Anthony (1988).   [167] Hugo Reyne (pers. comm.).

[168] Like the majority of French chamber works that followed, this collection was written 'en symphonie', for generic treble and bass instruments. The 'en symphonie' concept is discussed in Ch. 3, §G.1.

[169] Some of these are found in other collections of Lully's dramatic works arranged for instruments.

better quality). The bass is unfigured, but the Marais basses are figured in his edition of 1692, suggesting they were originally played with realizations.

By 1668, the Abbé de Pure may have been describing the new developments when he wrote

Les Haut-bois ont un chant plus élevé, & de la maniere dont on en Joüe maintenant chez le Roy, & à Paris, il y auroit peu de choses a en desirer. Il font les cadences aussi Justes, les tremblements aussi doux, & les diminutions aussi regulieres que les voix les mieux instruites, & que les instruments les plus parfaits. Nous en avons mesme veu le succez sur les tres, & en certaines Entrées particulieres: Ie ne doute point quils ne fissent un merveilleux effet dans une Pastoralle. Mais on ne peut Jamais s'ausseurer sur le vent,[170] l'halene manque, les poulmons sépaisissent, l'estomac se fatigue, & enfin on sent une notable difference de la fin & des commencemens, & on n'y trouve plus de Justesse.[171]

Hautbois make a stately sound, and, played as they are nowadays at the Court and in Paris, they leave little to be desired. They make cadences as well in tune, trills as sweet, and diminutions as regular as the best-trained voice and the most perfect instrument. We have seen their success on stage, and in certain specific scenes. I have no doubt they would have a marvellous effect in a Pastorale. But it is never possible to be certain of the wind supply: the breath fails, the lungs thicken, the diaphragm[172] tires, and finally a noticeable difference is evident between the end and the beginning; good intonation can no longer be found.

Pure's description is of an instrument not yet entirely established, and one that may not yet have been fully mastered by its players.

The court hautbois players who had been active in the 1650s and remained after the apparent rupture of 1664 were the following:

Jean (3) Hotteterre
Hilaire Robeau
Michel Destouches
Moïse Dupin
Michel Rousselet
Martin Toussaint
Elie Charles James
Nicolas Malloy
Jean Brunet
Nicolas Perrin
Antoine Pièche

[170] Pure is comparing hautboys with musettes, which are supplied with wind through a bag filled by bellows.
[171] Pure (1668), 274. Transcription kindly provided by Giovanni Caviglia.   [172] Literally 'the stomach'.

Nicolas (10) Hotteterre
Pierre Maréchal
François Descoteaux
Jean Philidor

These fifteen men were probably the players who worked with the new hautboy, gave it its reputation, and influenced its evolution.[173]

E. Music Played in the Formative Period

Before 1670, the musical contexts in which the hautboy appeared were as follows: (1) in double-reed bands, the treble hautboy probably together with various sizes of cromorne; (2) in Lully's *petite bande*, doubling the strings; (3) possibly in chamber ensembles, alone or together with other instruments *en symphonie*.

In this period, and especially in France, instrumentation was left ambiguous and determined according to the situation of the moment, such as the acoustics of the performing space, available instruments, etc. (cf. the *symphonie*, Ch. 3, §G.1). As Menestrier wrote in 1682 (see above), for variety winds could 'play intermittently, or mixed together' with the violins. Beaussant speaks of a *son français* in this period, a '*substance sonore* proprement française, celle de cette masse de cordes, corsée par les hautbois' (typically French *sound medium*, that of a mass of strings seasoned by hautboys).[174]

But since the type-instrument was not yet clearly defined, the term 'hautbois' was quite general. Not only could it include different sizes of hautboy as well as the bassoon (just as 'violon' meant all the instruments of the violin family), it could mean any double-reed instrument, like the cromorne and the bagpipe chanters (with or without their windcaps), and even in some cases wind instruments in general (including the musette de cour, recorder, and traverso).[175] 'Hautbois' in a score might be marked 'flûtes' or 'musette' at the same place in the libretto, or vice versa, as long as the instruments had similar poetic associations (all the woodwinds shared the pastoral attribute). Still, if 'hautbois' are mentioned, we know that the music was considered playable on the hautboy and would have been appropriate for it.

Prunières speculated that the earliest known performance that involved a proto-morphic hautboy was *L'Amour malade* in 1657.[176] The libretto of this *ballet de*

---

[173] Other woodwind players who were active at court in the 1660s and would have been among the first to play the new hautboy were Guillaume Granville, Jean Rousselet, Joseph Le Roy, Louis (7) Hotteterre, Jérôme Noblet, Jacques Philidor, de Bonnefonds, Nicolas (12) Hotteterre dit Colin, Sylvain Gayet, Jean (8) Hotteterre, André Langlois, Jean Laubier jun., Claude Allais, André Philidor, Gilles Héroux, and Nicolas Dieupart.

[174] Beaussant (1992), 120.   [175] Eppelsheim (1961), 117–20.

[176] Prunières (1931), p. xxii. As Eppelsheim pointed out (1961: 104), this was no more than a conjecture. But there seems to be no reason to dispute it. Cf. also Harris-Warrick (1990), 98.

cour gives the family names of the woodwind players who played in the last *entrée* called 'Concert champestre de l'Espoux' (a five-part movement with unspecified instrumentation) as Descoteaux (who would have been François), Pièche (Joseph or Antoine), Destouches (Jean or Michel), and 'Obterre le pere, Obterre fils aisné, Obterre le cadet' (presumably Jean (3) Hotteterre, Jean (8), and Martin). There is no way to be sure which instruments they played, but the title suggests double reeds because of the village wedding context. The ranges of the parts are g1–b2, f♯1–d2, c1–a1, and do–d1.[177]

Like many technological innovations, the military were among the first to try out the remodelled forms of haut-bois. Lully specified 'hautbois' in a score in the 'Premiere Marche des Mousquetaires', dated 1658, a year after the performance of *L'Amour malade*.[178] According to Kastner, hautboys officially replaced trumpets and fifes in the musketeers' corps in 1663.[179] Brenet (1917: 348) cites an eyewitness account of the battle of Douai in 1667, claiming that the musketeers' victorious assault was made with 'drums beating, together with oboes'.[180]

Until the apparently critical year of 1664, Lully wrote for double-reed bands in five parts, in G1, C1, C2, C3, and F4 clefs. Five-part bands appear in *L'Amour malade* (LWV 8, 1657), *Alcidiane* (LWV 9, 1658),[181] *Ballet de l'impatience* (LWV 14, 1661),[182] *Ballet des arts* (1663),[183] *Les Nopces de village* (LWV 19, 1663),[184] *Le Mariage forcé* (LWV 20, 1664),[185] *Amours déguisez* (LWV 21, 1664),[186] and the 'Marche de Hautbois pour le dieu Pan et sa Suite' in *Les Plaisirs de l'isle enchantée* in May 1664 (LWV 22/3).[187] This changed after 1670, when the fourth part in C3 clef, the *quinte*, was consistently omitted. The band that played these early five-part pieces was probably a mix of hautboys and cromornes.

It is unclear whether winds played inner parts in tuttis. The tendency was to put many more instruments on the treble and bass than on the three inner parts, and it

[177] Semmens (1975), 71–2.

[178] 'Pour les hautbois et Tambours.' The *Mousquetaires* are described above, §C.5.

[179] Kastner (1837), 110, citing Mallet, *Travaux de Mars ou l'art de la guerre*, iii. 108. Furetière (1690), s.v. 'Hautbois' says that 'il est devenu depuis peu [!] un instrument militaire, le Roy en ayant mis dans les Compagnies des Mousquetaires'. (It is unclear when this was written.)

[180] There is of course no way to be certain that the musketeers were not using some kind of shawm.

[181] In a 'Concert Rustique', an *Air*, and a *Gavotte* in the second *entrée* of Part 3, for five parts. The last 'Petite Chaconne' for three parts may also have been for hautboys. Semmens (1975), 72–4.

[182] In the third *entrée*. The four upper parts (instruments unspecified, but not violins) are *dessus*, *hautecontre*, *taille*, and *quinte* (the latter with a range of co–e♭1). Semmens (1975), 74.

[183] Ritournelle to the Dialogue, written by Michel Lambert. Massip (1989), 33.

[184] 'Oboes' are specified in the libretto but not the score for the first *entrée* (and probably the preceding *ritournelle*) in five parts. The wind players for this production were four Hotteterres, Descoteaux, Destouches, and Pièche. Semmens (1975), 74–5.

[185] In 'Un Charivari grotesque'; cited as a suggestion by Prunières in Marx (1951), 14.

[186] In the sixth *entrée*, in five parts. The woodwind players were Pièche, François Descoteaux, three Hotteterres, and Michel Destouches. Semmens (1975), 76.

[187] This is illustrated (at least symbolically) in Israël Silvestre, *Les Plaisirs de l'isle enchantée*, 1664, at Paris (Estampes); Washington; New York: Pierpont Morgan Library (1876b), etc.

PL. 1.23. Nicolas Henri Tardieu, detail from fourth Tableau in the same series, soon after
25 Oct. 1722. Paris: Louvre, Cabinet des Dessins (26.315)

may be for this reason that several modern authors have stated that hautboys and
bassoons doubled only the outer voices of the string ensemble.[188] The illustration of
the twelve *Violons, Hautbois, Saqueboutes et Cornets* at Louis XV's coronation in
1722 (Pl. 1.23; see Ch. 5, §B.3) apparently includes six treble hautboys and two each
of the other three parts, which may indicate the normal division of parts. Using the
little information available on the size of Lully's orchestras and the divisions of the
parts,[189] it is likely that about thirteen violins played the upper part; since there were
ten hautboys available, the balance between wind and string would have been very
much in favour of the hautboys, had they all played the upper part in tuttis.

---

[188] See Eppelsheim. (1961), 103 and 204; Dean and Knapp (1987), 34; Zaslaw (1993), 12; Harris-Warrick and
Marsh (1994), 69. For an example of first and second hautboys doubling the soprano part together at the Dresden
court chapel in the early 18th c., see Horn (1987), 109.
[189] The only complete list of players that survives is for *Le Triomphe de l'amour* (1681). See La Gorce (1989),
109–10.

2

The Physical Characteristics of the Hautboy

A. Surviving Original Hautboys

It is difficult to estimate the number of hautboys that once existed. We know, for example, that at least nine members of the Hotteterre family made hautboys.[1] At a conservative estimate, if each of them made thirty hautboys in a lifetime,[2] they would have made a total of 270 instruments (the real number was probably much larger). Yet at the present time only two Hotteterre hautboys are known. There are a number of other hautboy makers by whom no instruments survive.[3] We know of the existence of some 134 makers of hautboys who were active between about 1625 and 1760. There were undoubtedly more. If each of 150 makers made thirty hautboys in a lifetime, there once existed 4,500 original hautboys; if each made 100 (which seems more likely), the figure would be 15,000. Of course, this number could have been even larger.

The number of known surviving hautboys is constantly changing. About a quarter of them are privately owned and they regularly change hands, and new ones are continually turning up. At the present time, probably fewer than 500 hautboys that could have been made before 1760 survive; 388 are known. That is in fact a relatively small sample—probably less than 3 per cent of the number that once existed. The other 97-odd per cent probably got thrown away. Not (as has sometimes been suggested) because they were worn out. Apart from the odd key spring, hautboys do not seem to suffer from long use; on the contrary, they sometimes get better. But there was an obvious reason for discarding old instruments: obsolescence. Hautboy design changed so quickly that it is unlikely that seventeenth- and eighteenth-century instruments were ever played more than a generation. And up until a generation ago, obsolete oboes were scarcely worth a pawnbroker's notice.

---

[1] Waterhouse (1993).

[2] The inventory on the death of Prudent included 885 instruments in his shop; see Giannini (1998), 9.

[3] For instance Adam Berger of Breslau, listed in Walther (1732: 87) as a maker of 'allerhand musicalische Instrumente, als *Violin*en, Flöten, *Hautbois*, Bassons, &c.' (Martin Kirnbauer (pers. comm.) suggests that Berger was only a 'semi-professional' maker). Becker (1961: 1792) mentions Descouteau and Doucet (Paris), Lissieu, François, and Lambert (Lyon), Perrin (Bourg-en-Bresse), du Buisson (Turin), and Ashbury (London). Moucherel (see Ch. 5, §B.5) and Wietfelt (Burgdorf; see Ch. 5, §D.4) also made hautboys.

TABLE 2.1. *Surviving original hautboys*

Country	1640–70		1670–1700		1700–30		1730–60		Total	
	no.	%	no.	%	no.	%	no.	%	no.	%
France	0	0.0	12	3.09	20	5.15	18	4.64	50	12.89
Italy	0	0.0	0	0.0	15	3.87	30	7.73	45	11.60
Germany	0	0.0	13	3.35	60	15.21	50	12.89	123	31.33
England	0	0.0	4	1.03	10	2.58	33	8.51	47	12.11
Dutch Republic	10	2.58	11	2.84	54	13.92	22	5.67	97	25.00
Spanish/Austrian Netherlands	0	0.0	0	0.0	0	0.0	12	3.09	12	3.09
Habsburg Empire[a]	0	0.0	0	0.0	3	0.77	1	0.26	4	1.03
Other	0	0.0	0	0.0	3	0.77	8	2.06	11	2.84
Total	10	1.58	40	10.31	164	42.27	174	44.85	388	100.01

[a] Besides Austria, the area referred to as the 'Habsburg lands' includes Hungary, Bohemia, Moravia, and parts of northern Italy and the Netherlands, all sharing the common government of the Holy Roman Empire that was traditionally led by the head of the house of Habsburg.

Of the survivors, it is also difficult to determine in which period they were made. Hautboys were rarely dated, and workshop dates frequently spanned two or three generations. Based on informed guesses, however, the breakdown could have been as shown in Table 2.1. Hautboys from Germany and the Dutch Republic are the most plentiful, between them making up over half the surviving instruments. The Dutch figure is remarkable, considering the relatively small size of the country.[4]

Our understanding of how these few surviving instruments were meant to play is as yet quite limited. Unlike strings, few old hautboys are regularly played nowadays. Originals are rare, expensive, fragile, and often in only partially playable condition. Most are now owned by museums, who severely restrict their use, in many cases not even allowing them to be repaired and made playable. Although the physical dimensions of some hautboys have been measured (as if that were enough, even when done accurately, to reproduce the sound and playing qualities of an original!), they are rarely allowed to be played long enough to yield more than a superficial appreciation of their playing qualities.[5]

[4] The relatively small number of surviving French hautboys is also remarkable. It is probable that more once existed.

[5] Although curators of public museums are generally helpful in responding to requests for information, it is not uncommon to be told that it is 'museum policy' not to allow certain old wind instruments to be played at all. Future generations will suffer from this short-sighted and fundamentally unmusical approach to 'preservation'. One large British collection, for instance, has treated many of its wind instruments with insecticide so that they are unplayable; little if anything of their playing characteristics is known, or will be known in this generation.

In any case, few modern players have the time to explore new models.[6] Until such time as they become more familiar with the original hautboys now locked away (as well as more different types),[7] we cannot claim to have a complete picture of how the instrument was generally played in the past.

1. Materials

The most important component of the hautboy, the reed, is made from a species of grass, *Arundo donax*, which is native to the countries surrounding the Mediterranean Sea, but has become widely dispersed throughout the world (see below, §E.2.a). By coincidence, the beautiful golden colour of the best quality *Arundo* cane is also the colour of the wood of which the great majority (about 85%) of surviving hautboys was made: Turkish boxwood, *Buxus sempervirens*.[8] Hautboys were also made of (in descending order of frequency) ebony, ivory, and fruitwoods (plum, pear, and cherry). Instruments in boxwood were sometimes stained dark, or in imitation tortoiseshell.

Box was the ideal wood for the smaller woodwinds. It was easy to turn finely and had a perfect balance of density and elasticity for resonance and projection. Ribock summed up the experience of many players and makers when he wrote

Ein Hoboe von Grenadill oder Ebenholze schreiet widrig. Buchs ist besser, und zwar recht altes besser als junges, und das pulpöse Elfenbein noch besser, wenn man blos auf die Eleganz des Tones sieht, und das zu leichte Aufquillen beiseitesetzt.[9]	An hautboy made of grenadilla or ebony is unpleasantly loud and bright. Box is better, older rather than younger. But softer ivory is even better, if it is strictly the elegance of sound that is considered, and one is not concerned with how it swells [when wet].

One could add that plumwood (used by the Denners, Königsberger, and Rÿkel, among others) yielded a warm and very responsive sound.

Hautboys were usually made from quartered logs.[10] Quartered wood presents two faces: the radial plane, which shows the growth rings as a vertical row of fine lines, and the flitch plane, showing flame grain. The flitch plane is the softer side and shrinks and distorts more than the radial, which is probably why makers normally put tone-holes on the more stable radial plane.

---

[6] Nor are most modern 'copies' indicative of how originals played; the bores and tone-holes are routinely altered, and modern wood is frequently denser. Most are designed to use anachronistic fingerings (much like the 'German-fingered' recorders of two generations ago), that oblige players to use these fingerings rather than the ones used in the past, and consequently obscure our understanding of original reeds and playing technique.

[7] Such as, for instance, those of Rippert, Bizey, the Lots, Palanca, Biglioni, Grassi, Christoph Denner, Gahn, Schell, Kress, Schuechbaur, Königsberger, Eisenmenger, Stinglwagner, Haka, and Rÿkel—as well as most of the apparently earliest hautboys, many by anonymous builders.

[8] For a description of this wood, see Record and Garratt (1925).   [9] Ribock (1782), 43.

[10] Bouterse (1999: 71) suggests that hautboy makers used timber about 130–40 mm in diameter.

Tenons were lapped with thread of the same kind as was used on reeds (see below, §E.2.b). Cork (which was in fact a better material for the job) was not in commercial distribution until late in the eighteenth century.[11]

B. *The Hautboy's External Form*

1. *Terminology*

The outside profiles of woodwinds were inspired by architectural moulding figures like the *ogee*, *bolection moulding*, *cove* or *flare*, *column*, *bead* or ring, *fillet*, *finial* or spool, and *baluster* or vase. The hautboy was usually turned with balusters on each of the joints. The top and centre joints both had columns, while the bell had a *waist* and a *flare*. The two extremities of the hautboy were usually the finial at the top and the *rim* at the bottom. The other elements of the outer profile were beads, smaller flat *fillets* often found on either side of beads, and *key rings*.

The terminology used for identifying the outward parts of the hautboy is shown in Figs. 2.1–4.[12] These diagrams represent the standard turning elements in use from the late seventeenth to the early nineteenth centuries, although many instruments differed in minor details (cf. also the variant Types B and C described in §B.4 below).

Bore characteristics that can be used as points of comparison are the *counterbore* (the section at the top that receives the reed staple), the *minimum bore* (a short cylindrical section located between the counterbore and the top of the main bore, the *widest bore*, and the bell *lip* (see Fig. 2.3).

Joint ends (usually the finial, balusters, and rim) were sometimes reinforced or ornamented with *tips* (also called mounts) of ivory, silver or brass; metal tips were also called *ferrules*. The phrase 'tip'd with Brass' was used by Talbot (*c.*1692–5) for the Schalmey.[13] In the early eighteenth century, Claver Morris, an English medical doctor and amateur hautboy player, wrote of 'a hoboy with ivory joints and tipped with same'[14] ('joints' here probably means sockets, and 'tips' the two ends).[15]

About half the surviving hautboys are tipped, most with ivory, a few with horn or bone, and even fewer with brass or silver. In works of art, ivory tips were mostly a feature of instruments made before about 1710. The ivory tips on the Dupuis hautboy (Berlin 2933), with their *mounting studs*, are the most elaborate of their type

---

[11] Wine could not be aged in the bottle until then, either, since cork stoppers were unavailable.

[12] This terminology has been developed together with Cecil Adkins.

[13] Baines (1948), 13.   [14] Morris (1934).

[15] 'Tippinges' was also used in an inventory of instruments owned by Henry VIII at the time of his death in 1547: 'Item. 8 Dulceuses couered with blacke leather, some of them havinge tippinges of Silver' (quoted in Lyndon-Jones (1996: 19)).

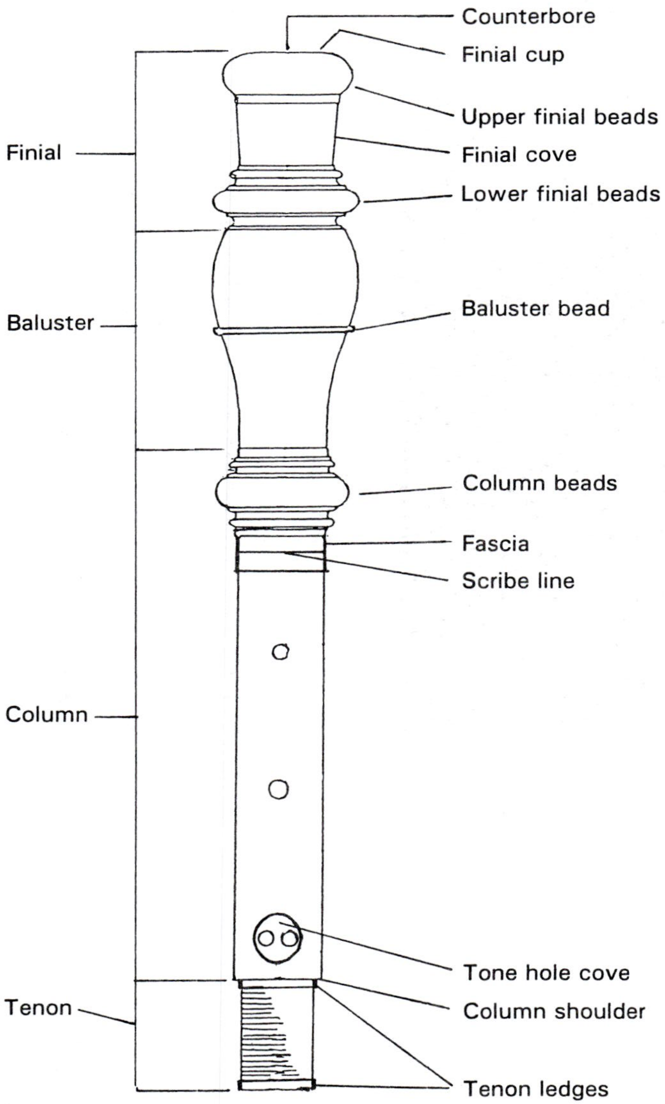

FIG. 2.2. Centre joint

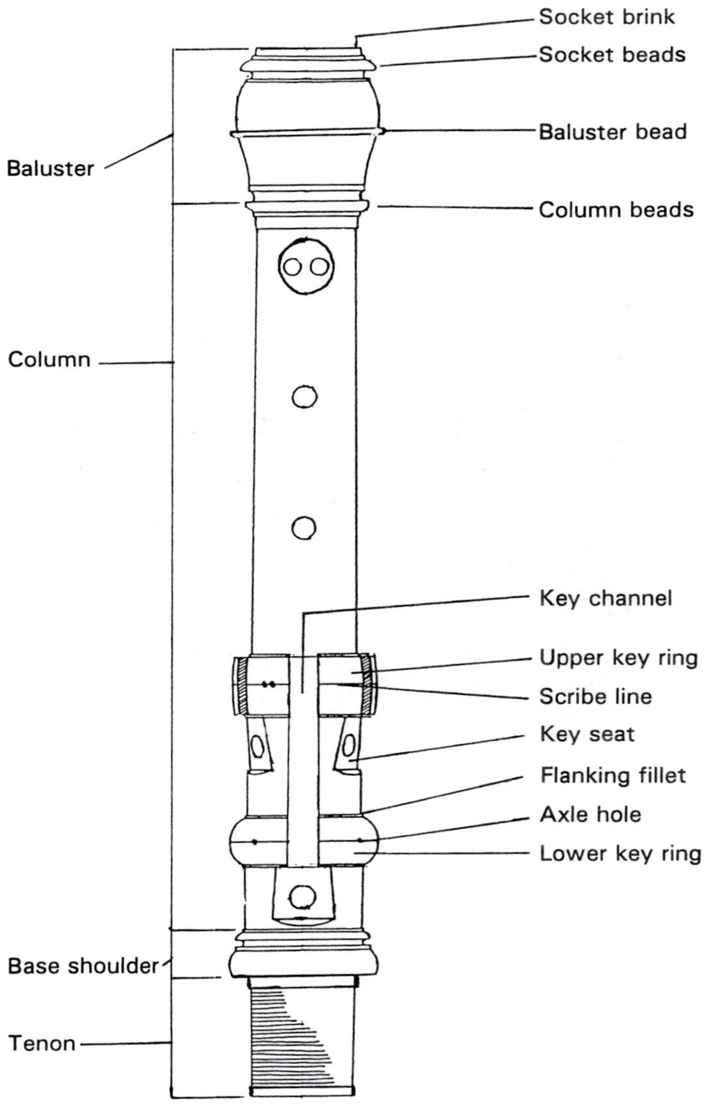

Socket brink
Socket beads
Baluster bead
Column beads

Key channel
Upper key ring
Scribe line
Key seat
Flanking fillet
Axle hole
Lower key ring

Baluster
Column
Base shoulder
Tenon

FIG. 2.1. Top joint

Counterbore
Finial cup
Upper finial beads
Finial cove
Lower finial beads
Baluster bead
Column beads
Fascia
Scribe line
Tone hole cove
Column shoulder
Tenon ledges

Finial
Baluster
Column
Tenon

UPPER AND LOWER GREAT-KEYS

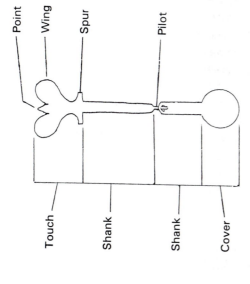

Point
Wing
Spur
Pilot

Touch
Shank
Shank
Cover

SMALL-KEY

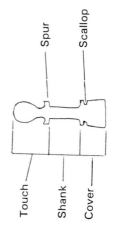

Spur
Scallop

Touch
Shank
Cover

FIG. 2.4. Keys

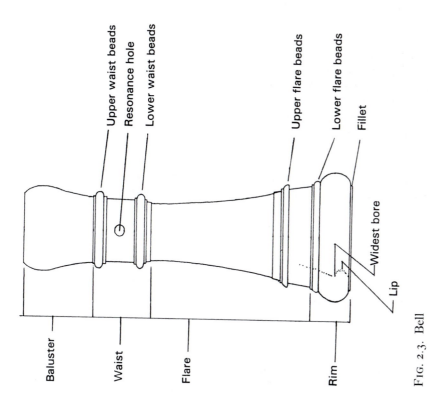

Upper waist beads
Resonance hole
Lower waist beads

Upper flare beads
Lower flare beads
Fillet

Widest bore
Lip

Baluster
Waist
Flare
Rim

FIG. 2.3. Bell

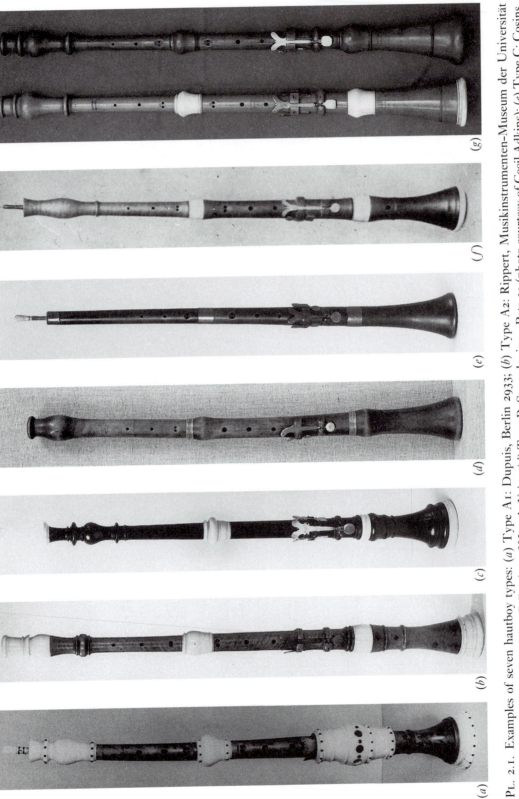

PL. 2.1. Examples of seven hautboy types: (*a*) Type A1: Dupuis, Berlin 2933; (*b*) Type A2: Rippert, Musikinstrumenten-Museum der Universität Leipzig, 1312; (*c*) Type A3: Haka, Collection of Han de Vries; (*d*) Type B: Stanesby jun., Bate 29 (photo courtesy of Cecil Adkins); (*e*) Type C: Cosins, Nuremberg MIR 375; (*f*) Type D1: M. Lot, Formerly Berlin 2947; (*g*) Type D1: Two hautboys by Palanca, Collection Alfredo Bernardini

Pl. 2.2. Edwaert Colyer, 1691, *Vanitas* (oil on linen). Castres:
Musée Goya

(see Pl. 2.1).[16] Mounting studs were dowels of dark wood inserted laterally like nails
into the ivory and wood, and spaced in a circle; they were probably originally meant
to help hold the ivory tips in place (ivory shrinks at a different rate than wood).
Plates 2.2 and 1.20 from the early 1690s are the only two pictures in which studs
appear.

2. Dating instruments

The obvious way to date hautboys is through their 'look', that is, the style of their
turning, their proportions, and other aspects of their outward form and structure.
But that is only possible if at least some instruments can be positively linked to real
dates, or can be attributed to a generation. This is difficult because Baroque woodwind makers did not generally date their instruments.

Biographical information on makers is of course useful, but is limited by the
fact that a maker's death dates do not necessarily indicate that his workshop stamp
ceased to be used. The workshop stamp (unlike the *Meisterzeichen* or master's

---

[16] Mounting studs are also used on an hautboy numbered 3636 at Brussels (name, in scroll, illegible).

initial) was analogous to modern company names like 'Ford' for automobiles, and instruments with the workshop stamp often continued to be produced by members of the founder's family or his successors long after his death. Christoph Denner's stamp, for instance, was used by his family for almost half a century after his death (see Ch. 5, §D.16).

There are several other possible kinds of evidence that can be used for dating: (1) the relatively few dated hautboys that survive; (2) a comparison of the instruments of particular workshops; (3) iconography. The first and most obvious source of information on dating hautboys are the rare dated instruments. Dates were sometimes added to workshop stamps or were stamped on the undersides of their keys.[17] There are at present thirteen known dated instruments from before 1760, the earliest by Beukers (1704), nine by Anciuti (from 1709 to 1738), two by Fredrik Richters (by 1731 and 1744), and one by Bizey (1749).

Another method of dating was recently used by Adkins in his study of the hautboys of the Milhouse family (1996). Adkins demonstrated how when sufficient instruments survive from a single workshop or family of makers, they can be compared morphologically, allowing a chronology to be established. Similar studies of a number of other workshops that are survived by enough instruments would be possible, such as those of the Stanesbys, Palanca, the Lots, the Denners, the Richters, Steenbergen, the Rottenburghs, and the Schlegels.

The most reliable indications come from works of art that depict hautboys, because these works themselves can often be dated accurately. Many pictures have careful chronological histories, and some have their dates written on them. They often appear in the context of other artefacts (such as clothes, furniture, music, and books) or specific people or events that are datable. Some are included in books. When pictures show hautboys together with players, and we know something of those players from other sources, we can even determine to what degree we are looking at what were considered state-of-the-art instruments.[18]

Original hautboys and artistic representations can complement each other, and the plausibility of iconographic evidence can be checked by comparing it with surviving original instruments. Where an instrument will usually give better information on details of construction, a picture may give a surer date (indeed, for certain stages of the hautboy's evolution, and certain kinds of instruments, nothing but pictures survives).

---

[17] Since keys on original instruments are sometimes difficult to remove, evidence from this source is often still unexplored.

[18] Although instruments were often used in works of art for their symbolic values, they had to be recognizable and therefore inherently realistic. Pottier (1995: 133) points out that Euterpe, the muse of music, was traditionally represented 'by the figure of a young woman crowned with flowers, holding sheets of music—a recorder, oboes, and other musical instruments near her'. Further depictions of hautboys may be discovered by searching for portrayals of Euterpe.

3. External features that can be compared

The outward physical features of hautboys that can be compared include the design of the keys, materials used, the presence or absence of twin holes and the shape of tone-hole coves, the turning profile, details of turning, and the form of the bell.

a. Keys Keys showed a number of possible variations: number, material, shape of touches and covers, and the presence of cross-spurs, for example.

The hautboy started life with one key, the *Great-key* (which on the treble hautboy is the C-key). E♭ was obtained on some protomorphic hautboys shown in the Gobelins tapestry of 1664 with a twinned sixth hole, as on some early recorders.[19] A close-standing key was soon added for this note as well, probably because the sixth hole was already too small even when it was single, and was even stuffier when twinned. A *Small-key* beside the Great-key was the solution.

Among the 266 surviving hautboys whose number of keys is known, there are about twice as many with three keys as with two. (The third key was a doubled Small-key on the other side of the Great-key, so the instrument could be played right-hand down or right-hand up.) Of the earliest hautboys (by, for instance, Christoph Denner and Haka) most have three keys.[20] Three keys appear to have been more common between 1670 and 1730 and two keys after 1730.[21] The eleven pictures that clearly show keys also indicate that the two-keyed option became more common with time. But early sources mentioned both two and three keys. One of the earliest tutors, Banister (1695: iii), included the following: 'Hold the *Hautboy* with your Left-hand uppermost, your little Finger of the Right-hand manageth the two [*sic*; the Great and Small] Brass *Keys* . . .'. And the *Compleat tutor to the hautboy* (*c*.1715) stated: 'there are eight holes on this Instrument besides two [!] under the Brass keys making ten in all'. Talbot, however, wrote in *c*.1692–5 (p. 14): 'On the same Joynt an 8th Hole on each side for right or left hand opened with a less Key.' Two well-known hautboys (the Bate Collection 'Galpin'[22] and the Dupuis[23]) have left-hand 'dummy' Small-keys, the holes under their covers having never been drilled.

The two most common shapes for the Great-key touch were *swallowtail* or *butterfly* (as in Pl. 2.3) and *winged*[24] (as in Pls. 2.4 and 2.5).[25] Mersenne's woodwinds in the 1630s showed the swallowtail key. Winged Great-key touches were more common in later periods. A winged Small-key touch is observable at the end of the

---

[19] Cf. also Pl. 1.9 (Gobelins, 1684), and the Haka (The Hague 20-x-1952), both of which lack the Small-key.

[20] Two of Denner's eight known hautboys have two keys. According to Jan Bouterse (pers. comm.), all Dutch hautboys have a doubled Small-key.

[21] One cannot be categorical about this because the instruments are not usually datable to exact periods.

[22] Oxford: Bate 200. Halfpenny (1949b), 22, (1949a), 358, (1953), 31.

[23] Paul Hailperin was told by the Museum that the right-hand key on the Dupuis was missing, and in 1950 the left-hand key was moved to the other side. Hand position is discussed further in Ch. 4, §B.4.

[24] Young (1993), under Van Aardenberg, called this shape 'Mickey-Mouse ears'.

[25] Early keys are described in Halfpenny (1949b), 13.

PL. 2.4. Anonymous, [? c.1750], portrait of an hautboist, ? French. Oil. Stockholm: Stiftelsen Musikkulturens främjande

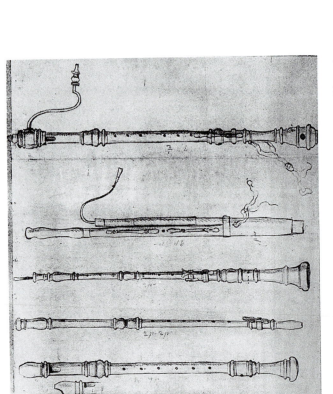

PL. 2.3. Anonymous, c.1705, early eighteenth-century French drawing of woodwinds, red chalk, 11½ × 12¼ in. Collection of Jill Croft-Murray

PL. 2.5. Hautboy by Martin, E.210, C.470. Paris: Collection Musée de la musique

seventeenth century, but the round and scroll ('spoon') shapes were much more common then and later. Although there were exceptions, Great-key covers were generally round in all periods and Small-key covers square.[26]

b. Twin holes and coves   Hautboys survive with single third and/or fourth holes,[27] but twin or doubled holes are somewhat more common, and are the rule on French instruments. After 1684 (Pl. 1.9, still with a single third hole), almost all the early pictures on which these holes are visible show twin holes.[28] But Halfpenny (1949b: 16) noted that Type C hautboys had a single fourth hole, and many of the best surviving hautboys (like those of Jacob Denner) were made with a single fourth hole.[29] Twin holes were usually (but not always) drilled the same size and straight (that is, at 90° to the direction of the bore), so they could be played by right- or left-handed players.

The tone-hole *cove* is the indentation made on twin tone-holes.[30] The earliest seventeenth-century hautboys often have square or rectangular coves on the twin holes,[31] as does one of the hautboys in panel F of the Gobelins tapestry 'L'Air' (Pl. 1.6). Later hautboys (the first datable one being Mignard, 1691, Pl. 2.6) have oval tone-hole coves.

c. Turning proportions and shapes   Turning style is difficult to describe in words, but one factor that can be objectively compared is the depth or shallowness of the profile; that is, the difference between the narrowest and widest points along the instrument's length. Two proportions that are useful for comparing profiles are the narrowest and widest points of the top joint (often both on the baluster), and the diameter of the bell rim (the widest point on the hautboy) compared with the instrument's total length.

---

[26] Although there were examples of round Small-key covers (the so-called 'dumbbell E♭') in the period 1685–1725. No chronological pattern can be traced from the few pictures that show cross-spurs on keys. According to Halfpenny (1949b: 16), the spurs were not present on Type C hautboys.

[27] Jacob Denner is survived by one hautboy, Nuremberg MI 90, with single third and fourth tone-holes.

[28] An exception is Simonneau (Pl. 2.13).

[29] Of the two hautboys by Johann August Crone in Han de Vries's collection, the older Type A2 has twin holes, while the Type D2 (classical model) has a single fourth hole. This suggests that single holes became more common towards the end of the 18th c.   [30] It is also sometimes called a *dimple*.

[31] Dupuis; Anon Paris E.108; Martin; Anon Nuremberg MIR 373.

PL. 2.6. Pierre Mignard, 1691, detail from *Sainte Cécile jouant de la harpe* (oil painting, *c*.1 × 1 m). Paris: Louvre (Inv. 6641)

As time went on, the trend was for *bolder* top-joint profiles. In pictures of haut-boys, shallow profiles (15% or less difference between smallest and largest diameters) are common in the seventeenth century and up until 1750;[32] bold profiles (17.5–20%) became common after the 1760s. *Proud* bell rims, on the other hand (that is, rims with a diameter of over 13% of the total length of instrument), were generally characteristic of the seventeenth and early eighteenth centuries.

Although the *bobbin* or *spool* is the finial shape commonly associated with the hautboy (as in Fig. 2.1), all the earliest finials were straight upward flares (see Pls. 1.9, 2.1(*a*), 2.5–8) or columns with parallel sides, in neither case with a bead or ring at the top. The first dated bobbin finial appeared in 1688 (Bismantova) but was exceptional; the shape is not seen again until *c*.1705 (Pl. 2.3); it became common only in the 1710s.[33]

The similarity between the shapes of the balusters on the three joints acted as a unifying design factor. But the earliest pictures to show balusters indicate that the typical shape, a graceful inverted 'vase' (the quirk ogee), did not become standard until the late 1680s.

d. Bead complexity, shapes of key rings Figures 2.1–3 show the typical early eighteenth-century beading above and below the upper two balusters, at the base of

---

[32] As Martin Kirnbauer (pers. comm.) notes, shallow profiles can be caused by the small size of the original piece of wood: 'there are several instruments by Denner and Oberlender where you can see still the marks of the saw'.

[33] The straight finial without bead continued to appear as late as 1795 (Verscheure-Reynvaan), but was unusual in pictures after 1725. The sides of the bobbin were slightly flared upward until the 1760s (Pls. 2.3, 2.14), when they became parallel (Pl. 2.11).

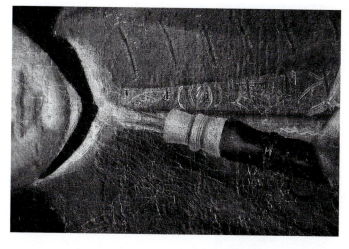

PL. 2.8. Anonymous, 1754, detail from portrait of the Family Parguez. Oil on canvas. Musée Municipal de Pontarlier, France. Photo: J. Guiraud

PL. 2.7. Anonymous, c.1725–32, portrait of hautboist, oil. c.1 × 1 m. Berlin: Staatliches Institut für Musikforschung

PL. 2.9. Anonymous, 1688, detail from title-page to N. Derosier's
La Fuite du roi d'Angleterre (Amsterdam). NL-DHgm

the centre joint, at the bell waist, and the bell rim. This was the norm, although some early hautboys show more (Rippert, for instance, added beads at the centre of the balusters, and the instruments in Pls. 2.9 and 2.2 have extra beading above the bell rim). Dutch hautboys often have an extra straight fillet (or *fascia*) below the top column beads.

Figure 2.2 shows the standard shape for the two key rings at the bottom of the centre joint (square-sectioned upper, rounded lower).[34] There were a number of exceptions to this pattern (see Pls. 1.6, 1.7, 1.10, 1.5, 2.10). Cut-away key rings, or *bosses*, were associated with the simplified turning of the mid-eighteenth century (Types B, C, and E; see §B.4 below).

---

[34] Key rings are elegantly described in Halfpenny (1949b), 13.

PL. 2.10. Hautboy, type A1. Paris: Collection Musée de la musique, no. E.108

e. Bell form   Bells presented several variables. The most obvious was the sharpness of the flare, which varied throughout the period under study (compare Pls. 2.9 and 2.3). Generalizations based on date are difficult, but the flare was often sharper in the seventeenth century than later.

The presence of a bell rim separated by beads, sometimes substantial and numerous ones (as in Pls. 1.9 and 1.19) was normal until the 1760s (see Pl. 2.11, which shows only an outward flange with no bead). The rim was to disappear altogether by the 1790s.

A factor that can indicate date is the number of waist beads on the bell. Instead of the classic symmetrical pair (as in Pl. 2.6), from the 1760s the bottom bead became rare.[35] The two beads are still seen in Pl. 2.11.[36] By 1767, the lower flare bead had also disappeared on some hautboys (Pl. 2.11).

[35] The change in number of waist beads was remarked in Piguet (1988), 84.
[36] But are missing in Piguet's Lot hautboy, number 7 (cf. Piguet 1988: 84).

PL. 2.11. Anonymous, 1767, portrait of Sante Aguilar. (? oil). Bologna: Sala Bossi,
Civico Museo Bibliografico Musicale G. B. Martini

Sand Dalton (pers. comm.) has suggested that one purpose of the bell lip was to
hold a mute in the bell (the standard mute was a wad of paper, which would have
fallen out without the lip).[37] The bell lip is missing on at least four early hautboys.[38]

4. *Types by turning style*

One of Eric Halfpenny's most important studies, published a half-century ago,
involved classifying hautboys by the style of their outside shape, or turning profile.[39]
Although his study was based on English models, it is now clear that there was no
particular distinction between English and Continental types, so his classifications
are valid for hautboys all over Europe. Because they make it easier to describe hautboys quickly, and to compare styles in different periods, I shall continue to use his
classification here with a few additions.

---

[37] Bell lips were absent on contemporary clarinets, even though their outside profiles were modelled on the hautboy; clarinets at the time had no need of mutes, as they were already considered soft.
[38] Bauer [*c*.1730, Leipzig], Nuremberg MIR 376; Anon. [17th c.], Paris E.108; Rouge [*c*.1700], Paris E.979.2.12.
[39] Halfpenny (1949b).

Both Halfpenny's Type A and his Type D can be divided into three variants. He isolated two other types, B and C, to which I propose adding one more, Type E. These categories are described below. Our knowledge of dating hautboys is still meagre, so it is not possible to assign surviving types to specific periods with complete assurance, but it seems likely that Type A was generally made in the period before 1730, while the others were made later; Type D2 seems to have belonged exclusively to the Classical period. Extant examples of seven of the nine categories described below are shown in Pl. 2.1, placed next to each other for comparison.

Observing these types, the original trend seems to have been towards simplification: Type A2 was less complicated than A1, B less than A2. From about mid-century, however, designs again became more complex. Type E, which may have derived from B, again had more beading, and the classical hautboy (Type D2), evolving from Type D1, was almost as complex in profile as A2.

a. Type A1　Type A1, apparently the earliest true hautboy, was probably current at the end of the seventeenth century in France. It is shown in works of art from 1684 to 1704,[40] but may have been made later. It shows certain external features that did not persist, such as the lack of a bell lip and square or rectangular tone-hole coves. The baluster was not necessarily a quirk ogee (the inverted 'vase') as it was later to become. Mounting studs are associated with this type. Some specimens are exceptionally short, while aggregate tone-hole size (explained in §C below) is relatively large, averaging 18.8. Examples:

> Dupuis (Berlin 2933)
> Martin (Paris E.210, C.470)
> three anonymous instruments (Brussels 423, Paris E.108,[41] Paris E.980.2.149)

This type is shown in Pls. 1.9, 2.1(*a*), 2.5, 2.9–10, 2.12–13, and 5.1.

b. Type A2　Type A2 is generally thought of as the standard hautboy shape, and with good reason. It is by far the most common, and seems to have been in vogue among makers from the very beginning (about 1670) right through the entire period covered by this book. It is shown in works of art from 1672 to 1763.[42] It includes rich beading, often with complex curves on the centre and bell balusters. The finial was turned both with and without a surmounting ring. The turning profile of the top joint was shallow, but the bell flare was frequently sharp. Although box was normal, other woods were used. The earliest instruments of this type typically show

---

[40]　Pl. 1.9, and below, Pl. 5.1.
[41]　This instrument shows interesting resemblances to the hautboy in Pl. 1.9.
[42]　Pl. 1.3; Halle (1763), iii. 378.

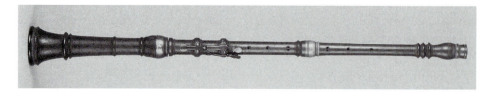

PL. 2.12. Anonymous seventeenth-century tenor hautboy, E.980.2.149. Paris: Collection Musée de la musique/Cliché J-M Billing

PL. 2.13. Charles Simonneau, title-page to Marais's *Pièces en trio* (Paris, 1692). Collection of William Waterhouse

abundant use of ivory tips and occasional tortoiseshell stain. Type A2 hautboys include:

Anon. (? Bressan) (Oxford: Bate 200)
Anon. (Paris: Musée de l'Armée)
Colin Hotteterre (Brussels 2320)
Debey (Bate 2)
Rouge (Paris E.979.2.12)
Rippert (Leipzig 1312, Geneva [La Ménestrandie])
Stanesby sen. (Horniman 232, Horniman 277)
Stanesby jun. (Honma, Horniman 1969.683)
Bradbury (Piguet)

Rottenburgh sen. (Pourtois, Piguet)
Naust (Haynes)
Anciuti (Pistoia, Bernardini)
Jacob Denner (Nuremberg MIR 370)
Desjardin[s], Jean-Baptiste (Winston-Salem, NC 0-113)
Rouge (DCM 423)
Stanesby sen. (Hamamatsu ex Rosenbaum A-0166R)
Rottenburgh sen. (Brussels 2608)
Scherer (Munich 66-88)
Anciuti (Rome 0827 and 0828)
Christoph Denner (Nuremberg MI 155, x Nürnberg MI 153, Berlin 2942, St Petersburg 508)
Jacob Denner (Nuremberg MI 90, Vienna 332 [7289], Yale 3411.78, MMA 89.4 1566, St Petersburg 1135, Nuremberg MI 89, Nuremberg MIR 371, Nuremberg MIR 372)
(David?) Denner (Venice Cons. 34)
Paulhahn (Vienna: Harnoncourt)
Gahn (Milan: Cons.)
Oberlender sen. (de Vries)
Königsberger (Nuremberg MIR 368)
Eichentopf (Halle MS 420, Lisbon MIC-0106)
Schuechbaur (Venice Cons. 33)
Haka (Dombrecht)
Aardenberg (de Vries)
Terton (Smithsonian 208.185)
Steenbergen (de Vries)
Schlegel (Basle 1878.16)

Type A2 hautboys are shown in Pls. 1.3, 2.1(*b*), 2.3, 2.6–8, 2.14–18, and 5.5.

c. Type A3   Type A3 was a profile used by some Dutch makers, current from the end of the seventeenth century and persisting until possibly as late as the 1760s. It shows unusually sharp flares at the finial and short bell and an 'emphatic round-ness'[43] at the balusters. Aggregate tone-hole size is typically on the small side, aver-aging 15.8, but bores are relatively wide; the length is standard (AL about 328).[44] Examples (selection):

---

[43] Adkins (1990), 46.

[44] The AL is the distance from the top of the instrument to the middle of hole 6; it is defined and discussed in §D.2.

PL. 2.16. David Teniers (the Younger), *The Painter and his Family*, detail. Oil painting. Berlin: Staatliche Museen, catalogue number 857

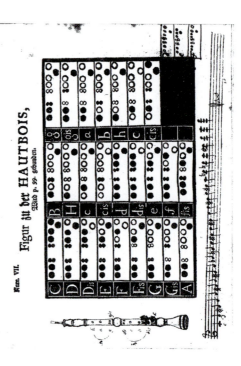

PL. 2.17. Eisel, fingering chart from *Musicus autodidactus* (1738), copy at F-Pn

PL. 2.14. After Domenico Zampieri, 1726, detail from title-page used for Handel's *Alexander*, *Rodelinda*, and *Tamerlane*. F-Pn (Rés. V.S. 125–27)

PL. 2.15. Louis Boullogne le Jeune, *c*.1711, detail of a putto on a ceiling panel of the tribune in the Chapelle Royale, Versailles. Photo RMN: Gérard Blot

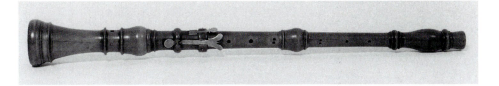

PL. 2.18. Hautboy by Naust. B. Haynes, Montréal

Haka (Stockholm 155, x Berlin 936, Amsterdam: de Vries)
Heerde (Brussels 177)
H. and F. Richters[45]
Rÿkel (The Hague Ea 6-x-1952)
Wijne (v.d. Grinten)
This type is shown in Pl. 2.1(*c*).[46]

d. Type B   Type B probably appeared in the 1730s or 1740s, but there are too few
survivors to date it securely. It is not shown in any known works of art. The
Stanesby jun. in the Bate Collection is a beautiful example (Pl. 2.1(*d*)), and the
shape of the top joint of this hautboy resembles the bell of a Stanesby jun. bassoon
dated 1747.[47] Survivors are known from France, Holland, and England. In Type B,
beading is simplified or absent, the bulge that takes the place of the top baluster is
symmetrical and unframed by beads. Type B represented an abandonment of the
traditional unity of design turnery between the three joints. The walls of the top
column are unusually thick (giving it a particularly warm tone). The centre 'baluster' is similar to the corresponding point on Stanesby's traversos. The Stanesby jun.
has key bosses instead of rings. Aggregate tone-hole size is large, averaging 18.1.
Examples (selection):

Deschamps (London: T. Bingham, Berlin 2934)
Van de Knikker (NL-DHgm Ea 14-x-1952 and Ea 3-x-1993)
Thomas Lot (Bate 24)[48]
Martin Lot (x Berlin 2947)
Schuchart (Glasgow A42-68ao)
J. Crone (Markneukirchen 1116)

e. Type C   Type C is commonly known as the 'straight-top'. The top joint was
turned without finial, baluster, or beads, but slightly conical in profile. The sockets

---

[45] The Richters apparently used this type exclusively. See Adkins (1990).
[46] See Langwill (1980), 80, Adkins (1990), 46, and Haynes (2000) for an interesting photo of some of the
double reeds in NL-DHgm, showing a progression of designs.
[47] In the possession of William Waterhouse (6). A picture of this instrument is published in Young (1982),
pl. VI.   [48] Shown in the oboe article of *New Grove*.

PL. 2.19. Sebastiano Lazzari, detail of a painting, [1752]. Oil on linen, 76 × 91 cm, detail.
Sold in 1992 by Finarte, Milan

of the centre joint and bell were reinforced with ivory tips or metal ferrules. The
first datable indications of the existence of Type C come from northern Italy;
Anciuti began making Type Cs possibly as early as *c.*1709;[49] one is dated 1738.[50] It
has brass ferrules similar to a painting by Lazzari done at Venice in 1752 (Pl. 2.19)
and may have been made for Venice, as it is stamped with the Lion of S. Marco.
Plate 2.20 by Ghezzi, showing a Type C, was probably made before 1730. The other
country where this type was made was England (Halfpenny, in fact, considered the
straight-top model 'typically English'[51]); it was apparently in use in the 1740s (see
Pl. 2.22) and popular there into the nineteenth century. It is shown in works of art
from *c.*1746 to 1789.[52] Straight-tops were evidently common in Italy by the 1740s
and 1750s. Tirabosco's portrait of Bissoli (Pl. 2.21) shows him holding a very thin,
straight-topped hautboy. Another unstamped early straight-top is preserved in the
cellar of the instrument museum at Rome. Examples (selection):

Anciuti (Victoria and Albert, Y3; Rome, Y6)
Cosins (Nuremberg MIR 375)
Palanca (Vindelle: Écochard)
Stanesby jun. (Hamamatsu A-0243R)
Gedney (Vermillion 5298, Christie's sale, 12 June 1996)

---

[49] Cf. London: V & A 23/2.   [50] Rome 1094.   [51] Halfpenny (1949b), 16.
[52] See Pl. 2.22 and Ignase Colombo, Portrait of the oboist Domenico Scolari, Trieste, 1789 (Milan: Civica
Raccolta di Stampe Bertarelli, Castle Sforzesco).

PL. 2.22. Anonymous, c.1746, frontispiece for *The Compleat Tutor for the Hautboy*. GB-Lbl

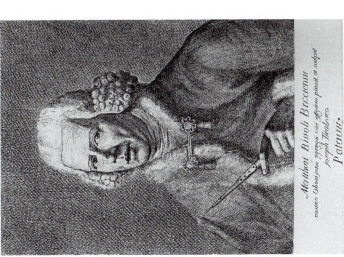

PL. 2.21. Joseph Tirabosco [2nd half 18th c.], portrait of Mattheo Bissoli of Brescia. Amsterdam: Collection Alfredo Bernardini

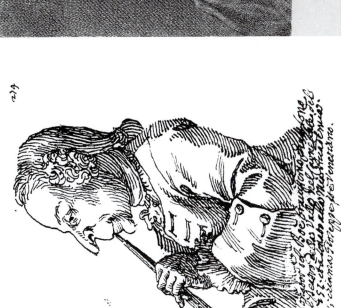

PL. 2.20. Pier Leone Ghezzi, caricature of Gioseppe, hautboy player. Rome: Gabinetto dei disegni e delle stampe (vol. 2606, n. 4654)

PL. 2.23. Hautboy by Anciuti (formerly owned by Rossini). London: Victoria & Albert Museum 23/2

> Cahusac sen. (Horniman 14.5.47/88)
> Miller (Bate x20, Brussels 964)
> Milhouse (Bate 26, Hamamatsu A-0244R)
> Goulding (Edgware: Boosey & Hawkes 203)
> V. Panormo (Piguet)

This type is shown in Pls. 2.1(*e*), 2.18, and 2.19–23.

f. Type D   Halfpenny called this 'the final form of the simple hautboy, and the type to which additional keys were subsequently added'.[53] The earliest examples probably date from about the middle of the eighteenth century. Three variants are contained in this type.

Type D1 first appeared in the so-called Rococo period, a profile that uses elements of both Type A2 and Type D2. Type D1 had fewer beads than Type A2 (the lower bell waist bead disappeared, for instance),[54] and those it retained were very thin and fine. The profile of the top column was often concave rather than straight. It had a centre baluster like Type A whose shape was rounded and whose widest point was nearer the middle than in Type D2 (whose widest point was close to the top of the baluster and was often sharp-edged or hooked). The bell formed a single simple flare from top to bottom below a symmetrically centred baluster; there were normally only two beads or bead complexes on the bell, one at the waist and the other about where the upper flare beads were placed on Type A2. The slightly expanded rim blended into the flare. Most had narrow minimum bores. Extant hautboys of Type D1 were made all over Europe into the nineteenth century. Examples:

> Palanca (Bologna 1800, Brussels 422, Musashino A720, Bernardini, Berlin 5336)
> Crone (Utrecht: Ehrenfeld 8, de Vries)
> M. Lot (Brussels 1980)
> A. Grenser, dated 1790 (Leipzig 3524)
> C. W. Sattler (Piguet, Linz Mu 115)

---

[53] Halfpenny (1949b), 16.   [54] Cf. Piguet (1988), 84.

Mason (Honma)
Astor (de Vries)
Rocko Baur (Linz Mu 45 [117], Milan Cons. 117)
Lempp (Linz Mu 120 [116])
Schlegel (de Vries, Piguet)
Delusse (de Vries, Burgess, Piguet no. 9, Paris 1186/1113, Paris C.479,
    E.367, Paris C.480, E.387, Paris C.481, E.263, Paris E.1807)
Goulding (Horniman 14.5.47/18, 1969/682)

This type is shown in Pls. 2.1(*g*) and 2.11.

Type D2 is the form generally thought of as the 'classical hautboy'. It is shown in works of art from *c*.1770 to *c*.1828.[55] One of its principal characteristics was the placement of the bulge on the balusters, which was clearly higher than previously. The centre baluster was also sharply hooked. Most turning gestures were proud and thin (e.g. Floth). The top baluster was quite pronounced compared with that of A2 models (such as Jacob Denner's or Paulhahn's). The bell had a complex double flare, the portion below the flare beads being less flared and almost vertical. The rim was quite prominent. Minimum bores vary between 4.4 and 5.0 with an average of 4.7. Examples:

Rocko Baur (Kremsmünster: Preiss)
Hammig (Linz Mu 121)
Cahusac (RCM 326 o/1)
Collier (Maunder, Piguet)
Goulding (Halfpenny, Hamamatsu)
W. Milhouse (Hamamatsu, Victoria)
J. Crone (de Vries, Lisbon OB.15, MIC.0615)
Engelhard (Leipzig 1324, Piguet)
A. Grenser (Piguet, Leipzig 3524)
H. Grenser (New York, Leipzig 1317, Hamamatsu)
Grundmann (Berlin, Vermillion, Piguet, RCM 75, Leipzig 3499, 1330,
    Hamburg 1912.1551, 1912.1552, etc.)
Floth (Gävle, Yale)
Kirst (Piguet)
C. Sattler (Linz)
Doleisch (Prague)
Hammig (Vienna, Linz)
Delusse (Paris C.1114, E.1187, de Vries)
Prudent (Brussels 3116)

---

[55] Pl. Int.1; L. A. Vény, fingering chart in *Méthode complète pour le hautbois* (*c*.1828).

This type is shown in Pl. Int.1.[56]

Type D3 differed little from D2, and the difference was in the very high top baluster bulge, which was even more extreme than those of Grundmann and Floth, being in a higher position and using a sharper swelling, and comparable to the high hooked centre baluster bulge on Type D2. It is not shown in any known works of art. The centre baluster of Type D3 could be either rounded or hooked. The bell flare was complex. The known examples probably date from 1760–90:

> Biglioni Y3 (Bernardini)
> Panormo (Vries)
> Schlegel (Leipzig 1322)

g. Type E   Surviving examples of Type E, which are fairly common, were made in francophone cultures (France, the Austrian Netherlands, and Switzerland) in the decades before 1750 until the end of the century. It is shown in works of art from *c*.1750 to 1761.[57] The instrument gives the impression of a Type A2 that has been stretched: Type E's are among the longest hautboys that survive, and the swellings at the balusters and bell flare are very gradual and 'streamlined'; beads are present but the smaller flat fillets that in Type A2 accompanied them on either side are often missing. Tone-holes and bore are relatively small. Examples (selection):

> Bizey (Boston 17.1910, Brussels 424, Paris C.1112, E.1047, Bate 201)
> Gilles Lot (de Vries, Paris E.2181)
> Thomas Lot (Piguet, St Petersburg 512)
> Martin Lot (formerly Berlin 2947)
> L. Hotteterre (Toho Gakuen)
> Lott (NL-DHgm Ea 13-X-1952)
> J. H. Rottenburgh (Ann Arbor 667 [52], Brussels 4360, Brussels 966,
>   Brussels 2609)
> G. A. Rottenburgh (Brussels 2610)
> Schlegel (Piguet)
> Prudent (St Petersburg 516, Cottet)

Type E resembles Type B, and may have derived from it; some hautboys are in fact hybrids between the two styles.[58] The minimum bores of Type E are generally small, like those of other later models, whereas Type B bores can be quite large. See Pls. 1.17 and 2.4.

---

[56] Also Thomas Gainsborough, Portrait of Fischer, 1774–88 (Buckingham Palace); Katherine Levin, 'The clarionet player' (Coll. B. Haynes); A. Vanderhagen, fingering chart in *Méthode nouvelle* (*c*.1790); F. J. Garnier, scale drawing of a Delusse hautboy in his *Méthode raisonée* (1802); A. G. Vogt, fingering chart in *Méthode pour hautbois* (MS, 1816–25); H. Brod, illustrations in *Méthode pour le hautbois*, 1826   [57] Pls. 2.4 and 1.17.
[58] Anon. (Oxford: Bate 292) and Thomas Lot (Bate 24).

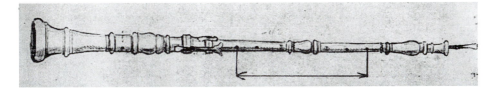

PL. 2.24. Diagram, tone-hole spread. Cf. Pl. 2.3

5. *Proportions*

Recently, it has been noticed that length dimensions of the joints and placement of tone-holes of early woodwind instruments show proportions that strongly suggest they were purposely designed with numerical relationships in mind.[59] These proportions sometimes correspond to simple numbers in length standards that were current at the time.[60] The top and centre sections of hautboys were usually of about equal length, for instance, and the bell was about 3/5 of that length, a proportion of 5:5:3.[61] Proportional relationships can be observed in the placement of tone-holes. On hautboys, the *tone-hole centre* (that is, the distance from the top of the instrument to the middle point between the two groups of three tone-holes) was generally placed at 3/5 to 2/5 of the total length. The *tone-hole spread* (the distance between the middle of hole 1 and hole 6) was usually about 1/3 of the total length[62] (see Pl. 2.24).

Surviving hautboys show that when practical necessities demanded it, makers modified the basic proportional scheme. Examples are the positions of holes 3 and 4 (which are too close respectively to the centre-joint socket beads and column beads) and the placement of resonance-holes on the bell, which are often below their ideal position in the middle of the waist beads. On original hautboys, hole 2 is often higher than the exact centre between 1 and 3, whereas hole 5 is lower than it should be. These holes would have 'looked' better if they had been placed differently. Since their position must have been known beforehand, it would have been easy to move the beads to accommodate them, had it been considered important. General proportions were thus evidently in a separate 'compartment' from acoustical considerations.[63]

---

[59] Cf. Heyde (1986), 187 ff.; Adkins (1999).

[60] An interesting 'TABLE of the Foreign Measures, carefully compared with the English', which first appeared in Stone's *New Mathematical Dictionary* in 1726 (under ME) is reproduced in *FoMRHIQ* 81 (Oct. 1995), 6.

[61] This applies to the visible parts of the joints when the instrument is assembled, so the tenons are invisible. The proportions are often even simpler (2:2:1) when the tenons are counted.

[62] Heyde (1986), 173, 179–80. These two concepts were termed the *Grifflochlagezentrum* and *Grifflochspanne* by Heyde.

[63] Heyde's suggestion of a relation between the dimensions of original instruments and local length standards is complicated by the fact that makers copied instruments from other places (as for instance Christoph Denner, who

C. Bores and Tone-holes

Appendix 2 gives the the rough acoustic profiles of ninety-eight original hautboys. The profile includes four parameters: the acoustic length (or AL; see §D.2), the minimum bore, the *bore scaling* (the ratio of bore diameter to length, in this case, the AL divided by the minimum bore), and the *aggregate tone-hole sizes* (that is, the total of the diameters of holes 1, 2, 5, and 6).[64] Instruments whose 'acoustic' dimensions are similar will probably feel similar to play and be at close to the same pitch.[65]

There was little reason for anyone to have written anything down about tuning adjustments to woodwind instruments in this period. These were the domains of craftsmen low on the social and artistic scale, and in any case the important information was regarded as secret (see §E.1). But a set of random notes on adjustments to the tuning and response of an oboe survives, made in about 1850 by Carl Golde, a Dresden maker.[66] Although Golde was making a key-system oboe, the relationship between bore and tone-holes he describes seem similar to that of the hautboy. Golde's adjustments were made in two ways: by *undercutting* the tone-holes (that is, enlarging the end of the tone-hole that enters the bore), and *chambering* (widening the bore by reaming at specific points). The effect of these operations was to raise the pitch of given fingerings. Undercutting on seventeenth- and eighteenth-century instruments was usually somewhat oval, being heaviest on the upper and lower sides of the tone-hole (the reed side and the bell side). Chambering was done above, below, and at the tone-holes.[67]

For any fingering in the fundamental register, it was the size of the first open hole (counting from the top) that had the primary effect on tuning. This was true for both cross- and simple fingerings. The tuning of open holes further down the bore had less effect.[68] Most fingerings were the same for the fundamental and its octave. Since the upper register was more sensitive than the fundamental to changes in the tone-holes,[69] undercutting affected the octave more than the fundamental.

---

probably began with French models). In examining surviving instruments by some Nuremberg makers, Kirnbauer and Krickeberg (1987: 263, 265, 274, 275) found significant differences between real dimensions and Nuremberg measurement standards. They also found variations in length standards between instruments by the same maker; such variation is also observable in Appendix 2 (and is in some cases caused by differences in pitch).

[64] The eighth tone-hole is purposely avoided because it may have been enlarged to accommodate later pitch rises. Cf. Talbot's measurements of the seventh and eighth holes of the Bressan hautboy he examined (below).

[65] These data are far from complete, of course. Graphed bore profiles would be more revealing. The tone-hole sizes do not take into account the amount of undercutting, but that was relatively standardized.

[66] Cf. Karp (1978), 19–21.

[67] Marc Écochard (1996), an hautboy maker, wrote a commentary on Golde's text and developed diagrams that show the main points along the bore at which adjustments of both bore chambering and undercutting occur in hautboy tuning.   [68] See Myers (1981), 12.

[69] According to Myers (1981), 43, 'bore perturbations have their greatest effect on the lowest mode, while tone-hole dimensions have their greatest effect on higher modes'.

Undercutting the upper side raised the fundamental more than when both the upper and lower sides were undercut.[70] When only the lower side was undercut, almost all the effect was to the octave. By contrast, chambering above a hole raised the fundamental but not the octave, whereas chambering below or at the level of a hole had the opposite effect. To put this schematically:

	Fundamental	*Octave*
Undercutting above only	↑	↑
Undercutting below only		↑
Undercutting both above and below	↑	↑̠
Chambering above tone-hole only	↑	
Chambering at and/or below tone-hole		↑

Undercutting affected notes in other ways as well. It made a note louder and brighter in tone colour, and (as Sand Dalton (pers. comm.) points out) made it easier to push up or down in pitch. It also made it respond more easily; if a tone-hole had sharp edges where it entered the bore, it spoke less easily, thereby causing the player to blow harder than usual to overcome the initial inertia, like a stiff accelerator on a car.

Much of the playing quality of an hautboy depended on its bore profile and size, which was a result first of its original design and second of the tuning and adjustments just described. These adjustments affected basic pitch, tone quality, resistance, and 'play', both in volume and pitch. The subtle interplay between these variables was the personal signature of each maker, and their general features fluctuated with time and place.

Appendix 2 shows a broad range of aggregate tone-hole sizes. The average is about 16.6, but the range is from 14.0 to 19.65, suggesting that hautboys can be characterized as small-holed (about 14.0–16.4) and large-holed (about 16.5–19.65). The contrast in playing qualities between hautboys with smaller or larger tone-holes is quite noticeable. A small-holed instrument will have a more defined basic pitch level, crisper intonation, and sharper differentiation of notes. Larger tone-holes produce a more fluid intonation. Undercutting of course affects these differences. Two outstanding examples of large-holed hautboys are by Jacob Denner (Nuremberg MIR 370) and Stanesby jun. (Bate 29), with holes at 19.25 and 18.3 respectively. Among the good smaller-holed instruments are the Brussels Hotteterre (16.0), the Bate 'Galpin' (16.17), and the Piguet Rottenburgh (16.3). Aggregate tone-hole size also affects pitch: for a given AL, hautboys with larger tone-holes will be higher by about a quarter-step.

---

[70] Cf. van der Heide (1983).

Tone-hole size is not linked to bore size. Of the two large-holed instruments mentioned above, Denners are almost always narrow-bore (this one is 5.8), while the Stanesby jun. is unusually wide (6.5).

It is of course difficult to know if the tone-holes of original instruments have been altered, an operation that might have been performed to raise pitch. Talbot (who was very precise in his measurements)[71] wrote in *c*.1692–5 of a Bressan hautboy: 'Dia. of 1st, 3d & 4th holes, 1″ 1/4; of 2d 1″ 1/3; of 5th, 6xth, 7th & 8th, 1″ 2/3.'[72] In other words, a report by a reliable contemporary on a good representative hautboy of the time observed only three sizes of tone-holes on hautboys, and the lowest four holes were all the same size. In surviving instruments, the general pattern is not unlike this, although the sixth hole tends to be a little smaller than the fifth, and the eighth (which is suspect because of later attempts to raise pitch) is much bigger than either. The averages of fifty original instruments are as follows:

Hole:	1	2	5	6	8
	3.2	3.6	5.0	4.8	7.5

Talbot's measurements were:

	4.0	4.2	5.3	5.3	5.3 [!]

The dimensions of the minimum bores shown in Appendix 2 range from 4.4 to 7.15 mm (mid-point 5.78), and average 5.95 mm. An excellent maker like Jacob Denner could have a range from 5.55 to 6.3, straddling any obvious cut-off point, and French hautboy makers used both wide and narrow bores. Among the early French makers of wide-bore hautboys were Rippert, Naust, Hotteterre, and Debey. Wide-bore instruments are also typical of Haka, Richters, Rottenburgh sen., and both Stanesbys.[73] French narrow-bore instruments include those by Rouge, Anon. (Paris: Musée de l'Armée), Anon. (Paris E.108), and Desjardins,[74] and elsewhere by (among others) Bradbury, Jacob Denner (frequently), Paulhahn, Eichentopf, and Castel.

A general, systematic, and comparative study of the internal dimensions (bores and tone-holes) of surviving hautboys has yet to be made. It is possible that the way an hautboy plays is influenced by bore scaling, since on original instruments bore

---

[71] As Baines noticed (1948: 23), Talbot measured from edge to edge between holes on the hautboy. A comparison of his total lengths with the linear placements of his tone-holes confirms this, as they match to a tenth of a millimetre. This indicates the care with which Talbot made his measurements.

[72] The aggregate tone-hole size of this instrument is relatively large at 18.8 mm.

[73] These bores range from 6.2 to 6.5. The average minimum bore (5.95) is used as a cutoff point between wide-bore and narrow-bore hautboys.

[74] This instrument may have been made by Pelletier; see Ch. 5, §B.5.

diameter appears to vary independently of bore length. But this is speculation and no study has as yet been made.[75]

Adkins (1996) made a comparison of the bores of thirty Milhouse hautboys made in the late eighteenth century, referring briefly to the bores of some earlier Dutch instruments. Powell (1996, 1997), studying traversos, has demonstrated how useful it is to be able quickly to compare bore profiles and tone-hole locations and sizes.

D. Hautboy Pitch

1. The difficulty of identifying accurately the pitches of original hautboys

Museum catalogues sometimes confidently report the pitches of the hautboys in their holdings as if they could be determined with the same certainty as those of recorders, clarinets, and traversos. It would be very helpful if this information could be taken seriously, but unfortunately there are physical factors that make it impossible to ascertain precisely the original pitches of hautboys. The most basic problem is that the reed is missing, and the only way to play the instrument is to use a reed made for some other hautboy. Players use their judgement based on what they are used to, and what therefore feels comfortable, and they make certain unconscious assumptions about how the instrument should sound and respond, based on past experience. These affect the reed they choose to use on the instrument, and the way they play it.

On the hautboy (unlike the recorder and clarinet), notes can quite plausibly be 'bent' to accommodate pitch levels as much as 40 cents apart on the same instrument. Not only are there differences between players, but the same player can alter the pitch of an instrument by using reeds of different dimensions.[76] Hautboys that are normally played at A−1 can be played reasonably convincingly by the same player a quarter-step higher and a half-step lower, and an hautboy that normally plays at A−2 can be played at A−1½ by using reeds for an instrument at A−1.[77]

This flexibility naturally increases as instruments get larger, and it is not surprising to learn from Halle (1763: 370) that 'englischen Waldhörner' (by which he probably meant oboes da caccia) could be played at different pitches (*Cammerton* and *Chorton*) by altering the dimensions of the reed:

Die Rohrmundstücke werden weiter, oder enger genommen, um ein Instrument aus dem Chortone blasen zu können.	Wider or narrower reeds are used in order to be able to play an instrument at *Chorton*.

---

[75] I include bore scaling (in this case, the AL divided by the minimum bore) in Appendix 2.

[76] In this case, the internal intonation requires adjusting the size of the lowest tone-holes: as pitch goes up, they must be enlarged.

[77] Cf. also Piguet's remark (1997) on his experience playing the same instrument at 415 in 1963 and 405 in 1982.

Based on the physical qualities of the instrument itself, there is in fact no objective method of being certain of the historical pitch of an hautboy. The nearest anyone can come is to say that an hautboy plays comfortably at a certain pitch level for a specific player, but may play at a different level for someone else.

There are, however, ways to estimate an instrument's original pitch, by comparing: (1) known historical pitch standards of the time and place where the instrument was made and/or played; (2) recorders, traversos, and clarinets made by the same hautboy maker; (3) acoustic profiles; and (4) hautboys by the same maker that differ in length.[78] This information can then be combined with the pitch produced by the instrument to arrive at a plausible guess.

Historical pitch standards and the reliability of pitch evidence from other woodwinds are treated in detail in Haynes (1995) and Haynes (forthcoming). Background information on sixteen representative makers can also be found in Appendix 3. The factor of hautboy length needs further discussion.

2. Lengths

As a rough indication of pitch, original hautboys can be sorted into categories according to their bore lengths. The easiest measurement to obtain is the *total length* (TL). But since bells vary significantly in length, the AL (the *acoustic length*, or distance from the top of the instrument to the middle of hole 6)[79] is more indicative of pitch. Pitch estimates of original hautboys based on their ALs can only be approximate and tentative, as other factors can influence pitch: the size of the bore,[80] the length from the top of the instrument to the first hole, and the possibility that toneholes are drilled at angles (so they enter the bore at a different length than they exit the exterior). Above all, the general size of the tone-holes is important for determining pitch: two hautboys of similar acoustic length with an identical reed set-up can vary a quarter-step in pitch because of their aggregate tone-hole sizes.

As can be seen in Appendix 2, original hautboys whose AL is known show a range from 263 to 344 mm. They can be sorted into four categories:

> AL 263–288 mm (5% of those known at present)
> AL 289–314 mm (5%)
> AL 315–329.8 mm (57%)
> AL 329.9–344 mm (33%)

The shorter hautboys of the first two categories account for 10 per cent of surviving original hautboys whose lengths are known. Logically, we would expect the shortest and longest hautboys to correspond respectively to the highest and lowest

---

[78] The two Prudents at St Petersburg, for instance, are at AL 323.8 and 340.2, a difference that corresponds to about a semitone in pitch (these and other measurements from St Petersburg are thanks to Christian Schneider).

[79] The distance from the top of the instrument to hole 8 (the hole closed by the Great-key) would be more accurate, but is less reliable historically because hole 8 may later have been enlarged to accommodate pitch rises.

[80] Re-reaming new hautboys after they have been 'played in' raises their pitch, for instance.

normal pitch standards of the period; the highest commonly used pitch level was A+1, the lowest was A−2. It would be convenient if these four categories could be attached to the pitches A+1, A+0, A−1, and A−2; but length is not the only factor that determines pitch. Some instruments in the third group that might be expected to play at A−1, for instance, seem to play best at A−1½ or even A−2.

a. The shortest hautboys (AL 263–288 mm) Five original hautboys (all Type A2) are remarkably short; the gap between their lengths and that of the next-longer instruments (at 300.7) is conspicuous:

263.1	Schuechbaur (Venice Cons. 33).
272.1	Christoph Denner (Nuremberg MI 155)[81]
274	Schell (Berlin 5250)
274.2	Eggl (Salzburg 13/1)
276	Gahn (Milan: Cons.)

The Schuechbaur plays well at A+1, and I played the Denner (MI 155) at the same pitch; it has a delightful squeaky little sound. These hautboys were made in south Germany and Austria, and could have been used in churches with organs at *Cornet-ton* (which was A+1), or for customers in Italy, where this pitch was sometimes used (and known as *Corista di Lombardia*).[82]

There is documentation of hautboys in *Cornet-ton*. On 16 July 1708, the great Abbey of Kremsmünster took delivery of '2 buxbaumene Hoboa, Cornetton 6 fl' (2 boxwood Hautbois in *Cornet-ton*, 6 *fl*); in 1707 they bought '12 Hoboa Rohr, als 6 Cornett Ton' (12 Hautbois reeds, 6 in *Cornet-ton*), and in 1710

Von Wienn empfangen 24 Hoboa Rohr vnd 12 Fagot Rohr, Cornet- vnd französisch Ton per 6 fl.[83]	Received from Vienna, 24 Hautbois reeds and 12 bassoon reeds, at [both] *Cornet-ton* and French pitch, 6 fl.

A list of instruments at the court at Stuttgart in 1718 included '2 *hautbois* [!] von Cornetthon' as well as three others[84] (presumably at another pitch). An inventory of instruments at Ulm in 1744 lists, among other hautboys, a 'Cornet Hautbois'; this name suggests it was at *Cornet-ton*.[85] The Munich court also purchased a 'Cornet Fagot und Hoboé' in 1750.[86] The Denner hautboy, MI 155, that apparently plays at A+1, is thought to have been used originally at St Sebald-Kirche in Nuremberg.[87]

---

[81] As Reine Dahlqvist (pers. comm.) points out, two other hautboys by Christoph Denner, MI 153 and MI 154, lost in the Second World War, were also about the same length (see Kirnbauer 1994: 126–7).

[82] See Haynes (1995), §3-2.

[83] See Kellner (1956), 302, 299, 304. According to Paul Hailperin, a surviving hautboy by Deper (? Vienna, now in Melk) is pitched no lower than A-460.   [84] Owens (1995), 206.

[85] Krause-Pichler (1991), 214, 232. The same list contains a 'Zincken', so the 'Cornet Hautbois' was probably not a type of cornett.

[86] Nösselt (1980), 95. Many other instruments bought in the same period were destined for chamber use, while these were probably used for playing with a church organ.   [87] Kirnbauer (1994), 128, 209.

Christoph Denner may have supplied high-pitched hautboys to Prince Ferdinando de' Medici of Florence. He finished building and repairing a set of instruments (probably hautboys and bassoons) for Ferdinando only three days before his death in 1707. Ferdinando's agent wrote

Stato un soprano solo . . . il maestro mi fece un altro in medesimo modo del concerto, e duoi altri *più acuti* . . .[88]	Instead of a single treble . . . the *maestro* has made me another in the same pitch as the consort, and two others that are *higher* . . .

It has been suggested that short hautboys in France were considered transposing instruments in D rather than C.[89] But there is no sign that musicians at the time thought in this way. Sources that name the lowest note consistently call it c_1 for hautboy (Talbot *c.*1692–5, Freillon-Poncein 1700, Hotteterre 1707). Likewise, from the 1680s the recorder's lowest note was always f_1, not g_1 (Loulié *c.*1685–90, Freillon-Poncein, and Hotteterre).[90] It is more likely that shorter woodwinds were regarded as in the usual C (or F) but at *Ton d'Écurie*, a pitch standard a tone higher than usual (A+1). Although some of the oldest surviving hautboys are at A+1 (as the treble shawm had been), far from all early hautboys are short; they are fairly well divided over all the length categories. Nor are all short hautboys early.

AL 289–314 mm. Five other instruments are relatively short, and a gap exists between them and the previous group:

300.7	Jacob Denner (Nuremberg MI 90).[91] Type A2
306.5	Rouge (DCM 423). Type A2
307	(David?) Denner (Venice Cons. 34). Type A2
310	Haka (Amsterdam: de Vries). Type A3
313.4	Martin (Paris E.210, C.470). Type A1

Players have associated hautboys of this length with A+0. It is possible these instruments were made for use in Italy (where this pitch was common and known as *Corista Veneto*).[92]

b. The longest hautboys (AL greater than 329 mm)   Most hautboys have a length between 315 and 329 mm, and were probably meant to be played at A−1 or A−1½. Hautboys that have an AL of 329 mm and longer play somewhat below A−1, either at A−1½ or A−2. About a third of the surviving hautboys whose AL is known come

---

[88] Letter from Cristoforo Carlo Grundherr to Ferdinando, 4 May 1707, quoted in Ferrari (1994), 211. Italics mine.   [89] Piguet (1988), 82–3.

[90] Two English recorder tutors of the 1680s (Salter, *The Genteel Companion* (1683), and Carr, *The Delightful Companion* (1684)) speak only of the recorder in f_1 (Eppelsheim 1961: 71). As Eppelsheim reasons, since these books treated a 'French' instrument, the custom was probably also common in France.

[91] This instrument is stamped '2' at the bottom back of the top joint. A traverso by Jacob Denner (Thalheimer collection) which is also higher than usual (in f_1 at 420) has the same '2' above the maker's stamp. This number may indicate that the instruments were originally part of a pair. But since both instruments are pitched high, it is possible that the number is an indication of pitch. Other instruments made in Nuremberg also used the number '2'; see Kirnbauer and Thalheimer (1995), 91–4. There is no indication another joint stamped '1' ever existed.

[92] See Haynes (1995), §3-3.

under this category; the longest is 343.8. When pitch is lower than A–1, hautboys can be adjusted to play at a range of levels, so in this length range a definitive classification of hautboys by pitch is not possible. Some hautboys, like the Denner Nürnberg MIR 370 (AL 328.8), will play convincingly at A–2, A–1½, and A–1.[93] As instruments become larger, they offer more leeway in tuning. In any case, the difference between A–1½ and A–2 is only a quarter-tone, and with so many other factors at work, a difference of that relatively small degree may not be reflected in length measurements.

3. Alternate top joints

An hautboy by the Milanese maker Anciuti dated 1722 has alternate top joints.[94] It is likely that Giuseppe Sammartini, who came from Milan, played such an instrument (see Ch. 5, §C.2). Hawkins included the following anecdote about Sammartini:

About the year 1735 an advertisement appeared in the public papers, offering a reward of ten guineas for a hautboy-reed that had been lost. It was conjectured to be Martini's, and favoured the opinion that he had some secret in preparing or meliorating the reeds of his instrument, though none could account for the offer of a reward so greatly disproportionable to the utmost conceivable value of the thing lost. It seems that the reed was found, and brought to the owner, but in such a condition as rendered it useless.[95]

It is difficult to imagine that Sammartini could have lost a reed (which would either have been in his mouth, the end of his instrument, or in its case); hautboists rarely lose reeds. What he could have lost is some part of his gear that was not regularly in use, the most obvious being an extra top joint. And considering the reward, this would not have been the product of a local maker and thus easily replaced. As it turns out, part of this speculation is confirmed by Redmond Simpson, a London hautboist of the next generation, who added in the margin of his copy of Hawkins, now at the Public Library in Minneapolis:

In the note which says a reward of 10 Guineas was offered for a Hautboy reed that had been lost, it was the upper joint of his Hautboy, for which he was inconsolable 'till he got one that suited him. The later [*sic*] was purchased at his sale by the late D. of Ancaster for 20 Guineas who gave it to me. It is still in my possession.

Sammartini would have had good reason to use alternate top joints to compensate for the pitch differences between Milan/Venice and London.[96]

---

[93] To play as high as 415, however, it is necessary to open the lowest tone-holes.

[94] Milan, Castello Sforzesco (information kindly supplied by Alfredo Bernardini). When they appeared on hautboys in the latter half of the 18th c. in Austria, alternate top joints were called *Muttationen* or *Motazionen*. See Hellyer (1975), 54, 55, 57 and Maunder (1998), 188.   [95] Hawkins (1776), v. 370 n.

[96] In a forthcoming book on pitch history, I speculate that Sammartini played at about A–423 in the three virtuoso opera arias he played for Handel two years later in 1737, rather than at his usual pitch of A+0 (about A–435).

In a 'Concert affetuoso l'haubois a 9 part' in the Rostock library,[97] the string and continuo parts are in E, the *Hautbois 1* and *Hautcontre* parts, marked *Tieff Röhre*, are notated in F, thus sounding a semitone lower. Owens suggests the piece is by Brescianello, which would date it between 1716 and the 1750s. *Tieff Röhre* may thus have been alternate joints pitched a semitone lower. The joints would have allowed the players to use a more appropriate tonality (see Ch. 4, §H.2).

Several of Telemann's Frankfurt cantatas also call for *Tief(f)-Rohr* in the hautboy parts.[98] Although none of these cantatas was performed before 1716, many had repeat performances, some as late as the 1750s. Ff.Mus.1497 has at the top of the hautboy parts: 'Mit tieffen Rohren [and above this in a lighter ink:] bey d. hochstimmenden Orgel' (use longer joints with the higher-pitched organ). There is reason to think that here, too, the purpose of using *tieffen Rohren* was to give the player a better tonality (in this case, B♭).[99]

On 5 December 1766 Josef Haydn, recently appointed Capellmeister, wrote in a letter to Prince Esterházy:

Übrigens melden mir die zwey hautboisten (gleichwie ich auch selbsten eingestehen mus) das ihre 2 hautboi alters halber zu grund gehen, und den rechtmässigen Tonum nicht mehr geben, wesswegen *Euer Durchl*: den schuldigsten Vortrag mache, das ein Meister Rockobauer[100] in Wienn sich befinde, welcher meines erachtens dissfahls der kündigste ist. weillen nun dieser Meister mit derley arbeith zwar stätts beschäfftiget ist, dermahlen aber sich besondere zeit nehmete, ein Paar gute daurhaffte hautboi mit einen extra stuckh auf satz (womit alle erforderliche Toni genohmen werden könten) zu verfertigen, dauor aber der nächste Preyß in 8 Ducaten bestehet. als habe *Euer Durchl*. hohen Consens zu erwarthen, ob besagte 2 höchst nöthige hautboi um erstgemelten Preyß eingeschaffet werden dürfften . . .[101]

Furthermore the two oboists tell me (and I myself must take their part) that their two hautboys are disintegrating with age, and no longer possess the proper pitch, wherefore I would like to report, that there is a craftsman named Rockobauer in Vienna, who in my opinion is the most skilful in such things. Because the master always has a waiting list for such work but would take time on special occasion to make a pair of good durable hautboys with an extra joint to each set (in order that all the necessary pitches can be played), for which, however, the minimum price would be 8 Ducats. I therefore hope for your Excellency's permission to obtain the above-mentioned two sorely needed hautboys at the stated price . . .[102]

---

[97] Mus. Saec. XVII: 51.38, described in Owens (1995), 213 ff.

[98] Ff.Mus.1078, Ff.Mus.1497 (written by 1727, when Telemann was in Hamburg; see Schlichte 1979: 367), and Ff.Mus.1105.   [99] See Haynes (1995), §6-3b.

[100] Rocko Baur (fl. Vienna, a1764–p1777). See Waterhouse (1993) and Maunder (1998), 181, 187.

[101] Haydn (1965: 56, c.1767). Bartha writes (Haydn 1965: 56) that evidence that the new instruments requested were ever ordered or received has not been found in the Esterházy archives. If they were purchased, it is likely they would have been used by Haydn for a considerable time afterwards.

[102] My thanks to Paul Hailperin for help in translating this passage.

In 1773, da Silva wrote from Lisbon:

Da Torino se desiderano due oboe di Palanca, ed approvati dal S^r. Besozzi, e basta che tenga ogn'uno due pezzi; ciò'è il primo pezzo che sia il tono naturale, e l'altro pezzo più basso . . .[103]

From Turin we would like two hautboys made by Palanca, approved by Mr Besozzi, and it is sufficient if they each have two joints; that is, the first joint should be in the natural pitch and the other lower . . .

Palanca is survived by three hautboys with alternate top joints.[104] Alfredo Bernardini (pers. comm.) observes that the two centre joints and bells found with six top joints of different lengths[105] at Musashino may be, in a sense, 'just one oboe at 6 pitches'. The two sets of centre bells are quite different in length. He speculates that Palanca determined that a given centre joint-bell combination could be well in tune with no more than a range of three top joints, and thus in order to support six top joints, it was necessary to supply two sets of centre-joints and bells.

E. *'L'anche qui donne la vie': Reeds*

1. Sources of information

Written information on reeds and reed-making is rare before about 1780, and most descriptions begin in about 1800. For Baroque reeds, this material is of limited value, because reed-making went through a process of evolution parallel to changes in hautboy design, and the instrument in use after 1780 was in many ways closer to the modern key-system oboe than to the hautboy.

There are several reasons for the scarcity of early sources of information on hautboy reeds. Apart from the difficulty of describing reed-making on paper, tutors generally addressed amateur players, who would have bought their reeds. Students preparing for professional careers would no doubt have learned reed-making directly from a teacher.

There was also a tradition of secrecy, since reeds were made either by professional players or instrument makers, and the process was screened, like thousands of other crafts, by the traditional protectionism of the guilds. One of Denis Diderot's great frustrations in writing his *Encyclopédie* was his attempt to gather technical information directly from craftsmen, an activity that was unheard-of in the pre-Enlightenment atmosphere of the mid-eighteenth century. With a tone that was almost bitter, he remarked

---

[103] Letter to Piaggio (Genova). Quoted and translated in McClymonds (1978), 42.
[104] Bologna 1800 (Y11) and Musashino A720 and A721 (Y14 and Y15).
[105] The difference in top joint lengths is 24.3 mm (203.5 to 227.8).

Les Artistes . . . vivent ignorés, obscurs, isolés; ils font tout pour leur interêt, ils ne font presque rien pour leur gloire. Il y a des inventions qui restent des siècles entiers renfermées dans une famille . . . Il y a des circonstances où les Artistes sont tellement impénétrables, que le moyen le plus court, ce seroit d'entrer soi-même en apprentissage . . .[106]

Craftsmen . . . live isolated, obscure, unknown lives; everything they do is done to serve their own interests; they almost never do anything just for the sake of glory. There have been inventions that have stayed for whole centuries in the closely guarded custody of single families . . . There are trades where the craftsmen are so secretive that the shortest way [of gaining the necessary information] would be to bind oneself out to some master as an apprentice . . .[107]

For earlier reeds, the best sources of evidence (the Talbot MS excepted) are not written but rather painted and drawn. We can always wonder how literally graphic representations were meant to be taken, since art had other intentions besides mere photographic accuracy. But for our mundane purposes, it is easy to see when objects were intended to be portrayed realistically. In the case of reeds, the accuracy of the instrument to which they are attached is the best criterion. Pictures give not only a good idea of proportions and shapes of reeds, but also real dimensions that can be derived by comparing the instruments in the pictures with similar surviving instruments.

a. Surviving examples of reeds   The role of the reed on the hautboy has been compared to that of the bow on the violin. Unlike bows, however, few early reeds have survived; they were made of a perishable and easily breakable substance, and had less obvious value and importance.[108] Since old oboes were virtually worthless until two generations ago, any reeds that happened to survive with them were at great hazard. To date, all that is known probably made before 1760 are three staples:

Haddon Hall, Derbyshire. Unsoldered staple, before *c*.1700 (cf. Burgess and Hedrick 1989: 60)[109]

Rome, Museo degli strumenti musicali. Staple together with hautboy by Anciuti, dated 1718.[110]

---

[106] Diderot and d'Alembert (1751–72), s.v. 'Encyclopédie', p. 647.

[107] Trans. J. Barzun and R. H. Bowen.

[108] I know of at least one old reed that was thrown away recently.

[109] Peter Hedrick (pers. comm.) writes: 'must be before *c*.1700 because the building fell into disuse then'. He notes that it could be for hautboy or shawm. Burgess and Hedrick's 1989 article gives some idea of the nature of surviving hautboy reeds, but is a specific study of nineteen English reeds of the period *c*.1788–*c*.1848 (!); it includes a general listing of all known surviving reeds, with some measurements. It also includes observations on differences between modern and late 18th-c. reed-making based on indications from these examples. There is some general information on reed-making for curtals, shawms, and crumhorns in the *Instrumentälischer Bettlermantl* (MS *c*.1645–50) described in Campbell (1995).   [110] Y7. Rome 0828 (1368).

PL. 2.25. Musette reed, Copenhagen (2 views)

London, Horniman Museum. Staple with Stanesby jun. hautboy 1969.683. Meas. P. Hailperin.[111] For dimensions of these staples, see below, §2.c.

Clues as to how hautboy reeds were made are also available from the reeds that chance has spared in the interior of a number of old musettes de cour (although they were probably not of the same exact dimensions).[112] Reeds found on grand chalumeaux (chanters) closely resemble pictures of hautboy reeds, and those on the petit chalumeau and the bourdon (or drone box) are similar to pictures of early bassoon reeds (Pl. 2.25). Musette reeds were enclosed and protected inside a cap, and since they were played dry (as moisture causes deterioration in cane),[113] they are often well preserved.[114]

[111] See also the reed in the Leipzig Musikinstrumenten Museum under §E.3.c below. Several reed cases have survived (some with reeds still in them):

  Munich, Stadtmuseum, Mu 147. Photograph in Prinz (1985), 308. 4 surviving reeds
  Chesham Bois. Edgar Hunt
  Musashino. Reed case with reeds and Palanca hautboys

All appear to be late 18th-c. and use the same principle of storing the reeds vertically in lozenge-shaped slots. Walther (1732: 285) called a reed case a *Glossocomium* (from the Greek *Glottis* for reed).

[112] In 1723, Hotteterre included advice on reeds for the chalumeaux of Uffenbach's musette: 'Il faut que l'anche soit fort petite et vous servir du meme tuyau ou cuivret si vous l'avez conservé pour monter la canne dessus . . .'. This warning would have been unnecessary if Uffenbach could have used a standard hautboy reed on his musette.

[113] Borjon (1672) wrote in his musette tutor: 'Il ne faut jamais soufler avec la bouche ny dans le chalumeau, ny dans le porte-vent, pour quelque sujet que ce soit, parceque le vent qui vient de la bouche estant gras & humide enroüille l'anche, & la corrompt tost ou tard.' Cocks and Bryan (1967), 25 write of Northumbrian bagpipes (which are similar to musettes): 'Well made reeds will last almost indefinitely (accidents excepted) with careful use, and cases are known where a chanter reed has still been in perfect condition after thirty years' playing; drone reeds may last even longer.'

[114] Reeds have been found in the following musettes:

  Chambure (grand chalumeau and bourdon)
  Claudius (grand chalumeau and bourdon)
  Berlin (petit chalumeau and bourdon)
  Paris E.571, C.520 (bourdon)
  Waddesdon Manor (Britain; see Halfpenny (1977), 447 for photo)

2. Historical components

a. Cane Hautboy reeds were made of the material still used on key-system oboe reeds, *Arundo donax*. Theophrastus (372 to 287 BC) described a cane used for musical instruments that was probably *Arundo donax*.[115] Borjon wrote (1672: 34) that

L'anche qui donne la vie au chalumeau, & celles qui anime le bourdon sont faites de canne . . .	The reed, which gives life to the chanter, and those that quicken the drones, are made of cane . . .

and elsewhere in his book he used the word *Arundo*.[116]

In his section on the bassoon, Talbot, writing in the 1690s, observed that the 'best reeds [are] from [the] Marshes of Spain and Provence'. Musical sources from the early nineteenth century spoke of the superior qualities of the cane in Fréjus, in the neighbourhood of Marseille and Perpignan,[117] the Departments of Bouches-du-Rhône, Var, and the Alpes-Maritimes.[118] These are areas from which most reed players still get their cane.

The process of cutting and drying cane was not described prior to 1802. But in the preceding centuries it was not likely to have been much different from the descriptions of Garnier (1802), Brod (1825), Sellner (1825), Bate (1956, 1975: 21–2), Ledet (1981: 87), and Perdue (1958: 381 ff.).[119]

b. Thread Thread was used for tying the cane to the staple, sealing the staple's open lengthwise seam, and making an airtight seal in the counterbore of the hautboy. Surviving early reeds and written sources indicate that the usual material was waxed hemp or linen.

Mersenne (1636: 302) mentioned 'fil, ciré, ou que l'on rend humide' (thread, waxed or made moist) on the reed of the shawm. Hotteterre wrote of the thread on musette reeds (1737: 78–9):

Au reste on peut encore quand les Anches sont trop hautes, les baisser, en mettant autour du bout de leur Cuivret un peu de fil de chanvre fin & ciré, ou bien un peu de papier mince, afin qu'elles entrent moins avant dans leurs trous. Au contraire quand elles sont trop basses, on ôte un peu de fil du même endroit, afin qu'elles entrent plus avant; ce qui les hausse.	Also, if the reeds are too sharp, they can be lowered by some fine, waxed hemp thread, or else a bit of thin paper, placed around the ends of their staples, so that they are not inserted as far in their holes. If, on the other hand, they are too flat, remove a bit of thread from the same place. This allows them to be inserted further and thus sharpens them.

---

[115] Girard (1983), 14.

[116] Borjon (1672), 19. The reeds in the musette formerly owned by the Comtesse de Chambure were made of a material that was very brown and looked like a combination of Dutch rush and *Arundo donax*.

[117] Brod (1825).   [118] Ozi (1803).

[119] Relevant extracts from Perdue are reprinted in Haynes (1984), 21–2 (which examines and discusses the written historical evidence on hautboy reeds).

One of the reeds in the musette formerly owned by the Comtesse de Chambure that I examined in 1971 was tied with thick hemp string, another with heavy linen. The thread on the grand chalumeau reed of the Claudius Collection musette no. 485 was pale red in colour, and could have been cotton, with a thicker white thread underneath, heavily waxed.[120] The thread on the bourdon reed was 0.7 mm thick, was double-wound, white, and possibly hemp, painted over with a red lacquer or paint.

Burgess and Hedrick (1989: 41–2) suggest that the most likely source of thread for the single wrap used on the staples they examined from the end of the eighteenth century was the linen thread commonly used to bind books.[121]

c. Staples   The reeds of bagpipes are generally bound permanently onto the staple, whereas it is thought that shawms used a staple separate from the reed. Either system could work satisfactorily on a treble hautboy.[122]

The staple (or tube, i.e. the lower, metal part of the reed) was cut from a piece of sheet metal, trapezoidal when flat, and hammered around a mandrel so the sides abutted, forming a cone with an open lengthwise seam. To make it airtight, the staple was then lapped with thread along its entire length (perhaps with gold-beater's skin underneath).

Brass was the most commonly mentioned staple material, although silver was also used.[123] Gug (1988) pointed out that the alloy now usually called brass, and the way in which it is forged, is somewhat different than it was in the early eighteenth century.[124] On a staple lapped with thread over its entire length, this difference is of no musical significance.[125] The thickness of surviving staples (dating from the late eighteenth century or early nineteenth) varies between 0.30 and 0.50 mm.[126] Staples were apparently sometimes soldered and left uncovered, as in Pl. 2.26 (a detail from Pl. 2.7).

The term *cuivret* (which probably meant 'brass tube') was used by Mersenne (1636: 302) in connection with shawm reeds, and by Hotteterre (1737: 78–9) for musette reeds; Hotteterre (1723) also called it a 'tuyau ou cuivret' (tube or brass staple). Talbot (*c*.1692–5: 12–13) mentioned 'brass Staples' on reeds for the three

---

[120] Examined by me in June 1974.

[121] According to them (68 n. 52), this thread is still produced as 'no. 18, 3 cord (plies)', by Barbour's of Lisburn, Northern Ireland.   [122] The historical evidence on these systems is discussed in Haynes (1990), 115.

[123] Some players of the key-system oboe find that silver staples have a brighter sound.

[124] The components of brass (copper and zinc) were extracted differently, and the making of sheet brass was done by hammering and scraping rather than milling. The crystalline structure was therefore different, which would have affected the metal's vibratory behaviour.

[125] Differences in materials would influence sound only by their smoothness and/or porosity (cf. Benade 1976: 500). Staples were also probably annealed (by heating to red hot and dropping immediately in cold water) to help bend them around a mandrel, and this would have affected the structure and vibratory qualities of the metal.

[126] Cf. Haynes (1990), app. 2, p. 119.

PL. 2.26. Detail from Pl. 2.7, showing reed

TABLE 2.2. *Dimensions of early staples*

	Total length	Top ID	Bottom ID	Taper[a]	Comments
Haddon Hall	33.9	?	about 5.0	—	Top crushed. For shawm?
Anciuti (1718)	43.7	1.5/3.0	about 5.6	.077	Bottom badly deformed[b]
Stanesby	43.0	1.5/3.5	5.0	.058	Brass, lapped in string[c]

[a] On taper, see §E.3.a below.
[b] Information from Alfredo Bernardini.
[c] Information from Paul Hailperin.

types of oboe he described. Douwes (1699: 114–15), describing 'Schalmeijen', mentioned a reed 'Met een draad omgewonden ende soo over een koperen pijpje geset' (lapped with thread and placed over a little brass pipe).[127] On his death in 1727, the hautboy maker Hendrik Richters left a great deal of musical material, including 'Drie kopere riette doosies . . ., een ritie met een silver pijpie' (three brass reed boxes . . . , a reed with a silver staple).[128]

The dimensions of the early staples mentioned above, found with hautboys by Anciuti and Stanesby jun., are similar (see Table 2.2).

[127] *Koper* in Dutch can mean either copper (*rood koper*) or brass (*geel koper*).
[128] Dudok van Heel and Teutscher (1974), 56.

Squeaking on the hautboy is caused by leaking air, usually at the point where the reed is coupled to the instrument. Talbot's hautboy informant (probably La Riche) expressed his concern about leaks: 'The reed must be well moistened before the Instrt. will sound well to preserve itself the Wind within.'[129] One way to avoid leaks is to design the staple to extend as far as it can into the instrument's (tapered) counter-bore. Yet the two (? original) hautboy staples just described are relatively short and could probably have extended downwards at least another centimetre into the bore. Talbot's reed was 'inserted' only 17.5 mm. Fischer (*c.*1770: 5) implied that staples were sometimes short enough that they could go in too far; he advised: 'When you put your Reed in the Hautboy you should be careful not to put it in too far, as it will be difficult to blow, and probably be out of Tune: if the end of the Reed is too small, to prevent it's going too far into the Hautboy, put some thread round it.'[130]

3. *Dimensions of early reeds*

a. 1640–1670   The reeds Mersenne showed in 1636 had the fan or fish-tail shape typical for a shawm;[131] these included reeds for an instrument that was in mutation towards the hautboy (Pl. 1.2). His most carefully drawn reed is shown in Pl. 1.4. It was not flared but was relatively wide at the throat, and had what appears to be a removable tube. A similar shape can be seen on the reeds of five of the proto-morphic hautboys in the Gobelins 'L'Air' of 1664 (Pl. 1.11),[132] which have short, wide reeds.

b. 1670–1700   The Gobelins tapestry shown in Pl. 1.9 (1684) shows a longer and apparently narrower reed, probably tied on a staple. It is placed on an instrument that has evolved beyond those shown in the Gobelins 'L'Air'.

A wide and very flared reed is shown in a sketch in Holme (*c.*1688) (Pl. 1.19). The inaccurate proportions of the hautboy make the relative dimensions of the reed less than useful.

The reeds on two of the hautboys shown in Simonneau's engraving of 1692 are also relatively long, and quite wide at the tip (Pl. 2.13). The proportions of the instruments are not accurate in this picture, however, so no reliable dimensions can be deduced from it.

Another very wide reed for a tenor Schalmey (by Haka?; see Ch. 3, §H) can be seen in Pl. 1.15.

---

[129] Talbot (*c.*1692–5), 14.

[130] The carelessness with which the bottom of the staple in the grand chalumeau of the Claudius musette was made (clearly not round) suggests that it was not intended to extend all the way to the walls of the counterbore.

[131] Smith (1992), 26. This book deals primarily with reeds for pre-Baroque instruments, based on empirical experiment. It is the best general explanation of how these reeds work, and includes a good survey of reed-making techniques, types of tools, and reed design.

[132] Two on panel A, one on panel C, one on panel F1, one on panel G.

The Talbot reed. In the last years of the seventeenth century James Talbot, a fellow at Cambridge and friend of Purcell,[133] made detailed notes on a number of musical instruments.[134] It is thought that he was preparing a book on music that was never completed. Talbot's notes included two fingering charts for the hautboy, given him by François La Riche (then in London),[135] and careful dimensions of an hautboy by Peter Bressan (which closely resemble those of a number of surviving instruments).

Talbot also gave dimensions for a reed (presumably La Riche's), which makes the Talbot Manuscript a unique and invaluable source because of its early date, its completeness, its apparent reliability and accuracy, and the likelihood that it came from an influential and well-travelled player. The reed Talbot described was probably representative of the sort of thing some hautboy players were using in France, England, and Germany from about 1685 to 1700 (or somewhat later). The direct and indirect dimensions Talbot provided (together with the fingering charts and specifications for an instrument) allow a workable reconstruction, which is described in Haynes (2000a).

Converted to mm, Talbot gave the following dimensions:

Breadth of Reed at Mouth	9.5
Length	98.4
whereof 5½″ inserted	17.5
Dia. at brass end	6.35

With this information, it is a relatively simple matter to deduce complete dimensions for the reed as follows (those given or implied by Talbot are in *italic*; the others are explained in Haynes 2000a):

tip width	*9.5*
total length	*98.4*
inserted length	*17.5*
total exposed length[136]	*80.9*
bottom outer diameter	*6.35*
brass thickness	0.5
bottom inner diameter	5.35
cane length	21.4
staple length	77.0
top staple opening	2.5
taper	0.037

---

[133] Unwin (1987), 59.   [134] See Baines (1948).   [135] On La Riche, see Ch. 3, §D.
[136] The amount the staple extends beyond the top of the instrument.

These measurements result in a relatively narrow taper in the staple that produces high notes that are too flat to be usable—that is, if one uses the usual modern long fingerings. The reed plays well, however, using La Riche's fingerings ($b\flat2 = 1\ 3$, $b2 = 2$ (!), $c3 = $ 'all open'; these are the 'short' fingerings discussed in Ch. 4, §G.6). The Talbot reed was probably meant to be played on the Bressan; using it on a similar instrument, I play it at $A \approx 401$. On a French late seventeenth-century hautboy like my Naust, with somewhat smaller tone-holes, it plays at $A \approx 388$ (A−2).[137]

It is not yet known how long this kind of reed was in use. Most players in the 1710s and 1720s would have begun their careers on late seventeenth-century models, on which they would have learned to make their reeds. Short high-note fingerings were the only option in published charts until the Classical period (*c.*1770; see Ch. 4, §G.6). But for later models, the best high-note response seems to be achieved with a much more tapered staple, very different from the Talbot-type staple that works on earlier instrument models.[138]

Mignard. The Talbot reed was not used universally; the reed shown in Mignard's painting from the same decade (1691; Pl. 2.6) is quite different. Mignard's reed looks somewhat stylized and carelessly rendered, but the hautboy to which it is attached is thoroughly convincing, and suggests that the reed should be taken seriously.

The dimensions of Mignard's reed are improbably large if the hautboy he painted was a low one at, say, 600 mm total length:

tip width	18.0
cane length	27.7
exposed length	30.6

But if the hautboy is assumed to have been short, like the Martin (which it strongly resembles) or the Rouge,[139] the reed's dimensions would be:

tip width	15.1
cane length	23.2
exposed length	25.6

Although this is more believable, the reed is still remarkably wide at the tip.[140]

A reed is also shown on the hautboy in the Teniers family portrait, Pl. 2.16, datable to before *c.*1695 (see Ch. 1, §A). Although the tip width cannot be determined, if the instrument is taken to be similar in dimensions to the 'Galpin Oboe'

[137] Cf. my 1998 recording (Atma) using the Naust and a reconstruction of the Talbot reed.
[138] See Haynes (1997c).   [139] See above, §D.2.a.
[140] The recorder shown with the hautboy is proportionally shorter than it should be if the hautboy is a normal C-treble and the recorder an F-alto.

(Bate 200), the reed would be quite short, with a cane length of 16.6 and an exposed length of 21.3.

c. 1700–1730   An anonymous family portrait made about 1700 includes an hautboy player holding an hautboy that resembles surviving Ripperts (Pl. 2.8).[141] The reed is fat and squat, and its dimensions were probably as follows:

tip width	10.9
cane length	19.6
exposed length (of staple)	19.7

A similar reed was attached to the hautboy held by a *putto* in a ceiling panel in the Chapelle Royale, Versailles, done about 1711 by Boullogne (Pl. 2.15). The reed is short and very wide.

Bouys's portrait made in 1704 (see below, Pl. 5.1) shows a reed. Using as references the distance from the top to hole 1 as well as the largest diameter of the top baluster, and comparing it with the Hotteterre hautboy (at 138 and 31.8 mm respectively), the dimensions would be about as follows:

tip width	16.7
total exposed length	46.1

A French chalk drawing of woodwinds, done *c*.1705, shows an hautboy with its reed (Pl. 2.3). A pencil inscription on the back mentions 'Dupuis' and 'Peutier/ Pentier'. Dupuis was listed by Du Pradel in 1692 as 'Maître pour le Jeu et pour la Fabrique des Instruments à Vent' (a master of playing and making wind instruments), and Charles Pelletier made woodwinds in the same generation.[142] The instruments shown in this drawing were evidently intended to be shown to scale. The hautboy was given as *2 p* long, presumably *2 pieds de roi*, and although this makes its total length an improbable 649.68 mm,[143] the AL is quite plausible at 333.64. The reed would have the following dimensions:

tip width	9.22
cane length	24.15
exposed length	22.39

---

[141] A reed has recently been noticed at the Musikinstrumenten Museum in Leipzig that was inserted in the Rippert hautboy there (1312) and plays well with it. A report on this reed by Georg Corall is now in preparation. It has the following dimensions:

tip width	8.6	(when dry)
Cane length	25.8	
exposed length	33.2	

The narrow tip width and long exposed length resemble the dimensions of reeds of the next period (see below, §d).

[142] See Waterhouse (1993), 98 and 297.

[143] This is 33 mm longer than the longest known surviving hautboy from this generation.

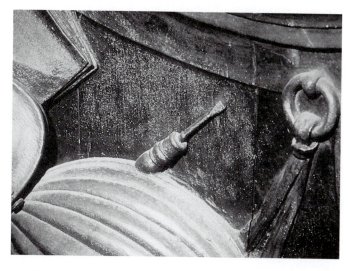

PL. 2.27. Anonymous, 1722, detail of hautboy and reed on the organ façade
of the Oud-Katholieke Kerk in Delft, half-round carving, full size.
Photo courtesy of Joh. and Eva Legêne

A very careful reed appears in an anonymous oil portrait of an hautboy player in
Pl. 2.26 (on this painting, cf. App. 4). Brush-marks show that the artist retouched
the cane shape, presumably to make it as accurate as possible (it is a very credible
shape). The cane has parallel sides for most of its length. The reed appears to have
been made on a soldered silver staple, as there is a short section between the tied
cane and the thread at the bottom of the staple that is not lapped with thread.
Dimensions that can be estimated are as follows:[144]

tip width	10.2
cane length	23.5
exposed length	26.1

A three-dimensional, real-size depiction of a reed and part of an hautboy is preserved in a trophy carving of musical instruments made in 1722 for the organ façade
of the Oud-Katholieke Kerk in Delft (Pl. 2.27). In profile, the hautboy resembles
Type A2 Dutch instruments. The EL is rather long (although not as long as the
Talbot reed's) and the cane is fairly short and wedge-shaped. Although it is difficult

---

[144] These dimensions are based on a comparison of the dimensions of the hautboy in the painting with a similar surviving instrument, the Rippert at Geneva.

to reach, I managed with the kind help of church staff to measure the total length of the reed, which produces the following dimensions:

tip width	14.0
cane length	22.5
exposed length	47.0

Zampieri evidently borrowed Mignard's motif (see Pls. 2.6 and 2.14) for the title-pages used for Handel's operas *Alexander*, *Rodelinda*, and *Tamerlane* (1726 and later). But the reed he used was not the same; Zampieri's looks as if it has a little 'turk's head' of thread like a bassoon reed, and may be detachable from its tube.

Long-stapled reeds appear to be the norm in this generation. Tip width shows a divergence from about 9.2 to 16.7, cane length from 19.6 to 24.15.

d. 1730–1767   The copy of Eisel's *Musicus αυτοδιδακτοσ* (1738) at the Bibliothèque Nationale, Paris, contains a hand-drawn hautboy with a reed (Pl. 2.17). The note names on the fingering chart are written in German, and the hautboy looks like a Denner or Eichentopf. The staple is fairly long, and the cane appears to have a wire. Using the dimensions of surviving instruments, this reed would have the following dimensions:

tip width	11.4
cane length	22.8
exposed length	30.6

An oil portrait of an hautboy player made about 1750, now in Stockholm, carefully depicts a reed mounted on a Type E instrument (Pl. 2.28). The angle of the reed does not allow for a measurement of its tip width, but it is clearly wide and the shape is fish-tail. The thread wrapping is thick. The length of the cane can be from about 26.5 to 27.6; the EL about 32.0 to 33.4. (These dimensions depend on the real size of the depicted instrument; surviving Bizeys vary between 576 and 617 mm in length.)

A realistic painting by Lazzari (Venice, 1752; Pl. 2.19) also shows a reed. The instrument resembles to the smallest details an hautboy by 'N. Cosins' (a name that could possibly have been Venetian) now at Nuremberg (MIR 375; Pl. 2.1(*e*)).[145] Based on the width of the brass ferrule of this instrument,[146] the dimensions of the reed are approximately:[147]

---

[145] This relation was noticed by Giovanni Caviglia (pers. comm.).

[146] The brass ferrule on the Cosins instrument measures at its very top 16.54–16.55 mm on the outside (my thanks to Dr Frank P. Bär, head of the musical instrument collection at the GNM, for this information).

[147] The reed is depicted at an angle so its dimensions are slightly distorted.

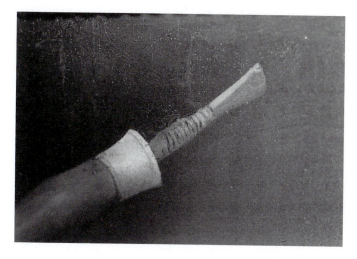

PL. 2.28. Detail of Pl. 2.4 showing reed. Photo: Alfredo Bernardini

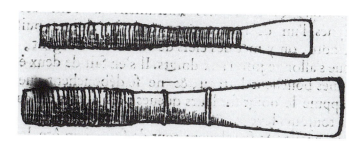

PL. 2.29. Garsault (1761), hautboy and bassoon reeds, p. 627

tip width	11.8
cane length	18.5
exposed length	22.8

This is both the widest tip width and shortest cane length known from this period.

Garsault's *Notionaire* (1761) showed a fairly good hautboy reed (see Pl. 2.29). If the real tip width of the reed was 10.0, the cane length would be 20.6, which is relatively short.

Finally, the remarkable portrait of the Bolognese player Sante Aguilar, done probably in 1767, quite explicitly (and apparently accurately) shows both his instru-

ment and its long thin reed (Pl. 2.11). The instrument looks like a typical Type D1
Palanca. As a basis for comparing measurements, the reeds at Musashino, associated with two hautboys by Palanca, show a tip width of about 7.5 and a cane length
of 21. Alfredo Bernardini measured the reed in the painting,[148] and the dimensions
he gives are:

tip width	7.2
cane length	24.0
exposed length	34.0
scrape length	12.0

Even in this period, moving towards the classical instrument, our best information indicates that hautboy reeds were often wider and shorter than has been previously thought. The range of widths is 7.2 to 11.8, of cane lengths, 18.5 to 27.15.
This is a remarkably wide variation.

4. Historical reed-making

North wrote (*c*.1710–28: 229–30)

To begin with the reed, the materiall is shaved very thin and put together as 2. plates, the
one end (almost) closing flatt, which is for the lipps, the other lapped and made fast about
a quill,[149] which is to be inserted at the end of the tube or pipe. The reed of it self thus disposed is an Instrument of sound but very shrill; for ye air from ye mouth being smartly
urged thro the slitt between ye 2. plates into ye quill, Makes a [? compression] in the quill,
and almost at ye same time closeth ye plates, which makes a sudden stopp in the airs cours
into the quill, and consequently a [? recycling] which opens ye slitt; and so alternately by
pulses (as to frequency) governed by the spring of ye air in ye quill . . .

Quantz (1752: VI, suppl. §4):

A l'égard du son sur ces deux instrumens
[le Hautbois, le Basson], beaucoup dépend
de la bonté de l'anche, savoir, que le bois
en soit bon & mûr; qu'elle ait toute la
concavité nécessaire; qu'elle ne soit ni trop
large, ni trop courte; & qu'en la raclant elle
n'ait été trop amincie, ni laissée trop
épaisse.

As for the tone quality of these two
instruments [the hautboy, the bassoon],
much depends on the quality of the reed,
and specifically, whether it is made of
good, well-seasoned cane, whether it has
the appropriate diameter [lit. concavity],
that it is neither too wide, nor too short;
and that it is scraped neither too thinly nor
left too thick.

---

[148] Bernardini (1990), 40.

[149] The word 'quill' does not necessarily refer to the shaft of a feather. According to the *OED*, an obsolete meaning of 'quill' is 'a small pipe or tube; esp. a small waterpipe'.

Garsault (1761: 627–8) may be describing a bassoon reed, as he does not mention here the 'petite lame de cuivre' (staple; see below):

L'anche se fait avec une espece de roseau qui s'éleve très-haut, & dont les noeuds sont éloignés l'un de l'autre. On coupe ce roseau aux noeuds: on le fend en long par le milieu: on ôte une moëlle qui occupe l'intérieur, puis on le fend par-dessus en travers, à son milieu, sans le déjoindre: on le ploie: on joint les deux bouts qu'on lie ensemble sur un petit mandrin de fer: on finit par couper & séparer tout-à fait en travers les deux moitiés d'en haut, on les amincit vers les bouts, & l'anche est fait.	Reeds are made of a type of cane that grows quite tall, on which the knots are spaced far apart. The cane is cut at the knots, split lengthwise in the middle, the softer material of the inside is removed, and it is then scored on the exterior, crosswise in the middle, without cutting right through. It is then folded, and the two ends are tied together on a small iron mandrel. The reed is finished by cutting off the end of the two upper halves, separating them completely; they are then thinned towards the end, and the reed is ready.

Hotteterre (1737: 78–9) mentioned a device used on musette reeds that could have been helpful for hautboy as well:[150]

On y ajoute quelquefois une petite ligature détachée que l'on appelle une Bride, laquelle sert aussi à les adoucir en la poussant pareillement en haut.	A small separate ligature is sometimes applied to reeds that is called a *Bride* [lit. clamp]. It can also be used to soften them by pushing it higher up [that is, towards the tip].

A *Bride* can be seen on the Copenhagen musette reed (Pl. 2.25). It presumably acted like the wire sometimes used on modern reeds.

a. Reeds not made by the player   It seems players in earlier times often had their reeds made for them, either by reed makers or instrument makers. Most beginners and many amateurs would have bought their reeds, of course, but there were apparently professional hautboy players who did the same. Reeds were usually made or at least sold through woodwind makers' shops. Haydn made regular orders of hautboy and English horn reeds (by the dozen) from the maker who probably provided his hautboys, Rocko Baur.[151] In some cases, players serving at court had other

---

[150] Hotteterre's description of an hautboy embouchure (1707: 44) mentions a 'ligature de l'Anche', which Lasocki in his translation of 1968 (p. 86) called 'wire'; Hotteterre's use of 'Bride' here for wire suggests that his earlier 'ligature' referred instead to the thread wrapping.

[151] Haydn (*c.*1767, p. 56). Bartha writes (Haydn 1965: 56): 'Der Name des Wiener Instrumentenbauers *Mathias Rockobauer* kehrt in den von Haydn revidierten Rechnungen des Esterházy-Archivs immer wieder . . . zumeist werden Mundstücke für Oboen und Englischhörner dutzendweise von ihm bezogen.' A bill from Rocko Baur for 'ein Tutzert [Dutzend] Huboe Röhr' dated 30 Dec. 1766 and paid by Haydn is reproduced in Tank (1980), 246, and another purchase list for 27 June 1767 includes 2 fl 23 1/3 d for 'Hoboe-röhr' (ibid. 258). See Waterhouse (1993), 24 under 'Baur, Rocko'.

duties, as the post of musician was often combined with that of lackey. Such players probably had little time for making reeds.

As for prices, Morris records: 'The prices paid for instruments in those days is of some interest . . . in 1688 a Hoboy with ivory joints and tipped with same cost £1 7s. and four reeds 2s. in 1697 . . .'.[152] A reed would therefore have cost about 1/54th the value of the 'Hoboy'. Kremsmünster Abbey bought 'eine Hoboa' in 1697 for 6 fl, and paid the same price for 12 'Mundstuckh für die Hoboa', that year and the next; each reed would therefore have cost 1/12 the price of the hautboy, which in today's currency would amount to more than £60 ($100) a reed. The Abbey ordered reeds for 'einen Fagott französisch Ton' and 'eine Hoboa' in 1697. '18 Fagott und Hubuenröhrl' were bought the next year, and cane for hautboy reeds ('Holz zu Huben Rohren') in 1699. There were later purchases of hautboy reeds in 1700, and in 1701 from 'H: Pregler zu Wienn vmb Huben Rohr bezahlt 1 fl 20 kr'. Purchases from Vienna in 1707 and 1710 included hautboy reeds at both 'Cornet-vnd französisch Ton'.[153]

Richard Haka supplied four reeds for each of the four 'franse discant Haubois' he delivered in 1685.[154] He also included two reeds for a 'franse tenor Haubois' and four for a 'franse dulsian Basson'. The discant reeds cost 5 'Stuÿfvers', which amounted to 1/32 of the price of the instrument. Reeds for the Basson were 6 Stuÿfvers but the tenor reeds were the most expensive at 10 Stuÿfvers.

Christoph Denner was also a supplier of reeds. A bill survives from the Denner workshop dated 4 September 1705:[155]

> Auff den alhiesigen Music Chor habe verferdiget wie folget:
> einen Fagott reparirt......   fl 30 K.
> 6 Hautbois u. Fagottrohr a 7½ Kr......   45 K.
> eine Rohrbixe......   15 K.
> _____
>
> Summa......   2 fl 30 K.
>   Johann Christoph Denner.[156]

Other makers also supplied reeds. The letter quoted in §D.3 written by da Silva in 1773, ordering hautboys by Palanca, went on to say:

---

[152] Morris (1934), 41–2.   [153] Kellner (1956), 285, 292, 294, 295, 299, 303, 304.
[154] Haka (1685).   [155] Nickel (1971), 201, 452.
[156] Music (1983), 102 records that ' "Reads [!] for Haut-Boys" were advertised for sale by Edward Enstone in a Boston weekly in 1716, along with instruments.' (Cf. Scholes 1969: 36.) In about 1750 John Johnson in London advertised reeds for bassoons and hautboys (Rendall 1971: 56), and Mortimer (1949: 28) noted that Adam Goodman, whose address he gave, was 'eminent for making Hautboy and Bassoon Reeds'. Several reed makers are listed in Doane (1794). According to Eisel (1738: 104), the best bassoon reeds were made in Berlin; it is possible the unnamed maker also sold hautboy reeds.

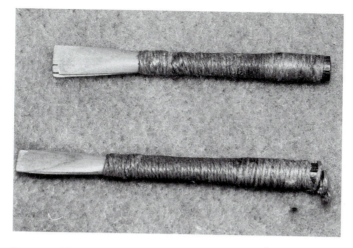

PL. 2.30. Two reeds with Palanca hautboys. Musashino Museum.
Photo: Masahiro Arita

che venga con mezza duzzine d'angie, e tutto sia fatta coll'intelligenza del Sᵣ. Besozzi, e con quella prestezza, che si puole.

and each must come with a half-dozen reeds, and all done with the advice of Mr Besozzi, and as soon as possible.

Reeds that would be similar to these are shown in Pl. 2.30. These reeds could well have been made by Palanca or Alessandro Besozzi (see Ch. 7, §A.1). There are many later eighteenth-century records of purchases of reeds.

But there are also early references to reeds made by players.[157] In 1713, Mattheson (p. 269) wrote that

Die beste *Maitres* pflegen sie sich selber nach ihrem Maul zu machen; weil ein gutes Rohr halb gespielet ist.[158]

The best *Maitres* usually make [their reeds] themselves, to fit their embouchures, as in a good reed is half the playing.

b. Tools   There are no surviving descriptions of hautboy reed-making tools until the beginning of the nineteenth century (Garnier 1802: 6), Froelich (1810: 53 ff.), and Brod (1825: 109 ff.).[159] Except for the gouging tool, scraper, and gouging bed, tools have changed little since that time.

c. Gouging and scraping   In a study of the reeds of eighty-one successful professional oboists from fourteen countries, Ledet (1981) demonstrated an astonishing variation in the measurements, gouge, and scrape of reeds made for the modern

---

[157] Cf. Vanderhagen (*c.*1790), 5.   [158] Repeated in Majer (1732), 34.
[159] They are shown in Haynes (1984), 27–30.

key-system oboe: 'It is evident from the photographs and measurements of individual reeds in Part II that seldom are the reeds of one player like those of another. Indeed, even separate reeds made by a single player are often quite disparate in appearance and measurement . . .'.[160] Yet all these players are using an instrument that is highly standardized in dimensions compared with the hautboy. If reeds differ with a single model of oboe, logic suggests that the variation in the seventeenth and eighteenth centuries, when instrument models were not only less standardized but changing rapidly, was at least as great. The personal nature of reed-making techniques (so eloquently established in Ledet's study) no doubt compounded the possible differences. The variations in the dimensions of the reeds described in §E.3 above speak for themselves; a striking example is the difference between the reeds of Talbot and Mignard, dating from nearly the same year.

Added to this is the unhappy fact that of the estimated 15,000 to 30,000 original hautboys that once existed prior to 1760, it is doubtful if any complete reeds have survived that can provide examples of their scrapes. Many surviving reeds (all probably made later than 1770) show a simple V- or U-scrape with no step or shoulder forming a separate tip and back (or heart). But considering the variety of scrapes used by modern players, the likelihood that all early eighteenth-century hautboy reeds were scraped the same way is rather small.[161] There is therefore no reason not to think that spines and hearts were used on some hautboy reeds.

There were probably significant differences in gouge thickness in the past. The wide disparity Ledet reports for players of the relatively standardized key-system oboe (the thickest, 0.94 mm, is more than twice the thinnest, 0.46)[162] suggests that variation in the early eighteenth century would have been at least as great. The late eighteenth-century reeds examined by Burgess and Hedrick (1989: 39) were 0.65 to 1.0 mm at the thickest part of the cane.[163]

It has been suggested[164] that early hautboy reeds were made with a *tapered gouge*, a technique that is described in late eighteenth-century and early nineteenth-century bassoon reed sources.[165] It is a technique that would not have been difficult when cane was hand-gouged (the gouging machine was not invented until 1847).[166] In tapered gouging, the gouge thickness diminished gradually from the throat to the tip and from the centre to the sides of the reed. The piece of cane was thinnest in the middle, at the point that became the tip.

---

[160] Ledet (1981), p. xi.

[161] Burgess (1997) gives the impression that 'early reeds' were generally scraped without a heart. This is a generalization that can only be based on the few surviving reeds, none apparently earlier than the late 18th c. It is questionable if it can be applied to Baroque reeds.   [162] Ledet (1981), 184.

[163] On gouging tools, see Haynes (1984), 28–30.   [164] Burgess and Hedrick (1989), 39.

[165] According to David Rachor (1998: 15), this is known as *contrepente* among French players.

[166] Waterhouse (1993), 404.

The result of longitudinal tapering, as White writes, was that the harder layers of the cane formed the tip: 'Early [bassoon] reeds, having less material in the blade prior to scraping, must, by default, have a shallower scrape which exposes considerably less of the soft inner cane and a greater expanse of harder, surface and sub-surface cane.'[167] This technique was documented for the bassoon by Ozi and Froelich, and described by Almenräder. The presence of harder cane at the tip probably produced a reed with a brighter tone (which may have been an advantage on the bassoon), and one that lasted longer.

It is possible that longitudinal tapering was also used by hautboists, although (other than the implication that hautboy reeds would have been made similarly to bassoon reeds) there do not appear to be any historical indications of it.[168] Burgess and Hedrick observed all strata of cane on the lays of the early hautboy reeds they measured; the parenchyma (the softest strata) generally appear on the last 2–5 mm of the tips of these reeds.[169] A tapered gouge would presumably have eliminated the parenchyma, however.[170]

The first source to describe the gouging of hautboy cane in any detail (Brod 1825: 113–14) described only lateral tapering, that is, making the sides thinner than the middle (a common practice on key-system oboe reeds). Brod (clearly a much later source) spoke of 'a thickness of 3/4 of a millimetre throughout the middle of the [reed's] width',[171] and of 'maintaining this proportion throughout the [reed's] length with perfect consistency'.[172] He also said

En regardant le grand jour à travers le roseau ainsi gratté, on doit voir dans le milieu et d'un bout à l'autre une ligne également opaque se fondant en demi transparant vers les bords.	In holding the gouged reed to the light and looking through it, one should see an equally opaque line in the middle from one end to the other, gradually tailing off to more transparency towards the sides.

It seems clear he expected the longitudinal thickness to be uniform from one end of the piece of cane to the other.[173]

On bassoon reeds, there was a good reason for leaving the 'tube' end of a piece of cane thicker. As Garsault wrote (1761: 627–8):

---

[167] White (1993), ch. 2. White's dissertation examines in detail the historical techniques of bassoon reed-making, many of which would also have been used for hautboy reeds.

[168] *Pace* Burgess (1997). The references he cites do not contain any concrete indications of the use of tapered gouging.

[169] Reedmakers call the *lay* of a reed the surface of the cane that has been scraped.

[170] Ozi (1803: 142) suggested that the tip of a bassoon reed should be gouged to a 'quart de ligne d'épaisseur' (= 0.56 mm); hautboy reeds might have been still thinner.

[171] 'l'épaisseur de 3/4 de millimêtre dans tout le milieu de sa largeur'.

[172] 'conserver cette proportion dans toute sa longueur avec une parfaite égalité'.

[173] Brod was at the forefront of the movement for 'rationalization', and may have consciously rejected such inequalities in reed-making.

Nota. Comme l'anche du haut-bois se met & s'enfonce dans un trou qui est au haut de sa tête; pour le faire, on roule sur le mandrin avant de lier, une petite lame de cuivre sur laquelle on lie le bas de l'anche, auquel elle reste, afin qu'il ne s'applatisse pas quand on l'enfoncera dans le trou, ce qui ne se fait pas pour l'anche B. du basson & celui du cromorne, parce que leurs serpentin ou boccal [!] entre dans la queue de l'anche.

Note. Since the hautboy reed is placed and inserted in a hole at the top of the upper joint, when it is being made a thin plate of copper is rolled on the mandrel before tying it, to which the base of the reed is attached, and on which it rests, so that it does not get crushed when it is inserted in the hole. This is not done on the bassoon reed at B, or on that of the cromorne, because their crooks are inserted into the tail of the reed.

Bassoon and cromorne reeds thus had more need for strength in the tube compared with the blades, unlike hautboy reeds tied on staples.

Burgess and Hedrick (1989: 39) noticed lateral tapering (from the centre to the sides) on some of the hautboy reeds they examined, though no longitudinal tapering. The reed that was dismantled (Ling no. 4) measured 0.7 mm at the centre and 0.54 and 0.56 on either side at 14 mm from the tip (beyond the end of the scrape). This reed was probably made in the early nineteenth century for a narrow-bore hautboy, possibly with extra keys.

d. Tying on   In the late eighteenth-century reeds they examined, Burgess and Hedrick (1989: 41) observed two tying procedures that contrast with the usual modern method:

- Sometimes the thread was not tied to the top of the staple, or continued on beyond the staple's end.
- In a few cases, the shape at the throat was bigger than the staple, leaving a gap.[174]

This allowed the shape of the reed to remain wider at the throat. If the staple was smaller than the cane shape, the cane would have cracked at the corners unless it was first steamed round on a mandrel (like modern bassoon reeds) and tied loosely.

e. Testing playing qualities   Reed dimensions affect intonation, and Quantz made two interesting remarks on this subject. On cane shape, he commented:

Si l'anche est par devant trop large ou trop longue, les hauts tons deviennent trop bas, à proportion des bas tons; & si elle est trop étroite ou trop court, les tons en seront trop hauts.[175]

If the cane is too wide or too long, the high notes become too low compared with the low notes; if it is too narrow or too short, the high notes will be too high.

---

[174] Cf. Haynes (1976), 177. Other reeds described in Burgess and Hedrick (1989) were bound as tightly as possible to the top of the staple, however (cf. reeds nos. 4 and 7, Burgess and Hedrick (1989), 49 and 51).

[175] Quantz (1752), VI, suppl. §4.

He also observed (1752: XVII, vii §7) that the octaves expand as the reed is shortened and contract as it is lengthened:

S'il falloit forcer à la hauteur par le
racourcissement des anches & des portes
voix (*) les Hautbois & les Bassons qui
sont construits suivant le ton bas, ces
instrumens seroient rendus tout à fait faux
par ce racourcissement. Les Octaves
s'étendroient, leur ton inferieur deviendroit
plus bas & le superieur plus haut; de même
qu'au contraire quand on tire dehors
l'anche & qu'on diminue[176] la porte voix,
les Octaves s'approchent & le ton inferieur
devient plus haut & le superieur plus bas.

(*) La porte voix est ce que les Allemands appellent l'S.

If it were necessary to force the pitch up by
shortening reeds and crooks (*), hautboys
and bassoons made to play at a low pitch
would be made quite out of tune. The
octaves would be expanded, the lower note
becoming flatter and the upper sharper;
just as if, on the contrary, one extends the
reed or [lengthens] the crook, the octaves
contract, and the lower note becomes
sharper and the upper becomes flatter.

(*) The crook is called the 'S' by the Germans.

This principle is confirmed by Cocks and Bryan (1967: 28), writing of the
Northumbrian bagpipe:[177] 'Supposing the reed to speak at a suitable pressure, but
sounding the top notes flat by the lower ones, it must have a few turns of wrapping
removed and be inserted farther into the chanter. The reverse process is used if the
top notes are sharp.'

An idea of the flexibility of reed pitch was given in the correspondence between
the Italian physicist Giordano Riccati and the composer F. A. Vallotti in Padua.[178]
On 28 November 1741, Riccati requested Vallotti's help in determining

qual mutazione di tuono egli sia capace di
cagionare in una pivetta separata dallo
strumento.

how much he is able to cause the pitch of a
reed to alter when it is separate from the
instrument.

The player in question was 'il gran Matteo', the famous Matteo Bissoli, a colleague
of Tartini's in the Cappella of Sant'Antonio at Padua (see Ch. 7, §A.3). Bissoli told
Vallotti that

il vero indicio che una pivetta sij perfetta è
questo di render le voci tutte di una intiera
ottava.

The sign of a truly fine reed is one that will
play all the notes of an entire octave.

At the moment he demonstrated this to Vallotti, Bissoli had a reed that would produce only a 'hexachord', or six notes (I find my own reeds will produce no more

---

[176] This word appears to be a mistake.

[177] The reeds for the chanter of this instrument are particularly interesting because they resemble hautboy reeds
but are played without an embouchure and its corrections. They thus offer the mythical 'objective' reed experiment, and generalizations about them are probably valid.

[178] Reported in Nalin (1991). Riccati's letter is also mentioned in Barbieri (1987), 32.

than this same interval). In his letter, Riccati mentioned a passage in Dodart (1700: 264):

J'ai vu M. Filidor pere [André Philidor *l'aîné*] parcourir de suite tous les tons & demi-tons d'une octave, & par-delà sur une anche de basson séparée du corps de l'instrument.[179]	I have seen Mr Filidor sen. play one after the other all the tones and semitones of an octave, and that with a bassoon reed separated from the body of the instrument.

The oboist's familiar reed 'crow' was mentioned in Fischer (*c.*1770), 5:

Before you put the Reed in your Hautboy you should spit thro' it, or wet it, as it will be easier and better Tone than when dry, and when you choose a Reed you must blow thro' it without pressing your Lips, & if it crows free, you are certain 'tis a good one.

---

[179] Dodart's article is discussed in Cohen (1981), 20.

3

1670–1700: The Spread of the 'French Hoboye'

By 1668 l'Abbé de Pure was writing that '*Les Haut-bois . . .* , played as they are nowadays at the Court and in Paris, leave little to be desired.'[1] At this date, the instrument was unknown outside of France. But almost immediately it caught on everywhere else: by 1673 it was being played in London, by 1677 in Turin, Amsterdam, and the Hague, Madrid in 1679, Celle and Stuttgart in 1680, Brussels in the 1680s, and Venice and Vienna by the 1690s. Halfpenny wrote:

The French hautbois . . . was something more than a mere literal improvement of the treble shawm. It possessed a range, fluency and a tone-quality which were entirely new in a reed instrument, and it took Europe completely by storm as soon as those qualities became generally known.[2]

By the end of the century, there were few places of political power in Europe where the hautboy was not familiar and established.

At the time of the hautboy's appearance, France was emerging as a strong power and a cultural exemplar.[3] Germany, by contrast, was recovering from the devastations of the Thirty Years War, and the monarchy in England had only just been restored after an appalling civil war.

All over Europe, musical institutions were being reorganized and were ready for changes, and French music was in vogue. Well-paid posts were thus on offer to French hautboy players willing to travel. At the same time, two forces tended to encourage French musicians to leave their native land.

One was Louis's revocation of the Edict of Nantes in 1685, discussed below in §C, which virtually expelled Protestant Frenchmen from France. The other was Lully's monopoly of power, which by the 1670s was so oppressive[4] that it forced a number of musicians to leave for other courts. In this way, Lully unintentionally contributed to the spread of the French hautboy. Cambert's move to London in 1673 after being outmanoeuvred by Lully brought with it the introduction of the

---

[1] Cf. Ch. 1, §D.   [2] Halfpenny (1949c), 149.
[3] Heyde (1993a), 593.   [4] Cf. Anthony (1973), 18.

French hautboy to England, and Farinel and Dumanoir, both strong anti-Lullists, brought an hautboy band to Spain in 1679 (see §D and §E.4).

The first performances that Europe heard on the hautboy were thus by Frenchmen, and, soon after, first-generation students of Frenchmen. By 1685, the Dutchman Richard Haka was making what he called 'franse Haubois', and they were being made in Germany and England in the 1690s. In some cases (like that of Christoph Denner and other Nuremberg makers) they were direct copies; in others, French makers (like Bressan) emigrated to other countries.

It was at the beginning of the 1670s that the hautboy took on its definitive form. The physical features of the 'French' hautboy of this period are seen in Pls. 1.9, 2.1(*a*, *b*, and *c*), 2.3, 2.5, 2.9–10, 2.12–13, and 2.15.

Being French (at least at the beginning), hautboys were first heard in French pitches: *Ton d'Opéra* at A−2 and *Ton de chambre* at A−1½.[5] In Germany, makers like Denner probably used these pitches for their first copies, calling it *tief-Cammerton* or *französischer Thon*. They also found a use for the French models at A+1 (*Ton d'Écurie*; A+1 was known in Germany as *Cornet-ton* and in Italy as *Corista di Lombardia*). In London, French *Ton de chambre* at A−1½ coincided with the standard English *Consort-pitch*.

The arrival of the new hautboy immediately inspired new music that explored its potential: solo sonatas and concertos,[6] chamber works for mixed instruments, and obbligatos with voice.[7] Excellent pieces were already appearing at the end of the 1680s and through the 1690s. Some were from French pens or in French style, but Italian, German, and English composers adopted the new instrument to their own styles and needs.

Over a dozen arias survive from the decade of the 1690s that call for a single hautboy with soprano and continuo. As early as the year of Lully's death, 1687, Steffani[8] was already writing arias with hautboy obbligatos; the first solos by Kusser appeared in 1692, and Keiser was writing them by 1697. These are beautiful pieces, and represent the earliest true solo parts featuring the hautboy. Germany is especially remarkable for the quantity of vocal music with hautboy obbligato, but this medium was also known by the 1690s in London and Venice (see below). In the early years of the eighteenth century the hautboy was given similar work in France. Some hautboy band music is still preserved from this period, but much that was played never got written down.[9]

---

[5] See Ch. 2, §D.

[6] Cf. the following in Haynes (1992): Anon. (10.3) Sinfonia [Concerto], D; Anon.(10.3) Concerto, C; Bononcini (1696); Fischer; Pignatta (*c*.1693); Rosier (1697); Anon. (10.3) Sinfonia con L'Oboe, C/D. ('10.3' refers to the classification used in Haynes 1992.)   [7] Cf. Index 4 in Haynes (1992a), 'Solos written between 1680 and 1710'.

[8] Braun (1987), 138. See under Munich below.

[9] Zaslaw (1993), 20 points out that a 'rather considerable iconographic evidence' suggests that musicians often played for dances without music in front of them.

Pl. 3.1. Bartolomeo Bismantova, from 'Regole . . . del Oboè' (1688/9). Bad Säckingen: Trompetenmuseum (Nr. 4017-002, fo. 67ᵛ)

The late 1680s also saw the first technical description of the new instrument (Bismantova: *Regole . . . del Oboè* (1688), which included a fingering chart as well as a sketch; see Pl. 3.1).

It was in this period that the torch was passed from the cornett, with its long and honourable history, to the hautboy. There are numerous indications that the rise of the hautboy and the demise of the cornett were connected by more than mere coincidence. Bismantova in 1677 gave the cornett extended treatment, whereas his few comments on the hautboy in the *Regole* of 1688 appeared only in a later manuscript version of his book. Just half a generation later, in the 1690s, the hautboy had taken over the cornett's functions at San Marco in Venice[10] (the city famous for its cornett makers). By 1703 Brossard (p. 16) wrote under 'Cornettino': 'On les peut supléer par nos Haut-bois' (the absence of them can be made up by using our hautboys). Mattheson (1739: 221) also stated clearly that the role of the cornett, at least in church music, was inherited by the hautboy:

Es wurden auch, wo es etwa irgend an diesem oder jenem Sänger fehlte, ihre Parteien bisweilen auf Zincken geblasen, welche damals die Stelle der Oboen vertraten.

Also, where a singer was lacking, their parts were sometimes played on cornetts, instruments that at that time occupied the place of hautboys.

[10] Selfridge-Field (1987), 118; Bernardini (1988), 374.

The story of Ferdinando de' Medici's order of cornetts from Christoph Denner[11] makes clear how quickly the transition occurred. Denner had made cornetts; he began his career in the late 1670s, before the general arrival of French woodwinds in Germany (indeed, he was to be one of the first, if not the first, Germans to start building the new instruments in the 1690s; see below, §C.9). The order from Prince Ferdinando came at the very end of Denner's life, in 1707, and in the event he died before the cornetts were completed. When one of his sons, Jacob or David, was asked in 1708 to take over the order, he explained that the instrument was by that time 'in poco uso', and it would be complicated 'a farli in quei toni così differenti' (to make them in those very different pitches—cornetts were normally at A+1). Ferdinando's agent wrote that

Il maestro solamente in questo lavoro non sia tanto pratico, come il Denner morto . . .	The [new] master is not as experienced in this kind of work as the late Denner . . .

The younger Denner eventually succeeded in producing satisfactory instruments, but it is clear that for him in 1708, it was a kind of 'museum restoration' work.

As might be expected, the shawm tradition did not immediately die away; both the Renaissance shawm and a new instrument with many of the shawm's attributes and functions continued to be played into the eighteenth century (see §H).

A. France

In 1672 Lully became head of the Académie Royale de Musique, or Opéra. In that same year, Blanchet's engraving appeared in Borjon's musette tutor; this is the first documentation of the hautboy's existence in its definitive form. But Borjon's text implies that the hautboy was by then already established (see Ch. 1, §B.1), and Cambert had used it in 1671 in two productions, his very successful pastoral *Pomone*[12] (described at the time as the 'first French opera to appear on the stage') and *Les Peines et plaisirs de l'amour*.

A year before *Pomone*, Lully had once again included the hautboy in *Le Bourgeois Gentilhomme*, produced for the court at Chambord in 1670. It was the first time he had asked for hautboys since May 1664 (see Ch. 1, §D). This was the period when the new castle at Versailles was being built, and change was in the air. *Le Bourgeois Gentilhomme* may thus represent the court debut of the new hautboy, developed in the preceding six years. Hautboys played in the trio of a Menuet;[13] immediately

---

[11] Ferrari (1994), 206 ff.   [12] Marx (1951), 14.

[13] In the fifth entrée of the *Ballet des Nations*. Both parts are in G1 clef (ranges a1–b2, g♯1–g2). Marx (1951), 14 suggested that this was for hautbois de Poitou, but Eppelsheim (1961: 105 n. 121) argues convincingly that the instruments involved were treble hautboys.

preceding it were a series of *récits* and *ritournelles* in trio form that may have involved hautboys alternating with violins.[14] *Le Bourgeois Gentilhomme* was probably played by the *Hautbois et Musettes de Poitou*, who in 1670 consisted of Michel Destouches, Martin Hotteterre, Antoine Pièche, Pierre Ferrier, Philippe Philbert, and René Descoteaux. The military debut of the new model may have occurred in the same year, 1670, with a new march and drum role by Lully (Sandman 10/M1, LWV 44) written by order of the King and played by the newly created *Régiment du Roy*.

Thus the definitive hautboy arrived in time for Lully's operas, the *tragédies lyriques*, the first of which was *Les Festes de l'Amour et de Bacchus* of 1672. He regularly called for hautboys in subsequent productions, although the instrumentation was not specific:

> 1672. LWV 47/11, a 'Symphonie pour les Hautbois et les Musettes' in *Les Festes de l'Amour et de Bacchus*. Final divertissement of Prologue[15]
>
> 1673. Trio in *Cadmus et Hermione* (LWV 49/14, marked 'tendrement'). Vocal trio followed by 'Menuet, air pour les Dieux champêtres', called in different sources 'Symphonie', 'Trio, hautbois, tendrement', and 'Air'[16]
>
> 1675. Trio, LWV 51/7, in *Thésée*. Called in different sources 'Menuet', 'Trio. Hautbois', 'Ritournelle', 'Prelude pour les flûtes'
>
> 1676. 'Entrée des Zéphirs' in *Atys*
>
> 1677. LWV 54/43, *Isis*. 'Marche' for 'Violons, musettes et hautbois', all on the upper part (of five parts). Called a 'Gavotte' in a later source
>
> 1680. Premier Air, *Proserpine*, LWV 58/44. 'Rondeau', 'hautbois', 'Prelude'
>
> 1682. Air pour les hautbois, *Persée*, LWV 60/5
>
> 1685. Menuet, *Roland*, LWV 65/63. 'Trio'
>
> 1685. Air with Coridon, 'J'aymerai toûjours ma bergere', *Roland*, LWV 65/69. 'Hautbois'

Lully called the purely instrumental trios in his theatrical works *ritournelles*, and they were generally for a trio of strings; occasionally, however, they specified *hautbois* (presumably two treble hautboys and bassoon or cromorne, though it is unclear how many instruments played each part).[17] It was apparently only after 1670, when he had the definitive hautboy, that Lully developed the hautboy trio as a contrast to a tutti orchestra. This was a texture used by many subsequent composers.[18]

---

[14] Semmens (1975), 80.

[15] Cf. Eppelsheim (1961), 106. First page of later printed score in Lindemann (1978), 165.

[16] This piece and the air in *Persée* are in Babel (1697), i. 12 (see Haynes 1992: 359).

[17] Herbert Schneider (1989: 113) writes: 'As a rule, it is in his *ritournelles* and preludes that Lully places the affective emphasis, presents the principal ideas and gives the signals needed for the understanding of the ensuing vocal passages . . .'   [18] Cf. Kleefeld (1899), 263, McCredie (1964), 170, 308, 310.

Lully's 'Heureux qui peut plaire' from *Cadmus* (LWV 49/14), performed in 1673, is a dialogue between three voices and two hautboys and bass. The piece includes both f and f♯2, e and e♭2, and a and a♭2. From this we can conclude that by the early 1670s the instrument was already at home with chromatic alternates that could be gracefully distinguished.[19] There is also an upward skip from g2 to c3, implying that the range easily extended at least this high.

Like other wind instruments, 'hautbois' were regularly called on in Lully's scores to evoke a pastoral atmosphere. They often depicted a mythical shepherd's life: peaceable, innocent, and untroubled, evoking idyllic nature.[20] The hautboy's bucolic image shaded into that of the flute, which was the principal instrument of *Amour*. Within the pastoral theme, however, when peace rather than love was the principal subject, it was hautboys that were called for.[21]

In the pieces for hautboy band that he wrote in 1670 and later, Lully normally scored for *dessus* in G1 clef, *hautecontre* (C1 clef), *taille* (C2), and *basse* (F4). These categories corresponded to the titles of members of the *Violons, Hautbois, Saqueboutes et Cornets*. Missing is the fifth part that was usually part of the string band, the *quinte* (just above the *basse*). As noted in Chapter 1, §C, five-part wind bands were the norm until 1664. From the 1670s, the *quinte* was generally omitted in wind ensembles (as for instance in the Philidor Manuscript and Philidor's *Mariage de la Grosse Cathos* of 1688). In the 'Entrée des Zéphirs' in *Atys*, for example, a five-part string group is answered by a four-part hautboy band. Harris-Warrick suggests that in seventeenth-century French theatrical music in general, when the typical five parts were reduced to four, it may have signalled a change from string scoring to winds, especially when the dramatic situation suggested it (as in pastoral scenes, or village weddings).[22] As we have seen, her observation is valid from 1670.

The *Opéra* performed from 1674 to 1763 in the Grande Salle of the Palais Royal, which, although it could hold over 2,000 people, was considered cramped and small. Single instruments would have been difficult to hear, and doubling was probably normal. Among the woodwind players in Lully's productions were:

Hotteterre, Jean (3) (regularly until at least 1677)
Hotteterre, Louis (7) (regularly until at least 1677)
Hotteterre, Martin (from a1658)
Philidor, Jacques (from *c*.1670)

[19] The reconstructions of treble protomorphic hautboys made by Marc Écochard in 1999 produce all the chromatic notes except c♯1 and e♭1.
[20] Eppelsheim (1961), 209–11 gives many examples in Lully's works of how hautboys were used to evoke the 17th-c. ideal of an *Arcadia* in ancient times. As he notes, the hautboy was not the only 'instrument champestre', merely the principal one.   [21] Cf. Lindemann (1978), 172.
[22] Harris-Warrick (1990), 101.

Descoteaux, René (from 1670)
Pièche, Antoine (1670)
Ferrier, Pierre (1670)
Hotteterre, Colin (from *c*.1670)
Du Clos, Jean (from *c*.1672)
Plumet, François (from 1674)
de La Croix (1674)
Philbert, Philippe (from 1670)
Rousselet, Jean (1677)
Hotteterre, Jean (6) (1677)
Hotteterre, Jeannot (? 14) (1677)
Hotteterre, Nicolas (10) (1677)
Philidor, André (from 1677)
Destouches, Michel (1664–at least 1681)
Monginot (1682)
Thoulon père (onstage) (1682)
Royer, Claude (1682)
Dieupart, Nicolas (1685)

Several drawings by Jean Berain survive that show costume designs for wind players who appeared on stage in Lully's *Thésée* (1675) and *Isis* (1677). They are excellent portraits, each showing different features; unfortunately, no names are given.[23]

At this period, success for any musician was a matter of gaining acceptance at court. Raynor (1972: 231) points out that 'the successful musician in Louis XIV's France was treated better than his equal anywhere else'. Court musicians not only had their regular salaries, but those who were outstanding were given special posts in the *Chambre* or yearly stipends in addition to their salaries, known as *pensions* or *gratifications* (these were not the same as retirement pensions).[24] The hautboists of the *Écurie* sometimes played in private concerts for the King, and supplemented the orchestra for Lully's special opera performances given at court.

The court musical establishment moved from Paris to Versailles in 1683, and many prominent players employed by the *Écurie* moved there as well (see Ch. 1, §C). Most of the names of French players of the hautboy in this period come from court records. But many other musical activities using hautboys continued to take place in the city of Paris. Orchestras existed there from the first years of Louis XIV's reign, and there was an active guild of minstrels, the Confrérie de St Julien-des-Ménétriers, that supplied music for weddings, social occasions, and formal concerts.[25] Parisian society, both the nobility and middle class, supported a busy

---

[23] See La Gorce (1989).   [24] Morby (1971), 95.   [25] Cf. Anthony (1973), 14.

private concert life. Several concert series (usually called *concerts spirituels*) thrived at the end of the seventeenth century, though little documentation on them survives. Charpentier's surviving music, for instance, is mostly for recorder, although his players would also probably have played hautboy. Among his twenty-eight volumes of *Meslanges* of instrumental music is a 'Prélude pour les flutes et hautbois devant l'ouverture', H520, dated 1679, probably written to introduce a stage work. It consists of an ouverture, menuet, and passepied. Each of the two treble parts is for recorder and hautboy in unison. Combining recorder and hautboy was evidently not unusual; Lully specified it in 1682 and 1685; the bass was for 'bassons'.[26] A document dated 23 June 1693 records the formation of a company 'for the purpose of performing various duties for and in the city of Paris' that included Nicolas Dieupart, Edme de Pot (Depot dit Dumont), Claude Royer, Louis Allais, and Philippe Breteuil,[27] all (then or soon thereafter) members of the *Cromornes et Trompettes Marines*.

The *Chapelle* was reorganized and expanded in 1683, from which time *symphonistes*, sometimes including hautboy players borrowed from the *Écurie*, began to take part in performances of grand motets.[28] The *Chapelle* was responsible for the music at the daily mass attended by the King (usually at midday) and often a separate service for the Queen, as well as performances for special occasions such as royal births, marriages, funerals, and the celebration of military victories. At Christmas, *Noëls* (sets of variations on Christmas tunes, such as those that survive by Daquin) were performed either on organ or with *symphonie* (see below, §G.1).

Before much music especially written for them appeared in print, hautboists played collections of airs and instrumental pieces that had originally been written for operas and royal balls. Many miscellanies for generic treble instrument survive in manuscript, like Philidor's *Recueil de plusieurs belles pièces de simphonie*, the *Pièces choisies*, and collections of Lully's airs arranged for instruments.

One of the earliest trio collections is entitled *Livre de Triôts appartenants à [Nicolas] Dieupart Fluste et Cromôrne ordin.ʳᵉ de la Chambre du Roy. 1680.*[29] It contains six 'suites' of movements excerpted from Lully's *tragédies* and *ballets*, some pieces by Louis Grabu, two *Trios* by Nicolas Lebègue (probably added in 1683, one of which has a concordance as one of four 'Simphonies' in his third book of organ pieces), and some other miscellaneous pieces.

As Ford points out, this collection was probably heard at court, not only because Dieupart was a royal musician, but because some of the pieces have added notes such as 'le petit coucher du Roy', 'les plaisirs du Roy', and 'la chambre du Roy'.

---

[26] Eppelsheim (1961), 203.   [27] Ford (1981), 48.   [28] Morby (1971), 145–7.
[29] Now held at Yale University (Filmer MS 33). See Ford (1981).

The 'Musique du Petit Coucher' was a ceremony that took place in Paris,[30] before the court moved to Versailles in 1683.

If the 1670s and 1680s were the zenith of the *Roi Soleil*'s career, twilight was already setting in by the 1690s. The King's mood was sombre, Lully was dead, and the court was strapped with debt. Grand spectacles were no longer needed to establish Louis's reputation,[31] and the repertoire that best suited the situation was chamber music. Trios and solos with bass, harpsichord solos, and small-scale cantatas became more common, and were often written by composers for the instruments they played themselves. The preferences of the King ensured that this music remained French in style.

The first solos especially written for the traverso and violin appeared in 1702 and 1704, but a specific music for hautboy never developed in France. The instrument was frequently heard, but it played the great body of pieces for unspecified treble instruments that began to appear in the 1690s. These were newly composed works, not derivatives. They were often organized by key, and movements could be selected to make suites.

Of the French trios of this type, Marais's are the touchstone by which all the others can be compared. A few (like Rebel's and Couperin's) come close; the rest, while often very good, are in a less majestic category. Even Lully's trios suffer by comparison. Fragments of Marais's six large trio-suites are found in the same manuscript as Lully's (some of which can be dated as early as the 1660s),[32] but Marais did not publish his trios until 1692. Almost everything is playable on hautboy; the instrument was not mentioned in the earliest print, but is specified in later ones; the title-page does show four hautboys (Pl. 2.13).[33]

Montéclair's *Sérénade ou concert divisé en trois suites de pièces* of 1697, 'propres à danser', is written so the violins, recorders, or hautboys specified in the title are in unison, except for the pairs of dances and a 'Sommeil'. The music is well written and interesting. A few other 'trios' had first and second parts in unison (cf. Lully's 'Gaillarde' and 'Boutade' and Jacques Aubert's trios).

Most trio collections were intended for performance *en simphonie* (see below, §G.1), but some were conceived for only one instrument to a part. The outstanding examples of the latter type are Couperin's early trios and the Rebel *Recueil*.

Couperin composed at least two trios in the 1690s: *La Pucelle* and *La Steinquerque*.[34] At the time, as Brossard wrote, Italian trios were all the rage in Paris:

---

[30] Ford (1981), 61 citing *l'Etat de la France* (1687), i. 240.

[31] House (1991), 13 suggests a number of plausible reasons for this change. [32] See Ch. 1, §C.

[33] Marais's trios originally specified only recorder, violin, and treble viol, but later editions expanded the instrumentation to include hautboy and even (like Books 2 and 3 of the *Pièces de violes*) 'toutes sortes d'instrumens'.

[34] Two other trios, *La Visionnaire* and *L'Astrée*, may also have been written in this decade (cf. Beaussant 1980: 232). Couperin later used these two, with *La Pucelle*, as the sonatas in three of the four sonata-suites of *Les Nations* (1726).

Tous les compositeurs de Paris, surtout les organistes, avoient la fureur de composer de Sonates à la manière italienne.[35]	All the Parisian composers, especially the organists, were seized with the passion to compose Sonatas in the Italian style.

Couperin confessed some years later that when his pieces first appeared, he had passed them off as the work of an Italian by rearranging the letters of his own name (Coperuni, Pecurino, or Nupercio).[36] The irony is that they are quintessentially French in style, and in fact, Couperin used *La Pucelle* as the 'Sonade' in one of the later *Nations* (1726) that he actually called *La Françoise*. He later wrote that *La Pucelle* 'was also the first [sonata] I composed, and in fact the first composed in France'.[37] It is an exquisite piece (*La Steinquerque*, a suite written to celebrate a military victory, is not—though it suits hautboys well).

Rebel, director of the *Vingt-quatre Violons* and *maître de musique* at the Opéra from 1716, composed the *Recueil de 12 sonates* by 1695, but they were not published until 1712. Brossard owned the copy now in the Bibliothèque Nationale de France; in 1724 he wrote quite accurately of these pieces, 'Elles sont toutes magnifiques . . .'. The first seven sonatas are trios (with occasional independent gamba *récits*), and the last five are solos with bass. The complete collection has yet to be republished; some of the trios have only just appeared.[38] Rebel, who was a famous violinist, did not specify which treble instruments (*dessus*) were intended. In their published keys, numbers 2 (*La Vénus*), 3 (*L'Apollon*), 4 (*La Junon*), 5 (*La Pallas*), and 6 (*L'Immortelle*) go well on hautboy (*La Vénus* is better on hautboys than violins).[39] *L'Apollon* and *La Pallas* seem written for two different kinds of instruments. Of the solos, number 9 in D minor is playable on hautboy with minor adaptations, and is worth the effort. Number 10 also works well when transposed from D to C.[40] Number 11 in B♭, possibly the best of the twelve sonatas, lends itself well to the hautboy with small adaptations; it includes a long Chaconne.

An interesting collection of solos probably assembled in the 1690s is the *Recueil des airs* (F-Pn Rés. 2060). It includes 'Airs' by a number of composers, including Desjardins, 'Couprain', 'Pecourt', 'Mathau', and Lully. These pieces are full of melodic invention and are quite satisfying to play. The bass line is not included, but many pieces are well-known opera airs to which the original basses survive, so they could easily be added. This manuscript is especially interesting because it is

---

[35] Quoted in Beaussant (1980), 69.
[36] Ibid. 68. Couperin did have a cousin in Turin who was sometimes called 'Coperino'.
[37] 'fut auscy la première [Sonade] que je composay, et qui ait été composée en France'.
[38] *Les Cahiers du Tourdion* (Strasburg), ed. Frédéric Martin.
[39] Numbers 1 (*La Flore*) and 7 (*Tombeau de Monsieur de Lully*) are string music. The names of the pieces are not included in the original publication, but come from the manuscript copy in Versailles.
[40] On transposition, see Ch. 4, §H.3.

heavily and carefully ornamented.[41] No specific instrument is called for, but the range and keys suggest hautboy.[42]

In 1716 Robert de Visée, guitar instructor to Louis XIV, published his *Pièces de theorbe et de luth*, 'mises en partition, Dessus et Baße'. The treble part was intended, he said, for violin; but in fact it goes well on wind instruments, including hautboy.[43] These are fine examples of pieces in classic Lullian style. Most or all of them had been written by the 1680s. Between 1694 and 1705 Visée frequently performed at court with René Descoteaux, who played from 1688 in the *Chambre* (hautboy and recorder, primarily the latter), and Philbert (with Descoteaux, the first player of the traverso in France, but an hautboy player as well). Descoteaux and Philbert may have performed Visée's *Pièces* on flute or hautboy.

Another type of solo that might have been used by hautboy players at the end of the seventeenth century was original dance music, such as the *Suite de danses pour les violons et haut-bois qui se joüent ordinairement aux bals chez le Roy* [Livre Ier], published by Ballard in 1699. According to the title-page, this collection was 'Recueillis, mis en ordre & composez la plus grande partie par Philidor l'aîné . . .'.[44] This compilation (one of many made by André Philidor) is set out for a treble instrument with bass; middle parts, if they ever existed, are now missing. Besides many movements by Philidor, a number of other composers are represented, including Lully, Toulon, 'Forcrois' (probably Antoine Forqueray), Plumet (François ?), Madame la Dauphine, Madame Leance, and Pecourt (Louis Pécour). Dance types include the Branle, Contre-Danses Angloises, Menuets, and Passe-Pieds. The quality and interest of this collection make it rewarding to play, and suites can easily be selected from the sixty-two movements.

As for the instruments on which all this music would have been played, few survive. But there were many makers of hautboys active in France between 1670 and 1700. They included Rippert, Jaillard (alias Bressan), Dupuis, Jean Rousselet, Rouge, Pelletier sen., Fremont, Naust, and seven Hotteterres (Jean (3) and (8), Nicolas (4) and (10), Martin, Louis (11), and Colin). According to Sauveur, 'Sieur Ripert' was one of the best woodwind makers in Paris in 1701.[45] Rippert had been working 'a long time' by 1696. About the end of his career we only know that it was between 1716 and 1723. If he worked for forty or forty-five years, he would not have

---

[41] That the ornaments are carefully marked in this manuscript can be seen from the corrected mistake for a trill in the next-to-last bar of 'Esprits solets', fo. 10^v.

[42] The part never goes below f2, suggesting that it might be for recorder, except that it does not exploit the high register (never going above d3, and that only rarely), the Airs are at the bottom of the range for an F-instrument but lie comfortably for a C-instrument, there are pieces in D major, which is not a typical recorder key, and f♯1 is required, an awkward note on recorder. The collection is probably not for solo traverso because so few pieces are in sharp keys. If it is for violin, it fails to use the G-string. Thus by default it is probably for hautboy.

[43] The best suites are those in G minor, E minor, C major, A minor, and C minor.

[44] Collected, organized, and for the most part composed by Philidor *l'aîné*.

[45] Sauveur (1700–13), 335. See Ch. 4, §F.1 for Sauveur's text.

started before about 1675. His career was thus probably between about 1680 and 1720. Naust married Pelletier's daughter Barbe in about 1686, and in about 1692 took over Fremont's workshop on the rue de l'Arbre Sec. Under the sign of the lion rampant, it was one of the most important French woodwind ateliers of its time.[46]

Plate 2.16 is a portrait by David Teniers of himself and his family, and shows an hautboy on a table. The work has an interesting history that concerns the hautboy. It was originally painted in 1645/6, but the hautboy cannot be that old because of its form. According to the museum,[47] another signed version of the painting exists in London with a standing woman playing lute; the hautboy was thus added later. A print by Jacques-Philippe LeBas based on this painting (which by that time was apparently in France)[48] includes the hautboy. Since the print is dated *c.*1695, the hautboy must have been added by this date. The long baluster and flare of the bell are unusual, though the profile is similar to French instruments of the time.

B. Italy

The hautboy arrived in Turin in the 1670s, and by the 1690s was in Milan, Venice, Florence, Naples, Bologna, Parma, and Rome. That the instrument had come to Italy from France is indicated by the Italian words used to describe it. 'Oboè, Obbuè', etc. are phonetic transliterations of the French 'hautbois'.[49]

By 1672 the court of Savoy in Turin, which from early in the seventeenth century had strong ties to the court of France,[50] had a violin band similar to the *Vingt-quatre Violons du Roi*. From 1677, it also had a 'Scuderìa' (or *Écurie*) of six hautboy players, some of whom appear to have had French names.[51]

The first known instructions to appear anywhere for the hautboy are Bismantova's brief *Regole* for hautboy (1688; cf. Pl. 3.1). Bismantova, who was a cornett player living in Ferrara, may have got his information on the hautboy from someone else. That the source may have been French is suggested by Bismantova's use of the words 'anso o linguetta' instead of the more current Italian term for reed, 'piva, pivetta o linguetta';[52] 'anso' would have come from the French 'anche'.[53]

---

[46] Cf. Giannini (1993b), 4, 6.

[47] Frau E. Stielow, Bildarchiv Preußischer Kulturbesitz, 5 Oct. 1987.

[48] The print states that it came from the 'Cabinet de Mr le Duc de la Vallière'.

[49] In Italy, the oboe was called *oboè* (plural *oboè*) until the beginning of the 20th c. At the time the French diphthong *oi* was pronounced as the Italian *uè* or *oè*. Bernardini notes many 18th-c. Italian variations: *abboè, aboè, abuè, boe, obboè, obbovè, obbuè, obuè, obrè, obria*, etc. (Bernardini 1985a: 1).

[50] Lindemann (1978), 24 citing the *Mercure de France* (Apr. 1678.) Cf. also Owens (1995), 224.

[51] Cf. App. 1 under Mosso, Perino, Ricardo, Rion, Mattis, and Morand. Sources: Bouquet (1969), 13, Bernardini (1985a), 3 and Wind (1982), 16–17. The Besozzi family was to have a long and distinguished relation with the court at Turin. The first member of the family to play there was Giovanni Battista Besozzi, who served from 1697 to 1719.   [52] Cf. Riccati's statement is quoted in Ch. 2, §D.1.

[53] Giovanni Caviglia (pers. comm.).

A description of an opera performance in Milan in 1707 singled out one player for particular praise:

L'Orchestra è questa: 10 p[ri]mi v[io]li[ni]; 8 2.i, 8 Viole, 6 Hautbois, ma uno che sona all'ultimo grado de perfettione . . .[54]	The orchestra consists of: 10 1st violins, 8 2nds, 8 violas, 6 hautbois, including one who plays to the most extreme degree of perfection . . .

The player in question was probably Aléxis Saint-Martin, a Frenchman who had been in Milan since about 1690. Saint-Martin occupied a pivotal position in the development of the hautboy in Italy. He married Gerolama Federici; several Federicis were later active hautboy players at the royal ducal theatre in Milan (cf. App. 1). Saint-Martin played at Novara in 1711 with his eldest son Giuseppe, who was to become a famous player under his Italianized name, Sammartini. Another of Saint-Martin's sons also became an hautboy player. Sammartini's younger brother Giovanni Battista was later a well-known Milanese composer.

Besides his sons, Saint-Martin may have been responsible for training several individuals who were later to play significant roles in the progress of the hautboy in Italy: Cristoforo Besozzi (the first of many hautboists with this famous name), Giovanni Maria Anciuti (possibly 'the earliest Italian to make French-style wood-winds'),[55] and Onofrio Penati, who originated in Milan[56] and later became an import-ant player in Venice.

It was probably Saint-Martin who played 'Veggo in voi che l'alba pose', an aria by 'R.C.' for soprano, two hautboys, and Bass that was performed at the 'Milano Teatro' in 1700.[57]

An instrument of some interest now at Paris (E.210, C.470; see Pl. 2.5) is signed 'Martin'. It resembles the one shown in Mignard 1691 (Pl. 2.6). It is possible that Saint-Martin was the maker. The instrument's elaborate decoration suggests it was a presentation gift to someone rich or influential, and was thus probably not made for a professional musician (it shows little sign of having been used). Its length (532 mm) and the four large resonance holes in the bell suggest that it played at A+0.

There must have been two hautboists in Venice by 1694, because Pollarolo used 'Hautbois' in his *Ottone*, produced in that year. The instrument had already appeared in operas by Pollarolo and Perti in 1692.[58] It entered the *cappella* of San Marco played by Penati, who had made his Venetian debut at the same festivities as the young Antonio Vivaldi, on Christmas Day 1696.[59] The earliest regular player

---

[54] Letter to Perti from Pistocchi, quoted in Schnoebelen (1969), 45.
[55] Waterhouse (1993), 43.   [56] Talbot (1990), 162.   [57] Berlin (Mus MS 30 345, p. 14).
[58] Wolff (1937), 102.   [59] Talbot (1990), 162.

in Venice, Penati was the only hautboist permanently employed by the orchestra of San Marco, and his salary was by far the largest of any of its members.[60]

It is unclear who was playing in Venice before Penati's arrival. Both Saint-Martin and Ignazio Rion are possibilities; Saint-Martin had been in Milan since about 1690, and nothing is known of Rion before his engagement as hautboy teacher at the Pietà in 1704. In any case, there was a good deal of activity and even training: by 1700 there were already good hautboy players among the orphan girls of the *ospedali* (Barbara, for instance).

It is a pity that Arcangelo Corelli in Rome does not seem to have written solo music for hautboy.[61] But his violin music was so influential and well known that (although there is no historical indication of it) it is likely that hautboy players all over Europe would have tried to adapt it for their instrument. Three of the solo sonatas in Opus 5 (his best known, 1700) work on the hautboy and might have been performed by hautboists. The first six are impractical: many movements have two voices, and others are without rests. Even by transposing, the range is sometimes too large for the hautboy. In the second half-dozen, it is possible to adapt 8/1, transposing it from E to D minor, and combine it with 7/2, 3, 4 (already in D minor). Sonata 9 can be played intact by transposing it from A to B♭, and 10 can work in its written key of F (it is the best piece of the collection, except for the last one, the famous set of variations on *La Follia*, which is unplayable on the hautboy as it uses many virtuosic string techniques). Some of Corelli's trios are also playable on the hautboy.

C. *Germany*

In the aftermath of the Thirty Years War, most of Germany was devastated, while at the same period France was emerging as a strong power with immense cultural influence.[62] In rebuilding their musical infrastructures after the war, German aristocracy looked to the new developments at the French court. In 1685 Louis XIV obliged them by revoking the Edict of Nantes, thereby depriving the Huguenots (his Protestant subjects) of their religious and civil liberties. Within a few years, more than 400,000 people—artists, craftsmen, intellectuals, and the cream of the most industrious commercial class in France—had left the country for courts all over Europe. Berlin was especially receptive of Huguenots, so that 'by the end of

---

[60] Bernardini (1988), 378. Selfridge-Field (1987: 120) suggested that Antonio Caldara's *Confitebor tibi Domine*, which includes an interesting hautboy obbligato, was written to celebrate Penati's appointment, but since this piece notated the hautboy a tone below the rest of the group (see Ch. 5, §C.6), it was probably written for Rome.   [61] A sonata for two hautboys survives by Corelli's pupil, Montanari.

[62] Heyde (1993a), 593.

the 17th century every fifth person in Berlin was of French extraction . . .'.[63] Among these exiles, working in Roman Catholic as well as the many small Protestant principalities of Germany, were many woodwind players and makers. One of the main centres of the Huguenot faith, Poitou, had become by the early seventeenth century a centre of woodwind making and playing; with Louis's revocation, that industry ended.[64] France's loss was Germany's gain.

The new instrument quickly became 'de riguer' in German courts. Court wind players, including *Capellknaben*, were sometimes commanded to learn the new hautboy.[65] German shawm players, already versatile on many kinds of instruments, quickly took up the 'Hautbois', getting help where possible from French players. German musicians were also sent to France for training.[66]

A number of German writers (not yet agreed on the instrument's gender)[67] ascribed the hautboy to the French. Mattheson wrote (1713: 268)

Der gleichsam redende *Hautbois, Ital.* Oboe, ist bey den Frantzosen, und nunmehro auch bey uns, das, was vor diesem in Teutschland die Schalmeyen (von den alten *Musicus Piffari* genandt) gewesen sind, ob sie gleich etwas anders eingerichtet.

The eloquent *Hautbois* (*Ital.* Oboe) is to the French, and now also to us, what shawms (which were called *Piffari* by the old musicians) used to be in Germany, although it is constructed somewhat differently.

Majer elaborated on this (1732: 34)

Der . . . *Hautbois* . . . ist bey den Franzosen auch sonsten überall bekandt, und ein aus Buchs=Baum, oder anderm guten Holz verfertigtes Blas=*Instrument*. Dergleichen vor diesem in Teutschland die Schallmeyen gewesen, ob sie gleich etwas anders eingerichtet . . .

The . . . Hautbois . . . is familiar to the French and now everywhere else, and is a wind instrument made from box or other good wood. Before it appeared, something similar (although constructed somewhat differently), called a Schallmey, was used in Germany.

Eisel (1738: 96) said that

Das *Hautbois* . . . ist ein blasendes *Instrument*, welches von den Frantzosen zu uns Teutschen kommen, und an statt der teutschen Schalmeyen getreten . . .[68]

The Hautbois . . . is a wind instrument, which came to us Germans from the French, and replaced the German shawm . . .

---

[63] *Encyclopaedia Britannica*, 15th edn., xx. 49. As a result, 'the Berlin dialect still employs many terms of French derivation'. Cf. also Hortschansky (1996), 437. [64] Pierre (1893), 414.

[65] Owens (1995), 169. [66] See §C.10 below.

[67] Cf. the three quotations here. Quantz (in 1752 and 1755) consistently used a masculine article ('der') for the *Hoboe* (rather than the modern 'die Oboe'); this corresponds to the French 'le hautbois'. Matthes's sonatas (1770) are 'für die Hautbois'. In 1732, Walther (p. 304) wrote that 'Hautbois' was both masculine and feminine.

[68] This is copied in Albrecht (1761).

In 1721 Mattheson (1721: 432, 436) wrote of the 'Frantzösischen Blas=Instrumenten, als *Hautbois, Flutes, Bassons*' (French wind instruments, such as hautbois, flutes, bassons).

Until late in the eighteenth century, the hautboy was usually known in Germany by its French name, *Hautbois*.[69] The word 'Oboe' or 'Obboe', borrowed from Italian, was less frequently used, and seems often to have implied an hautboy at A–1 (as distinguished from one at *tief-Cammerton*; cf. Ch. 6, §A).

In France, the name of the new hautboy did not change (shawm and hautboy were both called 'Hautbois'). But because the Germans distinguished the new hautboy from the shawm by its French association (calling it *französische Schallmey, französische Hautbois*, or *Hautbois* instead of *Schallmey/Schallmeye* and *Pommer*), it is possible to determine the date of the introduction of the new instrument.[70]

Quantz's description in 1752 of the circumstances in which the French woodwinds were first introduced into Germany shows that even then, less than a century after the fact, historical knowledge was sketchy. Gerber in 1812 (p. 854) rather thought the 'Hoboe' was a new instrument in Germany in 1700. In fact, it arrived in Germany on the tide of a new interest in French instrumental music that had developed in certain courts by the 1660s.[71] By the early 1680s, the hautboy was established in a number of German courts (see Table 3.1).

By 1700, 'almost every [German] court of consequence possessed the "new" instrument and maintained bands of *Hautboisten*'.[72] The fact that Steffani's solos for hautboy were written for various localities (Munich, 1687; Hannover, 1689, 1692, 1694; Hamburg, 1695) attests to the existence of accomplished players at a number of courts and opera houses in Germany by the late 1680s and early 1690s.

French influence was also strong in German military circles, and officers took up the custom of sponsoring hautboy bands. Regimental *Hautboisten* were retained in peacetime as well.[73]

In this period, the most common music played by instrumental ensembles and small orchestras in German courts was in the Lullian style, and consisted of orchestral suites, French dance movements, instrumental concertos, cantatas, and opera arias often brought back from trips to France.

1. Hamburg

Hamburg was a large and prosperous city by the end of the seventeenth century; during the Thirty Years War, it had escaped the fate of most other German cities

---

[69] Leopold Mozart wrote in 1778 of the Divertimento in D, K.251, by his son, '. . . mit Hautb: solo'.

[70] Hildebrand (1975), 26. In German-speaking lands, references to shawm-playing are found in 1676 (Leipzig), 1682 (Saxony), and 1683 (Vienna) (Becker 1961: 1801). As late as 1687, Speer (p. 117) mentions only the shawm and does not register the French hautboy. Praetorius-type instruments are shown in pictures into the 1660s (Bega 1663, Gabron, Lauwers by 1651).   [71] Cf. Owens (1995: 12) on Stuttgart.

[72] Braun (1983), 130.   [73] Ibid. 143.

TABLE 3.1. *Earliest records of the existence of hautboys in Germany*

Date	Place	Comments
1680	Celle	Beauregard (see §C.2)
1680	Stuttgart	*Hautboisten*-Bande[a]
1681	Hannover[b]	
1681	Berlin	Beauregard and Potot
1684/5	Munich	Four players sent to Paris
1686	Hamburg	Militärkapelle[c]
1687	Darmstadt	French hautboist, Fairint, engaged[d]
1689	Nassau-Weilburg	3 *Hautboisten* (possibly regimental)[e]
1690	Zeitz[f]	
1690	Braunschweig-Wolfenbüttel	
1692	Arnstadt	Bought a number of *Hautbois*[g]
1694	Ansbach	3 *Hautboisten* appointed[h]
1694	Nürnberg	Denner and Schell
1695	Weißenfels	
1695	Dresden	
1697	Gotha	
1698	Leipzig	Französischen Schalmeien[i]
*c.*1700	Arolsen[j]	
1701	Weimar	

[a] Sittard (1890a), 13.
[b] Lindemann (1978), 25.
[c] Braun (1987), 136 citing L. Krüger.
[d] Noack (1967), 157.
[e] Hildebrand (1975), 27.
[f] Werner (1922), 89 (also for Weißenfels and Gotha). Cf. Johann Stadermann in Zeitz, who in 1689 was a Schalmeipfeifer, in 1690 was 'Hoboiste und Kunstpfeifer', and in 1694 was 'Kunstpfeifer der französischen Hoboe'.
[g] Heyde (1987), 29.
[h] Hildebrand (1975), 34 citing Schmidt (1956), 67–8.
[i] Schering (1921), 47; Schering (1926), 290.
[j] Rouvel (1962), 10.

by remaining neutral. As a city-state only loosely connected to the German Emperor, it was exceptional in being free of control by aristocracy. With its wealthy foreign visitors, it was one of the most cosmopolitan cities of Europe.

Hamburg had an active Stadtpfeifer corps consisting of fifteen members called *Ratmusiker* and *Rollbrüder* (the latter a lower rank of musician comparable to the *Kunstgeiger* in Leipzig). They had the usual Stadtpfeifer duties in the Hamburg churches and private entertainments; four of the six *Ratmusiker* were authorized to perform *Concerten*[74] (that is, probably chamber and orchestral concerts).

[74] Sittard (1890b), 11, 14.

By far the largest number of hautboy solos written in Germany in the seventeenth century came from Hamburg, mostly in the form of opera arias. A public opera house had been established in 1678, the first outside Venice. The Hautbois is first recorded in Hamburg in 1686, when a 'Militärkapelle' with hautboys was formed.[75] Two years later, in January 1688, the instrument appeared in an opera by Förtsch, now lost.[76] By the early 1690s, the hautboy was being called for regularly in operas by Conradi, Kusser, and Steffani,[77] and in 1692 Lully's *Achille et Polychème* was performed with Hautbois. In about 1695 the Opera established fixed posts for hautboy players. The names of the players are unknown, but they must have been exceptional to inspire the many splendid obbligato parts in the works produced in the next few years by Graupner, Steffani, Kusser, Handel, Mattheson, and especially Keiser. Johann Sebastian Bach visited Hamburg several times in the first years of the eighteenth century, and may well have heard performances at the Opera that influenced his own approach to instrumental arias.

Braun (1987: 136 ff.) ascribes the interest in the 'Oboen-Arie' to French influences. Conradi, director of the Opera from 1690, introduced French operatic style to Hamburg. Hautboys were part of his orchestra, and one piece in *Ariadne* (1691) has two hautboys answering two voices. Later composers like Kusser started using a single instrument with a single voice in dialogue and imitation, in a relationship similar to the two treble voices of a trio sonata. In the words of a witness to the effects in 1703 of this newly invented phenomenon,

On a composé des airs expres pour être récitez dans l'Opera avec le seul Hautbois & une seule voix de femme qui charmoit. La voix & le son de cet Instrument étaoient si bien mêlez ensemble qu'on auroit crû que ce n'étoit qu'une seule voix.[78]

Arias were composed especially to be declaimed in an opera using a single hautboy and single female voice. They were charming, and the sound of the voice and instrument blended together so well that it seemed but a single voice.

The 1690s thus saw two new stars appear in opera: the new singer (for the first time a woman), and the new hautboy.[79] The fledgling genre of the obbligato accompaniment to voice was to become a major part of the new hautboy's solo repertoire, both in opera and religious vocal works.

Reinhard Keiser began producing operas at Hamburg in 1694. 'More than any other, [Keiser] was the composer who gave Hamburg its illustrious reputation for having one of the great opera houses in Europe.'[80] He was enormously popular and

---

[75] Braun (1987), 136, citing L. Krüger.   [76] McCredie (1964), 84.
[77] Documentation for this period is scanty (Braun 1987), and there may have been other pieces, now lost.
[78] Nolhac, *Voiage historique et politique* (Frankfurt, 1737), ii. 166, quoted in Braun (1987), 137. As Braun observed, 'Die Klangverwandtschaft ermutigte zur Klangmischung.' For an enlightening analysis of the forms used in the 'Oboen-Arie', cf. Braun (1987), 138–9.   [79] Braun (1987), 139.
[80] Buelow (1993a), 195.

greatly admired; Handel often borrowed from him. We shall follow his Hamburg activities after the turn of the century in Chapter 5, §D.2.

2. *Celle/Hannover/Osnabrück*

The court at Celle was particularly inclined to Lullian influences through its French duchess, Eleonore d'Olbreuze. The Duke, Georg Wilhelm, hired a Frenchman, Philippe La Vigne, as his Capellmeister in 1666. La Vigne directed music at the court, mostly with French personnel, until the Duke's death in 1705. Through his regular trips to France, he was able to keep the court up to date with the latest developments at Versailles.[81]

On one of those trips, La Vigne arranged to engage four French hautboists for the court, who arrived in Celle in 1681. They had been preceded by François Beauregard, who visited the court in 1680, later settling in Berlin. By 1683, the orchestra was sixteen strong, seven of whom were 'hautboisten' (that is, woodwind players). Three other hautboists were part of the 'Dragoner Guarde'. A 'Flötenmacher' named Stephan Crusta was also associated with the court. The Celle orchestra was visited by Sebastian Bach in 1703; he probably heard primarily French repertoire.[82]

Johann Ernst Galliard, who was later to be one of Handel's important soloists in London, grew up in Celle and learned the flute and hautboy there. He studied with a French hautboist at the court, Pierre Maréchal. Maréchal had been one of the original players of the new instrument in France in its first years. From 1693 the court paid him 100 Rthlr. annually to instruct Galliard. Galliard was himself a member of the Celle orchestra from 1698 to 1705.[83]

Georg Wilhelm shared with his brothers, the dukes of Hannover and Osnabrück, the services of a number of French performers. It was thus no coincidence that these courts employed the hautboy relatively early (Osnabrück had a French-oriented orchestra from about 1679).[84]

In Hannover too the Capelle was staffed with French instrumentalists. The first hautboy was engaged in 1681.[85] Hannover had a short but brilliant period of opera performances starting in 1678. Duke Ernst August's council eventually found it cheaper to build an opera house than to pay for his lavish, extended stays in Italy.[86]

An excellent collection of French airs that may have been played by Ernst August's *Hautboisten*, perhaps alternating on wind and string instruments, is the *12 Suittes (Concerts)* 'mise [*sic*] en partition par Mr. Barre à Hanover' in 1689.[87] It is in four parts (the eighth suite has two added flutes).

---

[81] Linnemann (1935), 57, 74. [82] Ibid. 61, 75. [83] See further Ch. 5, §E.1.
[84] Cf. Sievers (1961), 30–3. [85] Lindemann (1978), 25. [86] Linnemann (1935), 65.
[87] Darmstadt (Mus MS 1221; some pages missing). A certain 'van der Perre' was employed at the court before 1698, according to Sievers (1961), 58, and the similarity of names is striking.

Steffani was hired in 1688 as Capellmeister at Hannover, and for the opening of the new opera house in 1689 he wrote *Enrico Leone*, which has a fine hautboy solo in Mechtilde's bittersweet air, 'Blumen, so die Kälte bricht'. Steffani produced a new opera each year, many of which included beautiful hautboy obbligatos.[88] There are three obbligatos with solo hautboys in the opera *Briseide*, produced in 1696.[89]

The Hofcapelle was distinguished by excellent hautboy players. Matthieu Des Noyers and a certain de Loges were engaged at the court some time prior to 1698, and in that year, three more French players were hired for the orchestra,[90] one of whom was François Des Noyers (perhaps the son of Matthieu), who was later to distinguish himself in Milan (see Ch. 5, §C.1).

The Capelle was enlarged after 1698. Telemann, who heard it frequently in these years, commented:

Hier ist der beste Kern von Franckreichs Wissenschafft zu einem hohen Baum und reiffster Frucht gediehen.[91]

Here the finest seed of France's science has grown into a high tree with the ripest fruit.

3. *Braunschweig-Wolfenbüttel*

Even before the new opera house was opened, Braunschweig had produced a number of Lully's works. Duke Georg Wilhelm of Celle, who hired loges for performances at Braunschweig, had heard *Thésée* there in 1687. Members of his orchestra (possibly hautboists) occasionally played in opera performances there.[92] The Braunschweig opera company opened its new theatre in 1690, and 'Hautbois' were included in the list of expenses for the house's opening.[93] Braunschweig's first known hautboy solo, by Kusser, was performed in 1692.[94] From the large number of obbligatos for hautboy that survive (by von Wilderer, Österreich, and Schürmann), it is clear that there were good players there.

4. *Weißenfels*

Weißenfels, near Halle, had Johann Philipp Krieger as Capellmeister from 1680 to 1725. From 1685 opera was performed at the new theatre built in the duchy's residency, the Augustusburg.

The Duke of Weißenfels created a 'Bande Violons und Hautbois' in 1695, consisting of six players, probably playing both instruments.[95] All six had German names,[96] and at least one (Hilsefunck) had earlier served as a player of shawm.

---

[88] Cf. Haynes (1992a), 295 ff.   [89] This opera may have been by Torri rather than Steffani.
[90] Sievers (1961), 58.   [91] Telemann (1718).   [92] Linnemann (1935), 65, 66.
[93] Lasocki (1977), 29 citing [F. Chrysander], 'Geschichte der Braunschweig-Wolfenbüttelschen Capelle und Oper von 16. bis 18. Jahrhundert', *Jahrbücher für musikalische Wissenschaft*, 1 (1863) 189, 194.
[94] McCredie (1964), 159.   [95] Werner (1911), 95, (1922), 89.
[96] None of the numerous hautboy players in the court records at Weißenfels had French names.

Krieger had written a piece for shawm as late as 1688, but by 1696 he was writing for hautboy (his cantata *Träufelt, ihr Himmel, von Oben*, written in that year, is for soprano, two hautboys or violins, and continuo).[97] Besides the *Hautboisten* band that was used in chamber music, there were *Regimentshautboisten* in Weißenfels. The city was also visited by *Hautboisten* from other courts.[98]

5. Berlin

The first two players of the new French hautboy in Berlin were Pierre Potot and François Beauregard. From 1681 they both held well-paid posts as *Hautboiste* and *Kammer-Musikante* at the Royal Prussian Court.[99] Beauregard was still there after 1701, Potot until about 1702.

In the reign of Friedrich III (Elector from 1688, King from 1701 to 1713), music and the dramatic arts were well supported, and numerous grand parties, masquerades, ballets, balls, and sumptuous spectacles took place, in the style of Louis XIV. The court orchestra was relatively large, and had four hautboys.[100] Karl Rieck was the Capellmeister until 1704; he wrote two concertos involving hautboy that are now lost.

From 1693 to 1700, the Brandenburg court had a royal wind band directed by Pierre de La Buissière.[101] Ludwig Erdmann (who was later an important player in Italy) was in Berlin in the 1690s, and may have been taught by La Buissière (part of whose job was to train young players).

6. Eisenach

Sebastian Bach's father, Ambrosius Bach, was a Stadtpfeifer in Eisenach. It is unclear if by the time of his death in 1695 he had taken up the new French hautboy. In 1691 an *Hautboistencorps* had been founded in the town, which supplemented the court Capelle.[102] The Capelle, which had been organized in 1672, also employed the town's Stadtpfeifer. Thus Bach played frequently at court, as did his successor, Heinrich Halle. According to Telemann, who was Capellmeister at Eisenach from 1708 to 1712, the Capelle was excellent, and 'oriented to the French style'.[103]

Halle was evidently an hautboy player, as it was he who trained Johann Sebastian's elder brother Jacob Bach to play the instrument. Jacob was appointed to the court of Sweden in 1704;[104] he died at the early age of 40 in 1722.

---

[97] Werner (1911), 95.

[98] Such as that of Weimar in 1701, and the six *Hautboisten* of 'Die Zeitzer Pfeiffer' once during Carneval in 1698 and later in July 1708. Werner (1911), 101.   [99] Schneider (1852), 48, 52; Sachs (1910), 61, 172.

[100] Allihn (1994), 1420.   [101] Sachs (1910), 182; Braun (1983), 129.

[102] Oefner (1995), 1703 and 1704.   [103] 'nach frantzösischer Art eingerichtet'; Telemann (1740), 361.

[104] It has been traditionally thought that on that occasion Bach wrote his *Capriccio sopra la lontananza del suo fratello dilettissimo* (Capriccio on the departure of his most beloved brother, BWV 992). This idea has been challenged by Wolff (1992).

7. *Dresden*

Traditionally, German church music was the responsibility of the Stadtpfeifer, and in the seventeenth century the Dresden *Stadtmusici* played regularly in the Sophienkirche, Frauenkirche, and Neustädter Kirche.[105] The magnificent procession that was part of the *Hoffest* of 1695 (Dresden specialized in festive celebrations) included thirty-five double-reed players, amongst whom were evidently both shawms and hautboys[106] (the court had four shawm players on its roles until at least 1694).[107] Again in the *Hoffest* of 1709, both shawms and hautboys appeared.[108] The music of the *Stadtmusici* in the eighteenth century, along with that of the amateur Collegia Musica, has not survived.[109] The players were sometimes asked to supplement the court musicians.

Friedrich August I became Elector in 1694 and in 1698, the Saxon court Capelle was reorganized, making the switch to French instruments. The two Capelle hautboists, Charles and Jean-Baptiste Henrion, were part of a famous 'Bande Hautboisten oder Kammerpfeiffer' that Friedrich August had engaged while visiting Vienna in 1696.[110] Compared with many other German courts, 1698 was a relatively late date (see Table 3.1), but by 1709 the Dresden Capelle had become one of the finest orchestras in Europe.

In 1699, the court secured the services of François La Riche (who had earlier supplied James Talbot with information on the hautboy). La Riche is one of the more interesting hautboy players of this period. Born in 1662 in Tournai, by the age of 23 he was in England. Although there is much we do not know about La Riche, an unusual amount of documentation on him survives: notes on the fingerings he used, possibly on his reed and instrument (from the Talbot Manuscript), aspects of his life, and even a piece of music.[111]

La Riche had a dual appointment as *Hautbois de la Chambre* and as agent for the Elector in purchasing items such as jewellery and horses from abroad; his salary (3,200 Thaler per year) was much higher than even that of the leaders of the Hofcapelle orchestra.[112] At Dresden, La Riche probably taught several young players who were to become important hautboists of the next generation: Christian Richter, Michael Böhm, and perhaps Caspar Gleditsch (Bach's solo hautboy player at Leipzig).[113]

---

[105] A piece they probably performed was the cantata *Der Todt ist verschlungen in den Sieg* by Schulze, which includes two hautboys, two tenor hautboys, and bassoon.   [106] Buelow (1993b), 220.

[107] See Oleskiewicz (1998), 18–20. According to Becker-Glauch (1951), 85, one of the 'Schalmeipfeifer' in this procession was the court player Christian Elste.   [108] Hildebrand (1975), 58–9.

[109] Steude in Steude, Landmann, *et al.* (1995), 1529.

[110] Fürstenau (1861–2), ii. 12, 19; Landmann (1982), 49; Oleskiewicz (1998), 20–4. The band consisted of twelve players: four hautboys, five flutists, and three bassoonists.

[111] The fingerings are discussed in Ch. 4, §G and the reed dimensions in Ch. 2, §E.3.b.

[112] The average was 250–600 Thaler; even the Capellmeister, Heinichen, only got 1,200.

[113] Richter and Böhm are described in more detail in Ch. 5, and Gleditsch in Ch. 6. La Riche probably taught Glösch in Berlin as well (see Ch. 5, §D.6).

Johann Fischer's *Musicalisch Divertissement*, written for 'Violen, Hautbois oder Fleutes douces', was published in Dresden in 1699/1700, possibly with the collaboration of La Riche. Although the music was generic in instrumentation, it is the earliest known German chamber collection that mentions the hautboy as a possibility. It uses both A♭s and does not go above b♭2; the movements are short.

8. Darmstadt

Darmstadt had a brief 'French' period in the 1680s, when its ruler, Ernst Ludwig, Grand Duke of Hesse (r. 1687–1739), put on several opera performances, including Lully's *Acis et Galatée* (the première of which the Duke had attended in Paris in 1686). Ernst Ludwig had probably had composition lessons while he was in France; he later composed orchestral music. A French hautboy player named Fairint was attached to the court from April 1687 to October 1688. But soon afterwards, musical activities were curtailed and not renewed until 1709.

9. Nuremberg

Being Protestant, Nuremberg suffered less in the Thirty Years War at the hands of the Swedes than most of Catholic Bavaria. The city had traditionally been a centre of instrument making, and it was the first (or one of the first) to begin making the new French woodwind instruments. Its importance is indicated by the fact that more than two-thirds of the earliest surviving hautboys were made there.[114]

Christoph Denner and Johann Schell were key figures in this development. Both were players as well as makers; Denner was praised for his virtuosity on hautboy and other instruments. He had begun his career in Nuremberg about 1678, making traditional 'Renaissance' wind instruments. It may have been contact with the woodwind players appointed to the court at nearby Ansbach in 1694 (probably Pertelle and Erdmann) that led Denner and Schell in 1696 to request permission from their guild to make and sell the

. . . französische Musikalischen Instrumenta, so mainsten in Hautbois und Flandadois bestehen . . . die ongefehr vor 12 Jahren in Frankreich erfunden worden.[115]	French musical instruments, that is, hautbois and flûtes douces . . . that were developed about twelve years ago in France.

Twelve years before 1696 is 1684. It is unclear why this date was specified, as French hautboys were being played in Germany before then (see Table 3.1). But Denner or Schell may have been in communication with the players in Munich

---

[114] More than two dozen hautboys by Gahn, Denner sen., Schell, and Oberlender sen. survive.
[115] Nickel (1971), 206, 199.

who had been sent to Paris in that same year, 1684, to study woodwind-playing with Hotteterre (see below). In any case, by the year of this official request, 1696, orders were already being made to Nuremberg for 'französische Schalmeyen' (see §E.3 below), and Denner had been commissioned by the town Council to make two 'frantzesische Fletten' or 'Opera-Flöten' in 1694.

In outward turning details, Denner's hautboys resemble the one shown in Mignard 1691 (Pl. 2.6). To judge by the relative size of its reed, Mignard's hautboy was short and high-pitched. Many early Nuremberg hautboys, including about half of Denner's, were apparently at A+1.[116] A substantial fraction of Denner's other kinds of surviving instruments are also at this pitch, a holdover from the old traditional instrumental *CammerThon* described by Praetorius in 1618 and still common on most church organs in Germany in the early eighteenth century.

10. Munich

The Munich court under Maximilian II Emanuel, Elector of Bavaria from 1679, is of special importance in the history of the hautboy, both at the end of the seventeenth century and after 1715.

Steffani's *Alarico* was performed in Munich in 1687, and included an aria with hautboys, 'Care soglie a voi mi porto', a sweet little largo that goes up to c3; it has simple figuration, and the hautboy parts move in parallel. This date qualifies it as the earliest known hautboy solo. It is no accident that Steffani wrote for the hautboy so interestingly and so early. In 1678 the Munich court (by whom he been employed since 1667) sent him to Paris to master Lully's style of composition.[117] He must have become acquainted there with the hautboy and its possibilities. Several years later (1684/5), when Steffani was director of chamber music, the Munich court sent four young and promising musicians to Paris to study with one of the Hotteterres. 'Care soglie' was probably written for them on their return.

A *Sonata a 6* by Melchior d'Ardespin for '4 Violons, 1 Hautbois, Basson et Basse continue' also probably involved these woodwind players. D'Ardespin was Max Emanuel's music teacher, and director of the court orchestra from 1687. He is credited with the introduction of the French style to Munich.[118]

One of the four musicians sent to study in Paris was Felix Teubner, who from 1684 held an appointment at the Munich court as hautboist, flutist, and violinist. It may have been Teubner who was the recipient of Christoph Pez's remarkable

---

[116] Among the Nuremberg makers, three (total) lengths are discernible for hautboys, centring on 499, 538, and 571 mm. (The ranges are 490–505, 536–39.2, and 560–78.4 mm. The sample is twenty-five hautboys.) These presumably correspond respectively to A+1, A+0, and A−1 or lower. The shortest instruments were made by Gahn, Schell, Christoph Denner, and Oberlender. The younger Denners worked at the longest length (except for two instruments at 538). Christoph Denner and Oberlender also made a number of hautboys at the longest length.

[117] Nösselt (1980), 61.   [118] Münster (1993), 298.

Symphonia in G minor for hautboy and bass.[119] The melodic turns of phrase are seventeenth-century in style, and for that reason the piece might qualify as the earliest solo for hautboy and continuo that has survived.[120] But the numerous alternate readings in pencil on different pages, added after the manuscript was copied, suggest that it was originally written for violin and later adapted to the hautboy.[121] It also requires a virtuosity that seems improbable at this stage of the instrument's development. The alternative readings make the piece easier to play by eliminating all the high d3s, all but one of the c3s, and some of the fast runs at the end of the 'Passagaglia'. Another indication that the piece was not originally conceived for hautboy is the ample proportions of the second and fourth movements, which are unusually long for a wind instrument.

Max Emanuel became governor of the Spanish Netherlands in 1691. He moved to Brussels in 1692, taking most of his court musicians with him, among them at least three hautboy players, including Teubner (see below, §E.2). One of these players, Franz Schuechbauer, returned to Munich in 1696. Schuechbauer was active at the court throughout the troubled years of Austrian occupation. We shall follow this history further in Ch. 5, §D.17.

D. *England and 'Babtist's vein'*

But during the first years of Charles 2d all musick affected by the beau-mond run into the French way . . . and all the compositions of the towne were strained to imitate Babtist's [Lully's] vein . . .[122]

As a result of political intrigue between the courts of France and England, London unintentionally received the new French hautboy almost simultaneously with its development in Paris. The medium for this exchange was Robert Cambert, the composer who had used the new hautboy in the two theatre works he produced in Paris in 1671, before Lully seized control of the Opéra.

Cambert moved to England in 1673, it is now thought, on orders from Louis XIV. The English King Charles II had a taste for French music and French women.

---

[119] The manuscript is now in Rostock but originated in Stuttgart (where Pez worked from 1706). But to judge from its style, the piece was probably written before 1706.

[120] Thus antedating Fischer's *Musicalisch Divertissement* of 1699/1700, and Konink's 12 Sonates (Amsterdam, by 1700), which are the earliest known solos.

[121] Because of the alternate readings and the fact that the surviving manuscript is carelessly written, the piece requires a good deal of editing to be playable (cf. the edition by Christian Schneider, UE, 1994). Bars 79–80 of the 'Passagaglia' were subject to several corrections and the final version is unclear. There are three places where accidentals appear to be missing in the manuscript (II: 38: 11 f♯1, IV: 25: 9 and 29: 9 e♭2). As often in manuscripts, the original slurring is ambiguous and could be read in different ways, especially in the Gigue. Schneider includes all the alternative readings in the foreword to his edition.

[122] North (1959), 350, from *The Musicall Grammarian*, 1728. Cf. also Cudworth (1957).

His mistress was a young Bretonne noblewoman named Louise de Kéroualle, whom he had ennobled as the Duchess of Portsmouth.[123] As a means of re-enforcing France's influence on the English court, Cambert was to act as the Duchess's *Maître de musique*, leading a group of French musicians, including three of Louis's singers (who may have had secondary jobs as spies) and 'cinq ou six hommes qui jouent fort bien de la fluste'.[124]

Among these flutists were Paisible, de Bresmes, Guiton, and Boutet, who had probably come to England with Cambert in 1673.[125] They took part as 'French Hoboyes' in Cambert's *Ariane*, which he produced in 1674,[126] as well as a very elaborate court production of the masque *Calisto* in 1674/5.[127] They may have been involved in other performances in 1674 as well.[128]

The three singers went home after only five weeks in England. In the meantime, Cambert and his band had entertained Charles and members of his court with Lully's latest compositions that had been on the Paris stage less than a year.[129] In the process, they also (at Louis XIV's bidding) introduced London to the latest, most up-to-date instrument used at the Paris Opéra: the hautboy.

Although at the time there were strong anti-French feelings, the English public evidently liked the new instrument.[130] Cambert's players were hired by one of the two London theatres, the King's Company, in 1674–5. By 1676 the following lines appeared in a stage play: 'What, you are of the number of the Ladies whose ears are grown so delicate since our Operas, you can be charmed with nothing but Flute doux, and French Hoboys.'[131]

A revival in 1676 of the play *Volpone* by Jonson included the lines

> Did Ben now live, how would he fret, and rage,
> To see the music-room outvye the stage?
> To see French hautboys charm the listening pit
> More than the raptures of his God-like wit!

The players of these French hautboys were probably the same four who had played for Cambert.[132] From then on, there are regular references to public performances on the hautboy.[133]

---

[123] Kéroualle had been sent to England by Louis in 1670. Cf. Ashley (1971), 187.

[124] Buttrey (1995), 205.

[125] Lasocki (1983), 319. De Bresmes had been a 'joueur d'instruments' in Paris in 1671–2 (Brossard 1965: 46). 'Bouttet' may be the Jean Boutet, 'joueur d'instruments' who lived in Paris in 1694 (Lasocki 1983: 830 and Lasocki 1988: 340).

[126] Lasocki (1983), 321 and forthcoming, [14]. Halfpenny (1949c: 152) supposed they probably played as a consort of two trebles, tenor, and bassoon. Another possibility is Holman's suggestion (1993: 368) that since the orchestra was divided into two parts, it consisted of two pairs of treble winds.   [127] Halfpenny (1949c).

[128] Lasocki (1988), 340.   [129] Buttrey (1995), 209.

[130] For background, cf. Ashley (1971, esp. p. 234) and ch. 17 of Lasocki (1983).

[131] Etherege, *The Man of Mode* (11 Mar. 1676), Act II, Scene i, p. 21.   [132] Lasocki (forthcoming).

[133] Cf. Lasocki (1983), 330 ff.

In England, the word *hoyboyes* or *hautboiz* was used for waits or shawms as early as the mid-sixteenth century;[134] this spelling reveals the French origin of the word, and hence probably of the instrument. Without a difference in name, distinguishing the shawm from the hautboy is more difficult in England than in Germany. Between 1671 and 1707, references to the instrument in English theatre pieces and elsewhere refer to it variously as 'Hoboy', 'Haut-boyes', 'Hoe-boys', 'Haught Boys', 'Hooboys', 'Hoyboys', etc.[135]

The traditional shawm continued to be used for some time after the introduction of the French hautboy. Talbot (*c.*1692–5) described three oboe-type instruments that were then current in England: the 'English Hautbois or Waits treble' (= shawm), the 'Schalmey' (see below, §H), and the 'French Hautbois/treble'. The qualification 'French' for the latter instrument is significant. Talbot also offered a clue to when the new French instruments began to take root: 'Chief use of Sackbutt here in England is in consort with our Waits or English Hautbois. It was left off towards the latter end of K.Ch. 2d & gave place to the Fr. Basson.'[136] King Charles died in 1685, so the 'French' bassoon (and thus presumably the hautboy as well) had apparently been adopted by the Waits (or municipal bandsmen) in the early 1680s.[137] Banister seems to suggest that the 'French Hautbois' was not generally familiar even in 1695: 'Indeed it looks strange at first sight: But on the other hand, if a Man considers the Excellency and Use of it, this Wonder will soon vanish . . .'.[138]

The court engaged Paisible and three other French woodwind players in 1677, and they were still being paid in 1684.[139] By 1678 (if not earlier), De Bresmes, Guiton, and 'Cir Felix alias La Montagu Cir' (perhaps another of the 'cinq ou six hommes qui jouent fort bien de la fluste') were engaged at the Chapel Royal.[140] They probably played woodwind parts as needed. Positions in the Chapel Royal were demanding, as the personnel were required to be in constant attendance on the sovereign, and to travel with the royal household. After Charles's death in 1685, the regular use of 'musick' (that is, concerted music with instruments) was discontinued in the Chapel Royal.

Lasocki notes the presence of hautboys, and particularly of Paisible, in concerts given in *c.*1676–86 by the Duchesse de Mazarin, Hortensia Mancini, another mistress of Charles II and sometime rival of the Duchess of Portsmouth. It is unclear whether Paisible continued to play the hautboy as well as the flute, but he

---

[134] Becker (1961: 1800) notes the use of 'Hautboiz' in England in 1575. Praetorius (1618a: 15) pointed out that the English used the term 'Hoboyen'. [135] Price (n.d.) and Tilmouth (1961), 18.

[136] Baines (1948), 19.

[137] Waits were probably still used for certain outdoor performances, however, such as music on the Thames, through the 1680s. Cf. Wood (1995), 561. [138] Banister (1695), page following title-page.

[139] Lasocki (forthcoming). [140] Lafontaine (1909), 322; Ashbee (1986–), i. 179.

did compose for it (see below). He is not survived by any hautboy solos, but his recorder sonatas give an idea what the woodwind solo sonata in England was like at this time.[141] They have little resemblance to the solos being published in France by La Barre and Hotteterre le Romain.

New French hautboy players continued to arrive in England.[142] In 1678, six 'hoboys' were attached to the Horse Grenadiers (which were modelled on the French *Mousquetaires*);[143] a piece for the Grenadiers, written by André Philidor in about 1692, survives in the Philidor Manuscript.[144] In the 1680s, the new dragoon regiments also used them (one hautboy and two drums), and a company of twelve 'hautbois' were part of the King's Regiment of Foot Guards in London in January 1684/5[145] (John Ashbury, a maker of woodwinds before 1698, was 'Major Hautboy' to William III's own Regiment of Foot Guards). Many civilian hautboy players in London worked part-time in military units.[146] On 6 October 1685, four French players were lent money by Martin Hotteterre so they could go to England to join the Fusiliers as 'haubois'.[147] These players may have been Protestants forced to leave France, since just twelve days later Louis revoked the Edict of Nantes.

Because of the situation at court, organized public concerts began very early in London. At the restoration in 1660, the powers-that-be reinstated the monarchy but 'carefully arranged to keep it hamstrung for want of money',[148] so that musicians could seldom make a full living from court work. The result 'was an enrichment of public music in London. The presence of a number of highly skilled, under-paid and under-employed musicians meant that they had to go outside their official posts to make money, and this, in turn, meant the growth of the public concert.'[149]

Public concerts began in London in the 1670s[150] and became increasingly frequent. Musicians could hold a secure though never well-paid post at court while doing primarily freelance work: 'Charles II knew, as Elizabeth I had known, that to deny the freedom of his musicians to earn money outside court would have been to make it impossible for any first-rate composer or instrumentalist to accept

---

[141] Paris (Rés. Vma MS 700, 'Solos by Mr Pesible'), Detroit (RM 788.1191/S698), Cambridge (MS 122, 41 and 46). The lowest notes of the bass parts (D1 and C1) do not allow these pieces to be transposed down to hautboy range, a fourth lower.

[142] Among French or probably French woodwind players documented there before 1700 were Aubert, Granville, La Tour, Bressan, Le Fevre, Le Roy ('Baptist'), Chevalier, Colmack, and Paulin. Cf. Lasocki (1983), 361. Giannini (1993a: 378) uncovered evidence suggesting that a Jacques Hotteterre was employed at the English court in 1675. As she points out, there is no confirmation of this fact in any of the English documents studied by Lasocki and others. Jacques (-Martin) Hotteterre ('Le Romain') was born in 1674, so this Jacques would have been an older relative. He might have been the Jacques-Jean Hotteterre noticed by Thoinan (1894: 43, cited by House 1991: 32) in French court service from 1692 to 1705, who signed a document in 1694 (House 1991: 33). The later Jacques (-Martin) Hotteterre may have added 'Le Romain' to his name to avoid confusion with Jacques-Jean.

[143] Farmer (1912), 47 and (1950), 51.   [144] Sandman (1974), 86.   [145] Hamilton (1874), i. 267.
[146] Farmer (1912), 52.   [147] Lasocki (forthcoming).   [148] Raynor (1972), 255.
[149] Ibid. 256.   [150] Cf. Holman (1993), 349.

a position in the king's service.'[151] The state monopoly on music-making that was typical of Continental courts was absent in London, and, for the period, musicians enjoyed exceptional freedom to organize public concerts in any way they wished.

Concerts took place after the playhouses were finished for the night. They were usually financed by subscription and (according to ancient tradition) often took place in taverns. They were also held in 'Music Rooms', such as Hickford's and the room in York Buildings, which held about 200 people. By the 1690s, musical performances to a paying public had become as important in the musical life of London as the theatres. The hautboy took an active part in these concerts, 'to which for the reputation of the musick', as Roger North wrote, 'numbers of people of good fashion and quallity repaired'.[152] They were no doubt a means of livelihood for some of the French wind players, probably Catholic, who after 1689 were denied posts at court for religious reasons.

When James II became king in 1685, as well as hiring Paisible (apparently as a bass violinist), he engaged François La Riche (see above, §C.7), recently arrived in England. Both players were members of the band of twenty-four violins as well as James's Roman Catholic chapel.[153] La Riche went on to have an active career in England, but (perhaps because of religious intolerance) moved in 1699 to the Catholic court of Dresden.

King James fled the country in December 1688, and his successors, William and Mary, disbanded his 'Popish' chapel and cut back on musical activities at court. The anti-Catholic climate was renewed. As a result, hautboy players like La Riche must have depended even more on public concerts and the theatres. Until 1695, the United Company employed two hautboy players to play in Henry Purcell's operas and other large works.[154] A complete hautboy band appeared in Purcell's *Dioclesian* in 1690. Since he had no employment at court, and was obviously an exceptional player, it is quite possible that La Riche served as Purcell's hautboy soloist.

Purcell's song 'O let me weep' (or 'The Plaint') from *The Fairy Queen* (1692), with soprano and continuo, is published in the Purcell Society edition with an obbligato part for violin, but was evidently originally for hautboy. As Bruce Wood points out, not only is the slurring in the part idiomatic for hautboy rather than violin, but in the theatre where the music was first performed, a single violin would not have been well heard.[155] Wood and Pinnock (1993: 55) describe it as 'Six or

---

[151] Raynor (1972), 257.   [152] North (1959), 352.

[153] Sadie suggested (1993: 147) that some of James's French musicians were repatriated when he fled to France in 1689; Paisible and La Riche remained in England.

[154] I have since discovered that the entry '11.1' under Purcell in Haynes (1992a), 257 is neither by Purcell nor an hautboy solo.

[155] According to Bruce Wood (pers. comm.), the original editor of the PSE found a manuscript of the air in 1900 or 1901 at the Royal College of Music with the obbligato part specifically designated for hautboy. This manuscript is now lost. Wood writes, 'I think the "violin" designation is simply the best guess of whoever edited *Orpheus Britannicus*—the earliest source in which it is to be found.' Cf. also Wood and Pinnock (1993), n. 29.

seven minutes of very slow music in Purcell's best melancholy manner . . . the obbligato part was played by solo oboe, not violin, making it the very first song of this uniquely colourful and expressive kind in English musical history.' The piece also has many traits in common with two other hautboy obbligatos with soprano, 'Bid the virtues' in *Come, ye sons of art, away* (1694), a song full of happiness, with ingeniously contrived voice and hautboy parts that weave around each other, and 'Seek not to know' from *The Indian Queen* (1695).[156] A number of hautboy solos are peppered through Purcell's odes, all (except *Swifter, Isis*) from the 1690s.[157]

In his ode for St Cecilia's Day, 1691, John Blow called for 'Hautboys' doubling both violin parts as well as the viola. The latter part was presumably for tenor hautboy; indeed, Blow wrote the earliest documented appearance of tenor hautboys anywhere in the anthem 'Sing unto the Lord, O ye saints of his', written for the Chapel Royal between 1681 and 1683.[158] The players were de Bresmes and Guiton. Purcell used a tenor hautboy in *King Arthur* (1691) as well as *Dioclesian*; Holman (1994: 177) suggests he used a double-reed band in *The Yorkshire Feast Song* (1690) as well.

In the relatively early year of 1688, a curious *Collection of several simphonies and airs in three parts* (eight suites) for two violins, flutes, or 'Hoe-boys' and bass was published anonymously in London by Nott.[159] The music is of considerable interest, with a character not unlike Purcell. Ford (1981: 53) points out that five of these pieces were ascribed to Louis Grabu in another manuscript (Filmer MS 33), and suggests they were all by him.[160]

From 1692, Princess Anne (who became Queen in 1702), together with her Consort, Prince George of Denmark, maintained a chamber band of six hautboys and recorders at the court. Besides chamber music, this band would probably have played music for parades and military ceremonies. Several surviving works by Keller and Finger may have been written for this band. Among them would have been Keller's Sonatas, the last three of a collection of six published in 1699, for two recorders, two hautboys, and bass.[161] These pieces are quite beautiful, exploiting the tone colours of the four wind instruments; it is likely they were also performed in Thomas Britton's Music Club in about 1700, as he owned a copy of them.[162] There are other extant sonatas by Keller involving hautboy. Among Finger's many excellent chamber works is a Sonata in B flat (*c.*1700) for two hautboys or violins;[163] it is quite simple technically but full of musical surprises, and the last movement is excellent.

---

[156] Z 323/7 and Z 630/15 respectively.

[157] Holman (1994: 182) noticed on the basis of manuscript parts that hautboys, when they do not have their own parts, sometimes double the trumpets rather than the violins in large concerted works. See also pp. 185–6 on *Come, ye sons of art, away* and *Who can from joy refrain?*.   [158] C3 clef, range fo–b1 (Holman 1993: 408).

[159] GB-Lbl K.2.e.4; US-DW, 203.

[160] Peter Holman notes (pers. comm.) that the political situation at the time made it unwise to register the work as by a Catholic. Ford (54–6) lists other concordances of the Nott collection.

[161] The dedication copy is in the British Library.   [162] Lasocki (1983), 405.

[163] GB-Lbl Add. 49599/7. The parts are labelled 'Hautboy 1mo & 2do'.

Some of the repertoire of this chamber band may be contained in two interesting but incomplete collections preserved in manuscript part-books at the British Library.[164] The first, MS 39565, contains sixty-two pieces (mostly suites) by Paisible, 'Pourselle', 'Talott', Morgan, 'Finguor', etc. The MS is copied in a French hand; a 'tenor volume' (the third part) once existed, but is now lost. MS 30839 is a separate collection; it resembles 39565 but is shorter, containing a total of only ten suites (7 anon., 2 by Paisible, 1 by Keller). The instruments mentioned are 'flute', 'haubois/hobois', and 'Trompette'.[165]

In 1694, in *Come ye sons of art, away*, Purcell set to music the following lines:

> On the sprightly hautboy play,
> all the instruments of joy,
> that skilful numbers can employ,
> to celebrate the glories of this day.

The following year saw the publication of the first English instruction book for the hautboy, called *The Sprightly Companion*. At the end of the preface, the author (or compiler, a 'J.B.' who was presumably John Banister jun.), refers readers to 'above a Hundred Tunes proper for [the hautboy]' in *Apollo's Banquet*, an instruction book for violin that was published repeatedly from 1669 onwards. Copies of the two works at the British Library are in fact bound together. *Apollo's Banquet* itself never mentions the hautboy. Banister went on to praise the hautboy for its 'Majestical and Stately' character, and remarked that 'the greatest Heroes of the Age (who sometimes despise Strung-Instruments) are infinitely pleased with This for its brave and sprightly Tone'. Holman (1994: 178) remarks that this may have referred to King William, the Dutch Hero of the Age, who 'did much to promote oboe bands and trumpeters in the army and at court, to the detriment of the "strung instruments", the Twenty-four Violins'. Holman makes the case that the latter group were virtually 'superseded at court by oboe bands'[166] in the 1690s.

Queen Mary died on 28 December 1694, and Paisible's 'Queen's Farewell', a funeral march in four parts for two hautboys, tenor, and bassoon, was played at her funeral, probably by the six 'hautboys' of the first Regiment of Foot Guards.[167] It contains chromatic movement ($b\natural$ to $b\flat2$) and suspensions; played slowly, and muted,[168] it is quite moving. The piece appeared in *The Sprightly Companion*.[169]

---

[164] This idea was originally suggested in Tilmouth (1959), 383–4.

[165] The Premier Dessus is in G1 clef and later G2. The *Indian Queen* is mentioned (either Banister's of the late 1660s—cf. Holman (1993), 334—or Purcell's semi-opera of 1695). The library dates these manuscripts to *c*.1690; John Shore was attached to this ensemble, but only apparently from 1699 (this is the implication of Lasocki 1988: 355 n. 53). If these manuscripts were the repertoire of the royal band, since they contain both trumpet parts, they were probably made after that date.   [166] Holman (1993), 434.

[167] Lasocki (1988), 344.

[168] Mutes were associated with mourning (see Ch. 4, §E.2.b). The suspensions would have invited the use of the flattement (see Ch. 4, §K.3).   [169] A second march by Tollett, in three parts, appeared with Paisible's.

The United Company split into two in 1695, and hautboys were used in both the new companies.[170] Hautboys were also mentioned in productions at Drury Lane, Dorset Garden, and the Lincoln's Inn Fields theatres, playing martial and pastoral music. They were sometimes called for on stage,[171] and probably doubled the string band as well.

La Riche was Steward for the St Cecilia's Day festivities in London in 1697, and music he wrote for the event survives: an overture and nine Dances entitled 'Mr Le Ruch's Tunes on St. Cecilias Day 1697'.[172] The music, which is quite agreeable, is not assigned to any specific instrument. It is too low for the recorder and never goes below c1 (as violin music usually does). It is thus appropriate for hautboy. If it originally had a bass, it is now missing; Peter Holman thinks the Tunes are likely to have been originally in four parts. In that case, the parts would probably have been played *en symphonie* (see below, §G.1) with a group of winds and strings.

There were several makers of hautboys in England before 1700. Peter Bressan (originally Pierre Jaillard) had moved there from France in 1688.[173] He was the leading London recorder maker of his day, and his instruments were probably played as far away as Germany.[174] None of his hautboys is extant, although detailed measurements of one, made in the 1690s, have survived (see App. 3).

Shortly after Bressan's arrival in England, two English hautboy makers set up shop: Joseph Bradbury (p1689) and the elder Thomas Stanesby (1691). Both are survived by excellent hautboys, and both had been apprenticed in the 1680s to Thomas Garrett (who may himself have been a maker of French-type instruments).[175]

E. Other Areas

1. The Dutch Republic

In the Dutch Republic, three of the most important institutions through which the hautboy functioned (court, church, and military) were for various reasons unavailable. The performance of music was severely restricted in the Calvinist religion that predominated there and music was not cultivated by the stadtholders of the House of Orange until late in the eighteenth century.

In the same year that Lully became head of the Académie Royale de Musique, 1672, Louis XIV invaded the Dutch Republic and was narrowly repulsed. Even this

---

[170] Lasocki (1988), 343.   [171] Lasocki (forthcoming).
[172] According to a note on the manuscript, this particular copy was already owned by John Channing in 1694.
[173] Cf. Byrne (1983) and (1984). Bressan came originally from Bourg en Bresse, and Borjon (1672) mentioned a 'Perrin de Bourg en Bresse' as a musette player and teacher. He could have been Bressan's teacher. There were several important hautboy players at the court in Paris at the time named Perrin.
[174] Cf. Böhm's letter quoted in Ch. 5, §D.13.   [175] Waterhouse (1993), 42, 128.

failed to dull the appetite of the Dutch for Lully's works, and it was probably through the performances of Lully's operas in Amsterdam and the Hague starting in 1677 (when *Isis* was given, probably by French musicians) that the French haut-boy first became known in the Republic.[176] Lully's operas were frequently staged in Amsterdam in the 1680s, and complete operas, libretti, and collections of *airs* and instrumental pieces were published there. Lully's works were produced at the Hague until about 1730.[177]

Richard Haka, a Dutchman with English antecedents, is survived by five intact hautboys and nine Schalmeys; since he was working as early as 1661,[178] some of his surviving oboe instruments could predate 1670; it is certain he was making 'franse Haubois' (as he called them, 'French hautboys'), both 'discant' and 'tenor' sizes, by 1685.[179]

As prosperity gradually returned in the 1680s and 1690s (reinforced, as Rasch points out, by the special link with Britain through the Stadtholder William III, who became King of England in 1689), 'there was a conspicuous and definite shift in musical activities: foreign musicians arrived, operas were performed, musical set-tings of Dutch texts received a new impetus and there was a rapid rise in the inter-national music trade'.[180] William was back in Holland for a visit in 1691, and took with him an hautboy band that included La Riche, Bressan, and Michel Granville[181] (the latter had been a member of the *Douze Grands Hautbois*). It is also possible that René Descoteaux visited Holland at some point before 1687;[182] as we have seen, Descoteaux was an important woodwind player and maker at the French court.

Many Huguenots arrived after the revocation of the Edict of Nantes in 1685, and French, German, and Italian traders and craftsmen settled in Amsterdam, with its liberal religious and commercial climate. The Dutch have never been particularly chauvinistic, and have a tradition of accepting newcomers; as Rasch put it, 'the musical history of the Netherlands is in some large part the history of musical foreigners'.[183] In this period, the important composers and players of the hautboy were Hendrik Anders from Thuringia, Servaas de Konink from Flanders, and Elias Bronnemüller from Germany. In the eighteenth century, a number of foreigners, attracted by the wealth of the republic, contributed to the musical activities in Holland. Some settled there, while many passed through on concert tours.

For lack of court patronage, instrumental concerts were normally sponsored by city authorities, often in combination with Collegia Musica. These Collegia usually

---

[176] Cf. Rasch (1993), 398.
[177] A Dutch musical theatre was cultivated towards the end of the 17th c. (the *zangspel* or *muziekspel*) by such composers as Hacquart, Schenk, Anders, and de Konink, and probably included hautboys in the orchestra.
[178] See Waterhouse (1993).   [179] Haka (1685).   [180] Rasch (1993), 395.
[181] Jeans (1958a), 185 and (1958b), 92.   [182] Jonckbloet and Land (1882), p. clxxiii.
[183] Rasch (1993), 401.

PL. 3.2. Jan de Lairesse, ? 1687, title-page to Anders's *Trioos*, Opus 1, 1697–8

combined good amateurs with musicians employed by the city churches, and were often supported financially by city councils and better-off individual citizens. The Collegia Musica also served as concert organizers.

Anders's *Trioos* [sic], Opus 1 for 'toutes sortes d'instruments' appeared in 1687, unusually early. Jan de Lairesse's decorative title-page to this collection shows a shawm-hautboy hybrid similar to those that survive by Haka (Pl. 3.2). The music is good, and consists of dances (not arranged by suite of keys) and short 'Sonatinas'. There are some Lully airs at the end. Probably in deference to the recorder, the range is rather high: there are frequent c3s and d3s.

Anders founded a Collegium Musicum in Amsterdam in 1698, made up of professional players. This ensemble included Carl Rosier, Nicolas Desrosiers, and Michiel Parent.[184] Parent (d. 1710) was a maker of woodwinds. In 1697 Rosier published a curious collection of fourteen sonatas for trumpet or hautboy and strings ('ou tous hautbois' [!]). One of Desrosiers's Airs appeared in the Philidor Manuscript. He published collections of trios and quartets in 1697, 1703, etc.— unfortunately now lost—that included hautboy (Pl. 2.9). Anders, Parent, and two other members of this Collegium (Le Grand and Cockuyt) were employed at the Stadsschouwburg (the municipal theatre) in Amsterdam.

De Konink published two books of trios in Amsterdam in the 1690s (Pl. 3.3), and his *12 Sonates* for flute, violin, or hautboy and continuo were published around 1700. The only known surviving copy of the latter collection is a manuscript

[184] Rasch (1993), 398, 401.

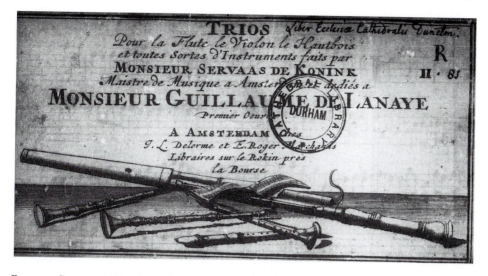

PL. 3.3. Servaas de Konink, 1690, title-page to de Konink's *Trios*, Opus 1. The Dean and Chapter of Durham

in Wolfenbüttel dated '1.ix.1700'. The solo part is marked 'Flute', and the last six sonatas are too high for hautboy; if the hautboy uses treble recorder finger-ings (so that F becomes C, and everything is transposed down a fourth), the range is more appropriate.[185] Sonatas 6 and 12 have movements using *tremolo*, an orna-ment that is rarely marked (see Ch. 4, §K.2.a). The most interesting sonatas are 3 and 8.

2. *The Spanish Netherlands*

The southern Netherlands (now Belgium) was governed by Spain in the sixteenth and seventeenth centuries and Austria in the eighteenth. The first opera house in Brussels, the Opéra du Quai du Foin, was opened to the public in 1681. Lully's tragic operas were the main repertoire.

The most important figure in the musical history of Brussels in this period was the Elector of Bavaria, Maximilian II Emanuel, who had inherited a thriving Capelle in Munich in 1679. He became Governor of the Spanish Netherlands in 1691, and moved to Brussels with most of his musicians the following year, resid-ing there until 1709.[186] During that period, the Elector produced operas by Lully with a combination of his own Capelle and musicians and dancers from France.

---

[185] It seems likely that this was a common key relation between the two instruments; see Ch. 4, §H.3.a.
[186] Münster (1993), 299 ff.

Max Emanuel's hautboy players at Brussels were Teubner, Schuechbauer (see above, §C.10), and Normand, who had all come from Munich in 1692. Teubner left the Elector's service in 1703. Schuechbauer, as noted, was back in Munich from 1696. Normand stayed with Max Emanuel, returning with him to Munich in 1715 (see further Ch. 5, §D.17).

3. The Habsburg Lands

There may not yet have been 'Hautbois' players in Vienna in 1687. Steffani's *Alarico* (mentioned above in §C.10) is preserved in a MS at A-Wn, but the aria for hautboys, 'Care soglie', is given in this version to 'Flauti'.

Soon afterwards, this apparently changed. 'Hautbois' and 'Flautae ex B' (i.e. French hautboys and flutes a tone lower than normal) were owned by Prince-Bishop Liechtenstein at Kroměříž by about 1695,[187] and in 1697, Friedrich August of Saxony, while on a visit to Vienna, engaged a 'Bande Hautboisten' from there.[188] In that same year, Ferdinand Richter produced an opera at the court in Vienna that included 'Hautbois' (that is, the new French hautboy).[189] And in 1698 and 1699 Fux, Badia, and Bononcini performed pieces involving hautboy.[190] But hautboists did not officially join the court Capelle until 1701. The court was slow to take up the new hautboy both because of political differences with France and because of the personal taste of Emperor Leopold I (d. 1705), who seems to have had an aversion to French music.[191]

Records from Kremsmünster Abbey indicate that it ordered 'ein ganzes Spill Hubua' (a complete set of hautboys) from Jacob Fux, and three 'französische Schalmeyen' from Stephan Melßhamber of Nuremberg in 1696.[192] That same year, the Abbey sent two of its players to Passau to learn 'Hubua und Fagot';[193] there were two players of those instruments at that court, probably Frenchmen.[194]

In Salzburg, Heinrich von Biber included 'Piffari' (in A, with clarini) in a *Requiem à 15*.[195] Vejvanovsky's *Balletti per il Carnevale* (Kroměříž, 1688) has parts for 'Schalamia ô Piffara', and Schmelzer in Vienna used Piffari in a *Balletto di Centauri* (Schönbrunn, 1674) and a *Balletto della Serenissima de more* [sic]. These were probably Renaissance shawms, to judge from their pitch and range (cf. below, §H). They are notated in the same keys as trumpets, trombones, violins, and organs, which means they were at the same pitch, A+1. There are normally two 'treble' parts and one 'tenor', with a range of a ninth or tenth.

---

[187] Otto (1977), pp. xv–xvi.   [188] Fürstenau (1861–2), ii. 12.   [189] Wellesz (1919), 59.
[190] Seifert (1987), 11–13.   [191] Antonicek (1980a), 718.   [192] Kellner (1956), 291.
[193] Puechers and Copisi (cf. App. 1).
[194] Kellner (1956), 285, 292, 294, 295. The players' names were 'Hali' and 'Morizen' (perhaps Hallé and Maurice).
[195] A *Muttetum Natale* also includes 'oboes', according to Chafe (1987), 175–7 (see also pp. 64, 109).

Biber's *Missa Salisburgensis* included 'Hautbois'. The French name indicates that the instruments in question were hautboys rather than shawms. This piece is sometimes thought to have been performed in 1682, but that would be an exceptionally early date for the appearance of hautboys in this area; the first records in other parts of the Empire are in the 1690s. The hautboy parts were in G2 clef in C major, the same key as everyone else, including the trumpets; this indicates hautboys in A+1. Biber's connections with Munich suggest the possible use of instruments by Schuechbauer; equally likely are hautboys by the Nuremberg makers of the time (Christoph Denner, Schell, and Gahn). All these makers are known for their high-pitched instruments at A+1.[196]

4. Spain

French hautboy players arrived in Madrid in 1679, together with a large company of musicians who accompanied Marie-Louise d'Orléans, daughter of 'Monsieur' and niece of Louis XIV, when she married King Charles II of Spain.[197] This troupe was organized by Henry Guichard, a secretary of Marie-Louise d'Orléans's father. Guichard had been involved with the first opera performances by Cambert and Perrin, and had thus run afoul of Lully (a trait shared by all the principals Guichard employed in this project). The group's musical director was the violinist and composer Michel Farinel, who had worked in England from 1675 to 1679, and had married there Cambert's daughter, Marie-Anne.[198] Farinel chose for his principal violin Guillaume Dumanoir, the famous leader of Louis XIV's twenty-four violons, *Roi des violons* of the Ménétriers, and a strong anti-Lullist.[199]

Among the instrumentalists were four hautboy players: Alais, Auger, Bonpar, and Griffon. It is possible that (just as in the case of the four French hautboists who went to England in this same decade) one of these players was primarily a bassoonist. Since the company was made up of singers and instrumentalists, it was able to mount many kinds of productions. The hautboy players could have been involved in cantatas, divertissements, ballets, operas, vocal concerts, 'concerts de symphonie', and music for hautboy band. Some of this music was probably by Farinel, and pieces by Cambert were also probably performed.[200]

By 1688 Farinel had returned to France; one of the hautboy players, Alais, was serving at Versailles by 1691 as an hautboy in the *Plaisirs du Roi*. Spain was not disposed to accept foreigners, including foreign musicians, nor did Spanish musicians travel abroad for education. Marie-Louise d'Orléans 'was criticized, rebuked, and even accused of treachery for introducing French customs':

---

[196] On Denner and Schell, see above, §C.9. On hautboys in *Cornet-ton*, or A+1, see Ch. 2, §D.2.a.
[197] Kenyon de Pascual (1984), 431; cf. also Benoit (1953).   [198] Cf. Benoit (1980), 396 (art. on the Farinels).
[199] It is unclear, as Benoit (1953–4), 55 ff. points out, if the Dumanoir in question is the son or the father.
[200] Ibid. 53, 59–60.

If the French consorts of the Spanish monarchs found the Spanish court austere, its etiquette severe and their new surroundings somewhat cold, the reception given their musical employees was even colder. The isolation of foreigners at court . . . is demonstrated by the experience of the 38 French musicians who accompanied Marie-Louise . . . For the short period they spent in Spain (less than a year), the French musicians aroused the envy of their Spanish colleagues because they dressed well and the queen regularly and liberally rewarded them with expensive gifts and money, as was the French custom.[201]

The preference of most of the Spanish court was for Italian music, and because the hautboy was associated with France, the instrument was at first received with less enthusiasm. French opera, the medium that allowed the most obvious entry for the hautboy, was evidently never performed there. Nor has any evidence been found of the use of hautboys in Spanish sacred music of the seventeenth century.[202]

F. The Hautboy Band

In modern music, oboes are not common instruments, compared with violins or guitars. But in the Baroque period, hautboys were quite as numerous as violins, and probably heard more often. Nowadays the oboe's environment is the orchestra, and even there, only four or at most five players are used. In the seventeenth and eighteenth centuries, by far the greatest number of hautboy players never played in an orchestra; most of them played in bands (see Pls. 1.22, 1.23, and 3.4).

Hautboy bands provided much of the musical background that is today the job of the radio and *Muzak*. If there had been shopping malls in the eighteenth century, hautboy bands would have played there. Their job was often simply to create 'atmosphere', and what they did was rarely listened to with complete attention. Most historical evidence on hautboy bands and bandsmen comes from Germany, but bands were common in all countries.

When we think now of historical hautboy players, we tend to think of the ones who played the music that has come down to us, the sonatas and concertos played by court chamber musicians, the *Hofmusici*. Or we think of the Stadtpfeifer who played obbligatos with voice in church. But in fact there were relatively few prime players of this type. With a few exceptions, wind/hautboy bands were made up of players of the least accomplishments, either beginners or failures. Players in the military had the lowest pay and hardest life in the field, so the best players no doubt avoided these jobs. Besides *Hautboisten*, who worked in regiments, for municipal governments, or for courts, an even lower rank of hautboy player existed who was

[201] Stein (1993), 413–15.   [202] Kenyon de Pascual (1985), 97, 95.

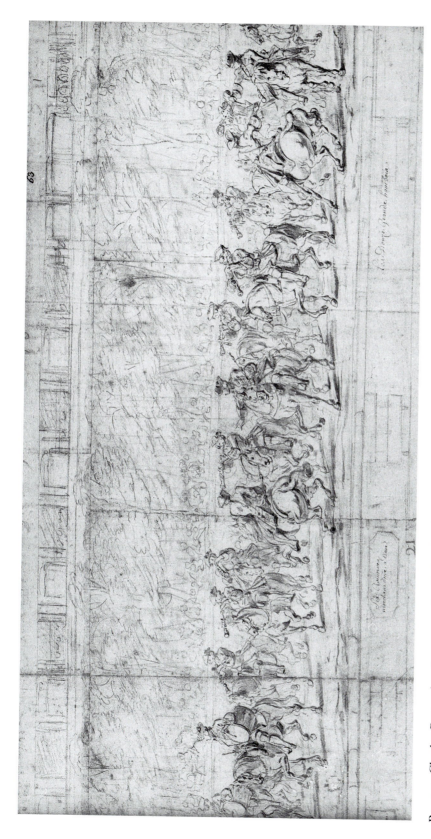

PL. 3.4. Charles Parrocel, 1 June 1739, detail showing 'Les Douze Grands Hautbois' in *L'Ordre de la marche pour la publication de la paix*. Painting 39 metres long (*sic*). Paris: Musée Carnavalet. Photothèque des Musées de la Ville de Paris

usually called a *Spielmann* or *Musikant*; he was a freelancer, playing for weddings, funerals, etc. whenever he could avoid the jealous watchfulness of the city musicians who normally covered these events.[203] It was to the poorer sort of *Hautboisten* that Johann Mattheson was referring when he wrote

Werden aber die *Hautbois* nicht auff das aller *delicat*este angeblasen, (es sey denn im Felde oder *inter pocula*, wo mans eben so genau nicht nimmt) so will ich lieber eine gute Maultrummel oder ein Kamm=Stückchen davor hören, und glaube, es werden ihrer mehr also verwehnet seyn.[204]	If however the Hautbois is not played in the most delicate way (as for instance in the field or at a drinking party, where it is not always taken too punctiliously), then I would rather hear a good Jew's harp or musical comb instead, and would, I think, be better entertained.

Fleming (1726: 20) also noted

Die Trompeten, Hautbois, und andere dergleichen, die einen allzugroßen Allarm machen, sind dem Kopf und der Gesundheit nicht allzu zuträglich, sie nehmen die Lunge mit und machen das Gesicht ungestalt, die Bachen und die Augen werden aufgeblasen.	It is not good for the health of Trumpeters, Hautboisten, and suchlike to play too loudly. They weaken the lungs and deform the face, inflating the cheeks and distending the eyes.

This is not to say that all hautboy bands were of mediocre quality. As noted in Ch. 5, §D.4, Mattheson described a group in Hannover that he heard in 1706 as a 'most exquisite band of wind players'.

The hautboy band was a continuation of the Renaissance tradition of similar instruments played together in consorts. One of the reasons for its success was acoustic. A group of hautboys played out of doors sounded much gentler than indoors, yet carried remarkably far; the sound changed little in quality or volume even at several hundred yards. The effect of this carrying power was enhanced when the performance was on water, as in Lully's music for *Plaisirs de l'île enchantée* or Handel's *Water Music*. Douwes (1699: 114) had noticed the same acoustic attribute in shawms, which he said

voornamentlijk by stil ende mooij weeder, buijten huis, van verre seer soet en aangenaam is.	out of doors and from a distance is very sweet and pleasant, especially in calm and agreeable weather.

---

[203] See Krickeberg (1971).   [204] Mattheson (1713), 268.

1. *Types of bandsman: the regimental* Hautboist, *the* Stadt-Hautboist, *and the court* Hautboist

Hautboy bands were first used in the military, but were soon adopted in civilian settings. The employers of *Hautboisten* were regimental officers, city governments, and almost any aristocrat who maintained a court.

In the standing armies that were established in the middle of the seventeenth century, drums and pipes were the symbols of the infantry, trumpets and drums of the cavalry. In the newer mounted infantry (often called Dragoons),[205] the instruments of choice in France, England,[206] and Germany were double-reeds and tambours (tympani). Unmounted infantry regiments also adopted bands of *Hautboisten*.

Shawms (two trebles, a tenor, and a curtal) were used in military music in Germany from the early seventeenth century.[207] German, Italian, and English armies later adopted the French hautboy. There is documentation of 'französischen Hautboisten', French hautboists, attached to German shawm bands in the 1680s and 1690s, probably as instructors in the new instrument. Wolfgang Caspar Printz wrote in his novel *Musicus vexatus* of 1690

Zu unserer Zeit noch hat der Fürtreffliche Held, Herr Graf von Sparr, Generalmajor, den Gebrauch der Schallmeyen und Fagotten in den Krieg eingeführt. Vor wenigen Jahren sind die französischen Schallmeyen, Hautbois genannt, aufkommen und im Krieg gebräuchlich worden . . .[208]

In our time, the great hero Major General Graf von Sparr introduced *Schallmeyen* and *Fagotten* in battle. A few years ago, the French *Schallmeyen*, called 'Hautbois', appeared and became common in war.

Since hautboys were not as loud as trumpets and drums, their principal functions involved military ceremonies, parades, regimental funerals, and concerts for officers (who were often their employers).[209] Fleming wrote

Es machen die Hautboisten alle morgen vor des Obristen=Quartier ein Morgen=Liedgen, einen ihm gefälligen March, ein Entree, und ein paar Menuetten, davon der Obriste ein Liebhaber ist; Und eben dieses wird auch des Abends wiederholet, oder wenn der

Every morning the *Hautboisten* perform a little morning piece in front of the officers' quarters, a march which is pleasing to them, a little *Entrée* and a few minuets, for which the commander has a special liking. This is also repeated in the evenings or whenever the commander has guests or

[205] Dragoons and hautboys are associated by more than one source (cf. Weigel 1698: 238). Dragoons fought as light cavalry on attack and dismounted infantryman on defence. The name comes from the weapon they used, a type of carbine or short musket. *Encyclopaedia Britannica*, 15th edn., iv. 210.
[206] Hautboys are described as 'Gay Hoyboys, the Dragoons Delight' in Motteux's play *Farewel Folly* (1707).
[207] Hildebrand (1975), 4, 6–7. Cf. also Hind and Baines (1980), 311. [208] Printz (1690), 179.
[209] Hildebrand (1975), 8 and 20–1.

Obriste Gastgebothe oder Assembleen anstellt, so lassen sie sich auf Violinen und Violons, wie auch Fleuten doucen und anderen Instrumenten hören . . .[210]

parties. At these they like to hear violins and cellos as well as the recorder and other instruments . . .[211]

In France, small bands like the *Fifres et Tambours* at court and privately sponsored military officers' field bands, as well as large ceremonial ensembles like the *Douze Grands Hautbois*, were heard in outdoor ceremonies, on military campaigns, as background music for social occasions, as dance bands, and in dramatic works (sometimes even as quasi-actors on the stage). Apart from entertainment, French hautboy players actually participated in battle campaigns until their presence among infantry troops was categorically forbidden by royal edict in 1683.[212]

Besides 'Hautboisten', military hautboy players were also called 'Oboisten', as well as the 'Feldmusik'.[213] Within the musical groups employed in military formations, hautboy players were generally of higher status than fife and drummers or even regimental drummers.[214]

The four-part setting that had been common for shawms was also the pattern for hautboys. Although there had been five-part hautboy bands (see Ch. 1, §E), the norm after 1670 was four parts. Both of Jacob Denner's surviving bills for Graf Gronsfeldt (1710) and Göttweig Abbey (1720) included four-part hautboy 'choirs'.

The number of players per part is not well documented. Bands usually varied between four and eight members. In the second half of the seventeenth century, the number of hautboys in French regiments varied, three to four being usual.[215] In Germany, the standard formation for *Regimentsoboisten* consisted of six players: two trebles, two tenors, and two bassoons. In 1713, Friedrich I's infantry regiments in Prussia, for instance, each consisted of six Hoboisten. The same is true of Bavarian and imperial Austrian infantry regiments, and it is documented for Munich in 1695.[216] Fleming wrote (1726: 181)

Nachdem aber die *Hautbois* an deren [der Schallmeyen] Stelle gekommen, so hat man jetzund sechs *Hautbois*ten, weil die *Hautbois* nicht so starck, sondern viel *doucer* klingen, als die Schallmeyen. Um die Harmonie desto angenehmer zu *complet*iren, hat man jetzund zwey *Discante*, zwey *la Taillen* und zwey *Bassons*.

Since the time the hautboy replaced them [shawms], the number of *Hautboisten* is six, because the hautboy is not as strong and sounds much more *douce* than the shawm. To round out the band in the most pleasant manner, there are now two trebles, two Tailles, and two bassons.

---

[210] Fleming (1726), 181.　　[211] Tr. based on Braun 1983: 143.

[212] Sandman (1974), 90 ff. Hautboys also played immediately after an artillery attack at the siege of Mons in 1691 (Kastner 1837: 103 n. 1). This is nine years after the royal suppression of hautboys in infantry regiments, which evidently did not affect the king's own ensembles. In 1692 the *Fifres et Tambours* (the 'fifres' were usually hautboy players) were ordered to prepare to follow the king on a military campaign (Benoit 1971b: 133).

[213] The latter term was also used for musical pieces; see Unverricht (1980), 456.　　[214] Braun (1983), 145.

[215] Sandman (1974), 88.　　[216] Hildebrand (1975), 51–2, 8–10.

The most practical deployment would have been to double the top and bottom voices.

Krieger published the six suites of *Die Lustige Feld-Musik* in 1704. They are full of spirit and interesting harmonies, and quite amusing to play. The collection was written

Auf vier blasende oder andere instrumenten im Marchiren vor denen Compagnien blasen und sonsten denen Officieren aufwarten.	For four wind or other instruments, to be played while marching at the front of companies of soldiers or else while serving their officers.

Krieger provided three copies of the first treble part, two of the second treble, one for the tenor, and three for the bassoon, implying a group made up of multiples of nine.

Many rich and independent German cities employed a special category of hautboy players, often called *Stadt-Hautboisten*, who were separate from the Stadtpfeifer, and belonged to the city militias that defended the city in emergencies.[217] Their duties were generally ceremonial, however; they performed the watch, took part in municipal festivities, provided entertainment at the city towers, etc. They were frequently made up of retired regimental hautboy players.[218] As might be expected, *Stadt-Hautboisten* were frequently involved in disputes over rights and privileges with the local Stadtpfeifer. *Stadt-Hautboisten* are documented in Leipzig and Frankfurt; Telemann's 'Frankfurter' Marche written in 1716 for three hautboys, two horns, and bassoon[219] was probably written for the *Stadt-Hautboisten*.

By the early eighteenth century, almost every court in Germany, large or small, maintained a non-military *Hautboistenbande*. A German court *Hautboist* was of considerably lower status than a *Hofmusicus*. He was not a member of the elite court chamber music, but was often regarded primarily as a soldier who happened also to be a musician. The kind of music he played was generally not as technically demanding as that played by *Hofmusici*,[220] and his salary was correspondingly lower. In some cases, *Hautboisten* also acted as servants or lackeys when they were not playing. Like the other court musicians, the court bandsmen were normally under the direct authority of the court *Capellmeister*.[221] Bands served as a pool of young talent for replacing personnel in the chapels, and players were often promoted to a court appointment after having served as *Hautboisten*, a period when they frequently continued their training and lessons (they were sometimes called 'Hautboistenjungen', or hautboy apprentices).[222] In Schwerin, some players had the title of 'Hofmusikant und Hautboist' and apparently served in both roles.[223] In Stuttgart, two of the nine *Hautboisten* were also members of the *Hofmusici*.

---

[217] Braun (1983), 145 ff.   [218] Hildebrand (1975), 70.   [219] Haynes (1992a), 312.
[220] Hildebrand (1975), 38–41.   [221] Owens (1995), 344, 346, 348.   [222] Hildebrand (1975), 36–7.
[223] Meyer (1913), 38.

Since the players were many-handed, they provided a basis for instrumental music of all kinds. Bands played for daily music at court other than that played by the Capelle: *Tafelmusik*, ceremonies, processions, weddings, dances, hunts, etc., and (like *Hofmusici*) were sometimes expected to travel with their noble employers.[224] Throughout the eighteenth century, many poorer courts had only a small wind group that doubled on strings and was relatively inexpensive to maintain, since (though they were better paid than military *Hautboisten*) the players did not have the status of *Hofmusici*.[225] A *Bande des Leibregiments* might double as a court hautboy band, or serve as a relatively inexpensive source of wind and string players to add to chamber music when needed. Mattheson (1722–5: 169) wrote disdainfully of every miniature 'Grand-Seigneur' and 'Dorff-Herrscher' who wanted to have his band of 'Kunst-Pfeiffer' kept at lackey's accommodation and pay, instead of professionally trained musicians.

In France, the distinction between bandsmen and chamber players was never sharp. Court players all had titles based on their membership in the bands of the royal *Écurie*, such as the *Douze Grands Hautbois*. With the exception of a few players, any chamber or orchestral playing they did came unofficially in addition to those duties. In 1688, a miniature opera-masquerade, *Le Mariage de la Grosse Cathos* by André Philidor, was actually built around an hautboy band, whose nine members provided all the instrumental music, and all appeared on 'stage'.[226]

2. Band music

Hautboy bands played marches, dance-suites, processions, funeral-music, calls and fanfares for the hunt, etc. Music of this kind was often played by heart and little of it found its way into court libraries.[227] What survives is therefore probably a fraction of what was played.

Hautboisten also played in church, sometimes replacing the cornett/sackbut ensembles that had previously been used to support choirs. Owens (1995: 354) reports that the Württemberg court *Hautboisten Bande* was regularly used for church music in the early eighteenth century. Four- and five-part bands were included in cantatas by Liebe (in Zschopau), Kegel (Gera), Schulze (Meissen), Zachow (Halle), and Boxberg (Görlitz).[228]

According to Fleming, the *Premier* player of each group was expected to be able to compose for all kinds of impromptu situations,[229] and much of the repertoire was probably written by such players.[230] The line between music for string bands and

---

[224] Owens (1995), 320.   [225] Hildebrand (1975), 55 and 33–5.
[226] Harris-Warrick and Marsh (1994).   [227] Hildebrand (1975), 53.
[228] Koch (1980), 56 ff.   [229] Fleming (1726), 181.
[230] Heinrich Simon was such a *Premier*; cf. Braun (1983), 151 ff.

wind bands was not strict, and *Hautboisten* were normally expected to be able to switch from one kind of instrument to the other. Many surviving multi-part suites now assumed to have been for strings were probably played by hautboy ensembles, separately or together with strings.[231]

In hautboy band music, the harpsichord was rarely if ever required. There were several reasons for this: the group had to be movable, there was a tradition of reed ensembles without continuo, and the harpsichord had a higher social status.[232] An ensemble that included hautboys with harpsichord was quite different: the tenor hautboy was normally absent,[233] and the parts were not doubled (as they usually were in pure hautboy ensembles).[234]

Over 500 pieces for hautboy band[235] are known to survive, about one-third of them written between 1670 and *c*.1710, and most of the rest between *c*.1710 and *c*.1740. Very few pieces appeared after the latter date. Composers include Fasch, Finger, Förster, Handel, Lully, Pierre Philidor, and Telemann. Among the more interesting pieces are

> Desmazures, *Pièces de simphonie à quatre parties* (1702)
> Erlebach, *Ouvertüre à 4* (1710)
> Fischer, *Tafelmusik* (1702) and *Musicalische Fürsten-Lust* (1706)
> Müller, *12 Sonates* ('Hautbois de concert' with hautboy band, *c*.1709)
> Paisible, 'The Queen's Farewell' (1695)
> Pez, *Pièces pour la Musique de Table*
> Prin, *Concert de Trompettes haubois et Viollons* (1724)
> Wieland, *Ouvertüre à 4* for '2 Houbous, 1 Lataille und 1 Basson' (*c*.1700)[236]

The Philidor Manuscript, mentioned in Ch. 1, §C, is one of the largest collections (as well as the earliest) of hautboy band music.

An important compilation of German hautboy band music is preserved at Herdringen.[237] It is in the form of six part-books in a leather folder stamped in gold with the initials 'G v L', and from this it is assumed that the collection originally belonged to Georg von Lillien, a Prussian general who died in 1726. There are fifty-two multi-movement pieces for two to three hautboys, one taille, and two bassoons. The instrumentation usually consists of six separate parts with an added trumpet in twelve pieces and two added trumpets in two others. The musical quality is

---

[231] For examples, cf. many of the pieces listed in Haynes (1992a), 374 under '09.1' to '09.3'.
[232] Hildebrand (1975), 46–7.
[233] The right hand of the harpsichord served the same function as the tenor hautboy in bridging the gap between bassoon and hautboys.
[234] A confirmation of this tradition is Philidor's *Mariage de la Grosse Cathos* (1688), which uses only bassoon continuo for the *récits*.
[235] That is, music probably intended for hautboys only, without other kinds of instruments.
[236] For exact sources and editions of these works, see Haynes (1992a).   [237] Herdringen, Fü 3741a.

consistently high. None of the pieces can be ascribed to specific composers, and many were evidently arrangements.[238]

3. *Hautboy players doubling on other instruments*

In the seventeenth and eighteenth centuries, a wind player was an hautboist who might by circumstance be led into a concentration on some other type of instrument. The modern idea of a musician who would limit himself to one instrument, and become a virtuoso on it, took hold at the Dresden court at about the beginning of the eighteenth century,[239] perhaps as a result of the numerous Italian musicians who worked there, and who tended to specialize.[240] But it remained unusual in Germany for some time. Some Stadtpfeifer did have 'Hauptinstrumente', however; in an active place like Leipzig, specialization became a necessity—Bach's hautboy players (who were Stadtpfeifer) must have been too busy to play other instruments very often.[241]

The life of a Stadtpfeifer is described in Wolfgang Caspar Printz's novel of 1690; he wrote that a Stadtpfeifer was expected to be a master of the trumpet, shawm, cornett, sackbut, and curtal, and to be proficient on the 'Hotboe' (probably the new hautboy) and string instruments.[242] Schering (1926: 100) observed that in pictures of musical performances of the period, wind instruments such as horns are sometimes shown hanging from the stands of string players. Hautboy players also doubled as organists.[243]

The chalumeaus in the Hamburg opera orchestra in 1732 were in the hands of an hautboy player and a bassoonist.[244] In Keiser's operas, flutes and hautboys never appear at the same time, and their entries are separated by passages with voice and strings to allow time for a switch. Arias that used more than two bassoons usually excluded hautboys, suggesting that the additional bassoons were played by the hautboy players.[245]

Bach also expected his woodwind players to play several instruments. In the final chorus of BWV 46, for instance, the two oboe da caccia players play *Flauto* (recorder).[246] In judging between two candidates for *Kunstgeiger* in 1748, Bach had them both play violin as well as hautboy.[247] In a testimonial for Carl Pfaffe (24 July 1745), Bach noted that he

---

[238] According to Moore (1981), 7, the combination of trumpet and hautboy suggests that the works were assembled after the Prussian 'reforms' by Friedrich Wilhelm I in 1713 (see Ch. 5, §D.6). On band repertoire, cf. also Altenburg (1979).

[239] Landmann (1989), 19–20 and (1993), 179. Based on archival evidence, Oleskiewicz (1998: 49) believes woodwind doubling 'completely disappeared sometime between 1717 and 1719'.   [240] Owens (1995), 21.

[241] There is evidence that hautboy players in bands in the early 18th c. could not necessarily switch to bassoon. Cf. Owens (1995), 47.   [242] Hildebrand (1978), 11.

[243] Braun (1983), 147.   [244] Lawson (1981), 318.   [245] McCredie (1964), 162, 185.

[246] Dahlqvist (1973), 61 and Prinz (1979), 168.   [247] *Bach-Dokumente* (1963), ii. 452.

auf jedem *Instrumente*, so von denen Stadtpfeifern pfleget gebrauchet zu werden, als *Violine, Hautbois, Flute Travers. Trompette, Waldhorn* und übrigen *BassInstrumenten*, sich mit Beyfall aller Anwesenden gantz wohl habe hören laßen . . .[248]

played quite well and to the satisfaction of everyone present on all the instruments that the Stadtpfeifer normally use, such as violin, hautboy, traverso, trumpet, horn, and the other bass instruments.

Colleagues of Bach's at Leipzig in 1750 remarked that the three 'haupt *Instrumenten*' of a Stadtpfeifer were (1) trumpet, (2) horn, and (3) *Hautbois*.[249] Terry wrote (1932: 10) that 'Johann Schneider, Bach's pupil, and organist of the Nikolaikirche, explicitly directed his horn and oboe players in certain movements of a wedding cantata of his composition to put down those instruments and take up their violins'.[250] As late as 1769, Bach's successor Doles examined two candidates for a vacant post as Stadtpfeifer. Among other things, they were asked to play the violone part of a concerted Chorale, a simple Chorale on four different trombones, a violin trio, a concerted Chorale on the Zugtrompete, and a horn, hautboy, or flute concerto.[251]

In 1755 Quantz wrote (p. 200) that the *Kunst-pfeifer*'s instruments were the violin, hautboy, trumpet, cornett, sackbut, horn, recorder, bassoon, 'deutsche Baßgeige',[252] cello, gamba, and many others. He commented that

Wegen der Menge so verschiedener Instrumente, welche man unter die Hände bekommt, auf jedem insbesondere ein Stümper bleibt.

Because of the great variety of instruments that come into one's hands, one remains a bungler on each one in particular.

One way players could avoid spreading themselves too thin was suggested by an audition for a Stadtpfeifer post in Dresden in 1766: the candidates had to demonstrate complete mastery of three main instruments and merely skill on the others.[253]

Gottlieb Görner of Leipzig was commissioned by the city of Zeitz to write an unusual piece especially to be used for Stadtpfeifer auditions; it is a concerto with separate movements for trumpet, trombone, cornett, horn, violin, and hautboy, presumably all to be played by the same candidate. Sebastian Bach was commissioned in the same year to write a similar piece 'auff alle Stadt-Pfeiffer *Instrumenta* gesetztes Kunst-Probe-Stück' (an audition piece set for all the instruments played by Stadtpfeifer).[254] It does not survive.

---

[248] Ibid. i. 147.   [249] Schering (1921), 44–5.
[250] This is from Schering (1926), 100, who further noted that the same kind of thing happened in the 'Großen Concert-Gesellschaft 1746–48'.   [251] Terry (1932), 18.
[252] 'Deutsche' here may refer to high pitch (see Haynes, 2000b).   [253] Techritz (1932), 20.
[254] *Bach-Dokumente* (1963), ii. 407.

There are many other recorded instances of doubling by hautboy players. Jacob Loeillet, Max Emanuel's highly paid hautboy soloist, apparently had a particular talent for playing on various instruments as well as singing and acting, to judge from a remarkable concert he performed before the Queen and King of France in 1727, in which he played bassoon, violin, traverso, recorder, voice-flute, and hautboy. He also hummed a bass while playing on two flutes, and simulated the effect of an entire choir.[255]

G. *Questions of Instrumentation*

1. *Generic instrumentation on treble lines: the 'symphonie' protocol*

Modern instrumentation is based on the assumption (enunciated by Berlioz) that an instrumental part should fit the nature of the instrument and thus be best served by that instrument. In the hautboy's time, musicians had a somewhat different attitude: the instrument was of secondary importance to the musical idea expressed, and if a given instrument could be made to perform it without sacrificing the piece's integrity, there was in principle no problem with adapting it.

The criteria for deciding whether a piece of music was 'originally' for hautboy are thus not as obvious as they might at first seem. To be included in my catalogue (1992), I required historical evidence that a piece might once have been played on the hautboy. I therefore included (1) pieces in which the title-page or parts indicated the use of hautboy, (2) music that was known to have been written for or played on the hautboy during the lifetime of the composer, and (3) pieces *en symphonie*. These criteria do not tell the whole story, however; it is likely that the real repertoire of the hautboy was much larger than that. Crossover instrumentation was common, and imaginative players would regularly have adapted music originally written for other instruments. This was a period when many players were composers, and musical notation was based on a different assumption of what it was meant to transmit: it was a shorthand 'cheat-sheet' for a general musical idea, not (as in music of the Romantic period) unequivocal instructions for performance. An eighteenth-century player would have had no second thoughts about altering details to suit his needs, and an enterprising hautboist would no doubt have taken music from wherever he could get it.

The term *symphonie* was purposely imprecise.[256] Bâton's *Suites* 'pour deux viéles, muzettes, flûtes traversieres, flûtes a bec, hautbois', and Chalais's *Sonates* 'pour

---

[255] Brenet (1900), 171.

[256] Cf. Diderot's definition of *symphonie* cited in Anthony (1973), 296: 'all instrumental music whether it be compositions designated for instruments, such as sonatas and concertos, or whether it be those works where the instruments are mixed with the voice as in our operas . . .'.

la flute, hautbois, et violon' were typical.[257] More nebulous instrumentations were also common: for 'Two trebles and Bass', or 'Pour toutes sortes d'instruments' (see Pl. 3.3). The instrumentation could be telescoped from as few as three players to a large orchestra, depending on factors like the occasion, the venue, and the available players. Even a violinist like Rebel went to some trouble in his *Recueil* of *c.*1695 to avoid specifying which *dessus* (treble instrument) was intended. Instrumental timbre and character, in other words, was not a specific concern of the composer, but was entrusted to the taste of the performers. This custom is well understood nowadays for the instrumentation of the continuo line; the *en symphonie* protocol, applied to the upper parts, is directly analogous.

This idea resembles the later concept of 'arranging' music for different instruments, although playing *en symphonie* was performed on the spot. 'Arranging' implies a corollary assumption that music is conceived for a specific instrument, and that assumption appears to have been less explicit in the hautboy's period. This is witnessed by the fact that a substantial portion of the hautboy's repertoire (more than 1,500 trios, countless solo sonatas and suites, and about 100 quartets) is written *en symphonie*. 'Arranging' also takes on importance in a context where each musician plays only one instrument, whereas in the Baroque period it was common for a musician to play several, and switch from one to the other, even in the same piece. Music *en symphonie* fell easily within the standard ranges of all the possible instruments (except, occasionally, the recorder), so it was a simple matter to switch.

There were other freedoms with instrumentation that seem surprising now. At the end of his collection of trios entitled *Sérénade ou concert* (1697), Montéclair wrote:

Le tout se peut joüer avec un Dessus & une Basse seulement, quand on ne pourra pas y joindre un Second Dessus, excepté le Sommeil.

If a second treble is unavailable, all this music can be played on only a treble and bass instrument, with the exception of the *Sommeil*.

In other words, not only could the instruments vary, but even one of the parts was optional. It is unclear whether Montéclair was describing here a practice that was general in playing 'trios'; if so, it would have had important consequences on their instrumentation.

The ambiguous nature of the *symphonie* protocol was also extended to a choice between solo instruments, as in Hotteterre le Romain's Opus 2, *Pieces pour la flute traversiere, et autres instruments, avec la basse-continue* (1708). Hotteterre wrote in the preface

---

[257] House (1991: 20) suggests that when pieces are advertised as for several different instruments, it is the first-named one for which the music is most suitable. That instrument is rarely the hautboy, and probably most often the flute.

Quoique ces Pieces soient composées pour la Flute Traversiere, elles pourront neanmoins convenir à tous les Instruments qui joüent le Dessus, tels que la Flute à bec, le Hautbois, le Violon, le Dessus de Viole &c. Quelques-unes pourront même se joüer sur le Clavecin . . .

Although these pieces are composed for the traverso, they may nevertheless work well on any kind of treble instrument, such as the recorder, the hautboy, the violin, the treble viol, etc. Some of them can even be played on the harpsichord . . .

The reverse instrumentation was offered by Gaspard Le Roux in his excellent *Pièces de clavessin* (1705), in which he provided a score under the harpsichord staves so they could be played on two treble instruments with bass, or even one treble instrument and obbligato harpsichord. Marais also extended his second and third books of *Pièces de viole* (1701, 1711) to other instruments:

Il est encore a propos d'avertir le public que la plupart des pièces qui composent ce troisième livre se peuvent jouer sur plusieurs instrumens comme l'orgue, le clavesin, le violon, le dessus de viole, le théorbe, la guitare, la flutte traversière, la flutte a bec et le hautbois: il ne s'agira que d'en sçavoir faire le choix pour chacun de ces instrumens.

It is also appropriate to inform the public that most of the pieces that comprise this third book can be played on various instruments, such as the organ, the harpsichord, the violin, the treble viol, the theorbo, the guitar, the traverso, the recorder, and the hautboy. In that case, it is important only to know which instrument to choose for a particular piece.

Solo concertos also used the *symphonie* protocol. While some published works were for specific instruments, many offered an array of possibilities for the solo part. All the surviving French concertos that mention hautboy as a possibility were also for other instruments. This meant that the solo part was not conceived in the first instance to exploit the special technical qualities of instruments; in fact, it was limited to the capacities of the most technically circumscribed (as for instance those that included the musette and vielle among the soloists).

More than two-thirds of the surviving *symphonie* pieces are French.[258] But generic instrumentation is also found in Italian, German, English, and Dutch music. Muffat mentioned Corelli's early concerti grossi, which could be played *a tre*, *a quattro*, or with a concertino and tutti orchestra.[259] The first surviving collections of *symphonie* trios came from England and Holland in the 1680s, and were compilations of older music, often airs from Lully's operas. The *symphonie* custom continued into the 1760s in Paris in 'orchestral' pieces by Blainville, Geminiani, Hasse, Carl Stamitz, etc.[260]

---

[258] 736 out of 1,093 trios and 79 out of 86 quartets are French.
[259] Cf. Harnoncourt (1988), 172 for an interesting discussion of this idea.
[260] Cf. Brenet (1900), 250–1.

In music that uses the *symphonie* principle, the operating criterion for whether it is hautboy music is whether it can 'work' on the hautboy—whether the hautboy is technically able to convey the piece's musical meaning without compromise. Some good *symphonie* pieces do not succeed on hautboy—Marais's solo viol music, the *Pièces de viole*, for instance (even though he says they can be played on hautboy), have a range that is too big (about four octaves), they frequently use chords, and they simply sound better on viol. Not all the pieces of Rebel's *Recueil* are playable on the hautboy either, although at least one (*La Vénus*) is more suited to hautboys than to other instruments. But in my experience, most pieces with generic instrumentation do indeed 'work' on the hautboy.

In this relatively early period, most of the hautboy's repertoire was generic.[261] It is therefore useful to consider which factors made a piece suitable to perform on the hautboy. As far as technique is concerned, they included breathing, choice of key, range, tessitura, and melodic motion. Many of these are discussed in detail in the next chapter (see §§C, H, F, and M).

On any wind instrument, the music must have allowed time for breathing. As discussed in Chapter 4, §H.2, music that worked best for hautboy tended to be in moderate flat keys. It rarely ascended higher than c_3 (in contrast to music for traverso, which was normally in sharp keys and used notes above c_3).[262] Violin parts usually included notes below the compass of both hautboy and traverso (c_1 and d_1, respectively), and often used double stops. Pieces that descended to c_1—and no lower—may have been conceived as hautboy music, since neither the standard traverso nor recorder of the period went that low, and the violin normally used a range from g_0 to at least e_3.[263] The presence of low $c\sharp_1$ was also significant, since it was difficult to produce on the hautboy. Many of these details could have been circumvented, however, by octave changes or the replacement of a few notes.

With so much of the hautboy's repertoire written or even primarily conceived for traverso or violin (both of which played better in sharper keys), hautboists probably considered the possibility of downward transposition of a step (see Ch. 4, §H.3).

To leave the instrumentation open seems to imply that the different characters of instruments were ignored or considered irrelevant. But that was not necessarily true. The same piece perceived through the different prisms of the flute, the violin, the harpsichord, or the hautboy was a piece with many potential facets, each with its particular colour and interest.

---

[261] There are, however, well over 2,000 parts that specifically require hautboy. Of the 7,748 surviving pieces written before 1760, 2,297 (30%) specify hautboy only. Of the 2,119 solo sonatas written in the same period, 454 (21%) specify hautboy only. Virtually every concerto, hautboy quartet, and obbligato with voice fall in this category, as well as many chamber works.

[262] In the late 18th c., the range went upward to f_3, of course. But even then, notes above d_3 seem to have been used for special effects and as markers of virtuosity, not as part of the normal usable range of the instrument.

[263] Cf. Fischer (1971), 64.

For the hautboy, the *symphonie* practice meant that the music it played in France was virtually never written exclusively for it, or specifically for its technique, which sometimes made it very demanding. It also meant that hautboy players, like other instrumentalists, could draw on a rich and abundant repertoire that included the best French composers of the day, like Marais (the trios, at least), Rebel, Couperin, and Lully, as well as many others.

2. The bassoon as continuo instrument for the hautboy

There is a traditional fraternity between the bassoon and the hautboy which is confirmed in countless pieces of music that combined the two instruments, as well as texts that associated them. The bassoon was often considered a 'bass hautboy'. Scarlatti called for a 'basso dell'oubuè' in bass clef (that is, probably a bassoon) in 1701 in *Il pastor di Corinto*. Brossard, under 'Basse de Hautbois', refers to 'Fagotto'.[264] Carlo Palanca's court title in 1719 was 'Suonatore di bassa d'Autbois'.[265] Mattheson wrote of 'der *stolze* Basson' (the proud bassoon) that it 'ist der *ordinaire Bass*, das *Fundament* oder *Accompagnement* der *Hautbois*' (is the normal bass and the continuo or accompaniment for the hautboy).[266] Jacob Denner's two bills for hautboy family choirs included the *Basson* with *Hautbois*. The notion of the bassoon as the 'true bass' of the hautboy continued into the nineteenth century.[267]

Certain bass instruments were naturally associated with certain trebles. In his Opus 37 (1732), which consists of five trios for a treble and bass instrument with continuo, plus a quintet, Boismortier indicated the standard associations at that time. On the title-page he suggested the trios could be played on violin with cello, traverso with gamba, or hautboy with bassoon (the final quintet was for everyone: traverso, violin, hautboy, bassoon, with gamba and harpsichord as Bass). Many pieces for hautboy specifically called for bassoon on the bass line. Sometimes the bass line, like the treble lines, is marked 'Hautbois', as if the bassoon was considered the bass member of the Hautbois family.[268]

But the connection was not automatic. Discussing music at the Württemberg court, Owens (1995: 395) points out that

In neither the compositions of Schwartzkopff, or Pez does the appearance of a bassoon (always doubling the harpsichord part) necessarily relate to the use of oboes ... Schwartzkopff does not utilize the Lullian double-reed trio combination, preferring to accompany solo passages for a pair of oboes with a harpsichord, rather than a bassoon.

[264] Eppelsheim (1961), Anhang 20.
[265] Bernardini (1985a), 3, 12. Palanca and a colleague were called 'oboè basso' in 1725.
[266] Mattheson (1713), 269. Mattheson was quoted by Majer (1732: 34), Walther (1732: 79), and Eisel (1738: 100).
[267] Cf. Béthizey (1754), 305; Burney (1771a), 70; Laborde (1780), 323 (quoted in Ch. 1, §B.1); Halfpenny (1957b), 36 quoting from the *Complete instructions for the bassoon* (Preston and London, *c*.1785); and John Marsh, *c*.1806, transcribed in Cudworth (1965), 65.   [268] Eppelsheim (1961), 112.

Brandt (1968: 65) argued that the assumption that the bassoon automatically played Bach's bass lines when the hautboys played, and at no other time, is not supported by historical evidence. There are a number of instances in Bach's music with hautboy where no bassoon is present, and vice versa. But the examples he gives indicate that the bassoon and hautboy played in different parts of the same piece, suggesting that only one player (who could play either) was available for the two instruments. This was the normal situation at Weimar, and it is likely that Gleditsch, Bach's hautboy soloist at Leipzig, could and did occasionally play the bassoon for Bach. Thus necessity often forced Bach to choose between the two instruments. That does not mean (as Brandt suggests) that in ideal circumstances Bach would not frequently have used both instruments together.

H. The Shawm after 1670

With the development of the new hautboy, the shawm's identity began to fragment. Because of its pitch, the old-style shawm continued to be used by municipal musicians like *Türmer*, or tower musicians, in combination with other traditional instruments at A+1 (called in the eighteenth century *Cornetton* or *Chorton*) like the brass and cornetts.[269] It also produced a 'hellen Laut'[270] (a sharp tone) that was effective in certain musical situations, such as parades, funeral processions, and military ceremonies.

But by the 1680s in Germany[271] (and perhaps considerably earlier in certain other places), a new and distinct model also came into use, slenderer, and smaller in bore and tone-holes. It evidently came in two sizes, treble and tenor, and was pitched at A−1 for the two-fingered note (thus about a major third lower than the older-model shawm). This instrument has been called the 'deutsche Schalmey' since Anthony Baines first drew attention to it in 1954 and defined its characteristics.[272] In a recent article,[273] I proposed calling it the 'Schalmey', following Talbot, who gave the most complete contemporary description of the instrument.

The Baroque Schalmey was clearly no longer the same instrument as the Renaissance shawm; it had a narrower bore, smaller tone-holes, and a lower pitch. But it retained some of the shawm's physical features, which thereby distinguished it from the hautboy:

- it was sometimes (although not always) still played with a pirouette;
- the treble member was without a key (like Praetorius's *Schallmey*);

---

[269] There are records (Hildebrand 1975: 58–9) of Stadtpfeifer playing shawm as late as 1709 (although it is unclear what kind of shawm was meant). Eisel declared the shawm obsolete in 1738 (see Thompson 1999: 49).
[270] Zedler (1741), 1844.   [271] Hieronimus Kynseker, who made a Schalmey, worked from 1662 to 1686.
[272] Baines (1954), 747 and (1957), 285.   [273] Haynes (2000).

- both sizes had a fontanelle;
- the bell was long, flared widely, and was without an internal lip;
- there were usually three resonance-holes on the bell;
- all fingerholes were single.

The bores of Schalmeys are also relatively slender, as shown in fig. 10 of Bouterse (1999), and the minimum bores are extremely small (4.0 to 4.6 mm)[274] compared with those of most Baroque hautboys (average 5.95).[275]

Some of Haka's Schalmeys show turning on the upper joint similar to the hautboy of the same period. Considering that Haka and other makers of Schalmeys are also survived by hautboys, this is not surprising. The two instruments shared other attributes, like the softer sound and lower pitch.

Talbot's fingerings for the Schalmey were similar to the ones he gave for the Waits, although the chart for the Waits only went up to b2, whereas the Schalmey had two octaves. Talbot did not offer chromatic notes in the Schalmey's scale except for B and B♭.

The playing technique and basic reed design of the Schalmey are so similar to that of the hautboy that the same players (who were usually comfortable on many kinds of instruments) could have played both, and probably did.

Baines suggested that the Baroque Schalmey was 'a German attempt at a quick answer to the new French oboe'.[276] But it is clear that the two instruments were not in competition in Germany; they were working in complement to fill different musical needs. The Germans had after all enthusiastically adopted French instruments and players, and at least one German maker made both Schalmeys and French hautboys.[277]

The Schalmey was evidently played into the second decade of the eighteenth century. To judge from the terminology in Serauky, the Schalmey was used in Halle until at least 1711 to accompany 'Psalmen und geistlichen Lieder' in the Schloß-Kirche and the Dom.[278]

With due allowance for variations in details, the similarities between surviving Schalmeys and the instruments represented in several Gobelins tapestries is striking.[279] It is likely these instruments were first developed in France, where the models shown in the Gobelins 'L'Air' (Pls. 1.5–7, 1.10, 1.13) already show evolutions like twin tone-holes and mouldings at the finial and baluster.

Given the evidence (which, it must be said, is meagre at the moment) it is not possible to distinguish the Schalmey from the hautboys being used in France in the early 1660s. The Schalmey could thus represent a survival of the protomorphic hautboy discussed in Chapter 1, §A.

---

[274] Bouterse (1999), 77.   [275] See App. 2.   [276] Baines (1957), 285.
[277] L. Walch.   [278] Serauky (1939), 389, 427.   [279] See Ch. 1, §A.3.

4

Playing the Hautboy

> The hautboy . . . , in my opinion, can suffer mediocrity the least of all the wind
> instruments . . .[1]

In a period when players often moved from instrument to instrument, techniques
were freely borrowed, and in a sense, individual instruments did not have their own
separate techniques. How the hautboy was played can often best be seen by looking
at how other instrumentalists and singers performed. It was the hautboy player
Galliard who commented on Tosi's *Opinioni de' cantori antichi e moderni* (which he
published in an English translation in 1742):

> The studious will find that our Author's remarks will be of advantage not only to vocal per-
> formers but likewise to the instrumental, where taste and manner are required; and show
> that a little less *fiddling* with the voice and a little more *singing* with the instrument would
> be of great service to both.

Any good instrumentalist of the time was a composer as well as a player, and a composer playing his own music looks beyond the details of the particular instrument
he plays to focus on the presentation of the music itself.

In matters of technique, however, each individual instrument has its own story.
An example is ornamentation: the concept of a trill must surely have been the same
regardless of the instrument a player had at hand. And yet, the same effect was produced in many different ways, depending on the kind of instrument; breathing and
tonguing, for instance, would not have concerned a harpsichordist or violinist. This
chapter deals with the particular means the hautboy used to realize general musical
conceptions, like trills. Section G.4 discusses trill fingerings for oboe, for instance,
including 'false trills'. But it does not discuss whether to begin with the upper
appoggiatura, because that is a matter that would have concerned players of any
kind of instrument.[2]

Most of the written information on playing the hautboy appeared just after the
period studied here, from about 1770. Most of it dealt with matters that had probably changed little since earlier times, so when earlier sources are not forthcoming,

---

[1] Vanderhagen (*c*.1790), 3: 'à mon avis [le hautbois] est de tous les instruments à vent . . . celui qui souffre le
moins la médiocrité'.

[2] A good survey of the general literature on Baroque ornamentation is Fuller (1989), 124–46.

or when a concept that can probably be applied retroactively is well expressed, I have cited later documents. But a warning is in order here: the hautboy after 1770 was a different instrument,[3] and the music it played had changed as well. Later information should always be considered in that light.

One of the limitations of historical source material about playing is its personal nature. Nobody felt the need to make sweeping reports about how things were generally done. The same is true today: playing instructions and reed books do not generalize on what everyone does; they express individual opinions about what is right to do. Writers in the past were also describing personal approaches, not (as it is so easy to assume) generalizations about how their contemporaries did things.

A. Training, Tutors, and Methods

Until the time of the French Revolution, teaching and learning music was usually based on the traditional relationships of father to son or master to apprentice.[4] In the French musical dynasties at court, musicians could get their training from various family members and, on the job, from colleagues. At courts like Turin, the celebrated players like Alessandro Besozzi or his assistants may have helped out the young beginners playing in the royal *Scuderia*. In Germany, the Stadtpfeifer used an apprenticeship system like a craft guild. Hautboy players were sometimes instructed by a Capellmeister; Schwartzkopff helped train young hautboists at Stuttgart in 1706.[5]

Public institutions devoted to the professional training of musicians were rare until the nineteenth century. There were a few; the conservatory/orphanages in Venice and Naples employed hautboy teachers. By the eighteenth century these institutions were accepting children of foreign nobility as students, and it may have been partly due to conservatories that Italian musicians became so dominant in Europe in that century.[6] More general musical training was sometimes available from schools attached to churches. Christian Barth, who became a well-known hautboy virtuoso in the late eighteenth century, was educated at the Thomaskirche at Leipzig and had been a pupil there of Sebastian Bach. An *Hautboistenschule* was founded at Potsdam in 1724 for the instruction of military players. It probably helped raise the standard of playing in the military.

With the new form of music education at the beginning of the nineteenth century, the objective of most instrumental instruction books changed. As they came

---

[3] Cf. the introduction to Ch. 7.
[4] For an interesting discussion of this subject, see Harnoncourt (1988), 24.
[5] Owens (1995), 71, 140, 143.   [6] Arnold (1980), 19.

to be used as teaching aids, they grew more substantial and were organized in an order of progressive difficulty. They thus became 'methods' that methodically and systematically developed technique, and were used for training professional musicians ('tutors' had been aimed at amateurs). The two methods of Garnier and Vogt, intended for use at the Paris Conservatoire (founded in 1795) are examples of this new approach. The tutors of the seventeenth and eighteenth centuries were something quite different; they often included a section of 'tunes', but they were all of the same general difficulty (even the 'traits' of Freillon-Poncein and Hotteterre were non-progressive).

A recent study of early recordings (Philip 1992) indicates the limitations of documentary evidence in understanding how music was played in the past. Comparing what was written about how to play in the early twentieth century with actual recorded performances shows that writings give a very different, as well as incomplete, idea of how musicians actually played: 'Musicians do not necessarily do what they say, or follow the advice of teachers or contemporary writers . . . in many cases it would be impossible to deduce everyday features of performance without the recordings.'[7] If the instruction books of the early twentieth century can be shown to differ significantly from the way people played then, the same is probably true of the Baroque period. Thus, no matter how detailed they may be, historical documents remain limited in the amount they can express about how music was really performed.

In any case, books would not have been an appropriate medium for the instruction of professional players, since their training was often so specialized and time-consuming that, although they were extremely literate musically, their general education was sometimes neglected. Many fine musicians knew no more of reading and writing than how to sign their names.[8] La Barre, conscious of his limitations in writing his famous *Mémoire sur les musettes et hautbois*,[9] excused himself to the Grand Écuyer with the apology

Je n'ay peu faire mieux; ce n'est point mon metier d'ecrire; je joue de la flute a votre tres humble service.	I was not able to do better, since writing is not my field; I am a player of the flute at your most humble service.

Tutors were less common for the hautboy than for recorder and traverso, instruments that were more accessible to the amateur. The hautboy was not an amateur's kind of instrument: it could not be played casually or occasionally, it was not easy to begin, and it involved a troublesome reed.

---

[7] Philip (1992), 2.   [8] See Benoit (1971a), 80, 'Un homme sans "culture"'.
[9] Partially quoted in Ch. 1, §A.1.

Being aimed at dilettantes, tutors varied in quality and completeness. The information on hautboy technique they offered was often rudimentary and general. Some of the early tutors were far from providing sufficient information to learn to play the instrument, and they insisted 'with emphasis on banal commonplaces';[10] in other words, they overstated the obvious while leaving many things unsaid that would have been useful (certainly to us today).

From the end of the seventeenth century, the instructions changed very little. The fact that the contents of *The Compleat Tutor to the Hautboy* (c.1715, itself possibly a copy of a lost tutor published in 1699) were repeated in seven other works appearing as late as c.1775[11] attests not to the static nature of hautboy technique (from other evidence, we know this was not the case), but rather to the superficial character of the books.

As Page points out (1988: 366), although the texts of English hautboy tutors changed little for more than fifty years, the musical content from book to book was quite different, and the instructions may have been a kind of 'publishers' convention, serving to introduce, if not merely to sell, the music that followed'.

Since information that was imparted orally in lessons never got recorded, the tutors, despite their shortcomings, are worth combing for hints and for information implied by reading between the lines. The substantive material found in tutors is treated in this chapter.

Not counting derivative works, there are eleven surviving self-help instruction books from the period 1688 to 1752 that include information on hautboy playing:[12]

Before 1700

> 1688. Bismantova
> 1695. Banister [ascr.]. W21
> 1699. Anon. *Second Book of Theatre Music*. W30

1700–1730

> 1700. Freillon-Poncein. W35
> 1707. Hotteterre. W42. Eng. trans. Anon. c.1729 as *The Rudiments or Principles of the German Flute* (omits hautboy chapter)
> c.1715. Anon. *The Compleat Tutor to the Hautboy*. W46
> 1719. Hotteterre. W52.
> 1722. [? Thomas Brown]. *The Compleat Musick-Master*. W56

---

[10] Bernardini, letter to Edward Tarr, 8 Jan. 1987.
[11] W126. 'W' numbers refer to the numbering used in Warner (1967).
[12] Surveys of woodwind tutors can be found in Warner (1964) and (1967). Additional information is offered by Vinquist (1974) (on recorder tutors) and Dijkstra [1996] (on traverso tutors).

1730–1760

1732. 2nd edn. 1741. Majer. W65
1738. [Johann Philipp Eisel]. W71
1752. Quantz (in French and German versions). W85[13]

The fundamental change in instrument design from long- to short-bore scaling that probably occurred about 1715, along with changes in pitch, no doubt affected technique, but the lack of tutors that discuss hautboy playing in this period makes it difficult to discern this process in any detail.

B. *Holding the Instrument and Body Carriage*

1. *Stance*

The first thing to consider is how the hautboy was held, and how players held themselves. Freillon-Poncein wrote in 1700 (7–8):

. . . que ce soit sans faire aucunes grimaces ny agitations d'aucune partie du corps. Je dis cela, parce que souvent sans y songer l'on tombe dans certaines habitudes & contortions, qu'il est presque impossible de reformer, ce qui paroîtroit tres-desagreable aux personnes devant qui l'on joüeroit.

[Play] without any unnecessary grimaces or movements of any part of the body. I say this because often without realizing it one adopts certain habits and contortions which are almost impossible to get rid of and are most disagreeable to one's audience.[14]

Hotteterre le Romain's advice on traverso playing was probably applicable to hautboy as well: 'If you play standing, stand firm, with ye left foot a little advanc'd, and rest the weight of your Body on the right leg, and all without any constraint.'[15] On the recorder, he said (1707: 34)

Il ne faut point lever les Coudes; mais les laisser tomber negligemment proche du Corps.

Do not raise your elbows, but let them fall loosely near your body.

---

[13] Five copies of W46 (sometimes with minor alterations) were also published in this period:

1730. [Peter Prelleur]. 'Instructions upon the Hautboy' in *The Modern Musick-Master*. W61
*c.*1745. Anon. *Instructions for the Hautboy*. W74
*c.*1746. Anon. *The Compleat Tutor for the Hautboy*. W77
1754. John Sadler. *The Muses Delight*. W88
*c.*1758. Anon. *The Compleat Tutor for the Hautboy*. W92

Minguet y Yrol's *Reglas, y advertencias generales* (W87) also contains a fingering chart for hautboy. It was dated 1754 until recently, but Joseba Endika Berrocal Cebrian (Universidad de Zaragoza) shows in a forthcoming article that the material on hautboy was not included until the second edition of 1774 (pers. comm.).

[14] Trans. Deakin.   [15] Hotteterre (*c.*1729), 2.

Quantz wrote about the hautboy and bassoon (1752: VI, suppl. §6):

Pour ce qui regarde la maniére de tenir ces deux instrumens, il faut avoir soin de tenir le corps dans une attitude convenable & naturelle. Les bras doivent être éloignés du corps & un peu étendus par devant, afin de n'être pas obligés de baisser la tête, ce qui serreroit le gosier, & empêcheroit de prendre haleine.

As far as holding these two instruments, take care to hold the body comfortably and naturally. Your arms should be held away from the body and extended forward a little, so that you do not have to lower your head, which closes the throat and hinders free breathing.

Vanderhagen (*c*.1790: 3):

ne point avancer la tête ni sur tout la baisser, par ce que cela empêche de respirer librement, il faut tenir la tête et le corps droit, sur tout sans affectation les deux bras écartés du corps a une distance raisonnable . . .

do not move the head forward, and especially do not lower it, since this hinders free breathing. Head and body must be held straight and without affectation; the two arms a reasonable distance from the body . . .

Garnier (1802: 9)

Il n'est point d'instrument qui dans l'execution détourne moins les parties du corps de leur position naturelle; aussi la meilleure attitude qu'on exige alors, est celle qui dénote extérieurement la liberté et l'aisance de tous les organes du joueur de Haut-bois. Son corps est droit; ses coudes doivent avec grace et souplesse s'éloigner un peu du corps . . .

There is no instrument that, in performance, contorts the parts of the body less from their natural positions. The ideal posture is thus one that demonstrates outwardly the freedom and ease of all the organs of the player of the hautboy. His body is straight, elbows held with grace and suppleness slightly away from the body . . .

2. Angle at which the hautboy was held

The hautboy was normally held fairly high. Hotteterre (1707: 44) suggested that

On doit tenir le Haut-Bois, à peu près comme la Flute à Bec, avec cette difference, qu'il doit être une fois plus élevé: par consequent on tiendra la tête droite, & on portera les Mains hautes . . .[16]

You should hold the hautboy more or less like the recorder, but with the difference that it should be held even higher. This will make your head level, and you will place your hands high . . .

If the hautboy was not held high enough, a player could drop it when he played the 'all open' high c3 (see below, §G.6). For this note, the fingers could not be used to hold the instrument; it was balanced only on the thumbs.[17]

---

[16] This passage is repeated in Diderot (1751) and Laborde (1780), 265.

[17] Although two charts, Bismantova and Hotteterre, indicated the use of *Stützfinger* (i.e. closing RH holes as a means of supporting the instrument) on the open c3.

Pl. 4.1. C. H. J. Fehling, detail of the orchestra, left, from 'Elevation du grand théatre roial, pris de face'. Shows the Dresden opera house 'am Zwinger' during a performance of Lotti's *Teofane* in 1719. Dresden: Kupferstich-Kabinett, C 6695 in Ca 200 I

Quantz (VI, suppl. §6) was concerned with the effect of the angle on sound:

Dans un Orchestre le Hautbois doit tenir son instrument aussi elevé qu'il lui est possible; en le fourrant sous le pupitre, les tons perdent de leur force.

In an orchestra, the hautboy player should hold his instrument up as much as he can. If he sticks it below the stand, the notes lose their force.

Quantz played hautboy at Dresden. Plate 4.1 shows an hautboist in the Dresden Hofcapelle (Richter?) performing Lotti's *Teofane* in 1719; he is clearly holding his instrument above his stand.

Garnier (1802: 9) specified that

Le Haut-bois doit être tenu de manière que sa direction fasse, avec la ligne perpendiculaire du corps, un angle d'à peu près quarante cinq degrés . . .

The hautboy should be held at an angle of about 45° from the perpendicular line of the body.

The fact that thumbrests are never found on original instruments also suggests they were normally held fairly high; holding the instrument between 45° and 90° to the vertical makes a thumbrest redundant. There are a number of pictures that show the angle of the hautboy relative to the body (see Pls. 1.15 and 4.2 and the hautboy players engraved by Van Florÿ on the keys of Richters hautboys, *c.*1700–50).[18]

[18] In Adkins (1990), 76, 81, 83–5.

PL. 4.2. C. H. J. Fehling, detail from a drawing of the Saxon *Hofjägercorps* performing on a float during festivities for the Kurprinz's marriage, 23 September 1719. Dresden: Kupferstich-Kabinett, C 6719 in Ca 200 I

3. Did players stand or sit?

Standing was evidently more common than sitting. In illustrations from the years 1672 to 1770, standing players outnumber sitting three to one (42:14), and among those sitting, many are playing in larger groups such as orchestras.[19] If the pictures are to be believed, it was also possible to play the hautboy reclining, marching, dancing, and riding a horse.[20]

4. Right or left hand below

Grassineau (1740: 103) wrote: 'This instrument [the Hautboy] is thus held; place the left hand uppermost next your mouth, and the right hand below; and the contrary with left handed people . . .'.[21] Since most people are right-handed, and the lower hand had more to do than the upper one, it was natural that the right hand was usually placed below. But left-handed players would have appreciated the option of switching positions offered by the duplicate Small-key.

Recorders and hautboys were played by the same musicians, so information on recorder hand position probably has direct relevance to the hautboy as well. Seventeenth-century iconography shows that recorder hand position was not yet standardized. Of fifty-two known Dutch examples, twenty-nine (only slightly

---

[19] Even more are shown playing alone in gardens.
[20] Adkins (1990), 83 sees two players on Florÿ's engraved keys sitting with crossed knees.
[21] Repeated in Coetlogon (1745), ii. 534.

more than half) have the right hand below, and one painting shows both.[22] Some recorders show signs of having been played 'left-handed'. Edgar Hunt points out that the twinned sixth holes on some Bressan recorders in the Grosvenor Museum in Chester are slanted and tuned for a left hand in lower position, and the thumb-holes are worn from use by a right hand. Dale Higbee also noticed that a Bressan voice flute has a thumb-hole that is placed off-centre apparently for a left-handed player.[23]

Speer (1697: 241) instructed the bassoonist to play with the right hand below, but acknowledged the possibility of the right hand above. At least one surviving haut-boy, the Gottlosbauer (Nuremberg MIR 376), has twinned holes at both 3 and 4 angled so that they must be played left hand below.

But from the earliest hautboy tutor (Bismantova 1688), written instructions on playing the hautboy consistently assigned the right hand to the lower position.[24] In his recorder method of *c.*1685, Loulié also assumed that the right hand was lowest. Hotteterre (1707: 4) called the method of playing the traverso with left hand below a 'mauvaise habitude' ('bad habit'). Freillon-Poncein (1700: 7) said the recorder was held like the hautboy, with the right hand below the left. Hotteterre (1707: 44) wrote of holding the hautboy

on les posera dans l'ordre que j'ay expliqué, parlant de la Flute à Bec, c'est à dire la Main droite en bas, la Main gauche en haut, &c.[25]	[The hands] are placed as I explained for the recorder, that is, the right hand below and the left above, etc.

When the duplicate Small-key was absent, one had no choice but to put the right hand below. In Chapter 2, §B.1 we observed that two-keyed hautboys (that is, instruments with a single Small-key for the right hand only) were made in all periods, but after 1730, they became a majority, suggesting that by that time (if not before) the usual position was right hand below.

Hotteterre (1707: 35) wrote further on hand position on the recorder:

On doit, autant qu'on le peut tenir les Doigts droits; principalement ceux de la Main d'en bas . . .	hold your fingers straight, as much as possible, especially those of the lower hand . . .
Il ne faut pas boucher les trous avec l'extremité des Doigts, mais il les faut avancer sur la Flute, ensorte que le bout du Doigt passe le trou environ de trois ou quatre lignes.	Do not stop the holes with the tips of your fingers, but place them further onto the recorder, so that the end of the finger extends about seven to nine millimetres beyond the hole.[26]

---

[22] Ruth van Baak Griffioen in Legêne (1995), 118. [23] Hunt (1984), 121; Higbee (1985), 143.
[24] Banister (1695), iii; Anon. (1699): next-to-last p.; Freillon-Poncein (1700), 7; Anon. (*c.*1715); Prelleur (1730), 1; Eisel (1738), 98; Diderot (1751–72), s.v. 'Hautbois', 70. [25] Diderot repeated this.
[26] A *ligne* was 1/12 of a *pouce* and = 2.25 mm.

Pl. 4.3. Hotteterre (1707), facing p. 34: hand-position for recorder

Pl. 4.4. Antoine Watteau (probably 1713–14), arms and hands of an hautboy player (Feuille d'études). Red chalk on ivory paper, 18.2 × 23.7 cm. London: British Library (1891-7-13-13)

I include here the illustration of recorder hand position from Hotteterre, and for comparison, the drawing by Watteau of an hautboy player's hands (Pls. 4.3 and 4.4).

C. *Breathing*

As David Ledet writes, respiration and support 'are the very foundations of oboe playing'.[27] Yet nowhere in the seventeenth- and eighteenth-century literature is there a detailed or systematic discussion of them. This section surveys the miscellaneous material on the subject that has survived.

1. The technique of breathing

a. Posture   As noted above, both Quantz and Vanderhagen wrote that lowering the head would impede free breathing. Ledet writes (1981: 7): 'Lowering the head can

---

[27] Ledet (1981), 3. Ledet gives a useful survey of breathing on the key-system oboe in the chapter 'Respiration' (pp. 3–19).

lead to bringing the shoulders forward, which tends to constrict the upper chest and cuts down the total potential capacity of the lungs by an amazingly high percentage.'

b. Exhaling   As Stössel wrote (1737: 171), '*Hautbois . . . erfordert aber viel Wind*' (but the hautboy requires much wind). Hautboy players rarely used all the air in their lungs because, although the instrument would not sound without '*viel Wind*', very little of it could actually pass through the small aperture in the reed. Denton points out 'the peculiar nature of the oboist's breathing': at the end of a phrase a player must expel stale air before he can inhale the needed fresh air.[28] As Brod explained (1825: 28),

De cet air comprimé dans la poitrine, une très petite partie est employée à passer dans l'anche, l'autre qui est bientôt altérée, nous devient à charge et nous fatigue; il est donc indispensable de l'aspirer et de renouveler . . .	Of this air, restrained in the chest, only a small proportion passes through the reed. The rest, which is quickly changed, becomes a burden and tires us. For this reason, it is imperative to exhale it and renew the supply . . .

Breathing on the hautboy thus involves two separate and opposite actions: exhaling as well as inhaling. 'It is vital to use every opportunity to get rid of the accumulation of carbon dioxide in your lungs, to renew the supply of oxygen in the body, and to relieve the pressure on the muscles while playing.'[29] No sources from the seventeenth and eighteenth centuries mention the obvious technique to answer this problem, namely, breathing only out or only in at alternate breathing places (but then, no source that dealt specifically with hautboy technique was ever very detailed). This technique is regularly used by modern players of the hautboy, so it may have been common then too.

c. Places to breathe   In his *Suittes* for treble instrument and bass published in 1717/18, Pierre Philidor used a comma-like sign, ')', that looks like a modern breath-mark.[30] The sign is found in several movements, including the 'Sicilienne' of the Quatrième Suitte and the 'Rigaudon en Rondeau' and 'Gigue' of the Neufième Suitte. Some four years later, Couperin (with whom Philidor played in the royal *Chambre*) explained his use of the same sign as an indication of a small silence at the end of a phrase.[31] It works well in this sense for Philidor, and if breath is also taken, is very effective dramatically. The sign appears to be concerned with expression, however, rather than simply gaining air. The Sicilienne is marked 'tres lentement' and some measures contain two of these marks.[32]

---

[28] Denton (1977), 50.   [29] Rothwell (1953), 7.

[30] Philidor's *Suittes* are exceptional in this period for the quantity of information on performance techniques they include (cf. below, §K.3).   [31] Preface to the *Troisième Livre de Pièces* (1722).

[32] A similar mark at the end of the 'Prelude' of Montéclair's second *Concert* for two treble instruments without bass is probably a mordent (as used by Hotteterre). Breath-marks (a lower-case 'h' for *haleine* or breath) are used in the *Petits airs, Brunettes, Menuets, &c.* (pieces by Blavet), published in the 1740s. Blavet's Opus 2 sonatas also have breath-marks.

An interesting general rule about taking breath in singing is mentioned by
Brossard in the 'Imprimeur au Lecteur' (*IVe livre d'airs*, 1696):

On peut prendre son haleine . . . quand la fin d'un mot se trouve sous une note pointée . . .[33]	One can take a breath . . . when the end of a word is located under a dotted note . . .

Ranum (1995: 219) suggests that 'A dot after a note was understood to be the equivalent of a punctuation mark and therefore to indicate not only the end of a word
group but also an emergency breathing place for singer or instrumentalist.'

Two points from Quantz's Chapter VII on the subject of breathing are of special
interest. In §3 he explains that, since the quickest notes of the same value in a piece
should be played a little unequally, breath should be taken between a long and a
short note rather than after a short note. §5 describes breathing on tied-over notes,
a case similar to Brossard's dotted notes.

d. Endurance   Endurance is connected to breathing. If a player has few chances to
breathe, he tires quickly, especially in longer movements. Telemann wrote in the
introduction to the *Kleine Cammer-Music* (1716), a collection particularly written
for the hautboy:[34] 'I have kept the *Arien* [movements] short, partly to spare the
strength of the player, and partly not to tire the ear of the listener.'[35] Being himself
an active hautboy player at the time he published this remark, he was no doubt
aware of the problem of endurance.[36]

Denton (1977: 114) observes that when Bach gave hautboys independent passages, he purposely allowed places for breathing. Movements in which hautboys are
doubled by violins or play parts similar to them have few rests, but independent
hautboy passages are made up of shorter passages with space between them. Denton
cites BWV 97/1 as an example.

2. Overblowing the octave

Sources from 1688 to 1792 speak of the need to blow harder and/or pinch the reed
to produce notes that overblow at the octave (that is, the notes from d2 upward).[37]
Bismantova (1688; cf. Pl. 3.1) wrote

Quando poi habbi intonato bene il primo C deve seguitare ascendendo, col crescere ogni volta più il Fiato, e ad ogni voce, che farrà più ascendendo, deve crescere sempre il Fiato; nel descendere poi, che si farà, deve anco calar il Fiato ogni voce che si farà . . .	After the first C is well placed, proceed upwards, increasing the air each time, and at every note, and as you ascend, continue to blow harder; and when you descend, diminish the air gradually at each note . . .

---

[33] Cited in Ranum (1995), 253 n. 40.   [34] See Hobohm (1975) and Haynes (1986a), 31–5.
[35] The introduction is quoted more completely, and in German, in §M.1 below.
[36] Cf. Telemann (1740), 357 and Ch. 5, §D.14.   [37] Cf. Wragg (1792), 5–6.

The last page of Anon. (1699) contains the remark:

Observe where you [see] this mark [n] over the heads of the Notes in the Scale which begins at *D-la-sol-re* and so on all ye notes in alt [= d2 to c3] [you] must Press the reed almost close between your lips and blow stronger than you did before and ye higher [you] goe still continue blowing somewhat Stronger.[38]

Roger North (*c.*1710–28: 230): 'If the lipps doe but constrain the plates a litle, and at the same time the breath is urged with more force into the pipe, . . . the Hautboys sounds an octave to whatever the tone of the pipe was before, . . . and withall the voice is also made more soft and sweet . . .'.[39]

With the lack of an octave key, the hautboy required a subtle and constantly changing combination of embouchure and breath support. Switching from the middle notes to the high notes was one of the arts of playing the instrument, distinguishing it from the recorder with its octave-hole. It is likely that many practice routines, especially for beginners, featured register changes (cf. also below, §G.6).

D. *Embouchure*

It is axiomatic in modern woodwind playing that instruments play in tune without embouchure corrections, and it is a criterion for judging their quality that they do so. By contrast, early woodwinds required a very flexible embouchure to achieve good intonation. The movements a traverso player had to make to correct intonation were easier to see, but similar adjustments, though less obvious, occurred on the hautboy by means of embouchure changes. Among these corrections were the notes produced by the two cross-fingerings on each hand (b♭1 fingered 1 3, and f1 fingered 123 4 6): both were too high if not lipped down. Hole 5 governed the pitch of both f1 and f♯1, and as these two notes were too close together using the fingerings given in most fingering charts[40] (even for the tuning models of the time), the f♯ was usually low and needed favouring.[41]

The 'rationalized' oboe that was developed in the first part of the nineteenth century[42] had as one its main goals the elimination of tuning corrections like this, and with them, the flexibility of embouchure they required. It is almost as if the new key-system oboe was designed around the premiss that embouchure should be

---

[38] Repeated in Anon. (*c.*1715), 5 and paraphrased in Prelleur (1730), 4 and Anon. (1758), 4. Passages to the same effect are found in Talbot (*c.*1692), 28, Banister (1695), p. iii, Freillon-Poncein (1700), 7, and Hotteterre (1707), 45. [39] He refers to the overblowing as 'the use of pinching, which gaines an octave'.
[40] 123 4 6 for f1 and 123 4 7 for f♯1.
[41] This is the note that usually causes traverso players to 'do the woodpecker', i.e. make sudden adjustments that involve moving the head. [42] Cf. Vény, quoted in the Introduction.

immovable. A fixed embouchure naturally discouraged the dynamic 'shaping' of individual notes, and the complex small-scale phrasing that had been part of the earlier hautboy technique (cf. §I.2 below on figural dynamics).

Freillon-Poncein and Hotteterre both discussed the question of how far to insert the reed between the lips: Freillon-Poncein wrote (1700: 7):

. . . prendre la moitié de la canne dont l'anche est faite avec les deux levres, & la tenir dans le milieu avec force . . .

. . . take half the cane of which the reed is made between the two lips, holding it firmly in the middle . . .

Hotteterre (1707: 44):

Il faut placer l'Anche entre les Levres, justement au milieu; on ne l'enfoncera dans la Bouche que de l'épaisseur de deux ou trois lignes, ensorte qu'il y ait environ l'épaisseur d'une ligne & demie de distance, depuis les Levres jusqu'à la ligature de l'Anche . . . [43]

As for the embouchure, the reed should be placed between the lips at precisely the middle; it enters the mouth only about 4–7 mm,[44] so that the distance from the lips to the thread is about 3–4 mm . . .

Quantz wrote (1752: VI, suppl. §4):

Mais quoiqu'on ait bien observé tout cela, les lévres & la façon de mettre l'anche entr'elles, sont encore toujours de plus grande importance. Il ne faut mordre les lévres ni trop ni trop peu; au premier cas, le ton en devient obscur, & au second il est trop bruyant & n'a aucune douceur.

But even if all these conditions have been met, the lips, and the manner of placing the reed between them, are of even greater importance. You should not take too much or too little lip between the teeth. In the first case, the tone is too dark; in the second it is too bright and without sweetness.

With the lighter reed that is necessary to play cross-fingerings, and generally less pressure, an hautboy embouchure required less muscle power than the key-system oboe. Since it could be formed more easily, the hautboy embouchure could be set and released frequently, so that players must have given the impression of being under less strain. This may be why so many early depictions of embouchures show relatively little tension. Plates 1.3, 1.21, 1.22, 2.20, and 4.5–7 give an impression of eighteenth-century embouchures that, while recognizable, would be characterized as very relaxed.

Credibility in art works is always a question, especially on a subject like embouchure. The particular tension in the body caused by blowing the hautboy, and the embouchure itself, are difficult to capture, not generally understood by non-players, and a particular challenge to artistic technique. Among the more

---

[43] Hotteterre's comments were copied by Diderot (1751: 70) and paraphrased by Laborde (1780: 266).

[44] The ligne = 2.25 mm (see above).

PL. 4.5. Anonymous, 1720?, playing hautboist. Oil.
Collection of Willi Burger, Zürich

PL. 4.6. Benoît le Coffre, 1709 or 1711,
detail from *Maskerade* (ceiling painting).
Copenhagen: Frederiksberg Castle, Rosen.
With permission of the Royal Army Academy,
Denmark

PL. 4.7. Peter Prelleur (1731), frontispiece to
Instructions upon the Hautboy

PL. 4.8. Antonio Baldi or Bartolommeo de Grado,
welcoming party at the dock with musicians serenading
Carlo Borbone during his triumphal entry into Naples, 10
May 1734. US-NYp, Spencer Collection (Ital. 1735)

PL. 4.9. Anonymous (late 17th-century Dutch ?), carving of a double-reed quartet on the bell of an hautboy. About 5 cm high. London: Victoria & Albert Museum

PL. 4.10. Anonymous, 10 June 1709, *Militär-musiker aus dem Grosser Aufzug zum Fuss-Turnier*. Dresden: Staatliche Kunstsammlungen (Sax. Top. Ca 195, Bl.7)

PL. 4.11. William Hogarth [?], *The Laughing Audience*. Collection Henk de Wit

PL. 4.12. Antoine Watteau, *c.*1714, head of hautboist, in *Huit études de têtes* (red, black, and white chalk; 26.7 × 39.7 cm). Paris: Louvre, Cabinet des Dessins

plausible attempts, there are also a number that show some physical effort (see Pls. 4.8–11). The most convincing representation of embouchure I have seen is by Watteau (1714, Pl. 4.12).

E. *The Sound of the Hautboy*

1. Tone

Tone quality cannot be adequately described on paper, but the hautboy's tone was sometimes compared to the voice and other instruments. Tosi's opinion (quoted in Ch. 1, §A.1) that a singer with poor diction was like an hautboy was not shared by everyone; James Ralph, writing in 1731 of plays in London, complained of 'that new method of filling the vacancies betwixt the acts with the choicest opera-songs improved by the additional excellencies of a hoarse hautboy, or a screaming flute, which by the strength of imagination, we are to believe S[enesi]no or C[u]z[zo]ni'.[45] 'Hoarse' may be an exaggeration, but it does convey an impression of the hautboy's tone quality, and reminds us of Parke's equally disparaging characterization of the tone of Vincent and Simpson as resembling a post-horn. In modern terms (and with a more positive outlook), this tone might be described as 'dark', 'hollow', or 'woody'.

The closest literal recording of historical hautboy tone may be preserved on some early organs. Burney, an organist, writing of the Martinikerk organ in Groningen (1773: ii. 283), claimed that 'The *vox humana* is very sweet, but resembles a fine hautbois or clarinet, more than a human voice . . .'. This organ still exists. Dom Bedos (1766: i. 57) also thought the resemblance to an organ stop worth noting:

Le *Hautbois* est un Jeu d'Anche, qu'on fait en étain & conique . . . Il a une harmonie gracieuse & imite assez bien le vrai Hautbois.[46]

The *Hautbois* is a conical reed stop made of tin . . . It has a graceful sound and is not unlike a real hautboy.

But Roger North (c.1710–28: 231–2) was not convinced that organ stops were literal imitations of other instruments:

In Organs . . . the operators have contrivances to imitate Cornetts and Trumpetts, as also the Voice Humaine; for which reason certein tubes are contrived and added [to the reeds] to caracterise the sound . . . but this, as the rest of that kind, [imitating] hautboy, violin, &c, seldome answers expectation.

---

[45] Ralph (A. Primcock), *The Taste of the Town* (London, 1731), 41, quoted in Lasocki (1983), 475.
[46] On p. 52, Bedos wrote 'Il en est deux autres [Jeux d'Anche] plus nouveaux qui font le *Hautbois* & la *Musette*'.

More might be learned about original hautboy tone by a systematic study of *Hautbois* and *vox humana* stops on surviving early organs.

2. *Volume*

This section considers the general strength of the hautboy's sound. For a discussion of expressive dynamics, see §I.2.a.

a. Compared with other instruments   In his article on the hautboy, Grassineau wrote in 1740 that 'its tone is louder than that of the Violin'. In orchestras, where violins and hautboys frequently played the same line, it was normal to have more than one violin for each hautboy, in ratios that ranged from 2:1 to as much as 11:1.

There is information on the instrumentation of twenty-six orchestras (or the same orchestra at different times) in the period 1700–30, and thirty-nine orchestras from the period 1730–60.[47] While there are some questions about this data (were all Capelle members playing all the time, for instance, and when did woodwind players switch to strings, or hautboy players to flutes, and what was the blend of tone qualities considered ideal?), the quantity of information and its general consistency offer a general impression of how the violin and hautboy compared in volume.

Before 1730 French and German orchestras tended to use fewer violins per hautboy (three or fewer, i.e. a band with two hautboys would usually have five to six violins); Italian and English orchestras used many more (five to eleven violins per single hautboy), and the Vienna Capelle usually used four. This could mean that the sound of the hautboy was more appreciated in France and Germany in this period; it could also mean that hautboists in Italy and England played louder.

Between 1730 and 1760 French orchestras, like those in Italy, were using about five violins per hautboy. German orchestras (Leipzig, Dresden, Braunschweig, Berlin, Gotha, Breslau, Zerbst, Schwerin, Rudolstadt) were still generally using three to four (except for Mannheim, where in the 1750s there were only two hautboys for twenty violins). London orchestras were usually at three to one, and the Vienna Capelle at four or five to one. In 1752 in Berlin Quantz was recommending two hautboys to eight or ten violins, and four for twelve violins.[48]

This was the situation in orchestras. In chamber music, the two instruments must have been considered approximately equal; trios for a single violin with hautboy and bass were not uncommon.[49] As Brady delightfully described a trio between woodwind and string,

---

[47] Sources I have consulted are Arnold (1966), 9; *Bach-Dokumente* (1963), i. 6; Becker (1961), 1804; Benoit (1971b), 377–80, *Diane et Endimion*; Dean (1959), 103–4; Helm (1960), 94; Lasocki (1983), 420; Marpurg (1754; cited in Donington (1963), 521 ff.); McCredie (1964), 303, 304; Mennicke (1906), 270, 272–7; Nickel (1971), 245–6; Pierre (1975), 77; Sachs (1908), 66–7; Schnoebelen (1969), 45, 46; Selfridge-Field (1987), 124; Selfridge-Field and Zaslaw (1980), 690.   [48] Quantz (1752), XVII, i §16.

[49] There are 157 known, written before 1760 (cf. Haynes 1992a).

Hark, each tree its silence breaks,
The box and fir to talk begin . . .[50]

Quantz implied that the hautboy sounded softer than the violin, cello, and bassoon, but louder than the traverso:

Contre un Violon [le joueur de la Violette] peut jouer presque dans la même force; contre un Violoncello ou un Basson également fort; contre un Hautbois un peu plus foiblement, le ton en étant plus mince que celui de la Violette; mais contre une Flute il faut qu'il joue très foiblement, surtout si elle joue dans des tons bas.[51]

Against a violin, [the violist] can play almost as strongly, against a cello or bassoon with equal strength, against an hautboy a little softer (since its tone is thin compared with that of the viola); but against a flute, he should play very softly, especially if it plays in the low register.

Elsewhere in his book, Quantz (VI, suppl. §6) implied that the hautboy's sound was not very loud (see quotation in §B.2 above).

Much of the hautboy's most important repertoire combined it with a single voice or other instrument, suggesting an approximate parity of volume.[52] There were a number of trios for traverso, hautboy, and continuo written before 1760.[53] Bonanni wrote in 1722:

Molto grato all'udito, e più strepitoso del Flauto è il suono dell'Oboè, istromento di moderna invenzione . . .[54]

Very pleasant to the ear is the sound of the hautboy, an instrument of modern invention that is stronger than the flute.

Bonanni probably meant the recorder. Banister also compared the two instruments in 1695 (ii), 'With a good Reed it [the hautboy] goes as easie and as soft as the *Flute*'.[55] He added that the hautboy was 'Majestical and Stately, and not much Inferiour to the Trumpet'. The hautboy's range of volume was evidently considered equivalent to these instruments, at least in a small chamber context.

In the case of the voice, Denton (1977: 55) noticed that in Bach's solo hautboy arias, it is rare to find dynamic markings in the hautboy part at the beginning, and 'most often the first dynamic indication in the oboe part is a piano at the point at which the voice enters'. The *piano* must have been more than a kind of habitual signal to the player that the voice was beginning, as this would have been obvious to

---

[50] Nicholas Brady, 'Hail, bright Cecilia' (set by Purcell in 1692; the 'box' in that case referring to the recorder and the 'fir' being the violin). [51] Quantz (1752), XVII, iii §14.

[52] Mrs Papendiek related the amazement of Fischer after a performance with Madame Mara (who could sing up to e3), 'Fischer in the greatest excitement said "her voice was louder than my oboe I heard it"' (Broughton 1887: 224).

[53] Forty-five survive. Zelenka paired a 'Flauta traversa sola' with an hautboy 'col sordino', however (Horn 1987: 200). [54] 2nd edn. (Rome, 1776), 81.

[55] There are forty-one surviving trios with recorder.

any musician (the vocal entrance normally followed the first exposition of the aria's subject, with its cadence). Since he rarely if ever wrote the obvious, Bach was evidently concerned that the hautboy might overshadow the singer (and/or his text), and he took the trouble in these cases to remind the hautboy player to temper his volume when the singer began. Denton (1977: 78) also noted that in obbligatos for two hautboys, Bach's parts 'are marked piano when accompanying the voice and forte when playing alone'. Bach's hautboists, we must conclude, were not shy and retiring players.

b. Muting Several hautboy pieces call for mutes (see App. 5). The earliest was composed in 1692, the latest in the second half of the eighteenth century. Most of the known examples, interestingly, were composed specifically for Hamburg or Dresden.[56]

Muting was accomplished in a variety of ways. The aria in the *Lukaspassion* formerly attributed to Bach called for an hautboy band 'mit Papier gedämpft' (muted with paper). Quantz (who had been an hautboist in Dresden) reported what appears to have been his own discovery (XVII, ii §29):

Les joueurs d'instrument à vent, sont mieux, de mettre un morceau d'éponge humectée dans l'ouverture de leurs instrumens, que de se servir de papier ou d'autres chose [*sic*], pour rendre leurs instrumens sourds.	When wind players wish to mute their instruments, they would do better to insert a piece of dampened sponge, rather than paper or other materials, into the opening of their instruments.

Fischer (*c*.1780: 7) suggested that 'To soften the Sound of the Hoboy, put some Cotton or Wool up the Bell of your Hoboy but be careful not to put it up higher than the Air holes for if you do it looses its effect: this Invention was made known in England by the famous Player, G. C. Fischer.'[57] Like Quantz, Fischer had also played at Dresden.

The use of mutes on wind instruments, including the trumpet, was often (though not exclusively) associated with death and mourning. Many of the pieces listed in Appendix 5 express sorrow, or are connected with death or ghosts. Fleming (1726: 376) described the burial of an officer, during which *Regimentshautboisten*

vor der Leiche gehen die Hautboisten mit gedämpften Hautbois und blasen ein Sterbelied.	marched in front of the casket, the hautboists playing a dirge with muted hautboys.

---

[56] An example from Rome involves Handel, who had recently arrived there from Hamburg.

[57] Repeated in Fischer (*c*.1790), 7 and (with slightly different wording) Fischer (*c*.1800), 1, as well as Holyoke (*c*.1800), 3 and Whitely (1816), 10. Fischer arrived in England in 1768. Wooden and leather mutes apparently date from the late 18th or early 19th cc.

Regimental *Hautboisten* in Austria played a funeral piece (a 'Sterb-Lied') with mutes in 1749.[58]

Fischer spoke of the use of cotton or wool simply as a way 'to soften the Sound of the Hoboy', a technical effect rather than an expressive device. Muting was often effective when playing with traverso, as well as in slow movements of sonatas and concertos. Mutes altered the tone, making it more diffuse, and more like that of an hautbois d'amour.

Page (1993) suggests that choice of tonality could also create an effect similar to muting. The aria 'O Golgotha!' from Keiser's *Passion nach dem Evangelisten Markus* was in F minor; the number of cross-fingerings in this key would have produced a somber sound like the effect of a mute.

c. The relation of forte *to* piano

Scarcely a work of [Baroque music] is altered in its essence whether played loudly or softly. In many cases, the dynamics can simply be reversed, playing *forte* passages *piano* and *piano* passages *forte*. If they are played well and interestingly, either approach makes sense. In other words, dynamics were not composed.[59]

Few players or pedagogues cared to commit exhaustive instructions on dynamics to paper; such details were the business of performers to decide, and to be over-specific would have seemed pedantic.[60] The musical examples in several tutors, especially the later ones,[61] contain some dynamic markings. But of the sources, only Quantz, in his encyclopedic zeal, went thoroughly into the subject (see below, §I.2.a).

Bach occasionally prescribed dynamics, the most interesting being for special effects, like the echo aria (BWV 213/5 for hautbois d'amour and BWV 248/39—the *Christmas Oratorio*—for 'Hautbois ordinaire'). The piece involved two singers, one (the echo) 'off-stage'; a single hautboy was expected to imitate this effect. The part was marked 'piano' and 'forte' (and occasionally 'pp'). It gives a good idea of the hautboy's possibilities for dynamic contrast.

Although Marshall (1985: 263) observed that Bach's dynamic markings appear to be 'skewed towards the soft end', he went on to show that *forte* was considered the normal and standard dynamic, so it did not need to be marked, while *piano* did. Walther (1732: 257), Bach's friend and kinsman, defined *forte* as

Starck, hefftig, jedoch auf eine natürliche Art, ohne die Stimme, oder das Instrument gar zu sehr zu zwingen.	Strong, intense, but in a natural manner, without forcing the voice or instrument too much.

---

[58] Page (1993). The two 'Queen's Farewells' by Paisible and Tollett in *The Sprightly Companion* were probably played with mutes. [59] Harnoncourt (1988), 47.

[60] Cf. Warner (1964), 117 and Boyden (1965), 484 ff.   [61] e.g. Wragg (1792).

and *piano* as

So viel als leise; das man nemlich die Stärcke der Stimme oder des Instruments dermassen lieblich machen, oder mindern soll, dass es wie ein Echo lasse.	In effect, soft; one should adjust or reduce the strength of the voice or instrument so that it may have the effect of an echo.[62]

If *piano* required 'adjustment', *forte* was evidently closer to the normal playing dynamic.[63] This seems to be demonstrated in Bach's hautboy obbligatos, where usually the first dynamic indication was not at the beginning (*forte* would have been understood), but at the vocal entrance, where (as noted above) a *piano* was often marked.[64] Denton suggests that 'for Bach, as for other Baroque composers, forte was the standard, piano or pianissimo the special effect'. If *forte* was generally regarded as normal, it was probably not thought of as particularly loud but merely comfortable and (unlike *piano*) produced without conscious effort.

F. Range

The hautboy's usual range throughout the eighteenth century was c_1 to d_3. The c_1 is documented from the 1660s, the d_3 from the 1680s. But exceptionally, the range was extended in both directions.

The development of an extended range seems not to have been a priority in most of the earliest solos written specifically for the hautboy. Telemann's *Kleine Cammer-Music* (1716) contains neither low c_1s nor high c_3s. The Dornel *Sonate*, written specifically 'pour un haubois' in 1723, rarely goes down to d_1, and there are only two c_3s (in the Gigue). Sammartini's Rochester collection regularly extends downward to use low c_1 (and also $c\#_1$ in V:3:49), but notes above $b\flat_2$ are rare; there are only five c_3s in the entire collection of six sonatas. Even in display movements, c_3 is virtually non-existent.

In terms of range, the Pez *Symphonia* mentioned in Chapter 3, §C.10 would be remarkable at its early date for including high d_3 as well as low c_1, and the two within a bar of each other in a fast movement.[65] But as noted there, the piece in this version was probably written for violin; the added alternate readings, which were probably adaptations for the hautboy, eliminate all the high d_3s and all but one of the c_3s in the second movement. The implication is that at the time, these notes were difficult to perform.

---

[62] Quoted and translated in Marshall (1985), 262.
[63] Marshall suggests this on p. 265.   [64] Denton (1977), 55.
[65] Cf. the Allegro, 39–40. This is the only place where the two notes appear, except at the end of the Gigue, where two other c_3s are probably the reason the bars in which they appear are given an alternate reading.

1. Highest notes

There was a c3 in a part that was probably for hautboy in Lully's 'Heureux qui peut plaire' from *Cadmus* (LWV 49/14), performed in 1673. Bismantova in 1688 gave a fingering for d3 (Pl. 3.1). Collections for instruments *en symphonie* frequently included the odd d3, even as early as Konink's Trios of 1690.

It appears that hautboys in England did not go beyond c3 until after the turn of the century. English seventeenth-century sources did not mention d3, giving c1–c3; c♯3 and d3 were not included in the English fingering charts of La Riche (in Talbot *c*.1692–5), Banister (1695), or the *Second Book of Theatre Music* (Anon. 1699). Roger North commented on the notes above c3 in (*c*.1710–28: 230): 'It is possible that by like means stronger enforced, the sound of the pipe might be made to break into a fifth higher, but it is not easy to doe it, and it would not pass in the harmony identically, as the octave doth; therefore the performers, if at all, very rarely offer at it.' North is speaking here of c♯3 and d3, which are a fifth above f♯2 and g2 and use the same fingerings, except that the topmost hole is leaked to make them speak.[66] He seems to suggest they would be out of tune.

In German opera arias, Keiser in *Janus* (1699) only went to a2. *La forza della virtù* (1700) reached c3. But the usual range for solos was e1–b♭2. Steffani was generally conservative in his hautboy solo ranges, but at least twice used c1–d3. Graupner used e1–b♭2 in his operas of 1707–15.[67] Walther (1708: 48) gave the hautboy's range as c1–c3. In 1732 (p. 304), he gave the same range but added 'auch wol ins d[3] . . .' (also sometimes up to d3).

In 1701, Sauveur wrote (p. 135):

Nous avons reglé les termes & l'étenduë de la plûpart des Instrumens à vent, selon la pratique du Sieur Ripert, & du Sieur Jean Hautetaire le jeune,[68] qui sont des plus habiles Facteurs de Paris: Ces termes changent quelquefois selon la volonté de ceux qui en joüent.

For the majority of the wind instruments, we determined the extremes of range with the advice of Mr Ripert and Mr Jean Hotteterre the younger, who are among the best makers in Paris. The extremes sometimes vary, depending on the aptitude of different players.

Sauveur's *Planche III* gives a range for the *Dessus de Hautbois* of c1–d3.

A fingering for d3 was included in Freillon-Poncein (1700) and Hotteterre (1707). Hotteterre (1707: 45) implied that the hautboy occasionally played higher than d3:

---

[66] Using reeds based on Talbot's measurements on my original Naust, I have not had the problems of response or intonation on c♯3 and d3 that North describes. Reconstructions of protomorphic hautboys by Marc Écochard based on the Gobelins 'L'Air' also play d3 easily.   [67] McCredie (1964), 161–3, 158, 165.
[68] This was probably Jean (6), one of the best-known instrument makers of the family. Cf. Waterhouse (1993), 183.

Ex. 4.1. BWV 35/1: 108

Il faut remarquer que l'on ne monte guere plus haut que le *Ré* en haut.	It should be said that one rarely plays higher than d3.

Lemaître (1988–90–3) reports that hautboy parts at the Paris Opéra between 1687 and 1715 never exceed d3.

An e♭3 appears in the first movement of a concerto in E flat by Sammartini now at Dresden. This piece may have been brought back to Dresden from Italy by Richter in the late 1710s.[69] A concerto in C minor by Graun also has an e♭3, and one by Hasse for two hautboys, written before *c*.1740, has several e♭3s in the first hautboy part (first movement).[70] Dreyer's third solo sonata contains e3 as well as low c1. Fasch (who died in 1758) is survived by a concerto with an e3 (K.48/3).[71]

Bach's obbligato hautboy parts exploited the entire range, c1–d3, but he generally preferred d1–b♭2. More extreme notes were usually brief and, since they were the result of sequential patterns, probably unintentional. BWV 35/1: 108 shows that Bach was unwilling to go beyond d3 for hautboy (cf. Ex. 4.1).[72]

More than two-thirds of Bach's hautbois d'amour solos go no higher than fingered c3, and only a few use d3 in any quantity. In some cases (37/5, 133/1, 151/1, 154/7, 195/6), Bach provided alternate notes or omitted the instrument when it went out of the fingered range of c1–d3.[73] But he did occasionally call for notes above d3 on the hautbois d'amour, perhaps to compensate for the fact that the instrument sounded a minor third lower than the treble hautboy (its fingered d3 was thus only a sounding b3). There was a solo e♭3 in 55/1: 20 (premièred November 1726).[74] And the secular Cantata 201 included e3s and f3s, the only examples in non-unison or solo passages. Movement 1 had both notes (within a large orchestra)

---

[69] In the modern edition by Töttcher, the e♭3 is in a sequence d2–d3–e♭3, which sounds more convincing than the Dresden manuscript, which reads d2–c3–e♭3 (the fourth note is e♭2, not a♭2 as in the edition, and the next beat is f2–e♭2 with no g2).   [70] Darmstadt, MS score 222/4.

[71] Küntzel (1965), 49.

[72] The upper line is for hautboy, the lower line for violin. Denton (1977), 48, 111–12.   [73] Ibid. 143.

[74] There are a number of e3s in unison with other instruments in 17/1 (2nd Hautb.; Sept. 1726), 49/1 (Nov. 1726), 115/2 (Nov. 1724), and 145/3 (Apr. 1729). There are also f3s in unison with other instruments: 120/2 (before 1729), 195/3 (before 1730), and 244/36.

and movement 9 had an e3 in a solo aria, totally exposed and impossible to fake.[75] This piece was performed in 1729, possibly by Bach's Collegium Musicum in Leipzig for Michaelismesse.[76] An outside player could have performed this exceptional part, since it was not for the church; Böhm, for instance, is known to have made trips to Saxony, and may have been between jobs at the time (see Ch. 5, §D.15).

The Paris copy of Eisel (1738: 97, 99 pl.) has added pencil notations to the fingering chart that extend the range up to f3 (the printed chart ends at d3; see Pl. 2.17). The pencil additions cannot be dated.[77]

The period when higher notes began to be regularly requested coincides with the development of the new smaller-bore instruments, originating in Italy, which produced high notes more readily. The earliest known appearance of f3 is in the Bissoli sonata (written probably *c.*1750), which also contains several e3s (Bissoli holds a Type C hautboy in his portrait, Pl. 2.21). This trend continued, and by about 1770 both the higher range and smaller bore had become the norm.

2. *Lowest notes*

The protomorphic hautboys shown in the Gobelins 'L'Air' tapestry of 1664 had Great-keys; they thus presumably played down to c1. The first known fingering chart (Bismantova 1688) includes c1 (Pl. 3.1). And c1 already appeared in German hautboy solos in the 1690s.[78]

Freillon-Poncein noted in 1700 (p. 9) that 'On peut faire le si d'en bas sous la Clef toute bouchée' (The b0 can be played under the key, all closed). 'Toute bouchée' presumably included the two resonance holes on the bell, which can be closed with the knees if the player is sitting.

A number of b♭0s appear in the solo part of one of Fischer's hautboy concertos in F, written by *c.*1760.[79] This is a mystery, since b0 is the lowest note the bell will

---

[75] It could have been obtained with the fingering +2̶3̶ ⧧56 7 or 12̶3̶ 56 7.

[76] *Bach-Dokumente* (1963), iv. 1617.

[77] The fingerings (which are in a German hand) are:

d3 2̶3 8
e3 12 456 7
f3 12 56 7

[78] McCredie (1964), 164 suggested that Keiser did not write lower than d1 for hautboy, but Eumene's aria 'Das Schmertzenvolle Scheiden' in *Adonis* (Hamburg, 1697) goes down to c1, as does the second hautboy in Krieger's cantata *Träufelt, ihr Himmel* (1696). Bach may have avoided low c1 in all his 'Oboe' parts at Weimar (see Haynes 1995: 310). Questions of dating and instrumentation make it impossible to be sure of this, but if it is true, it is apparently coincidence; the c1/c♯1 was already available in the 1660s, since the Great-key was present on the protomorphic hautboys shown in the Gobelins 'L'Air' (1664).

[79] 'Concerto in F à oboe Solo', Regensburg (Fischer 7); manuscript dated *c.*1760. This concerto is not the same as either of the hautboy concertos in F at the British Library. The notes appear in the first movement, twice in bar 79; second movement, bars 20, 74, and 84; third movement, bar 163. Except for the last two, which are unison with the violins, these b♭0s appear in solo passages. My thanks to T. Herman Keahy for bringing these notes to my attention.

TABLE 4.1. *Analysis of tessitura in ten movements for solo hautbois d'amour in Bach's cantatas*

BWV	Number	Note
75/5	14.64	d2
210/8	14.9	d2
213/5	13.5	c♯2
8/2	14.9	d2
248v/5	13.8	c♯2
243/3	12.9	c2
92/8	15.4	d2
115/2	14.2	c♯2
69/5	15.82	e♭2
124/1	14.81	d

give with both holes closed: the only imaginable way this note could have been obtained was with an extension key. Extra keys of any kind were rare in this period, and such a key is otherwise unknown until after 1800. Fischer's hautboy shown in the portrait by Gainsborough (done at least a decade later in 1774–88) has no extra keys beyond the standard two.[80] It is also likely that if Fischer had had such a key, he would have written the concerto in B flat and featured the b♭$_0$ more prominently.

3. *Tessitura*

Tessitura is the average of the lengths of time each note in an instrument's range is used. Tessitura is important as a factor in endurance and the general tone character of a piece. Playing in the high register requires more physical effort, so if a piece tends to be high in tessitura, it will be noticeably more difficult to play. It will also sound thin and squeaky if not enough of the middle and low registers are used.

Tessitura can be quantitatively analysed, although it is a time-consuming process. It is done by assigning numbers to each note in an instrument's range, multiplying by the length of time each note is used, and averaging the result. Doing this to ten movements for solo hautbois d'amour in different settings from Bach's cantatas, I found the mean notes shown in Table 4.1. The average of the ten is

[80] This painting is reproduced in *MGG* iv. 270, *New Grove* vi. 610, and Joppig (1981), 121, among other places.

14.59, between c♯2 and d2.[81] By contrast, the tessitura of the hautboy quartet by Mozart is about five semitones (a major third) higher.[82]

G. Fingerings

The *primary scale* of a woodwind instrument is the one that uses its 'natural' fingerings (as opposed to cross-fingerings, half-holes, and keys). On the hautboy, that scale was D major, beginning on its six-fingered note, d1.[83] From the point of view of fingering combinations, D major was by far the simplest and easiest scale on the hautboy.

Because fingerings form the unconscious base of one's playing technique, it is natural that eighteenth-century players would have been reluctant to adopt new ones. And yet, as instruments changed, fingerings mutated with them, and a player who was in the flower of his career in the 1770s (cf. Pl. Int.1) would have been using some different fingerings on his classical instrument than the ones that worked on the old A2 he had started on as a student, back in the 1740s or 1750s.

There is a definite break in fingering usage between the charts ending with Eisel in 1738 and the late eighteenth-century sources starting with Fischer in *c*.1770. The break is not completely clean, but the trend can be seen in the following fingerings:

1. The use of 1 with d2 was standard on earlier charts (with the exception of Hotteterre, who used the traverso 23 456, and La Riche, who gave +); from Fischer *c*.1770 onwards, most charts omitted 1.[84]

2. The distinction between enharmonic pairs (in particular g♯2/a♭2) was common in the early charts and rare in later ones.

The most fundamental change was the introduction of long high-note fingerings from *c*.1770,[85] which will be discussed in §G.6 below.

Fingerings also changed, of course, when more keys began to be added. They were not a factor in the period under study, however, as beyond the Great- and

[81] The figures required counting over 8,000 individual notes.
[82] The quartet's movements are 19.82, 19.45, and 19.0; the total mean for the three movements is 19.32, or somewhat above f♯2.
[83] Halfpenny (1980), 581 suggested that the primary scale of the hautboy was C, the seven-hole scale. If this was true, the fourth note, f1, was produced with a cross-fingering. If instead D is considered the hautboy's primary scale, low c1/c♯1 would be downward extensions.
[84] See App. 6.
[85] See Haynes (1978), 80–1.

Small-keys, hardware was rarely used on hautboys until the end of the eighteenth century.[86]

1. *Collation of fingering charts*

There are eight surviving fingering charts (plus their various derivatives) that date from 1688 to *c*.1758.[87] Earlier charts were frequently copied well into the eighteenth century.[88] They are collated in Appendix 6.

La Riche provided Talbot with two separate charts for hautboy, one called 'Hautbois Treble Mr La Riche' (here L1) the other called 'Tablature of Hautbois from Mr Lariche' (here L2).[89] The two charts differ in some ways, providing confirmation of some unusual fingerings, and probably indicating that when several fingering options existed, they could not always be expressed in the 'black and white' form of charts.[90] There is reason to think the chart in the *Second Book of Theatre Music* (1699), which was the model for all English charts until *c*.1770, was also provided by La Riche, and in fact represents his most considered views.[91]

2. *The low $c\sharp1/d\flat$*

Low $c\sharp1/d\flat1$ was regularly requested in exposed situations in hautboy music (see App. 7). Since compositions were normally written with specific players in mind, we may therefore assume that some players were able to produce the note.[92] On the other hand, there are instances where composers appear to have purposely avoided $c\sharp1$,[93] suggesting that it was regarded as difficult.

---

[86] Cf. Haynes (1994a). Bizey is survived by two hautboys with 'octave keys', one dated 1749. The key on the dated instrument (formerly Piguet) is mounted in an integral block, and is therefore certainly original.

[87] The last original chart before *c*.1770 is Eisel in 1738 (Pl. 2.17). For a more detailed discussion of hautboy fingerings, see Haynes (1978), which is here updated by the addition of the Bismantova chart shown in Pl. 3.1, then undiscovered, and the re-dating of Minguet.

[88] The fingering chart in *The Second Book of Theatre Music*, Anon. (1699) was repeated in anonymous English tutors in *c*.1715 (W46), 1722 (W56), 1730 (W61), *c*.1745 (W74), *c*.1746 (W77), 1754 (W88), *c*.1758 (W92), 1767 (W113), and *c*.1775 (W126). Hotteterre's fingerings were copied literally by Diderot.

[89] One of the fingering charts appeared in *GSJ* 6 facing p. 48.

[90] La Riche L2 contains a number of what appear to be mistakes, and it may be that Talbot noticed this and asked for La Riche (L1) as a correction.

[91] In general, the fingerings coincide remarkably with La Riche L1 and La Riche L2; two of the fingerings, $e\flat1$ (which appears to be a mistake) and $b2$, are the same but differ from most other charts. The charts differ in some details, however: the *Second Book of Theatre Music* used the *Stützfinger* on the LH notes of the lower octave, and used a different $f\sharp1$. It also differs from La Riche (L1 and L2) on $d\sharp1$ and the use of 1 on $d2$ and $e\flat2$, but these fingerings are also inconsistent between the two charts identified as by La Riche, suggesting he was ambivalent about them.

[92] For an unexplained reason, Becker (1961: 1794) wrote that the $c\sharp1$ fell into disuse from about 1730; this was repeated in Bate and Halfpenny (1954), 146. Cf. App. 7, which gives several later examples of $c\sharp1$.

[93] Cf. Vivaldi RV 28: II, mentioned in Ch. 5, §D.12 and the Besozzi concerto in G discussed below.

There are many c♯1s in Bach's hautboy parts, dating from 1708 until after 1740.[94] About a third of them are important, independent notes undoubled by other parts.[95]

a. Ways to obtain c♯1   The c♯1 could be obtained in a number of different ways:

- by lipping upward from the fingering for c1;
- with an instrument tuned to play c♯1 rather than c1;
- by half-closing the Great-key;
- by turning the bell upside down; and
- by lipping down the fingering 123 456.

It was the lowest notes of the hautboy that were the most difficult to push up in pitch. An hautboy with a reasonably well-tuned c1 could scarcely have been made to play higher in order to obtain a c♯1. Lipping down for the c1, on the other hand, was a possibility if the fingering 123 456 8 was tuned closer to a c♯1 than a c1. Many original hautboys are tuned in this way, so that the fingering 123 456 8 sounds somewhat higher than c1. In fact, if the c1 was not tuned a little high by the size of the bell resonance holes, the stability of cross-fingerings like f1 and c3 was affected. As Francoeur wrote sometime before 1772 (13):

[94] They are:

BWV 6/2 b. 94 has a fingered c1–d♭1 combination. The part is for oboe da caccia or cello piccolo, but was evidently originally for oboe da caccia.
BWV 28/1 bb. 40–1
BWV 34/1 (p1740) b. 64
BWV 44/1 2nd hautboy
BWV 71/1 (1708), 1st hautboy
BWV 80/7, bb. 30, 67 for oboe da caccia
BWV 149/1 bb. 96–8
BWV 151/3 b. 34, for hautbois d'amour. Both written a♯o and a♮o.
BWV 170/1 for hautbois d'amour. Both written a♯o and a♮o.
BWV 198/1 b. 47 2nd hautbois d'amour.
BWV 232 Kyrie I b. 27 2nd hautbois d'amour.

Despite noting Bach's 'aversion' to writing c♯1 for hautboy, Terry (1932: 95) lists fifty-one times that he used it. Cf. also Denton (1977), 122 n. 112. Movements 11–17 in the second hautboy part of BWV 245 (the St John Passion) look like they should be on hautbois d'amour because they are low, in sharp keys, and have occasional low written c♯1s (in pieces nos. 14, 15, and 17). But according to the NBA score, no. 12b, b. 13:3 is a c♯1 in violin II and f♯1 in hautboy II; no. 15, b. 14:1 is ao in violin II and a1 in hautboy II; bb. 16–17:3 is c♯1–bo in violin II and c♯1–d1–e1 in hautboy II. This seems to indicate that the part was especially adjusted for playing on an hautboy rather than hautbois d'amour, but (curiously enough) the player of the second part (only) does use hautbois d'amour in pieces 23b, 23d, 23f, and 27b. This being so, c♯1 is avoided in 12b, b. 13:3 but used in the other places. 15, for instance, is clearly for hautboy, since the corrections of range could have been played on an hautbois d'amour, and yet it contains 3 low c♯1s. Low c♯1s appear in movements 1, 2, 3 etc. Only one original hautboy II part survives, apparently used in at least the last three performances.

[95] Denton suggests that, since Bach was apparently aware of the difficulty of producing c♯1 (in BWV 245/12b, b. 13:3 he seems to have made an effort to avoid it), the cases where it was used without being doubled are 'over-sights'. But the number of independent c♯1s makes this difficult to believe. Prinz (1979: 171) gives a detailed account of the use of fingered c♯1 in Bach's taille/oboe da caccia parts.

L'Ut marqué A. est toujours faux: c'est à
dire trop haut pour être considéré comme
naturel, et trop bas pour être dièze, même
en forçant.

The *C* at letter A. [c_1] is always out of
tune; it is too high to be considered a $C\natural$
and too low to be $C\sharp$, even when it is
lipped upward.

Francoeur then indicated that both notes could indeed be played when there was
time to adjust them with the embouchure. An hautboy tuned in this way thus
allowed for lipping (mostly downward, presumably) to produce both notes, c_1 and
$c\sharp_1$, using the same fingering.

There are also original hautboys[96] that give a true $c\sharp_1$ rather than c_1 with the
fingering 123 456 8 (like many traditional folk bagpipes, which are tuned to play a
leading-note rather than a major second below the six-fingered note).[97] The tuning of this note depends on the size of the bell resonance-holes. The problem with
this option is that the low c_1, which appears much more frequently than $c\sharp_1$, is
awkwardly high.

Other instruments with an analogous key, such as the Denner traverso (Nuremberg
MI 566), and original tenor recorders in general, give clearly tuned Cs, not $C\sharp$s.

The Besozzi concerto in G (probably written by 1757) included $c\sharp_1$s, but the two
surviving versions (at the British Library and at Regensburg) indicate that not all
players were comfortable with this note. In the Regensburg version there are fewer
$c\sharp_1$s; they appear in situations that allow enough time to find them;[98] other passages
that include $c\sharp_1$s in the London version are given alternates at Regensburg that
avoid them.[99] The piece was thus probably adapted for two different players, the
London version for a player and/or instrument capable of handling quick $c\sharp_1$s
(probably for Besozzi himself, and perhaps Fischer), the Regensburg version (? for
Palestrini)[100] avoiding the note except when there was time to find it. There are no
$c\natural_1$s in this particular piece, so it is possible it was played on an hautboy tuned
to $c\sharp_1$ = 123 456 8; the instrument used for the Regensburg version was evidently
not tuned this way.

There is also the less than satisfactory method of half closing the Great-key, suggested by Banister, La Riche (L2), and Freillon-Poncein. The optimism of these
sources was not shared by later authors, only one of whom gave a fingering for this
note. Busby (*c*.1783–6) under 'Hautboy' wrote that 'its scale contains all the semitones excepting the sharp of its lowest note'.

Turning the bell upside down and wedging the centre-joint tenon into it can produce a $c\sharp_1$ with the fingering 123 456 8. It works better on some instruments than
others. This arrangement effectively displaces the resonance-holes longitudinally,

---

[96] Like the beautiful Klenig hautboy in Vermillion, the Deper alto hautboy, and high-pitched hautboys by
Denner, Rouge, and Martin.   [97] Marc Écochard (pers. comm.).

[98] Last movement, bb. 299, 300, and 320.

[99] Bars 108 and 112. The second cadenza for the first movement also contains a $c\sharp_1$.   [100] Cf. Ch. 7, §A.1.

raising their position on the bore. The same effect can be achieved by opening up the resonance-holes. The limitations of turning the bell upside down are that c1 is gone and that it is unwise to play standing up, in case the bell drops off.

Another dubious way to obtain c#1 was to use the fingering 123 456 (normally d1) and lip it down. This option is not found in early hautboy charts, and is uncertain because the distance between d1 and c#1 is so large, producing an unacceptable compromise in tone quality. But in his English translation of *c*.1729, Hotteterre described it for the traverso (whose lowest fingered note is d1): 'I have not in the Scale shew'd C Sharp, the lowest Note of all, because this Semitone requires no particular placing of the fingers, different from D the first Note, but is play'd by Artifice, (Viz.) by turning the Flute inwards, Sufficiently to lower the Sound by half a Note.'[101] Although lipping down was not reliable, it is difficult to imagine how else fingered c#1 could have been obtained on the hautbois d'amour, since the instrument had no resonance-holes in the bell, and thus gave a very decisive fingered low c1. Bach asked for both fingered c1 and c#1 for hautbois d'amour in BWV 151/3.

There were other situations when both c#1 and c1 were needed in the same piece. Freillon-Poncein asked for both of them in the series of 'preludes' in his hautboy tutor. Bach wrote c1 and c#1 consecutively in the second hautboy part to BWV 245/15 and 16b bar 21:5–6. BWV 6/2 bar 94 for oboe da caccia had a fingered c1–d♭ combination. The trio to the Menuet of Haydn's Symphony 38 (*c*.1766–8), written for Vittorino Colombazzi, had a concertante hautboy playing both d♭1 and c1 in bars 13–14.

When c♮1 was frequently used, and there were no c#1s in a piece, the fingering 123 456 8 could have been tuned lower by stopping one of the two resonance-holes in the bell either with wax or a removable peg.

At least two original hautboys have bell pegs, or did until recently. An Anciuti I examined in 1971 had an ivory peg in one of its resonance-holes.[102] The 'contrabass hautboy' by Heise,[103] built probably in the early eighteenth century, has an added hole below hole 8 that produces B1 when open and B♭1 when closed with a peg.[104] It is possible that other hautboys originally had such pegs that still exist or have been lost because of their small size and obscure use. The advantage of wax over a peg was that it was commonly available and required no special tools or equipment. But it could not be applied or removed as quickly and cleanly as a peg.[105]

Stopping the bell resonance-holes caused problems on other notes. There was a complex relation between the resonance-holes and the response and intonation of

---

[101] Hotteterre (*c*.1729), 12.

[102] When I saw the instrument, it belonged to Mme de Chambure; it is now in the Musée du Conservatoire, and is probably number E.980.2.138, dated 1719. [103] Cf. Ch. 1, §B.1.

[104] Schmid (1994), 104.

[105] This kind of peg serves a different purpose than the ones on instruments with a pirouette, like the Schalmey, where it held the reed/pirouette inside the bell when the instrument was not played (cf. Schneider 1985).

the two Fs. The lower F was sharper and less stable with a blocked resonance-hole (it was actually best when the bell was completely removed), and the upper F was flat. Also, closing a resonance-hole compromised the response of the short c3 and the d3. The disadvantages of having both holes open were the lack of a true c1 (which was often needed) and a certain wildness in the notes around b2 and c3. Players may have closed one of the two resonance-holes as a compromise between these conflicting demands, depending on the piece. In that case, pegs may have been commonly used, as they allowed the player to switch quickly from closed to open.

3. The low f1 and f♯1

The collation in Appendix 6 shows that sources were divided about the fingering for f1. It was played with an added 7 in four charts (La Riche L1, La Riche L2, the *Second Book of Theatre Music*, and Eisel), and without 7 in the other four. Later charts also show both fingerings. Adding 7 to the low f1 was a complication to fingering technique, so it would probably not have been done unless necessary. Reeds that were narrow at the throat (for the sake of high-note response) required an added 7 that was not needed with wider reeds. Alternating the two fingerings (with 7 and without) could have been a handy way to distinguish important and unimportant f1s, as the sound was different (bright and dark respectively).

There were also two different schools of thought on f♯1: whether to half-close 4 or close it completely. Hotteterre distinguished the two fingerings as G♭ and F♯:

Le *Sol Bemol* en bas . . . se forme, en débouchant le cinquiéme trou tout à fait, & la moitié du quatriéme; en bouchant tous les autres trous excepté celuy de la grande Clef: il se tremble sur le troisieme trou. Le *Fa Diézis* . . . se fait quelquefois de même, & se tremble sur la moitié du quatriéme trou, mais on le fait plus ordinairement, comme sur la Flute Traversiere.[106]

The low g♭1 . . . is produced by unstopping the fifth hole entirely as well as half of the fourth, and closing all the other holes except that of the Great-key [= 123 ♯ 6]. The trill is on the third hole. The f♯1 . . . is sometimes played the same way, and is trilled on half the fourth hole. But normally it is done as on the traverso [= 123 4 7].

As late as *c.*1802, Garnier (16) gave the full 4 for f♯1 and half-4 for g♭1 and f♯2. Corrette called these two different fingerings the 'Italian' F♯ (fingered 123 56 or 123 ♯ in both octaves) and the 'French' F♯ (closing hole 4 completely).[107]

Many instruments were made without twin holes on 4 (see Ch. 2, §B.3.b), implying that closing all of hole 4 was common. Denner's instruments all have a single fourth hole. An advantage is that many flattements are made by partly closing hole

[106] Hotteterre (1707), 45.
[107] Only in the second version (1773) of Corrette *c.*1740. The 'Italian' F♯ can probably be connected with some of the Italian players active in Paris at that time, and to their Type D1 or Type D2 instruments.

4, and this is easier to do when it is single. English tutors do not even suggest the existence of twinned fourth holes[108] until 1792, when Wragg wrote (1792: 4) 'As many Oboes, particularly the Italian Sort,[109] are made with two Holes in the second joint also,[110] it will not be amiss to inform the Pupil, that I have regarded those as a single hole only, they not being used separately as the others are.' Wragg's fingering for f♯1 was 123 4 7.

Two charts (Bismantova and Hotteterre) gave 123 4 (the latter with added 7) for the upper f♯2 as well. The advantages of the fingering 123 4 7 for the upper register were that it was easy to use in passagework, was clearly distinct from g2, gave a sound similar to the surrounding notes, and was closer to the ideal tuning (see below, §L) than the other two possibilities, 123 56 and 123 4̸.

Since the note was low with this fingering, there would also have been a temptation to make hole 5 larger or to undercut it, which would have raised the pitch of f♮1. The hautboy shared with the traverso and bassoon the problem that the fingerings 123 4 6 and 123 4 7 (F and F♯, or B♭ and B♮) produced notes that sounded too close together. If the F♯ was high enough, the F was too high; if the F was low enough, the F♯ was too low. In an article in 1777 discussing Quantz's traversos, de Castillon made an interesting comment on this problem:

. . . les flûtes de M. Quantz diffèrent encore des autres par le tempérament. Ordinairement le *fa* des flûtes traversières est tant soit peu trop haut & le *fa* dièse est juste; dans les nôtres, au contraire, le *fa* est juste, & le *fa* dièse un peu trop bas. . . . Rarement, ou plutôt jamais, on ne compose une pièce en *fa* dièse, soit majeur, soit mineur; mais on en compose très-souvent en *fa*, majeur & mineur. Le *fa* dièse ne paroit donc guère comme fondamentale, & il vaut bien mieux l'altérer que le *fa* qui est la fondamentale d'un mode, non-seulement très-usité, mais encore un des plus beaux pour la flûte; d'ailleurs, on peut forcer le *fa* dièse par le moyen de l'embouchure, mais le *fa* devient d'abord faux.

. . . M. Quantz's traversos differ from all others in their tuning. Usually the F on the traverso is not flat enough and the F♯ is correct; in his, on the contrary, the F is true and the F♯ a little flat. . . . Rarely, if ever, is music written in the key of F♯, either major or minor, but very often in F major and minor. The F♯ appears but seldom as a tonic, and it is much better to have the F in tune, since it is the keynote of a tonality not only much used, but one of the most beautiful on the traverso. F♯, when it appears, could easily be tempered by the embouchure; but as it stands, F♮ remains a bad note.[111]

By 1772, Francoeur (p. 14) was probably reporting a general impression of musicians that f♯1 needed to be higher than was possible using the fingering 123 4 7.[112]

---

[108] Evans (1963), 92.   [109] Cf. Corrette's 'French' and 'Italian' F♯s, mentioned above.
[110] i.e. at hole 4.   [111] Translation from Halfpenny (1956), 65–6.
[112] Corrette (1773) gave 123 4 7, Vanderhagen (*c*.1790) gave 123 4.

Cette note est toujours trop basse lors même en forçant le vent, c'est pourquoy elle ne doit être faite qu'en passant.	This note is always too low, even when it is pinched.[113] For this reason, it should be used only as a passing note.

That perception, based on a general abandonment of the low thirds of meantone tuning, would eventually lead to an added key for f1 (thus allowing hole 5 to be opened more to raise the f♯1; cf. below, §L).

4. Fingerings for trills and mordents

Trill fingerings were given in Banister (1695), Freillon-Poncein (1700), Hotteterre (1707),[114] and Anon (*c*.1715). They are collated in Appendix 8.

As Halfpenny pointed out (1953: 54), trill (shake) fingerings are of interest not only for making trills:

In some keys the quick alternation of two neighbouring notes is either difficult or impossible if the orthodox tablature is followed, because their respective fingerings are awkward to combine smoothly . . . In reality the problem goes deeper than the mere performance of ornaments, for if two notes are difficult to shake the chances are that any quick passage through them will be equally difficult to play smoothly . . . In much the same way, of course, the modern 'shake' key is not put on an instrument merely for playing the now comparatively unimportant trill, but simplifies many a quick passage through the note it controls.

Francoeur (1772: 15) said that all the notes on the hautboy could be trilled from a whole note or semitone, but pointed out several difficult trills, including c1–c♯1 (which was not even included in charts), c♯2–d♯2 (because of the two keys), and f♯2–g♯2 (given as 123 4 7 in Freillon-Poncein and Hotteterre). In his Opus 8/VI:3, Sammartini implied that this trill (f♯2–g♯2) was unplayable by omitting it in a sequence of trills on d2, e2, f♯2, and g2. Hotteterre, writing of the nearly impossible trill on c3 on the traverso, suggested a practical solution to problem trills, commenting that 'we commonly soften this Note [that is, play a flattement] instead of shaking it [trilling it]'.[115]

Quantz noted that 'trills in thirds', using the third above the principle note rather than the adjacent second,

a été en usage autrefois, & il se trouve encore aujourd'hui des joueurs de Violon & de Hautbois Italiens qui s'en servent; mais il ne faut pas l'employer ni pour le chant ni pour les instrumens, (si ce n'est pour la Musette).[116]	were used in the past, and are still the mode nowadays among some Italian violinists and hautboy players, but they should not be used in either singing or on instruments (except, perhaps, on the musette).

[113] Lit. 'when the wind is forced'.

[114] Hotteterre (1707: 88) advised hautboy players to use the trills he gave for the traverso in his chs. 4 and 7, except for those on c2, c1, g♭1, f♯1 sometimes, g♭2, f♯2, g♯1, g♯2, a♭1, a♭2, c♯2, d♭2.

[115] Hotteterre (*c*.1729), 9.   [116] Quantz (1752), IX, §4.

a. False trills   In the days before keywork, trills were often played with special fingerings that produced larger intervals than were appropriate in the diatonic scale. Hotteterre wrote 'Some shake [on d♯3] with the 4th. and 6th. fingers at the same time, but 'tis not well articulated, because 'tis difficult for a Shake made by two fingers so distant from each other to be very distinct; I am therefore of opinion that one shou'd always borrow the Shake . . .'.[117] He explained that what he called 'borrowed' trills,[118] or (as we will call them here) *false trills*, were 'those Shakes that don't end on the same hole where you make the *Port de voix* [= the first appoggiatura]'. Loulié in *c*.1685 had used a similar definition:

Les tremblements sont défectueux ou irréguliers lorsque le son qui sert d'appui n'est pas conservé dans le tremblement.	Trills are defective or irregular when the note that serves as an appoggiatura is not retained in the trill.

In other words, false trill fingerings were different from the normal fingerings for the notes involved. As an example, Hotteterre described the trill e♭1–d1, which began with a normal E♭ fingering using the key, but was trilled not with the key but on hole 6, exactly like an e1–d1 trill. He went on to comment on the trill f♯1–e1:

The shake on *E la mi* Natural [e1], taken from F Sharp [f♯1], is of this kind, 'tis begun by opening the 5th. 6th. and 7th. holes, to make F Sharp [f♯1; = 123 4], which serves it as a sigh, or Port de voix [appoggiatura], and 'tis ended by stopping the 5th. & shaking on the 4th. which removes the Superior Tone further off [that is, makes the upper note higher], and shews the Cadence [trill] more, instead of shaking on ye 5th. which wou'd not be sufficient.[119]

The reason for using false trills was (as Hotteterre explained) greater clarity. The fingerings in the trill charts often produced intervals larger than those that corresponded to the diatonic scale (as they would have sounded on a keyboard instrument). Apart from the sound that resulted, the fingerings involved the use of only one finger, which made them more effective than trills involving several fingers.[120] As Halfpenny commented (1949a: 361):

Many of the shakes in [*The Sprightly Companion*] as in later tutors are *falset*, that is to say, the fingering does not accurately represent the written notes because rapid rearrangements of cross-fingering are impossible . . . In such cases the upper note of the trill is correctly fingered as a long appoggiatura on to the written note, which is then trilled by moving a single finger.

For false trills in fingering charts for the hautboy, see Table 4.2.

---

[117] Hotteterre (*c*.1729), 14 (1707), 18–19.   [118] 'Tremblements empruntez' in the original French text.
[119] Hotteterre (*c*.1729), 13 (1707: 16).
[120] Unlike Hotteterre and other later sources, Loulié in *c*.1685 gave certain trill fingerings that involved closing two or even three holes.

TABLE 4.2. *False trills in fingering charts for the hautboy* (fingerings are given in Appendix 8)

Lower octave	Upper octave
	c–d♭
	c♯–d♯
	d♭–e♭
d–e♭	d–e♭
e–f	e–f
	e–f♯
f♯–g♯	f♯–g♯
g–a♭	
a♭–b♭	a♭–b♭
a–b♭	a–b♭
b♭–c2	
b–c2	
b–c♯2	b–c♯3

Loulié also classified some mordents (*battements*) as false ('irréguliers'):

lorsque le son inférieur n'est pas d'un degré plus bas, ou enfin lorsqu'il est trop haut ou trop bas.	when the lower note is not a [whole] degree lower, or actually, when [this note] is too high or too low.

Hotteterre's mordent chart contained a number of 'irregular' fingerings of this kind.

False trill fingerings could be disturbingly out of tune if they were not corrected.[121] But it is clear that they were not intended to produce out-of-tune notes; Hotteterre was obviously concerned enough about keeping trills in tune to remark 'There are some of them [trills] which must be begun by turning the Flute inwards, and ended by turning it out . . . there are others in which you must observe the quite contrary [*sic*] . . .'.[122] Loulié wrote:

Dans ces formes de tremblement [défectueux ou irréguliers] il faut très peu lever le doigt d'où on tremble, et diminuer le vent.	With this type of [defective or irregular] trill, one's trill finger should be raised very little, and the breath softened.

For the same reason, Quantz (1752: IX, §§9 and 10) advised when playing false trills to 'moderer le vent & faire en sorte que le doigt ne quitte presque pas le bois' (moderate the breath and barely allow the [moving] finger to leave the wood).[123]

---

[121] As Benade remarked (1994: 76), 'all that is necessary is to get the *important* notes of a passage in accurate tune within their context, while keeping the remaining ones plausible. Most listeners will find this quite acceptable and often will be unaware of the artifice.' [122] Hotteterre (*c.*1729), 13–14.

[123] See also IV, §22.

5. *Hole 1 and d2/e♭2*

There is no clear pattern of closing or opening hole 1 for d2 and e♭2, except that La Riche is the only source to suggest using a half-1, and all charts closed 1 for e♭2:

Hole 1 completely closed on d2:
> 1695 Banister
> 1699 *Second Book of Theatre Music*
> 1700 Freillon-Poncein
> 1738 Eisel

Hole 1 completely opened on d2:
> 1688 Bismantova
> 1707 Hotteterre

Hole 1 half-closed on d2:
> *c.*1692 La Riche (L1)

Hole 1 completely closed on e♭2:
> 1688 Bismantova
> 1695 Banister
> *c.*1692 La Riche (L2)
> 1699 *Second Book of Theatre Music*
> 1700 Freillon-Poncein
> 1707 Hotteterre

Hole 1 half-closed on e♭2:
> *c.*1692 La Riche (L1)

6. *High-note fingerings before c.1770*

One of the distinguishing characteristics of the Baroque hautboy was how the high notes were produced. Until the Classical period, all the charts gave 'short' high-note fingerings similar to the octave below (see the collation in App. 6). From about 1770 *long* fingerings were gradually introduced; these involved the fingers of both hands, and used a longer speaking length within the bore, tapping second harmonics of lower notes. The long fingerings varied but were often

> b♭2   12 456 7
> b2   1 3 456 7
> c3   23 45 7

Upward slurs to b♭2, b2, and c3 from beyond the register break (that is, from c2 downwards) could only have been played with long fingerings. But to my knowledge, the music written specifically for hautboy before *c*.1770 contains no slurs of this kind.[124]

The fine metal chains that were sometimes attached to hautboys may have had to do with using short high-note fingerings.[125] It was possible to drop the instrument when playing c3 'all open' (the usual fingering), especially if (as sometimes happened) the player was marching. The chain may have been meant to loop through a buttonhole to keep the instrument from falling.[126]

The trill fingering Hotteterre gave for the combination c3–b♭2 was 12 456 7.[127] This was in fact the long b♭2. Evidently, then (as we should expect), the long fingerings were known in the early eighteenth century. But for a normal untrilled b♭2, Hotteterre did not use that fingering, suggesting the short 1 3 instead. Thus, given the choice between long and short fingerings, the latter seem to have been preferred. Indeed, without exception, every known source until about 1770 chose the short fingerings. They were favoured, presumably, because of their obvious advantages: they were simpler, easier to finger, and clearer sounding. The short fingerings were used throughout the eighteenth century; the short b♭2 and b2 persisted until 1816,[128] the c3 until 1795.[129] The first chart to use long fingerings for all three notes did not appear until 1810.[130]

The short b♭2 and b2 were the same as their lower octaves (although the b2 was sometimes played by closing the second hole).[131] These notes work fairly well nowadays with almost any reed/staple set-up. But modern players find the short c3 capricious in response. For this reason, the history of fingerings for this note is worth a closer look.

The earliest hautboy charts are grouped between 1688 and 1707, a period when hautboys with longer bores and lower pitch were predominant. These charts almost always give c3 as 'all open', and this fingering (if we can call it that) works well enough on long-bored instruments in combination with the Talbot staple of the same period.[132]

---

[124] The last Allegro of Dreyer's sixth sonata, bb. 19–20, has octave slurs from a1 to a2 and b1 to b2; the slurs are casually placed and I prefer the musical effect when they are not slurred. The original score to Emanuel Bach's hautboy concerto in B flat (H466, *c*.1765) has upward slurs to b♭2 and c3 in bb. 52, 146, and 204 of the first movement that cannot be accomplished with short fingerings. But not only is this piece relatively late, it is probably an arrangement of a harpsichord concerto (see Ch. 7, §C.5). Bach's Christmas Oratorio of 1734 may be an exception, as it calls for octave slurs on b♭1–2 and c2–3 in the first hautbois d'amour part.

[125] Cf. the poem comparing the Schalmey with the hautboy in Weigel *c*.1722, quoted in Haynes (2000), which includes the phrase 'Thou art held by a penny-band; a golden chain graces me'.

[126] It is unclear how common the use of these chains was; like bell-pegs, they may have been part of the hautboist's standard equipment.

[127] This appears on the traverso chart; Hotteterre gives no hautboy chart as such, but merely refers to the traverso charts and mentions any differences.   [128] Whitely (1816).

[129] Verschuere-Reynvaan (1789).   [130] Froelich (1810).

[131] The latter sounded more open than 1 and offered better combinations with the adjacent notes (as, for instance, the trill from b2 to c♯3).

[132] Cf. Haynes (2000a) and my 1998 recording of Couperin using short fingerings on a reconstruction of the Talbot reed (ATMA).

Empirical experiment indicates that the Talbot dimensions do not work effectively on hautboys with shorter bores and higher pitch, however, nor is 'all open' for c3 very reliable with any kind of staple. Going back to the fingering charts, nothing is known after Hotteterre in 1707 until the appearance of Eisel in 1738. This is in fact the only new chart to appear until the Classical period. Eisel's fingering for c3 (Pl. 2.17) was no longer 'all open', but rather 2 7, like the octave below with a resonance-key added.[133] This fingering lowers the c3 considerably by adding 2, so it implies using a staple with a relatively sharp taper to raise the high register. With such a staple,[134] Eisel's fingering makes the c3 quite dependable. In both cases, the mechanism that helps the c3 to respond is the necessity to pinch and push: for the Talbot staple because it has such a small taper, for the Eisel because it adds a finger.

Reeds influenced the speech of the c3. But more important than reeds was a manner of blowing that was basically different from the less-demanding techniques of the late eighteenth and early nineteenth centuries that used long fingerings or octave keys. To control the highest register successfully and make it respond consistently, the Baroque player needed a more sophisticated diaphragm support, a firmer embouchure, and (though it did not necessarily result in louder b♭2s, b2s, and c3s) the ability instantly to 'urge the breath with more force' (cf. above, §C.2). The technique implied by the short high-note fingerings is thus distinct from that of later types of oboe.[135]

H. Choice of Key

One of the principal reasons key systems were developed on woodwinds in the nineteenth century was to eliminate (or at least reduce) the differences in sonority and finger technique between different tonalities, 'rationalizing' them by making them feel and sound more equal. Vény, writing in *c.*1828, considered the traditional two-keyed hautboy 'defective' and 'irrational'.[136]

The scales of woodwinds without key systems, like the hautboy, were indeed quite different from one another, both in the sound they produced and the technique they required. As for technique, the good keys (that is, those with few 'irrational fingerings' and 'uneven tones') were actually easier to finger without key mechanisms.[137] But each additional flat or sharp complicated the finger technique

---

[133] Bismantova had given almost the same fingering (2 6) in 1688, unlike all the other charts (see App. 6). Like Eisel (and unlike Banister, La Riche, Freillon-Poncein, and Hotteterre), Bismantova was probably dealing with a shorter hautboy at a higher pitch, on which this fingering seems to work best.

[134] Cf. Haynes (1997c).

[135] Short high-note fingerings did not become secure again until the introduction of the Barret/Triébert oboe design that appeared in 1865 (Geoffrey Burgess, pers. comm., Apr. 1999).

[136] Cf. the Introduction.

[137] The Mozart hautboy quartet and the concerto in C, for instance, are both easier to play on an oboe without keys.

and made the response less secure. Beyond four accidentals, eighteenth-century woodwinds were in trouble. The unevenness of sonority produced distinct characters in different tonalities. These differences were of course exploited for their expressive worth, but even so they remained special effects, and in practice the tonalities with fewer accidentals were the ones most often used.

1. Tonality and technique

a. Cross-fingerings and half-holing Passagework that used cross-fingerings and half-holing was obviously more complicated to finger. Borjon (1672: 11), comparing the musette with other woodwinds, wrote that

Ce qui fait la difficulté des autres Instrumens, comme la flûte, le flageolet, la traversiere, &c. ce sont les croisées des doigts qu'il y faut observer, desquelles la Musette est exempte . . .	The cause of problems on other instruments like the recorder, the flageolet, the traverso, etc. are the cross-fingerings that must be used, from which the musette is exempt . . .

Quick combinations of F–E or B♭–A, for instance, involved moving both weak fingers of the right hand (123 4 6 → 123 45) and left hand (1 3 → 12) respectively. The combination f1–a♭1 required alternating a cross-fingering with a half-hole (123 4 6 → 123). The technical difficulty of a given tonality was thus directly related to the number of cross-fingerings it used, both because of uneven response and awkward fingerings.

b. Other tonality-related fingering problems Other fingering problems that were a function of tonality were (1) the fingering 123; (2) the combination d♭2–e♭2, alias c♯2–d♯2, and; (3) certain trills. The fingering 123, which was always precarious, produced G♯/A♭, notes that first regularly appear in the tonalities of A major and E flat major.[138] Any fingering combination that involved slurring to the low g♯1/a♭ tended to have an awkward sound.[139] It was thus at the appearance of three sharps or three flats that the player had to deal with 123.

When the hautboy ventured into four sharps and four flats, it had to cope with the 'diabolus in hautboy', the sequence d♭2–e♭2 or c♯2–d♯2: 'The technical limit of the two or three keyed oboe is reached with a signature or musical situation which requires the player to cross the interval C-sharp to D-sharp, for which there is no provision as there is on the modern oboe.'[140] 'I.P.' explained in 1830 (p. 192): 'As C and D sharp [c♯2 and d♯2] are made by touching two keys with the little finger of

---

[138] g♯2 also occurs in A minor (melodic).
[139] Very like that of 'iro-iro-iro' as pronounced by modern Parisians.   [140] Grush (1972), 54.

the right hand successively, of course it requires an expert performer to produce them neatly, particularly if descending quick and legato.'[141]

The use of the 'all open' c♯/d♭2 is the usual alternative fingering in this situation, but it has an unsavoury sound, since it is flat. Trill fingerings for these two notes are offered by Freillon-Poncein and Hotteterre, but are of no help.[142]

Trills that were complex, poorly in tune, or unpleasant in sound were found in the following tonalities:

> A major (f♯1–g♯, f♯2–g♯)
> F sharp minor (f♯1–g♯, f♯2–g♯)
> A flat major (c2–d♭, d♭2–e♭)
> F minor (c2–d♭, d♭2–e♭)
> E major (f♯1–g♯, c♯2–d♯, f♯2–g♯)
> C sharp minor (f♯1–g♯, c♯2–d♯, f♯2–g♯)

From this, it is clear that the passage into difficult tonalities occurred at three sharps and flats, with E flat major/C minor being on the borderline.

The anonymous portrait of an hautboist that hangs now in Berlin (Pl. 2.7 and App. 4) includes a 'Concerto' in F minor under the player's elbow. That the piece is in this key was a flag: it indicated to contemporaries that the player was a virtuoso hautboist, and perhaps famous for his performances of this obviously difficult piece (which incidentally corresponds to no known surviving concerto).[143]

There are examples where a skilful composer could avoid the technical traps in inappropriate keys by judicious passagework. Telemann succeeded particularly well in his F minor hautboy concerto, as did Sammartini in the A major concerto, number 6 in his *6 Grand Concertos*, Opus 8.

One way around the problem of extreme sharp tonalities was the use of the hautbois d'amour, which was a 'sharp' oboe: its fingered scale of C major produced a sounding A major scale, automatically adding three sharps. This put pieces as extreme as B major (five sharps) within easy range of its technique.

2. Preferred tonalities

Going back as far as Lully's works, of the fifteen pieces that are thought to have been for hautboys, seven were in flat tonalities and six in sharps (including two pieces in *Le Bourgeois Gentilhomme* in D major).[144] The Philidor Manuscript went

---

[141] The combination c1–e♭1 involves the same problem, but was requested several times by Bach.

[142] The e♭2 is even poorer with this fingering ([1]23 45̲6̲ 8) than the 'open' d♭2; Hotteterre also suggested the traverso trill, 12̲3̲ 456 7, which works well on hautboy but is essentially the same 'open' d♭2.

[143] There are three concertos in F minor, two by Telemann, K Ob.f.(1) and K Ob.f.(2) in Dresden and Darmstadt, and one by Hertel, Brussels MS S 5563. [144] Two were in C major/A minor. Semmens (1975), 81.

no further than key signatures of one sharp and two flats, and the majority of pieces were in C major.[145]

In 1700 Freillon-Poncein went systematically through all the keys in his preludes: G A B C D E and F major and G A B C D E and F minor. This meant he had a range from one flat to five sharps in the major keys (the use of B and E major instead of B flat and E flat is surprising) and in the minor keys, four flats to two sharps. The point does not seem to have been to choose suitable keys, however. He wrote (p. 28)

Mon intention n'a pas esté en les composant de les faire bien chanter, mais seulement de les rendre tres-difficiles à executer par les longues & extraordinaires intervales où je les fais proceder . . .	My aim in composing these preludes was not to create beautiful melodies but only to make them very difficult to play because of the large and unusual intervals that I chose . . .

He added some other preludes for beginners (p. 37) in the more moderate keys of C G D A B flat and F major and C and A minor.

Georg Muffat, in the introduction to his *Auserlesene Instrumental-Music* (1701), implied which tonalities he considered suitable for hautboy. Although this collection was written primarily for strings, Muffat suggested the occasional addition of hautboys and bassoon

Wann aber unter deinen Musicanten einige die frantzösische Hautbois/oder Schallmey lieblich blasen . . . kanst du derer . . . anstatt . . . Violisten, und ein guten Fagotisten, anstatt deß Bäßl zur Formirung deß Concertino . . . löblich brauchen/wann du nur von solchen Thonen *Concerten* erwählest/oder in solche *Tonos* versetzest/die obgemelten Instrumenten taugen . . .	if among your musicians are some who can play the *Hautbois* (that is, the [new] French shawm) agreeably . . . you can use them profitably, in place of violins, together with a good bassoonist in place of other bass instruments, to form a *Concertino*, provided you choose only concertos in those tonalities, or transposed to those tonalities, in which the [hautboy and bassoon] work well . . .

The tonalities he suggested were D major, A major, B flat major, G minor, F major, and C major, a range of three sharps to two flats. It is interesting to observe Muffat's clear awareness that these new winds were sensitive to key choice.

Among early collections specifically conceived for the hautboy and written by an hautboist are the six suites of Telemann's *Kleine Cammer-Music*, in which flat keys were predominant: B flat major, G major, C minor, G minor, E minor, and E flat major. The six solo sonatas in Sammartini's Rochester manuscript also showed a clear flat bias: they were in C major, B flat major, E flat major, G major, and G minor. Sammartini wrote a concerto in the unusual key of E flat major as well, and was not averse to playing sharps, as the A major Concerto of Opus 8 shows.

Bach's favourite tonalities for hautboy and hautbois d'amour were A minor and D minor (twenty-three solos in each).[146] When he began composing a piece and had to decide the tonality to put it in, surely one of the most important considerations (if not the prevailing one) was how it would sound on the obbligato instrument. In his hautboy obbligatos that survive in alternative versions, Bach usually kept the fingered key, even when he switched sizes of hautboy.[147]

The central tonality of hautboy solos by the three most prolific composers for the instrument (Bach, Telemann, and Handel) was F major/D minor. More than half of all the pieces for solo hautboy written by these composers are within one accidental of F major/D minor, and almost all stayed within two accidentals of it. Tonalities were conservatively used: four-fifths used only two accidentals, and half were limited to no more than one. Finally, the hautboy's general repertoire (as much as is known at present and survives) shows like a mirror which tonalities were considered appropriate for the instrument. The relevant pieces, of course, are those written specifically and only for hautboy: solo sonatas (other than French, which were almost never for a specific instrument), trios for two hautboys and continuo, solo concertos, concertos for two hautboys, and vocal works with one and two obbligato hautboys. From the period 1670 to 1760, there are 1,361 pieces of this kind in the surviving literature.[148] The fingered tonalities are shown in Table 4.3. Almost all these pieces (96.19%) were written in a range of two sharps to three flats. The exact centre (calculated mathematically) is close to one flat. The most common tonalities were B flat major, C major, F major, G major, G minor, and C minor. The flat bias is clear.[149]

---

[146] Bach's surviving hautboy/hautbois d'amour solos are in the following fingered tonalities: A minor (23; 13.37%), D minor (23; 13.37%), B flat major (19; 11.05%), C major (19; 11.05%), C minor (17; 9.88%), G minor (17; 9.88%), F major (16; 9.30%), E flat major (11; 6.40%), E minor (11; 6.40%), G major (9; 5.23%), D major (3; 1.74%), F minor (2; 1.16%), A flat major (1; 0.58%), B minor (1; 0.58%).

[147] BWV 187/5 and 235/5, 248iv/4 and 213/5, 236/5 and 179/3, 68/4 and 208/7, 68/2 and 1040, 69/3 and 69a/3 (the first for hautboy in G, the second for oboe da caccia in C), 235/4 and 187/3, 120/1 and 120a/6. The exceptions are 233/4, in which he transposed 102/3 for hautboy and alto in F minor (!), putting it in C minor for hautboy and soprano, and several instances where he moved pieces back and forth between fingered C and D minor (BWV 21—see Haynes (1995), 304—243/3 and 243a/3, and 23/1—see Ch. 6, §B).

[148] There are 325 solo sonatas, 89 trios for two hautboys and continuo, 391 concertos (345 for solo hautboy), and 556 aria obbligatos. This information is based on the same (updated) database that was used in Haynes (1992a). For the purpose of the present discussion, works for hautbois d'amour use the fingered tonality rather than the notated tonality.

[149] Appropriate tonalities for the hautboy are described or implied in a number of other historical sources, and agree with the above. Cf. Francoeur (n.d.; a1772), 15; Laborde (1780), 266; McClymonds (1978), 279; Wragg (1792), 65; Vandenbrock (1793), 58; Fischer (c.1800), 10; and Gianelli (1801/30), 20.

TABLE 4.3. *Fingered tonalities in the hautboy repertoire, 1670–1760*

Key[a]	Number	Percentage
B flat	180	13.23
C	166	12.20
F	159	11.68
G	154	11.32
g	139	10.21
c	121	8.89
d	96	7.05
D	91	6.69
a	89	6.54
E flat	61	4.48
e	53	3.89
A	18	1.32
f	17	1.25
b	11	0.81
E	4	0.29
A flat	1	0.07
f sharp	1	0.07

[a] Lower-case letters indicate minor keys.

3. *Transposing to achieve more appropriate tonalities*

From the point of view of its particular technique and its historical repertoire, it is clear that a piece for solo hautboy in any tonality beyond two sharps or three flats was unusual. This was not true of other instruments, however. Bach's violin and traverso solos, for example, both had an average tonality of one sharp.[150] This put the hautboy about two accidentals flatwards of the other two standard treble instruments: F instead of G, for instance, or C instead of D. Given the physical nature of the instruments, this was logical. The violin, although more versatile than any woodwind instrument, usually succeeded better in tonalities that used its open strings (G D A E) on the important notes of the scale. This effectively made G and D the preferred tonalities.

Because the traverso was never too loud, it tended to play towards the upper end of its range (the part that was more audible) more frequently than the hautboy. It also kept close to D major, its natural scale, which avoided the darker- and softer-sounding cross-fingerings. Mattheson wrote (1713: i. 271) that the traverso's favoured tonalities were G, A, and D major and E minor. As Halfpenny (1948–9: 33) noted 'All the best solo utterances that one can call to mind, written for the

[150] See Haynes (1986c).

one-keyed flute, are in medium sharp keys, fairly high-lying and usually not very remote from the tonality of D major.'

Because much of the hautboy's solo literature was conceived (or at least published) for the traverso or violin (see Ch. 3, §G.1), it might not therefore have appeared in ideal keys for the hautboy. The traverso and violin differed from the hautboy not only in their preference for sharp tonalities; they both went easily up to e3, one note higher than the hautboy's top note. The hautboy also went a note lower than the traverso (whose lowest note was d1). A potentially useful strategy for the hautboy player was to transpose this music down a whole step, thereby producing a more appropriate range and moving the key signature flatwards.

Evidently, players had no difficulty transposing. Marin Marais, in the preface to a suite for gamba published in 1689, wrote that 'presentement en France chacun transpose si facilement sur tous les Tons et Demi-tons' (everyone in France now transposes with ease to all the whole- and half-steps). In his *Premier recueil de Brunettes* (1724: iii), Montéclair also reported that altering the key was an expedient used by 'experienced players'. After discussing the music in relation to flute range, he suggested that players might shift its tonalities for reasons of practical necessity:

Les habilles gens m'entendront pour peu de reflexion qu'ils fassent la dessus et conviendront qu'il y a des occasions ou il seroit necessaire de poser les clefs dans les espaces aussy bien que sur les lignes ou du moins de les y scavoir suposer. Chacun cependant fera sur cela ce qui luy paraitra le plus commode.

Experienced players of treble lines will understand my point immediately, and agree that there are instances when it might be necessary to place the clef signs on the spaces rather than the lines, or at least know how to do so. Each player will decide this according to what seems most practical to him.

By placing the clef signs 'on the spaces rather than the lines' he apparently means moving the tonality up or down a whole step. Montéclair also mentioned flute transposition in the third of his *Concerts* (1724) in C, which (according to the part) was for musette. He said the movements

conviennent a la Musette, a la Vielle, au Haubois, au Violon, au Deßus de Violle, a la Flûte-Traversiere, et a la Flûte-a-bec.

will work well on the musette, hurdy-gurdy, hautboy, violin, treble viol, traverso, and recorder.

He added that

Pour rendre ce Concert plus convenable a la Flûte-Traversiere, il faut le transposer un ton plus haut, sçavoir en D la re majeur, ou une 3ce plus bas, en A mi la majeur.

To make this *Concert* more appropriate for the traverso, it should be transposed up one step to D major, or down a third to A major.

Freillon-Poncein (1700: 38) also suggested transposing 'up or down a second, third, fourth, or greater interval' to adapt his preludes to different instruments.[151]

a. The analogy with recorder transposition   Transposing traverso music down a step for the hautboy was analogous to the transposition Hotteterre suggested for the recorder in his *Premier livre* of 1708 (which was principally for traverso but could be played, according to the composer, on any treble instrument):

Comme il y en a qui descendent trop bas pour la Flûte a bec, il faudra avoir recours a la transposition, lorsqu'on les voudra joüer sur cet Instrument; On transposera par exemple le D la re tierce majeure, en F ut fa naturel; le G re sol tierce majeure, en B fa si bemol tierce naturelle, et l'E si mi, en G re sol tierce mineure.	As some of them go too low for the recorder, it is necessary to resort to transposition if one wishes to play them on this instrument. D major, for instance, should be transposed to F major, G major to B flat major, and E minor to G minor.

This recorder transposition, up a minor third, seems to have been common:

1. Purcell's chaconne, *Three parts upon a ground* (Z 731), was written in D major for three violins or '2 notes higher [= F major] for Flutes'.[152]

2. William William's *Six new Sonatas, in three parts* were described in the *Post Boy* of 24 December 1696 as 'three design'd for Violins, and three for Flutes; those for the Flutes being writ three notes lower, will go on the Violins, and those for the Violins being rais'd will go on the Flutes, which will make six for each instrument'.[153]

3. Corbett's *Six sonatas with an overture and aires*, Opus 3, published by Walsh in 1708, was for trumpet, violin/hautboy, traverso, and continuo but was 'to be played with 3 flutes [= recorders] & a bass in the French key 3 notes higher' [that is, in French violin clef, or G1].[154]

4. In 1719 (p. 27) Hotteterre suggested playing exercises for recorder down a minor third on other instruments by moving the G clef from the first to the second line.

The recorder player transposing in this way would thus play an f1, fingered 123 456 8, when he saw a d1. The same fingering on the hautboy produced c1. By this logic, a piece for traverso in D would have been played in F on the recorder and C on the hautboy. In 1776 Hawkins suggested that this was indeed the natural relation between the three instruments: 'There is an objection that lies in common against all perforated pipes; the best that the makers of them can do is to tune them to some one key, as the hautboy to C, the German flute to D, and the flute à bec to F; and

---

[151] Transpositions also raise the question of displaced key characters. For a discussion of this, cf. Haynes (1995), 261.   [152] This beautiful piece, although not officially for hautboys, goes very well on them.   [153] Tilmouth (1961), 18. I owe this reference to Peter Holman.   [154] Lasocki (1983), 457.

to effect this truly, is a matter of no small difficulty.'[155] Quantz implied that this tonality relationship was common by suggesting in the introduction to his *Sei duetti* for traversos, Opus 2 (1759), that they could be played 'sur deux Hautbois un ton plus bas; et sur deux flûtes à bec une Tierce mineure plus haut' (on two hautboys, one step lower, and on two recorders, a minor third higher).

In terms of fingerings, the hautboy thus effectively transposed recorder music down a fourth. If other circumstances allowed it (for instance, the range of the continuo), it made sense to retain the fingerings, regardless of their note names, since not only the range but the placement of cross-fingerings would then have remained the same. It is what Sammartini did in a sonata that appears for hautboy in C major in the Rochester collection (no. 1) and for recorder in F major in a manuscript collection at Parma (no. XII).[156]

Since it was common for hautboy players to double on recorder, transferring fingerings would not have amounted to real *transposition*, but rather something analogous to what bilingual people do when changing languages; they do not *translate*, but simply switch 'modes'. Modern recorder players do this when switching from treble to tenor recorder; it is done with the fingers rather than the mind. It was probably common among woodwind players, who often switched instruments. It was the 'transposition' used on the voice-flute (sounding d1 is fingered 123 456 8), and it is also seen in Philidor (1717–18), 82; the beginning of the 'Réduction de la Chaße', notated in D, mentioned that 'this piece is played in G on the bassoon'.[157] The bassoon's G is fingered like D on the hautboy and traverso.[158]

b. The relation to the traverso   Most of the large number of eighteenth-century pieces that survive in versions for both traverso and hautboy show the whole-step relationship described above: the hautboy version is a tone lower than the one for traverso.[159] The best-known example is probably the Mozart concerto, in C for hautboy and D for traverso.[160] (Mozart's hautboy quartet in F, K. 370, also appeared in its first published form as a traverso quartet in G).[161]

---

[155] Hawkins (1776), ii. 739 n.

[156] McGowan (1978), 42. There is an indication that hautboy pieces were transposed for recorder in a letter written in 1705 by Captain Prendcourt quoted in Tilmouth (1973), 305: 'Never in my Lives Time I had such a Task as Mr Festin's Tunes did give me, for they being set for a Hautbois I was oblig'd to Transpose'm for the most Part . . .' (It is assumed the adaptation was for recorder, since Prendcourt mentions 'flute' in another letter, and transposition for other instruments would probably not have been necessary.)

[157] 'Cette Piece se joüe en G.re.Sol pour le Baßon.'

[158] It is interesting to find that a *symphonie* piece might also be played on the bassoon. For bassoons, by the way, Quantz suggested transposing his duets 'à la Tierce mineure de dessus' (a minor third higher, i.e. as for recorder).

[159] For lists, see Haynes (1979) and Haynes (1992a), p. xiv. Cf. also John Marsh's *Hints to Young Composers of Instrumental Music* of *c.*1806, discussed in Cudworth (1965), 64.

[160] The differences in technique and range between C and D are not of the same importance to players of the key-system oboe. Cf. Goritzky (1979), which suggests playing the flute version (in D) on the key-system oboe.

[161] Vienna: Hoffmeister, 1801. See Vester (1985), M627.

Although it seems an obvious solution in many cases, there is no direct evidence that hautboy players did indeed transpose traverso music down a step; no
sources are known that explicitly suggested it. Hotteterre did not mention the
possibility of transposing for hautboy, either in the passage from his *Premier livre*
where he advised recorder players to transpose or in *L'Art de préluder* (1719: 6),
where he said the traverso preludes could be played on the hautboy 'excepté ceux
qui regnent beaucoup sur les tons hauts' (except those that use many high notes).
This would have been the moment to suggest transposing downwards. Introducing his preludes for the recorder, he mentioned the G1 and G2 clefs and said
(1719: 27):

Plusieurs [préludes] conviendront außi au Hautbois sur l'une et sur l'autre clef [G1 or G2].	Some [of the preludes] will also work for the hautboy in one or the other of these clefs [G1 or G2].[162]

And some pieces sound better on hautboy in the same tonality as the traverso,
often because of the position of cross-fingerings. There was also a complication in
transposing down a step when a piece included d$\sharp$1, which became the problematic
c$\sharp$1.[163]

There are interesting implications to the whole-step tonality relationship
between the traverso and hautboy, since in fact the two instruments had virtually
identical fingerings. As Hotteterre put it 'As far as the arrangement of the fingers,
[the traverso and hautboy] differ in only a few notes.'[164] Although D major was by
far the easiest tonality to finger on the hautboy (as on the traverso),[165] it was not (as
we have seen) a common tonality in original music for hautboy, being used about
half as often as C and B flat. What worked well on the traverso in D was frequently
given to the hautboy in C.

The effect of dropping the tonality a step was to give the hautboy two more cross-
fingerings than the traverso (as there are none in D major, one in G, two in C, three
in F, etc.).[166] The hautboy was thus able to move easily into keys with the darker,
covered sound of cross-fingerings, whereas the clearer, more open sound of tonalities that required simple fingerings balanced better the relatively introverted sound
of the traverso. The hautboy's versatility in key choice (combined with an easily
audible low register) would explain why it was so commonly used in the orchestra.

---

[162] Hotteterre mentioned transpositions 'd'un Ton a un autre' on p. 56, and gave examples.
[163] An expedient that might often have worked was to substitute an e1.   [164] Hotteterre (1707), 44.
[165] This is based on a systematic analysis of the finger combinations of each diatonic scale.
[166] These two extra cross-fingerings meant that the same piece was somewhat more difficult to finger on the
hautboy than on the traverso, another reason amateurs would have been more likely to take up the traverso.

I. The Speaking Phrase Compared with the Romantic 'Long-line'

Nobody in the Baroque period bothered to write the obvious or describe the commonplace, whence comes the saying 'what everyone knew then, no one knows now'.[167] This has an opposite side, which is that what everyone knows now may not have been known by anyone then. Among the things oboists know very well now, for instance, are long-line phrases, continuous vibrato, trying to play in equal temperament, and playing four sixteenth notes with equal stress. None of these practices, as we shall see, seems to have been familiar to hautboists.

The most basic of these different concepts of performing has to do with phrasing. Phrasing is mainly expressed through a combination of articulation and dynamics; these are areas where the 'eloquent' hautboy and the 'sostenuto' key-system oboe parted company.

The hautboy reed had to be lightly scraped to respond smoothly on cross-fingerings and half-holings. This lightness gave it two of its special technical attributes. It was able to start and stop quickly, even abruptly, so it was easy to leave silences and breaks in its lines. It also had an extraordinary dynamic range and could change its dynamic level abruptly and extravagantly. North noted (*c.*1710–28: 218), 'This ['soft and lowd'; or dynamics] conduceth much to the delight of musick . . . The voice performes this best; next wind musick, as trumpetts and hautboys . . .' Being able to move instantly from very loud to very soft and vice versa gave the hautboy a particular ability to intensify points of harmonic and rhythmic stress. (The Baroque bow lent itself to the same effects for the same basic reason—less tension— as did the relative lack of force needed to activate the keys of a harpsichord.) These were probably the qualities that Mattheson was thinking of when he characterized the hautboy as 'eloquent'.

But these attributes brought with them the necessity to make constant minute adjustments of breath pressure and embouchure on individual notes, and the obligation to pay attention to separate notes was an impediment if one wished to produce an evenly contoured *sostenuto*, or long-line phrase.

The Romantic long-line phrase is essentially a dynamic shape, a single long crescendo–diminuendo superimposed over a short musical unit that has a melodic and harmonic independence. It is normally played in one breath, starting softly and building to one or more notes, often high and usually somewhere in the middle (designated as the important notes of the phrase, sometimes called 'goals' or

---

[167] Boyden (1965), 2.

'climaxes'), and then diminishing to the end. Besides 'long-line phrasing', it is also known as 'the arched phrase', the 'sweeping melodic line', the 'sostenuto', and the 'grande ligne'.

The mutation of the oboe from the later eighteenth century to the middle of the nineteenth is a gradual move away from a low-pressure, cross-fingered, essentially keyless hautboy to an instrument that was better adapted to producing the long-line. The new oboe had holes for every semitone as well as speaker holes. The extra holes, operated by keys, were intended to equalize tone quality, intonation, and blowing technique, so the player could more easily develop a smoothly arched phrase without needing to trouble with the minutiae of tuning and response on individual notes.

The embouchure cultivated in the course of the nineteenth century, as mentioned above, was relatively stationary, conceived to make minimal corrections to tuning (ideally, none—though this has never been achieved). The key-system oboe's reed is also much heavier than the hautboy's; so heavy in fact that it will not readily play cross-fingerings. This kind of reed inhibits quick dynamic change and discourages frequent stops, because it takes considerable energy and higher pressure to restart.

Reeds and embouchures of this kind were developed to work well with the gradual dynamic process of the *sostenuto* long-line phrase. But they are virtually incapable of the range, frequency, and speed of dynamic change implicit in Baroque melodic lines (cf. Quantz's Adagio discussed below), or the regular use of the *messa di voce*. The nineteenth-century oboe had different imperatives: the music it was designed to play was not articulated in musical 'words' and 'spoken', but was (as Harnoncourt describes it) 'painted' in larger legato surfaces.[168]

The long-line is a very appealing concept, and it is so generally accepted and assumed nowadays that it is often unconsciously applied to seventeenth- and eighteenth-century music as well. The idea of an overarching line was not strange to musicians of the Baroque, but it was less important than the many smaller components of phrasing. With the clear harmonic structure of eighteenth-century music, the longer unit that later became the long-line phrase was simply the passage between two cadences, so implicit and obvious that it needed no special attention.

The long-line assumes one or perhaps two crucial points in the phrase (the climax) rather than a series of hierarchically arranged points of emphasis, and because it is played on a wind instrument in a single breath (implying a *sostenuto* interrupted by tonguing, rather than real stops or silences in the line), it is fundamentally incompatible with the priorities of Baroque phrasing.

---

[168] Cf. Harnoncourt (1988), 39 ff.

1. Principles behind a speaking phrase

To demonstrate the spoken quality of musical performance, Mattheson (1739: 160–80) developed a system of 'Klang-Füsse' comparable to the foot accentuations of poetic metre. The musical scansion of a Baroque phrase involved 'good' and 'bad' beats, dissonances, and figures.

The first and most basic emphasis came on the beats of the measure, which formed an order of prominence among themselves.[169] First beats were the most important, followed in duple metres by third beats. Second and fourth beats were lighter. Reflected in dynamics, this made beats one and three louder than two and four; or, as Harnoncourt puts it,[170] the order was ONE–two–*three*–(four). A bar with differently inflected beats is in fundamental opposition to the long-line phrase, which becomes difficult to project when there are too many accents. In miniature, the four sixteenth-notes of a beat were also in the same relation, giving each beat the shape of a decrescendo—an effect that contrasts quite audibly with the four equally stressed 'sewing machine' sixteenths often heard in performances of Baroque music on modern (so-called modern!) instruments.[171]

Running across the principle of good and bad beats were the exceptions created by dissonance. Dissonance took precedence over beat, so a suspension, appoggiatura, 4–2 chord, etc. was emphasized even when it was on a weak beat. Its resolution was slurred and unstressed.[172] Babitz called this the 'interplay between the regular beat and the irregular melody'.[173]

Another factor that broke up the potential monotony of a repeated pattern were the *figures* that claimed melodic emphasis and ran sometimes counter to both the beats and dissonances.

Figures (*Figurae*, 'figures' of speech) were small patterns of notes, or melodic clichés.[174] By the late seventeenth century, most of them had become codified into a rich store of characteristic motifs or gestures. They were the building blocks out of which Baroque melodies were made, and the mark of a good composer was how well he could assemble them in new and effective ways. If a phrase was like a sentence, figures were the words; they were the principal units from which music in the Baroque period was constructed (and through which it can be most effectively

---

[169] Cf. Babitz (1967), 21 ff. Babitz described a number of phrasing practices (like fringing, pointing, and rubato) that have still not received much attention by performers. For an assessment of Babitz's articles, see Fuller (1989), 130 ff.　　　　　　　　　　　　　　　　　　　　[170] Harnoncourt (1988), 40.

[171] Taruskin (1989: 167 ff.) calls this 'the twentieth-century "geometrical" Bach style' and associates it with Stravinsky, who called it 'monometric' rhythm.

[172] Harnoncourt (1988: 41) mentions other exceptions to the beat pattern that received emphasis: a longer note following a short note (as in a syncopation or the typical chaconne rhythm), and the top notes of a melody.

[173] Babitz (1967), 26 n. 9.

[174] Examples of figures are given in Butt (1990), 19 ff. Cf. also Harnoncourt (1988), 55, 133 and Ratner (1991).

analysed). Clarifying and projecting figures was one of the main occupations of a Baroque musician. To achieve this, he called on every expressive technique he had, including dynamics, articulation, and vibrato.

2. *Performing the speaking phrase*

a. Dynamic nuance and the Quantz Adagio The hautboy's wide and flexible dynamic range suited well the demands of its music, which was built of thousands of these small, constantly changing gestures—a system where, as Quantz put it, 'Il faut donc observer un changement continuel du Forte & du Piano' (a continual alternation of the Forte and Piano must thus be observed).[175]

As examples of this 'changement continuel', Quantz (somewhat reluctantly, it seems) included two remarkable Adagios in his book, with detailed instructions on their dynamics: one of them contained twenty-two changes in the first two bars, and continued in the same manner.[176] Shortly after Quantz's book appeared, his pupil Johann Friedrich Agricola (who was the leading German singing teacher of the day) drew attention to this Adagio:[177]

Denen, welche sich aus abstracten Regeln, ohne die Beyspiele gleich vor Augen zu sehen, keine hinlängliche Begriffe zu machen wissen, zu Gefallen, hat sich Herr Quanz [sic], in seinem Versuche über die Flöte, die rümliche Mühe gegeben, bey vielen einzelnen Sätzen, auch bey einem ganzen Adagio, die Stärke und Schwäche fast jeder Note aufs genaueste vorzuschreiben . . . Es ist zwar alles eigentlich für die Flöte eingerichtet: allein ein angehender Sänger wird doch großen Nutzen davon haben, wenn er diese Exempel durchgeht, und das was seiner Stimme möglich ist, nach der Vorschrift in Ausübung zu bringen suchet.[178]

As a service to those who have difficulty making sense of abstract rules when no concrete examples are put before them, Mr Quantz has kindly provided many examples of the use of dynamics in his Essay on the flute. He even took the trouble to set down in minute detail the exact degrees of strong and weak for practically every note of an entire Adagio . . . Of course, it is actually conceived with reference to the flute, but any developing singer would surely profit greatly by working his way through this example, attempting to perform according to its instruction everything that is possible with his voice.

Agricola's advice to singers would have been equally valid for violinists (Quantz mentions the bow when discussing the dynamics) and hautboy players.

Quantz's Adagio is especially useful to us now, as heirs to a different concept of phrasing. That it is not better known nowadays is probably due to the format in

---

[175] Quantz (1752), XI, §14.   [176] Ibid. XIV, §41 and Tab. XVII, XVIII, and XIX.
[177] In more recent times, the significance of Quantz's Adagio has been pointed out by (among others) Dolmetsch (1915), appendix; Warner (1964), 124; Boyden (1965); and Babitz (1967).   [178] Agricola (1757), 146–7.

which he presented it. The dynamic markings were not set with the music notation, but were in the form of descriptive text placed in another part of the book. Of this problem, Agricola went on to say

Wobey es ihm [ein angehender Sänger] leichter werden wird, wenn er sich die Mühe nimmt, die Exempel aus den Tabellen weitlauftig abzuschreiben, und die Grade der Stärke und Schwäche . . . aus dem Buche, mit den daselbst befindlichen abgekürzeten Wörtern, selbst über die Noten zu setzen.[179]	To make it easier [for developing singers], they could take the trouble to copy the example out in detail from the *Tabellen*, marking over the notes the levels of strong and weak by appropriate abbreviations.

Following Agricola's advice, I have transcribed the Adagio with its dynamic markings (cf. Pl. 4.13).

Although Quantz made frequent use of the words *piano* and *forte* in his book, conceiving them as absolute levels of sound intensity (as we do today), the dynamic indications he used in this Adagio often meant something else.[180] The absolute *piano* and *forte* do appear, but most of the instructions are put in relative terms: 'stronger than before', 'weaker'—concepts that resemble the modern *crescendo* and *diminuendo*. He explained:

Les mots abregés doivent être entendus de la maniére suivante: *aug. augmentant*, ou en augmentant la force du ton; *dim. diminuant*, ou en diminiuant [*sic*] la force du ton; *f. fort*; *p.f. plus fort*; *d. doux*.[181] C'est le coup de langue ou de l'archet qui exprime le fort & le doux, pour que chaque note en soit plus ou moins marquée. Il ne faut aussi pas toujours prendre le dernier dégré de la signification de ces mots; devant en user comme dans la peinture, où l'on se sert des *mezze tinte*, demi-couleurs, pour exprimer la lumiére & l'ombre, & c'est par là qu'on passe insensiblement du clair à l'obscure.[182]	The abbreviated words should be understood in the following manner: *aug. augmentant*, or increasing the strength of sound; *dim. diminuant*, or reducing the strength of sound; *f.* = *forte*; *p.f.* = *più forte*; *d.* = *piano*. *Forte* and *piano* are expressed by the tonguing or bow stroke, so that each note has greater or lesser stress. There is no need to take these words always to their extreme degree of meaning; they can be used as in painting, where the *mezze tinte* or half-tints are employed to express light and shadow, and light converges imperceptibly with dark.

In the transcription here, I have used 'f' and 'p' for 'fort' and 'doux', and '<f' for *plus fort*. For the 'aug.' and 'dim.', I followed Geminiani's example and used black wedges analogous to *crescendo* and *diminuendo*.[183]

---

[179] Ibid. 147.   [180] Cf. Reilly (1966), 172 n.

[181] The corresponding German words were *wa. wachsend, abn. abnehmend, sta. starck; stä. stärker; schw. schwach*. In German, Quantz normally used *Piano* and *Forte* for absolute dynamic levels.

[182] Quantz (1752), XIV, §25.   [183] Geminiani (1751), 4. See also Geminiani (1739).

Adagio.

PL. 4.13. Quantz, Adagio (1752, Tab. XVII–XIX). Transcribed by B. Haynes

* Each note of this phrase with a crescendo.
** In a 'flattering' manner.

Other composers used dynamic markings as Quantz conceived them here, to indicate, not absolute decibel levels, but a contrast to what had just happened, as with the marking 'pp', which at the time often meant not *pianissimo* (very soft) but 'più piano' (softer).[184] There is an example of this in the tenor aria of BWV 95, where the second hautbois d'amour was marked 'più piano' when he repeated a short figure previously stated by the first hautbois d'amour (who had no dynamic marking).[185]

Examples as detailed as Quantz's were rare for two reasons: players were expected to know how to use dynamics, and such a quantity of markings was impractical in regular use. The eye can only take in so much information when it is obliged to keep moving. D. G. Türk commented in 1789:

Wie überhäuft würden aber diese Worte [*forte* and *piano*] beygefügt werden müssen, wenn jede einzelne Note, welche eine besondere Schattirung verlangt, damit bezeichnet sollte.[186]	How profusely, however, these words [*forte* and *piano*] would need to be added if every single note requiring a particular shading had to be so designated.[187]

b. Note shaping ('bulging')   The difference between long-line phrases and earlier ones based on the functions of individual notes is also manifested in the shape of notes. Leopold Mozart wrote that

Jeder auch auf das stärkeste ergriffene Ton hat eine kleine obwohl kaum merkliche Schwäche vor sich; sonst würde es kein Ton, sondern nur ein unangenehmer und unverständlicher Laut seyn. Eben diese Schwäche ist an dem Ende iedes Tones zu hören.[188]	Every tone, even the strongest attack, has a small, even if barely audible, softness at the beginning of the stroke; for it otherwise be no tone but only an unpleasant and unintelligible noise. This same softness must be heard also at the end of each tone.[189]

Boyden, who compares Tartini's similar description of note shape to Mozart's,[190] comments:

What Mozart and Tartini seem to be saying is that there is a small initial 'give' to the old bow which has to be taken up before a good tone can emerge; and this remark is perfectly consistent with the character of the old bow. The same 'give' also occurs in the modern bow, but it is much less because the concave construction of the modern bow stick does not permit it; and this fact, combined with a modern technique that cultivates the smoothest possible initial attack and bow change, makes this 'small softness' practically imperceptible to the ear in modern playing.

---

[184] Cf. Marshall (1985), 262–3.   [185] Denton (1977), 146.   [186] Türk (1789), 348.
[187] Cited and translated in Jackson (1995), 3.   [188] Mozart (1756), 103.
[189] Trans. Boyden (1965), 393.   [190] In a letter written in 1760 and quoted in Boyden (1965), 393.

Ex. 4.2. Examples of two ways of phrasing from Brod (1825: 10)

In the long-line phrase, by contrast, a note is a segment of a much larger shape, and goes essentially in a single direction (towards, or away from, the climax note). On this subject, Harnoncourt writes (1988: 41 ff.):

The individual tone in music after about 1800 appears to me two-dimensional in its *sostenuto*, while an ideal tone in earlier music had a physical, or three-dimensional effect because of its inner dynamics. The instruments also correspond to these ideals of *flat* or *speaking*, as can easily be heard if, for example, the same phrase is played on a Baroque oboe and on a modern oboe.

Quantz, too, described the 'small softness':

Chaque note, qu'elle soit une Noire, une Croche ou une Double croche, doit avoir son Piano & Forte, suivant que le tems le permet.[191]

Each note, whether it is a quarter, eighth, or sixteenth, should have its own Piano and Forte, to the extent that time permits.

This sounds very much, in fact, like what Henri Brod, in his *Méthode pour le hautbois* published in the 1820s, was to call 'papillotage'. Brod explicitly compared the older style using dynamic nuance (which he rejected) to the simpler long-line phrase.[192] He commented on the passage in Ex. 4.2:

Généralement, on doit *nuancer largement* c'est à dire ne faire plutôt qu'une nuance dans une phrase de trois ou quatre mesures, qu'une quantité de *petites nuances* les unes à côté des autres, lesquelles non seulement se nuisent entr'elles, mais encore détruisent l'effet de la musique et deviennent ce qu'on appelle du papillotage.[193]

Generally speaking, a player should make *broad nuances* (that is, no more than one crescendo or decrescendo in a phrase consisting of three or four measures) rather than many *small nuances*, one after the other, which is not only harmful to the smaller sections but also destroys the effect of the music, and becomes what is called 'fluttering'.

---

[191] Quantz (1752), XIV, §11.
[192] Hedrick (1974), 58 points out that in A. M. R. Barret's *Complete Method for the Oboe* (London, 1852), 'most of the dynamics look like this [second] example!'.
[193] Brod (1825), 10. Italics mine.

'Papillotage' is very much out of style nowadays, but it is interesting to observe that even on the key-system oboe, it almost happens by itself. Under 'Bad habits' in her book *Oboe Technique*, Evelyn Rothwell lists 'Bulging':

Beware always of the very common bad habit of making a 'bulge', i.e. a little <>, on each note, or over every few notes. It is a monotonous, niggling form of expression, which is unmusical, and maddening to the listener. Unfortunately, it seems fatally easy for oboe players to acquire this bad habit . . .[194]

Recent studies by Geoffrey Burgess have illuminated the process whereby the art of detailed dynamic shading was abandoned in the early nineteenth century.[195] He found it alive and well in the *Vocalises* (vocal studies without text) by the castrato virtuoso Girolamo Crescentini (1762–1846). Crescentini's *Vocalises*, which went through many editions in the first half of the nineteenth century, are full of detailed dynamic nuance, and he wrote that the dynamics, as marked, were obligatory and essential to bringing out musical syntax.

Probably around 1810, Gustave Vogt, professor at the Paris Conservatoire (and the father of modern oboe playing) transcribed ten of Crescentini's *Vocalises* for oboe. Vogt may have made his transcriptions for his students at the Conservatoire, including Brod and Vény. Burgess (1995a: 7) describes how Vogt 'ironed-out' the small-scale dynamic nuance on individual notes in favour of phrase units of about four bars. Burgess points out that Vogt's earliest compositions still contain considerable dynamic nuance similar to Crescentini's; in other words, Vogt's own taste on this question changed during the course of his career. We now find ourselves on the other side of this watershed.

Note shaping and complex dynamic nuance as shown in Quantz's Adagio probably represented the general practice of the period prior to the appearance of his book. But by 1770, when Burney met Quantz, he gave the impression of its being old-fashioned. Burney specifically commented that Quantz did not play in 'the modern manner . . . of gradually enforcing and diminishing whole passages, as well as single notes'.[196] This suggests that the kind of dynamic inflection described above was already yielding ground to larger more sustained dynamic shapes fifteen to twenty years after Quantz published his book.[197]

c. Silences within the phrase   The long-line phrase is played on a key-system oboe in a single breath into which tonguing is (as it were) inserted. Tonguing does not interrupt the long arch, but is incorporated into it, almost as an ornament. This of

---

[194] Rothwell (1953), 11.   [195] Burgess (1995a) and (1995b).   [196] Burney (1773), 158.
[197] Simpler dynamic shapes would have reflected the simpler architecture of the music that was in vogue almost everywhere outside Berlin at the time.

course creates a *sostenuto* effect. And because of the energy and pressure involved, players of the key-system oboe are often reluctant to interrupt the air flow or disturb their embouchures by stopping.

Yet silences between the notes were important in Baroque phrasing. Dynamic nuance, as discussed above, was not the only means of expressing emphasis and accents. In fact, a number of important instruments of the time (the harpsichord, recorder, and musette, for example) had virtually no dynamic range at all, but were still able to convey clearly the difference between important and unimportant beats. They did this by making the bad beats short and the good ones longer; upbeats were lifted (as on the upbow of a violin), downbeats were placed.[198] To the degree that there is silence before a note, it sounds more important. Harpsichordists and recorder players used the length of silence before a note to give it more or less emphasis.[199] This also happened naturally with the short, light violin bow of the time. And the hautboy, unlike the key-system oboe, could stop and start instantly, without special effort, so hautboists could integrate their own opulent dynamic range to the precise and frugal articulation of the harpsichord and recorder.

Babitz (1967) argued convincingly that the regular use of pointing (*notes inégales* in long–short pairs; see below, §J.3) was an integral component of how accents were clarified, since the long note was on the good part of the beat. Pointing also implies a complexity in the phrase that would have been incompatible with the simplicity of the long-line shape.

d. Irregular tempo   Irregularities of tempo flow, especially if they happen frequently, also tend to make broad phrasing less coherent. Yet slowing down and speeding up have often been used in the past to bring out detail within phrases. The notion that a tempo once established continues at a uniform, invariable pace, as if a metronome was beating somewhere in the wings, has in fact emerged only since the Second World War, as Robert Philip has demonstrated by studying early recordings.[200] This observation has interesting implications. If tempo did not operate as a kind of internal metronome in pre-industrial days, the connection between speed and tempo must have been less straightforward. Reducing tempos to mathematical calculations (as encouraged by the metronome) ceases to be convincing, as it implicitly assumes a twentieth-century regularity of tempo.[201] This assumption often leads

---

[198] See Babitz (1967), 24.

[199] This practice is common among players of these instruments, and is constantly implied by the music itself. But it is difficult to find it discussed in explicit terms in original sources, perhaps because it was self-evident at the time.

[200] Philip (1992), 7, 37. This book draws attention to the manifest differences between real musical performance (as documented in recordings) and the written instructions of players of the time. Composers sometimes ignored their own tempo markings when they performed their music.

[201] Cf. Miehling (1993), valuable as a study of sources on tempo, but weakened by a simplistic and mechanistic view of tempo as the equivalent of speed.

modern musicians to equate the little words written at the beginning of movements, like 'Allegro', with the *speed* of the movement. But anyone who knows how important the characterization of pieces was to eighteenth-century musicians, how important it was to evoke the affect (or mood) of the music, is aware that 'Allegro' meant a lot more more than where to set the metronome (in fact, metronomes were not yet in general use in the eighteenth century). 'Allegro' means 'jolly' in Italian, not 'fast'. Of course, a projection of 'jollity' might be effective at a quick speed, but that speed would have varied depending on the size of the room, the instrument, the weather, and what everybody had had for lunch.[202]

e. Slurs used for emphasis   The slur was a technical expedient (see below, §J.5). But its main use was expressive, as it could be used to bring out accents. The corollary of the principle that notes sound more important when there is silence before them is that they sound less important when there is none; that is, when they are slurred. This means that the first note under a slur normally sounds stronger because the other notes seem less important by contrast. On a violin, the slur represented a natural diminuendo, as the bow produced less volume as it approached the point. On the harpsichord, this was done with 'over-legato', holding notes down while playing others, so the attacks of the later notes were obscured. Instruments that could make little or no dynamic changes, like the harpsichord, recorder, and organ, depended on the slur to give the illusion of diminuendo. The slur was consequently regarded as a kind of ornament. Brown wrote in 1722 (p. 66), 'The usual *Graces* [on the HAUT-BOY] are three in number, *Viz.* a *Shake* [= trill], a *Beat* [mordent] and a *Slur*.' Many other writers at the time (Muffat, Rousseau, and Prelleur, for instance) described the slur as an ornament.[203]

Bach, 'to the astonishment and annoyance of his contemporaries',[204] marked slurs very thoroughly when he had the time.[205] This was unusual, because any competent eighteenth-century musician knew where to slur. By systematically studying the scores and parts Bach wrote out himself,[206] John Butt (1990) shows that it is possible to make generalizations that allow us to predict where slurs would normally be added, both in Bach's music and, by analogy, in that of his less fastidious contemporaries. Bach used slurs most commonly over figures, which were easily recognizable to performers; it was natural to slur them because they were usually elaborations of a single note (deriving originally from patterns of improvised ornaments added to melodies).[207] 'Figural slurring' was useful in marking appropriate accents and

---

[202] Cf. Philip (1992), 30.   [203] Muffat also included staccato among ornaments. See Butt (1990), 41, 45.
[204] Harnoncourt (1988), 41.
[205] He rarely marked wind parts very carefully, however. Butt (1990: 120) points out that one exception is the later parts to the Easter Oratorio. The articulation in the aria with hautbois d'amour solo is indeed elaborate: it contains many slurs, and suggests that Bach preferred his hautboy parts played that way.
[206] Bach's performance parts often clarify and amplify his autograph scores, showing how he 'interpreted his own music from the viewpoint of performer'.   [207] Butt (1990), 17, 19 ff., 113, 114, 140, 192 ff.

delineating musical lines.[208] Bach also used slurs as technical instructions (mostly for strings)[209] or with certain motifs whose essential character depended on their being slurred. He also occasionally used slurs as 'phrase marks' in the modern sense, as for instance the long slur in the hautboy solo at the beginning of the Adagio in the first Brandenburg Concerto, which includes a number of different figures.

f. The messa di voce, *or 'fine swell'* The *messa di voce* (lit. 'placing the voice') was originally a vocal ornament. Tosi (1723) thought it should be used infrequently, but later eighteenth-century writers encouraged its use on every long note, including fermatas and the beginnings of cadenzas. On woodwinds, it was associated with the flattement (see below, §K.3).

Several authors commented on the hautboy's ability to make this ornament. Fischer noted (*c.*1780b: i) that 'The Hoboy played well, has a delicacy superior to any Wind Instrument now in use; and when blown and fingered by a skilful Performer, you have the sweetness of tone, the fine swell, the pleasing grace, and every other beauty, necessary to charm the Mind and delight the Ear.' Wragg (1792: 13):

A Swell . . . is executed by touching the Note, over which it is placed, at the first gently, and by degrees increasing the tone till it arrives at its full pitch; then diminishing it almost imperceptibly, till it falls off to its first softness. This I cannot recommend too much, having one of the finest effects on the ear which the Instrument is capable of producing.

The hautbois d'amour part to BWV 201/9 (1729), an aria with tenor and continuo, begins with an effect similar to a *messa di voce*. The hautbois d'amour's long e2 is marked *piano* at the beginning and *forte* halfway through the bar. The effect is repeated on a g2 in bar 3, and later in the piece.

In the 1770s both Burney and Leopold Mozart were struck by Carlo Bezzozi's use of the *messa di voce*. Leopold Mozart wrote to his wife and son (28 May 1778):

sonderheitlich zeichnet er sich in den Aushaltungen aus, wo er mit einer unbegreiflichen Athemlänge anwachsend und abnehmend aushält, ohne auch nur im geringsten in der reinen Intonation zu wanken. Diese messa di voce kam mir aber schier zu oft, und machte mir die nämliche traurige Wirkung, wie die Töne des Glasinstruments oder der Harmonica, dann es war fast die nämliche Klangart.	What is particularly remarkable is his ability to sustain his notes and his power to increase and decrease their volume, without introducing even the slightest quiver into his very pure tone. But this *messa di voce* was too frequent for my taste and has the same melancholy effect on me as the tones of the glass harmonica, for it produces almost the same kind of sound.[210]

---

[208] Inconsistencies in articulation between hautboys and violins or voices in unison might reveal something of the character of articulation on the hautboy. Butt convincingly demonstrates, however, that such inconsistencies are rare, and when they do exist, differ only in details, while the accent pattern and general effect remain essentially similar. Cf. Butt (1990), 32, 89, 119–22, 129, 132, 163, 210. He cites also Dadelsen and Dürr, who came to similar conclusions.

[209] Butt (1990), 103.

[210] Trans. based on Anderson (1938), 798–9.

Burney wrote (1773: ii. 45–7): 'Bezzozi's *messa di voce*, or swell, is prodigious; indeed, he continues to augment the force of a tone so much, and so long, that it is hardly possible not to fear for his lungs.'

With the development of the key-system oboe, the *messa di voce* passed into the realm of a technical exercise, and was being used in that way by Sellner in his oboe method (1825: 4).

3. Conclusion

Given the eighteenth-century conception of music, the use of dynamics and articulation to bring out the hierarchy of beats, dissonances, and figures was only logical. And despite its lack of pertinence, it is no wonder the long-line is so pervasive in present-day performances of earlier music. The techniques of the Baroque (and Classical) periods that tended to bring out individual notes and small gestures rather than the sweeping line are the ones that are the least familiar and least used now: unequal tonguing, *notes inégales*, the emphasis given to 'good' beats, uneven tempo, extravagant dynamic changes, the *messa di voce*, note shaping, and flattements.

Every aspect of seventeenth- and eighteenth-century music seemed to combine, in fact, to break up the long-line phrase into points of greater and lesser emphasis. And each of the steps the key-system oboe took away from the hautboy helped it produce the later concept of broader phrasing, a concept that can thus be seen as the fundamental motive and cause of all the developments that eventually culminated in the key-system oboe, and all those characteristics that distinguish it now from the hautboy.

J. Paired Tonguing

It is ironic that with the enhanced ability of Baroque instruments to articulate, the signs for detaching and slurring ('articulation' in its more specific sense) were not regarded as essential to write down. Composers normally limited themselves to the odd slur, dot, and vertical stroke. Musicians were evidently expected to effect subtleties of articulation without specific advice from the composer. On woodwind instruments, the everyday act of tonguing had certain interesting nuances, because unequal, paired tonguing patterns were the norm during the hautboy's period.[211]

Paired tonguings already had a long history by the time the hautboy was developed.[212] The sources that described them were written all over Europe, and

---

[211] For further background on this subject, see Haynes (1997b).
[212] The first known printed instructions for woodwinds by Ganassi (1535) described several forms.

extended until well after the end of the period covered in this book.[213] Most of the information survives in traverso tutors, many of which stated that the syllables applied to woodwind instruments in general.[214]

Combining two contrasting tongue movements like *tu* and *ru* gave a woodwind player two technical possibilities that were difficult with the single tongue: first, a means of sustaining tempo in extended passages of quick notes through a rebounded tongue motion, and second, the creation of a pattern of repeated strong and weak stress. The two basic kinds of paired tonguing were *lombardic*, which put the accent on the first syllable (as in *tú-ru*) and *pointed*, where the accent was on the second syllable (as in *tu-rú*). Lombardic tonguing was used for quick tempos and was primarily meant as a technical aid. Pointed tonguing was used in slower movements as an expressive device; for obvious reasons, it died out when the long-line phrase became dominant in the nineteenth century.

The syllable *ru* (or *ri*) was pronounced in the French of the time with the 'lingual' or 'dental' *R*, similar to the modern Spanish and Italian *R*. The lingual *R* is essentially a quick, light *D* enclosed at its beginning and end by a vowel, as in *uh-dúh* or *ah-dóo*. Since *ru* thus effectively began with a vowel, it was impractical to use as the first syllable of a series. As Hotteterre wrote, 'You must only observe never to pronounce RU on a Shake, nor on two successive Notes, because RU ought always to be intermixt alternativly with TU.'[215] The *ru* worked well when preceded by *tu*, however (as in *tuh-dúh* or *too-dóo*). Quantz wrote:

Il faut s'appliquer à prononcer très fortement & distinctement la lettre *r*. Cela fait à l'oreille le même effet que lors qu'on se sert de *di*, en jouant de la simple langue: quoique il ne paroisse pas ainsi à celui qui joue.[216]

Try to pronounce the letter *R* very sharply and clearly. It produces the same effect on the ear as the single-tongue *di*, although it does not seem so to the player.

The use of syllables to symbolize these tonguings has tempted some modern writers to compare them with sung texts and even to suggest that they directly emulated the rhythms of the French language.[217] The connection between woodwind articulation and the French language is hardly automatic, however. While it is probably true that French was spoken by woodwind players, by 1700 most of them were not native Frenchmen and French was not their mother tongue.

That articulation syllables and unequal tonguing were associated with any national style or specific language is not indicated by the evidence. In a Largo by

---

[213] There are twenty-eight sources extending from Ganassi (1535) to Drouet (*c.*1827); the most relevant are the fifteen from Mersenne (1636) to Lorenzoni (1779). Most of the texts are included in the appendices of Castellani and Durante (1987).

[214] Figuratively this may have been true, although (as we shall discuss below) the articulation of reed instruments and flutes differs significantly.   [215] Hotteterre (*c.*1729), 20.

[216] Quantz (1752), VI, ii §2.   [217] Cf. Ranum (1992) and (1995).

Corelli, Hotteterre demonstrated pointing with no hesitation.[218] Quantz described pointing without a hint that it was particularly French. As discussed elsewhere, woodwind technique at this time was not yet as parochial as it was to become with the rise of nationalism in the nineteenth century.

In any case, one of the arts of the instrumentalist was to express metre without the help of words. It would have pleased people to hear instruments evoke the vocal model and then proceed to extend its technical possibilities, suggesting an impossible virtuosity in matters of range and articulation. As Mattheson pointed out (1739: 82),

Ein Spieler, oder der für Instrumente was setzet, muß alles, was zu einer guten Melodie und Harmonie erfordert wird, viel fleißiger beobachten, als ein Sänger, oder der für Sing-Stimmen componiert: dies weil man bey dem Singen die deutlichsten Worte zum Beistande hat; woran es hergegen bey Instrumenten allemahl fehlet.	An instrumentalist, or a composer of instrumental music, must more carefully consider all the necessities of good melody and harmony than a singer or vocal composer, since in singing one has the aid of the clearest words, which by contrast are missing with instruments.

This brings to mind Tosi's comment (quoted above, §E.1) on the resemblance of the hautboy to a voice without words. North (c.1710–28) even suggested that (although the hautboy could not pronounce words) it was superior to the voice in articulation:

Beside what the lipps performe by pressing or easing the plates [of the reed] under action, the tongue hath a notable office, of stopping the sound by touching the slitt, and of letting it goe againe, which distinguisheth the notes so precisely, that devision is performed as distinct upon the Haut-bois as upon any other instrument; which the mouth cannot doe neer so well, tho' the lipps are tormented to effect it.[219]

Direct imitation of vocal pronunciation was not the issue here, but rather a close relationship. It is unlikely that any letter of any alphabet accurately represented the real movements of the tongue in articulating music on woodwind instruments. Describing them by analogy to spoken syllables was merely a means of conceiving them; at the time, the letter *R* corresponded most closely to the bounce the tongue needed. The *ru* or *ri* was one side of the coin and had no meaning by itself; it was just the rebound in the linked tongue movement of *tu-ru* or *ti-ri*.

As Loulié (c.1685: 200) warned, sources that described tonguing patterns were not entirely consistent.

---

[218] Mather (1973: 6) wrote 'From Hotteterre in 1719 to Mussard around 1780 . . . , French theorists made no distinction between French and Italian music in regard to the unequal performance of sixteenth-notes [Mather suggests that eighth-notes may have been differently performed], and they freely mixed examples from both countries to demonstrate their rules . . .'   [219] North (1959), 230.

[Ceux qui enseignent] ont chacun leur manière particulière, et souvent un même maître se sert indifféremment de tu tu ru tu tu, ou de tu ru tu ru tu; Touttes ces manières peuvent être bonnes . . .[220]	[Each teacher] has his individual manner, and often the same musician will sometimes use *tu tu ru tu tu* and sometimes *tu ru tu ru tu*. All these ways can be good . . .

1. The hautboy and paired tonguing

The first known set of instructions for the hautboy, Bismantova (1688), mentioned the use of paired tonguing on the instrument:

E osservar bene anco in quest'Instrumento le Regole del Flauto, si per le Mani, e Dita, come per il Fiato, e Lingue Dritte, e Roverse et altre cose, che possono accadere.	The rules for the Flute apply also to this instrument [the hautboy], as much for the hands, the fingers, the breathing, the *Lingue Dritte*, and *Roverse*, as for everything else that may happen.

The *lingua roversa* or *riversa* (té-re-lé-re) had in fact gone out of style by this time;[221] the *lingua dretta* (or *lingua dritta*) was the lombardic tonguing, *té-re*, given in French sources as *tú-ru*.

The cornett, recorder, and traverso (for which most tonguing instructions were written) had the advantage over reed instruments in tonguing, because there was nothing projecting into the mouth. The *tu* and *ru* were thus performed very much like they were spoken. In hautboy articulation, the tongue did not actually touch the teeth or mouth in the way described in these tutors; the reed was in the way, and it was the reed that the tongue touched. Quantz wrote of players of the hautboy and bassoon

Il faut seulement remarquer à l'égard du coup de langue par *ti*, qu'au lieu de courber la pointe de la langue, & de la presser en haut au palais, comme cela se fait à la Flute, il faut étendre toute droite la langue, parce que l'on prend l'anche entre les lévres.[222]	For the tongue-stroke *ti*, I would like to say only that instead of curving the tip of the tongue and pressing it upwards against the palate, as is done on the flute, they should extend the tongue straight forward, since the reed is taken between the lips.

Except at very slow speeds, the only physical distinction that could be made between syllables on the hautboy was between *T* and *D*, and thus the audible difference was slight. That would explain why Hotteterre noted that ' 'twill be proper to observe, that tipping with the Tongue ought to be more, or less articulate,

---

[220] Loulié, MS 6355, fo. 200ʳ.
[221] It is documented as early as 1535, and Bismantova in 1677 is in fact the last source to describe it.
[222] Quantz (1752), VI, suppl. §2.

according to the Instrument on which you play, for 'tis soften'd on the German Flute, more distinct on the Common Flute, and very Strong on the Hautboy.'[223]

With these observations in mind, Garnier's conception of hautboy articulation as late as *c.*1802 might not have been very different from that of an hautboy player at the beginning of the eighteenth century:

Il n'existe qu'un coup de langue, puis qu'il n'y a qu'une maniere d'articuler le son sur un instrument à vent. mais cette articulation peut être forte ou floible [*sic*], nette ou molle, suivant le caractère de musique.[224]	There is only one kind of tongue-stroke. Furthermore, there is but one way to articulate sound on a wind instrument. But this articulation can be stronger or weaker, sharper or softer, depending on the character of the music.

Garnier then demonstrated five different shades of single-tonguing. Quantz also used the metaphor of shades in describing tonguing:

De même qu'il y a plusieurs diverses couleurs qui tiennent le milieu entre le noir & le blanc, de même aussi on doit trouver entre les coups de langue rudes & mols, plusieurs coups moderés, & que par conséquent on peut exprimer le *ti* & le *di* de plus d'une maniére.[225]	Just as there are several different shades between black and white, you should find several degrees of tongue-stroke between the roughest and the mildest. Thus *ti* and *di* can be expressed in more than one way.

Freillon-Poncein, who gave very precise instructions for unequal tonguing, nowhere suggested that the hautboy (which was the principal instrument handled in his book) could not use them. Diderot (1751–72: 70) wrote of the hautboy that

A l'égard des coups de langue . . . ils se font comme sur la flûte traversiere.	As for the tongue-strokes . . . they are done as on the traverso.

Quantz also noted that

Ceux qui s'apliquent à l'un de ces instrumens [le Hautbois & le Basson] peuvent profiter . . . des instructions qu'on a données pour l'usage des deux sortes de coups de langue par *ti* & *tiri* . . .	Those who apply themselves to one of these instruments [the hautboy or bassoon] can benefit . . . from the instructions provided on the two types of tongue-stroke, *ti* and *tiri* . . .

But for hautboy players, it is clear that the position of the reed changed the way paired tonguing was accomplished, and the instructions for flutists were sometimes useful only as technical metaphors.

---

[223] Hotteterre (*c.*1729), 20. This appears to be a general remark, not specific to the difference between *tu* and *ru*.
[224] Garnier (*c.*1802), 11.   [225] Quantz (1752), VI, i §12.

There were complex combinations, like the three-note dactylic pattern in equal rhythm (*tú-ru-tu*, as in the word 'desperate'), the dotted jig- or canary-type rhythm (*tú-tu-ru*), the anapest pattern (*tu-ru-* | *tú*, as in the phrase 'Are you well?'), the triple-tongue (*tí-tl-ti*, 'finally'), and four-note units. These patterns were variants of the two principal types of unequal tonguing, lombardic and pointed.

2. Paired tonguing and inequality

Tonguing in pairs could produce (if desired) a natural stress on one of the two notes. The accent could fall on either syllable, but in practice it usually came on the first syllable in faster tempos[226] and on the second in slower ones. Unequal tonguing on woodwinds had its analogies in paired string bowings (upbow–downbow)[227] and keyboard fingerings (using a pair of fingers) that all exploited a potential contrast in stress. It was sometimes explicitly connected with the playing of 'good and bad notes' (that is, notes that were stressed or unstressed based on their musical function) and with rhythmic inequality.[228]

Rhythmic inequality and paired articulation were clearly related, but they were not the same. Inequality was usually produced on the hautboy by using paired articulation. But a player could use paired tonguing without automatically playing unequally; he could choose how much lilt to apply. And at slow speeds, he could play notes unequally using a single-tongue.

Despite the efforts of Sol Babitz (1967), most players today use the term 'notes inégales' to mean the iambic swing represented by a word like 'enough', *tu-rú*. But in the eighteenth century, the concept of *notes inégales* was broader and included lombardic inequality (the 'Scotch snap'), which put the accent on the first syllable, as in the word 'forest'. French writers like Loulié, Freillon-Poncein, and Hotteterre all gave examples of both lombardic inequality and the slower, iambic kind.

3. Expressive articulation: pointing

Any degree of inequality in the iambic rhythm of the word 'baróque', from the mildest to the sharpest, was usually called 'pointing' (*pointer* in French). Barthold Kuÿken (pers. comm.) has observed that pointing is not an ornament (that is, an optional feature). We could add that, once it is established as a pattern within a piece, *not* pointing can act as an ornament, in the sense of an expressive device.

---

[226] On the basis of my own technique, I would define 'faster' as above about four notes = 116.

[227] Cf. Corrette's remark (*c*.1740: 20), reflecting a common opinion of the time, that 'Les coups de langue sont sur la flute ce que les coups d'archet sont sur le violon'. The elaborate system of bowings of the time is reviewed in Boyden (1965).

[228] For a discussion of the relationship between the concepts of 'good and bad notes' and inequality, see Hefling (1993), 35 ff.

Ex. 4.3. Example of pointing taken from Schickhardt's *Principes de la flûte*

In his flute book, Hotteterre introduced the concepts of pointing and the use of slow paired tonguing (*tu-rú*) at the same time, leading to the impression that the two practices were parallel and connected in his way of thinking:

You must observe that quavers are not always to be play'd equally, but that you must in certain movements make one long, and one short, which is also regulated by their number when they are even. You make the first long, the second short, and so on—when they are odd, you do quite the reverse, that is called pointing.[229]

Pointing can be approximately represented as a sixteenth-note pick-up followed by an accented dotted eighth. There were, however, many degrees of pointing. Whether pointing was explicitly written out (as in Ex. 4.3, taken from Schickhardt's *Principes de la flûte* (*c.*1710–12))[230] or automatically applied to equally notated notes, it used the *tu-rú* tonguing. *Overdotting*, as in overtures, was an extreme example of pointing.

Pointing cannot be either perceived or expressed beyond a certain tempo. Thinking of the violin, Hefling observed (1993: 143):

Very subtle inequality can be brought off only at a relatively moderate pace, while a stronger ratio of roughly 2:1 is manageable in quicker pieces. But at a certain point (particularly when sixteenth-notes predominate), the bowing becomes too awkward for string players to project much more than the ordinary stress that distinguishes 'good' and 'bad' notes, and down-bow from up-.[231]

When this juncture was reached, Quantz suggested adding slurs over two notes.[232] It is also at about this speed that lombardic tonguing begins to work well. Thus pointed articulation is necessarily associated with slow and moderate tempos.

Loulié (*c.*1685) gave five examples of pointed tonguing (Exs. 4.4–8), the first (Ex. 4.4) being similar to one of Freillon-Poncein's (Ex. 4.9) and one of Hotteterre's (Ex. 4.10). Freillon-Poncein noted that pointed tonguing was used for tempos below 'tres vite' (for which he used lombardic tonguing). Schickhardt (*c.*1710–12)

---

[229] Hotteterre (*c.*1729), 17.   [230] Quoted in Mather (1973), 36.
[231] It also begins to sound slightly ridiculous.   [232] Quantz (1752), VI, ii §8.

Ex. 4.4. Example of tonguing from Loulié *c.*1685

Ex. 4.5. Example of tonguing from Loulié *c.*1685

Ex. 4.6. Example of tonguing from Loulié *c.*1685

Ex. 4.7. Example of tonguing from Loulié *c.*1685

Ex. 4.8. Example of tonguing from Loulié *c.*1685

Ex. 4.9. Example of tonguing from Freillon-Poncein 1700

Ex. 4.10. Example of tonguing from Hotteterre 1707

Ex. 4.11. Hautboy part to BWV 243/3, first bar (1723 version)

Ex. 4.12. Hautbois d'amour part to BWV 243/3, first bar
(later version, 1732–5)

showed it in several musical situations. Quantz (1752: VI, ii) gave a detailed description of pointed tonguing (which he called *ti-ri*) as one of the three principal articulations (the other two being single-tonguing and *did'll*). He used pointed tonguing in 'passagework of moderate speed'.

Repeating Hotteterre's observation, Quantz noted that one cannot begin a passage with *ri*, so when the first note is on a down-beat, the first two notes are pronounced *ti* (*ti-ti-ri-ti-ri* etc.). *Tu* was often used as a neutral beginning, before the real tonguing pattern started (cf. Exs. 4.4 and 4.9). Ranum (1995: 221) compares the neutral first *Tu* to the lead-in word often found in songs; this word was normally unimportant, although it might exceptionally be treated as an accented monosyllable, like *Ah!* or *Oh!*.

Although earlier writers were reluctant to do so, Quantz did not hesitate to use pointed tonguing in arpeggios. He preferred *di-ri* rather than *ti-ri* for faster tempos.

The aria 'Quia respexit humilitatem' in Bach's *Magnificat* presents an interesting question related to pointing. In its first version (BWV 243a/3, performed at Christmas, 1723), the first bar of the hautboy part was dotted (Ex. 4.11), whereas in the later version (1732–5) for hautbois d'amour, it was notated evenly (Ex. 4.12). The dotting of the first bar presumably implied dotting throughout the aria. The dots resemble pointing, but in pointing, the short note was deliberately connected to the next long note, whereas Bach here added slurs from long note to short, so the passage became something quite different. However we interpret the slurs, either as instructions for tonguing or as indications of accents, by using them Bach made it clear that he was not thinking here of pointing.[233]

---

[233] Bach used the same articulation in the hautboy part to BWV 84/1 (of which an autograph score and original parts survive). The soprano, however has *tierces coulées* slurred from the short to the next long note. Cf. Butt (1990), 128, ex. 59.

4. Tonguing for fast tempos

Lombardic tonguing was used for speed. Two articulations when played as a pair were easier to express quickly than the simple *tu-tu* used in single-tonguing. As Drouet put it in *c*.1827:

E rimarcato per una lunga esperienza essere più facile pronunciare prestissimamente più volte di seguito due Sillabe che una sola.[234]	Long experience has indicated to me that it is easier to pronounce two syllables quickly when there are several in succession, than a single one.

Woodwind players use the modern double-tongue to avoid fatigue in extended passages of quick articulation. A few notes can be tongued quickly with single-tonguing, but if there are more than about three of them, the tongue begins to slow down. The speed at which a modern player switches from single- to double-tonguing depends on how rapidly the notes must be played; there comes a moment (for most skilled professionals, somewhere around four notes at 120) when an extended passage of quick notes can no longer be single-tongued. At this point, the player changes into a kind of 'articulation overdrive', using double-tonguing. It seems reasonable to assume that the same physical problem motivated the development and use of the earlier lombardic tonguings.

There were three varieties of lombardic tonguing. The most common form used contrasting movements of the tip of the tongue (for instance, *té-re*, *tú-ru*; Ex. 4.13). A second form involved the front and back of the tongue alternately (the early double-tongue, *did'll*; Ex. 4.14), and a third (which is the modern double-tongue, *té-ke*) alternated a tongue-tip motion with a throat constriction.

By 1700 (when *lingua riversa* was apparently no longer in use), the fastest pair given by Freillon-Poncein, 'quand le mouvement de la mesure est tres vite', was *tú-ru*. Quantz described the same tonguing in 1752, and it survived until well into the nineteenth century.[235]

Bismantova in 1677[236] used this pattern for two isolated smaller notes mixed with longer ones (Ex. 4.15); it was also used this way by Loulié *c*.1685/4 and 7[237] (but not nos. 11, 12, and 13, where it would be expected), Freillon-Poncein 1700/F, and Hotteterre 1707/5, 8, 11, 12, 13, and 14. The same pattern appeared in Quantz 1752/III/12, but instead of using lombardic tonguing, he made both sixteenths and

---

[234] Artusi in 1600 (fo. 4ᵛ, quoted in Castellani and Durante 1987: 130) implied that paired tonguings were fast by commenting that the single-tongue was an example of a slow articulation.

[235] It was discussed by Drouet in *c*.1827 (as *Deú-Reu* or *De-Re*).

[236] NB. These are not the hautboy instructions.

[237] Where many musical examples are given in a source, they are identified as here by their numerical order.

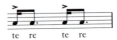

te   re   te   re

Ex. 4.13. First example of lombardic tonguing

did 'll   did 'll

Ex. 4.14. Example of the early double-tongue, *did'll*

te   le   re te

Ex. 4.15. Tonguing pattern by Bismantova

thirty-seconds pointed (Ex. 4.16).[238] He did use *dí-ri* for isolated sixteenths in III/30 and 31, however (Exs. 4.17 and 4.18). Hotteterre wrote: 'You understand that you must pronounce TU RU on the two first Quavers, or Semiquavers of an even number, which is frequently practis'd when two Quavers are intermixt with Crotchets, or else two Semiquavers with Quavers, 'tis done for a greater Sweetning, and 'tis the Ear that must decide it.'[239] Hotteterre 1707/10 used *tú-ru* for a series of thirds (Ex. 4.19). Quantz (1729–41: 70, Allemande) gave *tí-ri* for the same passage, which he called 'unegal aber nicht als Puncte' (unequal but not pointed—in other words, lombardic).[240]

The pattern eighth–two sixteenths–eighth (Ex. 4.20) inevitably incorporated lombardic tonguing on the two sixteenths.

If *tú-ru* or *dí-ri* was not fast enough, Quantz reserved *did'll* for the quickest passagework on the flute, devoting a long section to it (1752, ch. 6/iii). *Díd'll* was an articulation he had apparently invented himself,[241] and it involved using the front and back of the tongue alternately. The second half of this articulation, *d'll*, did not contain a vowel and was not done with the tip of the tongue. But as he wrote, it was not effective on the hautboy.

---

[238] Cf. Hefling (1993), 27, who describes certain sources for whom inequality 'descends' to lower note values.

[239] Hotteterre (*c.*1729), 19.

[240] Quantz (1729–41) distinguished 'ungleich' notes that were written unequally (using the pattern *ti-ti-ri-dl-ri-dl*, which, like *did'll*, cannot be done on the hautboy because it involves using the back of the tongue) from pointed notes ('Unegal'; *di-di-ri-di-ri*).

[241] He may have adapted it from the *lingua riversa* of recorder and curtal tutors (cf. Mather 1973: 48).

Ex. 4.16. Example of pointing from Quantz

Ex. 4.17. Quantz's use of *di-ri*

Ex. 4.18. Quantz's use of *di-ri*

Ex. 4.19. Hotteterre's use of *tú-ru*

Ex. 4.20. Example of lombardic tonguing on two isolated sixteenths

Le Basson a encore cet avantage sur le Hautbois, qu'il peut se servir, aussi bien que les joueurs de Flute, de la Double langue *did'll*.[242]

Like the flutist, the bassoonist has the advantage over the hautboy player in the possibility of also using the double-tongue *did'll*.

[242] Quantz (1752), VI, suppl. §3. Probably thinking of Freillon-Poncein and Hotteterre, Sellner in 1825 commented on articulation (p. 3) 'Es geschieht nicht, wie in einigen Schulen für dieses Instrument irrig gelehrt wird, durch Anlegen der Zungenspitze an die Zähne, sondern dadurch, dass die Spitze der Zunge gerade an die Öffnung des Rohres gesetzt, die Luft dadurch gespannt (zurück gehalten) und ungefähr die Sylbe *ti* ausgesprochen wird . . .'

The French sources *c*.1685–1707 had not mentioned *did'll* as a possibility for any instrument, using only the tongue-tip (lombardic tonguing, *tú-ru*).[243]

Just before discussing *did'll*, however, Quantz offered another, faster alternative to lombardic tonguing. If *tú-ru* or *di-ri* was not fast enough, he recommended a nuanced version of the 'slur-two tongue-two' pattern (or its reverse; cf. Pl. 4.14). After lombardic tonguing, this was evidently the hautboy player's normal resort for articulating the fastest passages. Vanderhagen (*c*.1790: 14) offered the pattern slur-two tongue-two as 'le Coup de langue le plus beau et le plus usité' (the most beautiful and most common tongue-stroke), and called it 'le Coup de langue ordinaire' (the normal tongue-stroke). But he too nuanced it as follows:

Il faut prononcer Té *a* Tu Tu car si vous prononcée [*sic*] Té Té sur les deux dernieres nottes, le passage seroit trop haché, il faut aussi que la premiere de chaque quatre reçoive une expression un peu plus marquée que les trois autres.	One should say 'Té *a* Tu Tu', because if you say 'Té Té' on the last two notes, the passage will be too chopped up. The first note of each [group of] four should also be stressed a little more than the other three.

Quantz and Vanderhagen are relatively late sources, and the earlier instructions do not include the slur-two tongue-two pattern. Denton (1977: 53) points out that this articulation never appears in Bach's hautboy parts. It has a tendency to create a regular (even mechanical) pattern that ignores the existence of figures and subtleties of melodic grammar, and it seems more appropriate in the simplified phrases of later eighteenth-century music. It is unclear whether it was used before the mid-eighteenth century.

The third kind of lombardic stroke was the modern double-tongue, *té-ke*, a cousin of which, *té-che*, was first mentioned in 1535 by Ganassi (although he called it an 'effetto crudo').[244] There is no historical indication that it was used on the hautboy. In 1677, Bismantova said it was no longer in use, and the next known mention of it (Devienne *c*.1794, as *dóú-gue*) criticized it because, being too regular, it did not allow articulation nuance or expression. Devienne implied that although it was used on the traverso, it did not suit other instruments such as the clarinet, bassoon, hautboy, and horn. Drouet in *c*.1827 was strongly against its use.

In the problematic situation of doubling violins in very quick orchestral passages, hautboy players were not apparently expected to be able to go as fast. Rousseau (1768: 130) proposed that the hautboys should 'be used to mark the principal notes' because of 'the velocity which is wanting, or which ill suits [the hautboy] in certain

---

[243] Cf. Freillon-Poncein 1700/F.

[244] Dalla Casa (1584, i. 1) said of it, '. . . è lingua cruda per sonatori, che vogliano far terribilità . . .'. It is mentioned also by Artusi (1600) and Rognoni (1620).

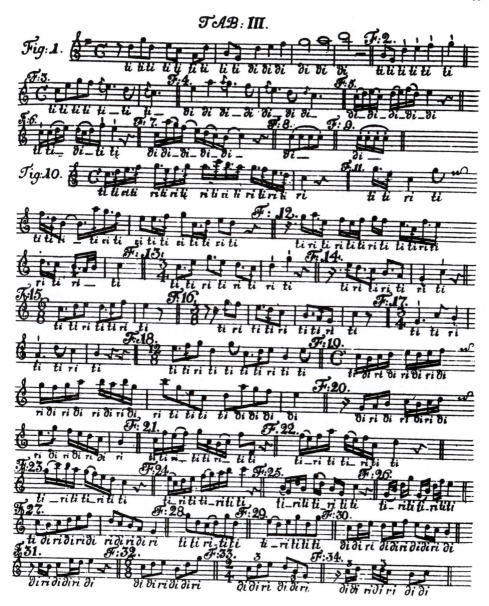

Pl. 4.14. Quantz (1752), parts of Tab. III

quick passages'.[245] This suggests that in groups of four sixteenth notes, the hautboys played only the first, or first and third notes of the group.

5. *The slur as a technical aid*

Quantz in 1752, Lorenzoni in 1779, and Gunn in 1793 continued to advocate pointed articulation. But with the comments of Corrette *c.*1740 (calling the syllables *tu ru* 'une chose absurde') and Moldenit's criticisms of it in 1753,[246] we see the beginnings of the end of the use of most paired tonguings. It is at about this time that the slur began to come into its own.

Slurs, even short ones of two notes only, were not described in wind sources until relatively late;[247] La Barre in his Opus 4 solos of 1702 felt obliged to explain the 'liaison' at length, as if slurs were an unfamiliar concept to his readers. Tosi/Galliard (1742: 53) noted that 'The Use of the *Slur* is pretty much limited in Singing, and is confined within such few Notes ascending or descending, that it cannot go beyond a fourth without displeasing.' This would presumably have applied to the hautboy as well, when it was playing cantabile lines. The technical impossibility of slurring certain upward leaps on the hautboy is discussed below, §M; slurs of intervals larger than a fourth on the hautboy are generally pleasing only for special effects.

If it is true that the popularity of slurring was in inverse proportion to that of paired tonguing, and longer slurring came in during the same period that most kinds of unequal tonguing were gradually going out of style, it would seem that slurring and unequal tonguing were both regarded as means of dealing with extended passages of notes at fast tempos. This in turn implies that hautboy players before the second half of the eighteenth century did not necessarily resort to the slur for its technical advantages.

K. *Vibrato*

1. *Vibrato as an ornament*

Two characteristics of woodwind vibrato have developed since the nineteenth century: (1) using it continuously, and (2) producing it with the breath. As Greta Moens-Haenen points out (1984: 1), there were a number of techniques that resembled modern vibrato in the period we are studying, some affecting the pitch of notes, others of changing intensity on the same pitch; these techniques could be slow, fast, or of changing speed.

---

[245] Text cited in Ch. 5, §A.1.c.

[246] Joachim von Moldenit, *Sei sonate da flauto traverso e basso continuo con un discorso sopra la maniera di sonar il flauto traverso.*   [247] Cf. Bismantova (1677) in Castellani and Durante (1987), 36.

PL. 4.15. Montéclair (1736: 85), examples of the use of flattements

The fundamental difference between the modern and Baroque concept of vibrato is its purpose. In the Baroque period, vibrato was used as an ornament and expressive effect—a spotlight on a particular note. The vibrato of the late twentieth century, by contrast, is seen as an attribute of tone and is therefore used continuously.[248]

Continuous vibrato was rare before this century, and none of the early wind tutors speaks of it[249] (this is logical, since it is of course absurd to apply an ornament continuously). Montéclair commented (1736: 85) that if vibrato was used on every 'strong note, it would become unbearable, as it would produce a wavering melody without contrasts'[250] (cf. Pl. 4.15).

Although the continuous vibrato seems normal to any musician born after 1950, it only became widely used in the 1940s. Robert Philip wrote:

It might come as a surprise to many [performers on period instruments] to learn that one only has to step back to the 1920s to find oboists and flautists playing without vibrato, and string players who use vibrato as 'an effect, an embellishment', rather than as a perpetual tone-intensifier.[251]

According to the distinguished oboist Leon Goosens, in the early part of the twentieth century vibrato 'was rarely, if ever used, and certainly not as a fundamental aspect of tone production'.[252] He himself introduced a constant vibrato in his playing in the Queen's Hall Orchestra in the 1910s, and remembered the disapproval of his colleagues. In recordings of the 1920s, Goossens is the only British

[248] Cf. Moens-Haenen (1984), 56, 57, 58 and Zaslaw (1979), 48. Goossens and Roxburgh (1977), 87, representing the modern approach, write that 'the soul of the sound can justifiably be said to rest in this quality [vibrato]'. Not all modern players agree on the continuous use of vibrato.

[249] Moens-Haenen (1988), 143, 272. Some sources from the second half of the 18th c. rejected continuous vibrato (thereby indicating its existence). There is a reference to 'zitterndem odem' in Agricola (1529, fo. 23), but none in the 17th or 18th cc.; cf. Dickey (1978), 102 and Moens-Haenen (1988), 83.

[250] Several later authors follow his text. Cf. Moens-Haenen (1988), 222.

[251] Philip (1992), 139. See also pp. 109–39 and ch. 5, 'Woodwind vibrato'.

[252] Goosens and Roxburgh (1977), 87.

oboist to use 'a real vibrato', according to Philip (p. 123). A recording of Georges Gillet made in 1905 displays little or no vibrato; Philip reports that recordings of some of Gillet's pupils indicate that they began to use it in the 1920s and 1930s, although rarely as a constant component of tone:

> The general adoption of almost continuous vibrato on strings and most woodwind has had a profound impact on musical expression . . . Vibrato has come to impose a uniform height-ened expression on most playing (and singing). The effect is to deny that any passages are 'unexpressive' or 'neutral'. The idea that 'the steady tone' should predominate, and that vibrato should be used only to intensify carefully selected notes or phrases, as Joachim, Auer, and others insisted less than a century ago, is quite alien to most late twentieth-century string-players and many woodwind-players.[253]

Michel Piguet noted that 'The Romantic period rejected vibrato as being tasteless . . . The late-nineteenth century flute tutor of Paul Taffanel (still in use today) remarks: "le vibrato est mauvais et réservé aux amateurs [vibrato is bad and reserved for amateurs]".'[254]

2. *Vibrato produced by breath*

Breath-vibrato is not mentioned in woodwind sources until the 1790s.[255] Quantz, whose treatment of every aspect of traverso technique was exhaustive, gave no hint of the existence of either breath- or lip-vibrato in 1752; he mentioned only finger-vibrato (which he called 'flattement' in the French version of his book and 'Bebung' in the German). Tromlitz in 1791 (239 ff.) minutely described the flattement (he also called it a *Bebung*), but he indicated that breath-vibrato was indeed being used on the traverso by 1791 (by strongly arguing against its use). But by 1803, Knecht (p. 53) was using the word *Bebung* to mean a breath-vibrato.

a. The tremolo   The *tremolo*, or 'breath stroke', was a group of repeated notes of the same pitch under a slur; it amounted to a breath-vibrato, but was unlike mod-ern vibrato in being rhythmic. Its use was indicated either with a word (usually 'Tremolo') or in musical notation (cf. Pl. 4.16). The corollary effect on the violin has been called the 'bow vibrato'.[256]

The defining characteristic of the tremolo was that it beat in the rhythm of the piece in which it was used (usually eighth notes). It had therefore to be slow enough to be heard as rhythmic, and thus was not as fast as the organ 'tremulant'

---

[253] Philip (1992), 120–7, 138.   [254] Piguet (1997). Cf. Philip (1992), 111.
[255] Moens-Haenen (1988), 83, 95 ff., 272.
[256] Harnoncourt (1988), 128. Cf. the 'slurred tremolo' in Boyden (1965), 266–8.

PL. 4.16. Servaas de Konink, by 1700, Adagio in the twelfth sonata of *XII Sonates*.
Wolfenbüttel: Herzog-August Bibliothek

(which had more in common with the flattement—although it was continuous, it was audible on the organ only on long notes).[257]

The tremolo was of course a type of repeated note. Harnoncourt (1988: 127–8) points out that the act of repeating the same note was a relatively recent invention at the time (he attributes it to Monteverdi), and therefore had a significance that is not obvious nowadays.

The earliest example of the tremolo in hautboy music is in de Konink's XII Sonates (Roger, by 1700). The twelfth sonata has an Adagio marked 'Tremolo' that includes two and four notes, usually at the same pitch, with slurs over them (Pl. 4.16); the bass part also has slurs on pairs of notes of the same pitch. Tremolos were also used in an aria for soprano and two hautboys by Österreich, written for Wolfenbüttel in 1717. Bach used the tremolo regularly for hautboy; examples include BWV 6/1, BWV 114/1, BWV 245/35: 80–1 (the oboe da caccia solo 'Zerfließe, mein Herze' in the St John Passion), and the remarkable Recit 'So geht denn hin', BWV 248/18, with two hautbois d'amour and two oboes da caccia playing *piano* tremolos.[258]

In texted music, the tremolo had a symbolic association with shivering,[259] and thus with cold, fear, awe, death, grief, sleep, and weakness. But with time, it seems gradually to have changed function from a rhetorical figure to a neutral, specialized form of articulation. Already in Sammartini's hautboy sonatas (at least one of which, Rochester MS no. 6, was written in the 1720s), it is used as an abstract technical effect.[260] At the end of Sonata 5/2, there is a bar with a wavy line over eighths on the same pitch, immediately followed by a bar with a slur over eighths on the same pitch (cf. Pl. 4.17); a distinction between the two notations appears to have been intended.[261] Quantz described two closely related effects that may be forms of it in his chapter on tonguing (1752: VI, i §11); later sources also classified the tremolo as a form of articulation.[262]

In 1752 Barbandt published a collection of trios that use the tremolo on single pitches in every sonata, sometimes on both eighth and quarter notes. Boccherini used the wavy line over notes at the same pitch in the first of his Opus 55 Quintets (G. 431), written in 1797.

At the extreme soft end of his articulation examples, Garnier (*c*.1802) showed a 'Fremissement de lévrès' (*sic*; trembling of the lips), consisting of four quarter notes

---

[257] The *vox humana* stop of the Martinikerk organ in Groningen, which Burney said 'resembles a fine hautbois or clarinet' (see above, §E.1), has or had a tremolo which would be interesting to hear on that account.

[258] There are many other examples in Bach; for a list see Moens-Haenen (1988), 242 n. 752.

[259] Moens-Haenen (1984), 2.

[260] Cf. Rochester MS 1/1, 5/2, 5/3, and 6/2. A wavy line appears over a diatonic scale in the hautboy part in bar 2 of the third movement of Gatti's Quartetto in F. See Meyer (1973), 58.

[261] According to Moens-Haenen (1988), 242, these two contrasting notations are used in the two versions of Bach's *Magnificat* (BWV 243a and 243, movement 6, b. 31).

[262] Cf. Dickey (1978), 107, Moens-Haenen (1984), 52 discussing Quantz; Delusse (1761), 10; Dard (1769), 17; Petri (1782), 478–9.

PL. 4.17. Sammartini, end of movement 2 in the 5th Rochester Sonata (MS US-R, p. 49)

with a wavy line above them. No. 13 of the fifty-five lessons (p. 17) shows the wavy line in the teacher's part, and the VIe Duo (p. 43) shows it over a long held a2. Whether this effect originated with the lips or the breath is a moot point, as the functions of the two are difficult to distinguish. But Sellner (1825: 3), in discussing shades of nuance in articulation by using *ti* or *di*, also suggested an articulation done with the lips.

b. The glissando   Moens-Haenen (1988: 242 ff.) draws attention to a specialized form of tremolo called the *glissando*, marked with a wavy line but distinguished by its appearance over progressions of half-steps. She noted that almost without exception, Bach's use of the wavy line was over such chromatic lines (in other cases, he used a slur over repeated notes of the same pitch).

It is unclear how the glissando was played, but the obvious method would have been to play it rhythmically like a tremolo, using some suitable subdivision of the time signature.

Although the glissando was rarely notated, an ornament that matches its features (a wavy line over progressions of half-steps) was described in several sources.[263] It may have been regularly applied to chromatic lines, even when it was not marked

---

[263] Rousseau (1687), Danoville (*L'art de toucher le dessus et basse de violle*, 1687), Montéclair (1736). Cf. Moens-Haenen (1988), 242 ff.

by the composer. A place it might have been effectively applied is in 'Aria 2' in the second Partia of Telemann's *Kleine Cammer-Music*, a long descending chromatic line that could have been marked with the breath in eighth notes, thus coinciding with the movement in the Bass. A striking case of a probable glissando is BWV 116/2: 43–4; it is not marked in the hautbois d'amour part, but only in the alto, which has the same figure two bars earlier: a wavy line over the word 'Angst', climbing on long notes chromatically.

3.　*The flattement (softening, finger vibrato)*

The flattement was called by both Hotteterre (1707: 29) and Loulié (c.1685) a 'tremblement mineur', or 'lesser trill'. It had different names in different countries; its English name was the 'softening', which exactly captures its effect of briefly unfocusing a note's tone quality.[264]

The flattement was already in use in the second half of the seventeenth century and is documented into the mid-nineteenth century. Hotteterre described it as follows:

> The Softening, or lesser Shake, is made almost like the usual Shake, there is this difference, that you always end with the finger off, except on *D-la-sol-re*, for the most part they are made on holes more distant, and some on the edge, or half the hole only, it participates of a lower Sound, which is contrary to the Shake.[265]

Hotteterre went on to explain that some flattements had to be produced in another way. For fingerings where no further holes could be half-closed (as on the six-fingered D), flattements were made by 'shaking the Flute' with the right hand (Corrette c.1740: 30 says the same).

The fact that shaking the instrument was used as a fall-back has interesting implications. First, since it 'imitates a usual Softening', it gives us an idea how the other flattements done with the fingers would have sounded. Second, it says something about the existence or absence of breath- and lip-vibrato in this period. Shaking is clearly a dubious recourse because it affects embouchure: this would have been the moment to resort to a breath- or lip-vibrato, had they been options. The resort to shaking thus implies that no one at this time was making a vibrato produced by the breath.

For us at the end of the twentieth century, raised in the modern tradition of breath-vibrato and the long-line phrase, the benefits of a vibrato operated by the fingers are not immediately obvious. But in fact, vibrato is easier to control with finger movements than with either the diaphragm or the throat. With fingers, vibrato can become gradually more intense (that is, faster, or wider, or both) as a

---

[264] For a more general survey of the use of the flattement on woodwinds, see Haynes (1997a).
[265] Hotteterre (c.1729), 22.

note becomes louder, and more relaxed as the note softens. This greater control of both speed and amplitude is more appropriate to music that involves many quick turns of direction, accompanied by complex dynamic shading, like that of the seventeenth and eighteenth centuries. Because of the way it is produced, the kind of vibrato used on modern instruments could not have accommodated such frequent and rapid changes. It was only with the simpler shape of the long-line phrase that a continuous breath- or lip-vibrato became effective.

Vibrato does not need to be notated now, because for most singers and players it is always 'on'. Signs for it were not common in eighteenth-century parts either,[266] but when it did appear, it was usually notated with a horizontal wavy line over a single note.[267]

Hotteterre in 1707 gave detailed instructions and fingerings for the flattement, and a generation later it was described in the traverso tutor attributed to Corrette (*c*.1740). This is of interest because Corrette was quite up to date, systematically rejecting techniques he considered old-fashioned (paired-tonguing syllables, for instance). The flattement thus evidently survived the change in French taste that Corrette's tutor reflects, as well as new developments in instrument construction.

Nowadays, the flattement is usually presumed to be exclusively French. But it first appeared in a Dutch tutor for the recorder published in 1654 (van Blanckenburgh). It was subsequently described in a number of early English sources.[268] And its most complete description came from Germany in 1791 (Tromlitz). The flattement was used all over Europe, and there is every reason to think that Bach, Handel, and Vivaldi heard it regularly.

Fingerings for flattements were given by (among others) van Blanckenburgh 1654 (recorder), Loulié *c*.1685 (recorder), Hotteterre 1707 (traverso and recorder), Corrette *c*.1740 (traverso), and Mahaut 1759 (traverso).[269]

As Hotteterre wrote, flattements could be made by touching the edge of a strategic hole, in a way similar to trilling. But he said that only 'some' were done 'on the edge, or half the hole only'. How were the others done? The anonymous *Compleat Flute-Master* of 1695 (and subsequent editions to 1765) remarked that the flattement (called an 'open shake or sweetning' [!]), was performed by 'shaking your finger *over* the half hole immediately below yᵉ note to be sweetned ending with it off'.[270] This technique is clearly different from touching the edge of the hole. Corrette (*c*.1740: 30) was more specific:

---

[266] As Corrette remarked (*c*.1740), 30.

[267] Loulié (*c*.1685), Paris MS Rés. 2060, Hotteterre (1707) and (1738), the manuscript version of Hotteterre's trios, Philidor 1717/18, Corrette (*c*.1740), Miller (*c*.1799), and Nicholson (*c*.1816 and 1821). Nicholson (1821) is cited in Boland (1996), 2. For other vibrato signs, see Moens-Haenen (1988), 283–4.

[268] Hudgebut (1679); Salter (1683); Carr (1686); Anon. (1695); Anon. (1706), all for the recorder. These sources are cited in Moens-Haenen (1988).   [269] All these charts are included in Moens-Haenen (1988), 97 ff.

[270] Italics mine. Quoted in Moens-Haenen (1988), 91.

Le Flattement se fait avec un doigt qu'il faut bien allonger *sur le bord, ou audessus du trou*[271] et audessous de ceux qui sont bouchés. Il faut observer que le doigt ne bouche point le trou sur lequel se fait le flattement, mais le baisser doucement et le tenir en l'air en finissant excepté sur le second ré.

The flattement is done with a well-extended finger, *on the edge or above the hole*[272] and below the ones already closed. Notice that the finger does not actually close the hole on which the flattement is made, but is rather gently lowered, and finishes by being held in the air (except on d2).

The flattement could thus be produced in several different ways. Since each fingering had its own sound and acoustic properties, the only way the same effect could be achieved on all of them was by adjusting the finger motion for each particular note. It was therefore necessary for the player to have a range of techniques to choose from.

As to speed, Loulié (*c*.1685) spoke of beating the edge of the hole 'slowly.' Hotteterre wrote in 1708:

On observera qu'il faut faire des flattements . . . aussi bien que les tremblements et battements, plus lents ou plus précipités, selon le mouvement et le caractere des Pièces.

Note that flattements should be made . . . like trills and mordents, slower or faster, depending on the speed and character of the piece.

When Hotteterre stated that the flattement 'participates of a lower Sound, which is contrary to the Shake', he probably meant that the flattement affects only the principal note, while the full trill involves two separate notes. The sources that describe the flattement give the impression that it was not intended to be perceived as a change of pitch. Loulié (who called the flattement a 'balancement' or 'flatté/flatter') wrote:

Pour faire le flatter ou balancement il faut commencer par jouer la note sur laquelle est marqué le flatté, battre aussitot lentement le bord du trou le plus haut de ceux qui restent ouuerts,[273] exceptez le Ier et le 2e qu'on ne bat jamais ensorte que le Ier son ne soit point changé.[274]

To play a flattement or wavering, begin by sounding the note upon which it is marked. Immediately beat the edge of the highest open hole slowly (except for the first and the second [holes], which one never beats) in such a way that the principal note is not altered in any way.

---

[271] Italics mine.   [272] Italics mine.
[273] Loulié (*c*.1685, fo. 202^r, quoted in Moens-Haenen 1988: 96) added that 'Il y a pourtant quelques flattez ou l'on bat d'autres trous'.   [274] Loulié (*c*.1685), fo. 181^r. Quoted in Moens-Haenen (1988), 96.

His description of the *balancement* (vibrato) for singers also warned about not vary-ing the pitch,[275] and various other sources made the same point.[276] Quantz (1752: XIV, §10) also discussed this question indirectly:

Hat man eine lange Note entweder von einem halben oder ganzen Tacte zu halten, welches die Italiäner *messa di voce* nennen; so muß man dieselbe vors erste mit der Zunge weich anstoßen, and fast nur hauchen; alsdenn ganz piano anfangen, die Stärke des Tones bis in die Mitte der Note wachsen lassen; und von da eben wieder so abnehmen, bis an das Ende der Note: auch neben dem nächsten offenen Loche mit dem Finger eine Bebung machen. Damit aber der Ton in währendem Zu- und Abnehmen nicht höher oder tiefer werde, (welcher Fehler aus der Eigenschaft der Flöte entspringen könnte;) so muß man hier die im 22.§ des IV. Hauptstücks gegebene Regel in Uebung bringen: so wird der Ton mit den begleitenden Instrumenten in beständig gleicher Stimmung erhalten, man blase stark oder schwach.

If you must hold a long note for either a whole or a half bar, which the Italians call the *messa di voce*, first tongue it gently, blowing almost not at all; then begin pianissimo, allowing the strength of the tone to swell to the middle of the note, and from there, soften it to the end of the note. At the same time, make a flattement with your finger on the nearest open hole. To keep the tone from becoming higher or lower during the crescendo and diminuendo (a defect which could originate in the nature of the flute), the rule given in §22 of Chapter IV should be applied here; the tone will then always remain in tune with the accompanying instruments, whether you blow strongly or weakly.

Section 22 of Chapter IV was concerned with tuning corrections for false trills (see above, §G.4.a); the same principle was thus applied to flattements (as 'lesser Shakes').[277] On a woodwind instrument, much could be done to influence pitch with embouchure and breath support. In any case, if the finger-movement was fast, the pitch of a flattement sometimes did not 'have time' to change; the same movement made slowly had more potential effect on pitch.[278]

On the flattement on c♯2 on the traverso, Corrette (*c*.1740: 31) suggested beating on the complete third hole, and commented:

Les anciens le faisoient sur le 2e trou mais il ne vaut rien et baisse le ton d'un Comma.

The old players made it with the second hole, but that is useless and lowers the pitch a comma.

---

[275] Loulié (1696), 73.

[276] See North *c*.1695, fo. 76ᵛ, quoted in Moens-Haenen (1988), 171, on the 'waived' note on the violin; Simpson (1659), 9 (quoted in Donington 1963: 167 and Moens-Haenen 1988: 57–8), describing gamba technique; and Montéclair (1736: 85), speaking of the 'flaté' for singers. [277] See also Quantz (1752), IX, §§9 and 10.

[278] My own experience is that flattements are more effective when there is no change of pitch. Played in this way, the flattement intensifies and excites the tone. Donington (1989: 124) has called vibrato 'the sparkle of the sound', and this phrase describes well the effect of the flattement when it does not alter pitch.

Hotteterre in 1707 did indeed give hole 2, which on a traverso drops this note much more than a comma (about 45 cents, or 2 commas) unless it is done quickly. Using hole 3, as Corrette suggests, has little or no effect on either pitch or tone. Evidently, then, if he was forced to choose, Corrette preferred virtually nothing to 'a comma'.

North[279] associated the 'waived' note on the violin with a 'swelling', and Quantz added (almost as an afterthought) that one added 'eine Bebung' to a *messa di voce*. Most woodwind sources coupled flattements with swells. In *c*.1740 Corrette wrote:

Le flattement se fait pour enfler et diminuer le son.[280]	The flattement is used to swell and diminish the sound.

Mahaut (1759) said something similar.

It is clear that in his *Suittes* of 1717/18 (cf. Pl. 4.18) Philidor related the flattement to a crescendo, since numerous notes that invited one (long notes held over a bar line or leading to a trill on the same note) were marked with the flattement. Philidor rarely noted dynamics in his *Suittes*, but he may in effect have used the flattement sign (which appears frequently in this collection) to indicate dynamic nuance indirectly.[281]

Marais frequently associated vibrato with the mark for 'Enfler' (*e*), which was essentially a *messa di voce*.[282] Leopold Mozart (1756: 104) described his long note with *messa di voce* as accompanied by vibrato, quite slow in the weaker parts of the note, somewhat faster in the stronger.

There was a technical connection between these elements on woodwinds. If the flattement tended to lower pitch, playing louder tended to raise it, and the two actions could counterbalance each other if combined.[283]

Hotteterre wrote: ' 'twou'd be hard to teach a method of knowing exactly all the Notes whereon these Graces are to be play'd, what can be said in generall thereupon, is that the Softenings are frequently made on long Notes . . . the Beats are made more commonly on the short Notes . . .'[284] He confirmed this in 1708:

On observera qu'il faut faire des flattements presque sur toutes les notes longues.	Note that flattements should be made on almost all long notes.

---

[279] (*c*.1695), fo. 76ᵛ, quoted in Moens-Haenen (1988), 171.

[280] Moens-Haenen (1988: 225) points out that Corrette said the same thing in his violin tutor of 1782 (p. 4), over forty years later.

[281] In the introduction to his *Recüeil de trio nouveaux* of 1699, Toinon lists an 'Enflez de Son' among his ornaments, indicated by three horizontal dots above a note; the ornament is used once on p. 5 on successive long notes, and may indicate the flattement. Three dots under a slur also appear on the last note of the first movement of Philidor's *Suitte* number 4 in A minor. According to Dickey (1978), 108, a similar sign (four dots under a slur) appears in Altenburg (1795), 118 as an indication of the tremolo.   [282] Cf. Moens-Haenen (1988), 205.

[283] Barthold Kuÿken (pers. comm.) has observed that 'giving slightly faster air' on the traverso makes it easier to keep the flattement steady.   [284] Hotteterre (*c*.1729), 22.

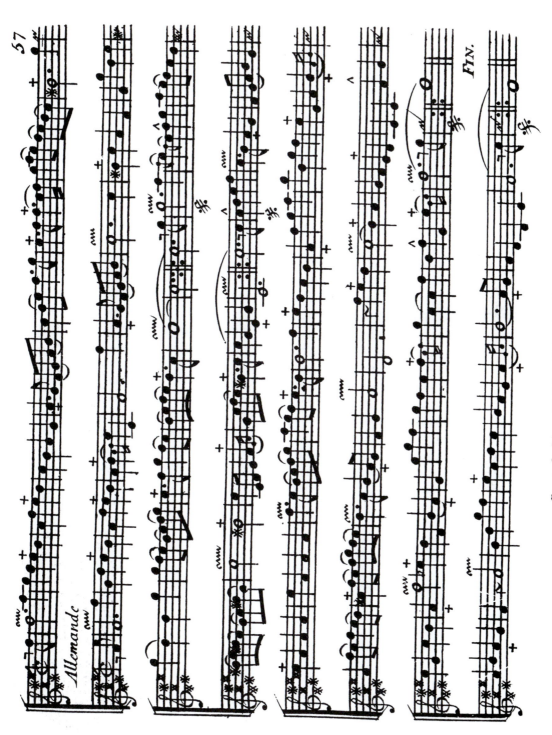

PL. 4.18. Pierre Philidor, *Suites* (1718), p. 57

The New Flute-Master (Anon. 1706: 6) was more specific, advising that all 'ascending long notes [must be] sweetned'. Geminiani (1748) described a wrist vibrato for the violin that he called a 'Close Shake'; although he encouraged violinists to use it 'on any Note whatsoever', he wrote that on the flute it 'must only be made on long Notes'.[285]

In his *Suittes*, Philidor marked flattements with a horizontal wavy line;[286] with the exception of the 'Neufième Suitte', they appear only a few times in most of the movements (see Pl. 4.18). The *Suittes* give a better idea of what Hotteterre meant when he said 'Softenings should be made on almost all long notes'. Most of the notes with flattement are longer than the general movement.[287]

The majority of Philidor's flattements indicate a continuation or reanimation of the line at points where it might otherwise be expected to come to repose. They appear most often on notes in the middle of phrases where emphasis would not otherwise be foreseen by the player; in these cases, they probably suggested a crescendo. Philidor also used them on certain kinds of final notes to indicate when the piece continued, such as the last notes of *couplets* in rondeaux (leading back to the rondeau theme), last notes of phrases moving on to the next, and on last notes that led into a repeat. In these cases, he did not indicate a flattement for the same note on the second ending (which did not lead onward; cf. Pl. 4.18).

Moens-Haenen (1988: 230) noticed that Philidor often used the flattement to emphasize syncopations, strong beats, and hemiolas, as well as the highest note of a piece. He also used it for the special effect of the 'Air en Musette' in the 4th *Suitte*. Flattements are scarce or entirely absent in movements of a light or peasant character; they are not found in two of the Gavottes, for instance. These were movements that invited less subtle dynamic nuance, and the flattement thereby emerges as a tool for expressing the more intimate, sophisticated effects. Danoville said in 1687 of the analogous two-finger gamba vibrato:

Il a de la tendresse & remplit l'oreille d'une douceur triste & languissant.[288]	It is gentle in character, and fills the ear with a melancholy, languishing tenderness.

Philidor's 'Neufième Suitte' was exceptional in its elaborate use of flattements, frequently in unexpected places (cf. Pl. 4.19). In the Courante, there are two vibrated

---

[285] Based on early sources, Moens-Haenen (1988), 175 reports that vibrato in general was used more sparingly on wind instruments and the voice than on the violin.

[286] There is no accompanying table that establishes that the wavy line is meant to indicate a flattement, but no other standard ornament would be appropriate, and the same mark is used for this ornament by Loulié and Marais.

[287] The flattement was not marked over several long notes that were obvious candidates; since there is no indication why they would be omitted, I take this to mean that Philidor marked the flattement only in ambiguous situations.

[288] Danoville, *L'Art de toucher le dessus et basse de violle* (1687), 41, quoted in Moens-Haenen (1988), 191.

PL. 4.19. Philidor, *Suittes* (1718), beginning of the 'Neufième Suitte', p. 58

PL. 4.20. Anonymous, 'Coeurs accablez', p. 5ᵛ in F-Pn MS Rés. 2060

long notes held over the measure, followed by trills, suggesting an excess of emotion. Philidor noted 'On peut perdre la mesure a ces deux tenuës' (the tempo can
be abandoned on these two sustained notes).

The wavy sign for flattement was also used in Paris MS Rés. 2060, a collection
probably written for hautboy in the 1690s (see Ch. 3, §A). Flattements were often
placed on last notes of sections, helping to suggest that the piece continued, as
in Philidor.[289] 'Coeurs accablez', fo. 5ᵛ, (cf. Pl. 4.20) included two flattements combined with mordents; this combination is found also in Philidor (1717–18), 12: 1, 9:
1 and 9: 2 (cf. Pl. 4.19).

---

[289] This manuscript also gave flattements on second endings (cf. 'Esprits solets', fo. 10ᵛ and 'Chaconne de
Gallatée', fo. 9ᵛ. In these pieces, the second-time bar is separately written out with a flattement. 'Eh! Vogue la
Gallere', fo. 9ʳ, on the other hand, has a flattement on the first ending but not on the second.

Flattements were also marked, sparingly, in the manuscript version of Hotteterre's trios.[290] They occur regularly on final notes, even in movements without repeats. In one case, flattements were used consecutively on a series of suspensions descending by step, and the final note of the phrase also had one. In general, they are found on suspensions, confirming their association with swells/crescendos.

The most complete and precise clues to where and how the flattement was used come by analogy from French works for viola da gamba, particularly those of Marais.[291] Gambists consistently indicated 'two-finger' and 'one-finger' vibrato with horizontal and vertical wavy lines respectively. The 'two-finger' vibrato corresponded to the flattement; it was used most often in slow pieces with singing lines (such as *tombeaus*, slow préludes, sarabandes, and *plaintes*), but rarely in quick movements, pieces with frequent chords, or those with disjunct passages.

Because of its status as a 'lesser Shake', the flattement could sometimes have been used effectively on notes that might otherwise have been trilled, even those marked with the trill sign (indeed, the cross + was sometimes used to mean a flattement).[292] Trills in the music of composers who were harpsichordists, like François Couperin, might often have been replaced with flattements (harpsichordists would have been unlikely to distinguish the 'tremblement mineur' from the 'tremblement majeur').[293] As mentioned above, Hotteterre wrote that awkward trills were sometimes replaced by a flattement. In systematically practising flattements, I find they are not easy to control and cannot be casually added to technique. I imagine young players in the past would have taken some years to master them.[294]

a. Fingerings for flattements on the hautboy In his brief chapter on hautboy, Hotteterre wrote:

A l'égard des Cadences, coups de langue, Flattements, &c. on lira les Explications que j'ay données sur ces agréments, au Traité de la Flute traversiere.[295]

For trills, tongue-strokes, flattements, etc., you should read the explanations I have given on these ornaments in the section on the traverso.

A fingering chart for flattements on the hautboy is fairly simple to construct, using the analogous fingerings Hotteterre provided for traverso and recorder (see Table 4.4).

---

[290] Paris 4° Vm. 848 [1–3]. [291] Moens-Haenen (1988) devotes a chapter to this subject (pp. 191–206).
[292] Cf. The *Compleat Flute Master* (1695), 6 (called there a 'sweetning'); cited in Moens-Haenen (1988), 170.
[293] Marais and de Caix d'Hervelois sometimes indicate a vibrato in their works for gamba after an appoggiatura (*coulé*), or on raised notes, where a trill might otherwise be expected. See Moens-Haenen (1988), 205.
[294] Cf. Quantz (1752), IX, §1. [295] Hotteterre (1707), 46.

TABLE 4.4. *Fingering chart for flattements on the hautboy*

Note	1st octave	2nd	3rd
C	Shake	♩ / ♯	4
C♯	—	Shake	5
D	Shake	Shake	
E♭	Shake	Shake	—
E	6	6	
F	5	5	
F♯	5	5	
G	♯	♯	
G♯	♯	♯	
A	♯	♯ / 4	
B♭	♯	♯	
B	♩	♩ / ♯	

Note. This table assumes the use of short high-note fingerings.

L. Hautboy Intonation and the Keyboard Temperaments

At the end of his long life, Telemann was prevailed upon to describe his ideal tuning scheme, and commented:

Mein System hat keine Claviermässige Temperatur zum Grunde, sondern zeiget die Klänge, so, wie sie auf uneingeschränkten Intrumenten, als *Violoncell, Violine* etc. wo nicht völlig, doch bey nahe, rein genommen werden können, welches denn die tägliche Erfahrung lehret.[296]	My system is not based on any keyboard temperament; rather, it displays the sounds found on unrestricted instruments like the cello, violin, etc., that can play purely (if not always entirely, nearly so), as day-to-day experience teaches.

Telemann's point was that melody instruments did not play in a closed tuning system based on a circle of fifths, like a keyboard temperament. Temperaments were a contrivance for instruments with immovable pitch, like the organ and harpsichord, an expedient designed to help make their intonation sound convincing. Singers and players of stringed and wind instruments had no need of such artifices, and

---

[296] Telemann (1744), 716. Sorge (1748: 61) said that 'Aufs Clavier wird sich dieses System [Telemann's] nicht appliciren lassen; auf der Geige aber, und einigen Blase-Instrumenten, möchte es eher thunlich seyn; denen Sängern aber ist es am leichtesten.'

'temperament' was too rigid a concept to apply to them.[297] Discussing intonation, Quantz commented (1752: III, §8):

Il est vrai que cette difference ne peut pas être exprimée sur le Clavecin, où l'on touche tous ces tons qu'on distingue ici, sur une même touche, ayant recours à la Temperature ou Participation.[298]	It is true that this distinction is impossible to make on the harpsichord, where each pair of notes we wish to distinguish are produced with a single key, making it necessary to have recourse to tempering.

'Tempering' in this sense referred to a compromise that attempted to make the best of the fact that only one note could be played when two were needed. Petit (*c*.1740: 24–5) explained that

L'Orgue, ou le Clavessin, sont après le Violon & le Violoncello, les Instruments les plus beaux & les plus complets, quoi-que défectüeux en ce qu'ils ne peuvent pas donner le Ton si vrai n'y si juste que le Violon, par la Raison que les Demi-tons qu'en Musique on nomme *Diésis & Bémols*, étant de leur Nature dans l'Harmonie différents l'un de l'autre, devroient par Conséquent être distinguez par deux Touches différentes, & que l'Orgue & le Clavessin n'ayant qu'une seule & même Touche pour les deux, cela est la Cause que le Cercle parfait de toute l'Harmonie, devient nécessairement imparfait.	After the violin and cello, the organ or the harpsichord are the most beautiful and complete of all instruments, though they are defective in that they cannot produce pitches as true and in tune as the violin. Since the semitones that are called in music *sharps* and *flats* are different one from the other by reason of their relationship in the harmony, they should therefore be distinguished by two different keys on the keyboard. But organs and harpsichords have but one key for two notes, so the perfect circle of harmony must necessarily be imperfect [on these instruments].

At Cambridge, Robert Smith wrote in 1749 (p. 239):

By a perfect instrument I mean a voice, violin or violoncello, &c, with which a good performer can perfectly express any sound which his ear requires . . .

The several parts of a concert well performed upon perfect instruments, do not move exactly by the given intervals of any one system whatever, but only pretty nearly, and so as to make perfect harmony as near as possible.[299]

The idea of 'tendency' tones, the practice of raising sharps and lowering flats to enhance their melodic function, is the reverse of the normal practice of seventeenth- and eighteenth-century musicians, for whom leading-notes were low.[300] Telemann wrote in 1767:

---

[297] For more background on non-keyboard tuning systems, see Barbieri (1991) and Haynes (1991).
[298] Cf. Castillon (1777), quoted above, §G.3.   [299] Smith (1749), 240, 'Proposition XXII'.
[300] See Boyden (1965), 186, 370–1; Cavallo (1788), 238 (quoted in Haynes 1991); Lindley (1987), 296.

Dass des[301] und és zween unterschiedene Klänge ausmachen, solches findet sich auch bey den Violinen, wo des mit dem 4ten, und és mit dem kleinen Finger gegriffen wird; desgleichen haben die Traversieren hierzu zwo besondere Klappen . . .[302]

That D♯ and E♭ are two separate sounds is demonstrated by the violin, where D♯ is played with the fourth finger and E♭ with the fifth; traversos are the same with their two separate keys . . .

It was Quantz who designed a traverso with separate keys for D♯ and E♭. He explained that

Ce qui m'a porté à ajouter à la Flute encore une Clef qui n'y a pas été auparavant, c'est la difference entre les Demitons majeurs & mineurs. . . . Le Demiton majeur a cinq Comma; le Demiton mineur n'en a que quatre. Il faut par consequent qu'Es (mi b mol) soit d'un Comma plus haut que Dis (re Diese).[303]

What led me to add another key not previously used on the flute was the difference between major and minor semitones. . . . The major semitone has five commas, the minor only four. For this reason, E♭ must be a comma higher than D♯.

The concept of major and minor semitones differing by a comma was the general 'rule of thumb' for tuning used by singers and instrumentalists in the Baroque period. It was described in 1723 by Tosi:

Everyone knows that there is a Semitone Major and Minor, because the Difference cannot be known [i.e. played] by an Organ or Harpsichord, if the Keys of the Instrument are not split. A Tone, that gradually passes to another, is divided into nine almost imperceptible Intervals, which are called Comma's, five of which constitute the Semitone Major, and four the Minor. . . . If one were continually to sing only to those above-mention'd Instruments [the organ and harpsichord], this Knowledge might be unnecessary; but since the time that Composers introduced the Custom of crowding the Opera's with a vast Number of Songs accompanied with Bow Instruments, it becomes so necessary, that if a Soprano was to sing D-sharp, like E-flat, a nice Ear will find he is out of Tune, because this last rises. Whoever is not satisfied in this, let him read those Authors who treat of it, and let him consult the best Performers on the Violin.[304]

What Tosi meant by a 'major semitone' was C–D♭ (or G–A♭, etc.); a 'minor semitone' was C–C♯ (or G–G♯, etc). An octave, as Francesco Geminiani wrote in 1751, could be divided '. . . into 12 Semitones, that is, 7 of the greater and 5 of the lesser'. Since the seven 'greater' or major semitones each contained five commas and the five 'lesser' had four, the octave consisted of a total of 55 commas. This '55-part octave' was a familiar concept in the seventeenth and eighteenth centuries. Sauveur wrote in 1707

---

[301] From the context, it is clear that Telemann means 'dis' here (i.e. D♯).
[302] Reproduced in Rachwitz (1981), 270.   [303] Quantz (1752), III, §8.
[304] Galliard's translation, 1742, ch. 2, 92–3. The words in brackets are mine.

Le systême temperé de 55 comma . . . est celui dont les Musiciens ordinaires se servent . . .[305]	The 55-part octave . . . is the one used by musicians in general [as distinguished from keyboard musicians in particular] . . .

Telemann's tuning system was also divided into fifty-five parts.[306] If we divide the 1,200 cents of an octave by 55, each part will be 21.82 cents. This is very close to the standard comma, the so-called 'syntonic comma', which is 21.5062896 cents.[307]

A temperament based on a 55-part octave was similar to what we now call '1/6-comma meantone'; it was produced by tuning eleven of the twelve fifths on the keyboard smaller than pure by 1/6 of a comma (whence the name). This system was associated with Gottfried Silbermann,[308] and is therefore sometimes called 'Silbermann tuning'. In this temperament, a major semitone = 109.09 cents and a minor semitone was 87.273.[309] The difference between them was therefore 21.817 cents, virtually identical to the comma of the 55-part octave, and about as close to a syntonic comma as it was possible to achieve in a keyboard tuning system. If a consistent system was implied in the use of major and minor semitones, 1/6-comma meantone was the temperament that it most resembled.

Compared with equal temperament, 1/6-comma meantone varied as follows:

<pre>
                    C +5 cents
      C♯ −8   D♭ +14
                 D +1
      D♯ −11   E♭ +10
                 E −2
                 F +7
      F♯ −6   G♭ +16
                 G +3
      G♯ −10   A♭ +12
                 A o
      A♯ −13   B♭ +9
                 B −4
                 C +5
</pre>

Here the principle of sharp flats and flat sharps is evident: as flattened notes became more distant from C, they became gradually higher, whereas sharpened notes became lower. F was 7c higher than in equal temperament, for instance, B♭ was 9c, E♭ 10c, A♭ 12c, etc. Going in the other direction, F♯ was 6c low, C♯ 8c, G♯ 10c, D♯ 11c, etc.[310]

---

[305] Sauveur (1707), 215.   [306] Adlung (1758), 317 (cf. Petzoldt 1974: 199).
[307] See Lindley (1980a), 591 and Sorge (1758).   [308] Barbour (1951), 42.
[309] See Lindley (1980b), 278.
[310] Note that synonymous sharps/flats are always approximately a syntonic comma apart (i.e. between 21 and 22c—the actual figure contains decimal points that have been rounded off on one side or the other).

For non-keyboard instruments, however, a strict 'temperament' was not possible. With flexible tuning, intonation was influenced by technical situations, subjective perceptions, even differences in dynamics.[311] And any instrument would have had to have enough pitch flexibility to be able to play both flats and sharps, depending on the musical context. The cross-fingered notes tended to be high on the hautboy, and it was no accident that they were 'flats' (F and B♭). Türk wrote in 1789 (p. 45):

Auf der Violine, Flöte,* Hoboe und vielen andern Instrumenten, auch im Gesange, können und sollen diese in Ansehung der Höhe und Tiefe verschiedenen Töne nach ihrem wahren mathematischen Verhältniß hervor gebracht werden. Daß es aber bey vielen Musikern blos beym *sollen* bleibt, liegt freylich nicht an den Instrumenten.	On the violin, flute,* hautboy, and many other instruments, as well as for singers, the observance of the distinction between higher and lower notes can and should be produced according to their true mathematical proportions. That it remains, however, for many musicians only a *should* [and not a *can*], is obviously not the fault of the instruments.
* . . . Auf der Violine greift man *cis* und *des, dis* und *es, gis* und *as* etc. ganz verschieden. Gute Hobospieler beobachten eben dasselbe.	* . . . On the violin, C♯ and D♭ are fingered quite differently; also D♯ and E♭, G♯ and A♭, etc. Good hautboy players observe exactly this same distinction.

Thus between the flexible tuning of melody instruments and the fixed temperament of keyboards, a working rapport had to be found, since they normally performed together. A keyboard temperament like 1/6-comma meantone would have operated as a frame of reference or model, from which singers and players of instruments could occasionally depart in the context of the moment.

Although embouchure adjustments made the hautboy's intonation relatively adaptable, hautboy charts indicated alternative fingerings for some sharps and flats (see Table 4.5).[312] Hotteterre advised beginners that

You need not much plague your Self at first about this nicety of adjusting these Semitones [that is, the enharmonic pairs like G♯ and A♭], as I have shew'd by turning the Flute in or out, till you are a pretty way advanc'd in Practice, and then 'twill be proper to observe it, to attain to a perfection on this Instrument.[313]

One of the first keys to be added to the hautboy was for the note F, and its appearance reflected an important aesthetic shift. As mentioned above, §G.3, the natural fingerings for F and F♯ were both tuned from the same tuning hole, the fifth, and

---

[311] A violinist will play on an open string up to 5c higher when playing *forte* than when playing *piano*.

[312] Freillon-Poncein systematically gave a fingering for every possible enharmonic note, but (with one exception that may be an oversight) he did not distinguish pairs. This is probably explained by the following remark (p. 9): 'Je ne parle point icy de la différence qu'il y a des demy tons majeurs ou mineurs, parce que aux Instrumens où l'oreille conduit les sons, on peut les faire tous égaux [i.e. probably: they can all be made equal]; ainsi la transposition sur toute sorte de demy ton se peut executer avec autant de justesse que sur le naturel.'

[313] Hotteterre (*c.*1729), 11–12.

TABLE 4.5. *Alternative fingerings for sharps and flats*

f♯1		123 4 7	Hotteterre
	g♭1	123 ♯ 6	
g♯1		123 ♯ 6	Bismantova
	a♭1	123 6	
g♯1		123	*Second Book of Theatre Music*
	a♭1	12 4	
g♯2		12 4 6	Bismantova
	a♭2	123 6	
g♯2		123	Banister, La Riche L1, La Riche L2, *Second Book of Theatre Music*
	a♭2	12 4	
a♯2		1 3 6 8	Bismantova
	b♭2	1 3 6	

these two notes were too close together. In meantone, where the interval between F and F♯ was small (F was at least 7 cents higher than in equal temperament and F♯ 6 cents lower), the problem was bearable (though sometimes an aggravation).[314] The trend towards equal temperament at the end of the eighteenth century induced makers to separate the hole governing the tuning of these two notes by adding another hole for F and providing it with a key (see §G.3). In this way, the two notes could be tuned independently: the F lower and the F♯ higher, to match equal temperament.

M. Technical Limitations

Contemporaries were not uncritical of the hautboy's technical limitations (a number of which have been touched on in the sections above). Several writers pointed out that the hautboy's positive qualities depended on playing it well.[315] Mattheson's sarcastic remark quoted in Ch. 3, §F ('I would rather hear a good Jew's harp or musical comb [than] . . . the *Hautbois* [when] not played in the most delicate way') is an example.

The French, having developed the hautboy, also coined a word for the 'split note' it sometimes emitted. According to Meude-Monpas (1787: 27),

---

[314] Cf. Castillon (1777), quoted in §G.3.
[315] See further Eisel (1738), 96–7; Froelich (1810), 36; Niedt (1700), 38; Schubart (1806), 320; and Whitely (1816), 10.

CANARDER. v.n. C'est produire un son qui
approche du cri du canard. Les mauvais
chanteurs et les médiocres joueurs
d'instruments à vent sont sujets à *canarder*.
Excepté le correct *BÉZOZZI*,[316] presque
tous les joueurs de hautbois ont *canardé*.

CANARDER. To split a note. v. To produce
a sound that resembles the cry of a duck.
Bad singers and mediocre wind players are
likely to split notes. Almost all hautboy
players split notes with the exception of the
precise Besozzi.

and Framery (1818: ii. 37) began his 'Hautbois' entry 'Son défaut est de canarder
quelquefois . . .' (Its defect is to split notes occasionally . . .).

The hautboy was included in two well-known indictments of the purity of wind
intonation. Perhaps stretching his point, Marcello wrote in his satire *Il teatro alla
moda* (*c*.1720):

Oboè, flauti, trombe, fagotti, etc., saranno
sempre scordati cresceranno, etc.[317]

Hautboys, flutes, trumpets, bassoons, etc.,
will be always out of tune, will be sharp, etc.

When he was introduced to him by Hasse in about 1725, Quantz recalled
Alessandro Scarlatti's comment (serious or in jest?):

Mein Sohn, . . . ihr wisset, dass ich die
blasenden Instrumentisten nicht leiden
kann: denn sie blasen alle falsch.[318]

My Son, . . . you know I cannot abide wind
instrument players; they always play out of
tune.

Francoeur (1772: 13) wrote of the hautboy

Cet Instrument n'est pas parfait dans
tous ses Tons: il y en a que l'Art de
l'Exécutant ne peut pas rendre
parfaitement justes . . .

This instrument is not perfect in all its
notes. Some [hautboys] exist that no
performer can manage to play perfectly
in tune . . .

1. Slurring upward leaps

Quantz (1752: VI, suppl. §3) described the difficulty of slurring ascending leaps
on the bassoon. The same problem applied to the hautboy, although on different
fingerings. Quantz wrote:

Il faut seulement remarquer qu'on ne peut
couler sur le Basson, comme sur la Flute,
d'un même coup de langue des sauts fort
éloignés de bas en haut; excepté ceux qui
ne sont pas au dessous du C sans ligne (*ut*

I should only note that on the bassoon,
unlike the flute, wide ascending leaps
cannot be made except up to C below
middle C. The upper of the two notes in
leaps from the bottom-most octave [of the

---

[316] Probably Gaetano Besozzi (1727–98), who played regularly at the *Concert Spirituel*. Burney admired his playing there in 1770.   [317] Page 54, quoted in Bernardini (1985), 13.
[318] Quantz (1755), 228.

de la seconde Octave du Clavecin [C]). Il faut au contraire pousser par un coup de langue, chaque ton qui saute de l'Octave la plus basse en haut. Dans la seconde Octave, c'est à dire, depuis le D sans ligne (*re second du Clavecin* [D]), on peut à la vérité couler quelques notes qui sautent; mais il ne faut pas qu'elles soient au dessus de l'A sans ligne (*la second du Clavecin* [A]); bien qu'à la vérité cela se puisse faire à l'aide d'une excellente anche, & d'une embouchure très ferme.

bassoon] must be tongued. A few notes can be slurred in the second octave (that is, from D below middle C), as far up as A below middle C, or farther with a particularly good reed and very firm embouchure.

Quantz's statement implied that the bassoon was not expected to be able to slur these intervals, as could be done on the traverso. Thus where such slurs appeared in parts that were also for traverso (or violin), they would presumably have been tongued by the bassoonist. It is reasonable to assume that the same applied to the hautboy player. The hautboy could slur upward to all notes except the following:[319]

g2 from c1, d1, and d♯/e♭1,
b♭2, b2, and c3 from e1 to c♯2,
b2 and c3 from d2 (the beginning of the second register)

Fake fingerings could be used to obtain g2, g♯2, and a2: g2 with added 456 8, and g♯2 and a2 with added 456 8. As late as 1816–24, Vogt wrote in his *Méthode*:

Quand on rencontrera donc . . . deux intervalles par degrés disjoints, qu'on sentira ne pas pouvoir lier facilement, il faut, lorsqu'ils se trouvent en montant, pincer un peu des lèvres au même instant où l'on force le souffle, et donner un coup de langue extrêmement doux pour que l'oreille ne puisse pas le distinguer . . .[320]

Thus, when you encounter . . . two [notes] that are disjunct and involve an upward leap, and it is unlikely they can be easily slurred, you should bite a little while at the same time blowing harder, and attack the note so lightly that it cannot be perceived by a listener . . .

Vogt may have been describing a technique that had been used much earlier.

Another reason large intervals were sometimes tongued rather than slurred on the hautboy, or avoided altogether, was the effect produced. The hautboy could produce many tongued leaps that nevertheless tended to sound like a fox in a chicken coop when played quickly. Such effects had a limited usefulness in music. Some slurred leaps were playable, but only at moderate speed. That was probably

---

[319] This list assumes the use of short fingerings for the high notes (see above, §G.6). Long fingerings offer more slurs, but were evidently not in general use.   [320] Vogt (1816–25), end of Article 4.

why Vivaldi was careful to rewrite certain passages in the bassoon concertos he adapted for the hautboy (see Ch. 7, §A.2), and may have been what Scheibe meant when he wrote:

In einem Solo für die Geige kann ein Componist, diesem Instrumente zu Gefallen, so weit ausschweifen, als es die Natur desselben verträgt. Ein Solo für die Hoboe aber muß allemal singender seyn, weil dieses Instrument sehr viel Aehnlichkeit mit einer Singestimme hat.[321]	In a solo for the violin, a composer can be as extravagant as nature will allow, in order to show off the instrument. But a solo for the hautboy must be more singing, because this instrument is very similar to the voice.[322]

Telemann referred to the hautboy's limitations in slurring (probably upward slurring) in the introduction to the *Kleine Cammer-Music* of 1716. In his introduction (writing from his personal experience as an hautboy player) he mentioned some of the criteria he considered appropriate for music for the hautboy:

[Zu dem Ende] habe den *Ambitum* so enge, als möglich gewesen, eingeschlossen, zu weit entfernte Sprunge, wie auch bedeckte und unbequeme Tone[323] vermieden, hingegen die *brilli*renden, und welche von Natur an unterschiedenen Orten in dieses *delica*te *Instrument* geleget sind, offt anzubringen gesuchet. Hiernächst habe mich in denen *Ari*en der kürtze beflissen, theils um die Kräffte des Spielers zu *ménagir*en, theils auch, um die Ohren der Zuhörer durch die Länge nicht zu ermüden.	[In order to make them suitable for the hautboy,] I have limited the range as narrowly as possible . . . [and] avoided leaps of large intervals and covered or awkward notes; but have always sought, on the contrary, to bring out the brilliance and distinctness of this delicate instrument. In addition, I have kept the movements short, partly to spare the strength of the player, and partly not to tire the ear of the listener.

The *Kleine Cammer-Music* was more varied and delightful than these remarks would lead us to believe. And, although there were many examples of large interval leaps,[324] few were slurred. The rare upward slurs were easy ones.[325] Thus when Telemann wrote of avoiding 'leaps of large intervals', he probably meant that he wished to avoid the slurred leaps that were not playable, that is, up to b♭2, b2, and c3 from any note between e1 and d2.

---

[321] Scheibe (1745), 682–3, quoted in Swack (1988), 9.   [322] Trans. Swack (1988), 9.

[323] Telemann appears to be describing cross-fingerings here.

[324] e.g. II: 1, II: 3, II: 5, V: 1, V: 2, and VI: 1.

[325] V: 1 has d1–c♯2–f♯2 and d♯1–c2, II: 6 has a1–e2, III: 5 has e♭2–a♭2 and d2–g2. Only VI: 4 has three upward slurs that are more complex: a1–g2, b♭1–g2, and c2–a2; but these can be played with fake fingerings.

5

1700–1730: The International Hautboy

By 1700 the hautboy had been adopted everywhere in Europe. Like the present-day pizza and its Italian origins, the association of the hautboy with France became in this period more a matter of tradition than fact.

If surviving repertoire is an indication, 1700–30 was the hautboy's Golden Age; the greatest quantity of solo and chamber music comes from this period, as well as some of the most profound and varied compositions in the instrument's history. Important works appeared in many different countries, and as in no other period, every genre of hautboy writing was well represented: solo sonatas, small chamber works, concertos, obbligatos with voice, and music for hautboy band.[1]

This is what has survived. We cannot be entirely certain, however, that hautboy music (like music in general) has been accurately transmitted to us. In eighteenth-century Italy and Spain, most music circulated in manuscript, whereas northern Europe supported many music publishers.[2] Music in manuscripts is ephemeral; only one copy may exist, easily lost. There is thus a natural bias that has favoured the transmission of northern music.

But there are other indications that before 1730, most of southern Europe had not yet embraced the hautboy to the extent of northern countries. In his writings, the well-travelled Joachim Christoph Nemeitz is generally well-informed, fair-minded, alert, and reliable. His comments on the wind players of his generation, published in Leipzig in 1726, seem to agree with other evidence:

Auf Blase=*instrumenten* . . . thuns die Teutsche und Frantzosen ihnen [den Italienern] weit zuvor . . . auf der *Hautbois* und *Flûten* halten sie sich einander die Waag=Schale.[3]

On wind instruments . . . the Germans and French are far ahead of them [the Italians] . . . on the hautboy and flute they balance each other equally on the scale.

Frenchmen and Germans certainly predominate among the players who (from our present vantage point) appear to have been the leading hautboists of this period: Bernier, Böhm, Anne Philidor, Pierre Philidor, Jacob Denner, Erdmann,

---

[1] The only exception is the hautboy quartet, which probably did not appear until the 1750s (see Ch. 7, §E.3).
[2] Cf. Brown and Sadie (1989), 120.
[3] From *Nachlese besonderer Nachrichten aus Italien*, quoted in Braun (1990), 280.

Freymuth, Galliard, Gleditsch, Glösch, Martin Hotteterre, Colin Hotteterre, Kytch, La Riche, the brothers Jacob and John Loeillet, Penati, Richter, Rion, Rose, Saint-Martin, and Schön. The oldest of these players was born in the 1650s, but most were from the 1660s and 1680s; their careers were contemporary with those of Bach, Couperin, Handel, Marais, Telemann, and Vivaldi.

Instrument design was volatile in this period. Having been trained in the seventeenth century or the earliest years of the eighteenth, many of these players first used instruments that were probably Type A1 or Type A2 hautboys with long bores built at pitches below A–1 (A≈415).[4] Hautboys at these pitches (A–1½ and A–2, or A≈403 and A≈392) played differently enough from shorter, higher-pitched models that even though the outward turning patterns did not change (A2 in both cases), we are probably justified in speaking of a new design of instrument. Shorter hautboys used a different fingering for c3 (see Ch. 4, §G.6), required a reed with a markedly different staple design,[5] and favoured technical agility over sensuous sound and voice-like melodic lines.

The higher pitch and the general use of hautboys with shorter bores occurred in Germany and Italy at the beginning of the century and by about 1715 all over Europe.[6] This was the same decade in which the new hautbois d'amour and oboe da caccia made their first appearances, and the leaner four-piece traverso replaced the elegant model in three pieces. Although there is little documentation to prove it (cf. Ch. 4, §A), it is likely that playing technique underwent some fundamental changes at this time as well.

Artistic depictions of the hautboy between 1700 and 1730 show that the straight upward-flared finial of the seventeenth century began to be replaced by the bobbin shape (the two types appear in about equal numbers). And the relatively sharp bell flare seen in late seventeenth-century pictures became noticeably less extreme.

A. Court Musicians and Stadtpfeifer

While the majority of hautboists in the Baroque period were bandsmen, the talented and/or fortunate players found more interesting work at courts as *Hofmusici*, or in cities as Stadtpfeifer. It was these players who were the original recipients of most of the solo music for hautboy. Hautboists who managed to secure these posts were usually among the highest-paid orchestral musicians of the seventeenth and eighteenth centuries.

---

[4] Cf. Ch. 2, §B.4.a and b.   [5] See Ch. 2, §E.3.b.
[6] See Haynes (forthcoming), ch. 4.

It is said that the Baroque sense of propriety found something disturbing about women doing things with their mouths in public to objects like reeds. But there is a more fundamental explanation for the fact that so few hautboy players were female: other than singers, women were rarely professional musicians of any kind. And among amateurs, the hautboy was not often the instrument of choice. The frontispiece shows a lady hautboy player, albeit a mythical one, Diana. The Venetian *ospedali* featured several famous girl soloists (who, however, were obliged to play behind a screen).

1. The court chamber musician (Hofmusicus)

In Germany, one of the predicaments of most cities during the terrible Thirty Years War was that they were unable to 'raise sufficient money to wage war on a seventeenth-century scale, so that for the sake of their security the cities were forced into dependence on the Princes . . .'.[7] As a result, the centre of musical activities moved to the courts. Only Hamburg and Leipzig, which had been less affected by the war, retained significant musical institutions at the end of the seventeenth century, and became important centres of hautboy activity in the early eighteenth. By the time the cities had recovered, the aristocratic courts had consolidated power. Modelling themselves on Versailles, courts were quick to adopt French music and along with it the new hautboy. Indeed, court ensembles governed by the whim and pride of a rich prince were the logical places for new and modish instruments to be adopted. Operas and orchestras belonged of necessity to the wealthy because of their cost—more than the average city could afford to pay.

A *Hofmusicus* in the eighteenth century, even a court composer, was a middle to upper servant at court, and had a deferential comportment not unlike that of a twentieth-century butler. The hierarchy of court servants was carefully worked out. At the Württemberg court in 1710, for instance, the *Capellmeister* was in the sixty-ninth place, 'Cammer-Musici-Virtuosi' in ninety-fourth, 'Musici ordinarii' at 104th, and bandsmen (*Hautboisten*) lower still, probably at about the same social rank as the stable boys.[8]

A court musician was normally involved in performances for the chapel, the chamber, theatrical productions, lighter entertainments (such as *Tafelmusik*, music for balls, dancing lessons for younger nobility), and official ceremonies.[9] His daily schedule would have been very full, and time for rehearsals correspondingly small. Court musicians were also frequently required to travel with their ruler when he moved to different residences or made trips. Some musicians held other

---

[7] Raynor (1972), 205, 307.
[8] Hildebrand (1975), 54. *Hautboisten* were associated with the trumpeters (who had a much higher rank), however, so they often had similar privileges, such as the wearing of livery. Cf. also Petzoldt (1983), 164–5.
[9] Owens (1995), 283 ff.

non-musical positions: menials (as in Esterháza), secretaries, administrators, purchasing agents, etc.

Players at the Württemberg court at the end of the seventeenth century were lent their instruments. But they were not allowed to take them home.[10] In such a situation, the better-paid players probably found it more practical to use instruments they owned themselves, on which they could practise and make reeds, and play other occasional music.

a. Chamber music with hautboy   The term 'chamber music' is now used to distinguish music for smaller ensembles from orchestral music, and I shall use it in that sense here. But in the eighteenth century, chamber music evidently meant something slightly different. In 1732 (p. 130), Walther defined it as

Diejenige, welche in grosser Herren Zimmern pflegt aufgeführt zu werden.	[Music] that is generally performed in the chambers of the upper classes.

Walther's definition, unlike the modern one, included orchestral music as well as smaller ensembles. By the beginning of the eighteenth century, special titles like *Cammermusicus* began to be bestowed on court musicians;[11] for hautboy players, this title distinguished them from mere bandsmen. But a *Cammermusicus* regularly played orchestral music.

There are nearly 6,000 surviving duets, solo sonatas, trios, and quartets written before 1760 that include hautboy.[12] A small percentage of these pieces was published and therefore available to anyone, but most were written for specific court ensembles and remained in manuscript. This music was not in the public domain: it was privately owned by the prince or monarch (in the way many paintings are still owned by individuals); it did not circulate and was unknown outside the palace circle. In some cases, the musicians themselves were not even allowed to borrow music to practise, let alone copy; it was part of the Capellmeister's job to keep—indeed guard—the parts.[13] The result was that virtually every piece was conceived for a specific player with his individual talents and abilities. It was not normally expected that anyone else would play it.

Being conceived for a particular place and for specific musicians, music was not written (as in the nineteenth century) to become 'classic' and be mastered, or understood, at some future time. A composer could not count on having a piece heard more than once: it had to succeed the first time, which might also be the last time. There was every reason, then, to write it appropriately for the performers at hand.

---

[10] Owens (1995), 64, 128, 164.   [11] Ibid. 311.

[12] There are 1,127 pieces without bass (solos, duets, etc.), 1,902 solos with bass, 1,919 trio sonatas, 440 quadro sonatas, and 396 quintets for mixed winds and strings written before 1760. This is a total of 5,784 chamber pieces.

[13] Owens (1995), 59.

We can thus be fairly certain that the pieces that have come down to us accurately reflect the real abilities of the instruments and players of the day.[14]

b. Opera   Although opera was the archetypical genre of Baroque music, and a vast number of them were produced, relatively few are known as yet. Many beautiful arias for voice and obbligato hautboy have thus still to be discovered.

Roger North wrote (1959: 274): '[In Operas], the hautbois in the superior [part] have a transcendent effect . . .' The hautboy obbligato was the instrument's first and arguably its most successful solo genre. There is a good reason the hautboy began to be used quite early in opera arias. Unlike a section of violins, a single player could use more expressive nuance, and spontaneously vary an obbligato in a way that was not possible for several instruments playing in unison. And if a single player was to be used on a solo line, the hautboy was more effective in the acoustics of most theatres than a solo violin or traverso.

Whether hautboys actually played solos in Lully's dramatic works, other than the famous instrumental *ritournelles* or 'trios' for double reeds, is unclear. By the time of Lully's death, as we have seen, Steffani was already taking the hautboy beyond these roles and writing beautiful full-fledged solo obbligatos for the hautboy in opera productions for Hannover and Munich; these are the first known solos for the instrument.

By the 1690s other composers, inspired but not bound by the Lullian tradition, began to experiment with the hautboy as a foil to the solo voice. Besides Steffani's, obbligatos appeared in Germany by Conradi, Keiser, and Kusser. In Italy, we know of solos in operas by Pollarolo, Scarlatti, Torri, and Petrobelli. In England, Purcell often featured the hautboy in vocal works. By the first decade of the new century, there were solos by French, Italian, German, and English composers. Vocal obbligatos in theatre works continued to be written in large numbers until about 1770.

Opera seria was organized as a series of *da capo* arias interspersed with recitative that carried forward the dramatic situation. The aria's function was to intensify that situation at particularly interesting points by pausing and considering a single specific *Affect*, a moment with poetic potential if appropriately handled by both composer and performers. There were several benefits to the occasional use of a wind instrument like a flute or hautboy in an aria: it provided variety of sound colour compared with the standard sound of continuo or string orchestra, it might conveniently recall affective associations, and it offered a chance to contrast and compare the potential of musical figures alternately played and sung. But since the purpose of the aria was to feature and contemplate a single emotion, the most important reason for the presence of the instrument was to enhance the evocation

---

[14] Cf. Libby (1989), 17.

of that emotion, either through the instrument's character or by the way it was played (or both together).

The vocal duet in the *opera seria* may often have served, consciously or not, as the model for dialogue arias between voice and hautboy:

Until the 1780s the duet was always sung by the primo uomo and prima donna and had a highly conventionalized format. It began (after the orchestral introduction) with a lyrical solo that was immediately repeated with different words by the other singer. A short passage of dialogue followed and then a lengthy session in which the singers shared material of various sorts, much of it involving florid passage-work, sometimes together in parallel thirds or sixths, sometimes in the overlapping alternation of short phrases.[15]

This formal layout applies to many arias that pair hautboy and voice, including most of the ones cited in this book.

c. Orchestra As Raynor (1972: 175) pointed out, there were never enough operas for the number of theatres. That meant that an opera travelled from theatre to theatre, and as a result, a more or less standardized ensemble of instruments became a basic requirement for every court and public theatre.

In orchestral music, the pattern established by Lully remained popular all over Europe through the first half of the eighteenth century: a basic string orchestra, often supplemented with hautboys and bassoons doubling the strings, strengthening them and varying the colour, and playing occasional exposed 'trio' passages. Other winds were sometimes added: horns, and for festive occasions, trumpets and drums. Flutes and clarinets (played by hautboists) were used exceptionally for specific purposes.[16]

Doubling hautboys to a string band gave a more 'tutti' character; it added bite and clarity, and changed the colour of the line, 'giving fullness and contour to a large ripieno, providing brilliance to the coloratura in virtuoso passages by their prompt attack on first and last notes', as Harnoncourt put it.[17] Double reeds were probably added to many scores in which their specific presence is not mentioned on paper. Many larger works have brief indications like 'con strom.', which may or may not have included hautboys.

Over the course of the eighteenth century there was a change in the hautboy's relation to the violin in the orchestra. Violin and hautboy parts were essentially identical at the beginning of the century, and the two instruments frequently shared melodic lines. Many of Bach's arias have unison parts for violins and hautboy, for instance, and whether these pieces are for a string section with an added hautboy or for a solo hautboy with added strings is often difficult to decide. But by mid-century, composers like Telemann, Hasse, and Graun were starting to give the

---

[15] Cf. Libby (1989), 18, 29.   [16] Cf. Kubitschek (1987), 109.   [17] Harnoncourt (1988), 173.

orchestral winds a more harmonic function, in the form of held chords against moving violin lines. That trend grew stronger with time.[18] While hautboy parts became simpler and more harmonic, the violin was gradually given more complex figuration, until by the Classical period the hautboys and violins had taken on quite independent functions. Rousseau wrote of copyists in 1768 (p. 130):

Les Parties de Hautbois qu'on tire sur les Parties de Violon pour un grand d'Orchestre, ne doivent pas être exactement copiées comme elles sont dans l'original: mais, outre l'étendue que cet Instrument a de moins que le Violon; outre les *Doux* qu'il ne peut faire de même; outre l'agilité qui lui manque ou qui lui va mal dans certaines vitesses, la force du Hautbois doit être ménagée pour marquer mieux les Notes principales, & donner plus d'accent à la Musique. Si j'avois à juger du goût d'un Symphoniste sans l'entendre, je lui donnerois à tirer sur la Partie de Violon, la Partie de Hautbois; tout *Copiste* doit savoir le faire.

The hautboy parts that are extracted from the parts of the violin for a full band should not be copied exactly, but, besides the smaller range [of the hautboy], besides the pianos that it cannot perform the same way, besides the velocity which is wanting, or which ill suits it in certain quick passages, the force of the hautboy should be used to mark the principal notes better, and give a greater accent to the music. If I had to judge the taste of a musician without hearing him, I would ask him to extract an hautboy part from that of the violin; every copyist should be able to do it.[19]

Barsanti's *Concerto Grosso* for trumpet and two hautboys (Op. 3, 1742) shows in its final Allegro how a common problem of this type was solved: while the violins have continuous sixteenth notes, the winds have an eighth with two sixteenths.

After the middle of the eighteenth century, the effect of combined hautboys and violins, used so successfully in earlier times, was rarely any longer exploited, and the hautboys served merely as re-enforcement rather than equal melodic elements. If occasionally the hautboy was given the principal material, it played by itself as a soloist.

Many eighteenth-century orchestra seating plans survive, and give indications of the relative strength and importance of instruments. In both orchestra seating schemes by Métoyen (1773),[20] for instance, the hautboys are seated forward. The musical implications of the spatial placement of instruments have not yet been seriously studied.[21]

Concertos. The hautboy's clarity and directness, its lyric qualities, and its range of character in slow movements were all advantages in a concerto setting. Although

---

[18] Cf. McCredie (1964), 152–6.   [19] Trans. partly based on that in W. Waring (London, 1771).
[20] J. B. Métoyen, 'Plan de la Musique du Roy au grand théâtre de Versailles' and 'Plan de l'orchestre du théâtre de Fontainebleau et du petit théâtre de Versailles', aquarelles in the Bibliothèque de Versailles, MS 131. Reproduced in Lesure (1972), 20–1.
[21] For the ratios of hautboys in an orchestra compared with violins, see Ch. 4, §E.2.a.

TABLE 5.1. *Concertos for solo hautboy with strings*

Period	Number	Percentage
1670–1700	31	3.60
1700–30	215	24.94
1730–60	256	29.70
1760–90	307	35.61
1790–1820	53	6.15

TABLE 5.2. *Hautboy concertos before 1760*

Country	Number	Percentage
France	0	0.0
Italy	92	43.19
Germany	101	47.42
England	20	9.39

its technique was less flexible than that of the violin, it offered a natural contrast in timbre that was difficult for a violin to achieve with an accompanying string group, and there were none of the balance problems intrinsic to concertos for harpsichord or traverso.

The earliest concertos for solo hautboy with strings began to appear in the 1690s, and by 1760 more than 500 had been written. The genre became increasingly popular as the eighteenth century progressed, tapering off only at its end (see Table 5.1). There were also numbers of concertos for hautboy with other solo instruments. Almost all the hautboy concertos written before 1760 came from Germany and Italy (see Table 5.2).

The solo concerto quickly developed into a medium for displaying virtuosity, and it is this that made it special. No player, no matter how good, could stand in front of an audience with the goal of impressing and surprising it without investing a substantial amount of time and energy in mastering the piece. It therefore made sense to perform a concerto many times, and the performances naturally got better as a result. Having invested time in learning it, it was also a good idea for a soloist to try to keep a concerto from being played by others (it is known that Mozart, for instance, took only rough notes of his own solo parts to concerto performances, 'so that the work would be meaningless to any outsider into whose hands the manuscript fell'.)[22] Concertos were thus associated with particular players, and it is

---

[22] Raynor (1972), 334.

easy to understand why Ramm, for example, made Mozart's hautboy concerto his 'cheval de bataille'.[23]

2. The municipal musician (Stadtpfeifer)

It might seem that the top of the ladder for an hautboy player was playing at court, and in some cases it was true. Certainly a court position had prestige. But there were advantages to the life of a musician employed by a city government. Municipal positions were relatively stable, and working conditions calm. Petzoldt (1983), by contrast, draws a shocking picture of the financial insecurity of the court musician's life: his pay was constantly in arrears and he might be dismissed from one day to the next without recourse. As Telemann (who had tried both systems) wrote, 'Whoever wants a secure post for life should settle in a republic.'[24] Although a Stadtpfeifer's pay was less than that of court musician, it was regular. While the lowest salary in the Dresden orchestra was 100 Thaler, the base salary of Bach's Stadtpfeifer (before extras) was 51 Thaler.[25] Stadtpfeifer had many other benefits, however: in Leipzig they were given a communal house on the 'Stadtpfeifergäßlein' (Town Piper's Alley).[26] The Stadtpfeifer's instruments, music, and clothes were sometimes bought for him, he was entitled to bonuses for certain yearly events, he received donations of food, and was often exempt from taxation. He was appointed for life, and his post could be passed on by marriage or inheritance within the family. He had a relatively high social status within the city, and for some (like, one imagines, Bach's hautboists), the musical rewards were considerable.[27] If a city and a court were connected, Stadtpfeifer sometimes played at court as well.[28]

Wind players were employed by German cities in two general categories: *Türmer* and *Stadtpfeifer*. In smaller cities, the same individuals filled both roles; in bigger ones, there was specialization. *Türmer*, or tower musicians, were responsible for *Anblasen* (blowing alarms for fire or the approach of strangers), *Abblasen* (sounding the watches, which might also include ensemble pieces, usually performed on brass instruments), and *Aufwarten* (performing for weddings, *Tafelmusik*, and other entertainments, much as at court). Stadtpfeifer were normally required to be more accomplished musicians than *Türmer*, and by the eighteenth century many of them, especially in larger cities, were excused from the *Abblasen*. In addition to the duties of the *Türmer*, Stadtpfeifer were expected to perform at civic ceremonies

---

[23] Hautboy concertos are discussed further in Ch. 6, §E.

[24] 'Wer Zeit Lebens fest sitzen wolle, müsse sich in einer Republick niederlassen.' Telemann (1740), 363.

[25] Bach, himself a municipal employee, calculated his total annual income in Leipzig at 700 Thaler. Petzoldt (1983), 175 ff., 181, 183.   [26] Schering (1921), 21, 38.

[27] Rouvel (1962), 148 n. 2 notes that, except for those protected by local laws, Jews were excluded from the trades and guilds in 18th-c. Germany, and were thus not allowed to take positions as Stadtpfeifer or become citizens of any town.   [28] See Hildebrand (1975), 55–6.

and festivities, as well as to provide the *Figuralmusik* in the city's churches. In larger cities, the Stadtpfeifer were sometimes supplemented by a lower rank of 'Kunstgeiger' or 'Rollbrüder', who performed similar functions but received less pay.

An important complement to the Stadtpfeifers' salary was their traditional and exclusive privilege to provide music for weddings, funerals, and other ceremonies within the city's boundaries, paid privately by individuals. Fees for these events were carefully regulated.[29] In order to guard their exclusive rights to play, the Stadtpfeifer were protected by imperial statutes dating from the mid-seventeenth century; these rights were jealously guarded against potential competition, including that of *Stadt-Hautboisten*, regimental *Hautboisten*, and freelance musicians.[30]

A traditional function of the Stadtpfeifer was to train new musicians through an apprenticeship system. Apprentices received 'on the job' training in playing all kinds of instruments, both winds and strings. An apprentice was trained over a five- or six-year period and then released as a journeyman, or *Musikant*. A journeyman could then choose whether to continue working for a master or travel to study with or listen to others. Journeymen could audition for posts as Stadtpfeifer.[31] The practical result of this system was that most hautboy players in Germany were trained by Stadtpfeifer.

Larger centres with commercial pre-eminence required more accomplishment, which was reflected in higher salaries. More candidates applied for the higher-paying jobs; there were four of them (!) for the auditions in Dresden in 1698, 1735, and 1766,[32] and eight at Celle in 1691.[33]

Wind instruments were the prerogative of the Stadtpfeifer, and in some places, Stadtpfeifer were the only ones allowed to play them professionally.[34] Wind instruments had traditionally had a higher standing than strings. In the eighteenth century, wind music was a reminder of princely pomp, churchly Te Deums, processions, and graduations; by contrast, string music brought to mind dance floors and beer halls. The air of the minstrel long clung to the average German fiddler. It is no surprise, then, that the Stadtpfeifer were of higher standing than the Kunstgeiger.[35]

Very little of the ceremonial music known to have been played by Stadtpfeifer has survived. Some part of the extant hautboy band repertoire, which consists mainly of suites of dances, may originally have been theirs. Two examples survive

---

[29] See Altenburg (1979), 25.   [30] Cf. Schering (1921), 46–9.
[31] Ibid. 37.   [32] Techritz (1932), 20.
[33] Linnemann (1935), 81. For more on the general working and living conditions of Stadtpfeifer (or
Ratsmusikanten), see ibid. 77–9, 83.   [34] Hildebrand (1975), 63.
[35] Cf. Schering (1926), 258.

of marches played by the Stadtpfeifer of Nuremberg at the *Pfeifergericht* held at the Frankfurt trade fairs.[36]

a. The Stadtpfeifer and church music   In Germany, the city governments were responsible for providing music in the churches, and it is they who hired the Cantor, who in turn directed the Stadtpfeifer and composed the music they played. Bach's role as director of municipal music at Leipzig was typical. The city musicians were under his authority and all of them were involved in providing music for the city's churches—elaborate 'figural' pieces in selected churches, and vocal music in the others. German church music adopted orchestral instruments like the hautboy early on, and used them much more extensively than other countries. This may have been partly because (like the voice) wind instruments are generally effective in the generous acoustic environment of churches. Also, new musical styles were easily assimilated into the Lutheran service 'because the old conservative safeguards built into the Catholic system were not part of Lutheran organisation, so that the only check on the sort of music provided was the civil authority which appointed both the clergy and the musicians of the church'.[37]

A cantor was expected to write new music regularly (as no one saw any point in repeating music, any more than they did in repeating sermons).[38] Since a cantata was required for the morning service and at Vespers, the number of German cantatas that were written in the first half of the eighteenth century was enormous. Although many of them have been lost, those that survive have yet to be surveyed. There are over 1,400 extant cantatas by Graupner, about 450 by Stölzel, three printed cycles and almost 1,150 manuscripts by Telemann, 236 by Römhild, 70 by Fasch, and numerous others by composers like Keiser, Kuhnau, Zachow, Österreich, Zelenka, Johann Ludwig Bach, Bokemeyer, Förster, Kirchhoff, Volckmar, and Hoffmann, not to mention those of Sebastian Bach.

It was the aesthetic of opera that served as the model for the new aria-type cantata after 1700, the type that included the hautboy and other 'figural' instruments. Apart from the subjects and texts, there was no essential difference between a da capo aria for voice and obbligato hautboy in an opera and a sacred cantata.

By the 1750s the cantata form was going out of style. And as the century progressed, the expense of putting on credible musical performances in church increased. Even in Bach's time, cantors were hard pressed to recruit minimum ensembles for the kind of music that was expected. Bach's son Carl Philip Emanuel took over Telemann's job at Hamburg in 1767, and had simply to reconcile himself

---

[36] These are printed in Moser (1935), 30–1 and Hofmann (1954), 85 ff. Cf. also Altenburg (1979), 23.
[37] Raynor (1972), 200.
[38] Cf. ibid. 209. Music was sometimes repeated (cf. Bach), but usually only after a number of years, and in a revised form.

to the inevitable mediocrity of church music with the limited funds available.[39] By the mid-1760s, arias using hautboy in church music had ceased to be written.[40]

At the same time concerted *Musique* was in decline in church, a new genre appeared: the *Choralbearbeitung* (chorale prelude) for organ with solo wind instrument, usually hautboy.[41] The first, by G. F. Kauffmann, appeared in 1733–6; they were written until well into the nineteenth century. Some three dozen chorale preludes with hautboy by Ebhardt, Gerber, Homilius, Krebs, Oley, and Tag are extant. The effect of the hautboy playing the chorale melody 'heimlich' (unannounced) amidst the density of organ sound was found 'angenehm' (pleasant).[42] Adlung implied that this was regularly done 'aus dem Stegreife' (extempore).

3. Mutation of the hautboy band during the eighteenth century

Starting early in the eighteenth century, the classic formation of two treble hautboys, two tenors, and two bassoons took on a new dimension with the addition of two horns which, when used, replaced the tenor hautboys, making a band of two hautboys, two horns, and one or two bassoons. Hildebrand (1975: 49–50) pointed out the significance of this innovation, as it marks a shift from the Renaissance concept of consorts of like instruments (in this case, double reeds). Even Lully's orchestra can be seen as the combination of a string consort with various complete wind consorts. This new ensemble was an early example of the practice that is now taken for granted of mixing together different kinds of wind instruments.

The earliest surviving music for this Baroque wind quintet (with two hautboy parts, two horns, and one bassoon) was written by Störl and was dedicated to the Württemberg court in 1711.[43] Telemann's suites for this combination, TWV 55, are also relatively early (*c.*1712–21); to judge from their present locations (the libraries at Rheda, Schwerin, Darmstadt, and Stuttgart), these courts were probably supporting bands of this kind by the first decade of the eighteenth century. The first written documentation of an ensemble with horns may be the report of the 'Hautboys' that Gottfried Pepusch brought to London from Berlin in 1704. This band played 'upon Hautboys, Flutes [= recorders], and German [or Hunting] Horns'.[44]

At Dresden this quintet formation inspired a piece by Vivaldi, the *Concerto* in F, RV 97. It is for two hautboys, two horns, bassoon, and continuo, to which is added a virtuoso viola d'amore solo (all the instruments except the basses are 'sordini').[45]

---

[39] Raynor (1972), 221.   [40] The last two were late works by Telemann (1762 and 1764).
[41] Cf. Held (1976) and Janson (1987).   [42] Adlung (1758), 687, quoted in Janson (1987), 101.
[43] MS Rostock, reproduced in Owens (1995), 352–3.
[44] Quoted in Tilmouth (1961), 54–5. Horns and hautbois alternated in Graupner's opera *Bellerophone* in 1708 (McCredie 1964: 86).
[45] This may have been written for Pisendel, who received a number of autograph scores directly from Vivaldi.

In 1726 Fleming mentioned the addition of horns to the Saxon infantry.[46] By the 1730s the wind quintet/sextet had become the norm, and had virtually replaced the group made up strictly of hautboys. Over 500 pieces survive for wind quintet, and almost all of them were written after 1730.[47] The bassoon part is usually single, but was probably intended for two players, not only because two bassoons were the norm in such bands but because there are a number of pieces where the predominantly single bass part temporarily splits into two.

In military bands starting in the 1750s, the hautboy itself was gradually replaced by the clarinet as the principal instrument.[48] Hautboys were used less and less in bands. In many cases, the players were probably the same but had simply switched from hautboy to clarinet. In France, Louis XV's minister of war signed an ordinance on 19 April 1756 that effectively banned the hautboy from the infantry:

La musique admise dans les régiments d'infanterie . . . serait désormais composés de cors, de clarinettes et de bassons.[49]	Music allowed in infantry regiments . . . will henceforth be composed of horns, clarinets, and bassoons.

4. Relative pay-scales of hautboy players

'The bottom line' was how much value was attributed to the instrument and its players by those who paid their wages.[50] The best-paid hautboists did very well in the eighteenth century, certainly better than any player today, and often better than their colleagues on other instruments. But in a society built on class differences, the second- and third-desk players did not come off as well.

While not all hautboy players were well off or even secure in their lives, it is striking to see how many did do well: Böhm was Concertmeister and 'Sekretair' at Darmstadt, and at the end of his career Alessandro Besozzi was 'Direttore Generale della Musica Strumentale' at the Turin court, and owned town and country houses and many fine paintings.[51] In a time when music had some of the public functions that sport does today, the best-paid players were probably regarded in a way not unlike the star athletes of today, hired by city teams. The salaries of some players suggest they were in this celebrity category:

---

[46] Fürstenau (1861–2: 68) reported that Saxon regiments in the early 18th c. contained eight *Hautboisten* (including a Premier), namely two discant, two taille, and two bassoonists, as well as two horns.

[47] Of surviving band music, only 9% (26 pieces) has added horns before 1730; after 1730, the figure is 95% (488 pieces). [48] Sadie (1956), 109.

[49] Cotte (1979), 316.

[50] This is a subject we can discuss now, as Benoit (1971a: 357) writes, 'avec l'indiscrétion qu'autorise le recul de temps'. [51] Burney (1771a), 72.

Penati's salary was by far the largest of any player in the orchestra of San
    Marco;

Jacob Loeillet likewise had a much higher salary than any other court
    musician at Munich;[52]

Kytch was paid £50 at Cannons 1719–20; the next highest salary was £40,
    earned by the first violinist;

Glösch at Berlin had the highest salary in the Capelle in 1713;

Rion's salary at Rome was much higher than that of the rest of the orchestra;

Böhm's salary at Darmstadt was close to the highest at court, at 600 florins;

Bissoli was paid 263 lire in 1754 and 1762, while the Maestro di Cappella,
    Vallotti, was paid 310 and the last violists got 34.[53]

The French players who began working at Berlin in 1681 were relatively well paid,
as were the 'Fratelli Martini: Aboè' in the orchestra of the Regio Ducal Teatro in
Milan. In Celle in 1682, Denis la Tourneur received a rise in salary from 180 Rthlr.
to 240 when he switched from violin to hautboy.[54] La Riche's position at Dresden
gave him a much higher salary than any regular musician. Prevost seems to have
done very well at Arolsen. Hautboy players employed in the *Chapelle* at Versailles
were better paid than any of the organists and violinists.[55] There are probably other
cases.[56]

    For the 1709–10 season and the next, the two hautboys in the Opera orchestra at
the Haymarket Theatre in London were John Loeillet (first, paid at the top level,
15s. per night) and La Tour (second, at 10s.). The principal hautboy and bassoon
were at the same level as the leading violinists; only the harpsichordist and principle cellists (who had to play all the time) were paid more.[57]

    As for court salaries, Dresden is an example: the composer and conductor
Antonio Lotti and his wife, the singer Santa Stella, received 10,500 Thaler, and
Senesino got 7,000. A construction worker in Dresden received less than 100 per
year.[58] Schmidt, the Capellmeister, was at 1,200, as was Woulmyer, the leader; good
instrumentalists like Pisendel (one of the best-known violinists of his day) were
paid 400, and the violists survived on 100; on special occasions, there were other
gifts both of cash and articles of value. Other German courts had similar or somewhat lower pay-scales. Later in the century, Fischer was getting 400 Thaler as an
absentee player in 1764, and Antonio and Carlo Besozzi were earning 1,200 and
1,000 respectively.

---

[52] Nösselt (1980), 80.   [53] Bernardini (1985a), 22.
[54] Linnemann (1935), 61.   [55] Pierre (1899), 13.
[56] At court, musicians were sometimes provided with personal servants (Linnemann 1935: 61).
[57] Milhous and Hume (1982), 133, 151; Burrows (1985), 352.   [58] Petzoldt (1983), 166–7.

The bandsmen employed by the court—the *Hautboisten*—got less than their colleagues in the chamber, and regimental players (normally paid by the officers) were the worst paid.

B. France

1. The contrasting styles of Louis Quatorze and Louis Quinze

Between 1700 and 1730 in France, there was a clear shift in the style of music being written and in the way it was performed. The event that was the symbolic watershed between these styles was Louis XIV's death in 1715; his influence in musical matters had been potent, and had caused many beautiful works to be created. But at the end so much dominance became restrictive and oppressive. When Louis XIV died, there was a general sense of change and renewal.

Until his demise, Louis's personal taste in music had preserved the classic French style at court,[59] though artificially. The Duc d'Orléans, who acted as Regent until the new King Louis XV came of age, and who moved the court back to Paris from Versailles, was partial to Italian music ('Italian', that is, as perceived by French ears). But because many of Louis XIV's musicians continued to hold positions of power and influence, the 'Louis Quatorze style' persisted at court for another decade, culminating in the great works of François Couperin, which were still quite close in spirit to the earliest chamber works he wrote back in the 1690s[60] (and those of Marais, written even earlier).[61]

Woodwind chamber music of this Louis Quatorze period was primarily in the form of suites, with some explorations into Italian style.[62] It was a good period for the production of music that could be played on the hautboy, and included some of the best music in the repertoire.

Louis XV was crowned in 1722, and soon afterward there was a clear shift to a new style of chamber music, in which suites gave way to 'Italian' sonatas. I shall discuss this Louis Quinze style in Chapter 7, and consider here the hautboy music of the Louis Quatorze period.

---

[59] Cf. Sadie (1993), 161.

[60] As discussed elsewhere, *Les Nations* actually combines some of those early pieces with newly written ones.

[61] Cf. Bowers (1972), 37 on the three periods into which French music of the first sixty years of the 18th c. can be roughly divided.

[62] House (1991), chs. 4 and 5, makes an exemplary and very useful analysis of French and Italian compositional style in chamber music (summary on pp. 173–8) that demonstrates that the two styles can be distinguished not only by their manner of performance but by many concrete methods of composition.

2. Music of the Louis Quatorze period (to c.1726)

In Louis XIV's lifetime, the most prestigious performances of chamber music were at court, but there were also regular concerts in the salons of musicians in Paris like Certain, La Guerre, Marais, Couperin, and Clérambault.[63] A good proportion of this music was published, so it was probably played frequently by amateurs as well as professionals. Couperin and Marais were the major composers of chamber music for hautboy in Louis Quatorze style, but woodwind players like La Barre, Hotteterre le Romain, and Pierre Philidor also produced fine pieces.

Our age makes a clear separation between the identities of the flute and oboe. But before about 1770 that distinction was blurred. The two instruments had virtually the same repertoire, functions, and players. It was very rare for a flutist to be anything other than an hautboy player by training who later specialized on 'flute' (that is, recorder and/or traverso). Quantz followed this pattern, and the French players most associated with flutes, like Destouches, Philbert, Descoteaux, the Pièches, La Barre, Hotteterre le Romain, Bernier, and Blavet, often continued to play what had been their first instrument, the hautboy, alongside the flute.

That was one reason, of course, for the generic 'symphonie' approach to instrumentation. The French music discussed here was not only for hautboy (as indicated or implicit on the title-pages or the parts), but was almost always for other instruments as well, especially flute (cf. Ch. 3, §G.1).

La Barre's first set of solo *Pièces* was modelled on Marais's splendid gamba solos. La Barre's first solo traverso collection, Opus 4, was printed in 1702 with reprints in 1703 and 1710; in the last edition he expanded the instrumentation to include the violin and 'autres instrumens'. He had been performing his *Pièces* for several years before they were first published.[64] With the collections of Hotteterre and Pierre Philidor, they were among the best solo pieces published in the first quarter of the century. La Barre's suites are sometimes technically challenging. Like other early collections, they contained eight or nine movements, from which a selection could be made.

Shortly afterwards, in 1708, the next important solo collection was published: Hotteterre le Romain's *Premier livre de pièces*. Hotteterre dedicated these pieces to Louis XIV, for whom he had played them. Although they were advertised for traverso, he said the *Pièces* were playable on any treble instrument. All of them

---

[63] Sadie (1993), 150.

[64] He wrote in his preface that they were the first solos to be published 'pour cette sorte de Flute' (meaning, presumably, traverso instead of recorder).

can be played on the hautboy in key except the third and fifth suites, which work better when transposed down a step.[65]

Hotteterre and La Barre were very nearly the same age, and their music is in many ways similar. Although La Barre published his solos first, there is no way of knowing if they were conceived before Hotteterre's. House (1991) points out that Hotteterre's solos, like La Barre's, were probably influenced by French chamber music of the 1680s (when both composers had been students and had come of age). That was the period of Lully's greatest power and influence.[66]

It is likely that French vocal technique influenced the conception of woodwind solo playing. As Raynor put it, 'Lully's melodic ideal was simplicity, grace, and dignity . . . A [French] singer's virtuosity was demonstrated by smoothness of style, sweetness of tone, elegance of phrasing and clarity of diction, rather than by vocal pyrotechnics.'[67] For woodwind players, these same qualities demanded precision and control of the fingers in executing ornaments, and clarity of articulation. The music is therefore often extremely demanding technically, although the listener is not (or should not be) aware of it. As Quantz remarked, 'les petits agrémens exigent bien plus de vitesse que les passages mêmes' (the small ornaments require an even greater speed than passagework).[68] This is in contrast to pieces in the Italian style that included passages often purposely meant to sound difficult.

In 1715 Hotteterre came out with a second superb book of *Pièces*, his Opus 5. Like the first book, this one consisted of suites, although the third and fourth pieces were also called 'Sonates' and showed Corellian influence.[69] All four of them can be played on the hautboy in their written keys except the fourth suite in B minor, which is better on hautboy down a step in A minor. Hotteterre was a skilled composer and careful craftsman, and his music is full of moving moments.[70] As House (1991: 265) put it, 'If his compositions are neither as numerous nor as uniform in quality as those of François Couperin, they nevertheless occasionally reach the same heights.'

Hotteterre also wrote some interesting duets for various treble instruments. He published two suites in 1712 and 1717, his Opus 4 and Opus 6. A third suite, Opus 8 (1722), is especially well suited to hautboys; it is in a lighter, more rustic style

---

[65] On transposing, see Ch. 4, §H.3. For a general description of the solo suites written in the first quarter of the 18th c., see Bowers (1972), 100–8. On pp. 108–71, Bowers describes the musical style of the works of La Barre, Hotteterre le Romain, and other composers.

[66] House devotes her fourth chapter to an analysis of chamber works of the 1680s by Lully, d'Anglebert, and Marais (summarized on pp. 126 ff.). [67] Raynor (1972), 231, 227.

[68] Quantz (1752), X, §10.

[69] Cf. House (1991), 180–2. Hotteterre's compositional style is excellently described in House (1991), ch. 6.

[70] Besides being an important theoretical work, Hotteterre's *L'Art de préluder* (1719) contains some fine music. The two preludes in the back with bass go well on hautboy (the first in the lower, alternate key suggested by Hotteterre, B flat).

similar to the music of the Chédevilles.[71] It was to be his last publication that involved the hautboy.

Couperin's *Goûts-réünis ou nouveaux concerts* (1724) are written mostly for a single treble line with bass, and they are 'a l'usage de toutes les sortes d'instrumens de musique'.[72] They succeed well with a group of instruments, sometimes playing together, other times playing movements (or parts of movements) alone. The *concerts* that best serve the hautboy are numbers 6, 7, 11 (the most complex, difficult, and fascinating), and 14. This collection is a continuation of the four *Concerts royeaux* published in 1722.[73] Like the *Goûts-réünis*, the *Concerts royeaux* are excellent on hautboy, either alone with continuo or together with other treble instruments.

Couperin wrote that the *Concerts royeaux* were performed in 1714 and 1715:

pour les petits Concerts de chambre, ou Louis XIV me faisoit venir presque tous les dimanches de l'année.[74]

at the small chamber concerts that Louis XIV had me come play almost every Sunday of the year.

These must have been among the last pieces Louis heard. Couperin named the performers of the *Concerts royeaux* as 'Messieurs Duval, Philidor, Alarius, et Dubois'; he said he himself played the harpsichord. Duval was a violinist, Alarius (Hilaire Verloge) a bass gambist. 'Dubois' was probably Pierre Dubois, a bassoonist.[75] The 'Philidor' in question might have been either André Philidor *l'aîné*, his eldest son Anne, or his nephew Pierre; all were close to the King.

Anne and Pierre Philidor, grandsons of Jean and sons of André and Jacques respectively, both had distinguished and remarkably parallel careers. They were born in the same house within months of each other and were brought up together. Both of them were appointed to the *Chapelle* as 'dessus de hautbois' in 1704, and both had the special distinction of being appointed to the *Chambre* in 1712.

Pierre Philidor held four important positions at court: he was a member of the *Douze Grands Hautbois*, an hautboy in the *Chapelle*, and both hautboist and gambist in the *Chambre*. His name is listed in court documents next to those of Couperin, Marais, and Forqueray, and at the same salary. He was singled out by Louis XIV in 1714 for the 'satisfaction His Majesty has of his services'.[76]

Philidor published a remarkable collection of *Suittes* in 1717–18. Both musically and technically, this collection is more difficult than those of La Barre and

---

[71] House (1991), 191, 218, 225.

[72] The *Apothéose de Corelli* attached at the end is (appropriately) only playable on violins. Many movements of the *Apothéose de Lully* of 1725 succeed well on hautboy; the work is most effective when played by a *symphonie*.

[73] 'Le haubois' is mentioned in the third *Concert* (along with the violin and traverso).

[74] Couperin, introduction to the *Concerts royeaux*.

[75] Presumably one of the better bassoonists of his generation, Dubois was first mentioned in court records in 1717 and called 'basson de sa Chapelle-Musique' in 1729. Cf. Benoit (1971b), 289, 392.   [76] Benoit (1971b), 260.

Hotteterre. The fourth suite contains an 'Air en Musette' that ranks with the best of Couperin's character movements; it is very difficult to play because of the flattements and downward slurs it includes. This movement is considerably easier on hautboy in G major than A; that, and the high notes at the end of the first movement, are good arguments for playing the entire piece down a step. Suites 5 and 6 in this collection are also more successful on hautboy transposed down. The fifth suite is almost as remarkable as the fourth in musical content. The ninth is best on hautboy in its written key, E minor.

Philidor's *Suittes* are unique in their detailed indications for ornaments and dynamics; suite 9 is the most dense in this regard: the first movement, fourteen bars long, contains thirteen flattements, six battements, and eighteen trills. These pieces are especially useful as training material, not only because they contain so many explicit directions, but because they are at the same time technically challenging and musically rewarding.

François Chauvon, apparently an hautboy player, was a pupil of Couperin; his collection of solos, called *Tibiades*, appeared in 1717, the same year as the first of Pierre Philidor's *Suittes*. Another notable solo collection in this style is Montéclair's *Concerts* with movements 'propre au Violon, Haubois, ou à la Flûte à bec' (1724–5). The fourth Concert, for an unspecified treble instrument and Bass, contains much interesting and beautiful *Affect* portrayal; curiously, it is in both B minor and B flat major (but works better for hautboy in A minor and B flat major, with a selection of movements).[77]

Among the earliest good *symphonie* collections to appear were those of La Barre and Charles Desmazures. In addition to the published versions of La Barre's three books of *Pièces en trio* (1694, 1700, 1707), there is a manuscript copy at Paris bound with Hotteterre le Romain's trios.[78] This manuscript has notated ornaments (such as the flattement) that are not included in the published versions. Desmazures's *Pièces de simphonie à quatre parties . . . rangées en suites, sur tous les tons* are also excellent. They were published in Marseilles in 1702, and were composed on the occasion of a visit to Marseilles by Marie-Louise of Savoy.

After Marais's collection, probably the finest trios in the classic Louis Quatorze style are Couperin's four *Nations*: La Françoise, L'Espagnole, L'Impériale, La Piémontoise. Few pieces in the hautboy's literature can match their nobility and depth of feeling. Each 'Nation' is divided into a 'Sonade' in Italian style and a French suite of dances. As mentioned above, three of the 'sonades' were composed in the 1690s; the rest of the collection first appeared in 1726.[79] The music is

---

[77] Fleurot (1984), 157 points out that the fifth *Concert*, being in a military vein, is also appropriate for hautboy.
[78] 4° Vm. 848 [1–3].
[79] For more complete descriptions of these pieces, see Anthony (1973), 314 ff. and Beaussant (1980), 229–47.

technically quite challenging on hautboy, but almost all the movements are play-able, sometimes with small adjustments. These pieces work well with either two hautboys or in mixed instrumentation with violin or traverso.

French pieces like the ones just discussed have plentiful and detailed indica-tions for ornamenting and articulation. It is clear that these markings are not meant merely for the benefit of beginners (like, for instance, the ornamented slow movements of Telemann's *Methodische Sonaten*). The French indications are not optional; they are what Quantz called the 'agréments essentiels'; the music would sound quite different without them. They reflect the French attitude (as expressed by Couperin and Leclair, among others)[80] that ornaments marked in the music were to be followed literally.[81]

3. Hautboy players at court

By this period, the members of the *Douze Grands Hautbois* performed only for important ceremonials. On the occasion of the coronation of Louis XV in 1722, they were depicted in one of the engravings in the series by Tardieu (Pl. 1.23). The members included many eminent players of the hautboy of the older 'classic' generation at its sunset:

Treble hautboys:[82]
      Gilles Allain (about 57 years old)
      Julien Bernier (about 57 years old)
      Pierre Chédeville (about 27)
      Jean Hannès Desjardins (about 53)
      Jacques Hallé (about 30)
      Pierre Philidor (41)

Hautecontre:
      Colin Hotteterre (69 [!])
      Anne Philidor (41)

Taille:
      Charles Bidault de Gardainville (about 46)
      François Philidor (27)

Bassoon:
      Jean (6) Hotteterre (74 [!])
      Jacques Hotteterre le Romain (48)

---

[80] Cf. Anthony (1973), 325.

[81] Evidently, rigorous consistency was not necessary, however; I: 4 and I: 16 in the fourth Philidor *Suitte* are otherwise identical but place the slur over the *tièrce coulée* differently.

[82] These six musicians had no special designation, so it is assumed they were treble players.

The official titles of the players (as given in numerous documents of the time)[83] indicate how the parts were divided in the ensemble: six on the top part and two on each of the other three. The ages of the players varied widely. Because a position in this band carried much prestige and its functions were minimal, the majority of its members were long established, and the average age was 48.[84] Two of the Hotteterres were 69 and 74.

A number of religious works written for the royal chapel required *symphonies*. The standard ensemble was two traversos, two bassoons, and a basse de *cromorne* in addition to five-part strings. Hautboys were sometimes used: three hautboys were part of the *Chapelle* from 1704 to 1708.[85] Although the combination was never common in France, the hautboy was sometimes given obbligato work with solo voice, as in La Lande's Récit 'Ego autem annuntiabo' for Hautecontre, violin or hautboy 'seul' and continuo in the motet *Confitebimur tibi Deus* of 1701.[86] The royal chapels were exceptional in using winds; these chapels were not part of the church system in France. In the rest of the country, the use of orchestral instruments in ecclesiastical music was discouraged by a strict code (documented in the *Caeremoniale Parisiense*, 1662).[87]

4. Hautboy players in the city

The court moved from Versailles back to Paris during the Regency starting in 1715; by that time many courtiers had already retreated to their town houses. Concert life thus gradually centred in the city, and although the court moved back to Versailles when Louis XV was crowned, the new king was not musical, and only 'a token semblance of tradition, clearly weakened by the tone of the Regency, was maintained at Versailles'.[88] Thus after 1715 most instrumentalists found their work in Paris, playing concerts, teaching, and publishing their music.

Although new works were produced regularly at the Opéra after Lully's death in 1687, his opera-ballets remained an important part of the repertoire of the Opéra until well after the mid-eighteenth century.[89] Hautboys in the orchestra of the Opéra from before 1704 were Colin Hotteterre (principal; a1704–27), Bernier (second and traverso; a1704–p1719), Jean Rousselet (third; a1704–11), Mangot (1720–38), Lucas (probably second, also traverso; a1726–p1738), Despréaux, and

---

[83] Cf. Benoit (1971b).
[84] A description of the playing protocol for this coronation is found in Écorcheville (1903), 613–14, also 626.
[85] Pierre (1899), 5–6.
[86] La Lande's hautboy solo 'Sustinuit anima mea' in *De profundis* is not part of the original motet of 1689, but was written for a version revised sometime between 1715 and 1726.   [87] Schneider (1995), 713.
[88] Sadie (1993), 177.   [89] Cf. Bartlet (1989).

Du Fresne (both from 1727). From 1709, Esprit-Philippe Chédeville joined the Opéra orchestra and remained until 1736, probably playing mainly musette.

Quantz was in Paris for seven months starting in August 1726, and heard the Opéra orchestra (whose hautboists at that point were probably Mangot, Lucas, Despréaux, and Du Fresne). He was not impressed:

Das Orchester war damals schlecht, und spielte, mehr nach dem Gehör und Gedächtniß, welches der mit einem großen Stocke vorgeschlagene Tact, in Ordnung halten mußte, als nach den Noten.[90]

The orchestra was in those days poor, and played more by ear and by memory than by reading the parts; it had to be held together by the beating of a large staff.

With the musical energy concentrated in Paris after 1715, there were regular concerts in the homes of the aristocracy and wealthy commoners, such as that of Antoine Crozat. Crozat and others also initiated a subscription concert series at the Tuileries Palace at which professional musicians performed;[91] it became known as the *Concert Italien*. The success of these concerts inspired Anne Philidor, who had extensive contacts, to open in 1725 the famous and influential concert series called the *Concert Spirituel*, using the services of court and Opéra musicians (see Ch. 7, §B.2).

5. Instruments

There were many Parisian hautboy makers at the beginning of the century; among those known at present are Naust, Rippert, Colin Hotteterre, Charles Pelletier jun., Klenig, Bizey, Rouge, Debey, and Moucherel.

The type of hautboy used in the early eighteenth century is shown in a beautiful portrait by André Bouys made in 1704 (Pl. 5.1). Accurate images of the bell and keys of one hautboy and the upper part and reed of another are included in the instrument trophy.

In 1713 Jean-Baptiste Desjardins, who was one of the *Grand Hautbois*, hired Pelletier to make instruments exclusively for him for several years. The surviving hautboy stamped 'Desjardin'[92] might therefore have been made by Pelletier.

An hautboy formerly at Berlin was stamped 'Peltier' with a lion rampant, and there must surely have been a connection with the Naust workshop, which also used the lion rampant. Naust had married Pelletier sen.'s daughter Barbe; after his death in 1709, Naust's shop on the rue de l'Arbre Sec was operated by his widow until 1726.[93] Pelletier jun. may have worked there during this time. After 1726

---

[90] Quantz (1755), 238.   [91] Sadie (1993), 177.
[92] Winston-Salem 0–113.   [93] Cf. Giannini (1993b), 8–9.

PL. 5.1. André Bouys, *Caecilia de Lisorez (Vide, & audi)*, 1704. Mezzotint, 34 × 24.5 cm.
London: Tony Bingham

the Nausts' daughter Jeanne ran the shop until 1734 with her husband Antoine Delerablée (who had worked at the shop from before 1717). The workshop inventories in the 1720s and 1730s, when Delerablée was foreman, list a number of well-known performers among its clients: Desjardins (probably François) for two flutes, Philidor (probably Pierre, who lived nearby) dated 1725 for about seventeen instruments, Pièche (probably Pierre or Joseph, both hautboists) for about eighteen flutes, and Blavet for about twenty instruments. The Munich court received 'flûtes' from the Naust shop in 1719 and 1721.

A recorder from Naust's shop cost 15 livres in 1721. By way of comparison, Jacob Denner asked 5 'fl. Kr.' for an 'Alt-Flauden' (treble recorder) in 1710, and asked the same price for each of four 'Hautbois, von Buchsbaum' (hautboys in boxwood). In 1720 he asked only 4 fl. for each hautboy and 2 fl. for a recorder.[94] If the relation was the same, Delerablée would have asked 12 to 15 livres for an hautboy. A generation earlier, in 1685, three hautboys provided by Martin Hotteterre had cost 22 livres each.[95] In 1721, Bizey charged the Munich court 45 livres each for two hautboys 'garnis d'argent' (with silver fittings).[96]

A remarkable maker was Christophe Moucherel (b. 1686), who also made harpsichords and several organs, including the famous one at Albi. In a 'Mémoire' he wrote in 1734, he states that he made hautboys and had studied instrument-making in 1711 with both Rippert and Colin Hotteterre.[97] He wrote that his maker's mark consisted of a 'mouche' (fly) plus the letters 'rel'. None of his hautboys appears to have survived.

With so many Hotteterres performing, there would have been a considerable number of their hautboys in use, although only two bearing this name are known to survive now. Indeed, French hautboys in general account for only about 12 per cent of the surviving instruments; to judge from the number of known players and the level of musical activity at the time, and the orders for woodwinds made from abroad (like Berlin and Munich), that number does not seem to reflect accurately the original situation. The hazards of fortune may be the explanation—and possibly the systematic vandalism of old musical instruments that took place at the time of the Revolution. Hubbard (1965: 115–16) remarked that surviving French harpsichords are improbably scarce as well; it is known that many were broken up and used to heat the classrooms at the Conservatoire during the early nineteenth century. Boxwood also burns well, especially when it is dry.

---

[94] Nickel (1971), 251–3.

[95] Lasocki (forthcoming), 11. In 1715, Hotteterre le Romain asked 100 livres (= 10 pistoles) for a musette with ivory pipes and silver keys (House 1991: 57).   [96] Schmid (1986), 33.

[97] Moucherel (1734). Moucherel wrote that he also trained his brother Sébastien, and there is other documentation (Jacquot 1882: 2) that Sébastien Moucherel was a maker of hautboys at Nancy in 1724.

C. Italy

1. Milan

In the earliest years of the eighteenth century, Milan was governed by Prince Charles Henry de Vaudémont (whose *maître de la musique* was Michel Pignolet de Montéclair). From 1703, an exceptionally good hautboist named François Des Noyers was in Vaudémont's service. Des Noyers, who a contemporary called 'le premier Hautbois de l'Europe', caused a sensation with his playing ('a brillé dans toute l'Italie').[98] He had been trained at the court of Hannover, probably by (? his father) Mathieu (it may have been for the two Des Noyers that Steffani wrote his arias at Hannover).

Milan came under Habsburg rule in 1706, and was thus linked closely to Vienna. Opera flourished, and Saint-Martin was probably the principal hautboy player (he may have continued to play until about 1720; he died in 1724). Giovanni Bononcini's *Griselda* was produced there in 1718; it contains a lovely aria, 'Nel caro sposo', with a fine hautboy part. By 1720, the orchestra of the Teatro Regio Ducale included two of Saint-Martin's sons, one of whom was Giuseppe Sammartini.[99]

A number of hautboy solos were probably written in Milan in this period. Besides opera, there were regular performances of oratorios and sacred cantatas in the churches, and frequent private concerts in patrician houses. Three pieces by Brivio 'Della Tromba' survive.

Sammartini was in Milan until 1728 or 1729,[100] and during this time he may also have played regularly in Venice. By 1716 (when he was 21) he had published an hautboy concerto. His six provocative sonatas for the hautboy contained in a manuscript now at Rochester were probably composed over a long period in Milan.[101] One unusual movement is duplicated as the last of both Sonatas 2 and 3. In it, the repeats are written out in 'Altro Modo' as if to make divisions (though the second version is only slightly more elaborate than the first).[102] Not only are they musically interesting, these sonatas are relatively rare examples of music from this period conceived specifically for the hautboy by an hautboy player.[103] The third, fourth, and fifth sonatas are among the finest in the hautboy's repertoire. The first two give the impression of being youthful works: there is an experimental

---

[98] Braun (1987), 137 citing Nolhac.

[99] A note indicates that the 'Fratelli Martini: Aboè' were relatively well paid. Bernardini (1985a), 15, citing Barblan. [100] See below, §E.1 for a discussion of Sammartini's possible visit to London in 1723–4.

[101] The first sonata is in one hand, the second in another, and the other four in a third. The composer is called 'Giuseppe St Martino' in the second sonata, while the other title-pages call him 'Giuseppe S. Martini'.

[102] The movement is generally more accurately written out and has more explicit ornamentation in Sonata 3, although there are more slurs in Sonata 2. [103] Cf. Houle (1984). On p. 95, Houle analyses the first sonata.

character about them, harmonic sequences are sometimes unconvincing, and the brilliant inspirations found in the other sonatas are rare. Sonata 5 is the most authoritative, most difficult, and best of the group. It uses several interesting techniques, including trilled scales, tremolo in the Andante (see Ch. 4, §K.2.a), quick articulated downward scales, and a continuous broken trill on g1 (Pl. 4.17). The third movement also uses tremolo, and includes a low c♯1 (see Ch. 4, §G.2; there are several c♮1s in the previous two movements). The sixth sonata, like the fifth, is late in style, but has fewer good ideas and is less worked out. These sonatas show what a creative and remarkable player Sammartini must already have been in his twenties.

Three of the sonatas in this collection, no. 6 for hautboy and nos. 7 and 12 (for other instruments), have concordances with another manuscript collection at Parma, CF-V-20, '[17] Sinfonie [Sonatas] for Flauto e Bc'. The title-page of this latter collection says they are by Sammartini of Milan, so they must predate 1729, when Sammartini moved to London. Although the Parma sonatas are for *Flauto* (that is, recorder), Sammartini may also have conceived them for hautboy.[104]

Anciuti continued to make beautiful instruments in Milan during this period. Many are dated (the years are 1718, 1719, 1721, 1725, 1727, 1730, and 1738).

2. Venice

Vivaldi's earliest dated piece that includes the hautboy, RV 779, is a sonata written in about 1707 for violin, hautboy, and organ, on the score of which the name of the hautboist is written: Pelegrina 'dall'Oboè'. Pelegrina was one of a number of orphan girls trained to very high standards by several of the *ospedali* in Venice. Performances of the *ospedali* orphans were famous. Pelegrina was an inmate of the Pietà, where Vivaldi taught. In August 1703, the *maestro di coro* of the Pietà, Francesco Gasparini, requested the governors to appoint teachers of violin, viola, and hautboy.[105] Ignazio Rion, Onofrio Penati, Ludwig Erdmann, Pelegrina herself (from 1707), and Ignaz Sieber took turns teaching hautboy at the Pietà from 1704 until 1722. Stable teaching posts existed for hautboists at the Mendicanti from before 1700 and at the Derelitti from about 1713.[106] At the Derelitti one of the girls named Anna (presumably Anna 'dall'Oboè') was teaching from 1718.

Penati and possibly Saint-Martin and Rion were playing in Venice in the 1690s. From March 1704, Rion was teaching hautboy at the Pietà; by 1705 he had moved to Rome. Rion was probably related to Luigi (or Louis) Rion, who was employed as

---

[104] Someone long ago made notes on the manuscript, classifying the sonatas as '*migliori, inferiori,* and *per esercizio*'.   [105] Selfridge-Field (1986), 381.
[106] Bernardini (1988), 374–5. Erdmann married one of the inmates and teachers of the Mendicanti; see Kirkendale (1993), 449.

an hautboy player in Turin from 1677. Erdmann, who had come to Bologna from Ansbach in about 1700, was in Venice by 1706, when he was appointed to the Pietà. Like Rion's, his stay was apparently brief; in 1709 he was engaged by the Medici court in Florence. Sieber (presumably a German) was in Venice from 1713 to about 1716–17, teaching hautboy at the Pietà.[107] At that point he apparently moved to Rome. By 1728 he was again in Venice, teaching traverso at the Pietà.[108] Sammartini is known to have been in Venice in 1726 (see below), and might have been there earlier. Another young hautboy player, Giovanni Platti (b. 1697), was in Venice from before 1715 to 1722. He was later to have a distinguished career in Würzburg.

Cities in the vicinity occasionally hired Venetian hautboists. Caldara performed two *Gloria*s at either Mantua or Venice in 1705 that included 'large-scale arias with oboe obbligatos'.[109] Since there is no indication of other hautboy activity at Mantua at this time, a Venetian hautboist may have been involved. Another *Gloria* in C that contains a solo hautboy aria was performed in Venice in September 1707.

It is surprising that no evidence has been found of woodwind makers in Venice at the beginning of the eighteenth century. Penati purchased two hautboys for the Pietà in 1705.[110] According to Vincenzo Coronelli, writing in 1706,[111] hautboys were sometimes obtained from Milan. The only known makers working in that decade in Italy were Saint-Martin (if indeed he was a maker) and Anciuti, both of whom lived in Milan. Anciuti sometimes added a winged lion holding the testament of St Mark to his workshop stamp, suggesting the instruments were made for some official Venetian institution. Penati's order was thus probably to Anciuti (whom he no doubt knew).

Besides instrumental concerts, Venetian hautboists would at least sometimes have been involved in church music (Penati worked at San Marco). And as the home of opera, Venice may have produced a number of early hautboy obbligatos. This literature is not yet explored to any extent.[112] Alessandro Scarlatti produced the opera *Mitridate* in Venice in 1707; it included two hautboy obbligatos, 'Bella gloria d'un gran rè' and 'Vado sì'. There is a fine hautboy solo with soprano, 'Pensieri, voi mi tormentate', in the second act of Handel's opera *Agrippina*, produced at Venice in 1709. An aria for soprano, two hautboys, and Bass by Lotti, 'In questo sen non scherzo', had its première (according to the manuscript) at the theatre 'S. Giov. Gris.mo', *c.*1708–16.[113] And (although they did not invent it) Venetians were probably responsible for starting the vogue for the solo hautboy concerto.

---

[107] In documents, his name is given as 'Ignazio'.

[108] It may or may not be significant that the period of Sieber's absence from Venice corresponds to what is known of Sammartini's activities there.   [109] Selfridge-Field (1987), 120.

[110] Bernardini (1985a), 18.   [111] Cited in Bernardini (1988), 383.

[112] Cf. obbligatos by Zuccari (14.1 in Haynes 1992a) and Lotti (15.1).   [113] Berlin (Mus MS 30 274).

Tomaso Albinoni's *Concerti a cinque*, Opus 7 (1715), were the first hautboy concertos to appear in print, and enjoyed a remarkable success. The medium itself was not new: more than a dozen solos for hautboy and orchestra from before 1710 are known, the earliest dating from about 1693.[114] Pieces in sonata form for an hautboy and strings had been performed at Modena and Bologna around the turn of the century (see Ch. 3, §B), and Handel's famous G minor concerto is tentatively dated 1703–5. Vivaldi wrote his first hautboy concertos around 1710. The four hautboy concertos in the Roger anthology that appeared a year after Albinoni's group (including one by Sammartini, two by Rampini of Padua, and the well-known Marcello) may have been in circulation before they were published.

Albinoni's Opus 7 consists of four concertos for strings with continuo, four with one added hautboy, and four with two hautboys.[115] The concertos for two hautboys imitate the style of Italian trumpet concertos, with their simple melodies built around arpeggiation of the tonic chord, and diatonic scale passages;[116] Vivaldi's three surviving double-hautboy concertos follow the same model. In Italy, as Talbot observed, the hautboy was for a time 'a prisoner of the trumpet idiom'.

The solo hautboy concertos, on the other hand, broke new ground. As Talbot suggests (1990: 164), the most obvious model for an hautboy concerto was the violin concerto: 'On the whole, Vivaldi assimilates the style of the oboe as much as he dares to that of the violin . . .' But an hautboy 'could not enter and leave the limelight as unobtrusively as a solo violin, nor could [it] be expected to play continuously without any opportunity for rest'.[117] Albinoni seems to have looked to the voice rather than the violin as a model for handling the hautboy: 'Though he may err on the side of caution, Albinoni gives his oboe soloists more grateful and idiomatic parts than Vivaldi, . . . [who did] not scruple to reproduce the arpeggiations and rapid changes of register of his string writing . . .'[118] As Bernardini observed, the relation Albinoni established between the soloist and the strings makes his concertos more 'with' than 'for' hautboy.[119]

Although Rion had left Venice in 1705 and Erdmann in 1708, these concertos could have been written for Penati, Sieber, or Platti, who were all active in the years prior to their publication in 1715; Sammartini may have been in Venice by this time as well.

---

[114] There are surviving concertos by Pignatta (c.1693), Rosier (1697), Anon. (? 1690s), Fischer (? 1690s), Sydow (? by c.1701), Handel (1703–5 and 1706–10), Rieck (by 1704), Bononcini (1706), Corbett (before c.1708), De Castro (1708), Müller (c.1709), and Manfredini (? before 1710). See Haynes (1992a).   [115] Cf. Talbot (1990), 160.

[116] Talbot (1973), 16.   [117] Ibid. 18.   [118] Ibid. 20.

[119] Bernardini (1988), 377. Interesting observations on Albinoni's hautboy concerto form are found in Talbot (1973) 19 and (1990), 165–6. Butler (1995) observed that in Albinoni's hautboy concertos the hautboy does not play the initial ritornello. (More work needs to be done on this question by examining original performance material to see when the solo part is written out (cf. Ewell 1997: 16).)

The best-known of the Venetian hautboy concertos is probably the Marcello which, despite the amount it is played, remains fresh and interesting. Bach transcribed it for harpsichord, adding elaborate written-out ornaments to the slow movement (BWV 974).

Vivaldi is survived by twenty-two solo hautboy concertos.[120] Besides the two published by Roger in *c*.1720, only one of them, RV 460, is dated (1729). His earliest hautboy concertos were written between 1709 and 1712,[121] perhaps for students at the Pietà. A later group was written in the 1720s;[122] since Vivaldi continued to supply concertos to the Pietà in that decade, these may also have been for its students.[123] On the other hand, Quantz tells us he heard Sammartini in Venice in 1726.[124] The most difficult of these concertos (RV 460, RV 449, RV 461, and RV 463) might have been written for Sammartini.

Heinichen was in Venice from 1710 to 1716, and in October of 1715 he wrote an hautboy concerto that is now preserved at Dresden.[125] Crown Prince Friedrich August of Saxony (who was to become Elector at Dresden in 1733) arrived in Venice a few months later. The prince was making his Grand Tour, which included Paris and Vienna as well as Venice, and he was accompanied by several court musicians who would later take important posts in his Capelle, including Richter, Zelenka, and Pisendel (Richter was later to become principal hautboist of the Dresden court orchestra, and Pisendel its leader). The trip also served these musicians as an opportunity for study; Richter had had lessons in Paris in 1714, and probably had contact with hautboy players in Venice at the time, possibly even Sammartini (four of Sammartini's hautboy concertos are now at Dresden). Heinichen may have prepared his concerto on the occasion of the Dresden party's visit, perhaps to show the prince (who preferred Italian music to French) his mastery of Venetian musical idioms, one of the latest being the hautboy concerto. Friedrich August's party stayed in Venice until December 1716, and during that time Heinichen was engaged to be Capellmeister at Dresden.

In 1722 Albinoni produced another set of *Concerti a cinque*, his wonderful Opus 9, substantially longer and more intricately worked out than Opus 7, though following the same pattern of instrumentation.[126] Opus 9 was dedicated to Maximilian Emanuel of Bavaria, and was published, like Opus 7, by Roger in Amsterdam.

---

[120] My favourites are RV 447, 451, 454, 455, 457, 460, and 461 (among these, the most difficult to play are RV 451, 460, and 461). [121] Cf. Bernardini (1988), 376. These may include RV 464 and RV 465.

[122] It includes RV 449, RV 454, RV 456, RV 460, and possibly RV 455.

[123] A visitor at the time reported that the most gifted hautboist at the Pietà in 1726 was Susanna (Bernardini 1988: 374).

[124] He commented (1755: 232): 'Von Instrumentisten fand ich außer dem Vivaldi und Madonis, Violinisten, und dem Hoboisten San Martino aus Mailand, eben nicht viel besonders in Venedig.' It seems Sammartini was playing in both cities (as his father may have done before him). [125] H I, 6a–c.

[126] Cf. Talbot (1990), 182.

Roger did a great service to the hautboy in publishing these concertos, for they became well known all over Europe as a result, and inspired many a fine adagio; Handel's glorious slow movement in the Concerto Grosso, Opus 3/2 (1734), for instance, seems like his own interpretation of the Adagio of Albinoni's Opus 9/2. Albinoni's music was popular in Germany: several pieces involving hautboy are or were in German libraries.[127] He was highly regarded in Munich, and his wife, the singer Margherita Rimondi, sang there in 1720. Albinoni himself went to Munich in 1722, the year of the dedication of Opus 9. On that occasion the solo concertos were probably played by Jacob Loeillet (see below, §D.17).

In Opus 9 Albinoni extended the strategies used in the solo concertos to the ones for two hautboys, making them considerably more interesting than the double concertos of Opus 7. The second chamber hautboy at Munich (and thus presumably the player of the second hautboy part) was Schuechbaur, from whose workshop had issued the short hautboy preserved at Venice mentioned above. Albinoni's visit to Munich might have been the link in the chain of circumstances that caused Schuechbaur's instrument to end up in Venice.

Two of the shortest surviving original hautboys, probably pitched at A+1, have ended up in Italy.[128] A+1 was a pitch standard known in Italy as *Corista di Lombardia*. In addition, of the surviving hautboys probably at A+0, or *Corista Veneto*, one is now in Venice and another was probably made in Milan.[129] Some Venetian hautboy parts also suggest that (at least sometimes) high-pitched hautboys were used there. This has interesting implications.

The hautboy parts to Vivaldi's Concerto in D minor, RV 566, for two recorders, two 'Hautbois', bassoon, two solo violins, strings, and continuo suggest that the hautboys fingered this piece in C minor. In the first movement (b. 54), there is an $e\flat3$ in the first hautboy part; that is already a semitone higher than Vivaldi took the hautboy in any of his solo concertos. But in the third movement (b. 31), the first hautboy goes even higher to e3. In addition, there is an extremely uncharacteristic passage in the second hautboy part of the third movement that would be much easier if played down a whole step.[130]

RV 566 survives in D minor, but if the hautboys involved in its original performance had been pitched at A+1, a tone above the strings, they would have played in C minor, thus resolving the aberrations of range and finger technique described above. The strings, pitched at A–1 (as they apparently sometimes were both in churches and opera orchestras at Venice), would have played in the notated key, D minor.

---

[127] Herdringen and Rheda; see Haynes (1992a), 2–3.
[128] Schuechbaur (Venice Cons. 33) and Gahn (Milan Cons.).
[129] (David?) Denner (Venice Cons. 34), Martin (Paris E.210, C.470).
[130] Bar 39. The notes are g♯1–f♯1–e1–f♯1–b1–a1–b1–c2.

RV 566 suggests the possibility that the solo parts to Venetian hautboy concertos might regularly have been conceived a tone lower than the keys in which they were published. The Marcello concerto, for instance, survives not only in its published form in D minor, but in a manuscript in Schwerin in C minor.[131] Apart from other interesting differences of detail, in bars 49, 106, and 126 of the third movement of the manuscript, the hautboy goes up quite logically and musically to c3. In the printed version in D minor, these three c3s would be d3s, notes that would have been difficult for amateurs, and they are replaced by b2, g2, and g2 respectively. It is plausible, then, that the piece was originally conceived for the hautboy in C minor, not D minor. It might originally have been performed in Venice on an A+1 hautboy, like Vivaldi's RV 566, and a manuscript copy of this version found its way to the Schwerin library.

In both these cases, the transposition in question was a whole step; this means the pitch difference between the instruments would also have been a whole step. What of other Venetian hautboy concertos of the same period? If the strings were at A−1 in Venice and hautboys normally a step higher at A+1, is it possible that the scores of other Venetian hautboy concertos (which are our usual sources now) were prepared in the key of the orchestra, a whole tone above the solo hautboy parts? And that, when they were published in the north, the solo hautboy parts were all transposed up a step? Were all these concertos originally fingered a step lower on hautboy?

There are indeed reasons to think that the hautboy concertos of Albinoni's Opus 7 and Opus 9 were originally played in Venice a step lower on higher-pitched hautboys. Talbot (1990: 165 n. 16) observed that the notes c1 and eb1 never appear in any of them. Had the concertos been played down a step, eb1 would have become db1, a troublesome note on the hautboy, and thus avoided. The written d1s would of course have become the missing c1s (in the C minor version, the Marcello does go down to c1). Bernardini (1988: 377) also commented: 'A peculiarity of most Venetian solo oboe parts of the first half of the century is the frequent use of the high register, up to the top note, d‴ . . . Albinoni and many of Vivaldi's works seem to avoid the low register.' The d3 would have become c3 if the part was played down a step.[132]

Penati, one of the most likely candidates as the original performer of the Marcello and Albinoni concertos, had good reason to be playing at A+1, since he had taken over the cornett's functions at San Marco in 1698. Not only had cornetts usually played at that pitch,[133] but the organs of this church had been built at a very

[131] Schwerin: 3530.
[132] On the other hand, preliminary experiments by Sand Dalton (pers. comm.) with short hautboys indicate that they play the high notes particularly easily, which might explain why Albinoni used them so frequently.
[133] Cf. Haynes (1994b).

high pitch; on the basis of present evidence, either A+1 or another whole step higher.[134]

In their published forms, Albinoni's concertos often produce an hautboy sound —in A–1—similar to the bright effect of higher-pitched hautboys. For the double concertos of Opus 9, the version that was heard at Munich during Albinoni's visit in 1722 probably involved Schuechbauer as second hautboy; most of Schuechbauer's surviving instruments are pitched very high,[135] so the performances at Munich may have been conceived for high-pitched hautboys. It is therefore imaginable that for the published version, in order to achieve the same brilliant sound at a lower pitch, Albinoni transposed the concertos up a step (at least those that resulted in good tonalities).

There is thus a good case for thinking that some Venetian hautboy concertos were originally played in lower keys than those of their published versions. But there is one caveat: downward transposition would in some cases produce unlikely keys. The solo parts to the solo concertos of Opus 7 would have been in A♭, C, E♭, and B♭, and those of Opus 9 in C minor, B flat major, F minor, and A flat major. As solo tonalities of extant hautboy concertos, F minor is very rare and A flat major non-existent (see Ch. 4, §H.2). The resulting keys would also have required a number of difficult and uncharacteristic trills.[136] Only Opus 7/6 benefits from the downward transposition of a whole step, sounding better in C than D, and avoiding high d_3s in the last movement. An explanation could be that Albinoni was selective: some of the concertos may have remained in their original keys in their published forms.[137] But in that case, some of them would have included high d_3s.

As for the surviving concertos of Vivaldi, exactly half do not go down to c_1. Since so few of his concertos can be dated with assurance, it is not possible to relate this characteristic to periods. Concertos that have c_1 tend to be late, but not all late concertos have c_1. Some concertos are easier when transposed down a step, others are not. No positive conclusions can be drawn from them.

As Bernardini noticed, the usual evidence for transposition of hautboy parts (of the kind found in Handel's Roman works and some of Bach's cantatas) is missing for these Venetian concertos: parts to the same piece in different keys. For the moment, then, the question of transposition of Venetian concertos must remain open.

[134] Haynes (1995), 66.

[135] Recorders Bogenhaus 6a, Miller 328, Nuremberg MIR 210, as well as the very short hautboy at Venice Cons. 33. The Schuechbaur hautboy at St Petersburg (510) is normal length, however (AL 325.2).

[136] Opus 9/2, for instance, if transposed down to C minor, would have in II: 11 and III: 67 trills on c_2–d♭, and g_1–a♭.

[137] Since A+0 was also a common Venetian pitch, it is worth considering the possibility that some concertos were transposed down a semitone. But the resulting keys are not good ones on the hautboy.

3. Parma

Hautboy playing is first documented at the cathedral in Parma in 1701.[138] The two players were Aurelio Colla and Cristoforo Besozzi. Besozzi, who had come from Milan, was the progenitor of many renowned players.[139]

In 1702, Duke Antonio Farnese of Parma created an hautboy band called the *Guardia Irlandese*.[140] Cristoforo Besozzi and his eldest son Giuseppe were members of this band in 1711; his other two sons, Alessandro and Paolo Girolamo (who were later to be famous in Turin), were appointed in 1714, at the ages of 12 and 10.

The *Guardia* was active until 1731. While in Parma in 1726, Quantz heard one of the Besozzis (probably Giuseppe) playing in an opera with Farinelli and Carestini, and gave him the lukewarm judgement 'sehr geschickt' (very capable).[141] In 1727, Giuseppe's son Antonio (who would later be a celebrated soloist at Dresden) also joined the band.

4. Bologna

When the *cappella* of San Petronio at Bologna was disbanded in the 1690s, some of its members, including Pietro Bettinozzi, found work at Ansbach; Bettinozzi was employed as a violinist there soon after 1696. Padre Martini wrote that it was in Ansbach that Bettinozzi learned the hautboy, flute, and bassoon, and that he introduced them to Bologna in 1702, when the *cappella* was reconstituted there.

It is probably no coincidence that at the time Bettinozzi was at Ansbach, Erdmann was also employed there, or that Erdmann's first appearance in Italy was at Bologna in about 1700. From that time, numerous pieces produced at San Petronio involved hautboy parts, often added to existing works.[142]

The presence of Bettinozzi and Erdmann evidently inspired other compositions and arrangements involving hautboy, such as a collection (now lost) of forty-four sonatas or ayres for two hautboys or violins by Vitali, published in London about 1702, and a solo hautboy concerto by Manfredini.

There were a number of theatres at Bologna, and opera was performed there privately. The Accademia Filarmonica, which was run by musicians, acted as a catalyst for many concerts, and organized the musicians of Bologna's churches. Aldrovandini, who was *principe* of the Accademia from 1702 to 1707, is survived by a cantata, *Son ferito d'un labro di ciglio*, for soprano, hautboy, and continuo.

In 1708 Padre Francisco De Castro published a series of concertos for hautboy in the style of Torelli; he wrote in the preface that 'alcuni di tali Concerti possano

---

[138] Bernardini (1985a), 17.
[139] The Besozzi family may have been active in music well before this. Holman (1993), 20 notes that a violin consort was founded by four members of the family 'Bisutzi' at Munich in the 1550s.
[140] Bernardini (1985a), 17.   [141] Quantz (1755), 235.   [142] Schnoebelen (1969), 52.

essere sonati da una Tromba in mancanza dell'Oboè' (some of the said concertos can be played on trumpet if the hautboy is not at hand). The pieces may have been written for 'Monsù Luigi dall'Abbuè', who was paid in 1708 for a guest appearance at San Petronio; Monsù Luigi no doubt being Ludwig Erdmann. Ferdinando de' Medici gave permission to 'Lodovico mio oboista' (Erdmann) to play in Bologna just two years later.[143]

It is possible that Francesco Barsanti worked as an hautboist in Bologna from 1717 to 1735 (see below, §E.1).

The reigning Duke of Modena lived at Bologna in 1702–7, while his city was being occupied by the French. An aria with hautboy obbligato by Grazianini was performed 'before the Highnesses of Brunswick and Modena' in 1705 (presumably in Bologna), and 'marvelously received'.[144] It was probably in this period that the Modena court obtained the concertos with hautboy by Bettinozzi and De Castro that eventually became part of the Este Collection, now in Vienna. Bettinozzi may also have been responsible for the arrangements for hautboy that are preserved in the Este Collection of trumpet pieces by Corelli and Torelli.[145]

5. Florence

Prince Ferdinando de' Medici (b. 1663), son and heir of the Grand Duke of Tuscany, was an active patron of music, supporting public and private performances and commissioning works from many composers. He employed a number of fine musicians, and in 1709 he acquired the permanent services of 'Lodovico' Erdmann. In that year, Ferdinando requested a motet from Giacomo Perti of Bologna, reminding him of the 'Oboè di abilità' in his service. Erdmann played operas by Perti in 1709 and 1710,[146] and was no doubt featured in the adaptation of Scarlatti's *Pirro e Demetrio*, with its hautboy solos, given at Florence in 1712[147] (the same solos, when the opera had been staged in London in 1708, had probably been played by John Loeillet).

Erdmann may have played for Ferdinando before his official engagement. As noted in Chapter 2, §D.2.a, Christoph Denner seems to have supplied hautboys to Ferdinando, finishing them just three days before he died in 1707. Erdmann and Denner may well have worked together, since Erdmann was at Ansbach, near Nuremberg, in the 1690s; Denner and Schell were copying French woodwinds by 1696 (see Ch. 3, §C.9). Erdmann may have been the one who recommended Denner's instruments to Ferdinando, particularly as Denner regularly made

---

[143] Kirkendale (1993), 448. Erdmann played as a guest at San Petronio in Apr. 1711 as well (Schnoebelen 1969: 52).   [144] Jackson (n.d.).

[145] See Haynes (1992a), 152, 248 under Pignatta.

[146] Schnoebelen (1969), 52; Kirkendale (1993), 447, 448, 496.   [147] See Haynes (1992a), 277–8.

woodwinds at the higher pitches common in Italy. Erdmann may thus have played on Christoph Denner's instruments, either when he was at Florence or before.

Although Prince Ferdinando unexpectedly died in 1713, Erdmann remained in Tuscan court service until 1757. Quantz wrote of meeting him in Florence in 1725, and described him as 'not a bad wind player, and what is more, in contrast to his countrymen, a very friendly man'.[148]

It is possible that Handel's *Sonata pour l'Hautbois Solo* [*sic*] in B flat, HWV 357, was written for Erdmann on Ferdinando's commission. The piece was written in Italy, *c*.1707–9, and Handel was at Florence in 1706 (where he produced *Rodrigo*), returning there each autumn until 1709. Erdmann may well have been hired for these events. Handel was a composer-in-residence at the Marquis of Ruspoli's Palazzo Bonelli in Rome during most of 1707–8, however, so the piece could have been written for one of the hautboy players working for Ruspoli at the time. The most likely would have been 'Ignatio', Ruspoli's principal hautboy[149] (who was probably Ignazio Rion). Another possibility, considering the quasi-French title of the Sonata, is the 'Monsù Martino' (who else could this be but Aléxis Saint-Martin?) who was in Rome in 1707 and 1709.

Scarlatti's cantata *Clori, mia Clori bella* was written in 1699. It survives in manuscript in two versions. The one in Berlin is for soprano, hautboy, and continuo; the other is for recorder instead of hautboy. The piece lies high for hautboy, and the manuscript contains ad hoc alternative passages (noted in German) that avoided the high d3s. Since Ferdinando was a patron of Scarlatti's, it is possible a copy of the piece reached Florence in its original form for recorder, and Erdmann later adapted it for hautboy. The manuscript may have gone to the Berlin library through Erdmann (who had started his career in that city).

Later, Erdmann probably played for Giovanni Gastone, who became Grand Duke of Tuscany, and was a patron of Robert Valentine in Rome. Since Valentine wrote a considerable amount of hautboy music (see below), Erdmann may have played some of it in Florence.

Hautboy players probably found work in the Teatro della Pergola in Florence, which from the late 1710s produced operas from all over Europe, particularly those of Neapolitan and Venetian composers.

Domenico Dreyer is survived by an excellent set of six *Sonate da camera a oboe solo col suo basso* that were probably written by 1727.[150] Dreyer, whose father was German, may have grown up in Florence. He is known to have played a concert in Lucca in 1726, and he may have learned the hautboy from Erdmann. In 1731–4

---

[148] 'ein nicht schlechter Hoboist, und dabey, gegen seine Landsleute, sehr freundschaftlicher Mann' (Quantz 1755: 231).   [149] Ignatio was paid the most of Ruspoli's four hautboy players.

[150] Paris Vm7 6489 (MS). According to Alfredo Bernardini (pers. comm.), a music catalogue by the publisher A. Silvani in Bologna dated 1727 lists *Sonate da camera*, Opus 1 by Dreyer. These could be the same sonatas.

he was engaged as a musician at the court of St Petersburg. The third sonata in his collection has an e3 as well as a low c1 (which means it was not originally for traverso, and not transposable down a step). The three-part chords in this collection that look like triple stops were probably short-hand arpeggios. The fifth and sixth are the best sonatas of this collection.

6. Rome

Opera theatres in Rome were not open during the first decade of the eighteenth century, due to political instability and the suspension of Carnival in the years after the earthquake in 1703.[151] This removed one of the hautboy's main solo settings. But after 1711 opera was being regularly performed in at least four theatres in Rome; Neapolitan repertoire was predominant. Feo's opera *Ipermestra* (1728) included an aria with two hautboys.

At the beginning of the eighteenth century Popes Innocent XI and XII forbade the use in church of a number of instruments, including the hautboy, because of their 'theatrical' associations.[152] Despite this, hautboys appeared in Antonio Bencini's music for Christmas Eve celebrations at the Vatican in 1730.[153] Although the ban may not always have been strictly followed, it was complete enough that Quantz knew about it, and wrote of it in 1752, including the catty remark 'Whether the unpleasant high pitch or the manner of playing the [hautboys] was the reason for this [ban] I must leave undecided.'[154] Quantz was evidently unaware of the quality and beauty of the solos Handel and Caldara wrote in Rome for hautboy, and the opportunities they present for musical expression. They were obviously inspired by fine players, the main one being Ignazio Rion, who had come to Rome from Venice in 1705.

Handel was writing for noble Roman families like the Colonna, Pamphili, and Ruspoli, with whom Rion also found employment until about 1713. 'Rion's salary in Rome was always much higher than that of the rest of the orchestra, and often equal to that of the first violin'[155] (who was none other than Arcangelo Corelli). Rion performed several times with Corelli, and Burney recounted a contemporary anecdote ascribed to Geminiani that 'It was soon after this [Corelli's return from Naples], that a hautbois player, whose name Geminiani could not recollect, acquired such applause at Rome, that Corelli, disgusted, would never play again in public.'[156] Corelli retired in 1708 or 1709, so it is quite likely the 'hautbois player' in question was Rion.[157] The hautboy parts to Handel's cantata *Laudate pueri*

[151] Boyd (1993), 55.   [152] Selfridge-Field (1988), 508.   [153] Boyd (1993), 42.
[154] Quantz (1752), 247.   [155] Bernardini (1988), 378.   [156] Burney (1776), iii. 440.
[157] Rion was often identified simply as 'Ignatio'. This was also Sieber's first name, and Sieber also played in Rome. But Sieber died in 1761, which means he would probably not have been born much before 1690. In that case he would have been too young to be playing as a solo hautboist in Rome in 1705–12.

Dominum (HWV 237, part of the *Carmelite Vespers*) are notated a whole tone below the other parts; this piece was performed in the church of the Madonna di Monte Santo in July 1707.[158] 'Io sperai trovar', no. 17 in *Il trionfo del tempo e del disinganno* (HWV 46a), is not credible on hautboy in B minor (the key of the other parts); it must have been in A minor. But in the autograph of this work, the hautboy part to 'Fido specchio', is in the same key as the other parts (A minor). The opening hautboy solo to *Il trionfo* (produced in 1707) was also used for the spectacular *La resurrezione* (HWV 47).[159] Although the original parts are lost, its very high range suggests that it too had hautboy parts notated a tone lower.

This difference in key would have been necessary if the hautboy being used for these pieces was pitched a major second higher than the other instruments. Quantz wrote that

à Rome . . . les joueurs avoient des instrumens, qui étoient un ton entier plus haut . . . ces instrumens hauts faisoient contre les autres qui étoient bas, le même effet que s'ils eussent été des Chalemies.[160]	in Rome . . . the hautboists had instruments that were pitched a whole tone higher . . . these high instruments, next to the others that were tuned low, produced an effect like that of shawms.[161]

Since there is reasonably clear documentation of a pitch standard at A−2 at Rome at this time (used with the strings), it seems players like Rion used hautboys pitched at A+0, a major second (or close enough to it to be usable) above prevailing Roman pitch.[162]

For *La resurrezione*, performed in 1708, we know only single names of the hautboy players: Ignatio, Giovanni, Valentini, and Nicolò.[163] 'Ignatio' was most likely Ignazio Rion. Giovanni was probably Giovanni Sicuro, documented at the Ruspoli court in 1710–11. Valentini was probably Robert Valentine.

Valentine is thought to have come from Leicester in England, but spent most of his career in Rome. A pirated edition of his *6 Sonata's of 2* [sic] *parts*, Opus 4, dated about 1715, calls him 'Mr Valentini liveing [sic] in Rome'. Valentine (like Schickhardt and John Loeillet) published a good deal of competent but pedestrian hautboy music. He is survived by several manuscripts, including twelve *Sonate d'Oboè con il Basso*, possibly copied in 1719, which contain some elaborate written-out ornamentation, although (with the possible exception of no. 5) they are not of much interest musically. The style is Italian, and not unlike Handel. Hotteterre le Romain arranged some of Valentine's duets (1721). There has been speculation that Valentine returned to London in 1731.[164]

---

[158] Boyd (1993), 42; Shaw (1994), 62.   [159] It exists separately in an earlier form as HWV 336.
[160] Quantz (1752), XVII, vii §7.   [161] Trans. based on Reilly (1966).
[162] Haynes (1995), 90.   [163] Kirkendale (1967) under '14.4.1708'.
[164] Medforth (1981), 812, 815. No documents have been found to confirm it. A probable descendant of Valentine named 'H. Valentine' of Leicester is listed in Doane (1794), 66 as playing hautboy.

Antonio Caldara was employed as *maestro di cappella* by Prince Ruspoli from 1709 until 1716, and his pieces often featured hautboy solos. These included the aria 'Il duol che tu senti' from the cantata *La costanza vince il rigore* for soprano, hautboy, and continuo, the cantata *Clori mia bella Clori*, the aria 'Al tesoro del tuo crin' from the cantata *La lode premiata*, and three arias, 'Redemptionem', 'Confitebor tibi', and 'Et in saecula', from *Confitebor*.[165] Many (if not all) of these pieces notated the hautboy a tone below the rest of the group.

There is also documentation of performances for the Pamphilj family in 1707 by 'Sig. Ignazio' on hautboy and 'Monsù Martino' on both hautboy and 'Flauto';[166] a 'Martino' also played for Ruspoli in March and April 1709. These players were presumably Ignazio Rion and Aléxis Saint-Martin.

Ignaz Sieber was in Rome, apparently from about 1716–17. Walther (1732) lists a Sieber without first name who published six solos for the flute in Amsterdam. Sieber was back in Venice by 1728.[167]

7. Naples

The hautboy may have arrived in the Kingdom of Naples from Venice by way of opera performers and composers who worked in both cities. It could thus have been heard in Naples by the 1690s. For the performance of *Il Pastor di Corinto* in August 1701, Scarlatti included a 'Sinfonia con Oubuè' for a band of hautboys in four parts.[168] There were thus probably a number of good players in Naples by the turn of the century.

Naples was famous for its many theatres and its performances of opera seria. By the 1710s good comic opera was also being performed. Hautboists were no doubt regularly employed in the theatres. Porpora's opera *Flavio Anicio Olibrio*, first produced in 1711, included an aria 'Pensa che sono amante' with hautboy solo. In addition, there were more than 500 churches in the city at the end of the seventeenth century, and twenty-three of them had permanent *cappelle musicali*.[169] Much of the music in public religious services, especially on the big feast days, involved instrumental as well as vocal music. There were also numerous private entertainments. Naples had four famous music conservatories that had been functioning since the sixteenth century, and which offered employment for teachers as well as training to students.

Rion is the first hautboy player in Naples whose name we know; he performed for the feast of San Gennaro in 1721, and was 'oboè e flauto' in the royal chapel in 1722.[170] It is possible he had arrived there by 1713, as he is last mentioned in the

---

[165] The present information updates Haynes (1992a), 85.   [166] Marx (1983), 109 and 114.
[167] Quantz does not mention Sieber, who was apparently still in Rome during Quantz's visit to Venice in 1726.
[168] Two hautboys in G2 clef, 1 in C3 [? = taille], 1 'basso dell'oubuè' in F4.   [169] Gianturco (1993), 115.
[170] Bernardini (1988), 379.

Ruspoli documents at Rome in December 1712.[171] Medforth (1981: 815) suggested that Valentine may also have worked in Naples;[172] it is possible that he worked both there and in Rome. In 1719, Sarro was writing for two *Obuè* and soprano in the cantata *Andate o miei sospiri*. Mancini's cantata *Quanto dolce è quell'ardore* for soprano and hautboy may also date from this decade.

As in Venice and Rome, there is evidence of transposing hautboys in Naples. Alfredo Bernardini (pers. comm.) found a piece at the conservatory in Palermo with an hautboy part in C notated a tone below the strings in D. It is a *Sinfonia* and part of a collection of Neapolitan music from the first quarter of the eighteenth century. In the eighteenth century, pitch in Naples was generally at A−1, so it is likely the hautboy that played this piece was at A+1.

D. Germany

In 1706, Fuhrmann wrote:

It is a shame that [the Viol di Gamba] is now used so little. The French *Hautbois* have submerged it; for now one can hardly say to a professional musician, 'Sir, play me a sonata on the viola da gamba' (as was the case 20 or 30 years ago), but rather 'play me a march or a minuet on the hautboy'. Thus times and instruments of music are changed, and men are changed with them.[173]

The first three decades of the eighteenth century in Germany were an active and creative period for the hautboy. Court composers were producing solos, trios, quartets, and concertos. Lutheran church music developed a genre of church cantata starting in about 1700 that created a wealth of beautiful hautboy music. Church schools like the Thomasschule in Leipzig were offering instruction on instruments by the beginning of the century,[174] and the Stadtpfeifer tradition was still strong.

In most cases, we do not know what specific brands of instruments German hautboy players used. Many of the hautboys that survive from this period (37%) were made in Germany, and of these, more than four-fifths were made in Nuremberg[175] and Leipzig.[176] There was probably some export and import (both Berlin and Munich are known to have received woodwinds from Paris), but it seems logical to assume that most German hautboys were used within Germany.

---

[171] Kirkendale (1966), 355.
[172] A concerto for recorder by Roberto Valentini in B flat is included in a Naples MS of 1725 published by Ut Orpheus Edizioni.　　[173] Fuhrmann (1706), 93, quoted in Snyder (1987), 368.
[174] Schering (1926), 60.　　[175] 60% of German survivors.　　[176] 21% of German survivors.

1. *Schwerin*

There is no record of the presence of the hautboy at the court of Schwerin until 1701, the year Johann Fischer, a pupil of Lully, was appointed Concertmeister of the Capelle. At that time, six hautboy players were appointed, and four others arrived in 1703. In that same year, the court ordered a number of wind instruments from an unnamed maker in Breslau.[177]

Fischer, like Muffat, was a convert who worked to educate his fellow Germans in the French style. His music was widely played. Although his stay in Schwerin was brief (1701–4), it was during that time that he published his *Tafelmusik* (Hamburg, 1702), which consists of six suites and further dances for three and four parts. Dedicated to Schwerin's Duke, Friedrich Wilhelm, this music was probably written for the *Hautboisten* at the court.

2. *Hamburg*

With a rich and engaged musical audience, the city-state of Hamburg could afford to hire the services of exceptional musicians, including Reinhard Keiser and Georg Philipp Telemann. Unfortunately, historical documentation for much of the musical activities in Hamburg in this period,[178] and much of the music played, is now lost; some of Telemann's music has survived because, on account of his fame, copies of it were also located elsewhere.

Sittard (1890b: 22–3) lists some of the municipal musicians (*Ratsmusiker* and *Rollbrüder*) from 1524 to 1818. Members continued to be active in the first decades of the eighteenth century. The *Ratsmusikdirektor* in 1682 had been Friedrich Bruhns (Bruhns is survived by six hautboy arias). By 1718, the official number of *Ratsmusiker* and *Rollbrüder* was only eight, and it had become normal to mix other independent musicians with them, including visitors to the city like Böhm (see below) and Schickhardt.

The Opera continued to be very active at Hamburg, running a non-stop season and producing four to six different operas each year, of which three to four were new. Keiser, who directed it, contributed at least one new opera each season until 1717, and reruns continued for another generation. Keiser was very popular: he was described as 'perhaps the greatest original genius in music that had ever appeared in Germany', and 'the greatest opera composer of the world'.[179] Of the

---

[177] Meyer (1913), 38. An hautboy by A. Schütze, probably of Breslau, that plays very well, is now in Geneva (Alfredo Bernardini, pers. comm.).   [178] Lasocki (1977), 31.
[179] Buelow (1993a), 196, quoting Scheibe and Mattheson.

sixty to sixty-five operas he wrote, only seventeen survive. Many of them contain superb and expressive solos for hautboy, in subtle interaction with singers. Johann Mattheson wrote of Keiser:

In Instrumental-Sachen, besonders vor Hautbois, war er recht angenehm . . .[180]	In his treatment of instruments, especially the *Hautbois*, he was quite pleasing . . .

His three 'eye arias' in *Octavia* (1705) give the hautboy several kinds of dialogue and unison movements with the singer. Livia's cheerful 'So manchesmal, forscht meiner Augen' contrasts with Octavia's two touching love-arias, 'Geliebte Augen' and 'Angenehmste Augen-Sonnen'. These arias all combine the hautboy with a single singer and continuo. Other excellent hautboy solos in Keiser's operas include 'Hoffe noch, gekränktes Herz' in *Croesus* (1710), 'Ich weiss es wohl, ihr falschen Sterne' in *L'inganno fedele* (1714), and 'Umwölke doch, Vergessenheit' with pizzicato strings in *Tomyris* (1717). 'Hoffe noch' is an unusual aria; the vocal line, when it enters, does not imitate what has happened in the instrumental parts, but adds a new element, while the instruments continue their 'music box' effect. 'Ich weiss es wohl' expresses gentle protest to fate, using the same dialogue/commentary relation to the vocal line that Bach was to adopt later in most of his hautboy arias (the hautboy flying about like a *putto*, decorating the vocal line with garlands of flowers). Policares's tragic 'aria affettuosa' 'Mein herbes Leid und scharfer Schmerz' from *Tomyris* (1717), with pizzicato cello, uses the hautboy to comment on each idea as it is expressed.

Several solos for hautboy survive in the operas of Johann Mattheson, Hamburg's prolific writer on music. Mattheson had sung in the Opera as a young man. In the Duetto with two hautboys 'Ich bleibe dein' in his opera *Cleopatra* (1704), the composer sang one of the roles, Antonius, with Handel conducting. In the performance, Mattheson returned to the orchestra after Antonius' suicide in the third act, intending to take his place at the keyboard, but Handel refused to yield it to him. This led to their famous sword duel. The two young musicians were apparently soon reconciled, as Mattheson sang a leading role in Handel's *Almira* the next year, the opera that contains more hautboy obbligatos (usually for one, sometimes two hautboys) than any of Handel's other operas. Clearly, Hamburg's opera hautboists pleased Handel.

As Werner Braun pointed out, already in *Almira* the simple soprano–hautboy dialogue had developed into a more elaborate form, the hautboy beginning an aria with figures idiomatic to the instrument rather than to the voice:

---

[180] (1740), 129. Keiser may have had a son who was an hautboist, named Johann Kayser (Keyser). Kayser was director of the Rathsmusik from 1725 to 1729. For the possible relationship, see Noack (1967), 173.

Die Sängerin . . . deklamiert dazu und dazwischen; nur in der Kadenz des B-Teils darf auch sie brillieren. Da das Instrument das erste und das letzte 'Wort' hat (Ritornell ans Nachspiel), begleitet die menschliche Stimme den Oboenpart, nicht umgekehrt. In latenten Wettstreit der Klangbereiche vokal-instrumental hat der letztere einen Sieg errungen.[181]	The singer . . . declaims to and around [the instrumental subject]; only in the cadence of the B-section is she also allowed to shine. Since the instrument has both the first and last 'word' (the ritornellos at the beginning and end), the singer accompanies the hautboy, not vice versa. In the veiled contest between singer and instrumentalist for the field of sound, it was the latter who won the victory.

Bach's arias also frequently begin with an idea inspired by an instrument, and the voice sings a simplified version when it enters.

Besides arias, as McCredie wrote, 'Some of the independent movements for orchestra that were a regular part of Hamburg and Braunschweig operas occasionally included trios for two hautboys with Taille (called 'viola') as *Bassätchen* (bass at the octave). One example is the Passacaille from Telemann's *Damon* (I, 1).'[182] This is an extension of the traditional hautboy–bassoon trio interlude in orchestral writing.

Keiser also wrote church music that included hautboy solos. The superb aria 'O Golgatha' from the *Passio Christi secundum Marcum* in F minor for soprano, hautboy, and continuo (1720)[183] is characterized by dramatic pauses, descending lines, chromaticism, and pulsating repeated notes.

The rich repertoire of hautboy solos from Hamburg points to the regular presence there from the 1680s of at least one major soloist, and perhaps several. The earliest of these players were probably French. By the first decade of the eighteenth century, one of the hautboists at Hamburg had evidently inspired Handel's well-known hautboy concerto in G minor, HWV 287 (apparently written in the same years as *Almira*). It could well have been an hautboist at the Opera for whom Handel wrote this concerto. The hautboy acts in this piece very like an opera singer in relation to the orchestra. Graupner, who composed five operas for Hamburg in 1707–9, was also inspired to write several solos for the principal hautboist.

In 1721 Telemann began an extraordinary career in Hamburg, reigning over the music there for four decades. As a composer, Telemann was exceptional in many ways, and one of them was that he found a way to work successfully outside the court system and its privately controlled repertoire. He found the atmosphere for music making in Hamburg favourable, writing in the 1720s:

---

[181] Braun (1987), 139.   [182] McCredie (1964), 308, 311.   [183] Berlin MS 11471.

Und glaube ich nicht, daß irgendwo ein solcher Ort, als Hamburg, zu finden, der den Geist eines in dieser Wissenschaft Arbeitenden mehr aufmuntern kann.[184]	I do not believe that there is anywhere such a place as Hamburg where the spirit of one working in this Science can be more encouraged.[185]

As the premier German composer of his day, much of his music (or music by lesser musicians with his famous name attached) was copied and circulated in multiple manuscripts that ended up in various palace libraries like Darmstadt, Dresden, and Herdringen.[186] Telemann himself published (and even engraved) an impressive number of his compositions, thereby making them available to the public at large, even outside Germany.

Since Telemann played the hautboy (among other instruments), it is not surprising that several writers have drawn attention to his particular fondness for the instrument.[187] Apart from the numerous chamber works in which he used it, the instrument appeared in many expressive solo situations with voice, in pairs alternating with violins, and as re-enforcement in orchestral settings.[188]

Telemann was director of the Hamburg Opera. His première in 1721, the comic opera *Der gedultige Socrates*, which contained three hautboy solos, was highly successful.[189] Before the Opera company went bankrupt in 1738, Telemann provided it with about a dozen major new operas. He also contributed to pasticcios, and adapted and arranged operas by other composers. Little of this material survives.[190]

As city Cantor, Telemann was also responsible for supplying music for Hamburg's five major churches:

For each Sunday he was expected to write two cantatas and for each year a new Passion. Special cantatas were required for induction ceremonies, and oratorios for the consecration of churches. Still more cantatas had to be written and performed to mark civic celebrations, of which there were many.[191]

Telemann's Passions were so numerous that they are identified by the year of their performance; many contain hautboy obbligatos. As for cantatas, Telemann eventually wrote over a thousand,[192] and published several complete *Jahrgänge* (yearly cycles), including two sets called *Der harmonische Gottesdienst* (1725–6 and 1731), one for single voice, treble instrument, and continuo, the other (the *Fortsetzung*,

[184] Letter to J. F. von Uffenbach, 31 July 1723, quoted in Grosse and Jung (1972), 213.
[185] Trans. Buelow (1993a), 206.   [186] On Herdringen, cf. Sonsfeldt Catalogue (Chrd).
[187] Maertens (1988), 99, who cites also R. Meissner, *G. Ph. Telemanns Frankfurter Kirchenkantaten* (1924), 14 f. and H. Hörner, *Georg Philipp Telemanns Passionsmusiken* (1933), 93 ff.   [188] Cf. Maertens (1988).
[189] Haynes (1992a), 322.   [190] See Peckham (1969).   [191] Ruhnke (1980), 650.
[192] Many of them involve hautboy. See Schlichte (1979) (who lists 854 of them now at Frankfurt) and Menke (1982).

PL. 5.2. Christian Fritzsch, 1719, *Konzert beim Jubelmahl der Hamburger Bürgerkapitäne*
(copper engraving, 27.3 × 46 cm). Hamburg: Staatsarchiv

only now being published in a modern edition) with two instruments. Each cantata
in the *Harmonische Gottesdienst* consisted of two arias plus recits. The first collection contained fifteen cantatas with hautboy,[193] the second twenty-two.[194]

Telemann's aria 'Brecht, ihr müden Augenlieder' in the cantata *Du aber Daniel,
gehe hin* (TWV 4: 17) is a touching piece. The cantrata is similar in character and
instrumentation to Bach's *Actus tragicus*, BWV 106.

As if his church and opera activities were not enough, Telemann also conducted a busy Collegium Musicum (for which he was responsible for hiring performers). Public concerts were frequent in Hamburg at the Drillhaus (an exercise
hall for the city militia and a popular concert venue; see Pl. 5.2) and elsewhere. He
frequently organized and managed concerts for paying audiences, often of his own
music.

---

[193] The most interesting musically are numbers 2, 26, 31, 35, and 55.
[194] Seven with two hautboys, six with hautboy and violin, six with hautboy or trumpet and violin, two with
hautboy and traverso, and one with hautboy and recorder. The *Fortsetzung* is consistently equal in quality to the
best cantatas in the first collection.

Telemann wrote over 100 small chamber works for hautboy, including duets, solo sonatas, trios, and quartets.[195] Of his forty-three surviving trios with hautboy, many are worthy of mention, such as the Trio from *Musique de table* II/4 with traverso (with its third movement Minuet in E major), the recorder Trio I from *Essercizii musici*, the Trio XII from the same collection with obbligato harpsichord (one of the few pieces for this combination that succeeds), and the many trios for violin with hautboy (or hautbois d'amour) and Bass. Many of the latter survive in manuscript copies in more than one library, an indication that they were frequently played. Of Telemann's many good violin–hautboy trios, all the best are in G minor. They are:

> TWV 42: g12, I. N. 25 Trio/Sonata à 3, MS parts, Dresden, 2392-Q-49;
>   MS Herdringen Fü 3597a
> Trio III from *Essercizii musici*[196]
> Sonata. MS Darmstadt 1042/56
> N.2 Trio. Dresden, 2392-Q-51

One of the surviving hautboy–violin trios, a *Cantata a 3*, is an arrangement from the *Harmonische Gottesdienst*.[197] The original is for voice, hautboy, and continuo, but in this version the hautboy plays the voice part and the violin takes the original hautboy part. (Replacing the voice with an instrument, especially a wind, may have been a common practice at the time; in his preface to the *Harmonische Gottesdienst*, Telemann recommended it.)[198]

At Hamburg, Telemann mostly depended on competent hautboy players, and several must have been available. For church music, he could use a number of players, either from the six *Ratsmusiker*, the *Rollbrüder*, or musicians from the Opera. Students were not available, as they were in Leipzig,[199] but compared with the limitations of personnel with which Kuhnau and Bach struggled, each of the five main churches of Hamburg employed from seven to seventeen instrumentalists.[200]

It is likely that many other chamber pieces involving hautboy that were performed in Hamburg are now lost.

The names of only a few hautboy players are known from this period of Hamburg's history. Michael Böhm was in Hamburg some time after February 1711, sent by the Darmstadt court. After his move to Hamburg, Telemann may also have occasionally invited Böhm to play there. Alois Freymuth was at the Hamburg Opera by at least 1722; he also played recorder and traverso. Mattheson

---

[195] Haynes (1992a), 304–10. Good recent studies of this material are Swack (1988) and Zohn (1995).
[196] Separate manuscript copies at Brussels (7115); Berlin (21785); Dresden (2392-Q-48); Darmstadt (1042/60). The Dresden copy is probably originally from Pisendel's private collection.   [197] At Schwerin.
[198] Telemann 1725-6: [vi]. He suggested violin, hautboy, and traverso to replace the soprano and tenor voices.
[199] Petzoldt (1983), 182.   [200] Buelow (1993a), 203.

praised his playing, and his erudition, in *Critica musica* (1722: 113). Schickhardt was in Hamburg from 1712 to perhaps 1717. His six Sonates, Opus 20/1, for traverso/hautboy/violin and continuo were published in 1715; they were probably written when he was in Hamburg. These pieces are well crafted if not inspired, and display the same *galant* lightness and simplicity of *Affect* as the music of Loeillet and Corrette. Schickhardt's Opus 22, six Sonatas for two recorders, hautboy, and continuo, was published sometime between 1716 and 1721; the first, in F, contains two exceptionally pleasing movements (the Largo and the Giga).

3. Braunschweig–Wolfenbüttel

There were close ties between the opera companies at Hamburg and Braunschweig, and besides repertoire, there may also have been occasional exchanges of personnel, including hautboists. Braunschweig's opera was very active, and from the works performed there hautboy obbligatos with voice and orchestra survive by Österreich, Schürmann, Bokemeyer, and Heinrich Graun. The principle hautboy in the royal Capelle from 1720 was Carl Fleischer. Other players from about the same time were Grüneberg, Schmidt, and Statz.[201]

By 1731 Freymuth had moved from Hamburg to Braunschweig. He may have been the soloist in one of Graun's most beautiful hautboy obbligatos with orchestra, the tenor aria 'Betrübtes Herz, zerbrich' in *Scipio Africanus* (1732). The subject (which is a good one) is introduced by the hautboy, and is often presented in dialogue and in thirds, the voice and hautboy trading the upper part.

4. Hannover

Hannover was wealthy enough to employ Italian singers in its opera, including castrati, as well as a good orchestra of eighteen players, some of them French (the French had higher salaries than their German colleagues).[202] In 1710 and 1711 Handel served briefly as court Capellmeister. It was in Hannover that he completed *Apollo e Dafne*, which he had begun in Italy. The two lovely hautboy solos in this work, 'Come in ciel benigna stella' for Dafne together with an hautboy and violin, and 'Felicissima quest'alma' with hautboy and pizzicato strings, were written at different times, to judge from the handwriting of the autograph. His cantata *Languia di bocca lusinghiera* for soprano, hautboy, violin, and continuo was likewise finished in Hannover in about 1710 (it consists of one recitative and aria and is possibly only a fragment). Like 'Come in ciel benigna stella', the hautboy part in *Languia* is untransposed; this suggests that these pieces were written in Hannover

---

[201] Sievers (1941), 60.   [202] Dean (1980), 87.

rather than Rome (whence Handel had come) since (as we have seen) he normally wrote his Roman hautboy parts down a whole tone.

There were a number of good hautboists at Hannover who might have played these pieces. The court had several French players on its roles, and in 1701/2, it engaged six young *Hautboisten* who had been trained by Pepusch at Berlin. At the same time, new instruments were ordered for them from the well-known maker Harmen Wietfelt of Burgdorf.[203] Mattheson, who heard this group in 1706, described it as an 'auserlesenste Bande Hautboisten' (most select band of wind players).[204]

5. Gotha

The first record of hautboy playing at Gotha is 1697.[205] From 1713 to 1716 the Capellmeister there was Christian Witt; several of his pieces for hautboy band survive. Gottfried Stölzel arrived as Capellmeister in 1719, and reorganized and enlarged the Capelle. Stölzel produced numerous operas, cantatas, and chamber music that included hautboy. His eight sonatas for hautboy, violin, horn, and continuo, which are light entertainment rather than profound art, are delightful to play and hear.[206] The only hautboy player documented in Gotha is Johann Andreas Bach, a nephew of Sebastian Bach.

6. Berlin

The court orchestra at Berlin was quite active in the first years of the century, and King Friedrich I established a 'Chor Hautboisten' in 1708.[207] Music was especially well patronized by Queen Sophie Charlotte (d. 1705), Friedrich's wife. Telemann (1740: 359) reported having heard an opera during his visit to Berlin in 1702, in which Sophie Charlotte played harpsichord; among other notable players, La Riche was playing hautboy. La Riche also performed in the Queen's chamber concerts at Lietzenburg Castle (from 1705 called Charlottenburg castle).

Although La Riche was officially a member of the Dresden court from 1699, he was in Berlin in 1700–2. He is known to have played with Laurent de Saint-Luc then. In 1707/8 Saint-Luc published an exceptional collection of solo pieces in the style of Lully, the *Suittes pour le luth avec un dessus et une basse ad libitum*. Walther mentioned these pieces in his *Lexicon*;[208] according to him, the 'dessus' part (which is provided as an adjunct to the lute—or other continuo instrument) was for

---

[203] Sievers (1961), 58; Waterhouse (1993), 429.   [204] Mattheson (1740), 195. See Braun (1983), 130 n. 28.

[205] Werner (1922), 89.

[206] An unpublished edition has been prepared by Charles Lehrer. Cf. also the excellent quartets of Meusel for hautboy, violin or gamba, cello, and obbligato lute, which may have been written in Gotha.

[207] Heyde (1994), 26.   [208] Walther (1732), 372.

traverso or hautboy.[209] Many pieces in the collection suit the hautboy, and may have been played by La Riche and the composer.

Sachs (1910: 67) noted that the Capelle ordered recorders from Paris in 1700. Since the players of recorder also played hautboy, it seems that connections between French players resident in Berlin and hautboy makers in France were maintained. No hautboys made in Berlin from this period are known, but it is likely that Johann Heitz made them. From before 1700 until 1737, Heitz is the only woodwind maker who worked in Berlin; the fleur-de-lys on some of his instruments suggests a connection with France.[210] Gundling in 1712 reported that 'Hautbois' came to Berlin 'aus Nürnberg';[211] so they would have been made by Schell, Jacob and David Denner, or Oberlender sen. (see below, §16).

The hautboists at court were Glösch (principal), Schüler (assistant principal), Fleischer (who was later principal at Braunschweig), and Rose (later principal for Bach at Cöthen). They formed part of a richly instrumented court orchestra that included ten violins, two violas, five cellos, four bassoons, and harpsichord. Glösch had been appointed to the Capelle in 1706, and may have taken part in performances for Queen Sophie Charlotte in the years before that (when, presumably, he had studied with La Riche). By 1713, he had the highest salary in the Capelle.

It was in that year that Friedrich Wilhelm I (the 'Barracks King') ascended the throne, and immediately disbanded the Capelle. All the musicians were fired, and the money went for armaments. The opera house was converted into an army supply depot.[212] For a generation, until Friedrich Wilhelm's death in 1740, there was little music at court except what was organized by his wife, Queen Sophie Dorothea. She sponsored chamber concerts at Monbijou castle, and may have maintained a musical establishment.[213] Glösch stayed on in Berlin, working as a private teacher and perhaps being discretely patronized by Sophie Dorothea. He was known and favourably described by Telemann (1718: 169) and Baron (1727: 85).

The build-up of a standing army in Prussia had already begun in the seventeenth century, and by 1713 Friedrich I was employing some 1,266 musicians in his infantry, cavalry, and dragoons, many of whom would have played the hautboy.[214] Friedrich's successor, the 'Barracks King', employed still more military musicians. According to Panoff (1938: 74), from 1713 Friedrich Wilhelm's 'Pfeifferkorps des Leibregiments', a twelve-member hautboy band, was made up exclusively of black players who had been brought to Potsdam as children. An *Hautboistenschule* was established in Potsdam in 1724 at which the sons of fallen soldiers could study. The school was directed by Gottfried Pepusch, who had trained wind players for court

---

[209] The Sarabande no. 4 goes down to c♯1, and there are b0s (however these notes are unplayable on either instrument, although players could have rewritten these passages).
[210] Heyde (1994), 55. Seventeen of Heitz's recorders are extant.   [211] Ibid. 56.
[212] Moore (1981), 22.   [213] Lasocki (1977), 32.   [214] Heyde (1994), 49.

and municipal posts since the beginning of the century. (Plate 2.7 may be a portrait of Pepusch; see App. 4.) The six young *Hautboisten* engaged at Hannover in 1701/2 and the five *Hautboisten* sent for instruction to Potsdam by the Margrave of Ansbach in 1703 were trained by Pepusch,[215] who appeared in London in 1704 with seven of his pupils (see below, §E.2).

7. Zerbst

The court at Anhalt-Zerbst was particularly known for its music through the work of Johann Friedrich Fasch, Capellmeister there from 1722 to 1758. As a composer, Fasch was one of Bach's most significant contemporaries. Zerbst must have had a pair of good hautboists, as Fasch was a prolific writer for the instrument.[216] The inventory of music at the Schloss, made up in 1743, lists an impressive collection of chamber music and numerous concertos for hautboy, not only by Fasch but by such composers as Telemann, Pfeiffer, Bomoliere, Freislich, Frey, Hundt, Morzini, Pichler, Giuseppe Sammartini, Stölzel, and Roellig.

Fasch was known far beyond the borders of Saxony. He was in close contact with many musicians, and regularly sent music to them: Graupner and Böhm in Darmstadt, Stölzel in Gotha, Bach in Leipzig, and Heinichen, Pisendel, and Zelenka in Dresden.

8. Merseburg

To judge from the music that survives from Merseburg, the court there must have had at least one good hautboist. Most of this music is by Christoph Förster, who was there from 1717 to about 1743. The works with hautboy include a solo sonata, fourteen solo concertos, concertos for two hautboys and two hautbois d'amour, and cantatas. Other composers associated with Merseburg who left hautboy works are Römhild and Kauffmann.

This music was probably performed by members of the active 'compagnie' of four Stadtpfeifer in Merseburg. From 1707 to 1716 Quantz got his first training on various instruments, primarily hautboy, from Johann Fleischack, a member of this band.

9. Weißenfels

It is thought that Bach wrote Cantata 208 for the birthday of Duke Christian of Weißenfels, and the piece was first performed there in February 1713.[217] The Duke

---

[215] Schmidt (1956), 73.
[216] See Haynes (1992a), 117 ff. Cf. also Engelke (1908), Schneider (1936), Küntzel (1965), and Sheldon (1968).
[217] Cf. Cowdery (1989), 52 ff.

maintained a 'Bande Violons et Hautbois' of six players, and it may have been this group that played the parts for three hautboys and 'Bassons' in this cantata. But the court also had a number of titled *Cammer-Hautbois*, two of whom (Unger and Pardoffsky) held posts in 1713. A band of eight hautboys was present at the court until 1736.[218]

Georg Linike, who was later to lead the orchestra of the Hamburg Opera, was also at Weißenfels from 1711 to 1721. He is survived by several chamber works involving hautboy which may well have been written at Weißenfels.

10. Halle

At the end of the seventeenth century, Michael Hyntzsch and his son Johann Georg founded an 'Hautboisten-Compagnie' in Halle that included a number of players.[219] Both Hyntzsches are documented as shawm players at the court in the 1670s. It is not known where or from whom they learned the hautboy.

The Hautboisten-Compagnie was granted a monopoly in 1702 by King Friedrich of Prussia. From that date, the Hyntzsches were employed by the city, and effectively replaced the local Stadtpfeifer. Friedrich's unusual edict (the motive for which is unclear) superseded the imperial regulations governing Stadtpfeifer, and made it illegal for the local Stadtpfeifer to play the hautboy. The edict was renewed by Friedrich Wilhelm in 1713.

The Hyntzsches played in the Schloß-/Domkirche,[220] and were thus associated with the young Handel, who played organ there. If in fact the 'early' set of trios attributed to Handel (HWV 380–5) are actually his,[221] they may have been written for the Hyntzsches. The surviving copy of these pieces (which, although they are called 'oboe trios', are actually for hautboy and violin)[222] was owned by Carl Weidemann; he noted that he had once shown them to Handel, who remarked laughingly 'I used to write like the Devil in those days, but chiefly for the hautbois, which was my favourite instrument'.[223]

Friedrich Zachow, with whom Handel studied in Halle, included many hautboy solos in the cantatas he wrote between 1684 and 1712 for the Marktkirche.[224] Examples are his humorous 'A und O bleibt ganz zurükke' for two hautboys from the cantata *Das ist das ewige Leben* and the lovely air 'Der Herr verstösst nicht ewiglich' from *Meine Seel erhebt den Herren*, with complex interweaving between

---

[218] Engel (1966), 188.

[219] For more information on the Hyntzsches and other hautboy players in Halle, see Serauky (1939), 387, 389, 403, 405, 410, 419, 420, 423–8, 553.   [220] Braun (1983), 148.

[221] Bernardini suggests they might have been written by Pfeiffer (cf. Ch. 7, §C.10).

[222] The second part is higher than the first, going to e3, and there are double stops.

[223] F. W. Chrysander in his introduction to vol. xxvii of *G. F. Händels Werke* (Hamburg, 1879), quoting from Charles Burney's *Commemoration of Handel* (London, 1785), 3.   [224] See Haynes (1992a), 348–9.

the hautboy and alto solo lines. The hautboy parts were written a minor third higher than the others, indicating that the hautboys were pitched at A–2.[225]

11. Düsseldorf

During the reign of the Pfalzgraf Johann Wilhelm (known as Jan Willem; 1679–1716), Düsseldorf's court was modelled on Versailles and there was much musical activity, especially opera. Hautboy players were probably present from the 1680s. An opera house was built in 1695. The director was Johann von Wilderer, by whom five operas are extant.

Steffani also produced three operas at Düsseldorf. He included one hautboy solo in *Arminio*, produced in 1707. *Tassilone* (1709) contains six solos: the dialogue 'Piangerete, io ben lo so' is a charming aria; the hautboy repeats motifs and trades phrases with the tenor (usually afterwards, which invites added ornamentation), occasionally becoming entwined with the 'filigree-like'[226] vocal line. 'Dal tuo labbro amor m'invita' is a 'courage' aria and is accompanied by both hautboy and bassoon. Gheroldo's tragic largo, 'In faccia a queste pompe funeste' is a fine vocal solo, the three obbligato instruments (hautboy, violin, bassoon) commenting on the song like a Greek chorus. This opera was expressly composed for Düsseldorf by Steffani, and indicates that the court must have had a good hautboy player on its rolls in 1709.

The court Capelle was large and well financed, and consisted of fifty-three members, not counting singers and trumpeters. At the death of Johann Wilhelm in 1716, it was disbanded, and most of the musicians apparently moved to Mannheim.

12. Dresden

The 'Augustan era' at Dresden (under Friedrich August I, r. 1694–1733, and Friedrich August II, r. 1733–63) was 'the most brilliant and extravagant period in the cultural history of Dresden'.[227] It has been estimated that the court's yearly expenditure on music was equivalent to £90,000 of English money of the same period.[228] Starting in 1709, the orchestra was perhaps the finest in Europe, and included many of the greatest performers then living.[229]

A French presence was an important part of Friedrich August I's musical establishment.[230] A troop of French actors, dancers, and musicians was in residence from 1709, and nine of his woodwind players were Frenchmen. The court orchestra was led by Jean-Baptiste Woulmyer (Volumier; he was educated and grew up in Versailles), and Pierre-Gabriel Buffardin was the principal traverso. Although he

---

[225] See Haynes (1995), §6-3a.   [226] McCredie (1964).   [227] Buelow (1993a), 219.
[228] Raynor (1972), 295.   [229] For an informative overview of the Dresden Capelle, see Landmann (1989).
[230] Cf. Landmann (1982).

did not play in the orchestra, François La Riche taught the hautboy to some of its players.

The primary court orchestra, or 'Große Capell- und Cammer-Musique',[231] was involved in the Catholic court church music, the Italian opera, and instrumental concerts at court.[232] Until 1717 it also accompanied Friedrich August during his regular sojourns in Poland (Kraków and Warsaw). In that year a second, smaller orchestra, the 'Kleine Cammer-Musique' (also called the 'Capella Polacca'), was created to fill that function, led by the composer and hautboist Giovanni Ristori.[233]

There must have been many hautboy players at Dresden. Besides the two orchestras, the court sponsored groups of 'Bock-Pfeifer' (later called 'Hof-Pfeifer') and 'Jagd-Pfeifer' who played for theatre troops, *Tafelmusik*, and balls. In addition, there were military hautboy bands in court service. Members of these bands and of the city's corps of Stadtpfeifer were sometimes used to supplement the Capelle in case of need, and served as a pool from which candidates could advance to service in the Capelle. Players would have specialized on the hautboy for some time in order to qualify for consideration.[234]

The high point of elaborate cultural display at the Dresden court occurred in 1719, on the occasion of the marriage of the Crown Prince (who had been in Venice in 1716) to the daughter of the Emperor (Pls. 4.1, 4.2). Preparations had begun years before: Heinichen had been engaged as Capellmeister and commissioned to hire many famous Italian musicians to take part in the festivities, including Lotti (who wrote a number of pieces for hautboy while he was at Dresden from *c*.1717 to 1719). No other event was ever to equal these remarkable celebrations at Dresden; among the visitors were both Telemann and Handel.

With the opulence of its music and the prestige of its Capelle, Dresden could and did own copies of virtually any kind of music that was being produced in Europe at the time. The court employed four to six full-time music copyists.[235] Pisendel was an active collector of music, and his collection eventually became part of the magnificent court library. Despite two serious bombings in 1760 and 1945, the surviving remnants still make this library one of the largest collections of eighteenth-century music in the world. It holds 335 solos and chamber music from the early eighteenth century that involve the hautboy.[236] This music gives an idea of the richness of the concerts that were heard at the court.

---

[231] 'Cammer-Musique' meant any kind of concert music, for large or small ensembles. Cf. Walther's definition above, §A.1.a.   [232] Landmann (1993), 182.

[233] An hautboy concerto by Ristori is preserved at Dresden.   [234] Landmann (1993), 180.

[235] Landmann in Steude, Landmann, *et al.* (1995), 1545.

[236] Including works by Stricker, Heinichen, Telemann, Zelenka, Vivaldi, Fasch, Finger, Lotti, Ristori, Blockwitz, Califano, Homilius, Linike, Pezold, Quantz, Stölzel, Adam, Christoph Richter, Taschenberg, Hasse, Brescianello, and Pepusch.

Among the hautboy concertos is a delightful piece by Telemann in C minor (K Ob.c[2]).[237] This is Telemann in one of his clever, audacious moods, and it is not unlike his excellent concerto for recorder and traverso (!). The Fasch hautboy concerto in G minor (K. 12, FWV L:g1) is also worthy of mention, as well as his interesting quartets for two hautboys, obbligato bassoon, and continuo (four of which are now at Dresden). An ensemble consisting of these instruments must have been more or less permanent, as there are other pieces for it, written at various times.[238]

As for the hautboy players, La Riche, who had arrived in 1699, was the senior hautboy player at Dresden.[239] It is unclear how active he was as a performer after Christian Richter's return in 1716; in that year La Riche would have been 54. His other occupations on behalf of the Elector (purchasing foreign goods) may have required considerable travel. He was for many years a good friend of Quantz, whom he helped with a letter of credit during the flutist's stay in England.[240] In 1709, the year Woulmyer was retained as concertmaster, there were four other hautboists on the Hofcapelle roster: the Henrions (Charles as principal first and Jean-Baptiste as principal second), Richter, and Reche (or Roger).[241]

Quantz's Trio in C minor (K. 36; QV 2:5) for violin or flute, hautboy, and continuo is also in the library. It is a good, clear, well-crafted piece, shallow in content but better than much of his surviving music. In 1718, Quantz, then a young and ambitious hautboist, got his first chance at court in the 'Kleine Cammer-Musique' or Polish Chapel. As it turned out for Quantz, the seniority of other hautboists at the court meant he could never advance very far on that instrument, and he was thus led (on the urging of Pisendel) to turn his attention to the traverso.[242] The ascendant hautboist in the *Polnische Kapelle* (and, as Quantz's senior, possibly the reason he became a flutist) was Ristori.

Perhaps as early as 1716, and probably by the early 1720s, Christian Richter was the principal hautboist in the Große Capell- und Cammer-Musique. He had been trained by La Riche,[243] and had had opportunities to study and/or compare notes with players in Paris and Venice when he accompanied the Crown Prince on his Grand Tour in the 1710s. It is easy to imagine that La Riche never moved over to the newer designs of higher-pitched hautboys, playing his entire career on instruments like those of Bressan. Richter, on the other hand, had probably been affected

---

[237] The Dresden copy (2392/Q/52) perished, an example of the losses due to war (in this case, 1945), but the piece survives in a copy at Darmstadt (1033/56).

[238] Two by Lotti, for instance, one by Heinichen, and a collection by Zelenka (ZWV 181).

[239] He was not paid his disproportionately high salary out of Capelle funds (Fürstenau 1861–2: 50).

[240] Quantz (1755), 239.　　[241] Cf. Oleskiewicz (1998), 42, 44.　　[242] Quantz (1755), 209.

[243] Fürstenau (1861–2), ii. 135 and Quantz (1755), 207. He is easily confused with two other Dresden musicians, the organist and composer Johann Christoph Richter (1700–85) and the composer and conductor Franz Xaver Richter (1709–89).

by the year he spent in Venice in 1716. It is quite conceivable that he came home with hautboys made by Anciuti. These instruments would probably have been at A–1 (a common level both at Dresden and of Anciuti's surviving instruments). Richter's position in the Dresden Hofcapelle would have been influential among hautboists in Germany in those years, and his adoption of a newer, Italian-influenced manner of playing would probably have had its echoes in other courts. The hautboist in Pl. 4.1 may well be Richter.

Because of Vivaldi's ties with Dresden musicians, some of his manuscripts found their way there and are still in its library, including the sonatas for hautboy and continuo, RV 34 in B flat, RV 28 in G minor, RV 53 in C minor, as well as the hautboy concerto, RV 184.[244] Bernardini (1988: 376) noticed that thematic material in the C minor sonata, RV 53, is similar to the sinfonia of the opera L'incoronazione di Dario, suggesting a date of 1716, the year Richter was in Venice. Since it is now preserved at Dresden, this sonata may well have been written for Richter.[245] Vivaldi's interesting oratorio Juditha triumphans, RV 645, was also written in 1716 and may have involved Richter, as there is a solo bass aria (Holoferne's 'Noli o cara te adorantis') with obbligato hautboy and organ.[246]

In the collected works published by Ricordi, Vivaldi's sonatas RV 28 and RV 34 are for violin. In that case, they would be Vivaldi's only pieces for violin that do not exploit the bottom of the G-string (they never go below c1, the hautboy's lowest note). It is also unusual for a string piece to provide places for a player to breathe, yet there are rests that seem to have no other purpose. Apart from the fact that the passagework lies naturally on the hautboy and never goes out of its range, RV 28 is in a characteristic key for the hautboy, G minor. In the second movement, Vivaldi avoided low c#1 in bar 51 by going up an octave (the octave d1–d2 is necessary in bar 53). This movement is also reminiscent of the contrapuntal second movement of the last sonata in Il pastor fido, a collection earlier ascribed to Vivaldi.[247] These pieces too may have been written for Richter.

Martin Blockwitz played second hautboy in the Capelle from c.1717 to 1733, doubling also on traverso. Blockwitz is survived by an interesting 'well-tempered' collection of fifteen suites (60 Arien) in every practicable key, for traverso, violin, or hautboy.

In 1728 the Elector appointed the hautboist Claude Aubry to the 'Kleine Cammer-Musique', presumably to replace Quantz. Aubry had been a member of the Cromornes et Trompettes Marines at Versailles (a group that was probably not very active at the time). The Kleine Cammer-Musique was disbanded in 1733, and Aubry was back in Versailles by 1736.

---

[244] Two other pieces now at Dresden are copies of works that were originally performed elsewhere: RV 779 and RV 107.   [245] Richter might also have played in L'incoronazione di Dario itself.

[246] Cf. Selfridge-Field (1975), 44.   [247] See Ch. 7, §B.1 under Nicolas Chédeville.

With such an active musical life at court, music thrived in the city of Dresden as well. Private ensembles were maintained by the nobility and foreign embassies. Documentation on these activities is unfortunately scarce.

13. Darmstadt

Duke Ernst Ludwig reactivated his Capelle in Darmstadt in 1709 and appointed Christoph Graupner as Capellmeister. In the next years, Graupner assembled an excellent court Capelle. Schickhardt was probably at Darmstadt in about 1710, and would have provided the Capelle with a treble woodwind player until Michael Böhm arrived from Leipzig.

Walther (1732: 99) called Böhm 'ein vortrefflicher [fine] Hautboist'. Böhm was trained in Dresden, presumably by La Riche, and afterwards played (with Pisendel) in Telemann's Leipzig Collegium. In February 1711 he and Pisendel, both by then well known in Germany, were invited to perform at Darmstadt in Graupner's opera *Telemach*. They were subsequently offered positions in the Capelle. Pisendel declined, but (perhaps because Richter had just got the important job at Dresden) Böhm accepted the engagement, and was given the title of *Concertmeister*.[248] It was soon after this that the court sent him to Hamburg to study the 'Opern-Spielart'.[249] When in 1712 Telemann settled in Frankfurt (which is near Darmstadt), Böhm often played for him there. The two men later became brothers-in-law through marriage,[250] and Böhm was one of the four hautboy players to whom Telemann dedicated his *Kleine Cammer-Music* in 1716.

The Darmstadt library is another rich repository of music for hautboy from this period, a monument to Böhm, since most of it was probably written for him.[251] The library holds 176 chamber works, concertos, or sacred pieces for hautboy from this period. Of these, fifty-three are by Telemann. Other composers are Pfeiffer, Kreß, Fasch, Endler, Hesse, Böhm himself, Heinichen, Lotti, Hasse, and Weiss, giving some idea of the repertoire of Darmstadt court performances.

Among the more interesting chamber pieces by Telemann at Darmstadt is a trio for hautboy and violin, TWV 42: F4, II, conceived (like many of Telemann's chamber pieces) 'auf Concertenart' (in the manner of a concerto).[252] It may originally have been played by Böhm and the violinist Johann Kreß. There is also an interesting group of trios for treble viol and hautboy, probably written for Böhm and Ernst Hesse, the so-called 'German Forqueray'.

---

[248] Noack (1967), 176–7, 180.

[249] Graupner had composed for the Hamburg Opera just prior to his appointment at the Darmstadt court. At Darmstadt he produced a series of large-scale operas.

[250] In 1720, Böhm married Susanne Elisabeth Textor, the sister of Telemann's second wife Maria Katherina Textor (whom he had married in 1714). See Noack (1967), 180.

[251] A mediocre sonata for traverso in E minor (no. XXXVI) by 'Bohmer' (? Böhm) is preserved in the well-known Brussels MS XY15.115. [252] Cf. Swack (1988), esp. p. 134.

One of Telemann's trios in E minor, TWV 42: E14A, survives in three different instrumentations, a sign of its popularity. At Rostock[253] it is for violin and hautboy; the version at Darmstadt[254] is for recorder and treble viol, again probably for Hesse and Böhm (Böhm was also a recorder virtuoso). Another version exists at Dresden,[255] reworked as an orchestral piece. This version, too, may have had a connection to Böhm, as he noted in a letter to his former employer, Ernst Ludwig, in 1729; Böhm stated that he had travelled several times to Saxony, 'meine *Studia* weiters zu *prosequir*en' (to further pursue my studies).[256]

In that same letter, Böhm included information on the instruments and music he had used at Darmstadt:

Die Münchischen Bücher vom *Abaco*, Ihro Durchl *dedicir*et, das Gräfl Erbachische Buch,[257] das *Concert* so der Mannheimer Weiß[258] Ihro Durchl daselbsten gegeben, die Vier großen Hell: Flöten, die *Hautbois*, und zweÿ Stück von einer Berlinischen *Traversiere*, wozu der seeliger Kreß[259] das mittelstück behalten, sind alles was Ihro Durchl wir, nebst den englischen Flöten . . . anvertrauet Selbsten haben . . .	The books from Munich by Abaco, dedicated to Your Highness, the Count Erbach book, the concerto by Mr Weiß of Mannheim that he gave there to Your Highness, the four large unstained recorders, the *Hautbois*, and two joints of a Berlin traverso, of which the late Kreß retained the middle joint, are everything that Your Highness yourself (in addition to the English recorders) had entrusted to our care . . .

The traverso would have been too early to be by Quantz or Kirst; the only known maker working at Berlin at this time was Heitz, who is survived by a three-piece traverso[260] (Böhm's wording—'das mittelstück'—indicates that the 'Berlinischen *Traversiere*' was also a three-piece type). It is interesting that Böhm said he played English recorders, showing how far woodwinds could travel.[261]

Telemann's well-known hautboy concerto in E minor (K Ob.e) is also at the Darmstadt library. Another intriguing piece in manuscript at Darmstadt is Telemann's excellent Trio I from *Essercizii musici* in C minor, for recorder, hautboy, and continuo. Telemann published this collection in Hamburg after 1740,

---

[253] XVII: 45.5.   [254] Mus 1042/64.   [255] 2392-N-15.

[256] 30 May 1729, p. 4; letter now at Darmstadt: HA IV, Konv. 356, kindly transcribed by Samantha Owens. La Riche, with whom Böhm probably studied, was at Dresden until 1731.

[257] Probably F. K. Erbach, Count of Erbach, for whom Böhm may have occasionally played. The book may have contained the pieces mentioned in Noack (1980), 224.

[258] Probably Sigismund Weiß (see Ch. 7, §C.8).

[259] Probably Jacob Kreß (see above). Kreß died in 1728. See Noack (1967), 177, 212. Why Kreß would have kept the middle joint of this flute is unknown. Possibly the joint was later replaced with two new ones in a higher pitch, and these were Böhm's property.

[260] This instrument, at Vienna, is an attribution. Young (1993), 123.

[261] An inventory of instruments at Darmstadt made in 1752 includes 'Ein paar Quartflöten' (Noack 1967: 256), which may be the same instruments.

but parts of it may have been written much earlier; Böhm may have used this manuscript when he was at Darmstadt. Another good Telemann trio with recorder in A minor is at Darmstadt. One wonders which of the parts Böhm played, and who played the other one. Carl Fleischer was briefly at Darmstadt in 1719 (he had been Principal second hautboy to Glösch at Berlin). There were other woodwind players present at the court in this period (Corseneck and Kayser); to judge from the surviving music, they would have been put to good use (playing, for instance, the wonderful concerto in B flat by Telemann for three hautboys, three violins, and continuo).

There was also regular music at the Schloßkirche, composed by Graupner and the harpsichordist Gottfried Grünewald. (Grünewald, who died in 1739, requested that all his works be destroyed after his death, a wish that was unfortunately respected).[262] Graupner's large cantata output has survived. His cantata *Wie wunderbar ist Gottes Güt* (1717) is mentioned in Chapter 6, §C.1.a as probably the earliest known piece for hautbois d'amour. Many of Graupner's cantatas are of high quality (he was considered after Telemann but before Bach for the Leipzig job, but Ernst Ludwig raised his salary and refused to let him go). A very interesting aria with beautiful obbligato work is 'Seufzt und weint ihr matten Augen' for soprano, 'Hautbois' solo, and strings in the cantata *Ach Gott und Herr*, performed in June 1711, when Böhm had been four months at court.

A personal connection existed between many of the Darmstadt musicians, who had studied and worked together in Leipzig during the first decade of the century.[263] Graupner and Böhm were part of a circle that included Telemann, nearby at Frankfurt, and Fasch, who was in Darmstadt for several months in 1713 to study composition with Graupner and Grünewald. From Zerbst, Fasch later sent a number of his works to Darmstadt, and they are still there. Among them is a delightful quartet, FWV N:F4, for violin, hautboy, bassoon solo (no doubt written for a good player at court),[264] and continuo. It shows the same light but competent touch as Telemann's better pieces. Fasch's *Sinfonia/Sonata a 4*, FWV N:d2, for two hautboys, obbligato bassoon, harpsichord/(bassoon in one version), is an interesting and difficult work. The Darmstadt library also has a wonderful concerto by Fasch for two hautboys and bassoon solo (FWV L:c2).

In the late 1720s the financial position of court musicians at Darmstadt deteriorated to the point that in about 1729 Böhm was forced to leave. There is a series of more than a dozen concertos and 'ouvertures' for solo hautboy or hautbois d'amour by Graupner, now in the library in copies datable to the years 1729–37.[265] Since no hautboy players were employed there between 1729 and 1738, it may be that

---

[262] Noack (1995), ii. 1089. [263] Noack (1967), 177.
[264] Corseneck, at the court *c.*1706–30, is known to have played bassoon. [265] See Haynes (1992a), 148–9.

these pieces were composed earlier, when Böhm was still at the court. One of them, the Ouverture No. 40 in A major,[266] is for three 'd'amore' soloists: flute d'amour, hautbois d'amour, and viola d'amour with orchestra; it concludes with an elaborate, majestic chaconne. It is a striking piece.

14. Frankfurt

During Telemann's tenure at Frankfurt, he wrote a good deal of hautboy music which was played by a rather distinguished set of hautboists. As mentioned above, he often depended on Böhm in Darmstadt. And sometime after 1711, another remarkable player, Jacob Denner of Nuremberg, began making regular trips to Frankfurt,

Ampts wegen von einem Hochlöbl. Magistrat allhier verschicket worden, daß er allezeit wegen seiner guten Conduite und schönen Kunst, womit er sich von vielen anderen Virtuosen distinguiret, mit vielem Ruhm u. Lob Zurück gekommen.[267]	Sent officially by our most praiseworthy local municipal government. Each time he returned, he was showered with fame and praise, thanks to his good bearing and beautiful playing, by which he distinguished himself from many other soloists.

Denner was presumably travelling in his position as Stadtmusicus for the ancient *Pfeifergericht* that was held each year in Frankfurt from the fourteenth to the early nineteenth century. In Denner's time, the music for this event was traditionally provided by three musicians from Nuremberg.[268] In August 1712 Denner (in modern times better known as a woodwind maker than hautboy virtuoso; see below, §16) supplied the *Pfeifergericht* with a 'Bompart' which, in line with the historical character of the event, was purposely made in old-fashioned style.[269] This is probably the instrument that still exists at the Historical Museum in Frankfurt (Nr. 437). It borrows traits of an hautboy while remaining shawm-like: the six single finger-holes are on one unseparated joint, and the bell is long and wide (as on a shawm); at the same time there is a rudimentary hautboy-like turning at the top, an exposed hautboy Great-key, and only two resonance-holes between the beads at the bell waist. A photo of this instrument is reproduced in Young 1982, pl. X, together with Frankfurt X436, a Praetorius-style shawm with the workshop-stamp 'I. C. Denner' and the master-stamp 'D/I' (the latter suggesting it was made by one of Christoph Denner's sons).

Denner may of course have played other concerts during his yearly visits to Frankfurt.

---

[266] Darmstadt 464/40.   [267] Kirnbauer and Thalheimer (1995), 85, quoting Doppelmayr, p1730.
[268] Hofmann (1954), 85.
[269] On the delivery of this instrument, see Nickel (1971), 247; on the old-fashioned nature of the instruments used by the players, see Hofmann (1954), 86.

This same year, 1712, Telemann arrived in Frankfurt, and it is thus likely that he and Denner were in contact. And since Böhm also visited Frankfurt frequently during this period, Denner and Böhm could have met, and perhaps even played together. Böhm may have ordered instruments by Denner for the Darmstadt court: a court inventory includes hautboys by 'Tenninger' (probably Denner).[270] Thus, it is even possible that Böhm regularly played Denner's hautboys.

Telemann was evidently a serious woodwind player. When his Brockes-Passion was performed in April 1716, he played flute and hautboy in the orchestra.[271] While he was at Frankfurt, Telemann wrote five cantata *Jahrgänge*, and after he moved to Hamburg in 1721, he continued to send cantatas.[272] He also directed a Collegium Musicum at the Frauenstein, a private club of wealthy merchants, which gave regular weekly concerts from 1713. A piece that might have been written for the Frauenstein is the Trio in B flat with violin (TWV 42: B1, I) that Telemann published at Frankfurt in 1718 in a collection called *Six Trio*. This piece is again in the form of a miniature hautboy concerto. Although it was published, a manuscript copy is at Darmstadt, no doubt through the offices of Böhm, for whom it may have been written.

Telemann also provided music for regimental *Hautboisten* at Frankfurt. A number of his pieces for wind quintet (two hautboys, two horns, and bassoon) survive from there.[273] And a contemporary account of a military parade on 10 August 1716 described a band performing after an artillery salute on the occasion of the Archduke of Austria's birth:

Bei dem die 6 Hautbois in ihrer sauberen Montur den Mannschaften voranschritten, die den zu Ehren der Frankfurter Artillerie aufgesetzten Marsch von . . . Telemann bliesen.[274]	The six Hautbois paraded before the troops in their neat uniforms, playing the march by Telemann in honour of the Frankfurt Artillery.

The same occasion led Telemann to put on several festive cantatas in May 1716, to which it seems he invited three eminent hautboy players: Böhm, Glösch from Berlin, and La Riche from the Saxon court. Telemann later wrote that the performance was 're-enforced by many first-rate, well-known soloists',[275] and a local report commented that one concert was enhanced by 'the incomparable performance of the Darmstadt orchestra, and also the celebrated Berlin virtuoso on

---

[270] The inventory was made in 1765. Noack (1967), 269.   [271] Cahn (1995), 649.
[272] Ruhnke (1980), 649. Many of these pieces were performed repeatedly; none before 1716, but some as late as the 1750s.   [273] See Haynes (1992a), 310–11.
[274] Braun (1983), 54 quoting C. Valentin. This may be Frankfurt MS 1588, a 'Frankfurter' Marche in F for three hautboys, two horns, and bassoon, dated 1716.
[275] 'von vielen trefflichen, verschriebenen Virtuosen verstärket'.

the *Hauptbois* [*sic*], Mr Peter Glösch'.[276] This visit evidently inspired Telemann to prepare the six Partitas of the *Kleine Cammer-Music* or *Petite Musique de chambre* (TWV 41) for continuo with solo treble instrument (violin, traverso, harpsichord, 'besonders aber vor die Hautbois').[277]

Published in September 1716, the *Kleine Cammer-Music* is the first known collection of solos to be published for hautboy;[278] it is of special interest because it was composed by an hautboist. The *Kleine Cammer-Music* was dedicated to Böhm, La Riche, Glösch, and Richter. It may owe its name to the Dresden orchestra called the 'Kleine Cammer-Musique', and in fact a *symphonie* version of the collection, made by Telemann, survives. Richter was unable to attend the ceremonies at Frankfurt, as he was in Venice during most of 1716.[279] Telemann had long been acquainted with La Riche, having heard him perform at Berlin (possibly together with Glösch) in 1702 and 1704.[280]

15. Stuttgart

Christoph Pez was Capellmeister of the Württemberg court at Stuttgart from 1706 to 1716. His solo *Symphonia* was described in Chapter 3, §C.10. The six 'Sonata de M. Pestz' for two trebles and continuo preserved in manuscript are worth noting.[281] Despite the French movement titles, Pez's sonatas are Italian in style. The chaconne in no. 3 is quite powerful (as is to a lesser extent the end of no. 6). The quality is uneven: nos. 4 and 6 are the most musically convincing. Technically, these pieces are very simple. Pez's Sonata *a 3* in G minor for hautboy and violin[282] now lacks the hautboy part; it must have been an interesting piece, as the violin part is quite elaborate.

The principal hautboist at Stuttgart from 1699 or before until sometime after 1722 was Eberhardt Hildebrand, who was affectionately called 'ein alter, stiller, und fleißiger diener' (an old, calm, and diligent servant) by Pez in 1714. Hildebrand had a salary of 400 Gulden; other hautboists at court were paid the so-called 'ordinary' salary of 247 Gulden. Both Capellmeisters, Pez and Brescianello, considered Hildebrand the best hautboy in the Capelle, and it was probably he who played most of the hautboy and recorder music in the Friedrich Ludwig Sammlung. This

---

[276] 'der unvergleichlichen Execution des Darmstädtischen Orchesters, auch des renommirten Berlinischen Virtuosens auf der Hauptbois, Mr. Peter Göschens [Glösch]'.

[277] 'But especially for hautboy'. See Haynes (1986a).

[278] Bronnemüller's single 'Solo pour la Hoboj' is the only earlier solo (see below, §E). On the *Kleine Cammer-Music*, see also Ch. 4, §M.

[279] Telemann's dedication is to 'Francisco' Richter. Although this name points to Franz Xaver Richter as Telemann's intended dedicatee, it seems unlikely, since Franz Xaver was born in 1709 and since Johann Christian was a well-known hautboy player at Dresden and closely connected with La Riche.

[280] Telemann (1740), 359.

[281] Paris, MS 4° 848(1–3). The manuscript also contains six trios by Hotteterre le Romain (the same as the published ones, Opus 3, 1712) and several by La Barre.   [282] Rostock, MS XVII:38.4.

collection, made by Crown Prince Friedrich Ludwig, who died in 1731, is now housed in Rostock. It contains a cross-section of the repertoire of the *Cammer-Music* of the Stuttgart Capelle.[283] Thirty-two pieces involve hautboy,[284] primarily trios, solo concertos, and concertos for hautboy with another instrument.

Giuseppe Brescianello, a virtuoso violinist from Venice who had come to Stuttgart via Munich (as had Pez) was named Capellmeister some time between 1717 and 1722. Brescianello was a good composer who has yet to be rediscovered; several important works for hautboy survive (see Ch. 7, §C.9).

In 1718 the court owned '2 *Hautbois* von *Cornet*thon' and three other hautboys (presumably at *Cammerton*). The hautboys at *Cornet-ton* might by that time have been obsolete, or have been used in the various bands of *Hautboisten*.[285] Band members were paid less than the musicians of the Capelle. They were expected to be proficient on a variety of instruments, and to perform for various types of entertainments, church music, and occasions of a military nature. There was some upward mobility from bands into the Capelle. Some of the band music performed at Stuttgart has survived, including pieces by Christian Störl (the wind quintet dedicated to Duke Eberhard Ludwig), Pepusch, and Telemann.

16. Nuremberg

Nuremberg maintained its position as the most important centre of woodwind making in Germany until nearly the middle of the eighteenth century. In this period, hautboys were produced in the workshops of Christoph Denner (until 1707), Johann Schell (until 1732), Jacob Denner (1707–35), David Denner (? 1707/[a1736] –1760s), and Johann Oberlender sen. (1705–*c*.1745).[286]

Christoph Denner's eldest son Jacob was, like his father, celebrated as a player as well as a maker. Although his are among the finest-playing hautboys that survive, in his own day he was better known as a

welt-berühmter Musicus in seinen und den anderen Instrument, absonderlich aber in der Hautbois . . .[287]	world-famous musician on his own and other instruments, and particularly on the hautboy . . .

Born in 1681, Denner studied with both his father and his godfather, Jacob Lang, who was the principal municipal musician, a title he would also later acquire. He

---

[283] Cf. Owens (1995), ch. 8, and pp. 28 ff., 211 ff., 220 ff., 293, 303, 313, 344.

[284] They are by Baridoni, Brivio, Fasch (four concertos for traverso and hautboy, probably played before Böhm's arrival), Friedrich Ludwig himself, Giosna, Grüneberg, Heinichen (a solo concerto), Linike (a trio), Jacob Loeillet (a solo concerto), Molter, Pepusch, Perroni, Theodor Schwartzkopff, Stulicke, Telemann (two trios, band music, and a solo concerto), Thielo, Valentine, and Zellerino.

[285] For an overview of the history of hautboy bands at the Württemberg court, see Owens (1995), 343–57.

[286] Other possible Nuremberg makers by whom no hautboys survive at present are Johann Georg Zick (until 1733), Wendelin Meisenbach (1708–61), and Nikolaus Staub (p1700–34).

[287] Doppelmayr, p1730, quoted and translated in Kirnbauer and Thalheimer (1995), 84–5.

became a Stadtpfeifer in 1706, and a Stadtmusicus in 1717.[288] From 1727 he was the 'erstgenannter Stadtmusicus'. By 1708 Denner was well known as a performer, and he travelled extensively. He was said to have played with 'radiant grace and sensitivity' in courts such as Ansbach, Bayreuth, Sulzbach, and Hildburghausen, and (as noted above) he performed regularly in Frankfurt.[289] Plate 5.3 may show Denner playing.[290] He was producing instruments by 1710,[291] and was named a master builder some time before 1716.[292] His surviving instruments range in pitch from A–2 to A–1, with one hautboy that looks to be at A+0. Evidence mentioned above suggests he could have supplied instruments to a number of important soloists, including Böhm, Glösch, Fleischer, and Rose. Denner died prematurely in 1735, probably of consumption.

Jacob Denner had a younger brother, Johann David Denner, who was also a maker of woodwinds. Doppelmayr wrote in 1730 that on his death, Denner sen.

hinterließe zwey Söhne, welche den Ruhm ihres Vaters durch eine weitere Ausübung . . . annoch bestens befördern.[293]	left behind two sons, who continued to advance with distinction the fame of their father through their own work.

Shortly after Denner sen.'s death, a law was passed in Nuremberg establishing the right of succession of a master's workshop stamp; it was inherited by his widow, followed by the second son.[294] In the case of the Denners, that would have been David.[295] This would explain why Jacob Denner, since he was the elder son, set up his own separate shop, using his own workshop stamp: 'I. Denner' with 'I (fir tree) D'.[296]

David Denner was not accorded a master's status until 1736,[297] a year after his brother Jacob's death. But Christoph Denner's workshop stamp, 'I.C. Denner', continued to be used on instruments until at least 1754. On surviving instruments, there are two other normal marks that appear with the 'I.C. Denner' workshop scroll: either a 'D' or a 'D/I' (Pl. 5.4).[298] Of the fifteen known hautboys with the 'I.C. Denner' workshop stamp, ten have (or had) only the 'D', one (Venice Cons. 34) has 'D/I',[299] and four are unknown. Of other woodwinds with the 'I.C. Denner' stamp, thirty-four have only the 'D', and nineteen have 'D/I'.[300]

---

[288] Nickel (1971), 245.
[289] Kirnbauer and Thalheimer (1995), 97 n. 6 suggest that the Frankfurt fairs would have given Denner access to the latest woodwinds from other places, and might thus have affected his own construction.
[290] Weigel worked in Nuremberg, and at this time, *c.*1722, Jacob Denner was probably the foremost hautboist there.   [291] Cf. the bill for instruments sold to von Gronsfeldt in 1710, quoted in Nickel (1971), 251.
[292] Ibid. 248.   [293] Doppelmayr, p1730, quoted and translated in Kirnbauer and Thalheimer (1995), 84–5.
[294] The decree is dated 31 July 1710, according to Wörthmüller (1954), 290.
[295] Heyde (1993b), p. xviii.   [296] See Young (1993), 55–7.   [297] Nickel (1971), 267 ff.
[298] On two instruments, there is also an 'ID'.   [299] Its stamp can be seen in Langwill (1980), 217.
[300] The information on stamps comes from Nickel (1971), 214–39 and Young (1993), 58–61.

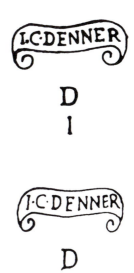

PL. 5.3. Johann Christoph Weigel, *c.*1720, *Musicalisches Theatrum*

PL. 5.4. Two Denner stamps showing the 'I.C. Denner' workshop scroll with the most common master stamps: 'D' and 'D/I'. (Stamps copied by Friedrich von Huene)

Kirnbauer (1992: 14) has shown that these single letters are in fact the most important part of the stamp, being the traditional *Meisterzeichen* or master's initial, conferred by the guild. Other stamps, including the 'I.C. Denner' scroll, were evidently used less as marks of authentication than as commercial additions that advertised the workshop.[301]

It is logical to assume that Christoph Denner would have used only the simple 'D' as his master's initial. And indeed, some instruments with the simple 'D' show early characteristics.[302] If that is true, then surviving instruments with the 'I.C. Denner' workshop scroll but other kinds of master's initial (such as 'D/I') were probably made by his sons after his death in 1707.

---

[301] The 'Werkstattzeichen', cf. Kirnbauer (1992), 17–18. Cf. also Heyde (1993b), p. xviii.

[302] Like the sopranino recorder, Brussels 434, in one piece and turned in early style, the basses, Salzburg CA 3/13 and Nuremberg MIR 213, and all the curtals. The recorder in Eisenach with the 'D' (115) is dated 1682. Another Christoph Denner stamp that 'is an unfailing feature of early Johann Christoph Denner instruments' has fluttering ends on its scroll; this stamp is always combined with the simple 'D'. See Kirnbauer (1995), 92–3.

Jacob Denner would have had no need to use his father's scroll, as he had his own workshop stamp, so it was probably David Denner who continued to use it. Thus all the instruments with the 'I.C. Denner' workshop stamp and more complicated master's initials than the simple 'D' may have been made by David Denner (in his mother's name or his own).

If this theory is correct,[303] Christoph Denner would himself have made some 49–59 known or surviving instruments, Jacob Denner 50, and David Denner 23–33.[304] Of surviving hautboys (whole or parts), Christoph would have made 10–14, Jacob 18, and David 1–5.

Two hautboys survive by Oberlender sen., considered by Nickel the most important woodwind maker after the Denners. Oberlender gained his master's title in 1705 (at the early age of 24), and is first documented as an instrument builder in 1710. His instruments closely resemble those of the Denners and Gahn.[305]

17. Munich

The Elector of Bavaria, Maximilian II Emanuel, had for political reasons been absent from Munich since 1692. When he re-established his court in 1715, he brought back to Munich with him Normand, Marchand, and Jacob Loeillet, the hautboy players of his Capelle-in-exile (see below, §F.2). There they joined Schuechbauer, who had remained at the Munich court (see Ch. 3, §C.10). Normand, who had been in the Elector's service since before 1692, retired from active playing in 1717. Marchand was a member of a band of *Hautboisten* called the 'Guarda' that existed from 1715 to 1726, and played for dances and balls.[306] The two chamber hautboists were Loeillet and Schuechbaur.

Max Emanuel's Capelle flourished until his death in 1726. Its opera was one of the most brilliant in Europe. Many of the operas performed there by Torri survive, and probably contain solos written for Loeillet (and, after his departure, for Schuechbaur).[307] The court's more extravagant productions (large-scale operas, tournaments, and balls) called on the services of the 'Guarda' as well as Munich's Stadtpfeifer for re-enforcements in the hautboy section.[308]

As the Elector attended daily Mass, sacred music was an important part of the work of the Capelle. Some of the smaller pieces (by Kerll, Ercole, Torri, and

---

[303] Applying this theory to recorder pitches means that the only surviving Denner recorders at A+o would have been made by David, which appears reasonable and supports the theory. That the A+o hautboy at Venice with a 'D/I' master's initial is by David seems likely because another high-pitched hautboy by Christoph Denner exists (Nuremberg MI 155), made using a different method (proportionally smaller than his standard model).

[304] There are ten instruments whose stamp is unknown.

[305] Nickel (1971), 289–90.   [306] Cf. Forster (1933), 25, 27.

[307] Torri is survived by a cantata for soprano, violin, hautboy, and continuo in Modena.

[308] Münster (1993), 304.

Giuseppe Bernabei) used obbligato instruments, probably including the hautboy. Most of that music is now lost.

Albinoni visited the Munich court in 1722, and dedicated his Opus 9 *Concerti* to Max Emanuel that same year. Loeillet, as Max Emanuel's 'vornembste Instrumental-Virtuos' (most distinguished instrumental virtuoso) with by far the highest salary of any musician at court,[309] no doubt performed the four solo concertos at that time, and the double concertos would have added Schuechbaur.

The court took delivery of woodwinds from Paris several times; in 1719 and 1721 from the Naust workshop (then run by Delerablée), and in 1721 two hautboys from Bizey 'garnis d'argent'.[310]

Evaristo Dall'Abaco was the most important chamber composer at court, which he served from 1704 to 1742. The music he wrote while the court was in the Netherlands and France (such as his *Sonate da camera*, Opus 3/2, for two hautboys or violins and continuo) is French in style, but after 1715 his music became more Italianate. His *Concerti à più istrumenti* (published 1717–19) contained a concerto for hautboy; this collection may have been the one to which Böhm referred in his letter of 1729 ('The books from Munich by Abaco, dedicated to Your Highness'; see above, §13). Dall'Abaco played in court concerts for Max Emanuel and his son, Carl Albrecht; he also organized 'academies' in his own house.[311]

Brescianello came to Munich from Venice in 1715, but left for Stuttgart the next year. He may have composed some of his surviving hautboy solos for the Munich hautboy players, as for instance the lost *Concertino* in C minor for hautboy or traverso, violin, bassoon, and harpsichord.

After the death of Max Emanuel in 1726 and the subsequent reduction of the Capelle, Loeillet left Munich and entered the service of the French court (see Ch. 7, §B.2). Schuechbaur became vice-concert master in 1735 and concert master in 1742. He was a composer[312] as well as an instrumentalist and instrument maker.

Max Emanuel's son, Carl Albrecht, who reigned from 1726 to 1745, devoted large sums to opera. Among the composers were Torri and Giovanni Battista Ferrandini. Ferrandini, a 'Wunderknabe', had first entered the service of Duke Ferdinand in Bavaria at the age of 12 in 1722. At that time he was an hautboy player. He had come originally from Venice in the same year as Albinoni (Albinoni may have brought the boy with him to Munich). It was probably in 1723 that Ferrandini entered the Elector's service. He rose to the rank of *Cammermusicus* and, in 1732, *Cammercomponist*. His first opera was produced in 1727 (at the age of 17); he was highly esteemed at court. Ferrandini is survived by three *Sinfonien* for two 'Oboe di Silva' and orchestra. Stefano Ferrandini (? his brother) also joined the court as *Hautboist* in 1723.

---

[309] Nösselt (1980), 80.   [310] Schmid (1986), 33.   [311] Münster (1993), 305.
[312] The lost *Concerto* for two tailles, two horns, and Bass listed in Selhof (1759) as by 'Schuch' may have been by him.

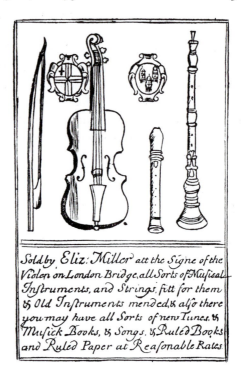

Sold by *Eliz: Miller* att the *Signe* of the *Violen on London Bridge, all Sorts of Musisal Instruments, and Strings, fitt for them & Old Instruments mended, & also there you may have all Sorts of new Tunes. & Musick Books, & Songs. & Ruled Books and Ruled Paper at Reasonable Rates.*

PL. 5.5. Elizabeth Miller, trade card, 1707–*c*.1727. Collection of Tony Bingham, London

E. England

There must have been considerable work for hautboy players in London in the first decades of the eighteenth century. A number of foreign players arrived on British shores (Galliard, Kytch, Mercy, Chaboud, John Loeillet, and Rousselet), and native players also appeared (Neale, Smith, Graves, and Denby).

The activities through which a musician could earn a living in London included the court, the churches, the theatres, and military bands. Few musicians specialized in only one of these categories, and public concerts served to fill in the gaps.

There were three important English hautboy makers in this period. Bressan and Stanesby made instruments until the early 1730s, and Stanesby's son set up shop in about 1713. Elizabeth Miller's trade card (Pl. 5.5, 1707–*c*.1727) presumably shows a typical English hautboy of the period; it is Type A2.

1. Opera

Performances of Italian opera began in London in 1705, the year the Queen's Theatre in the Haymarket opened. *Thomyris* (adapted from music by Bononcini and

Scarlatti) appeared at Drury Lane Theatre in 1706; it marked the first appearance of an Italian castrato in England, and featured two hautboy solos. Some of Purcell's larger works were also revived at Drury Lane in this period.

Opera sung in Italian by imported stars was a source of fascination to the London audience,[313] and in 1710 the Queen's Theatre put on two operas performed entirely in Italian (*Almahide* and Mancini's *Idaspe*). The Queen's had an orchestra of about twenty-five players, a group that was crystallizing into a regular, institutionalized entity just as Handel arrived there (Handel produced his first opera, *Rinaldo*, in February 1711).[314]

The arrival of Handel firmly established Italian opera in London. Handel produced operas during the next three decades, and the Opera orchestra was the most prestigious and probably the most interesting hautboy work in London in this period.

Since 1708 the hautboists at the Queen's had been John Loeillet, brother of Jacob Loeillet (as principal), and Pierre La Tour (2nd). In that year, Scarlatti's *Pyrrhus and Demetrius*, which contained a number of hautboy solos, was produced at the Queen's; the aria 'Thus in a solitary Grove' was sung by the famous Mrs Tofts, and the hautboist was presumably Loeillet.[315] The Opera band, and specifically Loeillet, was highly praised in 1709.[316]

There are no lists for the Opera orchestra between 1711 and 1717,[317] so it is unclear who was playing hautboy in most of Handel's early London operas. The list for Handel's first opera season (1710–11) no longer included Loeillet, who may have retired at that time to start a private concert series, his place being taken (at least temporarily) by Galliard.[318]

Johann Ernst Galliard had studied the hautboy at Celle with Maréchal (see Ch. 3, §C.2); he also studied composition with both Steffani and Farinel in Hannover. Galliard came to London in 1706, and his first employment was in Queen Anne's band. He also conducted public concerts (with, among others, Böhm's colleague, the gamba virtuoso Ernst Hesse, who visited England in about 1706).[319] Galliard became a well-known and prolific composer, and found time to translate 'the most influential singing treatise of the eighteenth century',[320] Tosi's *Opinioni* of 1723 (as *Observations on the Florid Song*, 1742). Galliard's Masque, *Pan and Syrinx*, included important hautboy work; written in the same year as Handel's *Acis and Galatea*, it was in much the same style. Galliard wrote several hautboy solos that are now lost. A reference to him in Roger North's 'What is Ayre?'[321] suggests he may have been North's informant on the hautboy.

[313] Milhous and Hume (1982), p. xxii.   [314] Burrows (1993), 361.
[315] The aria had been performed as 'Tortorella' in 1694 in Naples.
[316] By the English translator of Raguenet 1702 (who may have been Galliard).   [317] Burrows (1985), 349.
[318] Lasocki (1983), 878.   [319] Noack (1967), 166.   [320] Fuller (1989), 127.
[321] North (1959), [87].

Galliard was evidently close to Handel; as a fellow countryman and composer, who had spent some time in Hannover (whence Handel had just come), he may have befriended Handel on the latter's first brief sojourn to London in 1710 (when Handel's English was not yet good). Handel's C minor solo sonata, HWV 366 (one of his best), may have been composed during this visit, and it is easy to imagine that he wrote it for Galliard.[322]

When Handel produced *Teseo* at the Queen's in 1712, Galliard played the six (!) hautboy solos with soprano. Galliard, with his court position, may also have been the player of the hautboy obbligato in the Duet 'Kind health descends on downy wings' in Handel's ode *Eternal source of light divine*, written for the birthday of Queen Anne in 1713 (Handel used this same piece in *Esther*, performed at Cannons in 1718). Because of his proximity to Handel at the time, Galliard is also the most likely recipient of another of Handel's solo sonatas, HWV 363a in F, written in London *c.*1712–16.[323]

In about 1712, La Tour moved to the rival theatre, Drury Lane (perhaps to a first hautboy position), and Jean Christian Kytch (who had been playing bassoon in the orchestra probably since 1708) took over the second hautboy desk at the Opera.[324] Handel had written an obbligato bassoon part for Kytch in *Rinaldo*.[325] But it is unclear who was playing principal for Handel in the rest of his London operas produced between 1712 and 1718 (*Rinaldo*, *Il pastor fido*, *Silla*,[326] and *Amadigi*). It is quite possible it was Galliard; there is certainly a corresponding gap in his own stage productions in this period. Other possibilities are Loeillet (who might have returned to the orchestra) or Francesco Barsanti.

According to Hawkins (who would have had good reason to know) Barsanti was active in England from 1714.[327] Hawkins wrote that Barsanti played in the Opera in London for many years before moving to Edinburgh in the 1730s. But there are conflicting reports on Barsanti's career. Bernardini noted that he was the principal hautboy in Bologna 1717–35, when he moved to Edinburgh;[328] he was also reported in Lucca in 1735. Hawkins is the only source that suggested he was in the Opera, and there are no records of the orchestra at this time. Barsanti might have remained only three years and returned to Italy in 1717; he is not mentioned in the Royal Academy lists of 1719 (see below).[329]

---

[322] The incipit of this piece that appears in the Breitkopf catalogue (1766: 247) includes ornaments. David Lasocki's edition of the Handel solo sonatas for Nova is exemplary as a conflation of disparate sources, except for the addition of breath-marks (which no source includes). The last notes of IV: 17/18 in the C minor Sonata are reversed. The G minor Sonata (HWV 364a) was not written for the hautboy, although Walsh published it that way in the 1720s.

[323] Cf. Baselt (1986), 139. The version published in G for traverso is probably a creation of the publisher.

[324] Lasocki (1988).   [325] Lasocki (1983), 865.

[326] *Silla* (? June 1713) also has unusually elaborate hautboy parts (cf. Dean and Knapp 1987: 269).

[327] Barsanti came from Tuscany, and might thus have studied there with Erdmann.

[328] Bernardini (1987), 20, citing Luigi Nerici, *Storia della musica in Lucca* (Bologna, 1879), 340.

[329] Lasocki's suggestion that Barsanti was the 'Italian Master' who arrived in 1723 is contradicted by more convincing evidence that this was Sammartini (see below).

Barsanti published several solo collections in England in the 1720s, including his six solos, Opus 3. The fourth sonata in this generally undistinguished collection is truly inspired, and a pleasure to play (the sixth sonata is also charming, but in its written key of A minor has several e3s and is better on hautboy in G minor).

In Handel's early operas, the hautboists (Galliard and La Tour?) were playing instruments made by their opposite number in Paris, Colin Hotteterre, the first hautboy of the Opéra. This is documented in a letter written from London in January 1712[330] by a French hautboy player resident in London, Louis Rousselet:

Deux de mes amis . . . joue a lopera issy avec deux hautbois faits par Mr Colin Hotteterre . . .[331]	Two of my friends . . . play in the opera here on two hautboys made by Mr Colin Hotteterre . . .

The excellent Hotteterre hautboy that survives at Brussels (2320) is probably by Colin Hotteterre. In the same letter, Rousselet ordered two bassoons for members of this orchestra from the Parisian maker Rippert. He wrote:

Have the kindness to try [the bassoons] yourself, because it is for persons who know how to draw out of them all that one must when they are in their hands. It is necessary that the bassoons and the oboes be the same pitch we play here, almost ¼ tone higher than the pitch of the Opéra in Paris.[332]

Since French *Ton d'Opéra* was ±392, and a half-tone was either four or five commas, 'almost ¼ tone higher' than 392 would have been about two commas higher, or 403 Hz, exactly A−1½, called in England *Consort-pitch*, and the most common instrumental standard at the time.[333]

Rousselet evidently held the bassoonists in high esteem. One of them was probably Kytch, and the other could have been Thomas Vincent sen., who was born about 1680 and played either at the Opera or one of the theatres. Vincent had two sons who became famous hautboy players (see Ch. 7, §D.2).

A list of the orchestra for the Lord Mayor's Day festivities of 1714 included the names of many or all the most active hautboy players in London at the time. They were: Smith, Luly [John Loeillet], Clash, La Tour, Graves, Denbigh, Festion, Graves, and Cobson.

Nothing is known at present of Clash and Cobson.[334] William Smith, Humphrey Denby, and James Graves played at court in the Queen's hautboy band (see below). Smith was one of the assemblers of the orchestra on this list, and was active from

---

[330] 'January 1711' old style.

[331] Cf. Giannini (1993b), 45; Lasocki (1988), 348. Rousselet was the son of Jean Rousselet (a well-established hautboist and hautboy maker in France who had died the year before) and godson of Louis (11) Hotteterre (c.1645/50–1716). He was in London, c.1707–p1719. [332] Giannini (1993b), 45.

[333] See Haynes (1995), 339.

[334] Burrows (1985), 355. 'Clash' might have been Kytch, but a 'Mr Kitch' was listed among the basses (presumably bassoon). Bonnie Blackburn (pers. comm.) suggests the possibility that 'Clash' was Peter Glösch, who had been dismissed from the Berlin Capelle in 1713 and played in Frankfurt in 1716.

1703 to 1755. He played in the City of London Waits for a time. Graves was active in London by 1702, and until at least 1727. He published two collections of 'tunes' for hautboy in 1717 and 1718. Denby performed until at least 1742. He played a flute solo in a concert in 1709, and figured in a dispute over La Tour's will, 1735–8. John Festing was presumably younger than the others; he lived until 1772. He was considered for third hautboy at the Opera in 1720. Already by this time, his main instrument may have been the traverso.[335]

The Queen's Theatre (the King's from 1714) put on Handel's operas as well as those of other composers. The Drury Lane and Lincoln's Inn Fields theatres also had work for hautboy players; in the latter, a number of operas were produced in 1716–18.

There was a break in Handel's London opera productions between 1717 and 1720, and during this time he worked at Cannons,[336] the residence of James Brydges, Duke of Chandos. Handel produced a number of exquisite hautboy solos and chamber pieces for Chandos: a sonata for hautboy, two violins, and continuo (HWV 404), the 'Chandos Anthems' which include three obbligatos for hautboy, *Esther*, that had one hautboy, and *Acis and Galatea* with its prominent and delicate hautboy parts. *Acis* was for two hautboys doubling on recorders, although 'Sigr' Biancardi was the only hautboy on the payment lists for 1718.[337] Since Biancardi was paid relatively little, and the lists appear to be incomplete, he was presumably the second hautboy. The identity of the principal is unknown; it could well have been Kytch, who is documented at Cannons only from 1719 (when he was the highest-paid instrumentalist there).

The organ Handel used at Cannons survives at Gosport. It is at A-424, a common English pitch for organs known as 'Chapell-pitch', and a semitone above Consort-pitch (A–1½, or A-400/403), the usual standard for instruments.[338] The difference between these two pitches may explain why the opening Andante of Chandos Anthem 5A (HWV 250a, written for Cannons) is an hautboy solo in the improbable key of A major.[339] Handel used this same movement in several other pieces, including the 'Sonata a 5' (*c*.1707) and the third Concerto in *Select Harmony* (HWV 302a, published in 1740). In these alternative versions it is in the more natural key of B flat. The hautboy that performed Anthem 5A at Cannons may well have played in B flat, since it was probably tuned at Consort-pitch, the pitch of Handel's opera orchestra in London. In this key it would have agreed with the organ in A a semitone higher.

---

[335] John Festing is probably a relative of the 'Mr Festing' who performed in 1707 and 1708 and apparently wrote some 'Tunes' 'set for a Hautbois' that were in existence by 1705. 'Mr Festing' may have come to England from Germany with the French Marshall Tallard, taken prisoner at the Battle of Blenheim. See Lasocki (1983), 956 and Tilmouth (1973). Cf. Fischer's *Symphonie sur la bataille à Hochstad* (1706) for Hautbois ('Marlborough') and violin ('Tallard').   [336] Cf. Dean (1970), 29.

[337] Beeks (1985), 8, 17.   [338] See Haynes (1995), 329.   [339] See Hendrie (1985), 154.

After Handel's departure in 1719, the music director at Cannons was 'that eminent master Mr John Christopher Pepusch', brother of Gottfried Pepusch. An hautboy concerto by Pepusch is listed in a Chandos inventory of 1721, and was probably played by Kytch. It is now apparently lost.[340]

A new opera company, the Royal Academy of Music, was formed in 1719, and produced operas by Handel, Bononcini, and others during the next decade. There were two performances a week during the season (which was generally from November to June).[341] There are no surviving lists of the orchestra in the 1720s. But when it was first putting its orchestra together in 1719, the Royal Academy made up three lists, including the following potential hautboy players:[342]

List 1 (PwB 94)
Lulliet [Loeillet]	Category 2
Keitch [Kytch]	3
Festin [Festing]	5

List 2 (PwB 98), under 'Hautbois'
Luillet or Joseph	2
Ketch	3
Festin	5
Neal [Neale]	5

List 3 (PwB 97)
~~Lulliet or~~ Joseph	2
~~Ketch~~ Biancardi	3
Festin	5
Neal	5

In the margin is also added '[Mr Roussellet?]'

The categories were pay scales, the lower numbers being better paid. The Opera evidently used four hautboists, doubling the two parts, and (as the operas show) occasionally splitting them into pairs of flutes and hautboys who played together. The lists are reasonably consistent, and it seems clear that Festing and Neale were the third and fourth hautboy players; Neale was an active flute and hautboy player of whom there are documented performances until *c.*1744. About the other two hautboists there is some ambiguity.

Loeillet's name was the only one to appear at salary level 2 (indicating the principal hautboy player) on all three Academy lists. The only reason to think he did not hold that position in the early 1720s[343] is the presence of the name 'Joseph' beside his. Who was this?

---

[340] Unless it is the same as the one that survives at Herdringen.
[341] Lasocki (forthcoming).   [342] Milhous and Hume (1983), 158, 160.
[343] Loeillet also played and taught the harpsichord. He left a large estate on his death in 1730.

The sole English hautboist named 'Joseph' was a Joseph Woodbridge,[344] but he is unlikely. Woodbridge later became a kettledrummer, implying a less than full commitment to the hautboy. A player considered next to Loeillet for a high pay scale and a position demanding solo playing would surely have had more of a performing career than is documented for Woodbridge (even Kytch, who was an active performer in the 1710s, was not yet looked on at the Opera as a potential principal player). In any case, Woodbridge would no doubt have been called by his family name, as were all the other players. 'Joseph' was evidently someone unusual.

In this period, Italian musicians were often called by their first names, like French chefs and hair stylists today (cf. for instance the players of the *Resurrezione* above, §C.6). And there is a possibility that an Italian 'Joseph', none other than Giuseppe Sammartini, was in London shortly after this. Sammartini certainly did later play in the Opera, and the compilers of these lists may already have known of him and the possibility that he was planning a trip to London.

Sammartini settled permanently in London in 1729, but (like Handel in 1710) had apparently made an exploratory trip in 1723–4 and then gone back to Italy. Burney wrote of this visit:

The most memorable musical events of 1723, where [*sic*] the arrival of the admirable GIUSEPPE SAN MARTINI, whose performance on the hautbois and compositions were, afterwards, so justly celebrated . . . Martini's first public performance in England was at a benefit concert for Signor *Piero* [NB. again the first name], at the little theatre in the Haymarket, where he is called 'an Italian master just arrived'.[345]

The *Daily Courant* for 3 April 1723 announced that an 'Italian Master lately arrived from Italy' would play 'a solo on the hautboy' at the New Theatre, Haymarket, on the 4th.[346] Hawkins corroborated this with a remark that Sammartini was soloist for both Bononcini and Handel;[347] since Bononcini was not involved in the Opera after 1724,[348] Sammartini would have had to be in London by that year. Sammartini did not stay: he met Quantz in Venice in 1726, and witnessed his sister's marriage in Milan on 13 February 1728.[349]

Another indication that Sammartini was in London in 1723–4 is the existence of two arias, Guido's 'Amor, nel mio penar' in Handel's *Flavio* (14 May 1723),[350] and the second version of 'Sù la sponda del pigro' in *Tamerlano* (31 October 1724) that are in the unusual key of B flat minor.[351] The key was probably chosen for dramatic

[344] Milhous and Hume (1983), 160.   [345] Burney (1776), 997.

[346] Lasocki (1983), 846. Lasocki suggested that the player was Barsanti.

[347] Hawkins (1776), v. 369–71.   [348] Lasocki (1983), 887.

[349] Churgin (1980), 457. Sammartini may have been called back to Milan after October 1724 by the death of his father, which occurred in that year.

[350] I am obliged to Bruce Wetmore for bringing this aria to my attention.

[351] HG 153–4. There is an added part for 'Les Hautbois transposée in A' [A minor]. No other pieces surviving in Handel's autograph are written for hautboy in B flat minor, according to Möller (1993), 15.

effect: both arias are in highly emotional scenes. An hautboy is involved in the arias,[352] and in both cases, it is notated in A minor, a semitone lower than the rest of the band. For these arias, then, the hautboy would have been tuned a semitone higher than the strings. But the rest of both operas was evidently performed with hautboys and strings at the same pitch level (including 'Rompo i lacci' in *Flavio*, which has an hautboy solo in D minor in its B section).

This suggests that a special soloist with an hautboy pitched a semitone above the prevailing standard was invited to play these solos, while the rest of the two operas was performed by Handel's regular hautboists. The pitch level at Venice and northern Italy in general was commonly about a half-step above the Opera orchestra's Consort-pitch (see above), so this soloist was most likely from northern Italy. As Quantz suggested, Sammartini was the pre-eminent player of the hautboy in that area in the 1720s. Since Handel was later to write a number of solos for Sammartini, and since he was evidently in London at the time, it is conceivable that Sammartini was the invited soloist. Another aria performed in the same period that Sammartini might have played is 'Nel tuo seno' from *Giulio Cesare* (20 February 1724), which is in F minor; Sammartini would have played it in E minor, a much better key for the hautboy.

Putting this evidence together, the most likely principal player at the Opera in the early 1720s was Loeillet, with guest appearances by 'Joseph' Sammartini sometime between 4 April 1723 and 31 October 1724. Later in the decade, Kytch took over as principal.

Loeillet would thus have played 'Quando mai spietata sorte' in *Radamisto* (1720), one of the most beautiful examples of Handel's special way of combining a reflective vocal text with a lyrical hautboy in dialogue, accompanied by a warm, four-part string group. *Radamisto* also has the aria 'Deggio dunque'. The only other hautboy obbligato from the 1720s is 'Volate più dei venti' in *Muzio Scevola* (1721), for Bass with hautboy and bassoon (? Loeillet and Kytch). Although these are fine pieces, they are Handel's last from this decade that feature the hautboy in obbligatos. From this time onwards, in fact, no hautboy players except Sammartini seem to have been able to inspire Handel's muse. In the Opera orchestra, his hautboy parts were indifferent. To quote Winton Dean,

Much of Handel's scoring for oboes strikes us as unimaginative. Again and again they share the top line with the violins, in unison or alternation, and in choruses their role is to double the treble and alto voices. In some oratorios Handel confines them so rigorously to these duties as to raise a suspicion that he had little confidence in the players or their instruments . . .[353]

---

[352] The original performing score and a manuscript dated '*c*.1730s' both specify 'Hautb' and are notated in A minor. The part is for 'Flauto' (in A minor) in the version used for the revival in 1732 (Knapp 1993: 226).

[353] Dean (1959), 76

It is interesting that until the third decade of the century, none of the Opera haut-boy players was a native Englishman: Galliard was German, Kytch probably Dutch, Loeillet from the Spanish Netherlands, and La Tour from France. William Smith (fl. 1703–55) had been considered for second hautboy at the Queen's Theatre in 1707 but not hired. Richard Neale was apparently the first native son to join the section as fourth hautboy in 1720.

Kytch had probably rejoined the orchestra by at least 1724.[354] His position may have been ambivalent in 1721 because he was still in the service of the Duke of Chandos (Biancardi, his rival for the Opera job, had already left Cannons in 1720, and was probably in London and available).

Another list gave the names of hautboy players for the Lord Mayor's Day festiv-ities in 1727 ('all from the Opera and both Theatres'): Kytch, Neale, Woodbridge, Smith, Akeman, and Lowe.[355] A total of forty-seven musicians were listed, so there is no way to know which of these hautboys were from the Opera orchestra. Since Kytch and Neale figured on the Academy lists of 1719, however, there is a good chance that they (heading up the Lord Mayor's Day list) were in the Opera orches-tra in 1727.

Carl Friedrich Weidemann was a German who spent most of his career in London. He began playing in the Opera orchestra in 1725 in Handel's *Tamerlano*, presumably as player of both hautboy and traverso;[356] the latter was his main instru-ment. Quantz, who visited London from 20 March to 1 June 1727, and heard performances of Handel's *Admeto* and Bononcini's *Astyanax*,[357] mentioned both Weidemann and Festing as flutists. It may be that Weidemann joined the orchestra when Loeillet left, so that from 1725 the regular hautboists/flutists were Kytch, Neale, Festing, and Weidemann.[358]

2. Other kinds of concerts

At the court, Englishmen were listed for the first time in Queen Anne's chamber band in 1708 (Denby, Graves, and Smith). The band had eight players, including Galliard and La Tour.[359] A 'Solo pour la Hoboj' from *Fasciculus musicus*, published in Amsterdam in 1710–12 by Elias Bronnemüller, was dedicated to Queen Anne, and may have been played by members of this band.

The band was continued into the reign of King George I. George had come to England in 1714 from Hannover, where as the Elector Georg Ludwig he had employed a number of fine hautboists at his court, including an 'auserlesenste

[354] Lasocki (1983: 867–8) points out that he was playing arrangements of Handel's *Giulio Cesare* in March 1724; the opera had appeared only the month before and was not yet published; Kytch would have had trouble obtain-ing the music if he had not been close to Handel.   [355] Burrows (1985), 355.

[356] Drummond (1980), 295.   [357] Quantz (1755), 242.

[358] In 1729 Kytch was described as 'first hautboy to the Opera'.   [359] See Lasocki (1988), 348.

Bande Hautboisten' (see above, §D.4). George's English band may in fact have been involved in the first performance of Handel's *Water Music* in 1717.

Besides private concert series, like Loeillet's, concerts were still held in taverns (probably not unlike those Bach gave at Zimmermann's Coffeehouse in Leipzig). Tavern concerts were often organized by subscription or by music clubs like the Castle Concerts in the Castle Tavern, and the prestigious and wealthy Academy of Ancient Music (of which Galliard was a founding member) at the Crown and Anchor.

There were two types of public concerts, the 'music meetings' in concert rooms, and the 'act music' at the intervals of plays in the theatres. Hickford's Room next to the Opera house, which had been enlarged in about 1700, was the preferred concert venue of foreign virtuosi and opera stars. The Opera orchestra began performing there in 1719.[360] Public concerts were led by prominent professionals such as Geminiani, Loeillet, and one of the Festing brothers.

The music for hautboy heard at these concerts might have included solo sonatas by Handel, Pepusch (Pepusch's '26me Sonata, Mr Pebus [!]' in D minor at the back of a manuscript collection of recorder music[361] is an excellent piece) and Castrucci, trio sonatas by Handel, Pepusch and Steffani,[362] concertos by Handel,[363] and obbligatos with voice by Handel, Croft, Pepusch, and Bononcini.

From 1719, Kytch was active as a recitalist at public concerts, mostly at Hickford's Room. His concerts usually included a sonata or concerto on the hautboy (it is unclear from the wording of advertisements for these concerts whether Kytch was sometimes playing pieces of his own composition). The Babell solos (discussed below) were published and available by about 1725, and Walsh brought out Handel's solo sonatas soon afterwards; Kytch may have played these. For his concert in April 1729, he played arrangements of arias from operas by Handel and Bononcini 'on hautboy, also little flute and bassoon'.[364]

Setting vocal arias for hautboy or other treble instruments was evidently a common practice. Walsh in *c.*1717 published an instrumental arrangement of Mancini's *Idaspe* that calls for hautboy with four-part strings, 'The Hautboy performing the Song-Part, forms a complete consort, as if a Voice accompany'd'.[365] Walsh published many arrangements of current operas for 'a single Flute' or 'two Flutes'.[366] Probably in the 1750s, he also brought out two remarkable collections of 'Handel's

[360] Raynor (1972), 261.

[361] Rochester (MS Vault M 1490 B113, fos. 39ʳ⁻ᵛ, 40ʳ⁻ᵛ). Copied by Charles Babel.

[362] Cf. *Chomigioia* now at the British Library, which may have been brought to England by Galliard.

[363] Cf. HWV 301, 287, and the G minor concerto in Herdringen.

[364] Cf. Lasocki (1988), 350 and Haynes (1992a), 78. It is possible that the 'little flute' was the same sopranino recorder he used in the première of the now well-known aria 'Oh ruddier than the cherry' in *Acis and Galatea*.

[365] The part-books at the British Library include the vocal solo, the obbligato instrument, two violins, viola, and continuo.   [366] See Smith and Humphries (1968).

songs' from the oratorios and operas, arranged 'for concerts', 'the song parts for a Hoboy or German flute'[367] and four-part strings. The opera collection is a single volume, but there are five for the oratorios, containing about 400 arias.

Kytch probably played his own arrangements, combining the solo lines and tuttis, in the manner of the very attractive set of Handel's 'Airs for the Hautboy, from the operas' included in the back of Prelleur's 'Instructions upon the Hautboy' (1730). These pieces were quite effective in performance, and the tunes were already familiar. Arrangements of operas were no doubt popular in an age when recordings were not available, and listeners could be reminded of arias they had once heard in their original forms. The passage by Ralph (quoted in Ch. 4, §E.1) complaining of 'a hoarse hautboy . . . which by the strength of imagination, we are to believe S[enesi]no or C[u]z[zo]ni' may have been referring to Kytch's performances.

Both the Drury Lane and Lincoln's Inn Fields theatres maintained full-sized bands. The 'entertainments' or 'act music' at the intervals of plays were in fact short concerts and often consisted of the latest music, played by distinguished musicians like Paisible, La Tour, and John Banister. They were often as popular as the plays themselves. It was at Lincoln's Inn Fields that Gottfried Pepusch and his 'seven young Hautboys' from Berlin performed music written by Pepusch's brother Christoph, in April and June 1704.[368] At Drury Lane in 1722 (a larger space than the taverns and music rooms), Galliard accompanied Mrs Barbier on the hautboy in a new cantata he had composed.

There is evidence also of amateur hautboy playing, including the 'music meetings' organized by Claver Morris in Wells, which may have included professionals during the summer months, and the activities of Robert Woodcock, who is survived by three hautboy concertos (one of which is good enough to have been attributed to both Handel and Loeillet).[369]

The concert season of necessity took place when the landed classes were 'in town', and did not include the summer months when the richest patrons were at their country houses. For the sake of a large enough audience, concerts were usually placed on nights when there were no opera performances, and this made it possible to employ members of the opera orchestra, 'the best Hands in the Kingdom'.

It seems to have been unusual in England for aristocratic families to keep a band of musicians at their country estates or town houses, as was common on the Continent.[370] The newspapers in London in this period contained many advertisements for public 'benefit concerts' (in the older sense of commercial concerts of

---

[367] In the oratorio collection, 'the song parts with the words for voice, a hoboy, or German flute', which includes also the part for the original obbligato instrument.   [368] Tilmouth (1961), 54–5.

[369] Cf. Lasocki and Neate (1988); Haynes (1992a), 346.   [370] Cannons being a notable but brief exception.

miscellaneous pieces organized for the profit of the musicians).[371] Most were single events, although there were series as well.

3. Repertoire

A sizeable repertoire of chamber music and solos for hautboy was written in London in this period. Based on what we know of the dates of Handel's compositions, the decade between 1710 and 1720 was by far his most productive for music of this kind; forty-two pieces survive, all written in England (Cannons as well as London).[372] There are also solo sonatas by Babell, Barsanti, Giovanni Boni, Castrucci, Galliard (now lost), and Granom. Trios involving hautboy include those of Corbett, Galliard (lost), John Loeillet,[373] and Pepusch. Quartets and quintets survive by Charles Dieupart, Handel, and Pepusch. There are solo concertos by Alberti, Handel (for hautboy and violin, HWV 314), Pepusch, and Woodcock. Pepusch's *Six English Cantatas* contains a piece for soprano, hautboy, and bass.

The Babell solos 'for a violin, hoboy or German flute' with 'proper Graces adapted to each Adagio by ye Author' are the woodwind players' pale shadows of Corelli's famous solos. Babell's graces resemble those of editions of the Corelli solo sonatas that claimed to reproduce the ornaments as the composer himself played them on the violin. It may have been of Babell's collection that Galliard was thinking when he wrote that 'Many Graces may be very good and proper for a Violin, that would be very improper for a Hautboy; and so with every Species of Instruments that have something peculiar.'[374] Music can be a lot worse than Corelli and still be good enough, however. Babell's sonatas VIII and IX could both be played in a way that would make them well worth hearing.

A very good Italian-style four-movement sonata by Pietro Castrucci, for many years leader of the Opera orchestra, appears in the Chaboud collection of twelve *Solos* (c.1725). The sonata was obviously a success; it appeared in other publications variously for flute, violin, or recorder. Pietro Chaboud, who edited this interesting collection, was employed at Cannons on several instruments and as a composer, and was probably a bassoonist at the Opera.[375]

Handel's justly famous collection of trios, Opus 2, published about 1730, was not written as a unit. Walsh put it together from pieces conceived at different times.

---

[371] See Burrows (1993), 361 ff.

[372] These include four solos with continuo, four trio sonatas, five larger ensembles, a concerto, and nearly two dozen obbligatos with voice (most of them for soprano, hautboy, and orchestra). In the same decade, Bach produced thirty solos and Telemann twenty-four (though in the next decade they both far surpassed Handel). Twenty-four solos by Handel survive from the following decade, 1720–30. The decades 1700–10 and 1730–40 both produced twenty-two pieces.

[373] Although by all accounts Loeillet was a brilliant player, the published music he left is insipid and formulaic.

[374] Galliard, in an added comment to his translation of Tosi 1723 (1742: 159).

[375] His name appeared on all three of the Opera lists of potential players described above.

Only the first, third, and fifth trios, all apparently written about 1718, call for haut-boy. The first, HWV 386a, originally in C minor, has a higher tessitura than the other two; depending on which surviving manuscript one consults, the first voice is for traverso, hautboy, violin, or recorder; the second is specifically for violin. The third sonata (HWV 388 in B flat) and the fifth (HWV 390a–b in G minor) rarely stop—they have a breathless quality that is a challenge to a wind player. The third, if for hautboys, is for two of them;[376] the fifth can be either for two hautboys or haut-boy and violin.

F. *Other Areas*

1. *The Dutch Republic*

By the late seventeenth century, the Dutch Republic was supporting a thriving woodwind-making industry, based mostly in Amsterdam. Haka founded a school of makers that included Rijkel, Steenbergen, and van Aardenberg, all survived by a number of instruments. There were at least ten other makers, and the number of surviving Dutch hautboys from this period is remarkable.[377] The only other region with as many is Germany. Considering the relatively small number of players who were active in the Republic, it must be assumed that some German, English, and even French hautboists played Dutch hautboys.

The Republic owed its existence to trade, and specialized in obtaining raw materials, processing them, and selling them abroad. This included hautboys. The Richters brothers, for instance, imported not only ebony and ivory for their instru-ments from the Indies, India, and Africa, but coconuts and amber as well.[378]

Some of these instruments, especially the exquisitely worked hautboys of the Richters, made of costly materials (ebony, ivory, and silver), were probably bought by wealthy amateurs as much for their looks as how they played. The socket of the lower joint on an extant Fredrik Richters hautboy is engraved 'Pytter Heins Rol' and 'Anno 1731'.[379] The Rol family were well-to-do burghers in the town of Purmerend.

It is an irony that the most beautifully turned-out instruments were rarely made for everyday use by professing musicians, but rather for amateurs who could afford

---

[376] All the movements of the third appear elsewhere: the first three are a version of the Overture to *Esther* (HWV 50a), and the fourth appears in the organ concerto HWV 290/2.

[377] Cf. Ch. 2, §A. Since precise dating is not usually possible, assigning instruments to this period is only a best guess. Even here the numbers are deceptive: van Acht (1988: 5) believes that only a small fraction of the original number of woodwinds made in the Netherlands has survived. It could be argued that a disproportionate number of Dutch hautboys have survived compared with other countries owing to a lack of wars. But England has escaped invasion, and there the number of survivors is only about half that of the Dutch Republic.

[378] Van Acht, Bouterse, and Dhont (1997). [379] NL-DHgm Ea 439-1933.

them because they made their livings in more lucrative ways.[380] Richters hautboys are good examples. They are of course playable, but only a few of those I have played are really good,[381] and none are of the quality of the unpretentious-looking Rÿkel at the Hague.[382] I suspect the Richters made hautboys like the Dutch ceramic factories today make 'Delftware:' competently, and in great quantity, but principally for decoration rather than daily use. Such instruments are preserved today in large numbers because of their outward beauty, while many of the best-playing Dutch hautboys may have been discarded for their plainness.

Although Dutch makers are associated with Type A3, many are also survived by Type A2 hautboys,[383] and Haka and Rÿkel are survived by both types. Rÿkel's trade card, dated 1705, shows hautboys of Type A2.[384]

Few important pieces of music were composed in the Dutch Republic in this period, but (as Rasch 1993 points out) most of the great music from other parts of Europe was known there, if not printed there as well. Music printing and publishing was an important business in Holland, and over 500 hautboy solos first appeared in Amsterdam by such composers as Albinoni, Dall'Abaco, Handel, La Barre, Marcello, Pepusch, Sammartini, Schickhardt, and Vivaldi.

The most active music printer and publisher in Europe was Estienne Roger, a Huguenot working in Amsterdam from 1696 to 1722. One of Roger's 'house' composers was Schickhardt, who had lived in Holland, employed at the court of Henriëtte Amalia in Leeuwarden, until at least 1709.[385] Among the hautboy pieces produced by Roger and Schickhardt were four sets of sonatas for treble instrument and continuo, a set of trio sonatas, and two sets each of quartets and quintets involving hautboy.[386] This music evidently sold well, and was probably played all over Europe at the time. Schickhardt's tutor, *Principes de haut-bois*, published in 1730, has not been located.[387] Roger and his successor Le Cêne also published duets by La Barre and concertos for two hautboys by De Fesch.

Bronnemüller's 'Solo pour la Hoboj', the earliest known solo sonata to be published for hautboy, was mentioned above, §E. The six Sonates by Bronnemüller for hautboy or violin and continuo (the last two also for traverso) are interesting, and the hautboy part is written like the vocal line in an aria. They were published by Roger in 1710–12 but were composed *c.*1700. Walther mentioned them in 1732 (p. 116).

---

[380] The same is true of key-system oboes made today with gold-plated keys; it is rare for a professional player to own such an instrument.

[381] NL-DHgm Ea 286-1933, Ea 436-1933, Ea 584-1933, Ea 15-X-1952, and Ea 8-X-1952. I owned one of Hendrik Richters's hautboys for several years (now Young no. 17).

[382] Ea 440-1933. This is the best-playing Dutch hautboy I know.

[383] Van Aardenberg, Beukers sen., Boekhout, Haka, Rÿkel, Steenbergen, and Terton.

[384] Young (1988), 9–10.

[385] Schickhardt may have got his training on the hautboy from members of the opera orchestra in Braunschweig. See Lasocki (1977), 29. [386] Ibid. 45 ff.

[387] According to Geoffrey Burgess (pers. comm.), this tutor was frequently cited in 19th-c. sources.

Besides Schickhardt, hautboists active in this period in Holland include Johan van Nieuwenhoven (who sold and taught the flute, hautboy, and bassoon). Many of the Dutch hautboy makers were probably players as well.

2. The Spanish/Austrian Netherlands

From 1703 to 1709, Maximilian II Emanuel, Elector of Bavaria, was again in Brussels. As before, Rémy Normand continued to be one of the Elector's hautboy players, and in this period Jacob (Jacques) Loeillet was engaged. A new opera house, the Théâtre de la Monnaie, had been opened in 1700 (and still exists). Opera performances and numerous elaborate court festivals consumed great sums of court money (although musicians were sporadically paid).[388] Performances of new pieces for small chamber ensembles were also frequent. A number of chamber trios *en symphonie* (now lost) were written by composers resident in the Spanish Netherlands and published in Amsterdam in the early years of the eighteenth century.[389]

In the rest of the country, there was evidently a flourishing musical life. Churches had extensive music establishments (in sacred music, the French style was predominant in the early eighteenth century), and instrumental music was commonly supported by noblemen and wealthy bourgeois who formed 'academies' in various cities. It was from Ghent that the hautboy-playing Loeillet brothers came (Jean-Baptiste/John, who moved to London, and Jacob). In 1709, Loeillet and Normand accompanied Max Emanuel to France, and to Munich in 1715 (see above, §D.17).

In 1714 the Spanish Netherlands was ceded to the Austrian Habsburgs, who administered it for the remainder of the eighteenth century. Musical life in various parts of the country remained active, and foreign players and composers were prominent. The repertoire at La Monnaie in Brussels continued to feature Lully's works in the eighteenth century, along with those of other French composers and a few Italians. There was thus a regular call for hautboy players.

When Sammartini played a concert in London on 21 May 1729, the advertisement stated that he had 'just arrived from the Court of Brussels'.[390] He may thus have made a stopover there on his way from Milan to London.

Brussels housed the important workshops of the Rottenburgh family. Johannes Hyacinthus Rottenburgh worked from about 1700. His father was a violinist at the court of Maximilian Emanuel. Rottenburgh may have been in contact with Max Emanuel's hautboy players at Brussels; Schuechbauer, who made instruments, was there from 1692 to 1696. In the early years of the eighteenth century, Rottenburgh apparently supplied instruments to the court.

Rottenburgh's hautboys have a similar acoustic profile to those of Rippert and Naust (cf. App. 2): they are wide-bored and the tone-holes are relatively small.

---

[388] Münster (1993), 299.   [389] Alphonse d'Eve and Louis Le Quointe.   [390] Lasocki (1979), n. 5.

His surviving traversos and recorders range between A−2 and A−1½. Most of his hautboys are relatively long (with a range from 324 to 336.9 AL and an average of 331.5, thus in the A−1½ to A−2 class). Rottenburgh worked until about 1735, and his workshop was continued by his three sons (see Ch. 7, §E.2). At least three of the eleven surviving hautboys stamped 'I. H. Rottenburgh' are of Type A2, suggesting they were made by the father; these hautboys play very well (see Pl. 2.16). Jacob Loeillet may have played Rottenburgh's instruments, and one wonders if he did not later take them with him to France in 1709, Munich in 1715, and Versailles in 1727, thus spreading Rottenburgh's reputation. The five Type E hautboys stamped 'I. H. Rottenburgh' were probably made by his sons.

3. The Habsburg Lands

It may have been Joseph I, heir apparent to the throne, who invited Pierre de La Buissière to Vienna in 1700. La Buissière had been in Berlin since 1693, teaching the French hautboy. He brought six young students with him to Vienna (all apparently Huguenots, as they had French names). Joseph employed this band from 1701, and when he was crowned Emperor in 1705, employed four hautboists at the court. The Emperor was evidently fond of the new French woodwinds; he himself played traverso.[391]

The first hautboists had been appointed to the court Capelle in 1701.[392] In that same year, Johann Joseph Fux, already a composer at court, published a little microcosm of the contrast between French and Italian styles called the 'Nürnberger Partita'. It is for hautboy, 'Flauto' (recorder), and continuo. The third movement has the flauto playing an 'Aria Italiana' in 6/8 while the hautboy simultaneously plays an 'Aire françoise' in common time and in the style of an overdotted ouverture. The two contrasting styles are ingeniously combined to make a convincing movement (twenty-three years before Couperin wrote his *Goûts-réünis*). The piece requires a good technique on the hautboy and command of all the accidentals. Fux, who became the key musical figure at the Habsburg court in the first decades of the eighteenth century, was obviously no stranger to French woodwinds even at this relatively early date. The trio's title might be a reference to Christoph Denner (or one of his fellow Nurembergers) as the maker of the woodwind instruments for which it was written.

Court opera composers like Badia,[393] Ziani, and Bononcini started using hautboys during Joseph I's reign.[394] Ziani may have become acquainted with the new instrument at Venice, where he had worked in the 1690s.[395] He regularly used hautboys

---

[391] Seifert (1987), 9, 15, 14.   [392] Köchel (1869), 25. Selfridge-Field (1987), 124 makes it 1702.
[393] Cf. *Ercole* (1708).
[394] By at least 1706. Cf. arias in the operas *L'Abdolomino* and *Endimione* listed in Haynes (1992a), 78–9.
[395] Cf. Selfridge-Field (1987), 127.

in his opera orchestra, mentioning them only when they were to be omitted, and featuring them in concertinos contrasted with strings.[396]

When Charles VI became Emperor in 1711, he also appointed four hautboists to his Capelle.[397] Considering the amount of music performed in Vienna in Charles's reign, it is curious that it has been so little studied. We rarely hear the vast and superb repertoire that was played at court in this period, nor do we know much of the hautboists who played it.[398] An English eyewitness to an opera performance in 1716 wrote: 'Nothing of that kind ever was more magnificent; and I can easily believe, what I was told, that the decorations and habits cost the emperor thirty thousand pound sterling.'[399] This particular period was a 'golden age' for the Hofcapelle: the country was at peace and the Emperor was an educated musician. The court paid well, and was constantly looking for the best players available. We may be sure the hautboists in the service of the Vienna Hofcapelle, which has been called 'a virtuoso orchestra',[400] were among the best players of their generation.

Vienna was an important centre of *opera seria*:

A characteristic of Viennese Baroque operas is their attention to instrumental colour and detail.

Two features typical of Baroque opera generally are specially notable in the Vienna court operas. One is the ploy of using solo voices and instruments in virtuoso competition; the other, related to it, is the 'planting' of references in the text to evoke a particular instrumentation.[401]

An examination of the scores of the operas by the major composers of Charles's reign (Pancotti, Ziani, Fux, Caldara, and Predieri, for instance) might discover interesting hautboy obbligatos.[402] The hautboy parts in Fux's published operas are unremarkable. Compared with Keiser's and Steffani's creative and experimental use of the hautboy, Fux is conservative, rarely giving the hautboys parts independent of the violins, and frequently deleting them with the indication 'senza Hautbois'.[403]

---

[396] Antonicek (1980b), 674.   [397] Seifert (1987), 15.

[398] Köchel's published information on court players (1869 and 1872) is organized into a more intelligible form in Selfridge-Field (1987). Seifert (1987) supplements it by consulting additional sources.

[399] Lady Montagu, quoted in Wollenberg (1993), 342.   [400] Wollenberg (1993), 337.

[401] Ibid. 337–8.

[402] Of obbligatos with voice, there are pieces by Grimani, Porpora, and possibly Bononcini. According to table 7 in Selfridge-Field (1987), 138, the obbligato parts for hautboy in Caldara's operas and oratorios were not frequent. There is one for hautboy and bassoon in the opera *Ormisda* (1721), and another for two hautboys and bassoon in *Dafne* (Salzburg, 1719).

[403] It is evident that he had more than one player to a part, as there are indications for 'Hautbois tutti' and 'Due Hautbois soli' in *Pulcheria*, K 303 (1708), the opera with the most interesting hautboy material. One duetto in *Dafne in lauro*, K 308 (1714) has an unusual instrumentation, with the violins 'all'unisono' on one part and the hautboys 'all'unisono' on another.

Hautboys were not apparently used in the daily religious music at the Viennese court. None of Fux's published religious works includes hautboys,[404] but according to Wollenberg, hautboys were part of the orchestras involved in the many oratorios performed in Vienna, which included musicians from the opera and were often colourfully orchestrated.[405] Secular chamber cantatas were also frequently performed at court, and may have included hautboys. Hautboys and bassoons were also frequently used for Tafelmusik.[406]

Little solo music for hautboy has yet been discovered from Vienna in this period. An *Ouverture* for two hautboys and bassoon concertato with strings survives by Georg von Reutter, a court composer.

Table 3 in Selfridge-Field (1987) tabulates the number of hautboy players employed at court. From 1705 to 1730 there were never fewer than five, and occasionally as many as nine (see App. 1).[407] The player about whom we have the most information is Ludwig Schön (*c*.1695–1763), who had a court appointment from 1711 to 1740. Schön had been one of the students La Buissière brought to Vienna from Berlin in 1700 (his original name was Joli). He was involved in the performance of Fux's famous opera *Costanza et fortezza*, presented on the occasion of the coronation of Charles VI as King of Bohemia in Prague in 1723.[408] This was an especially sumptuous production, and involved many musicians from Dresden as well. Zelenka's awkward and difficult *Simphonie à 8 Conc.* for violin and hautboy solo with accompaniment of hautboy, violin, viola, cello, bassoon, and continuo (ZWV 189) was evidently written for these festivities, and the soloists were probably Pisendel and Richter. Richter would thus have been in contact with Schön and the three other Viennese hautboists who took part in the Prague performance: Daniel Hartmann, Roman Glaetzl (one of three brothers who taught the flute to several members of the royal family), and Ludwig Schulz.[409] To have been chosen to accompany the court, it would seem these four were the principal Habsburg hautboists in 1723.

Although Italian musicians were common at court, in this period no hautboy players with Italian names are to be found on court roles. It is possible their names were Germanicized, as was the case with many performers.

Besides the court, the city of Vienna was also active musically. The Kärntnertortheater opened in about 1709 and put on many operas in somewhat altered form, including those of Keiser and Handel. Whether court hautboists were used, or if there were other professional players in the city, is not known.

---

[404] They include 'fagotto' and sometimes trombones, so were probably performed at A+1.
[405] Wollenberg (1993), 333, 343.   [406] Seifert (1987), 15.
[407] Cf. Selfridge-Field (1987), 122–3 and Wollenberg (1993), 349.   [408] Cf. Nettl (1957), 5.
[409] Ibid. 954–5.

Four hautboys survive which may have been made in Vienna in this period, by Kohlert, Deper, Mischlinger, and C. Kilian. According to Paul Hailperin, the Deper is pitched no lower than A-460.

Eighteenth-century music in the cathedral and Peterskirche in Salzburg was notated with voices, strings, trumpets, trombones, and 'Fagott' in the organ key, while hautboys and sometimes one 'Fagott' were notated 'Trasposti', a major second higher (sounding, that is, a major second lower).[410] Many pieces show this notation until as late as 1780.[411] The higher parts were presumably for musicians from the court, who were playing at a correspondingly lower pitch.[412] The court musicians in Salzburg played in the cathedral and also at the university, where elaborate dramas (not unlike operas) took place.

The Abbey of Kremsmünster employed at least one player of 'Hubua und Fagot' named Sigmund Puechers, who was a teacher at the 'Musaeo' until 1722.

Musical activities in this period in Bohemia that involved hautboys include those of Count Šporck, who travelled frequently. His collection of fine art was spread over three palaces in Prague and two country seats.[413] Šporck was an important patron of opera, and he sponsored many performances in Prague from 1701 to 1737. Fux's lavish production of *Costanza e fortezza* in 1723 (mentioned above) involved many foreign players; it was surely an event of importance for the musicians of Prague as well.

4. Spain

Philip V, who came from France and was crowned in 1700, did his best to encourage music from abroad (which would often have involved hautboys). Although it was never very popular, he especially favoured Italian opera.[414]

Despite its title, Nassarre's massive book *Escuela música según la práctica moderna* of 1723–4 describes only shawms, as if the hautboy did not exist. Nassarre was a conservative, defending the Spanish tradition against foreign innovations.

The cold reception accorded the French musicians who accompanied Marie-Louise d'Orléans to the Spanish court in 1679 was repeated when a group of thirteen French players visited Madrid in 1702; they remained only until 1705. They

---

[410] Mendel (1978: 13–14, 34) cites unpublished research by Gerhard Walterskirchen.

[411] Walterskirchen cites a piece by Michael Haydn in the Dommusikarchiv dating from 1780, and Mendel (1978: 79–80) notes others by W. A. Mozart. Dahlqvist (1993: 39), lists six masses by Mozart written in Salzburg in which the hautboy parts are notated a tone above the voices and other instruments.

[412] A–1 is not quite a major second below the general pitch reported for Salzburg organs (454); A–1½ would have been closer. But a drop of a quarter-tone would not have been difficult, either with special reeds, or instruments tuned to that pitch.

[413] Hogwood and Smaczny (1989), 195.

[414] Cf. Stein (1993), 419. In an order of 1701, King Philip suppressed the court post of instrument maker as well as instrument purchaser (cf. Kenyon de Pascual 1985: 93), so potential players had a number of hurdles to jump in order to become hautboy players.

were directed by Desmarest and included the hautboy players Mangot, Huet, and Robert.[415]

During his brief stay in Barcelona from 1710 to 1713, the Habsburg Emperor Charles VI maintained a 'Hautboisten-Banda' there.[416]

By 1708, a player named Joseph Gesembach[417] had been appointed to the Madrid court chapel. Gesembach is first listed as a bassoonist and later as an hautboy player; his playing was highly praised in 1715.[418] He was on the court roles until 1749.

In the early 1730s, two more hautboists, both probably French, were officially added to the court roles at Madrid: Brienne (Voyenne) and Boucquet.[419] Both were playing in a royal Guards band in the 1710s and could have unofficially taken part in an orchestra at court if needed.[420] Among the music they would have played were cantatas 'según los nuevos inventos de la música', such as those of José de Torres.

---

[415] Kenyon de Pascual (1984), 432. According to Sadie (1993), 147, Jean-Féry Rebel and Michel de La Barre were in Spain in 1700.   [416] Seifert (1987), 10.

[417] Often spelled 'Jezebek', etc. Kenyon de Pascual (1984), 432.   [418] Kenyon de Pascual (1985), 95.

[419] Kenyon de Pascual (1984), 432. It is conceivable that at this point Gesembach went back to bassoon. According to Kenyon de Pascual (1985), 94, a bassoonist was appointed in 1739 named Juan Bautista Coulon, probably a Frenchman.   [420] Kenyon de Pascual (1985), 95.

6

Bach and the Hautboy

Bach gave the hautboy more solos in his vocal works than any other instrument. There are 216 surviving obbligatos for treble hautboy, hautbois d'amour, and oboe da caccia. Solos for violin, the nearest contender, number ninety-two; for traverso, twenty-nine. Chamber music is a different story, where it seems some works have been lost. In any case, it is clear that the hautboy was one of the most important elements in Bach's instrumentarium.

If the hautboy was important to Bach, the converse is also true. The hautboy's repertoire includes more solos by Bach than by any other composer.[1] It hardly needs to be said that this music is of consistently high quality, making it the largest single body of important compositions for the instrument that survives.

A separate chapter on Bach is therefore appropriate, the more so because his music involves special questions, such as choice of instrument, pitch, and pieces that are now lost.

A. Weimar, Cöthen

Hautboys were present at the court of Weimar from 1701, when the Capelle included thirteen instrumentalists. Bach was appointed *Concertmeister* in 1714, and in the ensuing three years he produced cantatas that included fourteen solos for hautboy.[2] They are among his most beautiful pieces for the instrument.

The hautboy player (or players) for whom Bach wrote these solos is not known. It has been suggested[3] that it could have been Bernhard Ulrich, who would single-handedly have covered the hautboy, bassoon, and sometimes cello parts at the Weimar court.[4] But this assumes that, since they were played by the same person,

---

[1] Except possibly Telemann (the exact number of whose solos in cantatas is not yet known). Bach's other nearest competitors are Handel (137), Keiser (45), and Vivaldi (52). See Haynes (1992a).

[2] Only two pieces with hautboy are known from before 1714, BWV 131 (see below) and 71. The BG transposed the *Obboe* parts to BWV 71 down a step from their original key (*Cammerton*→D) to *Chorton*→C to match the other parts. The *NBA* publishes it in both keys, C and D.   [3] Cowdery (1989), 171 ff.

[4] Dreyfus (1987), 124 points out that the accompanied recitative in Cantata 199 that precedes the first aria (no. 2) includes bassoon, while the aria (with obbligato hautboy) does not. Dürr (1987: 153) noticed that one of the surviving hautboy parts to Cantata 199 contains also the cello part when the hautboy is silent. Ulrich was employed from early 1714 or before (in a list of Hofcapelle members he is the only apparent woodwind player and is identified as a 'Fagottist').

the hautboy and fagotto never played together. In fact there are parts for both instruments in the *Sinfonia* of Cantata 12, in BWV 185 and BWV 132.[5] Evidently, then, another player was involved, at least occasionally. He could have been a member of the court band of *Hautboisten*.[6]

As for Cöthen, Prince Leopold had begun developing an orchestra there several years before Bach's arrival. In 1713 he engaged a number of the players from the Berlin court orchestra who had been fired by the 'Barracks King', Friedrich Wilhelm. Among the Berlin musicians was Leopold's principal hautboy player, Johann Ludwig Rose. Rose's son (of the same name) also played at court from about 1715.[7] There were two flutists, Gottlieb Würdig, in the Hofcapelle from 1714 to 1728, and Heinrich Freitag, Hofmusicus from before 1716. Since it would have been unusual for a flutist not to have also played hautboy, Bach probably had four potential hautboy players available. There is some reason to think that Schickhardt was employed as a woodwind player at Cöthen on an occasional basis in 1719–20,[8] and it is possible he replaced Freitag, who died in 1720 and may have been ill before then. Another occasional player was Gottlieb Jacobi, who is known to have played in 1724 and possibly earlier.

Augustin Stricker was the Capellmeister at Cöthen from 1712 to 1717. A solo sonata for unspecified treble instrument and continuo survives by him,[9] probably written in the 1710s,[10] that could have been written for Rose, Würdig, or Freitag. The piece is an excellent example of a classic early eighteenth-century sonata. Stricker is survived by a number of other hautboy pieces that may have been written at Cöthen.[11]

Bach arrived in 1717. Evidently, one of his functions was preparing pieces for small instrumental groups. In 1721 he presented six pieces of this kind in a fair copy to Margrave Christian Ludwig of Brandenburg. These 'Brandenburg Concertos' require the three to four woodwind players Bach had at his disposal at Cöthen.

One wonders what kind of hautboy Rose and his colleagues used. Considering the strong French woodwind tradition in Berlin (see Ch. 3, §C.5 and Ch. 5, §D.6), they might have played hautboys made in France. Other possibilities are Heitz (who worked in Berlin) and the Nuremberg makers (Schell, Jacob and David Denner, Oberlender sen.) who made 'Hautbois' for Berlin (see Ch. 5, §D.6). It seems the pitch at Cöthen was A−2.[12]

---

[5] There are also instances where hautboy and cello play together.

[6] A certain David Hoffmann was a 'Pfeiffer unter der Garde' from 1699 (Jauernig 1950: 52), and was appointed to the court in 1703, probably as an hautboy player.

[7] Rose was also a fencing master. His name sounds French, and a Jean Louis Joseph Roze (perhaps Johann Ludwig jun.) was employed at Versailles from 1749.   [8] Lasocki (1977), 33–4.

[9] 'Sonate 11', D, Brussels (MS XY 15,115).

[10] A number of other sonatas in this manuscript are known to have been written in the mid-teens.

[11] They include two solo sonatas, two trios, a quartet, a quintet, and an hautboy concerto. See Haynes (1992a).

[12] Cf. Haynes (1995), §7-3.

B. Leipzig and Gleditsch

At the age of 38, and by then an experienced professional nearing middle age, Bach was appointed Cantor and music director at Leipzig. There he began a musical relationship with one of the most remarkable players in the history of the hautboy, Caspar Gleditsch. The majority of Bach's solos for hautboy were written in his first years at Leipzig, between 1723 and 1726.

Next to Dresden, Leipzig was the largest city in Saxony. By the end of the seventeenth century, it was a vital commercial centre in close contact with the rest of Europe as a consequence of its three annual trade fairs, or *Messe*, each of which lasted several weeks and were the most important in Germany.

Hautboys were known at Leipzig by at least 1698, when there are references to 'Französischen Schalmeien'.[13] In the years leading up to Bach's arrival, Leipzig had become one of the principal German centres of woodwind makers and dealers.[14] Many outstanding players and instrument builders were attracted to the city and spent time there. By the turn of the century, the Bauers were at work, as were probably Ebicht and Noack. Poerschman arrived in Leipzig around 1700, Böhm in about 1705, Eichentopf by 1707, Gleditsch by at least 1712, Sattler in 1718, and Kornagel by 1719.

The dean of Leipzig's woodwind makers was probably Andreas Bauer (b. 1636), who was listed as a 'Schalmeyenpfeifer' in 1672 and a 'Fagott- und Schalmeyenmacher' in 1682. Like Christoph Denner in Nuremberg, Bauer made 'Renaissance' woodwinds first and later adopted the new French models. He worked until 1717. Given his age, he may have been the teacher of some or all the later makers of the city. His sons Gottfried and Gottlob are survived not only by treble hautboys, but hautbois d'amour and oboes da caccia. The existence of the larger instruments suggests that this family may have been responsible for, or at least closely involved in, their development (Gottfried's hautbois d'amour shown in Pl. 6.1 is dated 1719, a relatively early date).[15]

Johann Poerschman (*c.*1680–1757) was both a player and an important woodwind maker; he is the first hautboist at Leipzig of whom there are records. Poerschman later became solo bassoonist of the *Großes Konzert*, successor to Bach's Collegium Musicum. The occasional bassoon solos Bach wrote at Leipzig could have been for him. Poerschman's close association with Eichentopf, Noack, and Gleditsch is indicated by the fact that they were all godparents to various of his children.[16]

---

[13] Schering (1921), 47; Schering (1926), 290.
[14] Rubardt (1966), 411; Schering (1926), 393 ff.; Heyde (1993a), 593.
[15] It survives in Stockholm.   [16] Heyde (1985), 82.

PL. 6.1. Hautbois d'amour, Gottfried Bauer, Leipzig, 1719. Stockholm: Musikmuseet

Heinrich Eichentopf (1678–1769) was married in the Thomaskirche in 1710,[17] and records of godparenthood attest to his amicable relations with Gleditsch, Poerschman, and Hirschstein.[18] He worked in Leipzig from 1707 to 1749.[19] Among other instruments, Eichentopf is survived by two hautboys and many hautbois d'amour.

Cornelius Sattler (*c.*1691–1739) probably lived in Leipzig most or all of his life, together with his relative Gottfried Sattler (1707–55). Twelve of his instruments survive, including five hautboys and two hautbois d'amour. His family continued to work in the instrument-making trade until 1850.[20]

There was never an instrument-maker's guild in Leipzig, so there were no restrictions on setting up a workshop, materials, period of apprenticeship, etc.[21] The circle of woodwind instrument makers and players in Leipzig must have been close: Sattler, Poerschman, Eichentopf, and a daughter of Gleditsch were all godparents to children of another maker, Gottfried Ebicht (*c.*1681–1736), who was a player employed by the city; he may have worked for one of the other makers. Another Leipzig maker was Christian Noack (*c.*1682–1724) by whom one hautbois d'amour survives. Mathäus Hirschstein (*c.*1695–1769) was a dealer in musical instruments: two traversos and two hautbois d'amour have survived with his stamp (the instruments were probably made on commission by someone else).[22]

It seems unlikely that these instrument makers would have missed Bach's Sunday performances, or would not have had direct relations with him in his position as the city's music director.

Leipzig had no court of its own, but its connections with the splendid musical establishment at Dresden, the Saxon capital, were close, and the Elector Friedrich August made regular visits to Leipzig. He established a public opera house in Leipzig in 1693, which, it was thought at one time, might serve as a possible training school for musicians who could subsequently be employed by the Dresden court.[23] On

---

[17] Waterhouse (1993), 103.   [18] Heyde (1985), 81.
[19] Cf. Karp (1972), 85; Schering (1926), 296; Rubardt (1966).   [20] Heyde (1985), 82.
[21] Powell and Lasocki (1995), 17.   [22] Heyde (1985), 82–3; Waterhouse (1993), 177.
[23] Buelow (1993), 219.

his visits to Leipzig, the Elector was occasionally accompanied by members of his Capelle.[24] Such visits would have allowed Saxon hautboists like Gleditsch, La Riche, and Richter to maintain regular contact, and for Leipzig players to be in touch with the latest musical developments at Dresden (and through Dresden, Europe in general, especially France and Italy).

In the course of a generation (until 1720), the Leipzig Opera produced some eighty different German and Italian works, only a few of which have survived. The presence of hautboys would have been essential in those performances. Telemann became director in 1702, and members of the Collegium Musicum he founded in that year supplied many of the musicians.

The Collegium Musicum was one of a number of concert series in Leipzig, a city with a large music-loving public made up of prosperous businessmen, university faculties, and cosmopolitan visitors to the trade fairs. Johann Kuhnau, Bach's predecessor, had led a Collegium from 1688, and the new one begun by Telemann was made up of students and (for festive occasions) city musicians; it subsequently went through many different directors (including Bach; see §E below). The Collegium performed weekly, and its audiences were enthusiastic.[25] Another similar ensemble, run by Gottlieb Görner, was set up in 1723 and ran until 1756.

Among the musicians who played in Telemann's Collegium was Michael Böhm.[26] Böhm worked in Leipzig from about 1705 until he moved to Darmstadt in 1711, and it is likely he studied with La Riche in Dresden during this period.[27] He returned several times to Saxony for further lessons. Other hautboy players who may have been involved with Telemann's activities were Poerschmann and Gleditsch.

As Don Smithers has pointed out, without the special talents of the musicians with whom he worked, 'it is likely that many of Bach's best works would have been composed rather differently (if at all)'.[28] Bach worked regularly with two hautboy players, Caspar Gleditsch and Gottfried Kornagel, who like himself were employed by the city of Leipzig. Gleditsch was the principal.

Bach probably wrote more solos for Gleditsch than for any other musician except himself. Terry (1932: 101) noted that the hautboy is present in all but twelve of the surviving Leipzig cantatas. All the Leipzig solos for hautboy, hautbois d'amour, and oboe da caccia were tailored to measure for Gleditsch. A busy craftsman like Bach did not waste time writing pieces unless they had a specific purpose and there was

---

[24] Telemann wrote (1718, in Rackwitz 1981: 96) that the 'Herren Virtuosen' from Dresden 'honoured' his Leipzig Collegium Musicum by listening to it with 'approval' ('Approbation . . . beehreten').

[25] Cf. Neumann (1960), 410, 399.

[26] Telemann (1718), 165. As we saw in Ch. 5, §D.14, Böhm and Telemann were later to be in close contact at Frankfurt.   [27] Noack (1967), 180.

[28] Smithers (1990), 43.

a player who could make them succeed. His surviving hautboy solos can thus be seen as 'musical portraits' of his players. Through his playing, Gleditsch inspired Bach to write some 193 hautboy solos at Leipzig (he had written thirty-two before then). Taken together, these pieces represent the greatest single monument to the talent of an hautboy player in the history of the instrument. As a senior Stadtpfeifer, Gleditsch was among the best musicians in Bach's orchestra; Bach often marked his woodwind parts less completely than his string parts, suggesting that he gave Gleditsch unusual discretion in interpreting his part.[29]

Born in 1684 (a year before Bach), Gleditsch had risen through the ranks, starting as a Kunstgeiger in 1712 at the age of 28. The many cantatas produced by Kuhnau, who was Thomascantor at the time, would have included important parts for him.[30] From those that survive, it looks as if Kuhnau started writing solos for Gleditsch in the years just before he was promoted to Stadtpfeifer in 1719. The aria 'Kommt ihr Engel nehmt die Seele' in cantata *Lobet ihr Himmel* was written in 1717; two other solos survive from 1718,[31] and one from Christmas, 1720.[32]

Gleditsch must have begun playing in the late 1690s, when the hautboy was still a novelty in much of Germany. Nothing is known of his training or whereabouts before 1712; if he came from Saxony, he too would probably have studied with La Riche in Dresden. As a Stadtpfeifer, Gleditsch would have been trained to play many instruments when Bach needed them, including recorder and traverso.[33] The fact that bassoon and hautboy parts are often found in different movements of the same cantata[34] suggests that Gleditsch also played bassoon.

Telemann put on his opera *Damon* at the opera house in 1719. By then the Stadtpfeifer owned the Privilege for theatre performances.[35] As the premier hautboy player of Leipzig, Gleditsch probably played 'Ich suche mein geliebtes Leben', an obbligato with bass (Laurindo) in *Damon*. It is an unusual and interesting aria; the continuo line gives the introduction (to the bass singer). The hautboy comments on the solo line, using its same rising third and rising fourth motif. The singer stops first, followed by the hautboy (ending on the fifth), and finally, two bars later, the continuo (who began the piece) finish it.

Gleditsch was close to several Leipzig woodwind makers, and was at the forefront of the experiments in new instruments being made in the 1710s; he performed a solo on the new hautbois d'amour in 1722, and was thus in a position to inspire Bach's obvious interest in the new instrument when he arrived the next year.

---

[29] The solo hautboy part to BWV 56/3 has fewer articulation marks than the score. Butt (1990), 119, 86.
[30] Cf. Rimbach (1966).
[31] Cantatas *Ende gut und alles gut* and *Nicht nur allein* (the latter with two solo hautboys in the aria 'Denn wer dies Licht will beschauen'.   [32] In cantata *Uns ist ein Kind geboren*.
[33] The recorder part to BWV 69a/3, 'Meine Seele, auf! erzähle', was in the second hautboy part (Kornagel's part), and the oboe da caccia part was in the first hautboy part (Gleditsch's).   [34] Cf. Brandt (1968).
[35] Terry (1932), 16.

Gleditsch no doubt played elsewhere besides the Leipzig churches. Although he was no longer required for day-to-day *Turmmusic* duty after he was promoted to Stadtpfeifer,[36] the town council stipulated in his contract that he could not spend a night away from the city without written permission from the council.[37] Like Bach, Gleditsch may have occasionally performed concerts or tours outside of Leipzig. It is possible he was away on extended trips of several months at the end of 1725, in early 1726, and early 1727, when there are gaps in the hautboy solos in cantata performances.

When Bach performed his first and second yearly cantata cycles between mid-1723 and mid-1725, he was composing an average of three to four hautboy solos a month (a total of 42 and 52 for the two cycles respectively). In January, April, and May of 1725, Bach was producing an incredible seven to eight new hautboy solos each month. By mid-1725 and the beginning of the third cycle, he composed more slowly, and there was a relative lull in hautboy solos through 1727; during this period of thirty months, thirty-seven hautboy obbligati appeared, and fifteen of these months had none at all.[38] The fourth cycle, stretching over the years 1728 to 1729, produced only twelve solos (half of them concentrated around the end of 1728).[39]

It has been suggested that some of Bach's hautboy obbligatos might have been written for a player from outside Leipzig, but this seems unlikely. Music in the Leipzig churches was governed by strong guild traditions, and the use of an external player to replace the regular duties of the Stadtpfeifer would have contravened established privileges. In any case, the music itself shows that a strong player was regularly present; solos that are especially demanding either technically or musically are spread fairly evenly throughout the mid-1720s when Bach was composing solos for the instrument, and since some of them would surely have been played by Gleditsch, all of them could have been. There was thus no need of hautboy players from elsewhere.

On the other hand, visiting players like Richter or Böhm may have taken part in other types of music, such as solo appearances with the Collegia Musica, or specially arranged concerts.

Kornagel, Bach's second player, was appointed Kunstgeiger in 1719. He may have been a student of Gleditsch's, and taken over Gleditsch's post as Kunstgeiger when the latter was promoted to Stadtpfeifer. As a Kunstgeiger, Kornagel had a bad bargain: he had to work nearly as hard as Gleditsch, but his salary and social status were lower. In many of Bach's pieces, Kornagel's parts are of equal difficulty to

---

[36] In Leipzig from 1717, Stadtpfeifer were officially exempt from *Abblasen* duty. Schering (1921), 21.

[37] Stauffer (1993), 284.

[38] Butt (1990), 86 notes that the lack of care in marking and editing parts in late 1726 is striking, suggesting that Bach was preoccupied at this time with other projects.   [39] Pieces may be lost from this period, however.

Gleditsch's, and he too was expected to play all sizes of hautboy as well as other instruments. Considering Bach's realistic approach to composition and the large number of solos he wrote for two equally important hautboys, he must have considered Kornagel an excellent hautboy player whose talents could be put to good use. Bach's disparaging comments about the qualities of his municipal musicians, made in 1730,[40] did not apparently refer to his two principal hautboists.

Other *Hautboisten* were stationed at the military garrison at Pleißenburg castle. According to Petzoldt (1983: 183), Bach stood godfather four times to children of an unnamed regimental *Hautboist* at Leipzig. One wonders if this player was the recipient of any of Bach's music.

C. Larger Sizes of Hautboy

When he wished to distinguish the C-treble hautboy from the other sizes, Bach called it the 'Hautbois ordinaire' in the B minor Mass, 'Hautb. l'ordinaire' (Cantata 87/7), or 'Oboe ordinaria' (Cantatas 95 and 125). These names implied the more specialized nature of the other sizes of hautboy. In Leipzig, Bach frequently wrote for larger sizes of hautboy.

Because they are not always clearly distinguished from each other in this period, we shall describe here several types of alto hautboy, as well as the straight tenor and its curved counterpart, the oboe da caccia.[41]

1. Alto hautboys

a. The German 'Hautbois d'amour'   While it is often called the 'oboe d'amore' nowadays, the name by which this instrument was more usually known by German-speakers in its own time was 'hautbois d'amour'[42] (plural also 'hautbois d'amour'). The hautbois d'amour owes its reputation in our day to the works Bach wrote for it (which make up about two-fifths of its surviving solos and chamber music). But in the first half of the eighteenth century it was Telemann, then by far the most popular composer in Germany, who made it famous.[43] The instrument was essentially a German phenomenon, and its repertoire comes almost exclusively from Germany (see Pl. 6.1). Despite its name, there are no known pieces for hautbois d'amour written by Frenchmen.[44] The hautbois d'amour was rarely heard in England,[45] and the

---

[40] *Bach-Dokumente* (1963), i. 63 (23.viii.1730).

[41] A third type of tenor, the *Vox humana*, is not considered here as its career falls mainly after 1760. See Finkelman (s.v. 'lower oboes' in *New Grove II*, forthcoming).   [42] Cf. Koch (1980), 60.

[43] Telemann is responsible for about one-fifth of the hautbois d'amour's surviving repertoire.

[44] Cf. Schulze (1981), 14.

[45] An advertisement in a London newspaper in 1744 claims it was to appear then for the first time, together with the clarinet. Fitzpatrick (1971), 104.

one piece attributed to an Italian, Lotti, was probably written when he was at Dresden.[46]

Walther wrote (1732: 304) that the hautbois d'amour 'became known' in about 1720.[47] Although that was probably accurate, the instrument had already been in existence for several years. Unlike the treble hautboy, which developed in incremental stages, the hautbois d'amour seems like Minerva to have sprung fully grown and armed from the brow of Jupiter, and was immediately admitted to the assembly of the gods (that is, it was immediately used as a solo instrument). Mattheson's *Neu-eröffnete Orchestre* of 1713 did not yet mention the instrument. Nor is Christoph Denner, who died in 1707, and who made many kinds of woodwinds, survived by an hautbois d'amour.[48] So the instrument would seem to have appeared between about 1713 and (as we shall see below) 1717.

Removing the bell from an hautbois d'amour does not change the instrument's characteristic timbre, so the bulb-bell, distinctive as it is, is not the critical, defining factor that distinguished the hautbois d'amour from other oboe-type instruments. In fact, neither the bore diameter nor the size of the tone-holes of the hautbois d'amour were significantly different from those of the treble hautboy. How, then, did it sound three semitones lower? This was achieved by placing the tone-hole centre significantly lower. Another unusual feature of the d'amour is that, instead of a proportionally longer bore below these lowered tone-holes, it had a relatively short bell. And this bell was without the usual corrective resonance-holes. These three changes significantly affected the instrument's proportions, and created a special acoustical situation that made the hautbois d'amour sound and feel different from any other kind of hautboy, including other alto hautboys. The effect of the lack of bell resonance-holes was that the note produced by the fingering 123 456 8 was a decisive bottom note (the same fingering on the treble hautboy often produced a note a little higher; see Ch. 4, §G.2.a). It may be the existence of this authoritative low A that inspired Bach to feature the note so prominently in his concerto for hautbois d'amour, BWV 1055a; it is the first note of the piece.

The hautbois d'amour had an association with Leipzig. Most of the instrument's earliest music was written by composers closely tied to Leipzig. Gottfried Bauer's d'amour was mentioned above, and Heinrich Eichentopf is survived by ten hautbois d'amour, an unusually large number.

What may be the earliest surviving piece for the instrument comes from Darmstadt (it was written for Michael Böhm, who—as we have seen—had studied

---

[46] This piece is also attributed to Telemann in three of the five surviving versions. As for Holland, the hautboy maker Hendrik Richters owned a 'hobo de moer' of unknown provenance at his death in 1727 (Dudok van Heel and Teutscher 1974: 56). 'Moer' is pronounced in Dutch like the English word 'moor'.

[47] Later authors (Majer 1732: 34, Stössel 1737: 171, and Zedler 1732–54: H927) all paraphrase or copy Walther's description.   [48] Denner is survived by an Hautecontre, Linz 120.

at Leipzig and maintained connections with that city).[49] Christoph Graupner's cantata *Wie wunderbar ist Gottes Güt*[50] is dated December 1717. It has a part for 'Hautbois', but the notation of the part shows that the instrument was pitched in A.[51] Interestingly, Graupner's very next cantata, 1717/4, used both C-hautboy and A-hautboy, both in the same part. Other than the tonalities, there is no indication that different instruments are required, which suggests that at this time Graupner had as yet no special name for the A-instrument. Cantata 1718/2 also used an A-hautboy. Graupner did not begin to use the name 'hautbois d'amour' until 1724. Since Böhm would probably have been one of the first players to have used the new hautbois d'amour, it is quite possible that he and Graupner were using the instrument before it acquired its fanciful name.[52] How it got that name must have been somewhat arbitrary; the corollary recorder, for instance, (a minor third lower than the standard instrument and in sharp keys) came to be called the 'Voice Flute'.

Graupner was not the only composer sometimes to label his hautbois d'amour parts simply 'Hautbois'. Kuhnau is survived by a cantata (*Lobet ihr Himmel den Herrn* in the Bokemeyer Collection) that has two hautbois d'amour parts; the cover of the score says '2 Hautbois', but Österreich later added 'Oboe d'amour'. The score is thought to have been composed about 1717.[53] Bach also left out the name 'd'amour' in a number of cantatas that use it.[54]

The hautbois d'amour appeared in Kuhnau's cantata *Lobe den Herrn meine Seele*, a piece performed in 1722 (but by then at least a year old),[55] and presumably written for Gleditsch. Here a copyist called the part 'Hautbois Anglois A♮' (that is, in A major), and an organ part has the notation (perhaps added later) 'Zur Hautbois d'amour'.[56] The Hautbois part, which was technically quite straightforward, was in F, the other parts in D.

Telemann's first known piece for hautbois d'amour is dated 1718–20 (Ouverture, TWV 55: E2). Stölzel wrote frequently for the instrument from 1720–1.[57] The court at Anhalt-Zerbst (which appointed Fasch as its Capellmeister in 1722) made a payment on 31 August of that year for two Hautbois d'Amour (for 4 Rthlr).[58] Weimar (where Walther lived) purchased two hautbois d'amour by 1722.[59] It is also thought that Schürmann used the new instrument early on at Wolfenbüttel.[60]

---

[49] See Ch. 5, §D.13.   [50] Darmstadt Mus. MS 425/3.

[51] The 'Hautbois' part in the key of B flat is very simple. The real soloist in this aria is the bassoon. The aria is reproduced in Koch (1980), 65–6.   [52] Cf. Koch (1980), 67, 63.

[53] Dahlqvist (1973), 67.   [54] e.g. BWV 17, 29, 45, 94, 169, 193, 214, and 215.

[55] Dresden (MS parts, 2133-E-503). See Dahlqvist (1973), 67 and Rimbach (1966), ii. 504.

[56] The use of 'Hautbois Anglois' is interesting. It may be an indication that there was a debate about what to call the new instrument when it was first invented (it also contributes to the unsolved question of the origin of the term 'English horn').   [57] Hennenberg (1965), 117–21.

[58] *Bach-Dokumente* (1963), ii. 86.   [59] Grosse and Jung (1972), 170–1.   [60] Koch (1980), 68.

Telemann was casual about names for the instrument; in the 1720s and 1730s he used the term 'Oboe d'amour', in 1744 it was a 'Hoboe d'amour',[61] and in 1746 a 'Liebes Hoboe'.[62]

The d'amour's history is reflected in the solo and ensemble pieces written for it. Two-thirds of its surviving repertoire was written in the thirteen years between 1717 and 1730,[63] almost all the remainder between 1730 and 1760,[64] and less than 2 per cent after 1760.[65] Its most active period was thus the dozen years after its first appearance, and its career was effectively over in forty-odd years.

By the time Bach first used the hautbois d'amour in Cantata 23 in February 1723 for his audition for the post at Leipzig, the new instrument was obviously much in vogue; his erstwhile competitors, Telemann and Graupner, had already been writing for it for half a decade. Gleditsch and Kornagel must have convinced Bach of the instrument's potential when he arrived; to include it in an audition piece may have been a friendly gesture to the city of Leipzig and its musicians. For that performance, Bach put a special trust in the two hautbois d'amour players, who basically carry the entire, very long and sometimes difficult first movement of Cantata 23. This was evidently the piece with which Bach discovered the hautbois d'amour. His fondness for the instrument is unmistakable: he included it in his inaugural cantata in May (BWV 75) and at least eight other cantatas before the end of his first year at Leipzig.[66] Two concertos for hautbois d'amour, BWV 1053a and BWV 1055a, probably written in the mid-1720s (see below, §E), survive in his later arrangements for harpsichord.

The instrument appeared in other contexts, less known nowadays, such as Schürmann's beautiful opera arias,[67] and concertos for multiple 'd'amour' instruments (flute d'amour, viola d'amour, and hautbois d'amour with orchestra) by Graupner and Telemann.

The surviving chamber music and solos for hautbois d'amour give an idea where the instrument was heard. In the first bloom of the late 1710s and through the next decade, there are pieces from Berlin (by Graun), Braunschweig (Graun and Schürmann), Darmstadt (Graupner, Telemann, and Böhm), Dresden (Heinichen, Lotti, Telemann, Fasch, and Quantz), Frankfurt (Telemann), Gotha (Stölzel), Hamburg (Telemann), Leipzig (Kuhnau and Bach), Merseburg (Förster), Rheda (Telemann), Schwerin (Telemann), and Zerbst (Fasch).

Between 1730 and 1760, the hautbois d'amour was heard in Arolsen,[68] Dresden (Homilius and Quantz), Berlin (Carl Friedrich Fasch, Graun, Quantz, and Janitsch), Cassel (Chelleri), Darmstadt (Graupner), Hamburg (Prowo and

---

[61] St Luke Passion.   [62] Matthäus-Passion.   [63] 65% (167 pieces).
[64] 33% (87 pieces).   [65] Six pieces. Cf. Haynes (1992a).   [66] See Dürr (1957), 57–64.
[67] See Haynes (1992a), 285 ff.   [68] Rouvel (1962), 91.

Telemann), Limburg (Doemming), Rudolstadt (Förster), Sonsfeldt (Telemann), Stuttgart (Telemann), Wolfenbüttel (Graun), Zeitz (Krebs), and Zerbst (Fasch and Telemann). Copenhagen had compositions for hautbois d'amour by Scheibe, and Roman was writing for it in Sweden.

In contrast to the treble hautboy, composers used the hautbois d'amour primarily as a solo instrument, rarely requiring it to play unison with other instruments.[69] When it appeared at all, it seems to have been used as an important element and special effect.

Although it would have been valued for its special poetic attributes, one practical reason for the interest shown in the hautbois d'amour by Bach and his colleagues was its unusual key, A major. Bach wrote nearly half his 'oboe' solos for the hautbois d'amour. He was particularly fond of F sharp minor and B minor, and many hautbois d'amour obbligatos were written in these keys. He rarely required them of the treble hautboy, but on hautbois d'amour, F sharp minor and B minor were the relatively straightforward fingered tonalities of A minor and D minor.

Because the hautbois d'amour was played in a specific area and period, most if not all of them were pitched similarly, at A−1.[70]

The hautbois d'amour was sometimes used for its specific tone colour. Several composers (Bach, Graupner,[71] Roman,[72] Stölzel, and Telemann[73]) requested both treble hautboy and hautbois d'amour in the same piece. Telemann used hautbois d'amour and solo violin in unison in the aria 'Du, o ewiges Erbarmen' in the St Luke Passion of 1744; the range of the part was not low enough to have prevented the use of a treble hautboy, so he must have had a particular colour in mind. On the other hand, Telemann (probably for practical reasons) sometimes rewrote hautbois d'amour arias for treble hautboy.[74]

Although the hautbois d'amour and treble hautboy had an identical fingered range, their ideal tessitura was somewhat different; Bach occasionally wrote notes for hautbois d'amour above his normal treble hautboy range, mostly in unison with strings (probably because the d'amour's highest normal note, sounding b2, was relatively low for a violin). In 1729 he wrote a solo fingered e3 in BWV 201/9, a

---

[69] In Telemann's first known use of hautbois d'amour (Ouverture, TWV 55: E2, 1718–20), however, he has the hautbois d'amour double other parts (including, at times, the viola when it functions as *Bassätchen*).

[70] According to Piet Dhont (pers. comm.), incomplete hautbois d'amour by Poerschmann and Noack that survive in Poznań (Poland) appear from their dimensions to have been pitched lower than A−1; these might have been Hautecontre, however.

[71] Aria 'Gott wolle unseren David schützen', no. 5 in Cantata 1717/4, G.

[72] Concerto 45 . . . a 4. Parte, D. S-Skma. In the B-section of the first movement, the hautbois d'amour switches to 'Oboe ordinario'.

[73] The instruments change within the soprano aria 'Hamburg ruht in süßem Schlafe' in *Kapitainsmusiken, Einigkeit*, 1724/S13.

[74] e.g. the aria 'Aus deiner neuen Morgenröte' in the 1728 *Kapitainsmusiken*, later I/6 in *Emma und Eginhard*. Maertens (1988), 102.

piece that has many high notes. The tessitura of 115/2, written in 1724, was also abnormally high, and required an exposed e3.[75] Three weeks later, Bach wrote the remarkable aria 116/2, probably the most difficult of his arias for hautbois d'amour (appropriately titled 'Ach, unaussprechlich ist die Not'). This aria also included an unusual number of high notes. Telemann went as far as fingered e3 for hautbois d'amour in his operas *Miriways* and *Sieg der Schönheit*, but he generally stayed within a range of fingered f1–b♭2.[76]

Carl Philip Emanuel Bach was a small child when the hautbois d'amour first appeared, and he no doubt heard Gleditsch and Kornagel play it at St Thomas's when he was growing up in Leipzig. By the time he was in his 60s in Hamburg, and making notes on how to perform his father's cantatas there, the hautbois d'amour had not been heard in Hamburg for many years (the last time was in Telemann's *Tag des Gerichts* (TWV 6: 8) of 1762).[77] In notes made 1770–89, Bach (who was Telemann's godson) wrote next to his father's aria BWV 100/5 (for alto, hautbois d'amour, and continuo) 'NB. Must be done on the ordinary hautboy'.[78] In his performance of his father's B minor Mass, he had to eliminate hautbois d'amour in *Et in unum Dominum* and *Et in spiritum sanctum Dominum*, presumably because they were no longer available in Hamburg.

The musical catalogues issued by Breitkopf advertised pieces for hautbois d'amour up until 1763, but listings for the instrument ceased to appear after 1769. Michael Finkelman (pers. comm.) cites a performance on hautbois d'amour by one of the Parke brothers in London in 1781. The concerto for hautbois d'amour solo and orchestra by Carl Ditters von Dittersdorf may have been the last significant solo for the instrument; it is not dated, but to judge from its style was written rather late in the eighteenth century.

The hautbois d'amour must still have been played later in the century, however. Grundmann made one in 1774.[79] Some time before 1783, Kirnberger in Berlin, commenting on a work by Sebastian Bach, felt obliged (like Emanuel Bach) to explain to other musicians what an hautbois d'amour was, and why its part was transposed.[80] The hautbois d'amour was referred to by Verschuere–Reynvaan in 1795 (p. 370) and Koch in 1802 (p. 1083).[81] Koch said that it was 'seldom used anymore'. Eichentopf is survived by an hautbois d'amour with nine added keys;[82] since that

---

[75] This note is unison with the first violins, but cannot be faked or left out.   [76] McCredie (1964), 173.

[77] In 1759 Telemann had included a 'Grosse Hoboe' in his *Messias*, TWV 6: 4, and *Das befreite Israel*, TWV 6: 5.

[78] 'NB muß zur *ordin. Hautb.* gemacht werden'. *Bach-Dokumente* (1963), iii. 208.

[79] This instrument, which was dated, belonged to the Berlin collection before the war (Young 1993: 115). A copy made by Heckel survives. The two by Heinrich Grenser listed in Young 1993: 102 'are definitely no d'amores, but ordinary oboes!' according to Alfredo Bernardini (pers. comm.).   [80] *Bach-Dokumente* (1963), iii. 376.

[81] Meusel (1778–9), ii. 9 mentioned a certain Leonard Beck in Nuremberg who 'excelliret auf der Hoboe d'Amour'.   [82] Paris E.2178, Y7. The stamp is unusual, however, and may be fake.

number of keys was not in general use until well into the nineteenth century, this instrument appears to indicate a relatively late use of the instrument.

b. The 'Hautecontre de hautbois' as an instrument as well as a part   We are informed by J. G. Walther in 1732 that the term 'Haute-Contre de Hautbois' is French, and that it

ist in einem musicalischen Stück die zweyte *Hautbois* mit dem c-Schlüssel, oder auch wol die Alt-Partie.[83]	is the second *Hautbois* in C-clef in a musical piece, or else the alto part.

Walther's comment is ambiguous, but could be taken to mean that the 'Haute-Contre de Hautbois' was both a part and an independent instrument. 'Hautecontre de hautbois' was also the second of four official titles of posts in the *Grands Hautbois* at the French court, the others being 'Dessus de hautbois', 'Taille de hautbois', and 'Basse de hautbois'. Was the 'hautecontre' a mere part-designation and formal court title, or was it a separate type of instrument?

An anonymous drawing[84] datable to 1587–8 shows two shawms marked *Taille* and *Dessus*, and above the *Taille* is the remark 'hautecontre est de mesmes mais plus petite' (hautecontre is the same but smaller). So a distinct hautecontre shawm was apparently in use in the 1580s. This offers a precedent for the existence of an haute-contre hautboy.[85]

The term 'hautecontre', without the specific 'de hautbois' was used for string instruments and singers as well. But a number of pieces with hautecontre parts survive that appear to be for double-reed band (see App. 9). It can be assumed that in these pieces, the 'hautecontre' was neither a singer nor a string instrument, but a double reed.

If an instrument existed that was called an 'hautecontre de hautbois', these pieces would probably have been part of its repertoire. This music was either written by Germans or survives in German libraries. There was a part for *Hautboe-Contre* in C1 clef in Keiser's opera *Circe* (Hamburg, 1734), and apparently other Hamburg operas;[86] the Opera orchestra there included four hautboys, two hautbois d'amour, and one 'Hautbois-Contre',[87] (probably played by a total of four treble woodwind players). Brossard (1703: 78 and 167) twice mentioned the 'Haute-Contre de Hautbois', though what he meant by it is unclear.[88]

---

[83] Walther (1732), 304. Walther wrote in (1708), 49 s.v. 'Hautecontre': 'In Stücken so auf *Hautbois* gesetzet sind, ist es gemeiniglich der hohe *Alt.*'

[84] British Museum Add. 30342, fo. 145, reproduced in Oldham (1961), pl. 101.

[85] Mersenne (1636: 295 ff.; cf. Eppelsheim 1961: 101–2) indicated that both haute-contre and taille parts were played on tailles.   [86] Kleefeld (1899), 264.

[87] Mennicke (1906: 275), citing Kleefeld (1899), 219.

[88] Bach did not apparently use the term 'Hautecontre de hautbois'.

Based on the clef notation of its parts, it has been suggested that the Hautecontre was an hautboy in A, between the tenor in F and the treble in C.[89] When Lully used the famous 'trio' texture of two hautboys and bassoon in his orchestral scores, he put the two hautboys in G1 clef and the bassoon in F4 (bass clef). But in bigger four-part hautboy ensembles such as those found in Cambert's *Pomone* (1671), a number of Lully's works for hautboy band, and the Philidor Manuscript,[90] the first and second parts were in different clefs: the *Dessus* in G1 and the *Hautecontre* in C1 clef (as Walther had indicated). All the *Hautecontre* parts in the pieces listed in Appendix 9 also use the C1 clef. In addition, hautecontre parts frequently went below the lowest note of the treble hautboy, c_1;[91] in these cases, the two parts must have been played by different instruments.

The obvious instrument to cover the hautecontre part was the *Taille de hautbois* or tenor hautboy. This would be analogous to the three middle parts in the strings —hautecontre, taille, and quinte—played by various sizes of 'viola'.[92] But unlike the hautecontre in C1 clef, the taille part in hautboy ensembles was usually in yet another clef, C2. Clefs were frequently chosen to avoid leger lines rather than to indicate instrument changes. But in this case, for a player of an F-instrument like the taille, used to the treble clef (our modern G2 clef), the C2 clef of the third part was ideal, because a fingered G sounded C as it should have: it was equivalent to transposing the part. For the hautecontre in C1 clef, the same thing would have applied if the instrument were in A.[93] Bach, in fact, sometimes used the C1 clef for the hautbois d'amour in A.[94]

The clef argument is not entirely consistent, however, because the treble parts to these pieces were written in G1 clef. That does not suggest that anyone was expecting parts notated in G2 clef. If they were accustomed to reading in G1 clef on the treble hautboy, it would have been logical to have a part that required the fingering 123 for the note on the bottom line of the stave. 123 produces an e_1 on an A instrument, which is the bottom line in G2 clef, not the C1 clef; the same fingering produces c_1 on a tenor in F, requiring a part in C1 clef, not C2 clef.

There are other objections to the idea of the Hautecontre as a separate instrument, some of which can be answered.

The hautecontre part will fit on a taille. As far as ranges go, the four parts in the Philidor Manuscript are:

---

[89] This was first suggested by Marc Écochard, and was elaborated by Harris-Warrick in (1990), 101 ff.

[90] On this manuscript, see Ch. 1, §C.

[91] The Philidor Manuscript contains b_0 in the second part in 8% of pieces (Sandman 1974: 226), and also occasionally descends to a_0. The hautecontre part in the first entrée of *Les Nopces de village* (LWV 19, 1663), in which 'oboes' were specified in the libretto but not the score (Semmens 1975: 74–5), has a range of b_0–e_2. The 'Entrée des Zéphirs' in *Atys* (II.iv, p. 149) was for three upper parts labelled 'Hautbois', and bass; the second part descends to a_0. In *Le Mariage de la grosse Cathos* by André Philidor (1688), the second hautboy part sometimes goes to b_0.

[92] Eppelsheim (1961), 106 and Semmens (1975), 75.

[93] Making allowance, of course, for the key (C major for the treble in C would need to be E flat major for an instrument in A).

[94] Denton (1977), 127 and Crist (1985), 218–19.

Dessus	c1–c3
Haute-contre	b0–f2
Taille	f0–d2
Basse	C–f1

The taille, with a range of f0–g2,[95] (corresponding in fingering to c1–d3 on the treble hautboy), could easily have covered both hautecontre and taille parts, and is known sometimes to have done so.[96] But Marc Écochard (pers. comm.), who has tested the entire hautecontre part to the Philidor Manuscript on a taille, found that while it would be possible, the player is constantly in the highest register of the instrument, with frequent b2s and c3s; the parts would obviously be in a more comfortable range on an hautecontre in A.

We are also still ignorant of the types of double-reed instruments that were used in these ensembles; besides the treble hautboy, they may not have been hautboys as we usually think of them, but various sizes of cromorne (see Ch. 1, §B.1). Hautecontre parts in the Philidor Manuscript could originally have been played on a cromorne that descended to a0, but later copied into the manuscript without adjustments and corrected ad hoc by a player of the treble hautboy.[97]

Starting in the 1690s, there were a number of instances where tailles were mentioned but hautecontres were not. Corneille (1694) under *Hautbois* described the dessus and the taille, as well as the bassoon, but did not mention the hautecontre. Haka's bill of 1685 includes a set of 'Franse Haubois' that lists only the 'discant', 'tenor', and 'Basson'.[98] Talbot (*c.*1692–5) described the treble and tenor 'Hautbois' but mentioned no other size. In both of Jacob Denner's bills for choirs of woodwind instruments (1710 and 1720), the hautboy family included only *Hautbois, Taille*, and *Basson*; *Hautecontre* was absent.[99] Fleming (1726: 182) described hautboy bands used in the German army as consisting of 'Zwey *Discante*, zwey *la Taillen*, und zwey *Bassons*' (the Tailles were probably each on a separate part). The double-reed quartet carved on the bell of an hautboy at the Victoria and Albert Museum apparently has equal trebles (Pl. 4.9).[100] And at least some hautboy band music (like Krieger's *Lustige Feldmusic*, 1704) called for a second part that descended only to c1. These facts do not of course disprove the existence of the hautecontre, but they do establish that it was not always used in hautboy bands.

If the hautecontre was in A, it would have limited the tonalities in which the band could play. When a C-hautboy played in the key of F, for instance, the tenor would

---

[95] According to Sauveur (1701), 135, pl. 3, citing Rippert and Jean Hotteterre.

[96] The second part, called 'Hautcontre', was covered by a tenor hautboy in J. W. Glaser's cantata *Er ist allent-halben versuchet* (cf. Koch 1980: 82).

[97] That appears to have been what happened to the second part in the 'Entrée des Zephirs' in Lully's *Atys*, originally (1676) for five hautboys and three cromornes (range g0–g2), which descends to a0; apparently the piece was later (1689) played by hautboys only (see Ch. 1, §B.1).   [98] Haka (1685).

[99] Nickel (1971), 251, 253.   [100] See Halfpenny (1957a).

have been in C, and the hautecontre in A flat major, just about the limit of practical technique. A piece in B flat major would probably have been difficult on such an instrument. An Ouverture by Christoph Pez for two hautboys or violins, 'Haute-Contreè', taille, and Bass was written in D minor, for instance, which would have been F minor on an A-instrument.[101] But in fact, hautboy band music was often very conservative in choice of keys; seventy-eight pieces in the Philidor Manuscript are in C major, nine are in G, two in D minor, one in F, and one in G minor.[102] On an instrument in A, these keys would have been fingered E flat major (most of the time), B flat, F minor, A flat, and B flat minor. All the pieces in the manuscript would have been comfortable on an hautecontre in A except the *Folies d'Espagne* (10/M2) in fingered F minor and the *Marche du Régiment du Roy* (10/M1) in fingered B flat minor, which would have been playable but awkward. The written keys in the pieces in Appendix 9 were five times B flat, many times C and D, four times F, thirteen times G, A minor, and C minor, five times D minor and E minor, and four times G minor. C and G major predominate. Michael Finkelman (pers. comm.) suggested that hautecontres could have existed in B flat, that is, sounding a 7-fingered modern ao; considering the range of pitch standards in use, an instrument in this low register that played a semitone lower or higher is not at all implausible. Going up or down, a semitone difference could have solved tonality problems of this kind.

The case for the existence of the hautecontre as an instrument is confirmed, however, by surviving original instruments. The difficulty of identifying original hautboys that would have been used as hautecontres is that they were presumably built in an identical form to normal treble hautboys, the only difference being their larger size. In Chapter 2, §D.2 above, however, I suggested that acoustic length (AL) is a valid (if not complete) indication of sounding pitch. This is borne out by the ALs of seven hautbois d'amour, six of which were made in Leipzig, where pitch is known to have been at A−1 or lower.[103] As their lowest, 7-fingered note, these instruments should have sounded about modern a♭o. Their ALs are as follows:

380	Schlegel, Basle 1882.14
380.9	Eichentopf, Paris
382.8	Eichentopf, Brussels
384.1	Sattler, Munich DM 8868
384.5	Eichentopf, Venice
386.0	Sattler, 201
391.7	Eichentopf, Berlin 73

---

[101] Rostock (MS XVII: 38.24), transcribed in Owens (1995), 515–38. The range is d1–g2, too high for a tenor hautboy but possible on a treble.   [102] Sandman (1974), 137.

[103] Haynes (1995), §6.

The range of AL is 380 to 391.7, and the average is 384.3. The longest treble hautboys are a good 40 mm shorter than this. The ALs of tenors are appropriately distanced from the d'amours, being in the 420s.

Since we know that hautbois d'amour were in A (that is, their 7-fingered note sounded a modern a♭0 or lower), hautecontres, also in A, should have had a similar AL. At least three 'long hautboys' exist, that are otherwise built as treble hautboys with the normal flared bell. Their ALs are as follows:

393.6   Anon., Paris E.980.2.149
382   Deper, Vienna
393   Christoph Denner, Linz 120

The lengths suggest that these were hautecontres, and indeed, the Deper and Denner play well in 7-fingered A at pitches of A−1 or lower. The turning style of Paris E.980.2.149 (Pl. 2.12) looks very early, by the way, thereby suggesting that such instruments existed before 1670.

Music, texts, and instruments all offer cumulative evidence of the existence of the hautecontre as an instrument. How common it was, and exactly when it was used, are not yet clear. 'Hautecontre de hautbois' may have served as a catch-all term for alto hautboys of all kinds, just as 'taille de hautbois' would have served for the various kinds of tenor hautboys.

c. The Oboe Grande   The literature for hautboy also includes a number of pieces for an instrument called variously:

(1) Oboe Grande, Hautbous de Grand, Oboe le Grand
(2) Grosse Hoboe, Grosse Oboe, Groß-Hoboe, Oboe luongo, Obue bahse

These names appeared from at least 1720 to 1766 or later. For this discussion, I shall use the first term, 'Oboe Grande'.[104] As above, it is necessary to ask here if the oboe grande was a separate kind of instrument.

If the oboe grande possessed particular characteristics, they would probably be revealed in its repertoire, which is listed in Appendix 10. The keys, insofar as they are known, are all sharp (D, E minor, G, A, A minor). And its parts were normally notated a minor third below the general band. Thus the oboe grande, like the hautecontre and hautbois d'amour, was apparently an hautboy that sounded a 7-fingered A.[105] Was 'Oboe Grande' simply another name for the hautecontre or hautbois

---

[104] Terry claimed (1932: 108, without, unfortunately, citing a source) that Bach used the 'Grand-Oboe' in his aria 'Ich halte meinen Jesum feste', BWV 157/2. The aria is in fact for Tenor, hautbois d'amour, and continuo. The earliest sources are a copy of the score that dates from 1755–6 and calls the instrument an 'Oboe' on the cover, and the organ part (dating from 1760–7) that calls it 'Oboe et Oboe d'amore'. Cf. *NBA*, Neumann (1947), and Schulze and Wolff (1986–), ii. 716. The name 'Grand-Oboe' is plausible, however, and it would be interesting to know where Terry got it.

[105] The two exceptions are two late 18th-c. pieces: a Quartetto concertante in B flat (CS-K) by Johann Went for hautboy, 'Oboe Grande' in B flat, English horn, and bassoon, and a trio for hautboy, 'Oboe Grande', and English

d'amour, or was it yet again another kind of instrument? With the information currently at hand, this question cannot be conclusively answered.

Unlike 'hautbois d'amour', the terms used to indicate the oboe grande were not poetic, but merely descriptive of the size of the instrument. In physical terms, the oboe grande would presumably have been, like the tenor hautboy, simply a larger treble, whereas the hautbois d'amour was a separate design. Although the terms 'hautbois d'amour' and 'Oboe Grande' seem sometimes to have been considered interchangeable, Telemann, Carl Graun, Stölzel, and Homilius used the two different names in various pieces, implying a distinction between the two instruments. On the other hand, a Lübeck inventory included a 'Grant Hoboe', and a subsequent one referred to a 'Hoboe Amor',[106] suggesting that the two terms were used interchangeably. The Uhlig concerto for 'Grand Oboe' (see App. 10) is found in a section of the Breitkopf catalogue entitled 'Oboe d'amore'.

2. Tenor hautboys

a. The straight tenor or taille de hautbois   The tenor hautboy was a fifth below the treble. A synonym was the word 'taille' (which is the French word for tenor, or middle part). Talbot wrote in *c*.1692–5: 'The Tenor Hautbois differs not from Treble in shape, only in size & bore of holes which being at greater distance are bored more slantingly downwards that the tops may be covered with the Fingers.'

The development of a tenor hautboy that was outwardly identical with the treble except for its size was not as simple as it might seem. Apart from establishing a usable bore proportion, there was, as Talbot pointed out, the problem of tone-hole spacing, which was at the limit of the spread of the fingers of the hand (some modern players are unable to play the tenor because of its large finger-spread).

It has been generally assumed that the tenor hautboy was developed at about the same time as the treble. But the existence of the instrument cannot in fact be established before about 1680, a decade after the first documented appearance of the treble hautboy. In the original production of Lully's *Atys* in 1676, the double-reed band consisted of hautboys and cromornes, but at least one of the cromornes was replaced in a later performance in 1689 with the 'taille de hautbois', suggesting that the taille made its first appearance during the interval between 1676 and 1689.

horn by Joseph Triebensee (Finkelman, s.v. 'lower oboes' in *New Grove II*). These are the only known pieces for oboe grande in flat keys, and the reason may have to do with pitch standards. In Went's and Triebensee's time and place, instrumental pitch was generally at A≈430–435 (Haynes 1995, §9-2e). If this 'Oboe Grande' was an hautbois d'amour (by then old-fashioned) in its traditional pitch at A−1 (A≈415), the difference in pitch would have been about a semitone, and the instrument would have been regarded not as in A, but in A flat. It would then have been comfortable in flat keys rather than sharp. Michael Finkelman (pers. comm.) sees the evidence differently, postulating the availability of an Oboe Grande in B flat in Germany early on, used for playing the inner parts in Harmonie pieces. Evidence on this point is inconclusive at present.

[106] Finkelman, s.v. 'lower oboes' in *New Grove II*.

Two pictures that show different types of double-reed instruments, the Gobelins borders and Blanchet (1664 and 1672, Pls. 1.3 and 1.5), show the treble hautboy and cromorne but fail to register a larger size of hautboy.

As noted in Chapter 3, §D, the earliest known appearance of tenor hautboys is in an anthem by Blow from 1681–3. Since the instruments were played by Frenchmen and probably came from France, we can assume the tenor existed there by about 1680.

The problem of finger-reach was solved on the cromornes with extension keys (the ring mounts of which gave the instrument its typical profile). As long as a satisfactory solution existed, musicians may have felt less urgently the need for a larger hautboy.

To judge from surviving music, the taille was not a solo instrument. Its principal function was to play the tenor line in hautboy ensembles. And because much of the literature for bands was not written down or preserved, a significant part of the original music for tenor hautboy is probably lost. Of what is known, very little can be classified as solo music; apart from Philidor's exotic *Marche de Roy de la Chine* (no. 25 in the Philidor Manuscript), there are lost concertos by Telemann[107] and Beckurts, the first for treble and tenor hautboys together, the second for 'Hautbois de Taille'.[108] The other reasonably exposed parts for taille are found in German religious works by Schulze, Bach, Liebe, and Volckmar.[109] In France, a half-dozen pieces written before 1700 survive for taille in small ensembles. There are about 100 pieces from between 1700 and 1730 (mostly band music) from various parts of Europe, and thirty-eight from 1730 to 1760, the latter mostly in wind quintets.

Many tenors (such as the four that survive by Christoph Denner) have a flared bell like the treble hautboy, but some have bulbs, inside, outside, or both (like the Jacob Denner now in Berlin).

Whether the tenor hautboy was ever conceived as in 7-fingered G is a moot point. There were also treble hautboys pitched a step apart. This is in fact a question of semantics, depending on one's pitch reference; an F-tenor at *Chorton* was at the same time a G-tenor at *Cammerton*. Players were probably glad to have both possibilities, and used them in various combinations, when and as needed.

b. The oboe da caccia The oboe da caccia was a specialized form of tenor that, by a quirk of history, is probably better known today than it was in its own time. The instrument's fame is due to Bach, who wrote practically all the surviving solo literature for it (a total of about two dozen pieces, all written at Leipzig).

The instrument was known by a variety of names. Bach alone was responsible for calling it by ten different variations, including 'Hautbois da Caccia', 'Hautbois

---

[107] This is an attribution, and Michael Finkelman (pers. comm.) considers it spurious.   [108] Haynes (1992a).

[109] Finkelman (s.v. 'lower oboes' in *New Grove II*) lists other pieces that include the taille.

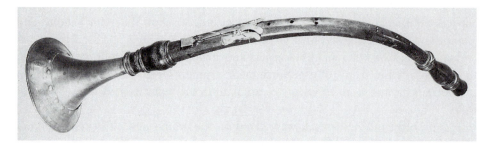

PL. 6.2. Oboe da caccia, Eichentopf, Leipzig, 1724. Stockholm: Musikmuseet

de la Chasse', 'Oboe da Caccia', etc.[110] Mattheson (1722–5, iv. 254) called it 'Hautbois de chasse', and it was also apparently known as the 'Hautbois de silve' (see below).

Physically, the oboe da caccia differed from the straight tenor by its flamboyant curve and widely flaring bell, leather covering, and faceted octagonal cross-section similar to the cornett (see Pl. 6.2). It was made in two parts, the curved wooden tube and a separate bell. The point of curving the instrument does not seem to have been to ease the finger-reach, as has often been suggested. Straight and curved tenors had similar tone-hole placement, and it was actually the straight models that were more comfortable to play.

I suspect the 'curve' was as much in the mind of its creators as in the instrument itself; the da caccia appears now as a poetic conceit, an unnatural adaptation of the attributes of a brass instrument into one made of wood. The instrument's name, as well as its shape and flared bell, suggest it was conceived as an imitation of the corno da caccia, the hoop-like trompe or hunting horn, which was just then being accepted as an indoor instrument.[111] In a like manner, the trumpet was coiled to form the tromba da caccia, and (like the oboe da caccia) probably had no other connection with 'the hunt' than its name.[112] This was the kind of intellectual artifice that produced painted marble, entire Handel operas arranged for a single recorder, and halls of mirrors. The curious look of the instrument was probably part of its appeal.[113]

If it was designed outwardly to resemble the hunting horn, it is ironic that the oboe da caccia was in fact a rather soft and retiring instrument: Bach often

[110] Cf. Prinz (1979), 162.

[111] Eppelsheim (1985), 77 n. 54 suggests that horns and oboes da caccia were associated in instrumentation. He points out that BWV 1 and BWV 65, both of which have oboe da caccia solos, also include horns.

[112] Eppelsheim's suggestion (ibid. 76 n. 53) that a curved taille would be more practical for mounted players is worth considering, however. One of the problems of playing wind instruments on horseback is the danger if the horse rears unexpectedly.   [113] Cf. Cron (1996), 26.

scored it with boy sopranos and traversos.[114] The leather covering (which acted as a kind of bandage to disguise and seal the kerf-cuts made along one side, for the sake of the curve) tended to dampen the sound. Bach used the da caccia fairly specifically; the texts of its solos usually expressed the affects of grief, tragedy, sin, or sorrow.[115]

The two best-known surviving oboes da caccia, both dated 1724, were made by Eichentopf (Pl. 6.2).[116] The oboe da caccia seems to have been a speciality of Saxony and Poland. It could have been invented by Eichentopf, who was also a brass-instrument maker. The thin brass bells he put on his instruments were more convincing as ersatz horns than the wooden bells of other makers. He even painted the inside of the bell (as was customary on the hunting horn, to prevent the glare of the sun's reflection from blinding the horseman behind).[117]

Eichentopf was not the only oboe da caccia maker in Leipzig, however. Two other da caccias by Gottlob Bauer, also dated 1724, are now in Prague, and Bauer's brother Gottfried is survived by a da caccia in the Berlin collection.[118]

Gleditsch had evidently been playing the oboe da caccia at least a year before Bach arrived in Leipzig in 1723, which was why Bach could immediately begin writing solos for the instrument. In 1722, Fasch had acquired for the court at Zerbst 'zwei Paar Waldhautbois', together with two 'Waldhörner' for a total of 14 Thaler.[119] These instruments were purchased through 'Gleditzsch [*sic*] in Leipzig'. As Dahlqvist noticed, the likelihood is strong that these 'Waldhautbois' were oboes da caccia, made (like the 'Waldhörner')[120] by Eichentopf. Gleditsch would have tested the instruments, and his association with this order suggests his central role in developing and promoting the da caccia.

The oboe da caccia was probably held in the same playing position as the hunting horn, that is, down and to the side (holding it up, 'pavillons en l'air', was obviously impractical). There is no historical evidence on this subject. Some modern players hold the bell between their legs, which suggests that the technique might have been used then as well.

The entire known solo and chamber literature for the instrument consists of:

1. 22 solo arias by Bach;
2. Fasch's Concerto [with added Menuets] for 'Hautbois du silve', two violas, two bassoons, and harpsichord (K. 44, FWV L: G11);

---

[114] In the middle of a vocal passage in BWV 101/6 (bb. 31 and 33), the traverso and da caccia are both marked *forte* (the traverso is low and the da caccia high).   [115] Denton (1977), 175–7.

[116] The instruments are described in Karp (1972).

[117] Friedrich von Huene (pers. comm.).   [118] Waterhouse (1993), 22.

[119] Dahlqvist (1976), 127, citing H. Wäschke, 'Die Zerbster Hofcapelle unter Fasch', *Zerbster Jahrbuch*, 3 (1907), 50.   [120] One of Eichentopf's horns dated 1722 survives in Munich.

3. an *Ouverture* written *c*.1735 for orchestra by Graupner with two 'Oboi di Selv.';[121]

4. Ferrandini's Sinfonien nos. 2, 3, 5 for two Oboe di Silva in F (on the transposed parts: 'Wald Oboe'), two violins, viola, and bass.

Fasch and Graupner both had close connections with Leipzig, and probably wrote their pieces for da caccias that had been made there.

When Bach added a third hautboy to his orchestra, it was sometimes a taille, in which case it usually shared the tuttis with the string viola.[122] But the instrument Bach called taille never played obbligato parts (except as the third hautboy in a double-reed choir): all his surviving solos for F-hautboy are specifically marked for oboe da caccia.[123] It is therefore tempting to assume that the instrument was called a taille when it played tutti and oboe da caccia when it played solos (all oboes da caccia being tailles, but not all tailles being oboes da caccia). Piet Dhont (pers. comm.) has pointed out that no straight tenor hautboys are known to exist by any of the numerous Saxon woodwind builders of the time.

Some of Bach's cantatas called for both taille and oboe da caccia, and in these cases the obbligato part for da caccia was written, not in the taille part, but in that of the first hautboy.[124] (This evokes the image of the student apprentice who was playing 'taille' passing the instrument over to Maestro Gleditsch, who played a solo on it—as an 'oboe da caccia'. One wonders if he used the same reed.)

Bach began writing for the oboe da caccia within a month of his arrival in Leipzig.[125] Gleditsch played the first solo aria (BWV 167/3) on 24 June 1723. In August of that year he performed three more cantatas with da caccia solos. Solos for the instrument were peppered throughout Bach's most active period of composition for hautboy-type instruments: four in 1723, three in 1724, five in 1725, three in 1726, and five in the St Matthew Passion of 1727. The most active months were August 1723, May 1725, and April 1727.

Throughout the period he wrote for it, Bach's da caccia solos were consistently as demanding technically as his solos for other kinds of hautboy.[126] With a few

---

[121] *Ouverture 15*; Darmstadt (autograph score).

[122] Because the taille normally had no independent line in the score, its part sometimes exceeded its range, and corrections were presumably made ad hoc. Denton (1977), 156 ff. discusses technical considerations of Bach's taille writing, including range, tonalities, dynamics, ornaments, phrase-lengths, and awkward passages.

[123] Prinz (1979: 179 ff.) lists a few cases where the da caccia doubles other parts, and others where the taille has an obbligato part (although always in the context of an hautboy choir).

[124] See Prinz (1979), 166–9, 180, 181 ff. Most of the distinctions between taille and oboe da caccia outlined here are based on Prinz. A complete table of da caccia and taille parts in Bach's works, with source, date of peformance, date of repeat performances, movement number, number of instruments, key, and range is located in Prinz.

[125] There is no evidence that Bach wrote for the instrument prior to his arrival in Leipzig. Alfred Dürr's proposed reconstruction of BWV 186/3 (1716) for oboe da caccia (*NBA* I/18, 1966) is problematic on the instrument, and unlikely historically.   [126] Cf. BWV 80/7, 13/1, 16/5, and 183/4.

exceptions notated in G2 clef, da caccia parts were usually in C3 clef (as were taille parts),[127] which entailed transposition for the player.[128] The range of Bach's da caccia parts was fo–a♭2 (= fingered c1–e♭3). The two highest pieces were BWV 176/6 (g2) and BWV 244/65 (a♭2), both involving doubling with strings. The highest solo note was f♯2 (= fingered c♯3; BWV 80/7). Notes lower than fo appeared in da caccia parts, but only when they were doubled, and corresponded to the odd notes down to go in doubled treble hautboy parts. But none appears in solo parts, and in some separate parts they were corrected (the ones that were not remained probably due to carelessness or lack of time).[129]

The *Hautbois du silve* in Fasch's Concerto in G mentioned above were in E flat.[130] If these were F-instruments, they would have fingered this piece in D. Since the parts were in E flat, the instruments would have been a fifth plus a semitone below the other instruments, which means they were probably in *tief-Cammerton* (A–2).[131] The range of their parts was f♯–e2 (= fingered d1–c3), which fits the instruments perfectly. Whether these were straight tailles or da caccias is unknown.

D. *Special Problems Involving Pitch*

When Bach's cantatas first came to be published at the end of the nineteenth century by the Bach Gesellschaft (BG), the scholars working on them found that Bach had sometimes notated the orchestral parts to the same piece in different keys. At that point it was no longer clear why this should have been necessary, and the editors resolved the question in a way that seemed reasonable at the time: they normally kept to the key of the greatest number of parts. That meant that the hautboy parts sometimes got transposed out of their original keys. The BG has remained the definitive edition of Bach's cantatas until recently, and as long as key-system oboes were used, this anomaly was (if not unnoticed) at least accepted.[132]

It was Harnoncourt and the Concentus Musicus who first ran up against the impractical side of this solution when they began the first recordings of the cantatas using original instruments. No longer was the problem theoretical: certain pieces were virtually unplayable on the hautboy in the keys to which the BG editors had transposed them.

An example is Cantata 131 (written 1707–8), which is virtually an hautboy solo from beginning to end. Bach wrote the 'Obboe' and 'Fagotto' parts in A minor and

---

[127] Prinz (1979), 162–3.
[128] C is fingered 123, which the hautboy player thought of as G; the two common hautboy clefs were G1 and G2.
[129] Prinz (1979), 169–71.
[130] Küntzel (1965), 49. [131] Cf. Dahlqvist (1973), 63.
[132] A detailed discussion of this subject can be found in Haynes (1995), §7.

the other parts in G minor.[133] The original parts in A minor fit exactly the range of the hautboy (c_1 to d_3). But in the BG edition, the wind parts got transposed down to G minor, which meant the hautboy part went a whole tone below its range, and that it included low $c\sharp_1$.

1. Weimar pitch

Bach's Weimar hautboy parts are unusual because at that time he was evidently considering the hautboy a 'transposing' instrument, much like the 'B♭ clarinet' today, whose parts are notated a tone higher than most of the rest of the orchestra because it sounds a tone lower. Bach's Weimar hautboy parts are also written higher than the other parts.

During the first year he wrote cantatas at Weimar, Bach included parts for a single 'Oboe' (his original name) notated a major second above the other parts. The organ, we know, was tuned at *Cornet-ton* (A+1),[134] and the voices and strings were written in its key, so they too must have been at *Cornet-ton*. The *Oboe*, pitched a tone lower, was thus at A−1, the normal German *Cammerton*. The solos from that year are as follows:

(pre-)1714 [? Dec. 1713]	BWV 21/1
	BWV 21/3
25 March 1714	BWV 182/1
	BWV 182/4
22 April 1714	BWV 12/1
	BWV 12/4
12 August 1714	BWV 199/2
	BWV 199/8

At this point, major repairs were carried out on the Schloßkirche, where cantatas were performed,[135] and during the Autumn of 1714 there was a four-month break in performances. When cantatas resumed in December, the 'Oboe' no longer appeared. From this time, Bach began using a number of new instruments, including a 'Basson', 'Flaut.', 'Viola d'Amour', and an instrument he consistently labelled 'Hautbois'. The parts for Hautbois, like those of the other new instruments, were notated a minor third above the organ and strings.

In 1732 (p. 130) Walther (who lived in Weimar) wrote of *Cammerton* as 'a whole-tone or even a minor third lower [than] *Chor-* or *Cornet-ton* . . .'.[136] He added later:

---

[133] Cf. his surviving autograph score.   [134] Haynes (1995), §7-2.   [135] Schrammek (1985), 102.
[136] 'entweder um einen gantzen Ton oder gar um eine kleine Terz tieffer [than] Chor- oder Cornet-Tone . . .'.

Mit einem aus dem *G.mol* gesetzten, und mit einer *Oboé* versehenen CHOR= STÜCKE . . . spielet die *Oboé*, aus dem *A* . . . ja, wenn dieses Instrument um eine kleine *Terz* tieffer als CHOR=TON stehet,[137] muß z.B. in einem aus dem *D moll* gesetzten Kirchen=Stücke . . . die *Oboé* ihrer *modulation* aus dem *F moll* . . . *formiren* . . .[138]

When a choral piece is in G minor and an hautboy is involved . . . the hautboy plays in A minor . . . and when this instrument plays a minor third below *Chorton*, for instance in a church piece in D minor, the hautboy must be in F minor . . .

It is evident from this that Walther was used to the idea of hautboys being available at both normal *Cammerton* and at a semitone lower, a pitch often called *tief-Cammerton*. Bach's new instruments were thus apparently pitched at *tief-Cammerton*, or A−2.

It is unclear why this change of instrumentarium occurred at the end of 1714; perhaps it was connected with the renovation of the Schloßkirche. Up until then, Bach had had only a single hautboy and bassoon (playing at A−1). But all the remaining works written for the Weimar chapel show instead the minor third pitch relationship. They include these hautboy solos:

30 December 1714	BWV 152/1
	BWV 152/2
21 April 1715	BWV 31/8
14 July 1715	BWV 185/3
22 December 1715	BWV 132/1
20 December 1716	BWV 147a/2[139]

The difference of a minor third between pitch standards can also be a source of confusion in distinguishing parts for the treble hautboy in C from those for hautbois d'amour. Since the hautbois d'amour sounded in A, a minor third lower than the treble hautboy in C, its parts were usually transposed up a minor third. A piece in C major for the string band, for instance, was in E flat for the d'amour. In this case, of course, all the instruments were at the same pitch standard, *Cammerton*. But a similar key relationship would also have existed where different pitch standards were in use simultaneously, as at Weimar, where as we have seen five cantatas have an *Hautbois* part notated a minor third above the band. In the case of Weimar, however, the band was at *Cornet-ton* (A+1) and the hautboy was a minor third

---

[137] Walther (1732) in at least two places referred to 'Chor- oder Cornet-Tone' and 'dem alten Chor- oder Cornet-Tone' as synonymous. Presumably then, his use of 'CHOR=TON' here refers to a level at A+1 (= *Cornet-ton*).

[138] Walther (1732), 162–3 under the term 'Chromatico'.

[139] BWV 208 and BWV 63 (including the hautboy solo BWV 63/3) were both probably performed elsewhere or under special conditions at Weimar, because (not only failing to use the regular instrument names) they show a different pitch relation: all the parts are in *Cammerton*.

lower at *tief-Cammerton* (A−2). Here, as for the hautbois d'amour, the *Hautbois* was sounding a minor third below the strings and was notated a minor third above them. Despite this, the hautboy in question was not an hautbois d'amour (which in any case had probably not yet been invented). This means that German works that use an hautboy and strings at a distance of a minor third were not necessarily for hautbois d'amour. That was only true when all the parts, wind and string, were at the same pitch standard (for Bach, that was the case in Cöthen and Leipzig).

2. Tief-Cammerton *at Leipzig*

For his audition for Leipzig, Bach performed his Cantata 23.[140] The genesis of this performance is revealing. Bach evidently arrived in Leipzig only a few days beforehand, and the surviving parts indicate that he suddenly decided on some last-minute changes, changes that involved juggling between normal (*hohe-*)*Cammerton* and *tief-Cammerton*.

The Leipzig pitch was identified by Kuhnau in 1717:

Ich habe aber fast von der ersten Zeit meiner Direction der Kirchen-Music[141] den Cornet-Ton abgeschaffet, und den Kammer-Ton, der eine Secunda oder kleine Tertia, nachdem es schikken will, tieffer ist, eingeführet . . .[142]	Almost from the moment I took over the direction of church music, I eliminated the use of *Cornet-ton* and introduced *Cammerton*, which is a second or minor third lower, depending on which is most convenient.

Cornet-Ton was a reliable and consistent name for the pitch at A+1.[143] After Kuhnau's reform of 1701, the organ remained at A+1 and was therefore notated a tone below the other instruments, or a tone and a half below when *tief-Cammerton* was used. Normal *Cammerton* was at A−1, and *tief-Cammerton* was A−2. A traverso by Eichentopf survives at A−2,[144] confirming that *tief-Cammerton* instruments were made in Leipzig.

Bach thus found he had a choice at Leipzig between *hohe-Cammerton* and *tief-Cammerton*. In order to include hautbois d'amour in his audition piece for reasons discussed above (see §C.1.a), he immediately found an ingenious way to use the difference between the two pitches. He had originally written this cantata for treble hautboys in C minor, but by having the strings tune down a semitone to *tief-Cammerton*,[145] the piece would have sounded in B minor.[146] He could then use hautbois d'amour—in *hohe-Cammerton*—playing parts written in D minor; the

---

[140] See Wolff (1978), 80.   [141] At Leipzig in 1701.
[142] Quoted by Mattheson (1722), ii. 235.   [143] Haynes (1995), §5-3.
[144] Leipzig Bachmuseum 1244. Powell (1993); Peter Noy and Courtney Westcott (pers. comm.); Heyde (1978), 84.   [145] See Dürr (1955), 35.
[146] In terms of *hohe-Cammerton*, of course.

result was that they sounded, like the strings, in B minor.[147] Bach quickly had the hautboy parts recopied in D minor, and this is the way the piece was performed.

During his first year and a half at Leipzig, Bach took advantage of the double-pitch option by writing several pieces at *tief-Cammerton* (Cantatas 22, 23, 63, 194, and the first version of the *Magnificat*).[148] The last known date that he used winds at *tief-Cammerton* was 4 June 1724, at the end of his first *Jahrgang*. From the second *Jahrgang* on, the notation of his parts shows that he used treble hautboys, hautbois d'amour, and oboes da caccia only at normal *Cammerton* (A–1), and it appears that at that point the *tief-Cammerton* winds were permanently retired from service.

E. The Lost Hautboy Repertoire

Having assembled a large body of church music that could be recycled in ensuing years (and in what was probably a conscious move in the direction of a court post at Dresden), in the spring of 1729 Bach took on the post of director of the Collegium Musicum that had been started by Telemann. From that time on, his production of church works decreased dramatically. For the Collegium project, he would himself have composed most of the music to be performed, and hautboys were of course an ingredient. Bach left a large quantity of instrumental music when he died, probably much of it written for the Collegium Musicum. But owing to the way his inheritance was distributed among his family, a large fraction of that music, much of it no doubt involving hautboy, is now lost.

A few smaller chamber pieces may survive now in arrangements for other instruments.[149] Chance has also preserved a number of concertos probably originally for hautboy or hautbois d'amour that Bach later adapted for his own use on the harpsichord. It is these concertos that will be discussed here.

Although no hautboy concertos by Bach have survived as such, there are indications that several once existed. Breitkopf's catalogue for the New Year 1764, lists 'Bach, G. S. I. Concerto, *a Oboe Concert. Violino Conc. 2 Violini, Viola, Basso.*'[150] The fragment BWV 1059 (to be discussed below) is entitled (in Bach's hand), 'Concerto a Cembalo solo, una Oboe, due Violini, Viola e Cont.' There are also three instrumental movements for solo hautboy and strings in cantatas BWV

---

[147] Again, in terms of *hohe-Cammerton*.

[148] Bach revised the *Magnificat* for performance in the 1730s, transposing it from E flat to D, probably because *tief-Cammerton* woodwinds were no longer available.

[149] As is suggested by the fact that a number of them can be adapted to the hautboy (possibilities are BWV 525–30, 817, 823, 1007–12, 1014–19, 1027, 1030, 1032, 1037, and 1039).

[150] Page 52. This was one of the 'non-thematic' catalogues not included in the reprint of Breitkopf (1760–87) (see Brook's introduction, pp. x–xi).

249a/2, 156/1, and 12/1 that Bach may have recycled from hautboy concertos that are now lost.[151]

Eight concertos arranged for solo harpsichord, BWV 1052–1059, survive in a score in Bach's hand.[152] At least some of them may have been made for a visit Bach made to Dresden in about 1738.[153] That they are not originally for harpsichord is apparent from the fact that the orchestral parts are virtually fair-copied, while the harpsichord part contains many corrections of a type that show that, as he wrote, Bach was adapting the solo part from earlier versions.[154] Could some of these concertos originally have been for hautboy?

It is clear that the violin was the solo instrument in some of them, but there are others that do not use typical violin figuration or the violin's complete range (as the authentic surviving violin concertos do).

Bach is known to have transposed movements when he recycled them,[155] and throughout his career he juxtaposed movements from different pieces to form new ones. So if these pieces were for hautboy, they might not originally have been in the same keys, and the individual movements might have been mixed differently.

The most effective method of discovering which of these concertos might originally have been for hautboy is to play them in various keys. Technical criteria the pieces would have to meet would include tonality, range, tessitura, and figuration. Tonality was discussed in Chapter 4, §H, range in Chapter 4, §F, and tessitura in Chapter 4, §F.3.

Some movements must be eliminated because, owing to limitations of range in either the solo part or the accompaniment, the line must be broken to the upper or lower octave in sequences. This is obviously not something a composer would normally have done when first writing a piece. There are other movements that cannot be played on the hautboy for technical reasons: their range is too large or their passagework is uncharacteristic. For these reasons, we can immediately reject

---

[151] Other movements involving solo hautboy(s) with strings in the cantatas are:

> BC A64 (incomplete 'Concerto', E minor, in its present state for two hautboys, strings, continuo). Seven bars survive; published in Marshall (1972), ii.
> BWV 124/1 (hautbois d'amour concertato; strings, chorus, continuo)
> BWV 21/1 (hautboy, violin; strings, continuo)
> BWV 182/1 (in one version for recorder, hautboy, strings, continuo)
> BWV 42/1 = BC A63/1 ('Sinfonia': two hautboys, bassoon, strings, continuo). In D. Although this is an improbable key for hautboys and even more so for bassoon, the combined ranges of the hautboy parts (d1–c♯3, c1–a2) exclude any transposition. Adjustments to one of these parts might restore a more convincing version. For a discussion of the origin of this piece, see section 3 of Rifkin (1999).

[152] D–B, Mus. Ms. Bach P234. I shall also discuss BWV 1060 below.

[153] Cf. Schulze (1981), 12 and Breig (1993), 433 n. 18, citing Kobayashi.

[154] See Fischer (1971), 11 and 16.

[155] The harpsichord versions of the concertos, for instance, are a step lower than the violin versions, and are sometimes a step lower than the corresponding organ solos. Bach raised BWV 156/1 for hautboy solo a minor third from F major to A flat for harpsichord (1056/2).

four concertos, BWV 1052, 1054, 1057, and 1058, as well as the 1st movement of 1056.[156] The others are discussed below.

1. BWV 1053

All three movements of this concerto exist in parallel versions in two cantatas, BWV 169 (in D major and B minor) and BWV 49 (in E major), which were first performed within two weeks of each other in 1726. In the cantatas, the solo instrument was the organ, with a range of f♯o–c♯3. But if two low passages are excepted that were not probably part of the original concerto,[157] the range becomes bo–c♯3. This is exactly a semitone lower than the standard range of the hautboy. The solo line also allows places to breathe.[158] Several writers have therefore suggested that this concerto was originally conceived for hautboy a semitone higher, in E flat major.[159]

Rifkin reconstructed the piece for hautboy in E flat and recorded it in May 1983 with Stephen Hammer playing the solo.[160] On the basis of copying mistakes in the original parts, Rifkin's argument for E flat is convincing.[161] Still, if an hautboy was the original solo instrument, it seems unlikely that the piece was originally conceived in this key because (with the exception of the second movement, which fits the hautboy well in C minor)[162] it is so awkward and difficult.[163]

E flat is a semitone removed from the hautboy's primary scale of D major, with all that that entails in the way of cross-fingerings, etc. It is a particularly challenging key on a technical level, notably because of the presence of A♭, produced by half-closing hole 3. It was no doubt because of its technical problems that E flat major was rarely used for hautboy solos in the eighteenth century.[164] Bach used it in less than 5 per cent of his hautboy solos,[165] and when he did, as in BWV 187/5, he exploited the key's unusual characteristics. In this concerto, however, E flat acts

---

[156] For comments on BWV 1054 and 1058, see Haynes (1992d).

[157] The organ part in II: 22 descends too low for hautbois d'amour in both fingered D minor and C minor. The lowest note of the solo line is f♯o (*pace* both Fischer and Siegele). But Siegele (1975: 139–40) believes that the concerto version, which omits bars 15–22, is closer to the lost original. [158] Joshua Rifkin (pers. comm.).

[159] Engel (1971), 337, Neumann (1971), 76, 179, and Siegele (1975), 142.

[160] Töttcher also published a reconstruction in F.

[161] The parts must have been copied from original versions in either E or E flat major; further considerations of harpsichord range narrow the possibility to E flat. See Rifkin (1999). [162] It also works well in D minor.

[163] There are awkward fingering combinations in the first movement in the opening solo entrance, bars 12, 22, 62–3, 69, 74–80, 88–9, etc. In the third movement, bar 55 contains a b♭o; this note can be plausibly played up an octave, however, and Siegele (1975), 142 believes the passage was probably originally written an octave higher. Bar 88 contains the combination e♭2–d♭2 (the 'diabolus in hautboy'), and the quick chromaticism of bars 161–75 and 243–58 is awkward in this key.

[164] E flat was used in only 1.25% of all known solos and chamber music written specifically and exclusively for hautboy in the period 1670 to 1760 (see Haynes 1992a, also Ch. 4, §H.2).

[165] There are eleven surviving solos in fingered E flat: eight for hautboy, two for hautbois d'amour, and one for oboe da caccia.

merely to create obstacles. It is difficult to see why Bach would have chosen this key when he originally conceived the piece.

On the other hand, there is a key that works well: F major, a step higher. In F, with two more natural fingerings per octave, the piece is freer in sound, and the difficulties caused by the presence of E♭s and A♭s are eliminated.[166] But there is a further twist.

The solo line sounds as good or better on an hautbois d'amour as on the treble hautboy. And when the hautbois d'amour plays in fingered F/D minor/F, it sounds in D/B minor/D, which are the keys of two of the three movements in the cantata versions. It is probably not a coincidence that the two fast movements in the cantata versions have prominent parts for hautbois d'amour.[167] From the beginning of the piece, the first violin's arpeggiated introductory figure sounds better (of course) in D than E flat.

In both extant versions (the concerto and the cantata), the last movement is in E.[168] If it is transposed down a step to D, there is a passage in the violin parts[169] that extends below the bottom note of the violin. But this passage succeeds equally well an octave higher; Bach had to keep it low in the organ version because an hautbois d'amour doubled the first violin, and would otherwise have ascended to fingered f3, beyond the instrument's range. In the harpsichord concerto, without the constraint of the doubling wind part, Bach rewrote this section in a lighter, airier manner, but understandably kept the strings in the lower octave in order not to cover the harpsichord (a consideration that was not necessary for an hautbois d'amour soloist).

In fingered F, there is one note in the organ version that exceeds the hautbois d'amour's normal upper range. The analogous measure in the harpsichord concerto takes this note down an octave, along with the first notes of the first and second beats. This is a curious anomaly; on a harpsichord, there is no physical or musical reason to have gone down an octave at this point. The answer is probably that the part was copied from an original for hautbois d'amour, where the octave break was necessary.

Bars 13–14, 23–4, and 66–7 in the first movement contain some independent (though unimportant) writing for winds that Bach probably added when arranging the movement for the cantata.[170]

---

[166] Another indication that the original solo part was in F is the close resemblance between the third movements of this piece and a concerto by Tomaso Albinoni, Opus IX: 3 for two hautboys, which is also in F. Butler (1995) suggested that Bach's movement is an adaptation of Albinoni's. Based on the date of appearance of Albinoni's Opus IX and other factors, Butler suggests the second half of 1726 as the period when BWV 1053a was composed. This is the same period that the cantata arrangements of these movements were performed (20 Oct. and 3 Nov. 1726).

[167] The 'oboe' parts to 169/1 are for hautbois d'amour rather than C-hautboys (see Haynes 1986b: 53).

[168] The organ part in the autograph score is in D because the instrument was in *Chorton*.

[169] Bars 223, 224, and 235.

[170] I recorded this concerto on hautbois d'amour in D (fingered F), along with BWV 1055, for ATMA in Apr. 1998.

2. BWV 1055

The original solo part for BWV 1055 in A major has a range of a0 to b2, and because it shows no particular violinistic traits, was probably originally for hautboy. But because of their range, the accompanying string parts cannot be transposed: the piece must have been originally in A. The solo instrument was therefore probably an hautbois d'amour, whose range exactly fits the solo part.[171] As an hautbois d'amour concerto, it has even found its way into one of the more daring ventures of the *NBA*, a volume of reconstructed concertos edited by Wilfried Fischer.

In the two outer movements, Bach evidently made a few octave shifts in adapting the piece from d'amour to harpsichord.[172] And I believe he must also have replaced the original second movement with the harpsichord Larghetto, because this movement, beautiful as it is, is not convincing on the hautbois d'amour: its tessitura is too high and it requires a number of unprepared high d3s. Evidently, another movement was used in the original concerto. A good candidate is available which is also an exquisite movement. This is the 'Adagio' of the *Schäferkantate*,[173] better known in its later form in the *Easter Oratorio*.[174]

This Adagio has long been thought to have been borrowed from a lost concerto.[175] In its surviving form, it was prepared for performances in February and April 1725. Although the movement is for hautboy and orchestra, it is in B minor, a key that is extremely rare in the hautboy literature and one used in no other hautboy solo by Bach.[176] Since it is audibly more comfortable on hautboy a step lower in A minor, it is a reasonable assumption that the *Schäferkantate* version derived from an earlier piece in A minor, presumably the slow movement of a lost concerto. Fingered A minor on an hautbois d'amour is sounding F sharp minor, the necessary key for the second movement of BWV 1055.[177] It is easy to see why Bach replaced this movement in his harpsichord arrangement: the many sustained notes in the *Schäferkantate* Adagio would have been difficult to make convincing on the harpsichord.

The articulation of the solo part in the outer movements of the *NBA* reconstruction is not particularly plausible on hautbois d'amour, since it is taken over directly from the harpsichord version.[178]

---

[171] Cf. Breig (1993), 433–4. Breig reports that the bass part to the harpsichord arrangement was originally begun in C and later corrected to A, indicating an original model in C, probably the solo part.

[172] In the first movement, bars 59–65 were probably up an octave. Bar 62 was probably like 54, but the d♯s were down, along with the last four notes of the phrase. The e2 at 39–40 might have been as in the harpsichord version.

[173] BWV 249a/2 and *BC* G2/2.   [174] BWV 249/2 and *BC* D8a/2.

[175] Schulze and Wolff (1986–), iv. 1457. See also Brainard (1981), 55.

[176] Of 843 known 18th-c. hautboy concertos, only one in Herdringen by an anonymous writer uses B minor. See Haynes (1992a). For his last performances of this piece in the 1740s, Bach replaced the hautboy with traverso, on which B minor is a much more appropriate key.

[177] The string parts of 249a/2 must then have originally been down a fourth, which presents no problems as they were written within a very narrow range.

[178] Legato playing, for example, is generally best used in soft passages on an hautboy, and the reverse on a recorder or harpsichord. Some examples of inappropriate articulation are noted in Haynes (1992b).

3. *BWV 1056*

BWV 1056 in its surviving form is a pastiche. The first movement is thought to have been originally for violin.[179] It is not convincing on hautboy, as there are some troublesome octave changes and uncharacteristic passagework.

But for an unclear reason, there is a general assumption that the third movement was also originally for violin. It is this third movement in G minor (which was apparently its original key)[180] that is, of all these concerto movements, the most successful on hautboy. The harpsichord version seems to have changed it very little, as it can be played comfortably and convincingly on the hautboy without change. The harpsichord's range (bbo–d♭3) is too large for hautboy, but Siegele (1975: 130) shows that the autograph part contains several octave changes: one of these, a correction upwards, is at bars 165–7. Bars 165–83 can be played an octave lower without changing the musical intent, thus putting the movement easily within the hautboy's compass (c1–c3), and incidentally making it unlikely that it would have been originally conceived for violin.

The second movement of the same concerto, 1056/2, survives as a well-known hautboy solo in F major (BWV 156/1), and can be played comfortably on the hautboy in G, the relative major of the last movement.

4. *BWV 1059*

It has been suggested that BWV 1059 (which survives only as a fragment) was originally for hautboy. The title of the piece reads 'Concerto a Cembalo solo, una Oboe, due Violini, Viola e Cont.'[181] The few surviving bars correspond to the first of two sinfonias with obbligato organ in Cantata 35, *Geist und Seele wird verwirret*, which naturally suggest themselves as the two outer movements of a concerto.

BWV 1059 is more elaborate and interesting than Cantata 35/1. But because the fragment ends in the middle of bar nine and more space was available on the page, it appears that Bach never completed the work. It is nevertheless interesting to explore what he may have had in mind.

The wording of the title of BWV 1059 makes the role of the 'Oboe' ambiguous. The piece could have been for harpsichord with an accompaniment including

---

[179] Cf. Fischer (1971), 81 ff. On pp. 84–5, he reasons convincingly that the second movement in the harpsichord version was not part of the original violin concerto. See also Siegele (1975), 129–30.

[180] There is compelling evidence that the harpsichord version of the first movement of this concerto was originally in G minor. See Fischer (1971), 86 and Siegele (1975), 129. Bach may have put the piece in F minor in order to dampen the string instruments and thus give the harpsichord an advantage in balancing with an orchestra.

[181] Bach used the term 'Oboe' at Mühlhausen, at Weimar during a specific period (see above), but only rarely at Leipzig (cf. Terry 1932: 96). In the notes to his 1983 recording, Rifkin suggests that the piece originated in Weimar, in which case (because of Bach's terminology; see above) it would have been written between the end of 1713 and the end of 1714.

hautboy, or it could have been for both harpsichord and hautboy as soloists. The first possibility seems unlikely, as the piece in this form would have been as good or better without the hautboy, as in all the other harpsichord concertos. No purpose would have been served by increasing the already delicate balance problem between the orchestra and the harpsichord. Not only is the presence of the hautboy unexploited in such an instrumentation, but the possibilities for dialogue are lost.

I find the solo part unconvincing for an hautboy alone. But I have played it a number of times as a double concerto for hautboy and harpsichord, and suggest that this was its original instrumentation, for several reasons. First, the solo line contains elements of question and answer that imply the presence of two separate voices in dialogue. With this in mind, one notices that some passages lend themselves to the hautboy's technique while others do not.[182] Second, the solo part in the last movement never stops, which is not typical of Bach's wind writing.[183] Finally, there are precedents for the combination of solo hautboy with solo harpsichord in chamber pieces by several of Bach's contemporaries, including Förster, Schaffrath, and Telemann.

There is no sinfonia in BWV 35 that could serve as a slow movement for a concerto.[184] As a solution, Rifkin (1978) suggested the sinfonia mentioned above under BWV 1056, which is an hautboy solo in BWV 156/1 (in the requisite key, F major) and a harpsichord solo in BWV 1056/2. But that is a solo for a single instrument. Two other possible solutions are an improvised double cadenza (as in the third Brandenburg Concerto) or the use of BWV 1063/2, which fits well with the other two movements, not least because it also contains an element of dialogue similar to that of BWV 35/5.

5. *BWV 1060*

BWV 1060 may have been the piece mentioned above in the Breitkopf Catalogue of 1764. In the surviving version, which is for two harpsichords, the two solo parts are different enough from each other in range and phrasing to suggest that the original was for two different kinds of instrument. As long ago as 1886, Woldemar Voigt

---

[182] Cf. the first movement in the passage starting in bar 68, which ventures into extreme flat keys and includes the combination $d\flat 2$–$e\flat 2$. In the last movement, the passage at 65 through 84 could not have been originally conceived for a wind instrument (at least not by a composer of Bach's competence): it features two unnatural finger combinations on $b\flat 1$–$c2$ and $a1$–$b\flat 1$, uses $e\flat 2$ in a position that can lead to squeaking, and requires skips of a seventh and ninth. Other dubious passages in the last movement include bars 17–20 and 47–50.

[183] Played on hautboy alone, as Rifkin (1983) put it, 'it ranks as one of the two most demanding works in the entire Baroque oboe literature'. The music is not particularly virtuosic, however; the demands in question are the result of the fact that certain passages are inappropriate for hautboy.

[184] Winschermann's use of the aria no. 2 with the hautboy taking the voice part is not convincing as a purely instrumental piece. See also Siegele (1975), 144 and Rifkin (1978), 145.

proposed that the instruments in question were hautboy and violin. The piece has been published in this form a number of times.[185]

None of the movements is possible on hautboy higher than D minor or lower than C minor. In general, the piece feels better on hautboy in d minor, but in this key each movement has several awkward high d3s that can be avoided only by making illogical octave changes in the middle of sequences. From the perspective of the hautboy, therefore, C minor appears to be the original key.[186] Siegele (1975: 131) came to the same conclusion on the basis of source evidence.

Rifkin makes some observations on this concerto that would have important effects on a reconstruction.[187] The main issue is that the second movement in the harpsichord version does not belong to the original concerto,[188] and there is no available piece in the appropriate keys of E flat or C that could replace it.[189]

6. *The case for concerto reconstructions*

A total of fifteen movements might originally have been part of hautboy concertos that are now lost. They could be played in the following possible (fingered) keys:

C major:	BWV 1055/1, BWV 1055/3
F major:	BWV 1053/1, BWV 1053/3, BWV 1056/2, BWV 1063/2
G major:	BWV 1056/2
B flat major:	BWV 1056/2
C minor:	BWV 1053/2, BWV 1060/1, BWV 1060/3, BWV 21/1
D minor:	BWV 35/1, BWV 35/5, BWV 1053/2
G minor:	BWV 1056/3, BWV 12/1
A minor:	BWV 249a/2

These movements can be combined to reconstruct the following complete concertos:

BWV 1053a in D/B minor/D for hautbois d'amour (fingered F/D minor/F)

BWV 1055a in A/F sharp minor/A for hautbois d'amour (fingered C/A minor/C)

BWV 1059a in D minor/F/d minor for hautboy alone or hautboy and harpsichord

---

[185] See Fischer (1971), 100–7. Earlier reconstructions were published by Breitkopf und Härtel (Schneider, in D minor) and Peters (Seiffert, in C minor).

[186] Violinists with whom I have played this piece are divided in their opinions about the technical advantages of C minor and D minor.   [187] Rifkin (1999).

[188] Rifkin noticed that in the first and last movements, the first ripieno violin part almost always doubles one of the other treble parts, and that the earlier form with hautboy and violin therefore probably included only one ripieno violin. The slow movement, by contrast, not only demands a four-part string group, but (unlike the outer movements) gives the two solo instruments the same range and the same thematic material.

[189] The *NBA* reconstruction includes some questionable slurs, noted in Haynes (1992b).

Movements are now missing that are needed to complete BWV 1056a (a fast movement in G minor to go with BWV 1056/2 and 3), and BWV 1060a (a slow movement in E flat or C major, to go with BWV 1060/1 and 3). If these two concertos could be completed, all the movements that work on hautboy (except BWV 21/1 and BWV 12/1, which may never have been intended as concerto movements) could be incorporated in plausible concerto reconstructions.[190]

No one has yet been able convincingly to date the origins of these concertos. The latest thinking puts four of them in the Leipzig period: BWV 1053a and BWV 1059a in the second half of 1726 (when, for unknown reasons, Bach's cantata production had slowed down),[191] and BWV 1056a (by association with BWV 156/1) in early 1729.[192] If the reasoning about the second movement of BWV 1055 outlined above is correct, that concerto must have predated February 1725.[193] No precise date can yet be ascribed to BWV 1060a. If these concertos were written in Leipzig, they might have been played by Gleditsch, Böhm, or Richter.

---

[190] The 'Italian Concerto', BWV 971 (in F), a piece probably written originally for harpsichord, also goes well on hautboy. (This might be called an 'extabulation', as it reverses the common practice of keyboard intabulation.)

[191] Butler (1995). The cantata arrangements of these movements were performed on 20 Oct. and 3 Nov. 1726. The cantata versions of BWV 1059a were performed on 8 Sept. 1726; cf., however, Rifkin's suggestion (cited in n. 182 above) that this piece was written in Weimar.

[192] Gregory G. Butler (pers. comm.) considers BWV 1055 a work of the Leipzig period.

[193] This is the date that the *Schäferkantate* movement derived from it was performed.

7

1730–1760: Italian Ascendancy and the Rise of the Narrow-Bore Hautboy

The period from about 1730 to 1760 troubles music historians. Although it has many names ('galant', 'rococo'), there is no single, universally accepted one, probably because its essential spirit and aesthetic is so difficult to characterize. It is hardly satisfying to call it either 'post-Baroque' or 'pre-Classical'. What is appealing about it is in fact the way it combines elements of both these styles. In the history of the hautboy, however, it has many characteristics that distinguish it from the periods before and after it.

First, it was dominated by great Italian virtuosos of the instrument, who 'swept out of Italy and conquered all of Europe'.[1] Wherever one looks, Italians were playing solos in important musical centres. In Paris, the appearance of the Besozzi brothers at the *Concert Spirituel* in 1735 changed the French hautboy world decisively. In Germany, Italians like Platti, Antonio Besozzi, the Ferrandinis, Schiavonetti, Stazzi, Carlo Besozzi, Secchi, Ciceri, and Colombazzi transformed the hautboy's image. At the court in Vienna (which was the major centre of Italian music outside Italy), there is little documentation of Italian players besides Gazzaroli and Colombazzi (at Esterháza), but Austrian hautboy makers, supplying a growing demand, were clearly reacting to developments in Italy. In England, Italians included Barsanti, Mancinelli, Giustinelli, and of course Sammartini, who left a lasting impression on players and audiences.

Naturally, there were fine players who were not Italian, and the dominance of Italians was far from complete. But it is a fact that in this period, no other country was represented by so many remarkable players of the hautboy. From our present perspective, the great players of this period seem to have been

Alessandro, Antonio, and Gaetano Besozzi
Matteo Bissoli
François Bureau
Esprit-Philippe and Nicolas Chédeville
Jean-François Despréaux
Nicolas Lavaux

---

[1] Zaslaw (1989), 1 (speaking in fact of Italian opera and instrumental music beginning in the 1740s).

Johann Christian Jacobi
Alexander Lebrun
Jacob Loeillet
Joan Baptista Pla
Ignazio and Filippo Prover
Nicolas Sallantin
Giuseppe Sammartini
Richard Vincent and Thomas Vincent jun.
Christian Ferdinand Wunderlich

The French, who had been at the forefront of players from the beginning, offered the only serious competition to the Italians. But none of the great French players seems to have gone further from Paris than Versailles. The Italians (who may have considered the French fortunate not to have had to leave home) were in key positions in every country.

Two other aspects that make the 1730s, 1740s, and 1750s unique have to do with the instruments that were used. This period saw the fragmentation of the general unifying concept of an archetypal 'French hautboy', personified by Type A2, into several distinct models.[2] Type A2 was abandoned by all but the more conservative makers and players. By the 1730s the Italians had developed the straight-top Type C and, probably somewhat later, the Type D1 (see Pl. 2.1). Type C became popular in England, along with Type B. The French developed the new Type E. Given our sketchy ability to date hautboys, it is not possible to be specific about dates, but the indications are that the music of this period was mostly played on these new models: Types B, C, E, and D1. Anciuti had made a Type C by at least 1738,[3] and many of Palanca's Type D1 instruments must have been made well before the 1770s.[4]

As different as these various new types were in outward turning style and pitch level, they generally had one important thing in common, which was the third characteristic of this period: a distinctly narrower bore. While Type A2 had an average minimum bore of 6 mm or larger, and Type B could also be quite wide, Type E and Type D1 instruments scarcely averaged wider than 5 mm.[5] This period thus saw the rise of the narrow-bore hautboy.

---

[2] For a discussion of these various models, see Ch. 2, §B.4.   [3] Y6, Rome 1094, dated 1738.

[4] Carlo Palanca's instruments are not dated, but by 1770 he was in his 80s; he had retired as a player in 1770. In his will there is mention of blindness ('la mancanza di vista'), which may have begun some years before (Bernardini 1985b: 22). Da Silva ordered two hautboys in 1773 (see Ch. 2, §D.3 and McClymonds 1978: 42), but only received one of them, partly old, in 1776, suggesting that Palanca was working only in a limited way by these dates.

[5] To put that into historical context, hautboys in the period 1760–1820 were at about 4.8; the modern key-system oboe is about 4.2. Of the eight Type E hautboys for which I have minimum bore dimensions, six (by Prudent, Lot, Schlegel, and Rottenburgh) average 4.94. Two others by Bizey and Rottenburgh are at 5.95 and 6.2. The minimum bores of Palanca hautboys range from 4.8 to 5.4 mm, and average 5.2 mm (Alfredo Bernardini, pers. comm.). Type D1 hautboys by Sattler and Baur are at 5.1 and 5.45.

It was not mere chance that two of these new models came out of northern Italy, or that they had such immediate success in the rest of Europe. They were of course brought out by the Italian virtuosos, who very convincingly demonstrated their qualities for the music they were playing. The thrust of much of the playing of Italian hautboists was virtuosic display and extension of the limits of technique; it was therefore logical that experimental instruments would be made by Italians. Italian music was also experimental, showing classical traits relatively early in the century (Pergolesi, for instance, who is often thought of as a classical composer, lived only until 1736).

London adopted Type B and fell under the sway of the Italian Type C (probably because Giuseppe Sammartini used it). In Paris the Type E was evidently the instrument in general use. The Germans do not seem to have been tempted by these models, but instead stayed with A2 models or went directly over to Type D1.

To players of these various mid-eighteenth century hautboy types, they were 'state of the art'. To us, removed from them by 250 years, they are as yet an enigma scarcely identified, much less copied and played.

It is clear that these models were abandoned relatively quickly. Type B has barely survived, suggesting that its history was relatively short-lived. Type E, apparently developed in France and used mostly there, has yet to be studied and understood. Type C, the straight-top, enjoyed great popularity in England until the end of the century. It gradually lost ground, as all these models did, to the 'classical' hautboy (Halfpenny's Type D)[6] that came to be the most popular everywhere after 1770.

The fragmentation of the period 1730–70 thus gave way to a relative uniformity throughout Europe at the end of the century. Also with hindsight, the model that appears to have been the direct antecedent to the classical hautboy was the Type D1, developed by Italian makers such as Carlo Palanca. Palanca's hautboys appear as midway between the extremes of the Baroque and the classical designs, being turned to the traditional pattern, but smaller in size, and showing fine attention to turning details and a concern for a more literal use of the classical principles of proportion.[7] Less obvious to the eye are the narrower bore and thinner walls.[8]

Thinner walls make the instrument sound brighter and cause the tone-hole chimneys to be shorter, thus producing a higher pitch.[9] As far as we can now tell, these newer models with thin sidewalls, a narrow bore, and using smaller reeds, produced a different sound than the Baroque A2 hautboys. The tone was narrower and more focused. They played more softly, especially in the upper register, and they were

---

[6] Halfpenny (1949b).   [7] Cf. Adkins (1999).

[8] Olivier Cottet (pers. comm.) also points out that classical hautboy bores have a narrower conicity, or taper; that tendency may have begun in the period 1730–60.

[9] This is parallel to the development of the mid-17th-c. hautboy, which had thinner walls than the shawm and thus shorter tone-holes.

extremely sensitive to intonation corrections and choice of fingering.[10] They also played the high notes more easily.[11] The hautboys of this period were built to be agile and mercurial rather than, as in earlier generations, rich and sensuous.

Palanca was not alone; there were other makers in Italy who produced instruments of this type. As Alfredo Bernardini points out (pers. comm.), Anciuti's hautboys already show thinner sidewalls than contemporary French and German instruments, and a number of other makers, including Panormo, Castel, the Biglionis, Grassi, Bertani, Cortellone, and Perosa, were active in this period. While there is a reasonable amount of documentation on Palanca, and as a maker he was probably known beyond the Alps, little has yet been found about other Italian makers and their role in developing Types C and D1. But we are fortunate in having nineteen of Palanca's surviving hautboys, a relatively large number, and his production can serve as a case in point.

Palanca was working closely with a great player, Alessandro Besozzi. In Turin, they played together for many years. It can be assumed that Palanca made hautboys for Besozzi, and that Besozzi advised him (cf. the order by Pinto da Silva quoted in Ch. 2, §D.3: 'From Turin we would like two hautboys made by Palanca and checked by Mr Besozzi . . .'). Whether or not he was the innovator he appears to have been, his instruments can be taken as representative of the Italian model of hautboy in mid-century (Pls. 2.11 and 2.1(*g*)). It is likely that other Turinese double-reed players used his instruments. And it is quite possible that Alessandro Besozzi's brother in Naples, Giuseppe, and Giuseppe's two sons Antonio and Gaetano, got their hautboys from Palanca.

Palanca's instruments may also have travelled with Italian players as they performed in other parts of Europe. Although Sammartini probably worked with Anciuti in Milan (Anciuti was active until at least 1740, Sammartini until 1750), the Besozzi brothers presumably used a Palanca hautboy and bassoon in the duets they performed in Paris in 1735. And if Antonio Besozzi had a Palanca in Naples when he played for Hasse, he would have taken it with him when he was hired by the Dresden court in 1738. When Giacomo Palanca performed an hautboy concerto by Besozzi at the *Concert Spirituel* in 1754, it is likely he played one of Carlo's hautboys, and Filippo Prover, who had had a post at Turin, probably took a Palanca hautboy to Paris in the late 1750s. The 'applaudissements' at the *Concert Spirituel* in 1757 for Antonio Besozzi and his son Carlo may also have been for their Palanca hautboys.

---

[10] Alfredo Bernardini (pers. comm.) is not entirely convinced of these comments, but writes 'What seems to me rather definite, is that their sound is more penetrating than that of baroque oboes.'

[11] A marked rise in tessitura is the technical element that most differentiates late 18th-c. hautboy music from earlier works. (A rise in tonality, i.e. towards sharper keys, can also be detected; see Haynes 1989: 10.) Cf. Ch. 4, §F.3.

A year after Antonio Besozzi was appointed principal hautboy at Dresden, Augustin Grenser moved to Dresden, and Jakob Grundmann followed him in the early 1750s. These two makers were to dominate the hautboy market in much of Europe during the last quarter of the eighteenth century. It is likely they went to Dresden to work with Besozzi and to learn more of his Italian instrument(s), which they then developed further together. The earliest surviving Grensers and Grundmanns closely resemble the instruments of Palanca and Panormo. Thus Italian hautboys probably served as the inspiration for the hautboys developed by these German makers, that were used extensively in Europe after 1770.

In terms of repertoire, there is a natural division around the year 1730. The most dramatic difference was in France, with what I call here the contrasting styles of Louis Quatorze and Louis Quinze (see Ch. 5, §§B.1 and 2, and below, §B.1). The solos of Alessandro Besozzi and Bissoli are examples of how different the Italian solo repertoire became after 1730; Sammartini's two collections, one before and one after this approximate date, are also in clear contrast. In Germany, Sebastian Bach had virtually finished writing hautboy solos by 1730, and his son Emanuel's 'Hoboe solo' (of 1731?) is the first early illustration of the new galant style in the German hautboy repertoire; Telemann's solos in the *Musique de table* (1733) also differ clearly from those in the *Getreue Music-Meister* (1728–9).[12] In England, Vincent's solos (1748) are in clear stylistic contrast to Babell's of the mid-1720s.

Two other important changes that mark the end of this period have to do with pitch and technique. Pitch was moving towards a relatively universal standard of A+0, which was achieved by about 1770. It was probably no accident that A+0 had been traditional in Venice and northern Italy; its adoption all over Europe was no doubt the result of the important role of travelling Italian virtuosos in the period just before. In addition, the decade or two before 1770 saw the general adoption of the new fingerings for the high notes, presumably connected with the instruments and reeds being played (see Ch. 4, §G.6).

The development into the Classical period was gradual, and there was no clear line of demarcation. This ambiguity is reflected in the music of the decade 1760–70. By this time, some music was already 'classic' in compositional style, but pieces like the Prover, Kirnberger, and Matthes sonatas, the Emanuel Bach concertos, Hertel trios, etc. were still in an older style, and often continued to use a figured bass (which had already been abandoned in some places).

Between 1730 and 1760 more solo and chamber music for hautboy survives than from any other single period. The kinds of music the hautboy played in these decades shifted somewhat. By 1760 the two original genres in which the hautboy had thrived in the seventeenth century, band music and arias with voice, had

---

[12] Cf. Haynes (1992a).

virtually disappeared. Very little hautboy band music is preserved from after 1730, in contrast to the abundance of the previous period. Many small chamber works were produced, however, and more than half of all the concertos written for hautboy come from after 1730. There were also many solo sonatas with continuo (a medium that was soon to be replaced by the hautboy quartet).

This period is also distinguished by the relatively large proportion of published music for hautboy. Nearly half of all the hautboy music that was ever printed appeared between 1730 and 1760 (well over 2,000 published pieces survive). A piece of published music was rather more expensive then than now. To judge from Walsh's prices and the amount musicians earned in the same period,[13] a set of six solo sonatas would have been about £32 or US$50 (as of the year 2000), and a concerto about £64 or $100.

The personal tragedy of a good locally established player replaced by an Italian virtuoso, and coming to a melancholy end a few years later, seems sadly similar in the cases of Kytch in London and Richter in Dresden, eclipsed respectively by Sammartini and Antonio Besozzi (see below). The Italian wave was irresistible, and these were signs of things to come.

A. Italy

Considering what happened afterwards, it is curious that Quantz met so few good hautboy players on his visit to Italy in 1726. He wrote of Milan:

Es fehlete aber auch hier, so wie in ganz Italien an Bässen, und, den guten Hoboisten San Martino ausgenommen, auch an Blasinstrumenten . . .[14]	Here too, as in all of Italy, no basses could be found; the same was true of wind instruments (excepting the excellent San Martino) . . .

Penati, Sieber, and several of the Besozzis apparently escaped Quantz's notice.[15] Wollenberg (1993: 345) notes that Austrian 'court agents acted on the Habsburgs' behalf in Italy, looking for suitable musicians to import'. They did not, apparently, find any hautboy players; at least, no hautboists with Italian names appear in Habsburg court documents.

It is possible that native players of talent could find little work in Italy itself, and had already left. Penati was the only hautboy player at San Marco in Venice, Bissoli the only one at Sant'Antonio in Padua. Besides these rare church positions, teaching at conservatories in Venice and Naples, and the courts in Naples, Florence, and Turin, there seem to have been few institutions able to offer regular financial

---

[13] Lasocki (1997), 353.   [14] Quantz (1755), 236.
[15] Quantz does mention both Erdmann and Besozzi elsewhere in his book.

support to woodwind players. With the exception of Milan, performances of instrumental music were rare in Italy in this period. Nor were there paid public concerts anywhere.[16] But considering the amount of opera, by the 1730s and 1740s there were probably many players who earned their livings playing in theatres in Milan, Venice, Florence, Rome, Naples, and elsewhere.

Alfredo Bernardini's pioneering and enlightening researches make clear how much more there is still to learn about the hautboy in Italy. As Bernardini's discoveries have indicated, there was a great deal happening there. Italy was a vast cornucopia of music in this period, and there are undiscovered virtuosos, probably a good deal of music, and some instrument makers about whom we have yet to learn.

1. Turin

The break-up in 1731 of the *Guardia Irlandese*, Duke Farnese of Parma's hautboy band, was to be of considerable consequence to other court musical establishments in Italy. The Duke's band had been staffed by members of the Besozzi family (see Ch. 5, §C.3). Two courts in Italy wealthy enough to support the presence of hautboy virtuosos were Turin and Naples. So at this point the family dispersed, and Alessandro and Paolo Girolamo (who played hautboy and bassoon) went to Turin.

Turin had had a long tradition of hautboy playing (see Ch. 3, §B), which was re-enforced by the arrival of the Besozzis, who were active there for many decades—Alessandro until the mid-1770s.[17] The two brothers made a speciality of playing duets together, which were evidently quite amazing to hear. Charles Burney, who many years later visited them in Turin and heard them play, wrote:

Their compositions when printed, give but an imperfect idea of [their style of playing]. So much expression! such delicacy! such a perfect acquiescence and agreement together, that many of the passages seem heart-felt sighs, breathed through the same reed. No brilliancy of execution is aimed at, all are notes of meaning. The imitations are exact; the melody is pretty equally distributed between the two instruments; each *forte*, *piano*, *crescendo*, *diminuendo*, and *appoggiatura*, is observed with a minute exactness, which could be attained only by such a long residence and study together.[18]

The Besozzis' spectacular success at the *Concert Spirituel* will be described in the next section. Apparently, they made no further tours. In 1775, Alessandro was appointed (together with Pugnani) 'Direttore Generale della Musica Strumentale' at court, at a high salary (Pl. 7.1).

[16] According to Libby (1989), 22, however, 'any respectable citizen or well-recommended tourist could attend the many concerts in private houses in celebration of weddings, baptisms, name days and other such occasions, often with specially composed music'.   [17] Ch. 3 of Wind (1982) is a biography of Alessandro Besozzi.
[18] Burney (1771a), 70 ff.

PL. 7.1. Charles Van Loo, portrait of Alessandro Besozzi (drawing).
Novara: Ex Collezione Trecate (present whereabouts unknown)

Alessandro Besozzi is survived by a number of hautboy compositions, including duets for two hautboys. Only one of his 'little conversations'[19] for hautboy and bassoon is known to survive (and that, of course, merely on paper). His *Six Solos with Continuo* were published in London in 1759; they are all good, especially the second and sixth.[20] Although they were advertised for the more commercially viable formula of 'German Flute, Hautboy, or Violin', they were probably conceived for hautboy. Considering the relation between traverso and hautboy tonalities (see Ch. 4, §H.2), it is likely he transposed at least some of them up a step for the edition. In these higher keys they are more difficult on hautboy, and even no. 6 in C sounds better in B flat (the only exception is no. 5, which lies better in D than C). Sonata 3 ascends to e3, and all of them have a high tessitura. It is clear from some of his other music that Besozzi could play the low c♯1s that are occasioned by transposing these pieces down a step for hautboy. (Incidentally, as in other later eighteenth-century music, a mute is effective in some slow movements.)

Italian hautboy solos often imitated the standard Italian vocal genres of the day. The convention in *opera seria* was that the *primo uomo* (that is, the first castrato) sang

---

[19] See the quotation by de Brosses in §B.1 below.
[20] No. 6 is preserved in a manuscript in DK-Kk as by 'Sigre Graun'.

his *aria di bravura* in the first act, the *aria cantabile* in the second, and an *aria grazioso* in the third.[21] As a metaphorical singer, the hautboy player often evoked (consciously or not) vocal styles like the *bravura* or *brillante*, the *cantabile*, and the *grazioso*; Italian hautboy sonatas and concertos regularly follow the same order in their movements, with a fast first (or second) movement full of technical display (the Allegro), a pathetic, touching slow movement (the Adagio), and a light, gracious menuet to end.

Besozzi also wrote sonatas for two hautboys and continuo, which until recently were known only by their incipits in the Breitkopf catalogue.[22] But they survive in versions for other instruments (sometimes as individual movements),[23] and it has been possible to reconstruct them by matching the Breitkopf incipits.[24] A number of his other surviving trio collections include hautboy.

Besozzi is also survived by several hautboy concertos. The fifth concerto in G from his six hautboy concertos was mentioned above in Ch. 4, §G.2.a. There are two surviving manuscripts. It is a pleasant, moderately interesting piece that never goes above d3. The title-page to the London copy states that it was performed by Fischer in Warsaw in 1757. The Regensburg manuscript contains ornamented readings of some passages and numerous cadenzas that were probably written by Palestrini, an hautboy player in intermittent service at Regensburg from 1774.[25]

The court orchestra at Turin was famous for its outstanding musicians. The pay lists for the theatre orchestra in 1747–8 show that the two top salaries (500 lire) went to Alessandro Besozzi and the concertmaster or leader, Somis; the next highest salaries were 300 lire. Plate 7.2 by Olivero shows the Turin orchestra performing an opera by Feo for the opening of the Teatro Regio on the day after Christmas, 1740. Two hautboy players and two bassoonists are visible. The court and theatre orchestras were not identical; the Besozzi brothers were members of both, while one of the hautboy players in the theatre orchestra, Ignazio Prover, played violin at the court.[26] In 1740, the bassoonists shown in Olivero's painting were probably Girolamo Besozzi and Carlo Palanca, the hautboists Alessandro Besozzi and Ignazio Prover.

Carlo Palanca learned instrument making from his father Giovanni (born *c.*1645), who was a woodwind maker working at Turin in 1705.[27] Besides Palanca, another member of the chapel, Carlo Antonio Ferreri, was probably an instrument maker.

[21] Libby (1989), 18.   [22] 1770: 22 (399).

[23] In a violin manuscript now in Berkeley and Opus 3 and Opus 4 (sometimes in other keys).

[24] Haynes (1992a), 67.

[25] The two alternative versions thus offer insights into how ornaments were added by hautboy players in the 1770s. The cadenzas are variants of one another in layers, the later ones being somewhat more elaborate versions inspired by ideas in the earlier ones. The cadenzas are transcribed in Lasocki (1972), 144–7, and they and the variant readings are included in the edition Lasocki prepared for Musica Rara.   [26] Wind (1982), 25.

[27] This information thanks to Alfredo Bernardini, citing Francesca Odling, 'La costruzione degli strumenti a fiato a Torino fra '700 e '800', *Quaderni della Regione Piemonte, Artigianato*, 2/11 (Oct. 1997), 45.

PL. 7.2. Pietro Domenico Olivero, 26 Dec. 1740, interior of the
Teatro Regio, Turin, during a performance of Feo's opera
Arsace. Turin: Museo Civico d'Arte Antica

Ferreri was also called 'Deiardin', 'Dujardin', and 'Giardini', and may originally
have been French. Two flauti d'amore survive with the mark 'Deiardin a Turin'. A
father and son 'Dujardin' were listed with the two Besozzis as playing in an opera
at Turin in 1736,[28] and Ferreri and his son may have been among the players shown
in an engraving of a performance of an opera by Fiorè in Turin in 1722.[29]

In 1755 Gioseffo Secchi temporarily joined the Turin Cappella. Secchi eventually succeeded Alessandro Besozzi as principal hautboy, but between 1765 and
1776 he had a distinguished solo career at Munich.

---

[28] Bouquet (1976), 133.

[29] Antoine Aveline (Dresden: Kupferstichkabinett, Staatliche Museen, A. 1050, 3, reproduced in Bowles (1989),
fig. 206). Three hautboists are visible (besides the Ferreris, they could have been Gio. Francesco Mattis or Daniel
Perrin).

PL. 7.3. Antonio Jolli, 1 Mar. 1740, detail from design for a stage
set at the Teatro Grimani a S. Giovanni Grisostomo, Venice.
Dresden: Kupferstich-Kabinett, C 1979-720

2. *Venice*

A number of players were active in Venice in this period. One of them was car-
icatured by Ghezzi (Pl. 2.20), who described him as '. . . bravissimo, performed at
the Teatro della Valle (Rome) in the Carnival of 1751 and has performed at my
Accademia. His name is Gioseppe and he is Venetian.' At least three hautboy
players are depicted in the orchestra shown with Antonio Jolli's spectacular stage
set at the Teatro Grimani at Venice in 1740 (Pl. 7.3).

Some players evidently earned their livings in the opera houses. From the 1740s
there were six theatres in Venice that presented opera.[30] There is an aria with hautboy obbligato in Nicolo Jommelli's *Semiramide*, performed in Venice in 1742, and
there may be many obbligatos still to be discovered in the operas of Leo, Vinci, and
Porpora.

Players may also have worked in churches. Even in this period, despite economic and political decline, Venetian church music was grand and impressive on
important feast days and special occasions. Penati and (after he retired in 1748) Sieber

---

[30] Libby (1989), 45.

were officially employed at San Marco,[31] but additional players would sometimes have been brought in; other churches may also have used hautboys occasionally.

The four conservatories performed Vespers on Saturdays and Sundays, which were one of the main tourist attractions of the city. Since they were not considered sacred services, instrumental solo concertos alternated with vocal music. An unusual aspect of these concerts was that all the performers were female (the girl orphans) in a period when few women except opera singers were professional musicians.

Bernardini points out (1988: 377) the scarcity of hautboy music from Venice in this period. Vivaldi adapted several concertos[32] 'Fag. ridotto per Haut.'[33] (reduced for hautboy from bassoon) in the 1730s. Some passages were rewritten to fit the smaller range of the hautboy compared with the bassoon, busy figures were sometimes simplified, and the large leaps that sound so good on bassoon were turned into more lyrical lines for the hautboy. The bassoon concerto RV 470, for instance, was 'reduced' in this way to make RV 448, which is a less successful piece on hautboy but fairly easy to play. In the first movement, octave and larger leaps in the bassoon became thirds for the hautboy. In fact, Vivaldi used the orchestral parts in the first and second movements but wrote an entirely new solo line over them. The third movement followed very closely the bassoon line, but condensed the octaves in both directions.

From one of these two sources, either directly from the bassoon concerto or as an elaboration of the hautboy version, Vivaldi created RV 447, which is among his most attractive hautboy concertos. It is more complex than either of the others, having many more notes in the first movement. Its last movement is a new piece, a delightful minuet with variations.

Three of the hautboy ateliers active in northern Italy in this period may have been located in Venice. Two good instruments by Castel are now in France and Germany. The differing stamps suggest that several makers were associated with this workshop, which probably existed from the second quarter of the eighteenth century.[34] The hautboy by Cosins was mentioned above. A three-keyed hautboy by 'Perosa' survives, and may have been made by Marco Perosa, an hautboy player at San Marco *c*.1760, or a member of his family.

3. Padua

Padua is very close to Venice, and Penati played there regularly from 1705 to 1721 and irregularly until 1745. Giacomo Rampini was from Padua, and his two hautboy concertos in the Roger publication of 1716 may have been written for Penati.

---

[31] Sieber was officially on the rolls until 1760, but had probably stopped playing by 1757 (Cf. Bernardini 1985a: 19).   [32] Cf. RV 447, RV 448, RV 450, RV 457, and RV 463.

[33] This description appears on Vivaldi's autograph score of RV 457. See Kolneder (1952), 45 and (1979), 151.

[34] Waterhouse (1993), 58.

In 1736, a full-time hautboy post was established at Sant'Antonio (the Santo) with the appointment of Matteo Bissoli. Bissoli played at the Santo until about 1780.[35] He was mentioned in a poem by Vincenzo Rota written in 1753:

Il gran Matteo più che uman diletto Presta nei cor col suo foruto bosso.[36]	The great Matteo gives more than human delight To the heart with his perforated boxwood.

His 'perforated boxwood' was, as can be seen in his portrait (Pl. 2.21), a Type C hautboy. Bissoli's excellent hautboy sonata in G minor, probably written about 1750, is a virtuoso display piece full of unusual harmonies, and the earliest known composition to use f3.

Bissoli was a close colleague of Tartini and the Maestro di Cappella, Vallotti. Vallotti's arias with obbligato hautboy were probably written for him. There was a correspondence in the 1740s between Vallotti and the physicist Riccati about Bissoli and his reeds (see Ch. 2, §E.4.e).

4. *Florence*

Erdmann continued to play at Florence, remaining on the ducal *ruolo* until 1757. Although principally an hautboy player, at his death in 1759 he was called 'un bravo virtuoso d'oboe et altri istrumenti di fiato' (a fine virtuoso on the hautboy and other wind instruments).[37]

With the death of the last Medici Grand Duke in 1737, Tuscany was ceded to Francis of Lorraine. Shortly afterwards (1739) there is documentation of the presence in Lucca of Nicolas Dôthel (Dôthel le fils), an hautboy player from Lorraine who later became well known as a flutist.[38] Dôthel was in Florence by 1746, and may have played both flute and hautboy together with Erdmann.

5. *Rome*

Jommelli put on the opera *Astianatte* at the Argentina Theatre in Rome in February 1741,[39] and included an aria with hautboy obbligato, 'O lieta saprò'. Ghezzi wrote under a caricature he made of Jommelli that one of the singers in *Astianatte* was 'Gaetano Basteri[, who] did the part of Pilade and has a tenor voice of such great agility that he sang like a soprano, and his father, who played the oboe in the orchestra, has no equal in Rome.'[40]

A number of other hautboy players were active in Rome in this period; they are listed in Appendix 1. Hautboys were also made there; three hautboys marked

---

[35] Bissoli was praised by Burney (1771a: 70). Cf. Bernardini (1987), 5, 15–16.
[36] From *L'Incendio del tempio di S. Antonio*, quoted in Bernardini (1985a), 22.   [37] Kirkendale (1993), 449.
[38] See Graziadei (1988).   [39] Bernardini (1985a), 29.   [40] Quoted in McClymonds (1978), 2.

/Biglioni/in Roma/ survive. The family consisted of players as well as makers, three of whom were active before 1760.[41]

6. Naples

Naples in this period was by far the largest city in Italy, more than twice the size of the next largest, Venice.[42] It was also the leading musical centre. While careers for hautboists were available in church *cappelle* or by teaching at the conservatories, the most prestigious work was at the court and the Teatro San Carlo.

When Antonio Besozzi moved to the Naples court in 1731, he was 17. He is probably the hautboist shown playing with the group of musicians welcoming Carlo Borbone to Naples in May 1734 (Pl. 4.8). By that year, Antonio's father Giuseppe also held an appointment at Naples. The delay in the appointment of Giuseppe may have been because of problems with his eyes, which four years later in 1738 forced him to retire from the orchestra at the age of 52; he remained in Naples, teaching, until his death in 1760. Giuseppe was probably the teacher of three of the most important players in the Besozzi family: his younger brother Alessandro[43] (at Turin) and his sons Antonio and Gaetano.

Giuseppe's blindness may have caused both his sons to take important positions as soloists at the court in place of their father at remarkably young ages. Pergolesi included an aria (Amoroso), 'Lieto cosi tal volta', for soprano, hautboy, and orchestra in his opera *Adriano in Siria*, produced in Naples in October 1734. It is unclear whether it was played by Giuseppe or Antonio. The aria features cadenzas for each of the soloists plus a double cadenza for both together. There is considerable chromatic writing, but the general *Affect* is light, and similar to Jommelli. Bird imitations appear in the hautboy part.

Hasse (soon to be appointed Maestro di Cappella in Dresden) was in Naples in 1732, and probably heard Antonio Besozzi play there. An hautboy concerto by Hasse survives (of not very impressive musical content), which may have been adapted[44] for Antonio in this period. In 1738 (at the age of 24), Antonio was engaged as solo hautboy at Dresden, and was to become probably the most celebrated hautboist in Germany.[45] Hasse no doubt had something to do with this appointment: the courts of Naples and Dresden were also allied by marriage that same year.

---

[41] Information from Alfredo Bernardini (pers. comm.), citing R. Meucci, 'La costruzione di strumenti musicali a Roma tra XVII e XIX secolo, con notizie inedite sulla famiglia Biglioni', in *La musica a Roma attraverso le fonti d'archivio: Atti del Convegno internazionale, Roma 4–7 giugno 1992*, ed. Bianca Maria Antolini, Arnaldo Morelli, and Vera Vita Spagnuolo (Lucca, 1994), 581–93. [42] Libby (1989), 20.

[43] Cf. Wind (1982), 20. Giuseppe was 16 years older than Alessandro.

[44] The probable slur from d2 to b♭2 in II: 49 suggests that the concerto was not originally written for hautboy.

[45] Alfredo Bernardini reports that Antonio was forced to leave Naples in 1736 because of a scandalous marriage with 'una donna di pessima fama'. He cites U. P. Giurleo, *La grande orchestra del R. Teatro San Carlo nel Settecento* (1927), 13.

The Teatro San Carlo, the court theatre and venue of *opera seria*, had opened in 1737. Although there were a number of other *teatrini* presenting comic opera that may have hired hautboy players, San Carlo became the city's most important theatre. Presumably, it was the court musicians who played in its orchestra. For reasons just mentioned, both Giuseppe and Antonio Besozzi had left this orchestra by 1738. Perhaps as early as 1736, Giuseppe's younger son Gaetano (who was later to become the premier hautboist of Paris) began playing at court, when he was all of 9 years old. He eventually became the court's principal hautboy, serving until 1765, when at the age of 38 he moved to Paris.

In the landscape of European hautboy players after 1730, members of the Besozzi family are prominent. It seems a remarkable coincidence that so many Besozzis —Alessandro and Paolo Girolamo in Turin, Giuseppe, Antonio, and Gaetano in Naples, and later Antonio and Carlo in Dresden and Gaetano in Paris and London—should have achieved such extraordinary success in a field teeming with competition. Their excellent reputations in different venues all over Europe attest to their qualities as players. Probably more was involved than genetics (and starting to practise at the age of 6, with Papa's old reeds). Perhaps they had the best instruments available. And their formula for approaching the instrument, the method of making reeds and developing a technique, must have been brilliant and something of a trade secret. This formula may owe a good deal to Giuseppe Besozzi, who passed it on to Alessandro, Antonio, and Gaetano. Antonio's son Carlo was later greatly esteemed as a teacher; he was the last major exponent of the Besozzi school (his *Études* are still studied today on the key-system oboe).

The hautboy concertos of Gianpaolo di Domenico, who wrote a number of comic operas in Naples and died in 1740, may have been written for one of the Besozzis.

By the eighteenth century, the schools of music in Naples that had originated as orphanages had become famous all over Italy and abroad, and eventually each of them offered a teaching position that would help stabilize a professional player's income. The names of a number of players and teachers who worked in Naples during this period are listed in Appendix 1.

As for instruments, the only known surviving hautboy possibly made in Naples in this period is by Joannes (Giovanni) Panormo. Through the connections with the Besozzis at Turin, Palanca's instruments may also have been played in Naples.

B. France

1. The Louis Quinze style (from c.1726)

As in all the other countries of Europe, the arrival of Italian hautboy players in France caused a sensation. The first were the Besozzi brothers from Turin, who came to Paris in the spring of 1735. This tour (which was apparently the only one they ever made) may have been organized with the help of Hotteterre le Romain, who was in Turin some time between 1730 and 1735.[46] The hautboy had not previously been regarded in France as an instrument on which to play solos of the new Italian type, conceived as vehicles for displaying dexterity and skilfulness. The Besozzis' approach (and no doubt their skill and sensitivity) were a revelation, and their success was spectacular.[47] They played repeatedly, and were rewarded by the Académie Royale with 100 gold Louis each. By the time they left for home, they had probably permanently changed the course of French hautboy playing. One contemporary description of their playing is as follows:

les deux Bezzuzzi, l'un hautbois, l'autre basson, qui eurent ensemble de petites conversations musicales dont il fallait pâmer d'aise. Je ne puis vous exprimer les ravissements où cela jette. Je n'ai rien éprouvé en ma vie de plus enchanteur . . .[48]	the two Bezzuzzi, the one oboist and the other bassoonist, who held little musical conversations together, which almost make one swoon with enjoyment; I cannot express the raptures into which one is thrown. I have never in my life experienced anything more enchanting . . .[49]

Their concerts were discussed forty-five years later in a music dictionary, the *Essai sur la musique*.[50]

The success of the Besozzis and the musical climate in Paris, represented by the 'Querelle des Bouffons', gave Italian music and musicians special interest. From 1735 Alessandro Besozzi's music was regularly published there.[51] And some of the rising stars of Italy began arriving. The great impression left by the Besozzis led to the engagement of Ignazio Cézar at the *Concert Spirituel* the next year. Cézar was hired as house hautboy by La Pouplinière. A set of trios by Tommaso Prota of Naples was published in Paris in 1751 (Prota's brother Giuseppe was later a well-known player). Other hautboy players from abroad performed in Paris in this period, and some stayed to have active careers.

In France, the vogue for things foreign was probably part of a reaction to the oppressive uniformity of the end of Louis XIV's reign. While in around 1730 the composer Jacques Aubert lamented the loss of 'les grâces, la netteté et la belle simplicité du goût Français',[52] others were enjoying the gossamer delicacy of a new aesthetic that was a direct backlash to the music of the older style. That explains how Couperin's noble and sage *Nations* could appear in the same year (1726) that

---

[46] See Bernardini (1985b), 24 citing Bouquet (1969), 27. [47] Pierre (1975), 98.
[48] De Brosses (1739–40), Lettre LVIII, 497.
[49] Trans. Scholes in his edition of Burney (1959), i. 58 (see Burney 1773).
[50] Cf. Wind (1982), 23 and 20. [51] Ibid. 23.
[52] 'The gracefulness, clearness, and noble simplicity of the French style'. In the preface to his *Première suite de concerts de simphonies*.

Boismortier was publishing his lighthearted *gallanteries*: French taste seemed to have skipped with no intervening stages from the exacting profundity of the Louis Quatorze style (in which the hautboy—a very different hautboy from Besozzi's—had first appeared) to the 'trifling, frothy Music'[53] of Corrette and Naudot. The end of the old era was clearly marked by the deaths of the three great Philidors: André (1730), his son Anne (1728), and his nephew Pierre (1731). Another key figure of the previous era, Colin Hotteterre, died at the end of 1727. Couperin himself died in 1733.

The new 'Louis Quinze' style combined lightness, nonchalance, and frivolity with grace, and was in direct contrast to the depth and sincerity of the earlier style. As Bollioud de Mermet bitterly put it in 1746:

Il n'est plus question de toucher, ni de plaire; il faut étourdir, étonner.	It is no longer a matter of moving the listener, or pleasing him; the player must stun and shock him.[54]

Despite its jaunty, breezy character, the Louis Quinze style had its rare moments of touching depth and occasional unforgettable themes. This period had its own special aesthetic priorities, epitomized by two of the five movements of Lavigne's Sonate *La D'Agut*, marked 'Gracieusement' (another movement is 'Légerement').

The shift from the court to the city favoured the younger composers who made their reputations at public concerts, and who taught and performed for wealthy aristocrats and bourgeoisie in Paris. Some composers of hautboy music (like Naudot, Braun, and Blavet) were players of woodwind instruments; others were not (Dornel, Boismortier, and Corrette).

Actually, an example of the new style had appeared as early as 1709 in Dornel's *Livre de simphonies*. Dornel's music does not strike one as French on hearing it, and in this sense he can be seen as the vanguard of the Italianate, *galant* spirit of the next generation. Dornel's *Concerts de simphonies* of 1723 is remarkable, by the way, in containing a 'Sonate pour un haubois avec la baße', which is the only known French solo from the first half of the eighteenth century expressly written for the hautboy. (Ironically, the piece seems inappropriate for the instrument. The second movement especially, a 'Fugue', ill suits the hautboy, with long-winded phrases and little obvious place to breathe, awkward skips, and a passage of quick sixteenth notes that contains G♯s and A♯s; see Ch. 4, §H.1.)

For the next decades, French woodwind music continued in the *galant* vein. New composers appeared: Chalais, the Chédevilles, Guillemain, Lavaux, and Mondonville. By the mid-1730s more than fifty concertos for wind instruments (a thoroughly Italian genre) had been published in France. The concerto and sonata

---

[53] Robert Price, 1760, quoted in Hogwood (1984), 38.   [54] Bollioud de Mermet (1746), 31.

became so popular by the late 1720s and 1730s that they seriously overshadowed the traditional suite.[55] It was in this period that Vivaldi became popular in France.

A great deal of hautboy music has survived from this 'Louis Quinze' period. The genres that were most fashionable were duets and trios.[56] Solos with continuo[57] and quartets[58] were also plentiful, and there were solo concertos and a few obbligatos with voice.[59] Most of it came from the early years of the period; there were 313 pieces in the 1730s, 141 in the 1740s, and only fifty-five in the 1750s.[60]

Of course, this repertoire was still being conceived *en symphonie*, so almost none of it was written exclusively for hautboy players. The vogue for the musette influenced most of the published woodwind music, and since extensive modulations were difficult to sustain on the musette (it had drones that fixed the key, and could not be turned off), the result was 'a certain melodic and harmonic monotony'.[61]

The best-known exponents of the musette were the brothers Esprit-Philippe Chédeville (*l'aîné*) and Nicolas Chédeville (*le cadet*). Esprit-Philippe had joined the orchestra of the Opéra in 1709 (at age 13). From 1723 he was a member of the *Violons, Hautbois, Saqueboutes et Cornets*, and he joined the *Hautbois et Musettes de Poitou* in 1738; he retained both positions until his death in 1762. Chédeville was a cousin of the woodwind maker Thomas Lot and was related by marriage to the Hotteterres. He lived in a house in Paris inherited from Colin Hotteterre. In about 1730 he began publishing collections of music in the pastoral style, principally for musette and vielle, but playable on hautboy. Some of the sonatas in Opp. 4, 6, and 10 are quite interesting. From 1734 Chédeville was *Hautbois de la Chambre du Roy*, so these pieces may first have been played at Versailles. Chédeville's performing career overlapped the great shift in French style, and his music personifies the best of the newer one.

Like his elder brother, Nicolas Chédeville was a member of the orchestra of the Opéra and the *Douze Grands Hautbois*; he played musette/hautbois in the première of Rameau's *Temple de gloire* (1745–6). It is now thought that he was probably the composer of a well-known collection of sonatas that appeared in 1737 known as *Il Pastor fido* (RV 54–9); until recently, this collection was attributed to Vivaldi, because it borrowed some of his themes.[62] Chédeville *le cadet* wrote another charming set of sonatas, his Opus 7, that appeared in *c.*1738–9.

---

[55] Bowers (1972), 174 n. 5. She notes that suites did continue to appear in three-part music by e.g. Aubert, Mangean, Mouret, and Corrette.   [56] 275 pieces and 218 pieces respectively survive from this period.

[57] 184 pieces survive from this period.   [58] Forty-nine pieces survive from this period.

[59] Other genres diminished, however. Bowers (1972: 277) points out the marked decline in solo and trio sonatas in the 1740s and 1750s.

[60] Haynes (1992a). But as Bowers (1972: 280) noticed, interest in the duet remained intense.

[61] Bowers (1980), 189.

[62] See Lescat (1990) and (1992). The sixth sonata in this collection may have more to do with Vivaldi than the others; it is noticeably better.

Lavigne's *Sonates*, Opus 2 (*c*.1739), are another good example of the Louis Quinze style; they list the musette and vielle as the first choices, with recorder, traverso, and hautboy as alternatives. 'Les Forgerons' is an unforgettable movement, and *La D'Agut* (mentioned above) is not bad. Like most other French pieces, Opus 2 can be played with either a single *dessus* or *en symphonie*.

A factor that influenced the nature of this music was commercial. It was in this period that publishers discovered a lucrative amateur market. As a consequence, woodwind music generally became less technically demanding than in the previous period, and it was aimed at middle-of-the-road tastes. Some of this 'tabloid' music was thus purposely mediocre, and not representative of the best the period had to offer.

Boismortier's works of the 1730s, like the *6 Sonates à 4 parties différentes*, Opus 34 (1731), and the *5 Sonates en trio + 1 Concerto à 5 parties*, Opus 37 (1732), are examples of the occasional pieces of solid merit that appeared in the midst of this trivial fluff. Opus 34, for three treble instruments with bass, offers the player opportunities for the expression of intense *Affects*. Opus 37 is the collection where Boismortier makes the classic pairing of appropriate continuo instruments for each treble instrument (see Ch. 3, §G.2); the first five pieces are trios, the last has four melodic lines plus a bass. Boismortier's Opus 35 (which is officially only for traverso, with or without bass, but is quite playable on hautboy) also contains much music of compelling beauty, especially the fourth suite. These are French suites rather than Italian sonatas, and Boismortier wrote that they were 'ornées de tous leurs agréments' (provided with all the necessary ornaments).

By this time, a good proportion of the music performed on the hautboy in France came from abroad, and the leading composers of the time were all foreign. In the 1730s Parisian publishers were bringing out works for flute by Quantz, Pichler, Telemann, Locatelli, Brevio, Mahaut, Handel, and Hasse,[63] indicating the French interest in foreign music, and probably both reflecting and influencing the shift of taste.

Besides the foreigners, Parisian hautboists would not have been indifferent to the new style of Leclair's violin playing, influenced as it was by his teacher, Somis (Besozzi's colleague at Turin). A new awareness of technique and its development is evident in D'Aquin's observation that several of the pieces in Montéclair's *Jephté* (1732) could not have been performed in Lully's day, because of their difficulty.[64] The electrifying playing of Michel Blavet on the traverso also affected the general woodwind performance style of the period. As Bowers wrote (1972: 59), 'Blavet was credited with the transformation of flute technique from something languorous and easy to an exciting, exact, and brilliant art.' Blavet rose to prominence in

---

[63] Bowers (1972), 177.   [64] D'Aquin de Chateau-Lyon (1752), cited in *New Grove* xii. 509.

the late 1720s, and was active into the 1760s. Bollioud de Mermet complained in 1746 that

La Flute, dont la propriété consiste à former de mouvemens affectueux, & des sons soutenus, est employée maintenant à articuler des batteries & des roulades. Les accens tendres & séduisans du fameux Marais semblent devenir insipides.[65]	The flute, whose proper qualities are to produce touching gestures and long, held tones, is now used to articulate fast runs and roulades. The tender and seductive strains of the great Marais now seem to have become dull and lifeless.

A change of this kind would not have occurred in a vacuum, and would have influenced hautboy players, many of whom also played traverso. Thus the style and presentation of performances on the hautboy probably moved in the same direction. An hautboy player who is known to have regularly performed with Blavet from *c.*1739 is Nicolas Lavaux (who was described as 'one of the best foreign [!] masters' of the instrument, and was a composer as well).

2. *Concert venues*

Louis XV's lack of interest in music caused musical activities at the court in Versailles to become increasingly ceremonial. The leading edge of musical developments was centred in Paris, sponsored by the public concert series and rich private patrons, and the most important musical events took place in their town houses and at public concerts. In the 1730s, there were many celebrated concerts at the Hôtel of the Prince of Carignan, and later at the home of La Pouplinière. La Pouplinière maintained an entire orchestra, and from about 1731 to 1762 put on regular concerts of instrumental music, conducted by Rameau, Carl Stamitz, and Gossec. The Baron of Bagge also held regular private concerts, in which many virtuosos made their Paris debuts. Some of the prominent players at Paris, native and foreign, were thus able to do well without official connection to the court, getting their financial support from wealthy sponsors.[66]

The Besozzis had appeared at the *Concert Spirituel*, the principal venue of non-operatic works in Paris. This series was originally intended to provide music on religious feast days when operas were not allowed, but the programmes quickly became mostly secular. The *Concert Spirituel* allowed the Parisian public to hear music and performers who had previously been heard only at court, and it introduced new genres and artists from abroad. The *Concert Spirituel* maintained its

---

[65] Bollioud de Mermet (1746), 33.

[66] Documentation is misleading for this period, as it is less systematic for players primarily involved in private concerts. Among known Parisian patrons of hautboy players (as far back as the end of the 17th c.) were Milord Montcassel, the Duke of Epernon, the Duchess of Maine, the Prince of Conti, the Duke of Orleans, and the Prince of Condé/Duke of Bourbon.

PL. 7.4. [Louis Carrogis] Carmontelle, *c.*1768, detail from painting showing Prover, Duport, Vachon, Rodolphe, and Vernier
(watercolour). Chantilly: Musée Condé

own *Symphonie*, which included five hautboists/flutists. Despite the fact that its
founder, Anne Philidor, was an hautboy player, its programmes did not include
solos on the hautboy until the famous arrival of the Besozzi brothers.[67] The Besozzis
were followed over the course of the century by twenty other hautboy soloists.[68]

Zollikofer ('Solicoffe'), apparently an Italian,[69] appeared at the *Concert Spirituel*
in 1748–9. Other hautboy players from Turin played there in the 1750s: Giacomo
Palanca in 1754, and Filippo Prover six times in 1756[70] (of Prover it was later written 'Jamais musicien ne joua plus agréablement de son instrument').[71] By the 1760s
Prover was in the service of both the King and the Prince of Conty (Pl. 7.4).[72] A

---

[67] Pierre (1975), 89.

[68] Relative to other instruments, however, the hautboy was hardly prominent: 307 singers appeared as soloists,
137 violinists, 29 each of harpists, hornists, and pianists, and 28 flutists (Pierre 1975: 222).

[69] Pierre (1975), 255.   [70] Pierre, ibid. 128, thought this was Ignazio Prover.

[71] 'Never has a musician played his instrument more agreeably than Prover'. Laborde (1780), 527.

[72] Prover published six sonatas for hautboy in Paris *c.*1767. The music is fragile, insubstantial, and inconse-
quential, not unlike the keyboard sonatas of Domenico Scarlatti. There are some e♮s as well as c♯1s. The third and
fifth sonatas are the most interesting.

generation later two other Besozzis, Antonio and Carlo, Hasse's soloists at Dresden, repeated the remarkable success of their relatives at the *Concert Spirituel*, playing to 'les plus grands applaudissements'.[73] Stazzi and Secchi also made guest appearances there. The success of the *Concert Spirituel*, which continued for sixty-six years, was partly due to the new kinds of music it presented. But there were other public concert series,[74] such as the *Concerts Français* (also founded by Philidor) and the *Concert Italien*.

Musical innovations may have come from Paris, but court recognition was still important to a musician's career. 'The prestige—and the salary—of a court appointment always remained a useful supplement to the applause of the Paris public.'[75] Between 1730 and 1760 the court employed some eighty-two hautboy players.[76] All the sections of the *Écurie* remained in place (at least in name) until 1784, surviving organizational reforms in 1715, 1761, and 1779. The *Fifres et Tambours* continued until the Revolution,[77] and the *Douze Grands Hautbois* until 1791.[78] The *Écurie* tended to serve as

avant tout, une réserve d'instrumentistes à vent appelés indifféremment à la Chambre, à la Chapelle, à l'Écurie ou au théâtre.[79]	above all, a stock of wind players to be used without distinction for music of the chamber, the chapel, ceremonial music, and the theatre.

Among court players, Jacob Loeillet, like Hotteterre le Romain, had the unusual distinction of being named official *Compositeur de la Chambre* at Versailles.[80] Loeillet had been hired away from the Munich court in 1727 (after Maximilian Emanuel's death) to become *Hautbois de la Chambre du Roy*. He was officially appointed to the *Chambre* and *Écurie* in 1733, and held those posts until his return to Ghent in 1746. He probably played principally for the Queen, who was responsible for hiring him, and who sponsored regular concerts.

If Versailles was not the centre of musical activities, many concerts were still held there. The Dauphine Marie-Josephe especially (daughter of Friedrich August of Dresden) organized several concerts a week in her apartments at Versailles. It was probably there that the famed Pla brothers from Catalonia (Joan Baptista and Josep) performed on the hautboy from 1752 to 1759 (perhaps reminding Marie-Josephe of the playing of Antonio Besozzi, which she must have heard as a child). At the *Concert Spirituel* in May 1752 Baptista Pla accompanied the famous soprano Marie Fel (who performed major roles in most of Rameau's works and was then at the height of her powers) in an 'Air italienne' of Pla's composition.[81] The piece is now apparently lost.

[73] Pierre (1975), 128.   [74] Anthony (1973), 21–3.   [75] Morby (1971), 49.   [76] Benoit (1971a).
[77] François-Sappey (1988–90), 158.   [78] Morby (1971), 84.   [79] Benoit (1971a), 221.
[80] Almost no hautboy music by Jacob Loeillet has survived.   [81] Pierre (1975), 262.

3. The Opéra

While the rest of Europe was obsessed with Italian *opera seria*, the mechanism of
the Paris Opéra kept France oblivious to the form. After Lully's death, the Opéra
had become a conservative icon of the French nation, an institution dedicated to
preserving a national tradition. Burney wrote in 1771a (p. 30):

> . . . the style of composition is totally changed throughout the rest of Europe; yet the
> French, commonly accused of more levity and caprice than their neighbours, have stood still
> in music for thirty or forty years: nay, one may go still further, and assert boldly, that it has
> undergone few changes at the great opera since Lulli's time, that is to say, in one hundred
> years.

The *tragédie lyrique* invented by Lully was the mould of French opera, pleasing an
audience still interested in Lully's works even into the 1770s.[82] Whatever the draw-
backs of this system, it did provide a forum for the exquisite works of Rameau,
which he himself (though not everyone) considered to be in the direct tradition of
Lully.

Rameau's operas contain a number of obbligatos for one or two hautboys with
voice, a genre that was rather rare in France at the time. One of the most remarkable is Mercure's air 'Tu veux avoir la préférence' in *Les Fêtes d'Hébé* (1739). One
of the characters, Palémon, who is in love with Eglé, 'plays' the hautboy part on
stage while Eglé dances. Mercure meanwhile taunts him, assuring him that he will
lose Eglé. At the end, in a fit of jealousy, Palémon breaks his hautboy. In the orchestra for the première, the two principal hautboys were Du Fresne and Monnot.[83]

Operas were performed in the Grande Salle of the Palais Royal until 1763; subsequent performances were in the Salle des Machines, which could seat nearly
8,000. (No wonder, in those days when there was no possibility of 'miking', there
were normally four hautboy players in the orchestra.)

D'Aquin in 1753 considered the Opéra orchestra to be composed of 'excellent
musicians'.[84] Among the hautboy players at the Opéra were Jean-François
Despréaux, François Bureau, and Nicolas Sallantin. Most of these players were
flutists as well as hautboists.

By 1727 Despréaux was in the Opéra orchestra 'grand chœur' at the top salary
level. He was described as a 'bon hautbois' at the court in June 1731. He attended
Thomas Lot's wedding in 1734, and at that time was also in the service of the Duc
de Bourbon. Despréaux's playing was praised in 1752; he also performed at the
Concert Spirituel in 1757.

---

[82] Rosow (1989).
[83] Cf. Cyr (1975). Monnot also played the première of Rameau's *Temple de gloire* in 1745–6.
[84] Morby (1971), 162.

Bureau was in the Opéra orchestra by 1730 and was still playing there in 1763. He was a member of the *Douze Grands Hautbois* at Versailles from 1731 to 1740. In the 1750s, he and his colleague Sallantin played several times at the *Concert Spirituel*. Bureau was the teacher of Sallantin's young son Antoine, who made his flute début at the *Concert Spirituel* at the age of 12 in 1768.[85] After the Revolution, Antoine Sallantin was to become the first professor of hautboy at the Paris Conservatoire.

Sallantin's father Nicolas was playing first hautboy at the Opéra by 1746. He appeared at the *Concert Spirituel* in 1750, 1754, 1755, playing with Bureau. He was called one of the 'premiers Maîtres' in 1752. In 1757 'Salentin & Bureau' were listed among 'les meilleurs Maîtres françois' for hautboy. He was still in the Opéra in 1763.

Many of the flutists/hautboists at the Opéra seem to have been exceptional players. Besides those already mentioned, there was the German Jean Daniel Braun, also 'Ordinaire de la musique' to the Duke of Epernon. Lucas (medium salary rung) was a soloist (on flute) at the *Concert Spirituel* in 1726 and 1736 and one of the flutists in Titon du Tillet's 'Orchestre du Parnasse' (1743).[86]

By this time there were other opera companies operating on the periphery of the Opéra's repertoire, including the *Comédie-Italienne* and the *Opéra-Comique*; their orchestras sometimes included hautboys.

4. Instruments

French makers of this period included Bizey, Boisselot *aîné*, Châsse, Jacques Delusse, Deschamps, Klenig, Gilles Lot, Martin Lot, Thomas Lot, Pelletier jun., and Villars.[87] It would seem that despite the vogue for things Italian, to judge from the number of makers and surviving instruments, most French hautboy players were getting their instruments locally.

The hautboy trade was dominated by Thomas Lot and Charles Bizey. Lot had worked for some years at the atelier on the rue de l'Arbre Sec that had been run successively by Fremont, Naust, and Delerablée. After Delerablée's death in 1734, his widow Jeanne Naust married Thomas Lot. Their wedding was attended by three woodwind players from the Opéra orchestra: Despréaux, Chédeville *l'aîné*, and Bernier.[88] Lot worked until 1787, a remarkable span of time. Five of his hautboys survive, of Types B and E.

Although the Type E has survived in relatively large numbers and its repertoire is being actively revived, the type itself has not as yet become very well known.

---

[85] Antoine Sallantin was the '1er flûtiste de l'Opéra' in 1784 when he played a new hautboy (!) concerto.
[86] Other flutists/hautboy players connected with the Opéra were Berault and Vincent (? = Vincent Breton).
[87] The locations and working periods of some of these makers are merely guesses. See Waterhouse (1993).
[88] Giannini (1993b), 14–16.

Like the Type D1, with which it was in competition, Type E hautboys were a new invention. Evidently the prevalent model in France in the mid-eighteenth century, the Type E differs sharply from the model of the previous generation, Type A2; tone-holes are quite small (averaging an aggregate of 14.65 mm), the bore is noticeably narrow (average 5.49, and many at 5.0). It is also drawn out much longer, the mean acoustic length being close to the longest of any type or period, 339 mm[89] (cf. Pl. 2.4). Charles Bizey could have been the maker who developed the Type E. Bizey had started working when the Type A2 was still in full fashion (1716), and some of his instruments show a transition, using elements of the two types.[90]

There is little evidence that the Type E was taken up beyond the borders of France, the reason probably being its low pitch (see below). And even within France, there was a countering tendency in this period. While the Opéra remained rigidly traditionalist, French instrumental music was being strongly influenced by Italy. It may be because these two trends could not easily be reconciled that there arose a dichotomy, a 'French' Type E hautboy and an 'Italian' Type D1, probably used for different types of music.[91]

It may be that the experimentalists, playing Italian music or music influenced by the Italian conception (at the *Concert Spirituel* and *Concert Italien*), got Type D1 hautboys directly from Italy. It is unlikely that such instruments were made in France before about 1760.[92]

The most noticeable difference between Type D1 and Type E would probably have been their pitches. Being Italian in origin, Type D1 hautboys tended to be higher than the usual French standards at A−1½ and A−2. By 1746, Bollioud de Mermet (p. 24) was criticizing French instrumentalists for 'la hauteur excessive du ton' (their excessively high pitch). In 1752, Quantz commented:

Anitzo aber fängt man an, den Pariser Ton dem venezianischen fast gleich zu machen.[93]	At present, however, the Parisian pitch is beginning almost to equal that of Venice.

(Venetian pitch had for some time been at A+0; if our speculation about *Flavio* and *Tamerlano* in Ch. 5, §E.1 is right, Sammartini was playing at A+0 in the early 1720s.) These comments may have been referred to playing at the *Concert Spirituel*, where pitch was probably already high.[94]

---

[89] Type E hautboys made outside of France, while relatively long, are a bit shorter; the average AL of Rottenburgh and Schlegel Type Es is 335.

[90] Bizey is survived by six hautboys. Those I have tried play very well.

[91] Cf. Corrette's 'Italian' and 'French' F♯ fingering (see Ch. 4, §G.3).

[92] Cf. the Martin Lot, Brussels 1980.   [93] Quantz (1752), XVII, vii §7.

[94] Pitch may have been high at the *Concert Spirituel* for some time before the bassoonist Pierre Cugnier, writing in Laborde's *Essai* (1780: 329), singled it out (see Haynes 1995, §4-8).

At the same time, the long ALs of instruments by Lot and Bizey indicate low pitches. There seems little evidence that these makers found their products marginalized during this period; they were obviously very productive and their businesses flourished. Concerts at Versailles may have maintained a traditional low pitch longer than in Paris (the principle of different pitches for different functions being long accepted). Any playing in churches would have been low to match the organs. It is known that Bizey supplied the Opéra, military players, and the Théâtre Italien.[95] Lot was evidently close to woodwind players at the Opéra, where pitch was traditionally low on account of the voice ranges Lully had used (his works being still performed regularly).

But even at the Opéra, high-pitched hautboys may have come into use. From the time instruments at A+o became common (by the 40s, as Bollioud de Mermet indicates), they may have been used at the Opéra within a prevailing standard of A−2. The wind parts in Rameau's operas are remarkable (and therefore suspect) for their use of extreme sharp keys and difficult high notes. A plausible explanation is that wind players sometimes used high Type D1 instruments when they played at the Opéra, transposing their parts down a whole step to the level of the voices. By doing this, they would have eliminated two sharps in their parts and rescued notes that would in some cases have extended above their reasonable range.[96] Most of Rameau's hautboy solos written for the Opéra[97] between 1739 and 1749 are easier and sound better when played down a tone.[98] By way of confirmation, the obbligatos Rameau wrote for other venues than the Opéra (as for instance motets and cantatas) were written in more typical tonalities and ranges for hautboy.

C. Germany

German chapels, especially in the more forward-looking courts, were quite susceptible to invasion by Italian hautboists; cf. Dresden, Würzburg, Stuttgart, and Munich. In these courts, new kinds of instruments were being used, and the style of music was quickly changing.

---

[95] Giannini (1998), 10.

[96] Cf. the b1 in the upper bassoon part to *Boréades* (first Gavotte, b. 16). A contemporary Prudent bassoon (a typical 'tenor' instrument perfect for Rameau's upper bassoon parts, which often double the violas) goes as high as a1. It is also true that the sources of Rameau's operas have yet to be systematically studied, and some high notes may be the result of alterations to the parts made as late as the end of the 18th c. (the e♭3s in *Zoroastre* of 1749, for example, were a later addition—1762 or later, according to Geoffrey Burgess (pers. comm.)).

[97] Rameau's dramatic works were normally performed at the Opéra (cf. Cyr 1980: 570).

[98] With the exception of 'Je ne sais quel ennui m'opresse', II/vi in *Naïs*, this is true of all ten solo arias in Rameau's operas. (For titles, see Haynes 1992a: 261 ff.). Traversos, already playing a basic scale in D, would not have had the same problem; they played higher notes and sharps more comfortably than hautboys (see Ch. 4, §H.3.b).

The German Stadtpfeifer, on the other hand, were insulated from the Italian onslaught, and for some time the same institutions continued to give them employment, and the same genres of music required their playing and composition. This may be why a number of German makers continued to turn out Type A2 hautboys (though probably with somewhat updated bore dimensions).[99] But by the mid-eighteenth century, the Stadtpfeifer gradually came to be seen as outmoded and redundant. A restructuring of the liturgy that minimized the place of music demanded less and less of their participation in church services. Many of these musicians were absorbed by the newer, more modish ensembles such as the *Collegia Musica* and 'Concerts spirituels', which came to be subsidized by public funds.

A typical German hautboy of the 1730s, of the type made in the major centres of Nuremberg and Leipzig, is shown in the Paris copy of Eisel 1738 (Pl. 2.17). It is a thinner, lighter Denner.[100] Few German hautboys from this period are extant, and we are without surviving examples of the earliest work of either Grenser or Grundmann (Friedrich II's bombardment of Dresden in the late 1750s may be responsible for this). But their earliest post-war instruments give an idea of what they were like, as they moved steadily closer to the classical model of the 1770s.

Compositional style underwent dramatic changes in this period. The most successful and respected composers in Germany during the last decades of Bach's life were Telemann and Hasse. The music they wrote after 1730 was in a new, simpler vein that avoided complex harmonies and long, complicated melodies.[101] Telemann's style of composition after 1730, for example, shows 'a decided turn towards simplicity and symmetrical thematic constructions, and an elimination of the unifying device of expressing only a single affection in each piece. Textures become generally uncomplicated, and the continuo line is frequently eliminated.'[102] Perhaps in reaction to this trend, another line of development during the same period that was characteristic of the Berlin school was the 'Empfindsamer Stil' (sensitive style) that featured frequent and sudden changes of direction, mood, dynamics, and harmony; these pieces were even denser in expressive content than the works of the previous generation of German composers.

With the gradual loss of the Stadtpfeifer option, even the best hautboy players had to be very agile on their feet to keep a decent job. Few of the top players were able to remain permanently at one post. Travelling was common in all the trades and professions, and it was assumed that musicians, music teachers, and opera companies had to make the rounds of various courts and cities to find employment, or better employment.

---

[99] The J. A. Crone in Han de Vries's collection is an example. Made in Leipzig after 1766, it is turned in a style popular before 1730, with relatively thick side-walls; its minimum bore is narrow, however, at 5.4.

[100] The Bauer (Y1, Nuremberg MIR 376) resembles this picture.   [101] Cf. Dahlhaus (1985), 71 ff.

[102] Buelow (1993a), 203.

1. Schwerin

After Johann Fischer's departure in 1704, it is unclear what became of the hautboy band at Schwerin. There are no records of court hautboy players there until 1739–43, when three players were appointed. Pieces in the Schwerin library indicate that they were playing wind quintets, chamber music (by Telemann) and concertos with orchestra (by Suhl). Adolph Kunzen became Capellmeister in 1749, and is survived by music for wind band and hautboy concertos. Wilhelm Hertel succeeded him in 1753; a number of Hertel's hautboy compositions still exist (wind/hautboy band, concertos, and opera arias). A charming collection of his pieces that work well in the ample acoustics of churches are the *3 Trii* for hautboy and organ (two keyboards + pedal). They are in a clear *galant* idiom; one of them is dated 1762. Three hautboy players were appointed at the same time as Hertel; one of them, Heinrich Selmer, was evidently an excellent musician and may have been a friend of Emanuel Bach (who owned a portrait of him).[103]

2. Hamburg

By the time the Hamburg Opera folded in 1738 for lack of audiences, Telemann had, as George Buelow wrote, 'devoted 17 years to its musical success. He was, however, to remain a major catalyst in the musical, educational, and cultural life of the city for another 29 years'.[104] Telemann, older than Bach, was active until his death in 1767 (by which time Mozart had already written eight symphonies). Besides his many church works, as the 'virtual concert manager for the city',[105] Telemann presented regular public concerts until shortly before he died. Virtually the entire contents of Hamburg's libraries have been missing since the Second World War.[106] We know not a single name of the many hautboists working in the city during these years, and can only guess at the instruments they played, or the solo and chamber repertoire they would have performed. Other than those by Telemann, only a handful of pieces for hautboy from Hamburg in the 1730s survive (by Linike, who was the leader of the Hamburg Opera orchestra from 1725, and Prowo, an organist in Altona).

For good reason, Telemann's *galant* Quatuor from *Musique de table* I (1733; TWV 43: G2) is well known. It is for traverso, hautboy, violin, and continuo, and the second movement is *auf Concertenart*, with the hautboy taking the solo role. The movement starts with a *devise*: a separate, repeated statement of the theme, as in the then already well-known hautboy concertos of Albinoni and Marcello.

---

[103] Wade (1981). The catalogue dates from 1790.   [104] Buelow (1993a), 199.   [105] Ibid. 205.
[106] However, some items are beginning to turn up again. See Charteris (1997).

Nineteen years later, in 1752, Telemann published in Paris a remarkable collection of *galant* duos for treble instruments without bass (TWV 40: 124–9). The music is brilliant and forceful; the collection is comparable in style and quality to Telemann's famous Paris Quartets.

Because it was a free city, Hamburg maintained its own standing army, an army that no doubt employed a number of *Hautboisten*. Each year, Telemann provided the 'Capitänsmusik', consisting of an oratorio and a serenata, to entertain the guests of the commandant of this army (Pl. 5.2). Several of the 'oratorios' for these 'Gastmahle der Bürger-Capitäns' contain hautboy obbligatos with voice.[107] In writing such pieces (with hautboy obbligatos), Telemann was continuing a tradition inherited from Friedrich Bruhns, who had written similar pieces in the decades before Telemann's arrival in Hamburg.

By 1740 Telemann's interests seem to have turned from instrumental and chamber music[108] to sacred works involving voice. Of his eleven solo and chamber pieces for hautboy written after 1740, nine were arias in religious works.

Although his name was not recorded, in 1753 'one of the finest virtuosos' on the hautboy and traverso was heard at the Kaiserhof in Hamburg.[109]

3. Zerbst

The only hautboy player associated with Zerbst whose name we know is Simeon Unger, who was appointed to the Hofcapelle in 1737–8. Unger had come from Weißenfels, where he had played since 1709. Fasch put on his opera *Berenice* at Zerbst in 1739, and Unger was probably one of the hautboists who played it, as well as one of Fasch's later hautboy compositions that is particularly good: a sonata in G minor for two hautboys and continuo (FWV N: g2). The fact that this sonata survives in two manuscript copies (Berlin and Brussels) indicates that it was also appreciated at the time. It is full of refreshing melodies, and exploits a number of interesting technical qualities of the hautboy. In form and character, this trio has a curious similarity to the solo sonata of Emanuel Bach (which is also in G minor).

4. Zeitz

Gottfried Lommer was appointed Stadtpfeifer at Zeitz in 1743, and was highly praised at his audition. Lommer played an unusual piece that the city had commissioned from Gottlieb Görner of Leipzig, especially to be used for such auditions: it is a concerto with separate movements for six (!) different instruments (see Ch. 3, §F.3). Sebastian Bach received a commission for a similar piece in the same year,

---

[107] Cf. also the popular 'Hamburger Admiralitätsmusik', an orchestral Ouverture with programmatic movements on maritime themes. Maertens (1988) and Haynes (1992a), 316–23.   [108] Cf. Swack (1988), 2.
[109] Sittard (1890b), 78.

but if he wrote it, it is now lost. As a condition for this commission, the piece was not to have been played before, and was to be communicated to no one beforehand. Lommer might also have played Bach's piece.

Zeitz is remembered as the place where Bach's distinguished pupil Ludwig Krebs became organist in 1744 (the year after Lommer's appointment). Krebs, who was there until 1755, is survived by fourteen interesting works for hautboy and organ (two keyboards and pedal). Probably the best piece that exists for this combination of instruments is Krebs's *Fantasia a 4, F♭ in g* (*sic*), generally known now in F minor. The original organ part is indeed in this key, but (as the title indicates) the hautboy part was conceived in G minor; the instruments obviously differed a whole step in pitch. In many ways, this piece resembles Bach's *Fantasia* for organ, BWV 651. It is published in three modern editions, two in F minor and one in G minor. None of them accurately reproduces the original situation, of course, as they all involve transposing one or the other part in order to put everything in the same key.[110]

5. Berlin

The Berlin court had been virtually without civilian music until the 'Barracks King' Friedrich Wilhelm's death in 1740. But as soon as his son Friedrich II ('Frederick the Great') was crowned, he ordered the construction of an opera house and established a large court orchestra that included four hautboys,[111] one of whom was Joachim Döbbert.[112]

Friedrich had maintained a Capelle before he became king, but it did not contain hautboy players. Glösch had remained in Berlin after 1713, active as a teacher and performer, and was mentioned by Walther (1732: 285). There is no indication that he ever played for Friedrich II, however. By 1754 Marpurg (p. 157) referred to him as deceased.[113]

There were several public and private concert series in Berlin, such as the *Musikausübende Gesellschaft*, the *Musikalische Assemblee*,[114] and the semi-public weekly 'Akademien' organized by Johann Gottlieb Janitsch; performances were ad hoc and featured current instrumental music. Among the more interesting chamber pieces in the hautboy repertoire from this period are the twenty-two trios and quartets by Janitsch, written from about 1750 to 1762.[115] Janitsch used hautbois d'amour in several of these pieces.[116]

---

[110] A concerto by Krebs in B minor for harpsichord and 'hautboy' that shows similarities to Bach's Fifth Brandenburg and BWV 51/1 is evidently for traverso, because of its key, its range (numerous e3s and nothing below d1), and its role (accompaniment to the harpsichord).   [111] Helm (1960), 94.
[112] Michel and Teske (1978), 95.
[113] The piece by 'Glösch' quoted in Quantz's *Solfeggi* must be by him.   [114] These two later merged.
[115] The two quartets by Riedel now preserved at Dresden resemble Janitsch's (although they are not as good).
[116] His last dated piece that specified the instrument is 1753.

At least some of the hautboy parts to Janitsch's pieces were written for Christian Jacobi, who had studied with Glösch. When he became a member of the court Capelle in 1746, Jacobi studied composition with Friedrich Riedt, a founder and director of the *Musikausübende Gesellschaft*.[117] At about the same time, Jacobi began attending Janitsch's weekly *Akademie*,[118] and his name appears on two original parts.

Jacobi was also one of the hautboists employed by Friedrich II's cousin, the Margrave Charles of Brandenburg (d. 1762), who maintained a Capelle. In 1754 Marpurg listed its members, as well as the hautboy players in the Opera orchestra; Jacobi, though a member of the Capelle, was not on the Opera list.

The 'Königliche Cammermusik', led by Quantz, was begun in 1747; these were daily performances in the *Musikzimmer* at Sans-Souci by members of the Capelle (including, presumably, some of the hautboy players).

The *Hautboistenschule* in Potsdam continued to be supported by Friedrich II, who even provided instruments for the students;[119] from 1736 it was directed by Samuel Peter Sydow.[120] Friedrich inherited an army that supported nearly 2,000 (!) regimental musicians, many of them hautboists, and the number increased during his reign.[121] It is no wonder that the court helped a Leipzig woodwind maker, Christoph Freyer, to move to Berlin in 1747.[122] Together with Johann Reinicke, active in Berlin from at least 1730,[123] Freyer (succeeded by Kirst in 1772) supplied the Prussian army with 'Hautboisten-Instrumente'. It is curious that no hautboys stamped by either of these workshops is known to survive. Some hautboys played in Berlin in this period could have been made by Heitz (who worked until 1737).

The balls that Friedrich often put on after opera performances in the 1740s and 1750s were accompanied by twenty-four 'Oboisten' (no doubt mostly playing strings) chosen from various regiments.[124] The music was composed by Janitsch; none of it survives. Friedrich also maintained an hautboy band with his *Leibregiment*, a tradition inherited from his father.

In 1752 Quantz published his encyclopedic *Essai d'une méthode pour apprendre à jouer de la Flûte Traversière*, full of eminently practical advice (it appeared in the same year in both French and German).[125] The book is much more than a flute tutor: only five of the eighteen chapters deal specifically with flute technique, the

---

[117] Riedt published a set of trios *c.*1754 that can be played on hautboy.   [118] Marpurg (1754), VI, 157–8.

[119] Heyde (1994), 31.

[120] Moore (1981), 16, citing Panoff (1938), 84–5. Sydow is survived by a concerto and a 'Simphonia à 4' for hautboys.   [121] Heyde (1994), 49.

[122] Ibid. 67, 354.   [123] Ibid. 73.

[124] Marpurg (1754), 156. Also Helm (1960), 107 citing Thouret (1898), 55.

[125] In German it was entitled *Versuch einer Anweisung die Flöte traversiere zu spielen*. The French version was prepared for the benefit of Friedrich, who was Quantz's patron, and who had difficulty reading and speaking German (cf. Mitford 1970: 20, 205). Although Reilly (1966), p. xxxv called the French version a 'translation', it appeared in Berlin simultaneously with the German edition and was in fact of equal authenticity. In some passages, as Reilly points out, the French text is clearer, in others, the German.

rest being on more general musical subjects. Quantz himself recommended it to hautboy players.[126] In 1770 Burney considered Quantz's taste 'that of forty years ago'[127] (= 1730); his writing can be assumed to describe the ideas of a gifted and thoughtful woodwind player of the 1730s, 1740s, and 1750s.

After the 1760s Berlin became in some ways a musical backwater, but the period from 1730 to 1760 provided an environment for the creation of the particular and very attractive *empfindsamer Stil* of composition. Many chamber and solo pieces for hautboy originated in Berlin in this period by composers such as Quantz, Janitsch, Johann Gottlieb Graun, Emanuel Bach, Schaffrath, Nichelmann, and Benda.

Because the Berlin style ossified, several pieces published a decade after 1760 are still very convincingly in the *galant* rather than classical style. Kirnberger's wonderful Sonata 'für die Oboe' from *Vermischte Musikalien* (Berlin, 1769) is an example. The piece is not unlike Emanuel Bach's solo sonata composed a generation earlier (see below); the last movement contains written-out crescendos (a novelty at the time). Bach also published two 'Sonate[n] für die Hautbois' by the hautboist Carl Ludwig Matthes in his *Musikalisches Vielerley* (1770). The style is similar to Bach's own. Matthes was only 19 in 1770, and was already 'Cammer-Musicus' to Friedrich's brother, the Margrave Henry of Prussia. Although both sonatas are good, the second in E flat is more interesting to play; these pieces require some technique, and both appeared elsewhere for traverso, the one in C transposed to D, the one in E flat to G.[128]

Emanuel Bach, who was in Friedrich's service until 1768, is survived by two concertos for either hautboy or harpsichord.[129] They are good pieces, of course, but since neither is particularly idiomatic for hautboy,[130] it is assumed they were originally written for harpsichord.[131] The great Christian Fischer, the only hautboy player known to have been in Friedrich's private employ (albeit rather briefly), was in Potsdam in 1763, and Bach may have arranged them for him.

6. Dresden

A musical revolution took place at the Dresden court around 1730. Woulmyer had died in 1728, Heinichen in 1729, and the old Elector Friedrich August I, who had always been more inclined towards French music,[132] in 1733. La Riche retired to his native home in Tournai in 1731, the same year that Hasse arrived.[133] (The

---

[126] Quantz (1752), VI, suppl. §1. Cf. also p. x of Reilly's introduction to his trans. of Quantz.

[127] Burney (1773), ii. 157.   [128] See Haynes (1992a), 224.   [129] H466 and H468 (W164 and W165).

[130] Cf. the frequent slurs up to c3, the trill on a♭2–g♭2 in the concerto in E flat (which is the better piece).

[131] The one in E flat is described in the Nachlaßkatalog of 1790 as for 'Clavier . . . auch für die Hoboe gesetzt'.

[132] See Landmann (1982).

[133] Tournai is now a part of Belgium but was then under French control. In that same year, Bressan died unexpectedly while visiting La Riche (see Haynes 1990: 114).

latter event doomed the chances of a number of musicians, including Sebastian Bach and probably Vivaldi,[134] who had hoped for the job of Capellmeister.) The new Elector, Friedrich August II, chose Hasse for that position in 1734. Hasse and his new opera style were to hold sway at Dresden, and indeed most of Germany, for the next thirty years. Reflecting the classical leanings of Neapolitan opera, Hasse's style 'had already in its formal and expressive character left behind any concept of the Baroque as a style'.[135]

Like his father, Friedrich August II (who began his reign in 1733) was a man of extravagant and luxurious tastes. Dresden outshone every other court (except perhaps Vienna) in the opulence of its musical productions, especially its Italian opera, which was internationally famous.

On Hasse's first visits to Dresden in 1731 and 1734, it was Richter who was playing solo hautboy (the other players were Henrion and Seyffert).[136] It is less clear who played solo hautboy for Hasse's third sojourn in 1737–8. The young Antonio Besozzi, arriving from Naples, was appointed principal in 1738. Besozzi held the post at Dresden with great success until 1764, and was much admired. One wonders how Richter, who had been principal hautboy, reacted to Besozzi's arrival. In 1738 Richter was 49, not yet of an age for retirement. But it was said that his health was not good; six years later, in a 'fit of melancholy', he took his own life.

Besozzi played one of Hasse's arias in such a 'heavenly' way that it inspired a verse in a local journal:

| Der Mann mit *Hautbois* er woll' die Leute zeigen | That man with the *Hautbois* wanted to show everyone |
| Wie mit sein Athem er kann biß in Wolken steigen.[137] | How on his breath he can ascend to the clouds. |

The aria, marked Andante, was the lovely, bittersweet 'Già sereno il disperai' in the opera *Solimano* of 1753, sung by the tenor Angelo Amorevoli. Already in Besozzi's long introduction there is a place for a cadenza, and a possible double cadenza for voice and player at the end of the A section. There are also cadenzas for Amorevoli in the middle of the very brief B section, and for Besozzi at the end of the B section. The piece often moves in thirds, the two soloists trading the upper voice; there are interjections from the hautboy going up to d3 between the singer's phrases. The audience, according to Fürstenau, was in raptures.

Soon after the performance of *Solimano*, Besozzi made one of several trips to Italy. One wonders if he came back with new instruments. In any case, he acted

---

[134] Landmann in Steude, Landmann, *et al.* (1995), 1538.   [135] Buelow (1993b), 228.
[136] Mennicke (1906), 270. Cf. J. F. Seyffart (Weissenfels, 1710–p1712).   [137] Fürstenau (1861–2), ii. 275.

as a link between developments in Dresden and Turin, making cross-fertilization possible between the makers in these two centres.[138]

For a brief period at the end of the 1750s the Dresden court had on its books not only Antonio Besozzi but his son Carlo (b. 1738) and Christian Fischer (b. 1733). These younger players were destined to become the two most famous European hautboists of the next generation,[139] and were both probably studying with the elder Besozzi, then in his prime.

The disastrous Seven Years War of 1756–63, during which Dresden was bombarded and occupied by the Prussians, destroyed the opera house and caused the breakup of the Capelle. Burney later wrote:[140]

In the year 1755, the late king of Poland had in his service . . . instrumental performers . . . of the first class, and more numerous than those of any other court in Europe; but, now, not above six or eight of these are to be found at Dresden *. . . It was from the dispersion of this celebrated band, at the beginning of the last war, that almost every great city of Europe, and London among the rest, acquired several exquisite and favourite performers.

* Signor Besozzi was so obliging as to furnish me with a list of the court and chapel musicians, now at Dresden . . .

Antonio and Carlo Besozzi (the latter then 19) escaped to London in early 1757 and went on to Paris, where they performed in December; they then spent the season 1758–9 at Stuttgart, playing under Jomelli. It is possible they afterwards waited in Turin for the war to end.

Fischer's position when he was first appointed in 1755 was that of *Jagd-Pfeifer*. Retreating from Dresden during the war, Fischer was in Warsaw with the Elector in 1757, and there is a record of his performance there of Alessandro Besozzi's G major concerto. He was regularly in Berlin in the 1760s (which must have strained his relationship with the Dresden court). He was still on the payroll at Dresden in 1764.

As principal, Antonio Besozzi was the highest paid of the four court hautboy players in 1764, and he and Carlo had special privileges. In his retirement, Antonio was evidently an active historian and scholar: on his trip to Italy in 1774 he visited Padre Martini in Bologna, and was described as 'expert in history and very contemplative, and you can speak with him about Grecian music'.[141]

In this period, two young makers, Grenser and Grundmann, who had both been students of Poerschman at Leipzig, set up separate shops in Dresden. Grenser

[138] Surviving chamber and solo works for hautboy that can be associated with Dresden in this period are by Adam, Antonio Besozzi, Califano, Fasch, Hasse, Homilius, Quantz, Reichenauer, Christoph Richter, Taschenberg, and Zelenka.

[139] According to Johann Gottlieb Naumann, 1776. Cited in Engländer (1922), 50 (Vtr. 6. März; V 45). Carlo Besozzi remained at the court until 1792, maintaining with honour the Besozzi name; Fischer was destined to travel, eventually settling in England. [140] Burney (1773), ii. 51.

[141] Bernardini (1985a), 7.

began working in 1744 and became the official purveyor of woodwinds to the Saxon court in 1753, the year Grundmann arrived in Dresden. As discussed above, §B, the presence of Antonio Besozzi and the Palanca/Panormo-type instrument he played may have been what originally attracted the two makers to the capitol. Their earliest instruments were probably a mixture of elements they had learned in Leipzig and the influence of the new Italian design. It may have been with the active collaboration of both Besozzis and Fischer that they developed the model that eventually became the prototypical European Classical hautboy. The two makers continued producing prolifically until the end of the century, and their instruments were played in Germany, Italy, the Habsburg lands, and (through Fischer) in England.

7. Leipzig

This period was the last in which Leipzig played a dominant role in woodwind making. From the 1760s on, although many instruments continued to be made there, the leading edge of hautboy design was the graft of the Leipzig tradition to the new Italian models, and that was happening in Dresden. Prior to 1760, however, Leipzig was extremely productive; makers included David Wolff, Caspar Grahl, Christian Haupt, Paul Otto, Christoph Hartwig, and Gottfried Zencker (only the last two of whom are survived by hautboys).[142] Instruments were also still coming out of the workshops of Eichentopf until 1749, Poerschman until after 1766, and the Sattler family and the Crones until well into the nineteenth century.

Having begun about 1700, Poerschman was evidently the dean of Leipzig woodwind players at this time. He must have been especially resourceful to have been active through so many changes in the design of the hautboy, from the French models at the beginning of the century through the classical models developed by his own Dresden students.

Gleditsch, as the senior Stadtpfeifer from 1734 until his death in 1747, remained the most prominent player in Leipzig; his partner Kornagel, who lived into the 1750s, must also have been honoured for his role in playing Bach's music. The newer generation of Leipzig hautboy players (in the shadow of Antonio Besozzi's playing at Dresden, and the instruments being produced there) included Caroli, Kirchhoff, Ofschatz, Gabriel Crone, the Pfaffes, Landvoigt, and Jonne.

In his memorandum of 1730 Bach did not name his third hautboy player, but it could have been Friedrich Caroli, who became a Kunstgeiger in that year. Gottfried Kirchhoff became a Stadtpfeifer in 1737, and Christian Ofschatz a Kunstgeiger in 1738. They were later to be the principal hautboy players in the Große Concert begun in 1746. Carl Pfaffe was a Stadtpfeifer; Bach certified him proficient on the

---

[142] Cf. Waterhouse (1993).

hautboy in 1745. In 1748 Bach was asked to audition Andreas Jonne and Michael Pfaffe, who had both applied for a post as Kunstgeiger; Bach recommended Jonne as able to play the hautboy 'weit reiner und wohlklingender' (much better in tune and with a better tone) than Pfaffe.[143]

Besides local players, Richter and Böhm may have visited Leipzig in the 1730s, and might have inspired Emanuel Bach's benchmark solo sonata, one of the masterpieces of the hautboy literature.[144] The piece was probably composed in the first half of the 1730s, when Bach was in his late teens and still in Leipzig,[145] and it might well have been performed at one of his father's Collegium sessions. It begins with a quasi fantasy with recitativo-like sections, suspensions, and seventh chords, in free rhythm. The second movement by contrast is very regular in rhythm (with strict repeated eighth notes in the bass), and the third is a brilliant minuet with variations. Stylistically, it is very daring for its period.

In the 1730s Sebastian Bach's production of new hautboy obbligatos in his church music was less frequent, averaging four to five solos per year; many of these solos were in the large works like the Christmas Oratorio and the Mass in B minor. After 1738 solos appeared only sporadically (two in 1741, one in 1744, and three in 1748). Bach's connections with Dresden grew stronger in the 1730s, when great changes were taking place there with the arrival of Hasse and the affirmation of Italian music and players. By the 1740s this movement was in full swing. One wonders what Bach thought of Antonio Besozzi's playing, which he probably heard on one of his trips to the capital.

Bach continued to direct the 'Telemann' Collegium Musicum until 1737, and then intermittently in the next years, with his pupil Gerlach. The other Collegium, directed by Görner, was also active. The Collegia normally met once a week (at fair-time, twice a week). Repertoire was varied, consisting of cantatas, concertos, instrumental suites, chamber pieces, and solo harpsichord works.[146] Collegia also performed music in honour of the Saxon Elector on various days of celebration, and when he visited Leipzig.

By 1747 there were three Collegia Musica in Leipzig, which all eventually merged into one 'Grand Concert' or 'Große Concert', with sixteen strings, three flutes/hautboys, and three bassoons. Friedrich Doles, an up-to-date pupil of Bach's, was the director (Doles was to become Bach's successor as Cantor at St Thomas's). Kornagel was involved, but Gleditsch, who died shortly afterward, was not.[147] Poerschman (by then in his 60s) was the regular bassoonist and an hautboy doubler in 1746–8. Landvoigt, the solo traverso, also doubled on hautboy when needed. This group eventually mutated, in 1781, into the Gewandhaus Orchestra.

---

[143] *Bach-Dokumente* (1963), ii. 452.
[144] H549 (W135).
[145] David Schulenberg (pers. comm.).
[146] Stauffer (1993), 287.
[147] Schering (1921), 50–1.

8. Mannheim

The large court of the Electoral Palatinate moved from Heidelberg to Mannheim in 1720. Some of the court musicians may also have come from the Düsseldorf Capelle, which had been disbanded in 1716. From 1723 to 1734 there were three hautboy players at Mannheim: Aloys Beck, Sigismund Weiß, and Martin Cannabich (father of the composer Christian Cannabich).

Weiß was a brother of the Dresden lutenist Silvius Leopold Weiß. He is survived by three solo sonatas, a trio with violin, and two hautboy concertos. The sonatas in G minor and B flat are excellent pieces. Böhm refered to Weiß's music in a letter quoted in Chapter 5, §D.13.

Of the woodwind players, by 1737 only Cannabich remained at court; Beck had left in 1734, and Weiß died in that year. This was a period when music was relatively dormant at the court, the Elector being involved in the War of Austrian Succession. Cannabich switched to flute in 1742, so the court was without hautboy players until 1745, when Bleckmann arrived. Anton Filtz was in Mannheim from 1754, and stood godfather to Bleckmann's son in the summer of 1757. Filtz, a highly-regarded composer, is survived by a solo sonata and a concerto for hautboy.

The opera house was dedicated in 1742, the year Carl Theodor began his reign. Carl Theodor spent great amounts on his Capelle, which 'for a brief period . . . represented a kind of musical Elysium unrivalled in many respects by larger and better-known centres'.[148]

The season 1747–8 marked the beginning of the brilliant opera and ballet productions that would continue at Mannheim for thirty years. It was the year the flutist Johann Baptist Wendling and the hautboist Alexander Lebrun were engaged at court. Lebrun, originally from Brussels, was solo hautboy of the orchestra and *Répétiteur* (Lebrun's son Ludwig August became a famous travelling hautboy virtuoso in the next generation). Johann Stamitz, leader of the Mannheim orchestra, wrote an excellent concerto for Lebrun sometime before 1757. The piece survives with three different middle movements, and the solo part has many notations for cadenzas. An hautboy concerto by the Capellmeister Holzbauer was also probably written for Lebrun.

The court musicians were involved in constant activities, including operas usually performed twice weekly, often followed by chamber concerts called *Kabinettsmusik*. 'Academies', or concerts featuring the fabled orchestra (which Leopold Mozart called 'undeniably the best in Europe'), were also given twice weekly (and included cards and tea for the audience). There were frequent gala days in honour of church festivals, royal birthdays and name days, weddings, etc., that included music.

[148] Wolf (1989), 213.

The Eisenmenger family had appointments as woodwind makers at the Mannheim court. Two hautboys survive made by members of this family. The elder Eisenmenger died in 1742; his son worked during the third quarter of the eighteenth century.

9. *Stuttgart*

From 1729 (at least officially, and perhaps before), Böhm had moved from Darmstadt to Stuttgart and was Concertmaster and principal woodwind player. He was in court service until 1755.

The presence of Böhm offered the possibility of exchanges of music with Pisendel at Dresden. It could have been through Böhm that the excellent Brescianello trio with violin is preserved at Dresden.

Pieces that Böhm may have played at Stuttgart that are now in the Friedrich Ludwig Sammlung (see Ch. 5, §D.16) include trios and a concerto by Bodinus, trios by Heinichen (H III 9b), Linike, Lotti, and Förster, a Telemann quintet for two hautbois d'amour, two violins, and bass, and a Brescianello hautboy–violin concerto (which may have been played by Böhm and the composer).

In 1744 Carl Eugen inherited the dukedom. He had been brought up at Friedrich II's court in Berlin, and had studied with Emanuel Bach. Until 1750 Carl Eugen's hautboy players were Böhm and Commerell (by 1750, Böhm was about 65 years of age). From 1750 Carl Eugen began spending vast sums on developing the Capelle and the Opera, and Stuttgart became one of the most important opera centres in Europe. Böhm was still on the rolls, but was assisted by Ignazio Ciceri. Commerell continued to play until 1772.

In 1755, the year that Jommelli took over from Brescianello as Capellmeister, both Böhm and Ciceri retired. For the 1758–9 season, Antonio and Carlo Besozzi were visitors at the court.

From 1759 Joan Baptista Pla was probably Jommelli's first hautboy; he was at Ludwigsburg until the end of 1768 (when the court cut back on its musical personnel).[149] One of the most interesting *galant* hautboy sonatas that survives, the *Sonata a due* in C minor, was written by Pla probably while he was at Stuttgart. There are melodic elements in the last movement that closely resemble arias in Jommelli's *La schiava liberata*, produced at Ludwigsburg in December 1768, suggesting that this piece was conceived at about that time. Pla cleverly chose technical effects that fit the hautboy like a glove but which sound 'difficult' to the ear because they are the kinds of passages that would be difficult on the violin (and most listeners used to hearing violin solos would consequently have heard them that way). Bar 26 of the first movement, bars 8–9 of the last, and the pyrotechnics at the

---

[149] Krauss (1908), 72.

very end of the piece are examples that actually lie easily on hautboy. (There are other passages, however, like the beginning of the second half of the last movement, that sound easier than they are.)

Another excellent sonata in C minor[150] that is in much the same style has been attributed to Giovanni Platti, a leading court composer at Würzburg and virtuoso not only as a tenor singer, but on the hautboy, violin, cello, harpsichord, and traverso. Platti is survived by a number of solos and chamber pieces for hautboy. The similarity of his name to that of Pla is the cause of the confusion of attribution of both this sonata and a wonderful concerto in G major that has been attributed to Platti in a modern edition.[151] Both pieces are probably by Pla.[152] The music by Platti that we are sure is his (for instance the trio for hautboy and violin in Wiesentheid) is less *galant* in style than Pla's.

10. *Bayreuth*

With the accession of Friedrich as Margrave of Bayreuth in 1735, musical activities, and especially opera, became intense at court. This was in large part due to his wife, the cultured and gifted Wilhelmine (favourite sister of Friedrich II of Berlin). Vivaldi dedicated two operas to Wilhelmine; Benda and Quantz were regular visitors to the court. The famous opera house was dedicated in 1748. In 1750 Wilhelmine wrote to her brother:

J'ai fait une grande acquisition d'un Hautbois qui surpasse pour l'Embouchure et l'execution touts ce qu'on en scauroit dire. Je n'ai jamais pu souffrir cett Instrument et l'avois banni d'ici. Mais cette homme scait le moderer et entirer si bien parti qu'il touche veritablement.[153]	I have made a great acquisition in an hautboy player whose control of embouchure and general performance is beyond the ability of words to describe. I have never been able to stand the instrument before and banned it here. But this man knows how to moderate and control it in such a way that it is truly touching.

There were no hautboys at court until 1738, when Christian Wunderlich was appointed (at the age of 16). By 1742 he was given the title Cammerhautboist and Cammervirtuoso, and he served the Margraves until at least 1786. It was probably of Wunderlich, then 28 years old, that Wilhelmine had written.

---

[150] Dresden (MS score), Mus 2782-S-2.

[151] A word of warning on this edition by Lebermann (Schott), which, though musical, differs in many details from the original. Almost all the changes make the piece more difficult to play (as for example the trills in the third movement, bars 80–3, which are Lebermann's invention).

[152] This is my opinion based on their musical style.

[153] Letter to Frederick II, 21 Mar. 1750, quoted in *MGG* ix. 1805.

PL. 7.5. Johann Friedrich Metzsch, performance of a concerto. Painting on porcelain bowl, *c*.1740. Courtesy of the Focke-Museum, Bremen (Inv. Nr. 29.17)

At some point before 1753 (when he left for Darmstadt), Christoph Metsch joined the Capelle, probably as second hautboy. He was replaced in 1754 by Joachim Döbbert from the Berlin Opera. One wonders if these players were using instruments from nearby Nuremberg or, with the close connections to Berlin, instruments from the north.

A painting on a porcelain bowl by an artist named Johann Friedrich Metzsch (fl. 1735–51) shows a performance of a 'Concerto Hautbois'[154] by five players (Pl. 7.5). Two hautboy players are shown, one left-handed. Metzsch worked in Bayreuth, and one wonders if he was related to Christoph Metsch, and the two players depicted on the bowl are not Metsch and Wunderlich.

The Capellmeister at Bayreuth from 1734 to 1761 was Johann Pfeiffer, who was also Margravine Wilhelmine's music tutor. Pfeiffer is survived by a number of chamber pieces and solos with hautboy, probably written after the appointment of Wunderlich. One of Pfeiffer's trios for hautboy and violin in B♭,[155] uses the same themes as three of the movements of HWV 380, a trio usually attributed to Handel.

---

[154] Claimed by the Museum to be by Johann Mathias Suhl, although no name is visible.
[155] Manuscript in Regensburg, dated a1748.

Pfeiffer worked them out quite differently after the first few bars. The flutist Jacob Kleinknecht, who joined the Capelle in 1743 (and later became Capellmeister), is survived by several fine trios with hautboy, in Berlin *empfindsamer* style. A collection of quartets (*c*.1743) also survives by Adam Falckenhagen, lutenist at the court from 1729.

Wilhelmine died in 1758, and with her, the period of Bayreuth's eighteenth-century musical glory.

11. Nuremberg

Like Leipzig, Nuremberg continued to be an important source of good hautboys during this period. With the death of Schell in 1732 and Jacob Denner in 1735, the responsibility for making hautboys in Nuremberg centred on David Denner and the Oberlender family.[156]

As suggested in Chapter 5, §D.16, David Denner evidently took over the 'I.C. Denner' workshop stamp. He worked into the 1750s or 1760s. Wilhelm Oberlender sen. was active until *c*.1745. Oberlender jun. may have taken over Jacob Denner's workshop in 1735, and have run it during Denner's last months (when he was ill). Oberlender jun. lived until 1779. He is survived by one hautboy.[157]

D. England

By 1750 London was a wealthy commercial centre and by far the largest city in Europe; its concert life was also probably the busiest. Although players continued to arrive from abroad, hautboy sections that had previously been staffed only by Continental players gradually admitted English musicians—probably pupils of the foreigners of the previous generation.

It is difficult to isolate a typical English hautboy of the period 1730–60 (cf. Pl. 4.7). Few instruments were dated, and most of the better-known makers (like Stanesby jun.) had careers that preceded these dates, or extended beyond them (Gedney, Schuchart, and Cahusac sen. for instance).[158] There are four extant instruments that can probably be attributed to this generation, however. John Schuchart is survived by one intact hautboy, a Type B.[159] Schuchart established his shop in 1731, and may have apprenticed with Bressan (Bressan died in that year). There is also an

---

[156] Other makers from this period by whom no hautboys have survived were Löhner, Meisenbach, Staub, and Zick. See Waterhouse (1993).

[157] Wendelin Oberlender, another son of Oberlender sen., was a player as well as builder. He was an instrument maker from 1738 and a member of the Stadtpfeifer from 1750; on his early death in 1751 he was called an 'Hautbois- und Flötenmacher' (Nickel 1971: 299–300). None of his hautboys is known to survive.

[158] An hautboy by Harris (owned by Tony Bingham in 1985) may also be from mid-century.

[159] Glasgow A42–68ao (Young Y2).

hautboy by Benjamin Hallet,[160] who worked from before 1736 to after 1753, and two examples by John Mason,[161] who was active in the 1750s. One of the Masons, now owned by Masashi Honma, is a Type D1, and sounds in his hands very much like later eighteenth-century hautboys, such as those of Grenser and Grundmann.

1. Sammartini's first decade and the fall of Kytch, 1729–1740

From the moment Sammartini moved to London in 1729,[162] hautboy playing in England was never the same. The 1730s and 1740s were dominated by this remarkable player, 'thought to be the finest performer on the hautboy in Europe'.[163] Sammartini's playing profoundly affected his audiences and was fondly remembered well into the next century. He performed as a soloist in the Opera orchestra at the King's Theatre, gave public concerts, and from 1736 was music master of the family of the Prince of Wales.

Hawkins's account of Sammartini (1776: 894), though limited by his ignorance of the world beyond London and the typical chronocentric perspective of late-eighteenth-century historians (in this respect, Burney was just as bad) shows genuine admiration: 'Giuseppe San Martini . . . was a performer on the hautboy, an instrument invented by the French, and of small account, till by his exquisite performance, and a tone which he had the art of giving it, brought it into reputation.' As Page (1988: 362) points out, Hawkins was 10 years old when Sammartini began playing regularly in London. His acquaintance with hautboy playing before then would have been fairly sketchy, and he was hardly in a position to make a reliable comparison from personal experience. But as the dominant hautboy player of the next two decades, Sammartini would have fixed Hawkins's ideas during his teens and 20s of what an hautboy could do (in his 20s, Hawkins was an active amateur musician). Though written a generation after Sammartini's death, his accounts are thus first-hand. He added:

As a performer on the hautboy, Martini was undoubtedly the greatest that the world had ever known. Before his time the tone of the instrument was rank, and, in the hands of the ablest proficients, harsh and grating to the ear; by great study and application, and by some peculiar management of the reed, he contrived to produce such a tone as approached the nearest to that of the human voice of any we know of.[164]

We will never be able to hear what it was that made Sammartini's playing so compelling, or how it differed from that of players already established, like Kytch.

---

[160] Oxford: Bate 21.   [161] Aylesbury 132.73 and Tokyo: Honma.
[162] The *Daily Journal*, 19 May 1729, cited in Lasocki (1988), 351.   [163] Hawkins (1776), v. 369–71.
[164] As late as 1827, an anonymous article in the *Quarterly Musical Magazine* (p. 468) echoed Hawkins: 'Martini . . . charmed his audience no less by the beauty of the tone and its near approximation to the human voice, than by its flexibility. His peculiar management and formation of the reed was supposed to have produced this difference.'

Sammartini's surviving music leaves no doubt of his technical virtuosity, and Hawkins singles out his tone; there must have been a strong emotional content in his playing as well. Kytch had his greatest success with his adaptations of Handel's vocal solos, a genre that succeeds effortlessly on hautboy, and it was probably he for whom Handel wrote his subtle and tender solos in *Acis and Galatea*. According to Burney, Kytch was sometimes 'engaged at two or three private parties of an evening to play opera songs, etc., etc., which he executed with exquisite taste and feeling'.[165]

It is likely that Sammartini's technique was more flamboyant than Kytch's, and that his style was more extroverted. The change in taste in instrumental performance—from intimate and delicate to energetic and exhibitionist—seems to parallel the one that occurred in Paris in the late 1720s and 1730s. Two years after Sammartini's death, and after two decades of his prominence in the musical world of London, Charles Avison wrote in 1752 (p. 112): 'The Hautboy will best express the Cantabile, or "singing style", and may be used in all movements what-ever under this denomination; especially those movements which tend to Gay and Chearful.'

For unclear reasons, after 'Volale più dei venti' in *Muzio Scevola* (1721), Handel wrote no further obbligatos for his regular orchestral hautboys. David Lasocki (pers. comm.) noticed that although hautboys doubled strings about half the time in Handel's operas, the hautboy had fewer solo obbligatos than traverso or recorder, and there was a gap between 1724 and 1737 in which no solos appeared. If it was indeed Sammartini who was the soloist in 1724 (see Ch. 5, §E.1), Handel evidently awaited his return before writing further hautboy obbligatos. Kytch seems to have been in the Opera orchestra at the end of 1734,[166] and was probably the principal hautboy until 1737.[167]

Sammartini was never a regular member of the Opera orchestra, but was featured as an invited soloist, much like the star singers. He appeared with Farinelli in February 1735 in the aria 'Lusingato dalla speme' in *Polifemo*, which Porpora had written for the two of them.[168] It is a remarkable piece, beginning with the hautboy accompanied by a bass played by the violins. It is in a slow tempo with figural imi-tation between the voice and instrument, usually staggered by a beat, and there are several opportunities for cadenzas.

In 1737 Handel featured Sammartini in three virtuoso opera arias at Covent Garden (two of which included two other ripieno hautboy players, presumably the regular members of the orchestra.) The obbligatos were 'Quella fiamma' in *Arminio* (produced in January),[169] 'Quel torrente che s'innalza sulla sponda' in Act II of

---

[165] Baines (1957), 280 citing Burney in Rees's *Cyclopaedia*.   [166] Lasocki (1983), 869.
[167] He played between-act music at the Haymarket Theatre in 1735 (Page 1988: 361).
[168] Burney mentions this aria (1776: ii. 797).   [169] Cf. Dean (1970), 198.

Giustino (February), and 'Chi t'intende?' from *Berenice* (May). What is striking about these arias is the role they give the hautboy as a true soloist; they offer as much latitude to ornament and 'grandstand' as is given to the vocal soloist (cf. Hasse's 'Già sereno il disperai', for Besozzi, performed sixteen years later). And when the hautboy plays at the same time as the singer, the two parts are often in thirds, or answer each other in similar phrases. This continued a tradition already seen in the earliest known solo hautboy arias, which Handel probably knew well in Hamburg. 'Quella fiamma' 'was a showpiece for the soprano castrato Conti and has three oboe parts, a spectacular obbligato for Giuseppe Sammartini and two ripieno parts as well'.[170] 'Quel torrente' showed off Sammartini's technique in many exposed passages, and even gave him a long solo cadenza (with written-out notes 'ad libitum'). 'Chi t'intende?' is a 'passionate address to the god of love',[171] and involves three separate sections in different tempos.

The arrival of Sammartini must have had an effect on the careers of the players he necessarily displaced. Loeillet died in 1730, at the early age of 50, a year after Sammartini's definitive move to London. Galliard was by then about 63, and considerably occupied with other affairs (although he did perform an hautboy solo of his own composition in his benefit concert of 1740). But Kytch was probably at the height of his powers when Sammartini arrived, and was the most celebrated hautboy player in England. Less than a decade later, he died insolvent, in sordid circumstances. This was shortly after Sammartini's triumphs of 1737. As Lasocki noted, Kytch 'would have found himself in financial difficulties again in the 1737–8 season when operas were produced only irregularly'.[172] Burney wrote of Kytch's end: 'He neglected his family, then himself; consequently he became totally incapable of appearing before any respectable assembly, and at last he was found one morning breathless [i.e. dead] in St. James's Market, in a deplorable condition . . .'[173] Drummond (1978: 269) describes how, in 1738, three London musicians, Festing (probably the hautboist/flutist John Festing),[174] Weidemann, and a member of the Vincent family (probably Thomas sen.)

were standing at the door of the Orange Coffee House in the Haymarket [perhaps on a rehearsal break] when they happened to see two boys driving asses and obviously in a desperately impoverished condition. On recognizing the children to be the sons of a former colleague—the oboe player Kytch who had died suddenly, leaving his family destitute—Festing and his companions contacted a number of musicians whom they thought might

---

[170] Ibid. 198.   [171] Ibid. 167.

[172] In a forthcoming book on pitch history, I speculate that the Opera orchestra had gone from its former pitch of A–1 (about A-415) to about A-423 (which I call Q–2) by the time Sammartini played these three arias in 1737. It is possible that Kytch never made this pitch switch, and was already no longer a part of the orchestra by this time.   [173] Lasocki (1983), 869 quoting Parke quoting Burney (presumably in Rees's *Cyclopaedia*).

[174] Drummond gives Michael Christian Festing, but on what basis is unclear. John Festing was one of the original Governors of the Royal Society of Musicians, as was 'Thomas Vincent'.

support their cause, and raised subscriptions to help the boys. They then conceived the idea of establishing a permanent fund to alleviate similar cases of distress.

Thus was founded London's Royal Society of Musicians (the RSM), on the initiative of three of Kytch's close colleagues. The Society still functions today, and as Lasocki (1983: 869) observed, is in a sense a memorial to Kytch.

Besides the Opera, there were in this period a number of other employment opportunities for hautboy players in London. Music remained an important element of playhouse performances into the 1750s.[175] There were many public concerts. Musicians who worked in the theatres continued to organize 'benefit concerts'. And the tradition of concerts held in taverns continued strong.[176] An important employment option was military bands, as this was work that could be done in the daytime, leaving the evenings free for concerts.[177] When in the summer the theatres closed, there was work at the pleasure gardens (see below). Page has found documentation for the continued functioning of the London city Waits until at least 1761. There were also private concerts in the homes of the wealthy. A number of large religious ceremonies took place during the 1730s that employed full orchestras.

Hautboy players in theatre orchestras normally doubled on other woodwinds like recorder and, from the late 1720s, traverso. Some hautboy players, like Festing and Weidemann of the Opera orchestra, were traverso specialists. Sammartini was also famous as a recorder virtuoso.

As a result of differences between Handel and his principal singers, an alternate company, the Opera of the Nobility, split away from the Opera at the King's Theatre. It opened in 1733–4 in direct competition to Handel's productions. The personnel of its orchestra is not known, but the split probably provided extra work for orchestral musicians for a few years. By 1737 some sort of unification between the companies had taken place.

The 1730s saw the first oratorios by Handel, starting with a revised version of *Esther* in 1732. Handel used his opera musicians for the oratorios. He wrote two important hautboy obbligatos in 1733 in the oratorios *Deborah* ('In Jehovah's awful sight') and *Athalia* ('What scenes of horror round me rise!') that may also have been for Sammartini, as they are both in the unusual key of F minor.[178] As noted above (Ch. 5, §E.1) in the case of 'Nel tuo seno' from *Giulio Cesare*, with Sammartini's hautboy pitched a semitone higher than the orchestra, he could have played these

---

[175] Page (1988), 361.

[176] Sammartini, with Burney and others, was a member of the Society of the Temple of Apollo, which may have organized concerts at the Devil Tavern (where the Apollo Society had had a weekly series starting in the 1730s).

[177] Page (1988), 359. For literature that might have been played in bands in this decade, see Handel 07.–09. and Carbonelli in Haynes (1992a).

[178] 'What scenes of horror round me rise!' is followed by a recitative and the same piece (with the same setting), but in C minor, with the text 'Oh Athalia, tremble at thy fate!'

solos in E minor (the texts of the arias explain Handel's choice of F minor for the orchestra). 'In Jehovah's awful sight' offers a potential double cadenza for soprano and hautboy at bar 23,[179] the kind of piece that would have been written for Sammartini.

Walsh came out with the first edition of Handel's Opus 3 *Concerti Grossi* in 1734; the second concerto has especially prominent hautboy parts, and the Largo for two solo cellos and solo hautboy with string accompaniment is one of the jewels of the hautboy's solo literature.

2. 'New Consort-pitch' and the rise of the straight-top, 1740–1750

Although Handel had other ideas, Italian opera continued to be performed in London in the 1740s; Galuppi worked at the King's Theatre from 1741 to 1743, and Gluck was there about 1745. But from 1743, when he returned from an extended visit to Dublin, Handel wrote no more staged Italian works, concentrating on oratorios in concert format instead. Several of these later oratorios, *Occasional oratorio* (1746), *Alexander Balus* (1747), *Solomon* (1748), and *The Triumph of Time and Truth* (1756–7) have hautboy solos.

In Sammartini's last decade, the 1740s, he and his pupil Thomas Vincent jun. performed as soloists at public concerts at Hickford's Room and at the Swan and Castle concerts. Sammartini may have written his Opus 13 solos in this decade (although it was not published until about 1760). Less interesting than the Rochester sonatas, they are still good pieces. The first movement of the second sonata has the same quick thirty-second-note downward runs as in Rochester V/2, clearly marked with wedges to indicate they were tongued; each place they occur is consistently marked 'dolce', and these may have been points where some leeway was taken with tempo.

Vincent's own six Solos, Opus 1, for 'Hautboy, German Flute, Violin, or Harpsichord', appeared in London in 1748. They are appealing, skilfully written, and fit the hautboy well. Vincent would probably have been using a Type C hautboy like his teacher (see below). He was in the King's/Queen's Band from 1735 to at least 1778, ran a concert series with Felice Giardini in the 1750s,[180] and was director of the King's Theatre, 1765–9. In 1784 he was solo hautboist at the Handel Commemoration Festival. His performances were praised by Burney, among others. Since his brother Richard, who died in 1783, was also a professional hautboy player, contemporary references to 'Mr Vincent' are ambiguous.[181]

---

[179] Cf. Spitzer (1988), 522.

[180] Giardini is survived by several hautboy quartets that may have been played by Vincent.

[181] Thomas Vincent jun.'s father was mentioned in Ch. 5, §E.1. He may have played exclusively bassoon, but if he played hautboy, he would probably have retired by about 1745.

The court was still an important source of employment for instrumentalists in the 1740s, and 'most of the prominent oboists of the period were members of the King's or the Queen's Band or held some other court position'.[182]

Richard Neale of the Opera orchestra played at Lincoln's Inn Fields Theatre from 1727 to about 1735. He performed in Arne's *Comus* in 1743 in Dublin, doubling on traverso, and was at Covent Garden from about 1738 to 1744. Neale's specialty was performing hautboy concertos. He was one of the first governors of the RSM.[183]

The pleasure gardens in London like Ranelagh (from 1742), Marylebone (from *c*.1659), and Vauxhall (from 1661, renovated in the late 1730s) were important concert venues of a more informal type. These concerts were among the most popular musical events in London, and were held three nights a week, from late spring to early autumn.[184] Programmes included vocal and instrumental music, usually with/for orchestra. Concertos were popular. The concerts at the pleasure gardens provided considerable employment for hautboy players, including soloists. Richard Vincent played frequently at Vauxhall, and John Perkins played an hautboy concerto between the acts of Pergolesi's *La serva padrona* in 1758 at Marylebone Gardens.

There were a number of large-scale outdoor performances that involved massed double-reeds. Handel's *Water Music* had regular performances into the 1760s, and the *Music for the Royal Fireworks*, involving at least twenty-four hautboy players, was premièred in 1749. As Page noticed (1988: 359–60), such performances were possible because of the large pool of players working part-time in bands supported by military units stationed in the London area.

Francesco Barsanti, who had moved to Edinburgh in 1735, published several works there in 1742. The most interesting of his solos for hautboy is the *Collection of Old Scots Tunes* with continuo. In 1743, then in his early 50s, Barsanti moved back to London. At this point, 'being advanced in years' (meaning perhaps that he was unable or unwilling to move on to a newer kind of hautboy), he opted for a viola desk in the Opera band and at Vauxhall, and continued to publish his compositions.

In the years before mid-century, it is clear that the prevailing orchestral pitch in London had become the so-called 'new Consort-pitch', about A-423, a pitch that appears to have been common in England until the second quarter of the nineteenth century.[185] The famous tuning fork left by Handel in 1751 at the Foundling Hospital is at 422.5, and is supposed to represent the pitch of the organ that Handel himself presented to the Hospital in 1750.

---

[182] Page (1988), 362.

[183] Under 'Bassoon', Coetlogon (1745) listed a player at Drury Lane Theatre named De Ricourt, described as 'A *Frenchman*, . . . who is one of the best Hautboys in *Europe* and plays extremely well on the *German* flute'. De Ricourt is otherwise unknown and is not listed in Hodges (1980).   [184] Weber (1989), 313.

[185] See Haynes (1995), 347.

PL. 7.6. Anonymous, *c*.1740, 'Concert Italien'. Lost; formerly
Manskopf Collection, Frankfurt a. M.

Along with this pitch level, it was apparently in the 1740s that the first straight-top hautboys, Type C, began to be made in England. Stanesby jun. is survived by a Type C,[186] and two by his apprentice Caleb Gedney are extant. There is a good chance that the straight-top model, which Anciuti was already making in the 1730s, was brought from Milan to London by Sammartini, and that (with its obviously different appearance) it was associated with him.

The player shown in the frontispiece to *The Compleat Tutor for the Hautboy*, brought out in about 1746 by John Simpson, is probably Sammartini, to judge from the resemblance of the subject to the picture of Sammartini in the *Concert Italien* (Pls. 2.22 and 7.6).[187] The player is holding a Type C hautboy.

Whoever this player was, it is clear that the Type C was in use in England in the 1740s, since Simpson's tutor is dated *c*.1746. Stanesby's straight-top (or others like it that have not survived) was most likely made before Sammartini's death in 1750 (Stanesby himself died in 1754). Soon afterwards, Type C became all the rage in England, and many of the hautboists mentioned below would have used such instruments.

3. *Sammartini's legacy, 1750–1760*

A list of orchestral players survives for a performance of *Messiah* conducted by Handel at the Foundling Hospital in 1754. It is in interesting contrast to the

---

[186] Hamamatsu A-0243R.

[187] Whether a relationship existed between John and Redmond Simpson (see below) is an interesting matter for speculation.

comparable list made up for the Lord Mayor's Day festivities in 1727, a quarter-century earlier (see Ch. 5, §E.1). Both lists include important London hautboists, but none of the same players is present. Sammartini had not yet settled in London in 1727, and was gone by 1754. One wonders, in fact, how many of the players on the 1754 list had been students of Sammartini. They were (probably in order of rank, to judge from their pay) 'Eyford' (Eiffert), Teede, Vincent (Richard or Thomas), and Simpson. In a similar list made in 1758 they were Eiffert, Teede, Vincent, and Weichsel.

Philipp Eiffert had an active career after 1754, and was apparently resident in Oxford. He was a member of the RSM from 1750. William Teede (Tiede) was a member of the RSM from 1739, and was listed as a teacher of flute and hautboy in 1763. Redmond Simpson was the lowest-paid hautboy on the 1754 list and was not rehired in 1758. Simpson rose to prominence and popularity as a soloist at the end of that decade, however, and was a member of the Queen's Band by about 1763.[188] Carl Weichsel became the principal hautboist at the King's Theatre in the early 1760s, and played the clarinet in that instrument's debut in English opera in 1760, possibly with Barbandt.

Carl Barbandt was probably in London by 1752, the year his Opus 1 trio sonatas were published by Walsh. One of the Vincents was among the subscribers to those pieces (which are good, and similar in style to Fasch). Barbandt was described there as 'Musician to His Majesty at Hanover'. He was an extremely versatile performer, playing woodwind and keyboard instruments.

Several hautboy concertos survive from the hand of Sir William Herschel, a distinguished astronomer who was posted to England from Germany as an infantry hautboist during the Seven Years War. After a successful career as a performer, composer, and conductor in various English cities, he eventually turned to astronomy. He discovered the planet Uranus in 1781, and the following year was appointed Astronomer Royal.

The great chess player and composer François-André Philidor[189] lived in England in the years preceding the publication of *L'Art de la modulation* (1755), his only instrumental work, and the use of the names 'oboe' on the part and 'haut-boy' in the title suggests that it was written for an English player.[190] *L'Art de la modulation* consists of six quartets for hautboy, two violins, and continuo, and is of considerable interest musically. Despite the date, the melodies and harmonies of these pieces are already very much in a classical idiom; they have the feeling of

---

[188] Simpson appeared as soloist at Covent Garden at least twenty-one times in 1763 alone (Page 1988: 361).

[189] Philidor was the best chess player of his generation and probably the next as well; his opening defence (he always played black) is still well-known. See Allen (1863).

[190] It might also have been written for Joan Baptista Pla, who was in England in the early 1750s.

hautboy quartets (see below, §E.3).[191] Philidor, who had a remarkable career, was the youngest son of André Philidor, born when his father was about 79 years old.

Stanesby jun. stopped producing in the early 1750s and was succeeded by Gedney, who worked until 1769. Schuchart's son Charles took over his father's workshop (probably in 1753), and maintained it until 1767.[192]

Two sets of visiting hautboy virtuosos appeared in London in the 1750s, both probably playing Type D1 instruments (and perhaps introducing them to English players). The Pla brothers performed a 'Duetto on Hautboys' at an interval in Arne's *Alfred* on 27 March 1754. Avison had written in 1752 that their playing 'excited the admiration of the town',[193] implying their presence in London in that year.[194] Their *Six Sonatas for two German-flutes, Violins, or Hautboys, with a Bass* was published in London by Hardy in about 1754. The brothers went on to Paris and later to Stuttgart (see above, §C.9).

Antonio and Carlo Besozzi, temporarily displaced by the bombardment and occupation of Dresden by the Prussians, performed a concerto (probably of Antonio's composition) in the interval of a performance of Hasse's *I pellegrini* in March 1757. Soon afterwards, they gave a benefit concert. It was probably no coincidence that Alessandro Besozzi's *Six Solos with Continuo* was published by Chapman in London two years later (see above, §A.1). Antonio or Carlo may have performed them there.

E. Other Areas

1. The Dutch Republic

No Italian hautboy players are known to have been active in the Dutch Republic in this period, although the violinist Pietro Locatelli moved to Amsterdam the same year Sammartini moved to London, 1729. Locatelli's presence probably generated concert activity there, and he is known to have written a solo and a set of trios for hautboy.

One gets the impression of regular musical activity in the Dutch Republic. Conrad Hurlebusch, originally from Germany, was the organist at the Oude Kerk from 1743; he wrote at least one quartet with two hautboys. In Amsterdam in the 1750s Antoine Mahaut and D. S. del Croebelis published several collections for

---

[191] Although the continuo is figured.

[192] It was then continued by Collier until some time after 1791.

[193] Page (1988), 363, quoting Avison, *Essay on Musical Expression* (2nd edn., 1753), 120.

[194] As noted above, Pla also performed in Paris in May of 1752.

amateurs that could be played on hautboy. As shown in two engravings by [? Jan] Punt made in 1752, hautboys were employed in military units in Holland.

Dutch hautboy makers continued actively supplying players in this period. There are numerous extant hautboys by Van Heerde, Steenbergen, Terton, Beukers sen. and jun., Van Buuren, Fredrik Richters, Wijne, Borkens, and Heller that were probably made between 1730 and 1760.

2. The Austrian Netherlands

Alexander Lebrun (d. 1771), solo hautboy of the famous orchestra at Mannheim from 1747, came originally from Brussels and may have begun his career there.

Henri de Croes was the royal chapel master at Brussels from 1749. There was an orchestra at court, which he may have led. He is survived by two concertos for hautboy or flute.

Prince Charles of Lorraine maintained an orchestra in Brussels whose principal hautboy player was a certain A. Vanderhagen. Vanderhagen's nephew Amand studied with him, and later wrote an excellent method for the hautboy (published *c*.1790).

Rottenburgh sen. retired in the mid-1730s, but his workshop continued to produce instruments until about 1775 under the supervision of three of his sons.[195] The shop moved several times. The surviving Type E hautboys with the 'I. H. Rottenburgh' stamp were presumably made after the father's retirement.[196] Probably after 1740, the second son, Godfridus Adrianus ('G. A. Rottenburgh'), began a separate workshop using his own name. Two surviving hautboys have his stamp.

3. The Habsburg lands

As we have seen, music at the court of Charles VI was well financed and highly developed. The last decade of his reign, 1730–40, was no exception. But political and military circumstances forced his successor, the Empress Maria Theresia, to reduce the strength of the Hofcapelle in 1740. Several hautboy players' careers at court ended in this year (e.g. Schön, who lived until 1763). Italian opera (the most expensive court spectacle) was even phased out for some time. In the 1730s, the court employed the hautboists Gabriel, Schön, Schulz, Hartmann, Widmann, and Gazzaroli. In the 1740s and 1750s, these last three were retained, but there were evidently no new appointments.

---

[195] Ottenbourgs (1989), 9.
[196] The fact that hautboys with the Rottenburgh stamp were probably derived from French models (either Type A2 or Type E) indicates the orientation of the shop, and probably its customers.

The Viennese theatre orchestras probably employed a number of hautboy players; their seasons ran throughout the year. Three whose names are known are Kühtreiber, Engelhardt, and Jauzer. At least one ballet, *La Force du sang* by Starzer (1757), featured an hautboy obbligato.[197]

The nobility from all over the Habsburg Empire resided in Vienna for much of the year (autumn and winter were the social season), and each household brought its Capelle or domestic musicians along.[198] At the Palais Rofrano, Prince Joseph Friedrich of Saxe-Hildburghausen had a standing orchestra and regular concerts in the 1750s. They were led by the court composer Giuseppe Bonno, who is survived by several wind quintets (for the standard combination, two hautboys, two horns, bassoon). One of the Besozzis (probably Antonio from Dresden or his younger brother Gaetano from Naples) appeared at the Palais Rofrano.[199]

It was common to have figural music (that is, music with instruments) in churches in Austria, and hautboy players were regularly involved except where there were strictures on wind instruments in church.[200]

By the 1760s, as suggested by Josef Haydn's letter to Prince Esterházy (quoted in Ch. 2, §D.3), the Habsburg Lands were self-sufficient in hautboy makers. Haydn saw no need to look further for new instruments than Vienna and the maker Rocko Baur, and it can be assumed that many other players in the Habsburg domains thought similarly (NB. Baur's waiting list). Baur evidently straddled the shift in style between Type D1 and the classical hautboy; two of his surviving instruments are the former (Y1 and Y3), and one (Y2) is classical.[201]

The Esterházy court at Eisenstadt employed the hautboist Carl Braun from 1737; it was probably for him that the previous Capellmeister, Werner, wrote the solo in *David* (1750). Michael Kapffer was appointed in the early 1750s. By the time Haydn wrote his letter, Braun had moved over to violin, and Georg Kapffer (perhaps Michael's brother) had joined the hautboy section.

In Prague, Italian opera was performed at the Kotce Theatre from 1738. This would have provided regular work for at least two good hautboy players. A few pieces survive by major composers from Prague, including Brixi and Habermann, evidently written for hautboy players there.[202] From the 1720s, there was an active musical programme at the Cathedral of St Vitus that involved at least one hautboy.[203] The Czech-speaking lands had a long tradition of wind music, and

---

[197] Brown and Sadie (1989), 114.   [198] Raynor (1972), 321.   [199] Brown and Sadie (1989), 119.

[200] Another restriction could have had to do with pitch. Winds were normally at A+o, and where organs were a semitone higher, transposition could be problematic.

[201] The identities of several makers with the name 'Baur' have not yet been sorted out. Cf. Waterhouse (1993) and Maunder (1998), 181, 187.

[202] Joseph Ignaz Flasska was an hautboist at Prague active from (? 1720s–1772) who composed concertos and other solos for hautboy, and a large amount of wind music, that has yet to be located. Hodges (1980), 233–4.

[203] Hogwood and Smaczny (1989), 203.

several wind quintets survive by composers working in Prague (cf. Cigler and Brixi). Burney in 1771 noted the particular excellence of hautboy players 'on the Saxon side of Bohemia', and the cultivation of the horn there is well known. Wind groups were regularly employed by aristocratic families, and Haydn wrote several Partitas for wind quintet in 1759–61 when he was Capellmeister at Lukavec near Pilsen.[204]

Wind quintets were evidently popular in Vienna as well, and from this period many Partitas by Asplmayer and Hofmann survive. The quintet eventually mutated into the wind octet with pairs of hautboys, clarinets, horns, and bassoons.

String quartets, often called divertimentos, began to appear in the 1750s, and with them, the earliest hautboy quartets for violin, viola, cello, and hautboy, a genre that after about 1770 replaced the solo sonata as the hautboy's main solo vehicle in chamber settings. In the hautboy quartet (which developed parallel with the string quartet, and was inspired by the same aesthetics), the cello no longer acted as a continuo (figured) bass, but rather as the lowest melodic part.[205] Early examples are Gassmann's *Sei Quartetti*, Opus 1, H.481–6, which survive in different printed and manuscript versions for flute or hautboy, and may have been written in the 1750s. In contrast to later hautboy quartets, Gassmann's *Quartetti* do not cast the hautboy consistently as the soloist but rather as an equal (if important) member of the ensemble, and the hautboy parts are not designed for virtuoso display. In this way they are similar to Philidor's *Art de la modulation* of 1755.

4. Spain

In this period, Madrid was the predominant musical centre in Spain. A post in the Real Capilla (the royal chapel) was prestigious and well paid, and allowed the player to participate in theatrical activities as well. The same three hautboy players are documented in the Real Capilla in 1736 as in the previous years; to judge from their salaries, Gesembach was the principal, followed by Brienne and Boucquet. A portrait of Philip V as an old man, with his family, was painted by Van Loo in 1743 (Pl. 7.7). The hautboy player depicted in the background may be Gesembach, who had probably been Philip's principal player during much of his reign.

There was evidently hautboy activity in other parts of Spain besides Madrid, as indicated by surviving music, such as a solo cantata by Gonima (1739), who was *Mestre de Capella* at Gerona (near Barcelona). A collection of *Canciones* (1751) also survives by Rodrigues de Hita of Palencia.

Ignazio Rion, who had been in Venice, Rome, and Naples, later came to Spain. Records at the Cathedral of Oviedo state that 'D. Ignacio Rión' entered its

---

[204] Cf. Hogwood and Smaczny (1989), 208–9.   [205] Cf. Tilmouth (1980), 276–8.

PL. 7.7. Louis Michel Van Loo, 1743, detail from *Philip V of Spain and his Family*. Madrid: Museo del Prado

service in 1731, having come from Madrid (how long he had been in Madrid is not clear). He died in Oviedo in 1734, leaving behind '163 sonatas' (perhaps of his own composition?) and some instruments, all now apparently lost.[206]

Kenyon de Pascual (1984: 434) also found evidence that Joan Baptista Pla was at the Madrid court in December 1738 to play an opera. By 1739, regular performances of Italian opera had ceased, probably because the medium never really appealed to a general audience. Orchestras played at the two main theatres only on an occasional basis.

Manuel Cavazza began playing in the court chapel as a supernumerary in 1742, and became the first Spanish hautboist appointed to the Capilla in 1744.[207] By 1749, all four of the court's hautboys (Cavazza, Mestres, López, and the composer Luis

---

[206] Casares Rodicio (1980), 117. I am grateful to Alfredo Bernardini for pointing out this information.
[207] Cavazza (Cabaza, Cavaza) was born in Spain to an Italian father. See Kenyon de Pascual (1984), 434.

Misón) were of Spanish origin. It is possible that these players had studied with Gesembach, Rion, or Pla.

Misón was a composer of considerable reputation, whose works were performed at the court of the Duke of Huescar. Huescar, like several other nobles of the time, frequently put on superb musical performances at his palace. The music performed at these concerts (much of which has since been destroyed by fires) may have included hautboy parts.

Music publishing was not encouraged by the crown, and as a result, 'Most Iberian music, regardless of merit, was imprisoned in manuscript form.'[208] Manuscript music was less well known, and of course more subject to loss.

During the reign of Ferdinand VI, 1746–59, Farinelli was director of royal entertainments, and organized musical events on a lavish scale. Many foreign virtuosos were invited (including, possibly, hautboy players).

[208] Russell (1989), 361.

Afterword

Although the history of the hautboy did not stop at this point, this book must, as it has already gone on too long. The instrument continued to evolve, and the next general form was the Type D2, the classical model, which served as the base to which a key-system was eventually applied in the 1820s.

'The rest', as they say, 'is history' (in this case, a history that has yet to be written in detail). The nineteenth century, seen through a glass darkly, still apparently too close and familiar to require much effort, will be an interesting challenge for historians of the oboe. To understand it better (and its direct precursor, the classical period) will be to gain deeper insight into the nature of both the period before and the one that followed; the Romantic oboe was created in reaction to the principles of the eighteenth century, a kind of 'negative image' of the hautboy. And of course it acted as the root of what was to become the ideal instrument of the twentieth.

Every age interprets history through its own eyes, and that view is constantly changing: 'We laugh at the mistakes of our fathers, as our descendents will laugh at us.'[1] The old assumption of straight-line progress to the supposed perfection of the present no longer seems useful. As Collingwood put it, 'Bach was not trying to write like Beethoven and failing; Athens was not a relatively unsuccessful attempt to produce Rome . . .'[2] The design of a musical instrument does not change for the same reason an automobile or toaster does. As a tool, its form is a direct result of what it is required to do. In a highly exacting atmosphere, it adapts—quickly—to the needs of its musical environment. As the music it must play changes, new techniques appear to accommodate it, while older ones atrophy. Thus each stage of the hautboy's evolution (in the neutral sense of adaptive change) represents an instrument closely and expertly adapted to the musical requirements of its age. I see the hautboy we have studied here as a series of brilliant responses to the demands of one of the more dynamic phases in the history of Western music.

---

[1] Friedländer (1942), 259.   [2] Collingwood (1946), 321.

Hautboy players 1600–1760, indexed chronologically by place of work

Amsterdam

1694–a1717. Nieuwenhoven, Johan van

Ansbach

1694. Erdmann, Ludwig
1696–1702. Bettinozzi, Pietro Lodovico
a1703–1703. Pertelle
a1703–p1723. Michel
1703–. Philipp
1703–at least 1707. Stollberger, Jobst
a1705. Kayser (Keyser), Johann (jun.)
1706–p1741. Voigt, Hans Jürgen
1708. Limppach, Adolph
1708–. Claup, Georg Friedr.
1726–65. Hummel, Joh. Friedrich
1737. Krezer (Kretzer), Johann Leonard
1737. Wieder, Albrecht Ernst

Arolsen

1699–. Neundorf, Georg
1699–c.1729. Prevost [Prévost], (? Charles)
a1700–1700. Jean
c.1700. Biano [Piano], Johann Hermann
c.1700. Liennard, Pierre
1712–45. Kehl, Vincenz
a1723–1734. Reinhardt (Reinhard), Franz
1723. Grünewald, Christoph Philipp
1723. Schmidt, Johann Henrich
1725–8. Grünewald, Christoph Philipp
1736–55. Schmidt, Johann Henrich
1741–c.1750. Lauterbach, Joh. Heinrich
1741–c.1750. Schäffer, Daniel

Bamberg

1714–54. Schnell, Johann Jacob

Barcelona

1710–13. Fasser, Johann Franz
1710–13. Hartmann, Daniel Franz
1710–13. Schindler, Johann Georg

Bayonne

1660. Boisson, Guillaume
1660. Davanta, Pierre
1660. Laroze, Jean
1660. Masson, Christophe
1660. Monjuif, Bernard
1660. Monjuif, Jean

Bayreuth

a1708. Claup, Georg Friedr.
a1708. Limppach, Adolph
1722. Enderle, Joh. Joseph
1738. Wunderlich, Christian Ferdinand
a1753. Metsch, Christoph
1754–. Döbbert, Joachim Wilhelm

Benthen on the Oder

c.1740. Kaeberle

Berlin

1681–p1701. Beauregard, François
1681–c.1702. Potot, Pierre
early 1690s. Erdmann, Ludwig

1692–. Pepusch, Gottfried

1693–1700. La Buissière (Laboussière),
Pierre de

1700–2. La Riche, François

1704–. Dümler, Gottfried

c.1704–*c*.1754. Glösch, Peter

1711. Fleischer, Carl Ludewig

1711–12. Schüler, Friedrich

1711–13. Rose, Johann Ludwig

1741–73. Quantz, Johann Joachim

c.1741–54. Döbbert, Joachim Wilhelm

1746. Jacobi, Johann Christian

1754. August, Carl

1754. Fischer, Georg Erhard

1754. Pauli, Friedrich Wilhelm

c.1754. Rodemann, Joachim Friedrich

Bologna

a1696, 1702–41. Bettinozzi, Pietro
Lodovico

c.1700, 1710, 1712. Erdmann, Ludwig

1712–22. Pierini, Pompeo

[? 1717–35. Barsanti, Francesco]

Bonn

early 18th c. Salomon, Philipp

Bordeaux

1711. Ferrier, Louis (fils)

Braunschweig

c.1720. Grüneberg, M. M.

c.1720. Schmidt, August

c.1720. Statz, Joh. Christian

1720. Fleischer, Carl Ludewig

1728–31. Tischer, Johann Nikolaus

1731, 1735. Freymuth (Freymut), Alois

a1749. Bode [Bodé], Johann Joachim
Christoph

Brussels

1692. Teubner, Felix

1692–6. Schuechbauer, Franz Simon

1692–*c*.1703. Normand (Lenormand), Rémy

c.1703. Loeillet, Jacob

May 1729. Sammartini, Giuseppe

Cannons

1717–20. Chaboud, Pietro

1718–19. Mercy, Louis

1718–20. Biancardi, [Sigr]

(?1718)/1719–1720/(?1721). Kytch, Jean
Christian

Cassel

1720–2. Hummel, Joh. Friedrich

p1742. Braun, Anton

Castel (near Darmstadt)

1717. Schickhardt, Johann Christian

Celle

1670–98. Tourneur, Denis la

1680. Beauregard, François

1680–3. Griffon, Nicolas

1681–95. Forlot

1681–1706. Courbesas, Le

1681–1706. Garenne, de la

1681–1706. Saint Amour

1682–91. Spannuht, Johann Heinrich

1683–98. Maréchal, Pierre

1683–1706. Mignier, Johann

1691–1710. Voigt, Ullrich Johann

1698–1703. Grimm, Ernst Heinrich

1698–1706. Galliard, Johann Ernst

1698–1706. Voigt, Hans Jürgen

a1706. Voigt (Vogt), Johann Georg

1752–7. Bode [Bodé], Johann Joachim
Christoph

1757. Ernesti

1768. Marckquardt, Wilhelm

1768–97. Seyfarth, Johann Justinus

Corbach

until 13 Jan 1699. Neundorf, Georg

Cöthen

1713–54. Rose, Johann Ludwig
a1714–28. Würdig, Johann Gottlieb
c.1715–. Rose, Johann Ludwig II
1716–20. Freitag, Johann Heinrich
1719–20. Schickhardt, Johann Christian
1724 and probably earlier. Jacobi, Gottlieb
   Siegmund
1754. Bahn, — (sen.)

Cremona

1739. Prover, Filippo

Darmstadt

1687–8. Fairint
c.1706–11; 1711–30 (afterwards Emeritus).
   Corseneck, Johann
1709–19. Kayser, Johann (jun.)
c.1710–12. ? Schickhardt, Johann Christian
1711–29. Böhm, Johann Michael
1719. Fleischer, Carl Ludewig
1738–62. Stolz (Stoltz), Jakob Friedrich
1748–79. Schön, Joh. Heinrich
1753–67. Metsch, Christoph

Dresden

a1696–1707. Steinberg, Charles
1696. Delveaux, Nicolaus
1696. Schwaiberger (Schweiberger), Anton
1696–1707. Gresle, Johann Wolfgang
1696–1707. Gresle, Tobias
1696–1733. Henrion, Jean-Baptiste
1696–1738. Henrion, Charles
1699–1731. La Riche, François
(? early 18th c.). Simon, Heinrich
early 18th c. Kummer
1709. Reche (Roger), Johann (? Christian)
1709–14. D'Huissé (D'Ucé), Jean Baptiste
1709–44. Richter, Johann Christian
by 1711 to 1733. Weigelt, Christian
c.1711–33. Blockwitz, Johann Martin
1714. Steinmetz, Johann Erhard

1717–53. Ristori, Giovanni Alberto
1718–*c*.1721. Quantz, Johann Joachim
1728. Aubry, Claude
1738–early 1770s. Besozzi, Antonio
1755–73. Fischer, Johann Christian
1755–92. Besozzi, Carlo

Edinburgh

1735–43. Barsanti, Francesco

Eisenach

c.1695. Bach, Johann Jacob
c.1695. Halle, Johann Heinrich

Erbach

a1738. Stolz (Stoltz), Jakob Friedrich

Esterháza

1 Mar. 1737 to *c*.1760. Braun, Carl
by 1753 to 1769. Kapffer [Kapfer], Johann
   Michael

Ettal

1730s. Klauseck, (Johann) Ignaz

Florence

1709–57. Erdmann, Ludwig
by 1746–*c*.1809. Dôthel, Nicolas

Freiburg

Fischer, Johann Christian

Freysingen

1727. Notrup

Gera

? 1708. Leonhardt, Johann Michael

Ghent

1702. Loeillet, Jacob
Loeillet, Pieter

Gotha

1733. Bach, Johann Andreas

Guben

1748. Schröter, Johann Friedrich

Halle

1676–. Hyntzsch, Michael
end of 17th c.–1724. Hyntzsch, Johann
   Georg I
1703–12. Müller, Christian
1707. Hyntzsch, Johann Georg II
c.1710–25. Nicolai, Christian August
c.1710–. Körbitz, Gottfried
by 1712. Hyntzsch, Joh. Samuel
1724, 1740. Zincke, Gabriel
1731. Ludwig, Joh. Philipp
1740. Hübner, Christian Wilhelm
1740. Körbitz, Joh. Christoph
1740. Schilling, Christoph

Hamburg

1710s. Böhm, Johann Michael
1712. Schickhardt, Johann Christian
by 1722. Freymuth (Freymut), Alois
1725–9. Kayser, Johann (jun.)
1757. Bode [Bodé], Johann Joachim
   Christoph

Hannover

a1698–1698. Des Noyers (Desnoyes),
   Matthieu
a1698–1698. Loges, de
1698. Des Noyers, François
? 1706–. Courbesas, Le
? 1706–. Garenne, de la
? 1706–. Saint Amour
1760–8. Seyfarth, Johann Justinus
a1767. Herschel, Isaac

Helmstedt

1749. Bode [Bodé], Johann Joachim
   Christoph

Königsberg

c.1700–32. Berwald, Johann Gottfried

Köslin

from 1735. Arsandt, D. S.

Kremsmünster

1696–p1697. Copisi, Gottlieb
1696–p1722. Puechers, Sigmund

Leeuwarden

before 1709. Schickhardt, Johann Christian

Leipzig

a1672–1717. Bauer (Bauermann), Andreas
c.1700–57. Poerschmann, Johann
c.1705–11. Böhm, Johann Michael
1707–30. Meyer, Christian Ernst
c.1707 and after. Fickweiler
early 18th c. Ebicht, Gottfried
[? 1712]–47. Gleditsch, Johann Caspar
1719–(?54). Kornagel, Johann Gottfried
1730–8. Caroli, Joh. Friedrich
1737–69. Kirchhoff, Joh. Friedr.
1738–63. Ofschatz, Joh. Chrn.
a1744–63. Crone, Gabriel
c.1745. Pfaffe, Carl Friedrich
c.1745. Pfaffe, Johann Michael
1746–8. Landvoigt
1748–63. Jonne, Andreas Christoph
1751–1800. Hiller, Johann Adam

Lisbon

1728. La Tour (Latur)
1728. Veith

London

c.1650. Banister, John
c.1650. Farmer, Thomas
c.1673–1721. Paisible, James
1673–5. Boutet, [? Jean]
1673–8. Bresmes [Breame], Maxant de

1673–8. Guiton (Giton), Pierre
1675. Hotteterre, Jacques[-Jean]
by 1685–p1698. La Riche, François
1685. Delestant, Louis
1685. Laurens, Joseph
1685. Le Brasseur, Toussaint
1685. Normand (Lenormand), Rémy
1687–91. Le Roy, Jean–Baptiste
by 1688. Bressan, Peter
1691. Granville, Michel
1691. Sutton, George
1692–9. Chevalier, Thomas
1692–1708. Aubert, John
a1698–p1704. Ashbury, John
by 1699–at least 1721. La Tour, Pierre
 (Peter)
1699. Colmack, John
1699. Paulin (Paulain), John
1699–1708. Le Fevre, Stephen
(? *c.*1700–p1727). Vincent, Thomas sen.
by 1702–at least 1727. Graves, James
by 1703–*c.*1755. Smith, William
1705–8. Festing, (not John)
1705–30. Loeillet, John
1706–47. Galliard, Johann Ernst
1707. Chaboud, Pietro
*c.*1707–p1719. Rousselet, Louis
1708. Mercy, Louis
1708–19, p1720–1738. Kytch, Jean
 Christian
1708–at least 1742. Denby, Humphrey
1714. Clash
1714. Cobson
[?1714–17. Barsanti, Francesco]
1714–p1744. Festing, John
1715–21. Roman, Johan Helmich
by 1720–*c.*1744. Neale, Richard
1720–at least 1735. Woodbridge, Joseph
1723–4. ? Sammartini, Giuseppe
1725–p1778. Weidemann, Carl Friedrich
by 1727 to 1783. Vincent, Richard
1727. Akeman
1727. Lowe

1728–55. Charles, [? J.]
1729–50. Sammartini, Giuseppe
1730s. Bothmar, [? Hans Caspar Freiherr,
 Baron]
1735. Mercy, Louis
*c.*1735–at least 1784. Vincent, Thomas jun.
*c.*1739–84. Teede (Tiede), William
1743–63. Stockton, Thomas
1743–. Barsanti, Francesco
1745. De Ricourt
1750s–76. Simpson, Redmond
1752. Cox, John George
1752–4. Pla, Joan Baptista and Josep
by 1753–5. Barbandt, Charles
1754, 1758. Eiffert, Philipp
1757. Besozzi, Antonio
1757. Besozzi, Carlo
1759. Young, Talbot
1759–at least 1763. Perkins, John

Lorraine

1702. Gabriel (Gabrieli), Jean
1702. Guery, Claude le (dela Guerriere)
by 1718–a1727. Des Noyers, François

Lucca

1709–30. Erdmann, Ludwig
[? 1717–35. Barsanti, Francesco]
1726. Dreyer, Domenico Maria
1735. Agnerè, Carlo
1739–. Dôthel, Nicolas
1746. Tulij, Elias

Lüneburg

a1691, 1710–. Voigt, Ullrich Johann

Lunéville (Lorraine)

*c.*1700–40. Dôthel, Nicolas (père)

Lyons

Loeillet, Jean-Baptiste ('Loeillet de
 Gant')

Madrid

1679. Alais, Louis
1679. Auger, Louis
1679. Bonpar, Jean
1679. Griffon, Nicolas
1701. Huet
1701. Mangot, Jacques Siméon
1701. Robert
1708–49. Gesembach (Jezebeck), Joseph
1712–p1736. Brienne (Voyenne, Boyenne), Claudio
a1715. Thomas, Joseph Niclas II
1716–44. Boucquet [Buquet], Luis
until 1731. Rion, Ignazio
1742–90. Cavazza, Manuel
1747. López Ximénez (de Elche), Juan
1747. Mestres (de la Bisbal), Francisco
1749–. Misón, Luis

Mainz

1755–60. Klauseck, (Johann) Ignaz

Mannheim

1723. Beyernmüller, Anselm
1723. Daniels, Johann Karl
1723–34. Beck, Joh. Gg. Aloys
1723–37. Weiss, Johann Sigismund
1723–59. Cannabich, Martin Friedrich
1745–64. Bleckmann, Joh.
1747–71. Lebrun, Jacob Alexander
1756–1802. Ritter, Georg Wilhelm
1758–78. Ramm, Friedrich
1759. Mifiti.

Mantua

a1731. Ratzenberger, Giorgio
1755–71. Livraghi, Luigi

Marly

1726. Mathieu

Meiningen

p1731–c.1768. Tischer, Johann Nikolaus

Milan

c.1690 (? until c.1720). Saint-Martin, Aléxis
before 1701. Besozzi, Cristoforo (3)
by 1703. Des Noyers, François
1711. Appiano, Giuseppe
1720–9. Sammartini, Giuseppe
1748–9. Federici, Baldassare
1748–65. Federici, Francesco
p1749. Borsani, Antonio
1750–p1765. Emanuelli, Tommaso

Moscow

p1726. Dreyer, Domenico Maria

Munich

1684–1703. Teubner, Felix
a1692, 1715–17. Normand (Lenormand), Rémy
1692–1743. Schuechbauer, Franz Simon
1715–26. Balthassar, Ignatz
1715–26. Loeillet, Jacob
1715–26. Maillen, Johann Christoph
1715–26. Marchand, Jean-Antoine (Johann Anton)
1715–26. Pourveu, Marino
1715–26. Sander, Gottfried
1715–50. Thomas, Joseph Niclas II
1722–55. Ferrandini, Giovanni Battista
1723–53. Ferrandini, Stefano
1750–65. Kösslinger (Koslinger), Franz
1753–77. Rummelsperger (Rumppelsperger), Georg Jacob
1755–68. Schilling, Johann Baptist

Münster

1750. Marometh, Johann Karl Andreas

Naples

1711. ? Valentine, Robert
1721–2. Rion, Ignazio

1731–4. Besozzi, Antonio
1734–60. Besozzi, Giuseppe (4)
1736–65. Besozzi, Gaetano (10)
1752–60. Buontempo, Francesco Saverio
a1762–1762. Corona, Cherubino

Nuremberg

*c.*1680–1707. Denner, Johann Christoph
1693–1732. Schell, Johann
1706–35. Denner, Jacob
before 1728. Enderle, Joh. Joseph

Oviedo

1731–4. Rion, Ignazio

Oxford

1754–73. Eiffert, Philipp

Padua

1701–*c.*1761. Zabile, Luca
1716. Semenzato, Antonio
1736–*c.*1780. Bissoli, Matteo

Paris (see also Versailles)

1607–48. Rousselet, Nicolas
1619–p1664. Boilly, Barnabé de
a1620–1645. Herbinot dit Destouches,
    Jehan (1)
*c.*1620–59. Danican dit Philidor, Michel
1625–. Bien, François de
1626–p1664. Dupin (Dupain), Moïse
a1629–1661. Herbinot dit Destouches,
    Jean (2)
*c.*1630s–a1685. Herbinot dit Destouches,
    Michel
a1631–by 1675. Andrieu, Félix
a1631–p1664. Hauteville (Houteville,
    Dhouteville), Pierre de
a1631–p1682. Rousselet, Michel
1632–48. Beranger, Étienne (Jean)
1632–p1677. Hotteterre, Jean (3)
a1634–p1664. Toussaint, Martin

1637–p1670. Malloy, Nicolas
a1638–p1672. Robeau, Hilaire
1640–p1650. Verdier, Abel
a1643–1664. Viam, François
a1644–1664. Verdier, Robert
a1648–1664. James (Jamme), Elie Charles
a1649–1664. Paisible, Louis
a1649–a1672. Brunet, Jean
1650–78. Maréchal, Pierre
a1657–1667. Pignon dit Descoteaux,
    François
?1657–1712. Hotteterre, Martin
1657–79. Danican dit Philidor, Jean
*c.*1657–94. Hotteterre, Nicolas (10) (*l'aîné*)
a1658–*c.*1706. Pièche, Pierre
a1661 (1666?)–95. Langlois, André
a1661–1667. Laubier, Jean I
a1661–1669. Le Boeuf, Claude
a1661–1708. Allais, Claude
a1661–1709. Brunet, Jean Louis
1661. Le Roy, Joseph
1661–1711 Rousselet, Jean
*c.*1661–*c.*1680 Granville, Guillaume
1664. Mazurier, Claude
1664–1725. Laubier, Jean II
a1665–1716. Hotteterre, Louis (11)
1665–8. Charlot, Louis
a1666–1667. Hotteterre, Jean (8)
1666–79. Héroux, Gilles
1666–82. Noblet, Jérôme
a1667–1676. Gayet (Gayen), Silvain
a1667–1700. Dieupart, Nicolas
a1667–1709. Marillet dit de Bonnefonds,
    Jacques
1667–1708. Danican dit Philidor, Jacques
1667–1716. Pignon dit Descoteaux, René
1667–1727. Hotteterre, Nicolas (12) (Colin)
1667–p1717. Rebillé dit Philbert, Philippe
1668–1728. Ferrier, Pierre
1669–83. Hotteterre, Jean
1671. Bresmes, Maxant de
1671–2. Guiton, Pierre
1672–86. Penhalleu dit Du Clos, Jean de

a1675–p1682. Pièche, Joseph

a1676–p1708. Buchot dit Duverger, François

1676–89. Arthus dit Plumet, François

1676–p1678. Deville, Hilaire

a1677–1693. Pièche, Pierre-Alexandre

1677–80. Malloy, Jacques

1678–1708. La Croix, de

1679. Lhomme, Claude de

1679–83. Danican dit Philidor, Alexandre

1680–1701. Royer, Claude

1680–1703. Depot dit Dumont, Edme

1680–91. Ludet, Jean

1680–*c.*1689. Granville, Michel

a1681–1730. Danican dit Philidor, André

1682. Monginot

1682. Thoulon père

1683–1725. Hotteterre, Jean (6)

1684. Adeline, Christophe

1684–1755. Bernier, Julien

1689. Revel, Louis

1689–92. Aubert, John

a1691. Hotteterre, Louis (7)

1691–5. Alais, Louis

1693. Bonnefont, Pierre Jacques de

1693. Faverolle, Jacques

1695–1706. Cochinat, François Jérôme

1695–1709. Anglard, Nicolas

1698–1719. Hotteterre, Jean (14)

1700. Berthélemy, Jean-Baptiste

1703–30. La Barre, Michel de

1704–46. Desjardins dit Fauchon, François Hannès

1706–16. Mercier de Villeneuve, Nicolas

1708. Olivier, Michel

1709–62. Chédeville, Esprit-Philippe

1709–18. Aubry, Claude

1716. Des Noyers, François

1720–38. Mangot, Jacques Siméon

p1720. Marchand, Jean-Noël

1725–81. Chédeville, Nicolas

a1726–p1738. Lucas

1726–69. Danican dit Philidor, Nicolas

a1727. Du Fresne, Louis François

a1727–a1768. Despréaux (Abram-Despreaux), Jean-François

1727–. Coulon, Jean-Baptiste

a1728–p1743. Braun, Jean Daniel

a1730. Desjardins, Charles Hannès

by 1730–p1767. Bureau, François

1730–49. Desjardins, Nicolas Hannés

1731. Le Roy

1733–51. Monnot (Moneau), Nicolas-Benigne

1735. Besozzi, Alessandro (5)

1736. Brunet

1736, 1763. Cézar, Ignace

a1746–p1763. Sallantin (Salentin), Nicolas

1748–9. Zollikofer

1748–70. Hotteterre, Jean-Baptiste

1749, 1757. Lavaux, Nicolas

1750/57–1781. Desjardins, ?

1751. Taillard

1752–9. Pla, Joan Baptista and Josep

1755–7. Berault ('Rault')

1755–74. Prover, Filippo

a1757. Berault, Jean-Baptiste

1757. Besozzi, Antonio

1757. Besozzi, Carlo

Parma

1701. Colla, Aurelio

1701–p1711. Besozzi, Cristoforo (3)

1711–31. Besozzi, Giuseppe

1713–31. Besozzi, Alessandro (5)

1727–31. Besozzi, Antonio

1729–70. Bocchi, Marco

1731. Ratzenberger, Giorgio

1751–70. Vettori, Gaetano

Passau

1698–9. Morizen

1699. Hali

Potsdam

1724–36. Pepusch, Gottfried

Prague

(? 1720s–1772). Flasska (Flaska), Joseph
Ignaz

Rastatt

1707. Cannabich, Joseph

Regensburg

1738. Nicolai, Christian August

Rome

1705–p1712. Rion, Ignazio
c.1706–10. Valentine, Robert
1708. Nicolò
1708. Sicuro, Stefano Giovanni Antonio
c.1717. Sieber, Ignaz
(? 1728–52). Mancini, Calisto
1741. Basteri
1751. Gioseppe

Rudolstadt

1732. Graff, Johann
1753. Barth, Christian Samuel

Salzburg

a1756–p1775. Burg, Christoph

Schleiz

1730–. Leonhardt, Johann Michael

Schleswig

Berwald, Johann Friedrich

Schmalkalden

1731. Tischer, Johann Nikolaus

Schneeberg

a1699. Schautzer, Joh. Michael

Schwerin

1701–3. Gessner, Hans Caspar
1701–3. Frick, Johann Heinrich

1701–3. Weichold, David
1701–13. Albrecht (Uhlbrecht), Gottfried
1701–13. Thieme, Philip Isaak
1701–14. Knöchel, Dobias
1701–14. Schmidt, Johann Gottfried
1703–. Mignier, Johann
1703–5. Hartmann, Johann Christoff
1703–13. Blau, Johann Jürgen
1703–15. Holler, Johann Joachim
1705–14. Walter, Johann Ludwig
1739–77. Schütt, Christoph Hermann
1742–88. Roschlaub, Markus
1743–85. Unbehagen, Johann Christoph
1753. Beissengrüll
1753–71. Daniel, Johann Benjamin
1753–71. Daniel, jun.
1753–88. Selmer, Heinrich Christoph
1755–63. Cords, C. J.
1755–85. Schmalz, Gideon

Sondershausen

1703. Kempe, Sebastian

Spain

18th c. Alvarez, Josef
18th c. Ballar, Juan
18th c. Boned, Luis
18th c. Camucha, Francisco
18th c. Cascante, Felipe
18th c. Casso, Blas
18th c. Deodato, Pascual
18th c. Escolaneta, José
18th c. Espinosa de los Monteros, Manuel
18th c. Fernandez Cruz, Sixto
18th c. Ferradellas (Terradellas), Pedro
18th c. Garcia, Antonio
18th c. Garcia, Manuel
18th c. Jardin
18th c. Julian, [—], José, Manuel
18th c. Izquierdo, Leandro
18th c. Jimenez, Teleforo
18th c. Masferrer, Carlos
18th c. Roig y Silvestre, Antonio
18th c. Torres, Antonio

St Petersburg

p1726. Dreyer, Domenico Maria
1731. Döbbert, Christian Friedrich
1742–59. Stazzi (Staggi)

Stuttgart

a1683–1684. Magg, Felix Friedrich
1688–p1722. Hildebrand (Hildenbrand), Johann Eberhardt
p1699–p1720. Bleßner, Georg Christoph
a1702–p1722. Nicolai, Johann Nicolaus
p1702–p1720. Castenbauer, Sigmund
p1702–p1731. Freudenberg, Stephan
c.1704/5–1722. Glockhart (Klockhart), Johann Michaël
1713. Kress, Georg Albrecht
1713. Thieme, Philip Isaak
a1717–p1722. Maÿer
a1721–p1736. Hetsch, Caspar Heinrich
1723–72. Commerell (Kommerell), Adam Friedrich
by 1726 to 1734. Schiavonetti, Giovanni
1729–55. Böhm, Johann Michael
1737–40. Stazzi
1750–5. Ciceri, Ignazio
1758–9. Besozzi, Antonio
1758–9. Besozzi, Carlo
1759–68. Pla, Joan Baptista and Josep

Sweden

[1704]–22. Bach, Johann Jacob
1721–58. Roman, Johan Helmich
1758–94. Grenser, Johann Friedrich

Turin

1674, 1679–a1694. Dupré
1677–a1694. Ghionot (Chionot), Pietro
1677–a1694. Mosso, Giacomo
1677–a1694. Perino, Filiberto
1677–a1694. Ricardo, Giuseppe
1677–a1694. Rion, Luiggi
1677–p1725. Mattis, Gio. Francesco

1677–p1725. Morand (Morano, Morando), Filiberto
1677–p1725. Ricardi (Ricardo), Vincenzo
1682–a1725. Perrin (Perino), Daniel
1694–. Chattelin, Nicolao
1694–. Guinneau, Renné
1694–. Souvage, Gianni
1695–1708. Chempli, Giuseppe (Joseph)
1697–1719. Besozzi, Giovanni Battista
a1719–1770. Palanca, Carlo
1719–p1742. Ferreri, Carlo Antonio (alias Dujardin)
1731–93. Besozzi, Alessandro (5)
1740–75. Prover, Ignazio
1742–3. Ascanio, Francesco
1742–4. Morano (Morando, Morand), Giuseppe Antonio
1742–4. Rossi, Gio. Battista
1743–4. Aimery (? Emery)
1743–4. Cholmayer
1743–4. Kays
1743–4. Mayr
1743–4. Racca (Racha), Antonio
1743–4. Schivinda
1743–4. Vaitseker
1744–56. Prover, Filippo
1751–4. Palanca, Giacomo
1755–6. Ellovi, Vitale
1755–6. Grosso (Grossi), Gaetano
1755–6. Otto, Giuseppe
1755–6. Pasquale
1755–6. Prover, Andrea
1755–6. Secchi (Sechi), Gioseffo

Ulm

1744. Kuttler, [jun.]
1744. Kuttler, [sen.]
1744. Unseld
1744. Weller

Venice

1696–1748. Penati, Onofrio
1700. Barbara [dall'Oboè]
1704–5. Rion, Ignazio

1706–8. Erdmann, Ludwig

1707. Pelegrina ('dall'Oboè')

1713–16, a1728–1760. Sieber, Ignaz

a1715. Platti, Giovanni Benedetto

a1718–. Anna [dall'Oboè]

1726. Sammartini, Giuseppe

1726. Susanna [dall'Oboè]

a1766. Perosa, Marco

a1766–at least 1776. Brizzio, Giovanni

Versailles (see also Paris)

1654–at least 1711. Perrin, Nicolas

(? a1657)–p1704. Pièche, Antoine

1672–1731. Herbinot dit Destouches, Marin (4)

1680–98. Desjardins, Antoine Hannès

1680–1732. Allain, Gilles

1689–1726. Dabadie dit Delisle, Jean

1689 (officially 1694)–1744. Desjardins, Jean Hannès

1689–1746/8. Hotteterre, Jacques dit 'le Romain'

1690–1721. Desjardins, Philippe Hannès

1692–1705. Hotteterre, Jacques[-Jean]

1695–1709. Danican dit Philidor, Jacques

1695–1713. Buchot, Pierre

1695–1715. Babelon, Claude

1695–1731. Danican dit Philidor, Pierre

1695–1737. Bernier, Julien

1698–1709. Breteuil, Philippe

1698–1728. Corbet, François Anne

1698–1728. Danican dit Philidor, Anne

1702. Freillon-Ponçein, Jean-Pierre

a1703–1736. Schwartzenberg dit Le Noble, Jean-Louis

1705. Leleu, Pascal

1705–6. Dupré, Jacques

1708–46. Desjardins, Jean-Baptiste Hannès

1708–. Danican dit Philidor, François

1709–10. Dumont, Aubin

1709–24. Ballois, Antoine I

1709–p1732. Matreau (Matrot), François

1709. Matreau (Matrot), Pierre.

1712–32/3. Hallé, Jacques

1713–31. Bidault de Gardainville, Charles

1714–25. Chédeville, Pierre

1714 (officially 1716)–1726. Danican dit Philidor, François

1714–56. Ferrier, Louis (fils)

(1714; officially 1717)–1724. Ferrier, François Antoine

*c.*1714–44. Brienne, Jacques Antoine de

1716. Verbe, Jean-Baptiste

1716–35. Charpentier, Jean Jacques

1720, 1726. Desjardins dit Monléry, Guillaume François

1722–7. Ballois, Antoine Barthélemy (II)

1723. Buisson, Claude

1723. Liennard, Pierre

1723–5. Perrin, (? Jean-Baptiste)

1724–46. Jouy, Valentin de

1725–7. Gouillart, Florent

1725–80. Marchand

1727. Le Maire, André

1727. Plumet Deselle

1727–30. Belleville, *l'aîné* [Laurent ?]

1727–46. Loeillet, Jacob

1727–50. Gouillart, Pierre Florent

1727–56. Daunates, Georges-Michel

1728. La Combe, Pierre

1728–32. Gillet de Valcour, Joseph François

1729. Martel, Denis

1729–31. Le Brun, Pierre

1729–58. Pajon, Pierre

1730–9. Chéron, Jacques-Michel

1731. Le Noir

1731–*c.*1742. Gaudichon de Bossé (Bessé), François

1732. David, Clément

1732. Gailliet, Christophe

1732–3. Jarry (Girard), Laurent Nicolas

1732–3. Morize, Toussaint

1732–47. David, Antoine

1732–p1735. Dueil, Antoine
1733–9. Coudray, Pierre
1734. Coutant, Jean-François
1735–42. Bidet, Nicolas
1735–57. Alexandre, Pierre
1736. Foissy
1736–40. Aubry, Claude
1736–55. Boquet, Pierre
1739. Cécile, Joseph
1739–41. Pin, Louis
1739–*c.*1752. De Selle, Jean Gaspard
1740. Rondin, Jean
1740–52. Gauthier, Jean Mathurin
1740–54. Breton, Vincent
1740–75. Machy, Thomas François de
1741–. Du Fresne, Louis François
1742. Corrard, Denis
1742–50. Touilliet, Charles
1742–75. Brunel, Jean-Baptiste
1743. Canivet, Antoine
1744–75. Charpentier, Jean François
a1745. Marchand, Claude
1745–. Pajon, Henry-Martial
1746. Hotteterre, Antoine Jacques
1746–8. Chardon, Nicolas
1746–9. Tremble, Guillaume François du
1746–9. Truteau, Jean
1746–80. Du Breuil (? Depriaux), Pierre
1746–p1788. Sallantin (Salentin), François-
  Alexandre
1747–. Boucher, Louis Pierre
1747–64. Feray, Pierre
1748. Collart, Pierre
1749. Robin, Michel
1749–52. Verlet, Antoine Nicolas
1749–p1752. Roze, Jean Louis Joseph
1749–p1788. Saint-Suire, Etienne
1750–76. Royer de la Cour, Claude
1750–80. Micolon
1751–60. Guérin de Vaucleroy, Joseph
  Benoist
1752–80. Duparc
1752–p1788. Bureau, Joseph-Gregoire

1754–. Pecoul, Laurent
1755–. Boquet, Pierre Jean
1756. Morizot, Jean
1756–63. Daunates, Esprit-Philippe
1756–76 (? 1778). Truguet, Jean Michel
1756–p1788. Souillard, Jean
1759–. Brucker (Bruches), Jean Pierre
1759–80. Rose de Wersigny

Vicenza

18.vi.1713. De Marchi, Domenico

Vienna

a1696. Delveaux, Nicolaus
a1696. Gresle, Johann Wolfgang
a1696. Gresle, Tobias
a1696. Henrion, Charles
a1696. Henrion, Jean-Baptiste
a1696. Schwaiberger (Schweiberger),
  Anton
1700–6. La Fourée, Johann
1700–10. La Notte, Ernst
1700–*c.*1715. La Buissière, Pierre de
1700–23. Schimann (? Chimene), Anton
1700–40. Schön, Ludwig (Joli, Louis)
1700–p1713. Beaufils, Joh. Anton
a1701–1705. Ledier, Johann
a1701–1707. Rosiers, Franciscus de
1701–17. Glaetzl (Glätzl), Franz
1701–27. Glaetzl, Roman (Romanus)
*c.*1701–*c.*1714. Leuttner (Leitter), Wenzel
*c.*1702–24, Lorber, Joseph Ignaz
*c.*1703. Muffat, Gottfried
a1705–1726, Glaetzl, Franz Xaver
1705–40. Gabriel (Gabrieli), Jean
1706. Achtsnit, Franz
1706. Redel, Adam
1710–11, Zechner, Johann Georg
*c.*1710–*c.*1713. Kreutz, Joh. Franz Ignaz
a1711–1759. Gazzaroli, Johann Zacharias
a1712–1767. Widmann (Widtmann),
  Andreas

1713–14. Fasser, Johann Franz
1721–40. Schulz, Johann Ludwig
1721–60. Hartmann, Daniel Franz
1721–. Hermann, Dav.
1722–6. Schindler, Johann Georg
*c.*1730–40. Müller, Franz Ferd.
1753. Engelhardt, Caspar
1753–5. Schaffarschek
1754–6. Kühtreiber, Franz
1756. Jauzer, [Georg?]

Waldeck

*c.*1750–. Schäffer, Daniel
*c.*1750–p1758. Lauterbach, Joh. Heinrich

Wallerstein

1747–51. Klauseck, (Johann) Ignaz

Warsaw

*c.*1755. Schröter, Johann Friedrich
1757. Fischer, Johann Christian

Weimar

1699–1703. Hoffmann, David
1727–30. Leonhardt, Johann Michael
a1714–p1716. Ulrich, Bernhard Georg

Weißenfels

1691–p1712. Hilsefunck, Johann Ludwig
1695–a1704. Buder, Christian
1695–p1709. Kühne, Johann
1695. Bötticher, Martin
1695. Schumann, Arnold
1696. Schautzer, Hans Caspar
1698–p1702. Garthoffen, David Heinrich
1699. Schautzer, Joh. Michael
1701. John, Johann Stephan
1701. Schubert, Balthasar
1707–p1712. Rosenbaum, John
1708–25. Prager, Joh. Jacob
1709–37. Unger, Joh. Simeon

1709–p1712. Köhler, Christoph Heinrich sen.
1710–p1712. Seyffart, Joh. Friedrich
1712–58. Pardoffsky (Bardowsky), Carl Leonhard
1712–p1720, ?1731. Köhler, Georg Wilhelm jun.
1712–p1726. Frisch, Johann Christoph
1712–p1733. Belldorff, Adam Friedrich
1715. Brage, Joh. Jac.
1723. Hoppf, Johann Valentin
1723. Nicolai, Christian August
1730–2. Oehler, Johann Wilhelm
a1733. Felber, Christoph
a1738. Volldorf, Ad.

Wertheim

1745. Klauseck, (Johann) Ignaz

Würzburg

1703–29. Orth
a1722–?1724. Schiavonetti, Giovanni
a1722–a1724. Pfister, Antoni
1722–5. Hummel, Joh. Friedrich
1722–at least 1761. Platti, Giovanni Benedetto
1735–79. Golz (Gölz), Joh. Georg
a1736. Brack, Joh.
a1736–1766. Cron, Joh. Peter
a1736–p1736. Bauer, Joh. Christoph
1736. Schweller, Jos.
1736. Fichtl, Mich. Jos.
1736–54. Burger
1736–56. Stadler, Joh. Georg
1736–61. Erdmann, Anton
1738–51. Plago, Ludwig
1757–82. Reinhard, Melchior
1757–85. Triebel, Anton

Zeitz

(? a1662–1701). Gebhardt, Martin
1680–94. Stadermann, Johann

1684–97. Pötzsch, Johann Martin
1691. Heynoldt, Gottfried
1694. Münch, Isaac
1697. Hermann, Jacobus
1698. La Buissière, Pierre de
1701–4. Winkler, Martin
1704–26. Dilesius, Christian
1704–p1734. Schulze, Tobias

*c.*1708–p1743. Lommer, Johann
1712. Meise, Johann
1716. Schumann, Adam Friedrich
a1738–p1794. Schnaucke, Johann Nicolaus
1743–64. Lommer, Johann Gottfried

Zerbst

1737/8. Unger, Joh. Simeon

APPENDIX 2

Acoustic profiles

The profiles include the acoustic length (or AL), the minimum bore, the *bore scaling* (the ratio of bore diameter to length, in this case the AL divided by the minimum bore), and the *aggregate tone-hole sizes* (that is, the total of the diameters of holes 1, 2, 5, and 6). For a discussion of these parameters, see Chapter 2, §C.

Mark and location	AL	M. bore	Scale	Tone-holes
M. A. Amsterdam: Han de Vries	338			15.98
Van Aardenberg The Hague Ea 438-1933	322.7			
Van Aardenberg Amsterdam: Han de Vries	320	6.0	53.33	17.80
Anciuti Rome 0827 (1709)	318.3	6.0	53.05	15.60
Anciuti Rome 0828 (1718)	318.5	5.9	53.98	14.40
Anciuti Berlin 5079 (1721)		6.2		
Anciuti Pistoia, Palazzo Rospigliosi (1725)	335.4	6.0	55.9	16.51
Anciuti Amsterdam: Bernardini (1730)	330.9	5.8	57.05	15.30
Anon. (? Bressan) Oxford: Bate 200	331.8	6.6	50.27	16.17
Anon. Edinburgh 1033	322	6.6	48.79	enl.
Anon. Paris E.108	331.6	5.7	58.18	18.45
Anon. Paris: Musée de l'Armée	331.5	5.9	56.19	17.2
[Mark unreadable], New York: Met 89.4.3132	321.5	6.15	52.28	17.3
Bizey Bate 201	334.4	5.8	57.66	14.55
Bizey Brussels 424	337.3	6.2	54.40	15.0
Bizey Paris C.1112, E.1047		5.95		
Boekhout Amsterdam: Han de Vries	320	6.0	53.33	16.0
Borkens Amsterdam: Han de Vries	334	5.9	56.61	16.0
Bradbury Piguet	331	5.8	57.07	15.2
Peter Bressan [Talbot MS]	329			18.8
Castel Nice: Musée instrumental	324.4	6.0	54.07	16.5
Gottlieb Crone Hildebrand	320.9			16.05
Gottlieb Crone Utrecht: Ehrenfeld 8	320.9			
J. A. Crone Amsterdam: Han de Vries (A2)	329	5.4	60.93	15.60
J. A. Crone Amsterdam: Han de Vries (D1)	322	5.2	61.92	15.70
Debey Bate 2	329.6	6.2	53.16	15.9
J. C. Denner Nuremberg MI 155	272.1	5.9	46.12	14.85
Jacob Denner New York: Met 89.4.1566	317.1	5.75	55.15	16.4
Jacob Denner Nuremberg MI 90	300.7	5.9	50.97	18.55
Jacob Denner Nuremberg MIR 370	328.8	5.8	56.69	19.25

Mark and location	AL	M. bore	Scale	Tone-holes
Jacob Denner Nuremberg MIR 371	321.8	5.55	57.98	18.2
Jacob Denner NY Met 89.4.893	320	6.0	53.33	17.05
Jacob Denner Vienna 332 (7289)	322.5	5.9	54.66	16.65
Jacob Denner Yale 3411.78	324	6.3	51.43	19.12
[? Jacob Denner] Nuremberg MI 89	320.4	5.7	56.21	16.55
[Johann David?] Denner Venice Cons. 34	307	5.25	58.48	14.5
Desjardin[s], Jean-Baptiste: Winston-Salem, NC 0-113	340.7	5.7	59.77	16.95
Dupuis Berlin 2933	316	7.15	44.20	17.8
Peter Eggl Salzburg 13/1	274.2	4.4	62.32	15.4
Eichentopf Halle MS 420	324.3	5.7	56.89	16.83
Eichentopf Lisbon MIC-0106	326.7	5.6	58.34	17.4
Gahn Milan: Cons.	276	6.0	46.0	16.2
Haka Leefdaal: Dombrecht	326	6.1	53.44	15.75
Haka The Hague Ea 6-1952	332.2	6.3	52.73	17.15
Haka Amsterdam: de Vries	310	5.9	52.54	16.9
Hotteterre Brussels 2320	330.9	6.4	51.70	16.0
Frederik de Jager Amsterdam: Han de Vries	330	6.1	54.10	
Klenig Vermillion (ex Kaltenbach) 3741	324.6	6.0?	54.10?	15.65
Klenig, Hamamatsu A-0062R	323.9	5.85	55.37	15.0
Joh. A. Königsberger Munich DM 25968	318.4	5.8	54.90	14.35
G. Lot Paris E.2181	337	5.0	67.40	15.5
G. Lot Amsterdam: Han de Vries	332.5	5.5	60.45	16.75
T. Lot Piguet	341.3	5.3	64.40	15.35
T. Lot St Petersburg 512 (A 254)	343.8			
Loth Hamamatsu (ex Rosenbaum) A-0229R	321.5	6.0	53.58	16.43
Martin (? Aléxis St-) Paris E.210, C.470	313.4	6.0	52.23	20.25
Naust Montreal: Haynes	329.9	6.35	51.95	16.8
J. W. Oberlender I Amsterdam: Han de Vries	324	6.0	54.00	17.80
Carlo Palanca, Amsterdam: Bernardini	329.7	4.8	68.69	15.2
Palanca Vindelle: Écochard	338.5			
Paulhahn Vienna: Harnoncourt	321.5	5.8	55.43	16.2
F. Richters Amsterdam: Han de Vries	331	6.2	53.39	15.80
H. Richters Bate 2037	329.4	5.6	58.82	15.85
H. Richters Piguet	328.6	6.35	51.75	15.67
H. Richters The Hague Ea 584-1933	327.3	6.3	51.95	
H. Richters Amsterdam: Han de Vries	329	6.3	52.22	15.80
Rippert, Geneva (La Ménestrandie)	329.8	6.5	50.74	16.3
Rippert, Leipzig 1312	331.6	6.4	51.81	15.9
Rottenburgh I Brussels 2608	326	6.25	52.16	15.9
Rottenburgh I formerly Piguet	332.5	6.2	53.63	16.3
Rottenburgh I La Louvière (B): H. Pourtois	336.9	6.4	52.64	16.7
J. H. Rottenburgh II Ann Arbor 667 (52)	331.5	5.0	66.30	14.0
J. H. Rottenburgh II Brussels 4360	332.4	6.2	53.61	14.0
J. H. Rottenburgh II Brussels 966	324	5.0	64.80	14.15
Rouge DCM 423	306.5	5.75	53.30	19.65

Mark and location	AL	M. bore	Scale	Tone-holes
Rouge Paris E.979.2.12	336.2	5.7	58.98	17.8
Rÿkel The Hague Ea 6-X-1952		6.4		
C. Rÿkel Amsterdam: Han de Vries	325	6.6	49.24	15.05
J. C. E. Sattler St Petersburg 506 (A 249)	326.5			
Schell Berlin 5250	274	5.8	47.24	15.7
Scherer Frankfurt: Spohr (1)	327.8	6.0	54.63	18.2
Scherer Frankfurt: Spohr (2)	330.2	6.0	55.03	18.5
Scherer Munich 66-88	323.1	6.25	51.70	
Schlegel Basel 1878.16	327.1	6.0	54.52	
Schlegel Piguet	329	5.0	65.80	
Schuechbaur Venice Cons. 33	263.1	6.45	40.79	14.0
Stanesby I Hamamatsu (ex Rosenbaum) A-0166R	328.2	6.55	56.90	14.1
Stanesby I Horniman 232	332.9	6.5	51.22	17.95
Stanesby I Horniman 277	333.5	6.55	50.92	17.05
Stanesby II Bate 29	325.5	6.5	50.08	18.3
Stanesby II Horniman 1969.683	332.5	6.3	52.78	15.9
Stanesby II Tokyo: Honma		6.3		
Steenbergen Brussels 2611	329.4	5.8	56.79	15.7
Steenbergen Amsterdam: Han de Vries	329	6.1	53.93	17.15
Terton Berlin 2941	327.8	6.4	51.22	15.85
Terton Smithsonian 208.185	323.8	6.27	51.64	16.5
Terton The Hague Ea 437-1933		6.22		
Zencker II Berlin 2937	331			15.1

Pitch information for sixteen representative hautboy makers

France

Naust (a1692–1709)[1]

Hautboy AL:

   329.9 (Haynes). Plays with a Talbot reed (see Ch. 2, §E.3.b) at A−2; the tone-holes are
      16.8 (the average for this period is 16.92).[2]
Traverso pitches: 392±, 400, 402±, 405, 412
Recorder pitches: 392, 408 (Flageolet)

Colin Hotteterre (a1692–1727)[3]

Hautboy AL:

   330.9 (Brussels 2320). Plays with a Talbot reed at A−2; the tone-holes are 16.0 (the aver-
      age for this period is 16.92). The bell is lost and is from another instrument.
Traverso pitches: (by Hotteterre, not necessarily by Colin H.) 390, 400, 402
Recorders (by Hotteterre, not necessarily by Colin H.) at 395, 395, 403, 404, 406, 406, 408,
      409, 415, 434, 461, 463

Rippert (a1696–p1716)[4]

Hautboy AL:
   329.8 Geneva
   331.6 Leipzig 1312
Traverso pitches: 396, 396, 400?
Recorder pitches: 392, 397, 397, 398, 406, 410, 460, 461, 466, 472, 471, 466, 469
Rippert does not appear to have made any instruments at A−1; his traversos are all at A−2
      and his recorders are at A−2, A−1½, and A+1.

Thomas Lot (1734–p1787)

Hautboy AL:

341.3 (ex Piguet)

343.8 (St Petersburg 512). This is the longest known AL for a treble hautboy.

Traverso pitches: 415 (early in career), 415±, 387/396/404/411/418, 387/396/404/411/
418, 390/?/?/?/420, 400, 401/415/423, 410, 415, 415±, 420, 435, 399/407/415/427/
433, 418–20, 417–20

Other Thomas Lot flutes with single joints play about 419.[5]

Italy

Anciuti (a1709–p1740)

Hautboy AL:

318.3 (Rome 0827, dated 1709)

318.5 (Rome 0828, dated 1718)

330.9 (Bernardini, dated 1730)

335.4 (Pistoia, dated 1725)

Traverso pitches: 410/420/435, 435

Recorder pitches: 413, 427, 430, 435, 437, 440, 443

Palanca (1719–a1780)[6]

Hautboy AL:

329.7 (Bernardini)

338.5 (Vindelle: Écochard)

Traverso pitches: 421, 430, 408/411/415, 414, 430/437/449, 417/427/435

Recorder at 435

These two hautboy ALs suggest lower pitches; the known TLs suggest three pitches in
semitone increments (presumably A+1, A+0, and A–1); exactly where the division falls
is unclear.

Germany

Christoph Denner (c.1678–1707)

Hautboy AL:

272.1 (Nuremberg MI 155). A+1 length range

Recorder pitches: 397, 397, 406, 409, 410, 410, 410, 410, 415, 415, 415, 415, 415, 415, 420,
421, 421, 455, 463, 466, 477, 484

---

[5] According to Masahiro Arita.

[6] Palanca's instruments are not dated, but they were probably made well before 1770 (cf. the introduction to
Ch. 7).

Clarinet pitches: 415, 425

The range of recorder pitches is from 392 to 479 (A−2 to A+1). The hautboy TLs suggest two pitches spaced a whole-step apart, A−1 and A+1.

Schell (1697–1732)

Hautboy AL:

274 (Berlin 5250). A+1 length range

Recorder pitches: 494, 494, 494, 494, 494, 408 (stamped also by Jacob Denner with the word 'corigirt'), 399, 420, 390, 392, 405, 406, 407, 409, 410, 411, 413

Johann Schell is survived by hautboys exclusively at the same short TL as three by his colleague, Christoph Denner.

Gahn (1698–1711)

Hautboy AL:

276 (Milan: Cons.). A+1 length range

Recorder pitches: 410, 414, 415, 417, 419, 431, 435

Oberlender sen. (1705–c.1745)

Hautboy AL:

324 de Vries

Traverso pitches: 390, 400/410/415, 405±, middle 411±, 392±

Recorder pitches: 392, 392, 392, 400, 404, 413, 415, 415, 415, 415, 417, 417, 417, 417, 420, 420, 423, 425, 430, 430, 440

Jacob Denner (1707–35)

Hautboy AL:

300.7 (Nuremberg MI 90). A+0 length range
317.1 (New York Met. MMA 89.4 1566)
320 (NY Met 89.4.893)
320.4 (attr.; Nuremberg MI 89)
321.8 (Nuremberg MIR 371)
322.5 (Vienna 332/7289)
324 (Yale 3411.78)
328.8 (Nuremberg MIR 370). Plays with a Talbot reed at A−1½; the tone-holes are unusually large at 19.25 (the average for this period is 16.92). Resembles Talbot Bressan (below).

Traverso pitches: 398/422, 402, 398/408/418, 408

Recorder pitches: 397, 409, 411, 413, 415, 415, 419, 420, 420, 421, 423, 425

Clarinet pitches: 415+, 415

Pitch centres represented by the traversos are 393, 397, 403, 413, and 417. The recorders are at 392, 404, 406, 408, 410, 414, 415, 416, 418, and 420 (corrected for shrinkage). There is thus a gamut in small increments from 392 to 420.

David Denner *(1707–p1735)*[7]

Hautboy AL:
   307 (Venice Cons. 34). A+0 length range
Recorder pitches: 400, 411, 415, 419, 420, 423, 428, 430, 434, 440, 440

Eichentopf *(a1710–1749)*

Hautboy AL:
   324.3 (Halle MS 420)
   326.7 (Lisbon MIC-0106)
Traverso pitches: 392–400
Recorder pitches: 415, 416, 425

England

Bressan *(1688–1730)*

Hautboy AL:[8]
   329 (Talbot). The tone-holes are unusually large at 18.8 (the average for this period is
   16.92). Probably played at A–1½, as does the Denner MIR 370, which it resembles.
Traverso pitches: 407, 412±, 418
Recorder pitches: 400, 401, 403, 404, 405, 405, 405, 405, 405, 405, 406, 407, 408, 408, 408,
   409, 409, 410, 410, 410, 410, 410, 410, 410, 410, 410, 410, 410, 410, 412, 413, 415, 415,
   415, 415, 415, 420, 422, 423
Of forty-two surviving flutes made by Bressan whose pitch is known, none is at A–2;
   his lowest surviving pitch is A-400. He probably changed the pitch of his instruments
   with time. He worked in London from 1688 to 1730, a time-span in which pitch
   went up from *Consort-pitch* at A–1½ to *new Consort-pitch* a semitone higher (about
   A-423).

Stanesby sen. *(1691–1733/4)*

Hautboy AL:
   327.2 (Hamamatsu (ex Rosenbaum) A-0166R)
   332.9 (Horniman 232)
   333.5 (Horniman 277)
Recorder pitches: 408, 410, 410, 414, 415, 416
The average of these pitches is 412, which would originally have been about 407, or A–1½.
Stanesby worked until 1733/4. Both his hautboy ALs and his recorder pitches suggest he
   made his instruments at *Consort-pitch* (A–1½) or lower.

---

[7] See Ch. 5, §D.16 for the rationale for attributing instruments to this maker.
[8] No Bressan hautboys survive, but Talbot made careful measurements of one in the 1690s.

Stanesby jun. (p1713–c.1754)

Hautboy AL:

   325.5 (Bate 29)

   332.5 (Horniman 1969.683)

Traverso pitches: 400, 410, 410±, 410±, 412, 413, 413–15, 415, 415±, 416–17, 416–17, 416–17, 417, 419, 424

Recorder pitches: 408, 409, 411, 412, 413, 415, 415, 429

The newer model hautboy, Bate 29, is probably at A–1; I have tried without success to play my copy of it at *new Consort-pitch* (A≈423), a level seen here on one traverso and one recorder. I have played the Honma Stanesby in concerts at A–2.

Plate 2.7. Anonymous oil portrait of an hautboist (Berlin: Staatliches Institut für Musikforschung)

Date

Because of the player's silk gown, which has a particular and well-known design based on a 'point' or 'mirror' repeat, this painting is 'extremely unlikely to pre-date 1720'. The wig-type 'came in during the 1720s, and remained popular for several decades'. Clare Brown (pers. comm.), Assistant Curator and specialist in European silks, Department of Textiles and Dress, Victoria and Albert Museum, would on this basis (having seen a photograph of the painting) date it to c.1725–32.

Player's age and status

Since the player is about 60 or a little more, he would have been born in the 1660s. He was clearly a virtuoso, as the concerto under his elbow is in F minor. Being a good player and having his portrait made, he was probably in the employ of a patron who both appreciated him and could afford to pay for the portrait. He was thus presumably a player of enough renown that we know of him now.

Nationality

The player's robe was of a material made and used in many countries in Europe (Clare Brown, pers. comm.). The handwriting of the concerto (which is presumably his) shows German traits (the capital 'C' and the treble clefs). That the part is for 'Oboe' argues against a French nationality.

Instrument and reed

The instrument matches the dates, although it could have been made as early as c.1700. The reed dimensions are discussed in Chapter 2, §E.3.c.

Hautboists who match this profile

The subject of this portrait was thus probably born in the 1660s and was a successful virtuoso of German nationality. He was possibly employed at a court. There are nearly a dozen hautboists who match this profile, including Blockwitz, Erdmann, Freymuth, Galliard,

Hetsch, Hildebrand, Leonhardt, Pepusch, Schuechbauer, Weiss, and Würdig. Considering that the portrait is now in Berlin,[1] Gottfried Pepusch (fl. 1692–1736) is the most likely candidate as a subject of this portrait. Although the court Capelle was inactive there between 1713 and 1740, Pepusch was actively employed in the royal service at this time as an instructor of hautboists. He had been master of the music corps of the King's bodyguard and had a title of general army music inspector at Berlin. From 1724 he was director of the Hautboistenschule at Potsdam.

[1] The Institut knows nothing of the painting's provenance.

APPENDIX 5

Partial list of hautboy music requiring mutes

This list is not complete, but is intended to give an overview of where and when mutes were used.

Kusser, thirtieth Aria in a collection called *Heliconische Musen-Lust* (1700) consisting of pieces from the opera *Ariadne* (Braunschweig, 1692). Voice, violin, hautboy ('Haubois con sordino'), flute, continuo. Owens (1995), 61 n. 29.

Handel, aria 'Per me già di morire' in *La Resurrezione* (Rome, 1708). Recorders and a muted hautboy in unison. Dean (1959), 526.

Keiser, aria V/6 in *Julius Caesar* (Hamburg, 1710) for 'gedämpften Clarinen, Hautbois und Pauken' before Pompei's grave. McCredie (1964), 74.

Anon., aria 'Laßt mich ihn nur noch einmal küssen' from *Lukaspassion* (BWV 246), T, two hautboys, Taille, bassoon, two violins, viola, continuo. 'Con molto lamento'. 'Piano, und zwar die Hoboen mit Papier gedämpft'. BG 45/2: 101. (Bach did not use the term 'Hoboen'.)

Telemann, cantata *Weiche, Lust und Fröhlichkeit* (? Frankfurt, 1712–21). Soprano/Tenor, hautbois [d'amour] 'surdinato' [ad lib.], violins, viola [d'amour] concertata, continuo.

Keiser, aria in *Fredegunda* (Hamburg, 1715) for violins and hautboys 'con sordini'. Hildebrand (1975), 72.

Lotti, aria 'Domine Deus, Rex coelestis' in *Missa Sapientiae* (D-Dlb Mus. 2159-D-4). Dresden? Solo traverso with 'Hautbois solo col sordino'. Horn (1987), 174.

Keiser, aria 'Ein Schäfferstock kan wenig nützen' from oratorio *Die durch Grossmuth und Glauben triumphierende Unschuld oder Der siegende David*, Hamburg, 1721. Traverso, muted hautboys, strings pizz., continuo. Page (1993).

Keiser, aria in *Otto* ([Hamburg ?], 1726) for two hautboys 'col sordino' in scene where ghosts appear. Kleefeld (1899), 263.

Telemann, aria 'Komm sanfter Schlaff', I/5 in *Miriways* (Hamburg, 1728). Soprano, two hautbois d'amour 'surdinata', two violins 'surdinata', viola, continuo (harpsichord 'pizzicato').

Heinichen, Concerto H I, 18. Traverso solo, three hautboys 'con sordini' and violins and violas 'pizzicati dolcemente'. Dresden. Hausswald (1937), 132, 138.

Zelenka, no. 9 in *Il serpente di bronzo* (cantata sacra), ZWV 61, Dresden, 1730. Alto, two hautboys (sordini), continuo.

Keiser, aria in *Circe* (Hamburg, 1734) including two hautboys 'col sordino' in a scene where ghosts appear. Kleefeld (1899), 263.

Zelenka, aria no. 13 in oratorio *Gesù al Calvario* (Dresden, 1735). Two hautboys 'con sord'. Page (1993).

Linike, *Mortorium à 5* (Hamburg, 1737). Trumpet, hautboy, traverso, violin, continuo (all muted except traverso in B-Bc version).

Gassmann, aria 'Occhietti cari del mio tesoro' in *L'amore artigiano* (1767).

Vivaldi, Concerto, RV 97. Viola d'amour solo, two hautboys, two horns, bassoon, continuo (all muted except bass instruments). Written for Dresden.

Vivaldi, RV 579, *Concerto funebre*. Includes muted hautboy. Selfridge-Field (1975), 259.

Platti, 'Stabat Mater Dolorosa' for Bass, recorder, hautboy (muted), two violas (muted), continuo. (Würzburg ?)

Galuppi, 'Crucifixus' in *Credo a quattro concertato*. All orchestral instruments 'con sordino'. ([Venice ?], 1752–82.)

Collation of fingering charts

The charts are identified as follows:

Bi	1688	Bismantova
Ba	1695	Banister
L1	c.1692	La Riche
L2	c.1692	La Riche
S	1699	*Second Book of Theatre Music*
F	1700	Freillon-Poncein
H	1707	Hotteterre
E	1738	Eisel

Note	Fingering	Sources
c_1	123 456 8	Bi Ba L1 L2 ('loud'),[1] S F H E
$c\sharp_1$	123 456 8	Bi
	123 456 $\bar{8}$	Ba L2 ('soft'),[2] F
	123 456 8	L1 ('louder')
$d\flat_1$	123 456 8	Bi
	123 456 $\bar{8}$	F
d_1	123 456	Bi Ba L1 L2 S F H E
$d\sharp_1$	123 456 7	Bi[3] Ba L1 L2 F H E
	123 45 7	S[4]
$e\flat_1$	123 456 7	Bi Ba[5] F H
	123 45 7	L1 L2 S[6]
e_1	123 45	Bi Ba L1 L2 S F H E
$e\sharp_1$	123 4 6	Bi F
$f\flat_1$	123 45	F
f_1	123 4 6	Bi Ba[7] F H
	123 4 6 7	L1 L2 S E
$f\sharp_1$	123 4	Bi
	123 4 7	S H

[1] The c_1 and $c\sharp_1$ fingerings are evidently reversed.   [2] The c_1 and $c\sharp_1$ fingerings are evidently reversed.
[3] Bi gives 123 456 8 but this is probably a mistake.   [4] Cf. S, L1, and L2 on $e\flat_1$.
[5] Unlike the $d\sharp_1$ fingering, 6 is mistakenly left open here.
[6] This appears to be a mistake, as it is the fingering for $e\natural$ and adding 7 raises it slightly rather than lowering it. It is interesting that the mistake (if it is one) is shared by these three sources.
[7] The f_1 and $f\sharp_1$ fingerings are transposed on the chart.

	123 ♮	L1 L2[8]
	123 ♮ 6	Ba F (H)
	123 5	E (also in upper octave)
g♭1	123 4	Bi
	123 ♮ 6	F H
g1	123	Ba L1 L2 H E
	123 6	Bi S F
g♯1	123 ♮ 6	Bi
	123♮	Ba L1[9] S H
	123♮ 6	F
	12 4	E
a♭1	123♮	Ba L1 L2 H
	123♮ 6	Bi F
	12 4	S
a1	12	Ba L1 L2 H E
	12 6	Bi S F
a♯1	1 3	F
	1 3 6	Bi
	1 3 4 6	L1[10]
	1 3 45	H
b♭1	1 3	Ba F E
	1 3 6	Bi S
	1 3 4 6	L1 L2
	1 3 45	H
b1	1	Ba L1 L2 H E
	1 6	Bi S F
b♯1	2 6	F
c♭2	1 6	F
c2	2	Ba L1 L2 H E
	2 6	Bi S F
c♯2	123 456 8	Bi[11]
	23 456 8	Ba L1 L2 S H
	+23 456 8	F
	3 7	E
d♭2	123 456 8	Bi
	23 456 8	H
	+23 456 8	F
d2	123 456	Ba (L2) S F E
	+23 456	L1 ('loud')[12]

[8] Given as 23 ♮, which appears to be a mistake as it produces c2.

[9] L2 gives 1 3 ♮ 6, but this is probably a mistake. Cf. L2 on a♭1.   [10] Not provided in L2.

[11] This produces g2 as a harmonic.   [12] L2 gives 123 ♮, which is probably a mistake.

Appendix 6

	23 456	Bi H (as on traverso)
		From this point on up the scale, L1, L2, and S require louder blowing
d♯2	123 456 7	Bi[13] Ba L2 S F H E
	+23 456 7	L1
e♭2	123 456 7	Bi Ba L2 S F H
	+23 456 7	L1
e2	123 45	Bi Ba L1 L2 S F H E
e♯2	123 4 6	Bi F
f♭2	123 45	F
f2	123 4 6 7	Ba L1 L2 S E
	123 4 6	Bi F H
f♯2	123 4	Bi
	123 4 7	H
	123 56	Ba L1 ('flat') S F H
	123 ‡	L1 ('sharp') L2
	123 5	E
g♭2	123 4	Bi
	123 56	F H L2
g2	123	Ba L1 L2 S H E
	123 6	Bi F
g♯2	12 4 6	Bi
	123	Ba L1 L2 S H
	123 6	F
	12 4	E
a♭2	123 6	Bi F
	12 4	Ba L1 L2 S
	123	H
a2	12	Ba L1 L2 S H E
	12 6	Bi
	12 6 8	F (possibly to help response)
a♯2	1 3 6 8	Bi
	1 3	F H
b♭2	1 3 6	Bi
	1 3	Ba L1 L2 S F H E
b2	1 6	Bi
	1	Ba H E
	2	L1 L2 S F
b♯2	2	F
c♭3	2	F
c3	2 6	Bi
	-o-	Ba ('all open', 'blow hard') L1 ('all open') L2 ('open all') S F H

[13] Bi gives 123 456 8 but this is probably a mistake.

	456	(H; this is not his traverso fingering)
	2 7	E
c♯3	6 8	Bi
	23 4 8	E
	23 4 6 8	F
	456	H (= c3, but 'en forcant le vent & serrant l'Anche avec les Levres')
		Note lack of ✚
d♭3	23 4 6 8	F
	23 456 8	H ('en forcant le vent & serrant l'Anche avec les Levres')
d3	23 8	F (E)
	23 456	Bi H

APPENDIX 7

Examples of independent c♯1s

The following list of c♯1s not doubled by other instruments is not meant to be complete but merely representative:

1688. Philidor, *Mariage de la grosse Cathos*, 'Entrée des filles de la nopce', Taille de hautbois, final of first half.

1690. Collasse, *Énée et Lavinie*, aria 'Chere ombre' (Act V, Sc. ii, p. 209), bar 4, Taille de hautbois.

1700. Freillon-Poncein, preludes. Three c♯1s as well as c♮1.

1735. Rameau, *Les Indes galantes*, trio for hautboys and bassoon, in second hautboy. (Geoffrey Burgess, pers. comm.)

Dreyer, Sonata 4, next-to-last note.

Sammartini, Rochester Sonata 5/3 (c♮1 appeared in the first and second movements).

Stölzel, quartets with horn and violin, no. 4, second movement, bars 39, 47.

Sher, solo sonata in F.

There are later examples, such as Gassmann's Quartetto (H.483/II) and the Prover Sonatas of *c.*1767.

APPENDIX 8

Collation of trill fingerings

Fingerings for trills on the hautboy were given in:[1]

Ba	1695 Banister
F	1700 Freillon-Poncein
H	1707 Hotteterre[2]
A	Anon. (c.1715)[3]

The finger to be moved (usually following an appoggiatura using the normal fingering) is underlined.

c_1–d	123 456 <u>8</u>	Ba H A
d_1–e♭	123 45<u>6</u>	Ba F H
d_1–e	123 45<u>6</u>	Ba[4] F H A
d♯$_1$–e	123 45<u>6</u> 7	F H A
d♯$_1$–e♯	123 4<u>5</u>6 7	H
e♭$_1$–f♭	123 45<u>6</u> 7	F
e♭$_1$–f	123 45<u>6</u> 7	Ba H A
	1<u>2</u>3 4 6 7	F
e$_1$–f	123 4<u>5</u>	Ba F H A
e$_1$–f♯	123 4<u>5</u>	Ba
	123 <u>♯</u>	F
	123 4<u>5</u>	H
e♯$_1$–f♯	123 <u>4</u> 6	F H
f$_1$–g♭	123 <u>4</u> 6	F
f$_1$–g	123 <u>4</u> 6	Ba F H A
f♯$_1$–g	1<u>2</u>3 4	Ba[5]
	123 <u>♯</u> 6	H A
	123 <u>4</u> 7	(H)
f♯$_1$–g♯	12<u>3</u> 4 7	F H
g♭$_1$–a♭	12<u>3</u> 4 7	F
	12<u>3</u> <u>♯</u> 6	H

[1] A comparative trill chart was published by Halfpenny more than four decades ago (Halfpenny 1953: 56).

[2] Hotteterre (1707: 88) advised hautboy players to use the trills he gave for the traverso in his chs. 4 and 7, except for those on c2, c1, g♭1, f♯1 sometimes, g♭2, f♯2, g♯1, g♯2, a♭1, a♭2, c♯2, d♭2.

[3] There are several copies of this source, including Prelleur 1730 and Anon. 1758.

[4] 8 is mistakenly added to the trill fingering.   [5] This produces a very large interval.

g1–a♭	123	Ba H
	123 6	F
g1–a	123	Ba H
	123 6	F A
g♯1–a	123 6	F A
	123 7	H
g♯1–a♯	123	F
a♭1–b♭	123	Ba[6] F
	123 7	H
	12 6	A
a1–b♭	12	Ba H
	12 alt 3	F
a1–b	12	Ba H
	12 6	F A
a♯1–b	1 3 6	F
	1 3	H
a♯1–b♯	1 3 6	F
	1 3 456	H
b♭1–c♭	1 3 6	F
b♭1–c	1 3	Ba
	1 3 6	F A
	1 3 45	H
b1–c	1	H
	1 6	F A
b1–c♯	123 456 7	Ba[7]
	+23 456 8	F[8]
	1	H
b♯1–c♯	23 456	Ba F
c2–d♭	23 456	F
c2–d	23 456	Ba F
	23	H
c♯2–d	23 456 8	Ba F[9] H A
c♯2–d♯	123 456 8	F
d♭2–e♭	123 456 8	F
	23 456 8	H or else as on traverso (123 456 7)
d2–e♭	123 456	Ba F H
d2–e	123 456	Ba F H A
d♯2–e	123 456 7	F H A

[6] The fingering for the b♭1 appoggiatura is mistakenly given as 123; probably the 3 was intended for the a♭1.

[7] This fingering produces the required notes but the b1 sounds strange and there is an unfortunate register break. [8] Actually given as +23 456.

[9] F adds 1, but probably a mistake.

Note	Fingering	Sources
d♯2–e♯	123 ♯56 7	F[10]
	123 456 7	H
e♭2–f♭	123 456 7	F
e♭2–f	123 456 7	Ba[11] F[12] A
e2–f	123 45	F H A
e2–f♯	123 45	Ba
	123 4	F
	123 45	H
e♯2–f♯	123 4 6	F H
f2–g♭	123 4 6	F
f2–g	123 4 6	Ba[13] F H A
f♯2–g	123 56	Ba F H A
f♯2–g♯	123 4 7	F H
g♭2–a♭	123 4 7	F
	123 56	H
g2–a♭	123	Ba H
	123 6	F
g2–a	123	Ba H A
	123 6	F
g♯2–a	123 6	F
	123	H A
g♯2–a♯	123	F
a♭2–b♭	12 4	Ba[14] A[15]
	123	F H
a2–b♭	12	Ba[16] H
	12 alt 3	F
a2–b	12	Ba[17] H A[18]
	12 6	F
a♯2–b	1 3	F
	1 3	H
a♯2–b♯	12 456 7	H
b♭2–c♭	1 3	F
b♭2–c	1 3	Ba[19] F A
	12 456 7	H

[10] Given as 123 4 6 7 but probably meant as here.

[11] Given as e2–f, but the flat sign was probably forgotten.   [12] Given as 123 4 6 7, but probably as here.

[13] Mistakenly given as g2–f♯2.

[14] The dot for closing hole 4 belongs on the trill fingering, not as here on the fingering for b♭2.

[15] The dot for closing hole 4 belongs on the trill fingering, not as here on the fingering for b♭2.

[16] Mistakenly given as b♭2–a♭2.

[17] The supposed b2 and g2 preceding and following this trill are mistakenly given with the fingerings 123 and 123 4 6 respectively.

[18] Moving on hole 2 is omitted.

[19] Mistakenly given as 'from B♭'. The a2 fingering is also mistakenly given as 1 3 instead of 12.

Appendix 8

b2–c   <u>I</u>   Ba[20] H

       <u>I</u> 6   F

       <u>2</u>   A

b2–c♯ <u>I</u>   Ba

       <u>I</u> 7   H

---

[20] Mistakenly given as 'B♯' to b2; actually c♮3 (hence the ♯ sign) to b2.

APPENDIX 9

Pieces possibly for *Hautecontre de hautbois*

Pieces probably for double-reed band

Förster, C. Concerto à 5, G. Two hautboys, [? Hautecontre ('Oboe', but has low c♯ and lies low)], two bassoons. By *c.*1728–45. D-HRD (MS)

Konink, S. de [?] 2 Ouverture à 4, Intrata à 3, g d B♭.[1] 'Dessus [G1 clef], Hautcontre [C1]: La Tajle/Tayle [C2], Basson/Bassong/Bassoun [F4]'. 21.x, 4.xii.1700. D-WD (MS Cod. Guelf. 139 Musica Hdschr, nos. 2–4)

Telemann. 6 Ouvertures à 4 ou 6. Dessus, haute-contre, taille, basse et 2 cors ad libitum. Hamburg, 1736. D-Bs

Venturini, F. Ouvertures Nos. 3, 4, 5, arranged from *Concerti di Camera*, g e a, [Op. 1]. Two hautboys, Hautecontre, Taille, two bassoons. [*c.*1714]. D-Bsb (MS). Arr. dated 25.vi, 10.vii, 6.vii.1723

Witt, C. F. Ouverture à 4, G. Violin/hautboy, viola/Haute contre, viola/Taille, violone/ bassoon, harpsichord. D-Kl (parts; Ms Mus 60b3)

Witt, C. F. Ouverture, d. Three hautboys [? Dessus, Hautecontre, Taille], bassoon. [1st half 18th c.]. S-SK (parts, 231: 27)

In addition, the following may also have been played by a double-reed band

Anon. Ouverture, B♭. Dessus, Haute contre, Taille, bass. S-Uu: IMhs 64: 13

Fischer, J. Ouverture a 5, F. Hautboy (G1), violin (G1), Hautecontre (C1), Taille (C2), bass. S-Uu (MS)

Fischer, J. *Tafelmusik* [6 suites + 3 groups of 'Pollnische Dänze'], B♭ C F C G g F B♭ G. Nos. 1–39 4-pt; nos. 40–64 3-pt; for 'Dessus, 2. Dessus, Haute Contre, Taille, [2x] F Basse'. Hamburg: Spieringk, 1702. D-SWl (part-books); S-Uu

Pez, J. C. *Lamento*, c. 2 Hautbouas [*sic*] Concert, 2 'Violas' in C1 and C2 clefs [probably hautecontre and Taille], continuo. D-ROu (MS XVII: 38.21, parts)

Pez, J. C. Ouverture 24 from *Pièces pour la musique de table*, d. 2 hautboys/violins 'concer:o' [same part], 'Haute-Contreè', Taille, bass/bassoon (4 separate F parts). [1706–16]. D-ROu (MS XVII: 38.24, 6 written parts)

---

[1] Lower case indicates minor keys.

Pez, J. C. Ouverture a 7 parts, B♭. 2 hautboys/violins; hautboy rip., Hautcontre [C1 clef], Taille [C3 clef], bassoon/violone, continuo. D-ROu (MS XVII: 38.9)

Pez, J. C. Ouverture à 5, C. Two hautboys/violins; hautboy rip., Hautcontre [C1 clef], Taille [C3 clef], bassoon/violone, continuo. D-Dlb (Mus 2026-N-1a)

Anon. Concerto affetuoso l'haubois a 9 part. D-ROu (XVII: 51.38)

Witt, C. F. 3 Kleine Märsche, F D C. Dessus, Haute contre, Taille, Basse. Gotha, 13 July 1714. D-Jever, Mariengymnasium (score)

APPENDIX 10

Music for *Oboe Grande*

1720–2. 'Oboe luongo' in an opera produced at Naples in 1720–2.

1727. 'Oboe luongo' in an opera produced at Naples in 1727.[1]

1728. Telemann. 'Capitänsmusik' of 1728. 'Groß-Hoboe'. Range a♮o–a2.[2]

1736. Biber, C. H. Sonata à 5, 2 'Obue bahse ex C', two violins, organ, cello, violone, bassoon.[3]

[Probably 1735–56]. Merseburg. Römhild, J. T. 'Grand Oboe' used in church cantatas.[4]

[Probably 1740–59]. Berlin. Graun, C. H. 'Grand Oboe' used in church cantatas.

Anon. Concerto a 5, A. 'Hautbous de Grand'. S-L (MS, Kraus 149).

[18th c.]. Hoffmann, J. G. [?] Cantata *Der starke Löw aus Juda Stamme*, a. Soprano solo, Grand Oboe, two violins, viola, continuo/organ. P-GD (parts).

1749, Gotha. Stölzel. Passionszyklus. 'Grand Oboe'.[5]

Anon. [? Weyarn]. 4 Deutsche Arien. 2 'Hautbois grand ex Es'.

MS 18th c. Leo, G. Sinfonia, A. Two 'Oboe le Grand', two violins Concerto; two violins, viola, continuo obbl, harpsichord. S-Uu (parts). 'Oboe le Grand' parts in C (= for instruments in A).

1755. Telemann. 'Capitänsmusik'. 'Groß-Hoboe'. Range a♮o–a2.[6]

1755. Finkelman (1998–2000) reports the use of an 'oboe luongo' in an opera produced at Naples in 1755.

1759. Telemann. Piece no. 5 in *Messias*, e, TWV 6: 4. Violin solo, 'Grosse Hoboe', two violins, viola, continuo. D-Bsb (autograph).

[a1776]. Wirbach, M. Two 'Grand Oboe' in eight Cantatas.

[a1785]. Dresden. Homilius, G. A. Two 'Grand Oboe' in seven Cantatas.

1762, Hamburg. Telemann. Aria 'Ich bin erwacht nach Gottes Bilde' from *Der Tag des Gerichts*, A, TWV 6: 8. Soprano, 'Grosse Oboe', bassoon, continuo. D-Bsb (MS).

---

[1] Finkelman (1998–2000). [2] Maertens (1988), 102–3.

[3] All the parts were in G except the 'Obue bahse' (which, as the title says, were in C). As Hubmann (1994: 378) explains, these were probably hautboys at A−1, sounding in A major; if the other parts were also at A−1, they would have been notated in A. The fact that they were in G indicates that they were a whole step higher, thus at A+1. Strings at Salzburg were normally notated at A+1 until the 1780s. Cf. Haynes (1995), §9-1a.

[4] This entry and the following, as well as those for Wirbach and Homilius, are from Koch (1980), 72.

[5] Cited in Koch (1980), 82, 232 (D-Bsb Mus. Ms. 21 401). According to Koch, the range for this entry and the following indicate a tenor hautboy. [6] Maertens (1988), 102–3.

1762, Hamburg. Telemann. Aria 'Seid mir gesegnet', no. 19 in *Der Tag des Gerichts*, a, TWV 6: 8. Bass, 'Grosse Oboe', two violins, viola, continuo. D-Bsb (MS). Range c_1–g_2 (g_2 = fingered d_3 on oboe da caccia, i.e. probably too high). Must be larger than an 'Oboe ordinaria'.

By 1766, Dresden. Uhlig, A. (Lost). Concerto, D. 'Grand Oboe'; two violins, viola, continuo. Breitkopf catalogue 1766: 49 (249); Gerber ii. 698.

BIBLIOGRAPHY

ACHT, ROB VAN (May and Aug. 1988). 'De bouw van houten blaasinstrumenten in Nederland in de periode 1670 tot 1820', *De Bouwbrief*, 49: 3–13; 50: 3–9.

—— BOUTERSE, JAN, and DHONT, PIET (1997). *Dutch Double Reed Instruments of the 17th and 18th Centuries*. Laaber.

ADKINS, CECIL (1990). 'Oboes beyond Compare: The Instruments of Hendrik and Fredrik Richters', *JAMIS* 16: 42–117.

—— (1996). 'William Milhouse and the English Classical Oboe', *JAMIS* 22: 42–88.

—— (1999). 'Proportions and Architectural Motives in the Design of the Eighteenth-Century Oboe', *JAMIS* 25: 95–132.

ADLUNG, JACOB (1758). *Anleitung zu der musikalischen Gelahrtheit*. Erfurt. 2nd edn. 1783. Repr. 1953.

AGRICOLA, JOHANN FRIEDRICH (1757). *Anleitung zur Singkunst*. Berlin. Repr. 1966. Translation of P. F. Tosi's *Opinioni de' cantori* (1723).

AGRICOLA, MARTINUS (1529). *Musica Instrumentalis Deudsch*. Wittenberg.

ALBRECHT, JOHANN LORENZ (1761). *Gründliche Einleitung in die Anfangslehren der Tonkunst*. Langensalza.

ALLEN, GEORGE (1863). *The Life of Philidor, Musician and Chess-Player*. New York. 1st edn. 1858.

ALLIHN, INGEBORG, et al. (1994). 'Berlin', *MGG*² i. 1417–86.

ALMENRAEDER, CARL (1829). 'Ueber die Erhaltung der Fagottrohre, für Fagottisten sowohl, als auch für Oboisten und Clarinettisten', *Caecilia*, 11/41: 58–62.

ALTENBURG, DETLEF (1979). 'Zum Repertoire der Türmer, Stadtpfeiffer, und Ratsmusiker im 17. und 18. Jahrhundert', in *Bericht über die Zweite Int. Fachtagung zur Erforschung der Blasmusik, Uster, Schweiz, 1977* (Alta Musica, Tutzing), 9–32.

ALTENBURG, J. E. (1795). *Versuch einer Anleitung zur heroisch-musikalischen Trompeter- und Pauker-Kunst*, 2 vols. Halle.

ANDERSON, E. (ed.) (1938). *The Letters of Mozart and his Family*. London.

ANON. (1695). *The Compleat Flute-Master*. London.

ANON. (1699). *The Second Book of Theatre Musick . . .* London.

ANON. (1706). *The Fifth Book of the New Flute-Master*. London.

ANON. (*c.*1715). *The Compleat Tutor to the Hautboy*. London.

ANON. (1827). 'The Rise and Progress of the Hautboy', *Quarterly Musical Magazine and Review*, 9: 464–74. (Ends with 'to be continued', but next issue contains nothing.)

ANTHONY, JAMES R. (1973). *French Baroque Music from Beaujoyeulx to Rameau*. London.

—— (1988). Review of *Trios pour le coucher du roy* by Jean-Baptiste Lully and Marin Marais, ed. Herbert Schneider, in *ML* 69: 437–9.

ANTONICEK, THEOPHIL (1980a). 'Vienna', §§2–3, *New Grove* xix. 715–19.

—— (1980b). 'Ziani, Marc'Antonio', *New Grove* xx. 673–5.

ARNOLD, DENIS (1966). 'Orchestras in Eighteenth-Century Venice', *GSJ* 19: 3–19.

—— (1980). 'Conservatories', s.v. 'Education in music', *New Grove* vi. 18–21.

ARTUSI, GIOVANNI MARIA (1600). *L'Artusi overo delle imperfettioni della moderna musica*. Venice.

ASHBEE, ANDREW (1986–93). *Records of English Court Music*, 4 vols. Snodland (Kent).

ASHLEY, MAURICE (1971). *Charles II*. St Albans.

AVISON, CHARLES (1752). *An Essay on Musical Expression*. London. Repr. 1967.

BABITZ, SOL (1967). 'Concerning the Length of Time that Every Note must be Held', *Music Review*, 28: 21–37.

Bach-Dokumente (1963, 1969, 1972) (supplement to *NBA*), ed. W. Neumann and H.-J. Schulze, 3 vols.

BAINES, ANTHONY (1948). 'James Talbot's Manuscript, I. Wind Instruments', *GSJ* 1: 9–26.

—— (1954). 'Shawm', Grove 5, vii. 747.

—— (1957). *Woodwind Instruments and their History*. London.

—— (1980). 'Shawm', *New Grove* xvii. 237.

BANISTER, JOHN JUN. [ascr.] (1695). *The Sprightly Companion*. Repr. 1987. London.

BARBIERI, PATRIZIO (1987). *Acustica, accordatura e temperamento nell'Illuminismo veneto*. Rome.

—— (1991). 'Violin Intonation: A Historical Survey', *EM* 19: 69–88.

BARBOUR, J. MURRAY (1951). *Tuning and Temperament, a Historical Survey*. New York.

BARON, ERNST GOTTLIEB (1727). *Historisch-theoretisch und practische Untersuchung des Instruments der Lauten*. Nuremberg. Repr. 1965.

BARTLET, M. ELIZABETH C. (1989). 'A Musician's View of the French Baroque after the Advent of Gluck: Grétry's *Les trois âges de l'opéra* and its Context', in Heyer (1989), 291–318.

BASELT, BERND (1986). *Händel Handbuch, Band 3. Thematisch-systematisches Verzeichnis: Instrumentalmusik*. Kassel.

BATE, PHILIP (1956). *The Oboe*. 3rd edn. 1975. London and New York.

—— and HALFPENNY, ERIC (1954). 'Oboe', Grove 5.

BEAUSSANT, PHILIPPE (1980). *François Couperin*. Paris.

—— (1992). *Lully ou le musicien du soleil*. Paris.

BECKER, HEINZ (1961). 'Oboe', *MGG* ix. 1772–1813.

BECKER-GLAUCH, IRMGARD (1951). *Die Bedeutung der Musik für die Dresdener Hoffeste bis in die Zeit Augusts des Starken*. Kassel.

BEDOS DE CELLES, Dom FRANÇOIS (1766). *L'Art du facteur d'orgues*, i. Paris. Repr. 1963.

BEEKS, GRAYDON (1985). 'Handel and Music for the Earl of Carnarvon', in Williams (1985), 1–20.

BENADE, ARTHUR H. (1976). *Fundamentals of Musical Acoustics*. Oxford.

—— (1994). 'Woodwinds: The Evolutionary Path since 1700', *GSJ* 47: 63–110.

BENOIT, MARCELLE (1953–4). 'Les Musiciens français de Marie-Louise d'Orléans, Reine d'Espagne', *Revue musicale*, 226: 48–60.

—— (1971a). *Versailles et les musiciens du Roi, 1661–1733*. Paris.

—— (1971b). *Musiques de cour: chapelle, chambre, écurie, 1661–1733*. Paris.

—— (1980). 'Farinel', *New Grove* vi. 396–7.

—— and DUFOURCQ, NORBERT (1966). 'Les Musiciens de Versailles d'après les minutes du Bailliage de Versailles conservées aux Archives départementales de Seine-et-Oise: 1661–1733', *Recherches*, 6: 197–226.

BERNARDINI, ALFREDO (1985a). 'Oboe Playing in Italy from the Origins to 1800' (diss., University of Oxford).

—— (1985b). 'Carlo Palanca e la costruzione di strumenti a fiato a Torino nel Settecento', *Il flauto dolce*, 13: 22–6.

—— (1987). 'Due chiavi per Rossini? Storia e sviluppo dell'oboe a Bologna prima del 1850', *Il flauto dolce*, 17/18: 18–32.

—— (1988). 'Oboe Playing in the Venetian Republic, 1692–1797', *EM* 16: 372–87.

—— (1990). 'Vier Oboistenporträts als Quelle zum Studium der Zwei-Klappen-Oboe', *Oboe-Klarinette-Fagott*, 1: 30–42.

BÉTHIZEY, JEAN-LAURENT DE (1754, 1764). *Exposition de la théorie et de la pratique de la musique*. Paris.

BILL, OSWALD (ed.) (1987). *Christoph Graupner, Hofkapellmeister in Darmstadt 1709–1760*. Mainz.

BIRSAK, KURT (1972). 'Die Holzblasinstrumente im Salzburger Museum Carolino Augusteum: Verzeichnis und entwicklungsgeschichtliche Untersuchungen', *Jahresschrift 1972/Salzburger Museum Carolino Augusteum*.

BISMANTOVA, BARTOLOMEO (1677). *Compendio musicale*. Ferrara. Repr. 1978.

—— (1688). 'Regole . . . del Oboè' (MS version of *Compendio musicale*). Printed in *Tibia* (1987).

BLANCKENBURGH, GERBRANDT (1654). *Onderwyzinge*. Amsterdam.

BÖHM, JOHANN MICHAEL (1729). Two Letters to the Landgraf of Hesse-Darmstadt, 30 May and 2 June, 1729 (D-DS: HA IV, Konv. 356).

BOLAND, JANICE DOCKENDORFF (1996). 'Charles Nicholson's Ornaments for "Roslin Castle"', *Traverso*, 8/1: 1–3.

BOLLIOUD DE MERMET, LOUIS (1746). *De la corruption du goust dans la musique françoise*. Lyon.

BONANNI, FILIPPO (1722); (Plates 1776). *Gabinetto armonico pieno d'istromenti sonori indicati e spiegati*. Rome.

[? BORJON DE SCELLERY, PIERRE] (1672). *Traité de la musette, avec une nouvelle méthode*. 2nd edn. 1678; repr. 1972. Lyon.

BOUISSOU, SYLVIE (1992). *Jean-Philippe Rameau: Les Boréades ou la tragédie oubliée*. Paris.

BOUQUET, MARIE-THÉRÈSE (1969). *Musique et musiciens à Turin de 1648 à 1775*. Turin.

—— (1976). *Il teatro di corte dalle origini al 1788*. Turin.

BOUTERSE, M. C. J. (1999). 'The deutsche Schalmeien of Richard Haka', *JAMIS* 25: 61–94.

BOUTERSE, JAN (2001). 'Nederlandse houtblasinstrumenten en hun bouwers, 1660–1760' (Ph.D. diss., Universteit van Utrecht).

BOWERS, JANE M. (1972). 'The French Flute School from 1700 to 1760' (Ph.D. diss., University of California, Berkeley).

—— (1980). 'Chédeville', *New Grove* iv. 189–90.

BOWLES, EDMUND A. (1989). *Musical Ensembles in Festival Books, 1500–1800*. Ann Arbor.

BOYD, MALCOLM (1993). 'Rome: The Power of Patronage', in Buelow (1993), 39–65.

BOYDELL, BARRA (1982). *The Crumhorn and Other Renaissance Windcap Instruments*. Buren.

BOYDEN, DAVID D. (1965). *The History of Violin Playing*. Oxford.

BRAINARD, PAUL (1981). Critical commentary to *NBA* edn. of BWV 249a, 57–8. Kassel.

BRANDT, KONRAD (1968). 'Fragen zur Fagottbesetzung in den kirchenmusikalischen Werken Johann Sebastian Bachs', *Bach Jahrbuch*, 65–79.

BRAUN, WERNER (1983). 'The "Hautboist": An Outline of Evolving Careers and Functions', in Salmen (1983), 123–58. Trans. from *Der Sozialstatus des Berufsmusikers vom 17. bis 19. Jahrhundert* (Kassel, 1971).

—— (1987). *Vom Remter zum Gänsemarkt: Aus der Frühgeschichte der alten Hamburger Oper (1677–1697)*. Saarbrücken.

—— (1990). 'Lully und die französische Musik im Spiegel der Reisebeschreibungen', in *Jean-Baptiste Lully: Actes du colloque, Heidelberg 1987*, ed. J. de La Gorce and H. Schneider, 271–84.

BREIG, WERNER (1983). 'Zur Chronologie von Johann Sebastian Bachs Konzertschaffen', *AfMw* 40: 77–101.

—— (1993). 'Zur Gestalt von Johann Sebastian Bachs Konzert für Oboe d'amore', *Tibia*, 2/93: 431–48.

BREITKOPF (1760–87). Thematic Catalogues (6 Parts, 16 Suppls.). Repr. New York, 1966 (ed. B. Brook).

BRENET, MICHEL [Marie Bobillier] (1900). *Les Concerts en France sous l'Ancien Régime*.

—— (1917). 'French Military Music in the Reign of Louis XIV', *Musical Quarterly*, 3: 340–57.

BROD, HENRI (1825). *Méthode pour le hautbois*. 2 parts; Part I 1825; Part II *c*.1830. Repr. 1835, 1890. Paris.

BROSSARD, SÉBASTIEN DE (1703). *Dictionaire de musique*. Paris. Facs. edn. 1964, 1965.

BROSSARD, YOLANDE DE (1965). *Musiciens de Paris 1535–1792* (Vie musicale en France sous les rois Bourbons, 11). Paris.

BROUGHTON, AUGUSTA MARY ANNE (1887). *Court and Private Life in the Time of Queen Charlotte, Being the Journals of Mrs Papendiek*. (Journals written in late 18th c.). London.

BROWN, HOWARD MAYER, and SADIE, STANLEY (eds.) (1989). *Performance Practice: Music after 1600*. London.

[? BROWN, THOMAS] (1722). *The Compleat Musick-master*. London.

BUCH, DAVID J. (ed.) (1993). *Dance Music from the Ballets de Cour, 1575–1651*. New York.

BUELOW, GEORGE J. (1993a). 'Hamburg and Lübeck', in Buelow (1993c), 191–215.

—— (1993b). 'Dresden in the Age of Absolutism' in Buelow (1993c), 216–29.

—— (ed.) (1993c). *The Late Baroque Era from the 1680s to 1740* (Music and Society). Englewood Cliffs, NJ.

BURGESS, GEOFFREY (1995a). 'Towards the Modern Legato-cantabile Style' (unpublished draft).

—— (1995b). 'The Louisquatorzien Oboe Band', *EM* 23: 714–16.

—— (1997). 'Historical Oboe Reeds: Avenues for Futher Research; or, Now what do we do with all these measurements?', in *Utrecht 1994*, 205–22.

—— (forthcoming). *'Le premier hautboist d'Europe': A Portrait of Gustav Vogt: Nineteenth-Century Oboe Virtuoso, Teacher and Composer*.

—— and HEDRICK, PETER (1989). 'The Oldest English Reeds? An Examination of 19 Surviving Examples', *GSJ* 42: 32–69.

BURNEY, CHARLES (1771a). *The Present State of Music in France and Italy: or the Journal of a Tour through those Countries*. London. Ed. Percy Scholes as *Dr. Burney's Musical Tours in Europe*, 2 vols. (1959). London.

—— (1771b). Journal of Burney's Travels in France and Italy (MS, GB-Lbl Add. 35122). Ed. H. Edmund Poole as *Music, Men and Manners in France and Italy 1770*. London.

—— (1773). *The Present State of Music in Germany, the Netherlands, and the United Provinces*, 2 vols. London. Ed. Percy Scholes as *Dr. Burney's Musical Tours in Europe*, 2 vols. (1959). London.

—— (1776). *A General History of Music from the Earliest Ages to the Present Period*, 4 vols. London. Repr. New York, 1935, 1957, 2 vols.

BURROWS, DONALD (1985). 'Handel's London Theatre Orchestra', *EM* 13: 349–57.

—— (1993). 'London: Commercial Wealth and Cultural Expansion' in Buelow (1993c), 355–92.

BUSBY, T. (*c*.1783–6) [inc.]. *An Universal Dictionary of Music*. London. 2nd edn. 1801; repr. 1973.

BUTLER, GREGORY (1995). 'J. S. Bach's Reception of Tomaso Albinoni's Mature Concertos', *Bach Studies*, 2, ed. Daniel R. Melamed, 20–46.

BUTT, JOHN (1990). *Bach Interpretation: Articulation Marks in Primary Sources of J. S. Bach*. Cambridge.

BUTTREY, JOHN (1995). 'New Light on Robert Cambert in London, and his Ballet et Musique', *EM* 23: 199–220.

BYRNE, MAURICE (1983). 'Pierre Jaillard, Peter Bressan', *GSJ* 36: 2–28.

—— (1984). 'More on Bressan', *GSJ* 37: 102–11.

CAHN, PETER (1995). 'Frankfurt am Main', *MGG*[2] iii. 643–64.

CAMPBELL, J. PATRICIA (1995). 'Musical Instruments in the *Instrumentälischer Bettlermantl*— a Seventeenth-Century Musical Compendium', *GSJ* 48: 156–67.

[CARR, ROBERT] (1686). *The Delightful Companion*. London.

CASARES RODICIO, EMILIO (1980). *La música en la catedral de Oviedo*. Oviedo.

CASTELLANI, MARCELLO, and DURANTE, ELIO (1987). *Del portar della lingua negli instrumenti di fiato*. Florence.

CASTILLON, FRANÇOIS DE (1777). 'Flûte traversière à deux clés', in *Encyclopédie* [D. Diderot], Supplément 1777, vol. iii. Paris.

CAVALLO, TIBERIUS (1788). 'Of the Temperament of those Musical Instruments, in which the Tones, Keys, or Frets, are Fixed, as in the Harpsichord, Organ, Guitar, &c.', *Philosophical Transactions of the Royal Society of London*, 78: 238.

CHAFE, ERIC THOMAS (*c*.1987). *The Church Music of Heinrich Biber*. Ann Arbor.

CHARTERIS, R. (1997). 'The Music Collection of the Staats- und Universitätsbibliothek, Hamburg', *RMA Research Chronicle*, 30: 1.

CHESNUT, JOHN HIND (1977). 'Mozart's Teaching of Intonation', *JAMS* 30: 254–71.

CHURGIN, BATHIA (1980). 'Sammartini, Giuseppe', *New Grove* xvi. 457–8.

COCKS, W. A., and BRYAN, J. F. (1967). *The Northumbrian Bagpipes*. Newcastle upon Tyne.

COETLOGON, Chevalier DENNIS DE (MD) (1745). *An Universal History of Arts and Sciences*, ii.

COHEN, ALBERT (1981). *Music in the French Royal Academy of Sciences*. Princeton.

COLLINGWOOD, R. G. (1946). *The Idea of History*. Oxford.

CORNEILLE, THOMAS (1694). *Le Dictionnaire des arts et des sciences*, iii. Paris.

[CORRETTE, MICHEL] (*c*.1740). *Méthode pour apprendre aisément à jouër de la flûte traversière*. Paris. Facs. edn. Buren, 1978 and (of 1773 reprint) Geneva, 1977.

COTTE, ROGER (1979). 'Blasinstrumente bei freimaurerischen Riten', *Tibia*, 2/79: 315–16.

COUPERIN, FRANÇOIS (1722a). Preface to the *Concerts royeaux*. Paris.

—— (1722b). Preface to the *Troisième livre de pièces de clavecin*. Paris.

COWDERY, WILLIAM (1989). 'The Early Vocal Works of Johann Sebastian Bach: Studies in Style, Scoring and Chronology' (Ph.D. diss., Cornell University).

CRIST, STEPHEN A. (1985). 'Bach's Début at Leipzig', *EM* 13: 212–26.

CRON, MATTHEW (1996). 'In Defense of Altenburg: The Pitch and Form of Foreign Trumpets', *HBSJ* 8: 6–41.

CUDWORTH, CHARLES (1957). ' "Baptist's Vein"—French Orchestral Music and its Influence, from 1650 to 1750', *PRMA* 83: 29–47.

—— (1965). 'Hints to Young Composers of Instrumental Music (by John Marsh)', *GSJ* 18: 57–71.

CYR, MARY ELLEN (1975). 'Rameau's *Les Fêtes d'Hébé*' (Ph.D. diss., University of California, Berkeley).

—— (1980). 'Rameau, Jean-Philippe, Work-List', *New Grove* xv. 570–3.

DAHLHAUS, CARL (ed.) (1985). *Die Musik des 18. Jahrhunderts*. Laaber.

DAHLQVIST, REINE (1973). 'Taille, Oboe da caccia and Corno inglese', *GSJ* 26: 58–71.

—— (1976). 'Waldhautbois', *GSJ* 29: 126–7.

—— (1993). 'Pitches of German, French, and English Trumpets in the 17th and 18th Centuries', *HBSJ* 5: 29–41.

DALLA CASA, GIROLAMO (1584). *Il vero modo di diminuir*. Venice.

D'AQUIN DE CHATEAU-LYON, PIERRE LOUIS (1752). *Lettres sur les hommes célèbres . . . sous le règne de Louis XV*. Amsterdam and Paris. 2nd edn. 1753.

DARD (1769). *Nouveaux principes de musique*. Paris.

DEAN, WINTON (1959). *Handel's Dramatic Oratorios and Masques*. London.

—— (1970). *Handel and the Opera Seria*. London.

—— (1980). 'Handel, George Frideric', *New Grove* viii. 83–140.

—— and KNAPP, JOHN MERRILL (1987). *Handel's Operas, 1704–1726*. Oxford.

DE BROSSES, CHARLES (1739–40). *Lettres d'Italie*. Ed. F. d'Agay (Mercure de France, 1986). Paris.

DE CASTRO, PADRE GIUSEPPE (Accademico Formato) (1708). 'Intenzione dell'Autore' in *Concerti accademici à quatro*, Op. 4. Bologna.

DELIUS, N. (ed.) (1997). *Sine musica nulla vita* (Festschrift Hermann Moeck). Celle.

DELUSSE, CHARLES (1761). *L'Art de la flute traversiere* [*sic*]. Paris.

DENTON, JOHN WILLIAM (1977). 'The Use of Oboes in Church Cantatas of Johann Sebastian Bach' (DMA diss., University of Rochester).

DEVIENNE, FRANÇOIS (*c*.1794). *Nouvelle méthode théorique et pratique pour la flûte*. Paris.

DICKEY, BRUCE (1978). 'Untersuchungen zur historischen Auffassung des Vibratos auf Blasinstrumenten', *Basler Jahrbuch für historische Musikpraxis*, 2: 77–142.

DIDEROT, DENIS, and D'ALEMBERT, J. LE ROND (1751–72; suppls. 1776–7, 1780). *Encyclopédie, ou Dictionnaire raisonné des sciences, arts et métiers*, 17 vols. Lausanne and Berne.

DIJKSTRA, JELLE [1996]. [Survey of flute tutors] (unpublished).

DOANE, JOSEPH (1794). *A Musical Directory for the Year 1794*. London.

DODART, DENIS (1700). 'Mémoire sur les causes de la voix de l'homme, et de ces différens tons', in *Mémoires de l'Académie royale des sciences*, 244–93.

DOLMETSCH, ARNOLD (1915). *The Interpretation of the Music of the XVII and XVIII Centuries*. London.

DONINGTON, ROBERT (1963). *The Interpretation of Early Music*. London.

—— (1989). 'The Present Position of Authenticity', *Performance Practice Review*, 2: 117–25.

DOUWES, CLAAS (1699). *Grondig ondersoek van de toonen der musiek*. Franeker. Repr. Amsterdam, 1971.

DREYFUS, LAURENCE (1987). *Bach's Continuo Group*. Cambridge, Mass.

DROUET, LOUIS (*c*.1827). *Méthode pour la flûte*. Milan.

DRUMMOND, PIPPA (1978). 'The Royal Society of Musicians in the Eighteenth Century', *ML* 59: 268–89.

—— (1980). 'Weideman, Carl Friedrich', *New Grove* xx. 295.

DUDOK VAN HEEL, S. A. C., and TEUTSCHER, MARIEKE (1974). 'Amsterdam als centrum van "Fluytenmakers" in de 17e en 18e eeuw' in *Historische blaasinstrumenten* (exh. cat.). The Hague. Eng. version (trans. Peter Bree) as 'From Flute Makers to Factories of Musical Instruments', *University of Victoria Loan Exhibition of Historic Double Reed Instruments* (Victoria, BC, 1998).

DUFOURCQ, NORBERT (ed.) (1946). *La Musique des origines à nos jours*. Paris.

—— (1970). *La Musique à la cour de Louis XIV et de Louis XV d'apres les mémoires de Sources et Luynes, 1681–1758* = *Recherches: La Vie musicale en France sous les rois Bourbons*, 17. Paris.

—— and BENOIT, MARCELLE (1963). 'Les Musiciens de Versailles à travers les minutes notariales de Lamy versées aux Archives départementales de Seine-et-Oise: 1661–1733', *Recherches*, 3: 189–206.

DU PRADEL, ABRAHAM [Nicholas de Blegny] (1692). *Le Livre commode des addresses de Paris pour 1692*. Paris.

DÜRR, ALFRED (1955). Kritischer Bericht for the Magnificat, *NBA* II/3. Kassel.

—— (1957). 'Zur Chronologie der Leipziger Vokalwerke J. S. Bachs', *Bach Jahrbuch*, 5–162.

—— (1987). 'Merkwürdiges in den Quellen zu Weimarer Kantaten Bachs', *Bach Jahrbuch*, 151–7.

ÉCOCHARD, MARC (1996). 'Tuning a Hautboy' (unpublished).

—— (1997). 'Hautbois in Mersenne's *Harmonie universelle*: Tuning, Classification, Evolution', in *Utrecht 1994*, 155–65.

ÉCORCHEVILLE, J. (1903). 'Quelques documents sur la musique de la Grande Ecurie du Roi', *SIMG* 2: 608–42.

[EISEL, JOHANN PHILIPP] (1738). *Musicus αυτοδιδακτοσ*. Erfurt.

ENGEL, HANS (1966). *Musik in Thuringen*. Mitteldeutsche Forschungen, 39. Cologne and Graz.

—— (1971). *Das Instrumentalkonzert*, i: *Von den Anfängen bis gegen 1800*. Wiesbaden.

ENGELKE, BERNHARD (1908). *Johann Friedrich Fasch: Sein Leben und seine Tätigkeit als Vokalkomponist* (diss., University of Leipzig).

ENGLÄNDER, RICHARD (1922). *Johann Gottlieb Naumann als Opernkomponist*. Leipzig.

EPPELSHEIM, JÜRGEN (1961). *Das Orchester in den Werken Jean Baptiste Lullys*. Tutzing.

—— (1986). 'Garsault's *Notionaire* (Paris 1761) als Zeugnis für die Stand der französischen Holzblasinstrumentarium um 1760', in *Beiheft zu den Studien der Aufführungspraxis und Interpretation der Musik des 18. Jh., Bericht über das VI. Symposium zu Fragen des Musikinstrumenten*, 56–77. Michaelstein.

EVANS, KENNETH GENE (1963). 'Instructional Materials for the Oboe, 1695–ca. 1800' (Ph.D. diss., University of Iowa).

EWELL, TERRY (1997). 'Het spelen van die "ontbrekende noten" in barok en klassieke concerti [1]', *Scrapes*, 4/3: 15–20.

FARMER, HENRY GEORGE [(1912)]. *The Rise and Development of Military Music*. London.

—— (1950). *Military Music*. London.

FÉLIBIEN, ANDRÉ (1676). *Des principes de l'architecture, de la sculpture, de la peinture, et des autres arts qui en dépendent*. Many later editions.

FENAILLE, MAURICE (1903). *État général des tapisseries de la manufacture des Gobelins*. Paris.

FERRARI, PIERLUIGI (1994). 'Cercando strumenti musicali a Norimberga: Ferdinando de' Medici, Cristoforo Carlo Grundherr, Johann Christoph Denner e Jacob Denner', *Recercare*, 6: 203–20.

FINKELMAN, MICHAEL (1998–2000). 'Die Oboeninstrumente in tieferer Stimmlage' [in 8 parts], *Tibia*, 4/98: 274–81; 1/99: 364–8; 2/99: 451–6; 3/99: 537–41; 4/99: 618–24; 1/00: 25–32; 2/00: 106–11; 3/00.

FISCHER, JOHANN CHRISTIAN [?] (c.1770). *The Compleat Tutor for the Hautboy*. London (Thompson).

—— (c.1780). *New and Complete Instructions for the Oboe or Hoboy*. London (Longman & Broderip).

—— (c.1790). *The Compleat Tutor for the Hautboy*. London (Thompson).

—— (c.1800). *The Hoboy Preceptor*. London (Astor).

FISCHER, W. (1971). Kritischer Bericht, Verschollene Solokonzerte in Rekonstruktionen, *NBA* VII/7. Kassel.

FITZPATRICK, HORACE (1971). *The Horn and Horn-Playing and the Austro-Bohemian Tradition 1680–1830*. Oxford.

FLEMING (FLEMMING), HANNS FRIEDRICH VON (1726). *Der vollkommene teutsche Soldat*. Leipzig.

FLEUROT, FRANÇOIS (1984). *Le Hautbois dans la musique française, 1650–1800*. Paris.

FOLKERS, CATHERINE (1998). 'Playing in Tune on a Baroque Flute', *Traverso*, 10/1: 1–3.

FORD, ROBERT (1981). 'Nicolas Dieupart's Book of Trios', *Recherches*, 20: 45–75.

FORSTER, KARL (1933). *Über das Leben und die kirchenmusikalischen Werke des Giuseppe Antonio Bernabei (1649–1732)*. Munich.

FOSTER, CHARLES (1992). 'The Bassanelli Reconstructed: Radical Solution to an Enigma', *EM* 20: 417–25.

FRAMERY, N. E., and GINGUENÉ, P. L. (i: 1791; ii: 1818). 'Musique', *Encyclopédie méthodique*, vols. 185–6. Paris. Repr. 1971

FRANCOEUR, LOUIS-JOSEPH. (n.d.). *Diapason général de tous les instruments à vent*. Paris. 2nd edn. 1772; 3rd edn. 1813.

FRANÇOIS-SAPPEY, BRIGITTE (1988–90). 'Le Personnel de la Musique Royale de l'avènement de Louis XVI à la chute de la monarchie (1774–1792)', *Recherches*, 26: 133–72.

FREILLON-PONCEIN, JEAN-PIERRE (1700). *La Véritable Manière d'apprendre à jouer en perfection du haut-bois, de la flûte et du flageolet*. Paris. Eng. trans. F. Deakin (unpublished).

FRIEDLÄNDER, M. J. (1942). *On Art and Connoisseurship*. London.

FROELICH, F. J. (1810–11). *Vollständige theoretisch-pracktische Musikschule*, Part II. Bonn.

FUHRMANN, M. H. (1706). *Musicalischer-Trichter*. Frankfurt an der Spree.

FULLER, DAVID (1989). 'The Performer as Composer', in Brown and Sadie (eds.), *Performance Practice*, 117–46.

FURETIÈRE, ANTOINE (1690). *Dictionnaire universel*, iii. Paris and Rotterdam. Repr. 1970.

FÜRSTENAU, MORITZ (1861–2). *Zur Geschichte der Musik und des Theaters am Hofe zu Dresden*, 2 vols. Dresden. Repr. Peters 1971.

GANASSI DAL FONTEGO, SYLVESTRO (1535). *Opera intitulata Fontegara*. Venice.

GARNIER, FRANÇOIS-JOSEPH (1802). *Méthode raisonnée pour le hautbois*. Paris.

GARSAULT, FRANÇOIS-ALEXANDRE-PIERRE DE (1761). *Notionaire, ou mémorial raisonné*. Paris.

GEMINIANI, FRANCESCO (1739). Preface to *Rules for Playing in a True Taste on the Violin, German Flute, Violoncello and Harpsichord*, Op. 8. London.

—— (1748). Preface to *Rules for Playing in a True Taste on the Violin German Flute Violoncello and Harpsichord*, Op. 8. London.

—— (1751). *The Art of Playing on the Violin*. London.

GÉRARD, MICHEL (1982). 'Hautbois, basson et instruments à anche double', in *Instruments de musique, 1750–1800* [Exposition organisée par Philippe Suzanne, Musée des Beaux-Arts, Echevinage-Saintes], 26–43.

—— (1983/4). 'Du hautbois à trois clefs au hautbois à treize clefs' (Ph.D. diss., Université de Sciences humaines, Strasbourg).

GERBER, ERNST LUDWIG (1790–2). *Historisch-biographisches Lexikon der Tonkünstler*, 2 vols. Leipzig. Repr. Graz, 1966–9.

—— (1812–14). *Neues historisch-biographisches Lexikon der Tonkünstler*, 4 vols.

GÉTREAU, FLORENCE (1984). 'Watteau et la musique', in Grasselli and Rosenberg (1984), 529–47. Paris.

GIANELLI, PIETRO (1801). *Dizionario della musica sacra e profana*. Rev. edn. 1820; 2nd edn. 1830. Venice.

GIANNINI, TULA (1987). 'A Letter from Louis Rousselet, 18th-Century French Oboist at the Royal Opera in England', *AMIS Newsletter*, 16/2: 10–11.

GIANNINI, TULA (1993a). 'Jacques Hotteterre le Romain and his Father, Martin', *EM* 21: 377–95.

—— (1993b). *Great Flute Makers of France: The Lot and Godfroy Families 1650–1900*. London.

—— (1998). 'A French Dynasty of Master Woodwind Makers Revealed: Bizey, Prudent and Porthaux, their Workshop in Paris, rue Dauphine, St. André des Arts, ca. 1745–1812: New Archival Documents', *AMIS Newsletter*, 27/1: 7–10.

GIANTURCO, CAROLYN (1993). 'Naples: A City of Entertainment', in Buelow (1993), 94–128.

GIRARD, ALAIN (1983). *The Singing Reed* [published simultaneously in French, German, and English]. Information und Versuche, 12. Basle.

GOLDE, CARL THEODOR (*c*.1850). 'Anweisung, die Oboe auszustimmen, nach wörtl. Aufzeichnung des Instrumentenmachers Golde' (now lost MS *c*.1850, formerly at Markneukirchen; repr. in F. Drechsel, 'über den Bau der Oboe', *Zeitschrift für Instrumentenbau*, 52 (1932), 258–9. Eng. trans. in *GSJ* 31 (1978), 19–21.

GOOSENS, LEON, and ROXBURGH, EDWIN (1977). *Oboe*. London.

GORITZKY, INGO (1979). 'Mozarts Oboenkonzert unter neuen Aspekten', *Tibia*, 2/79: 302–8.

GRASSELLI, MARGARET MORGAN, and ROSENBERG, PIERRE (eds.) (1984). *Watteau 1684–1721* (exh. cat.). Paris.

GRASSINEAU, JAMES (1740). *A Musical Dictionary of Terms*. London. Repr. 1966. Rev. edn. 1769, 1784.

GRAZIADEI, MARTA (1988). Introduction to *Niccolò Dôthel: Six sonates à trois flûtes*. Florence.

GRENSER, HEINRICH (1800). [Remarks on the writings of J. G. Tromlitz, 15 Mar. 1800], Intelligenz-Blatt zur *Allgemeine musikalische Zeitung*, 11: 44.

GROSSE, HANS, and JUNG, RUDOLF (eds.) (1972). *Georg Phillip Telemann: Briefwechsel*. Leipzig.

GRUSH, JAMES (1972). 'A Guide to the Study of the Classical Oboe' (DMA Project, Boston University).

GUG, RÉMY (1988). Comm. 893, 'Historic and Experimental Studies on Brass Used for Organ Reeds', *FoMRHIQ* 53: 51–69.

GUNN, JOHN (1793). *The Art of Playing the German-Flute on New Principles*. London.

HAAS, ROBERT (1927). *Die Estensischen Musikalien*. Regensburg.

HAILPERIN, PAUL (1970). 'Some Technical Remarks on the Shawm and Baroque Oboe' (submitted for the Diploma of the Schola Cantorum Basiliensis).

HAKA, RICHARD (1685). Statement for the delivery of an assortment of wind instruments to the Swedish Navy, June 1685. Amiralitetskollegium (Navy Board), kansliet, serie EIIa, 1685: 2.

HALFPENNY, ERIC (1948–9). 'The Tonality of Woodwind Instruments', *Proceedings of the Royal Musical Association*, 75th Session, 23–37.

—— (1949a). 'A Seventeenth-Century Tutor for the Hautboy', *ML* 30: 355–63.

—— (1949b). 'The English 2- and 3-Keyed Hautboy', *GSJ* 2: 10–26.

—— (1949c). 'The English Début of the French Hautboy', *MMR* 79: 149–53.

—— (1953, 1955). 'The French Hautboy: A Technical Survey' [2 parts], *GSJ* 6: 23–34; 8: 50–9.

—— (1956). 'A French Commentary on Quantz', *ML* 37: 61–6.

—— (1957a). 'A Seventeenth-Century Oboe Consort', *GSJ* 10: 60–1, pls. V and VI.

—— (1957b). 'The Evolution of the Bassoon in England, 1750–1800', *GSJ* 10: 30–9.

—— (1977). 'Musical Instruments [at Waddesdon Manor]', *Apollo*, 184: 446–51.

—— (1980). 'Fingering; Wind', *New Grove* vi. 580–2.

HALLE, J. SAMUEL (1763). *Werkstätte der heutigen Künste*, iii. Brandenburg and Leipzig.

HAMILTON, LIEUT. GEN. SIR F. W. (1874). *The Origin and History of the First or Grenadier Guards*. London.

HARNONCOURT, NIKOLAUS (1988). *Baroque Music Today: Music as Speech*. Portland, Ore. (trans. of *Musik als Klangrede*, 1982).

HARRIS-WARRICK, REBECCA (1990). 'A Few Thoughts on Lully's Hautbois', *EM* 18: 97–106.

—— (1993). 'From Score into Sound: Questions of Scoring in Lully's Ballets', *EM* 21: 354–62.

—— and MARSH, CAROL G. (1994). *Musical Theatre at the Court of Louis XIV: Le Mariage de la Grosse Cathos*. Cambridge.

HAUSSWALD, GÜNTER (1937). *Johann David Heinichens Instrumentalwerke*. Dresden.

HAWKINS, SIR JOHN (1776). *A General History of the Science and Practice of Music*. Repr. 1963; 1875, repr. 1969. London.

HAYDN, JOSEPH (1965). *Gesammelte Briefe und Aufzeichnungen*, ed. H. C. Robbins Landon and D. Bartha. Kassel.

HAYNES, BRUCE (1976). 'Making Reeds for the Baroque Oboe' [2 parts], *EM* 4: 31–4, 173–9. [Also in *The Double Reed* (1979) as 'Baroque Oboe Reed-Making'].

—— (1978). 'Oboe Fingering Charts, 1695–1816', *GSJ* 31: 68–93.

—— (1979). 'Tonality and the Baroque Oboe', *EM* 7: 355–7.

—— (1984). 'Double Reeds, 1660–1830: A Survey of Surviving Written Evidence', *JIDRS* 12: 14–33.

—— (1986a). 'Telemann's *Kleine Cammer-music* and the Four Oboists to whom it was Dedicated', *Musick*, 7: 31–5.

—— (1986b). Comm. 702, '"Temperamento per commune opinione perfettissimo": 18th-Century Tuning for Singers and Orchestral Instruments', *FoMRHIQ* 43: 56–68.

—— (1986c). 'Questions of Tonality in Bach's Cantatas: The Woodwind Perspective', *JAMIS* 12: 40–67.

—— (1988). 'Lully and the Rise of the Oboe as Seen in Works of Art', *EM* 16: 324–38.

—— (1989). 'The Oboe Solo before 1800: A Survey', *JIDRS* 17: 7–14.

—— (1990). 'Bressan, Talbot and the "Galpin" oboe', *GSJ* 43: 112–23.

—— (1991). 'Beyond Temperament: Non-keyboard Intonation in the 17th and 18th Centuries', *EM* 19: 357–81.

—— (1992a). *Music for Oboe: A Bibliography* (2nd edn.). Berkeley, Calif.

—— (1992b). 'Johann Sebastian Bachs Oboenkonzerte', *Bach Jahrbuch*, 23–43.

—— (1994a). 'The Addition of Keys to the Oboe, 1790–1830', *JIDRS* 22: 31–46.

—— (1994b). 'Cornetts and Historical Pitch Standards', *HBSJ* 6: 84–109.

—— (1995). 'Pitch Standards in the Baroque and Classical Periods' (Ph.D. diss., Université de Montréal).

HAYNES, BRUCE (1997a). 'Das Fingervibrato (Flattement) auf Holzblasinstrumenten im 17., 18. und 19. Jahrhundert' [2 parts], *Tibia*, 2/97: 401–7; 3/97: 481–7.

—— (1997b). 'Tu ru or not Tu ru: Paired Syllables and Unequal Tonguing Patterns on Woodwinds in the Seventeenth and Eighteenth Centuries', *Performance Practice Review*, 10/1: 41–60.

—— (1997c). 'Playing "Short" High Notes on the Hautboy', *JIDRS* 25: 115–18.

—— (1997d). 'New Light on Some French Relatives of the Hautboy in the 17th and Early 18th Centuries: The Cromorne, Hautbois de Poitou and Chalumeau Simple', in Delius (1997), 257–70.

—— (2000a). 'A Reconstruction of Talbot's Hautboy Reed', *GSJ* 53.

—— (2000b). '"Sweeter than Hautbois": Towards a Conception of the Schalmey of the Baroque Period', *JAMIS* 26: 57–82.

—— (forthcoming). *A History of Performing Pitch*.

HEDRICK, PETER (1974). 'Henri Brod's Méthode pour le hautbois Reconsidered', *Consort*, 30: 53–62.

HEFLING, STEPHEN E. (1993). *Rhythmic Alteration in Seventeenth- and Early Eighteenth-Century Music: Notes Inégales and Overdotting*. New York.

HEIDE, GEERT JAN VAN DER (1983). Comm. 457, 'Effects Associated with Tuning Instruments Having a Conical Bore and Rules of Thumb Concerning the Intonation of Historical Wind Instruments', *FoMRHIQ* 31: 48–50.

HELD, DAVID PAUL (1976). 'Chorale Preludes Composed in the Eighteenth Century for Organ and a Solo Instrument' (DMA monograph, University of Southern California).

HELLYER, ROGER (1975). 'Some Documents Relating to Viennese Wind-Instrument Purchases, 1779–1837', *GSJ* 28: 50–9.

HELM, E. E. (1960). *Music at the Court of Frederick the Great*. Norman, Okla.

HENDRIE, G. (1985). 'Handel's "Chandos" and Associated Anthems: An Introductory Survey', in Williams (1985), 149–59.

HENNENBERG, FRITZ (1965). *Das Kantatenschaffen von Gottfried Heinrich Stölzel*. 2nd edn. 1976. Leipzig.

HEYDE, HERBERT (1978). *Flöten: Musikinstrumenten-Museum Leipzig. Katalog, Band I*.

—— (1985). 'Der Instrumentenbau in Leipzig zur Zeit Johann Sebastian Bachs', in U. Prinz (ed.), *300 Jahre Johann Sebastian Bach*, 73–88. Tutzing.

—— (1986). *Musikinstrumentenbau*. Leipzig.

—— (1987). 'Contrabassoons in the 17th and early 18th Century', *GSJ* 40: 24–36.

—— (1993a). 'Die Werkstatt von Augustin Grenser d. Ä. und Heinrich Grenser in Dresden', *Tibia*, 4/93: 593–602.

—— (1993b). 'Makers' Marks on Wind Instruments', in Waterhouse (1993).

—— (1994). *Musikinstrumentenbau in Preussen*. Tutzing.

HEYER, J. H. (ed.) (1989). *Jean-Baptiste Lully and the Music of the French Baroque: Essays in Honor of James R. Anthony*. Cambridge.

HIGBEE, DALE (1985). 'A Left-Handed "Voice Flute" by Bressan', *GSJ* 38: 143.

HILDEBRAND, RENATE (1975). 'Das Oboenensemble in Deutschland von der Anfängen bis ca. 1720' (Diplomarbeit, Schola Cantorum Basiliensis).

—— (1978). 'Das Oboenensemble in der Deutschen Regimentsmusik und in den Stadtpfeifereien bis 1720', *Tibia*, 1/78: 7–12.

HIND, HAROLD C., and BAINES, ANTHONY C. (1980). 'Military Band', *New Grove* xii. 310–16.

HITCHCOCK, H. WILEY (1990). *Marc-Antoine Charpentier*. Oxford.

HOBOHM, WOLF (1975). 'Pädagogische Grundsätze und ästhetische Anschauungen Telemanns in der "Kleinen Kammer-Musik" (1716)', in *Telemann und die Musikerziehung: Konferenzbericht der 5. Magdeburger Telemann-Festtage vom 19. bis 27. Mai 1973*, 30–42. Magdeburg.

HODGES, WOODROW JOE (1980). 'A Biographical Dictionary of Bassoonists Born before 1825', 2 vols. (Ph.D. diss., University of Iowa).

HOFMANN, MICHEL (1954). 'Über das "Pfeifergericht" zu Frankfurt a.M.', *Fränkische Blätter*, 6: 76, 85–7.

HOGWOOD, CHRISTOPHER (1984). *Handel*. London.

—— and SMACZNY, JAN (1989). 'The Bohemian Lands', in Zaslaw (1989), 188–212.

HOLMAN, PETER (1993). *Four and Twenty Fiddlers: The Violin at the English Court, 1540–1690*. Oxford.

—— (1994). *Henry Purcell*. Oxford.

HOLME, RANDLE III (*c*.1688). Academy of armory. GB-Lbl Harleian MS 2034.

HOLYOKE, SAMUEL (*c*.1800). *The Instrumental Assistant*. Exeter.

HORN, WOLFGANG (1987). *Die Dresdner Hofkirchenmusik 1720–1745: Studien zu ihren Voraussetzingen und ihrem Repertoire*. Kassel.

HORTSCHANSKY, KLAUS (1996). 'Hugenotten', *MGG*[2] iv. 432–40.

HOTTETERRE, JACQUES-MARTIN (1707). *Principes de la flûte traversière ou flûte d'allemagne, de la flûte à bec ou flûte douce et du haut-bois*. Paris. Facs. edn. Kassel, 1942 (with German trans.) and Geneva, 1973. Eng. trans. by D. Lasocki as *Principles of the Flute, Recorder and Oboe* (London, 1968).

—— (1708). 'Introduction' to [Premier livre de] pièces, Op. 2. Paris.

—— (1719). *L'Art de préluder sur la flûte traversière, sur la flûte-à-bec, sur le haubois, et autres instrumens de dessus*. Paris.

—— (1723). Letter to Wilhelm von Uffenbach, 18 October 1723. Reproduced in House (1991), 273–5.

—— (*c*.1729). *The Rudiments or Principles of the German Flute* [Eng. trans. of parts of Hotteterre (1707)]. London.

—— (1737). *Méthode pour la musette*, Opus 10. Paris. Repr. 1977.

HOULE, GEORGE (1984). 'The Oboe Sonatas of Giuseppe Sammartini', *Journal of Musicology*, 3: 90–103.

HOUSE, DELPHA LEANN (1991). 'Jacques Hotteterre "le Romain": A Study of his Life and Compositional Style' (Ph.D. diss., University of North Carolina at Chapel Hill).

HOYLE, J. [= J. Binns] (1770). *Dictionarium musica*. London.

HUBBARD, FRANK (1965). *Three Centuries of Harpsichord Making*. Cambridge, Mass.

HUBMANN, KLAUS (1994). 'Vom rechten Ton am Fagott: Zur Frage von Stimmton-Verhältnissen im Barock', in M. Nagy (ed.), *'Musik muss man machen': Eine Festgabe für Josef Mertin*, 377–84. Vienna.

HUDGEBUT, JOHN (1679). *A Vade Mecum for the Lovers of Musick*. London.

HUNT, EDGAR (1984). 'Left-Handed Recorders by Bressan', *GSJ* 37: 121.

HUYGENS, CONSTANTIJN (1911–17). *De briefwisseling van Constantijn Huygens (1608–1687)*, iv, ed. J. A. Worp. 's-Gravenhage. See also Jonckbloet and Land (1882).

JACKSON, BARBARA GARVEY (n.d.). Preface to *Arias from Oratorios by Women Composers of the Eighteenth Century*, i. Fayetteville, Ark.

JACKSON, ROLAND (1995). 'Editorial: Performance Practice and Musical Expressivity', *Performance Practice Review*, 8: 1–4.

JACQUOT, A. (1882). *La Musique en Lorraine*. Paris.

JANSON, P. (1987). 'The Eighteenth-Century Chorale Prelude for Organ and Solo Wind Instrument: Its Repertoire and Historical Background' (MA diss., University of Victoria (Canada)).

JAUERNIG, REINHOLD (1950). 'Johann Sebastian Bach in Weimar', in *Johann Sebastian Bach in Thüringen: Festgabe zum Gedenkjahr 1950*, 49–105. Weimar.

JEANS, SUSI (1958a). 'Seventeenth-Century Musicians in the Sackville Papers', *MMR* Sept.–Oct.: 182–7.

—— (1958b). 'Bressan in 1690', *GSJ* 11: 91–2.

JONCKBLOET, W. J. A., and LAND, J. P. N. (1882). *Musique et musiciens au XVIIe siècle*. Leiden.

JOPPIG, GUNTHER (1981). *Hautbois et basson*. Lausanne.

KARP, CARY (1972). 'Baroque Woodwind in the Musikhistoriska Museet, Stockholm', *GSJ* 25: 80–6.

—— (1978). 'Woodwind Instrument Bore Measurement', *GSJ* 31: 9–28.

KASTNER, JEAN-GEORGES (1837). *Traité général de l'instrumentation*. Paris.

—— (1848). *Manuel général de musique militaire à l'usage des Armée Françaises*. Paris.

KELLNER, ALTMAN (1956). *Musikgeschichte des Stiftes Kremsmünster*. Kassel and Basle.

KENYON DE PASCUAL, BERYL (1984). 'El primer oboe español que formó parte de la Real Capilla: Don Manuel Cavazza', *Revista de musicología*, 7/2: 431–4.

—— (1985). 'Instrumentos e instrumentistas españoles y extranjeros en la Real Capilla desde 1701 hasta 1749', Istituto de las Artes Escénicas y de la Música; Ministerio de Cultura (Spain), 93–7.

—— (1990). 'Juan Bautista Pla and José Pla—Two Neglected Oboe Virtuosi of the 18th Century', *EM* 18: 109–10.

KIRKENDALE, URSULA (1966). *Antonio Caldara*. Graz and Cologne.

—— (1967). 'The Ruspoli Documents on Handel', *JAMS* 20: 222–73.

KIRKENDALE, WARREN (1993). *The Court Musicians in Florence during the Principate of the Medici*. Florence.

KIRNBAUER, MARTIN (1992). 'Überlegungen zu den Meisterzeichen Nürnberger "Holzblasinstrumentenmacher" im 17. und 18. Jahrhundert', *Tibia*, 1/92: 9–20.

—— (1994). *Verzeichnis der europäischen Musikinstrumente im Germanischen Nationalmuseum Nürnberg*, ii: *Flöten- und Rohrblattinstrumente bis 1750*. Wilhelmshaven.

—— (1995). '"No smoke without fire": An Approach to Nuremberg Recorder Making in the Seventeenth Century', in *Utrecht 1993*, 91–103.

—— and KRICKEBERG, DIETER (1987). 'Untersuchungen an Nürnberger Blockflöten der Zeit zwischen 1650 und 1750', *Anzeiger des Germanischen Nationalmuseums 1987*, 245–81. Nuremberg.

—— and THALHEIMER, PETER (1995). 'Jacob Denner and the Development of the Flute in Germany', *EM* 23: 83–100.

KLEEFELD, WILHELM (1899/1900). 'Das Orchester der Hamburger Oper, 1678–1738', *SIMG* 1: 219–89.

KNAPP, J. MERRILL (1993). Critical Report, *Tamerlano*, HHA. Kassel.

KNECHT, [JUSTIN HEINRICH] (1803). 'Über die Stimmung der musikalischen Instrumente', *Allgemeine musikalische Zeitung*, 32: cols. 529–33.

KOCH, H. C. (1802). *Musikalisches Lexikon*. Frankfurt am Main and Offenbach. Repr. 1964.

KOCH, HANS OSKAR (1980). *Sonderformen der Blasinstrumente in der deutschen Musik vom späten 17. bis zur Mitte des 18. Jahrhunderts* (Inaugural-Diss., Heidelberg).

KÖCHEL, LUDWIG VON (1869). *Die kaiserliche Hof-Musikkapelle in Wien von 1543–1867*. Vienna.

KOLNEDER, WALTER (1952). 'Vivaldi als Bearbeiter eigener Werke: Ein Fagottkonzert eingerichtet für Oboe', *Acta musicologica*, 24: 45–52.

—— (1970). *Georg Muffat zur Aufführungspraxis* (Collection d'Études musicologiques, 50). Strasburg.

—— (1979). *Antonio Vivaldi: Dokumente seines Lebens und Schaffens*. Wilhelmshaven.

KOPP, JAMES B. (1991). 'Notes on the Bassoon in Seventeenth-Century France', *JAMIS* 17: 85–114.

KRAUSE-PICHLER, ADELHEID (1991). *Jakob Friedrich Kleinknecht, 1722–1794*. Weissenhorn.

KRAUSS, RUDOLPH (1908). *Das Stuttgarter Hoftheater von den ältesten Zeiten bis zur Gegenwart*. Stuttgart.

KRICKEBERG, DIETER (1971). 'Zur sozialen Stellung des deutschen Spielmanns im 17. und 18. Jahrhundert, besonders im Nordwesten', in Salmen (1971), 26–42; trans. as 'On the Social Status of the Spielmann ("Folk Musician") in 17th- and 18th-Century Germany, Particularly in the Northwest', in Salmen (1983), 95–122.

KUBITSCHEK, ERNST (1987). 'Block- und Querflöte im Umkreis von J. J. Fux: Versuch einer Übersicht', in B. Habla (ed.), *Johann Joseph Fux und die barocke Bläsertradition*, 99–119. Tutzing.

KUHNAU, JOHANN (1717). Letter to Johann Mattheson, 8 December 1717, published in Mattheson (1722–5), vii. 229–39.

KÜNTZEL, G. (1965). *Die Instrumentalkonzerte von Johann Friedrich Fasch* (Diss., Goethe Universität, Frankfurt am Main).

LA BARRE, MICHEL DE (? *c*.1740). 'Mémoire de M. de la Barre: sur les musettes et hautbois, etc.', Arch. Nat. Maison du Roi (O'.878). In Benoit (1971b).

LABORDE, JEAN BENJAMIN DE (1780). *Essai sur la musique ancienne et moderne*. Paris. Repr. 1972, 1978.

LAFONTAINE, H. C. DE (1909). *The King's Music: A Transcript of Records Relating to Music and Musicians (1460–1700)*. London.

LA GORCE, JÉRÔME DE (1989). 'Some Notes on Lully's Orchestra', in Heyer (1989), 99–112.

LANDMANN, ORTRUN (1982). 'Französische Elemente in der Musikpraxis am Dresdener Hof des 18. Jahrhunderts', *Studien zur Aufführungspraxis und Interpretation von Instrumentalmusik des 18. Jahrhunderts*, 16: 48–56.

—— (1989). 'The Dresden Hofkapelle During the Lifetime of Johann Sebastian Bach', *EM* 17: 17–30.

—— (1993). 'Die Entwicklung der Dresdener Hofkapelle zum "klassischen" Orchester', *Basler Jahrbuch für historische Musikpraxis*, 17: 175–90.

LANGWILL, LYNDESAY G. (1980). *Index of Wind-Instrument Makers*, 6th edn. Edinburgh.

LASOCKI, DAVID (1972). 'The Eighteenth-Century Woodwind Cadenza' (Master's thesis, University of Iowa).

—— (1977). 'Johann Christian Schickhardt (ca. 1682–1762): A Contribution to his Biography and a Catalogue of his Works', *Tijdschrift van de Vereniging voor Nederlandse Muziekgeschiedenis*, 27: 28–55. (See also Lasocki 1979.)

—— (1979). 'Schickhardt in London', *Recorder and Music*, 6: 203–5.

—— (1983). 'Professional Recorder Players in England, 1540–1740', 2 vols. (Ph.D. diss., University of Iowa).

—— (1988). 'The French Hautboy in England, 1673–1730', *EM* 16: 339–57.

—— (1997). 'The London Publisher John Walsh (1665 or 1666–1736) and the Recorder', in Delius (1997), 343–74.

—— (forthcoming). *Woodwind Instruments in Britain, 1660–1740: Social History, Music, and Performance Practice.*

—— and NEATE, HELEN (1988). 'The Life and Works of Robert Woodcock, 1690–1728', *American Recorder*, 29: 92–104.

LAWSON, C. (1981). 'Telemann and the Chalumeau', *EM* 9: 312–19.

LEDET, DAVID A. (1981). *Oboe Reed Styles: Theory and Practice*. Bloomington, Ind.

LEGÊNE, EVA (1995). 'The Early Baroque Recorder', in *Utrecht 1993*, 105–24.

LEMAÎTRE, EDMOND (1988–90). 'L'Orchestre dans le Théâtre Lyrique Français chez les continuateurs de Lully 1687–1715', *Recherches*, 26: 83–131.

LESCAT, PHILIPPE (1990). '"Il pastor fido", une œuvre de Nicolas Chédeville', *Informazioni e studi Vivaldiani*, 11: 5–10.

—— (1992). '"Il pastor fido", une œuvre de Nicolas Chédeville', in A. Fanna and M. Talbot (eds.), *Vivaldi vero e falso: problemi di attribuzione*, 109–25 (a different article from Lescat 1990).

LESURE, FRANÇOIS (1955). 'Concerts de hautbois et musettes au milieu de XVIIᵉ siècle', *Revue musicale*, 37: 83–4.

—— (1972). *L'Opéra classique français*. Geneva.

LEWIS, E. J. (1964). 'The Use of Wind Instruments in 17th-Century Instrumental Music' (Ph.D. diss., University of Wisconsin).

LIBBY, DENNIS (1989). 'Italy: Two Opera Centres', in Zaslaw (1989), 15–60.

LINDEMANN, FRAYDA B. (1978). 'Pastoral Instruments in French Baroque Music: Musette and Vielle' (Ph.D. diss., Columbia University).

LINDLEY, MARK (1980a). 'Comma', *New Grove* iv. 590–1.

—— (1980b). 'Interval', *New Grove* ix. 277–9.

—— (1987). 'Stimmung und Temperatur', in *Hören, Messen und Rechnen in der Frühen Neuzeit* (Geschichte der Musiktheorie, 6), 109–331. Berlin.

LINNEMANN, GEORG (1935). *Celler Musikgeschichte bis zum Beginn des 19. Jahrhunderts*. Celle.

LORENZONI, ANTONIO (1779). *Saggio per ben sonare il flauto traverso*. Vicenza.

LOULIÉ, ÉTIENNE (*c*.1685–90). 'Méthode pour apprendre à jouer de la flûte douce', MS Paris, Bibliothèque Nationale de France, f. fr. n. acq. 6355. 2nd MS version *c*.1701, same location. Complete Eng. trans. by Richard Semmens in *American Recorder*, 24/4 (Nov. 1983): 135–45; corrections by P. Ranum, ibid. 25/3 (Aug. 1984): 119–21.

—— (1696). *Eléments ou principes de musique*. Paris. 2nd edn. 1698.

LYNDON-JONES, MAGGIE (1996). Comm. 1428, 'More Thoughts on the Bassanos', *FoMRHIQ* 83: 18–28.

McCLYMONDS, MARITA P. (1978). 'Niccolò Jommelli: The Last Years, 1769–1774' (Ph.D. diss., University of California, Berkeley).

McCREDIE, ANDREW D. (1964). *Instrumentarium and Instrumentation in the North German Baroque Opera* (Diss., Hamburg).

MACGILLIVRAY, JAMES A. (1961). 'The Woodwind', in A. Baines (ed.), *Musical Instruments through the Ages*, 237–76. London.

McGOWAN, KEITH (1994). 'The World of the Early Sackbut Player: Flat or Round?', *EM* 22: 441–66.

McGOWAN, RICHARD A. (1978). *Italian Baroque Solo Sonatas for the Recorder and the Flute*. Detroit.

MACHARD, ROBERTE (1971). 'Les Musiciens en France au temps de Jean-Philippe Rameau d'après les actes du Secrétariat de la Maison du Roi', *Recherches*, 11: 6–177.

MAERTENS, WILLI (1988). *Georg Philipp Telemanns sogenannte Hamburgische Kapitainsmusiken (1723–1765)*. Wilhelmshaven.

MAHAUT, ANTOINE (1759). *Nieuwe manier om binnen korten tijd op de dwarsfluit te leeren speelen*. Amsterdam.

MAJER, JOSEPH FRIEDRICH BERNHARD CASPAR (1732). *Museum musicum theoretico practicum*. Facs. edn. Kassel, 1954. 2nd edn. 1741. Schwäbisch Hall.

MARAIS, MARIN (1717). 'Introduction' to *Pièces de violes, 4e livre*. Repr. 1972. Paris.

MARCELLO, ALESSANDRO (1738). Foreword to *La Cetra, [6] concerti di Eterio Stinfalico*. Augsburg.

MARPURG, FRIEDRICH WILHELM (1754–78). *Historisch-kritische Beyträge zur Aufnahme der Musik*. Berlin. Repr. 1970.

MARSHALL, ROBERT L. (1972). *The Compositional Process of J. S. Bach*, 2 vols. Princeton.

—— (1985). 'Tempo and Dynamic Indications in the Bach Sources: A Review of the Terminology', in Williams (1985), 259–75.

MARX, JOSEF (1951). 'The Tone of the Baroque Oboe', *GSJ* 4: 3–19.

—— (1983). *The Writings of Josef Marx: An Anthology*, i. New York.

MASEL, ANDREAS (1995). 'Doppelrohrblattinstrumente: A. Europäische Instrumente', *MGG*² ii. 1349–404.

MASSIP, CATHÉRINE (1989). 'Michel Lambert and Jean-Baptiste Lully: The Stakes of a Collaboration', in Heyer (1989), 25–39.

MATHER, BETTY BANG (1973). *Interpretation of French Music from 1675 to 1775. For Woodwind and Other Performers*. New York.

MATTHESON, JOHANN (1713). *Das neu-eröffnete Orchestre*. Hamburg.

—— (1721). *Das forschende Orchestre*. Hamburg.

—— (1722–5). *Critica musica*. Hamburg. Repr. 1964.

—— (1739). *Der vollkommene Capellmeister*. Hamburg.

—— (1740). *Grundlage einer Ehren-Pforte*. Hamburg. Repr. 1969.

MAUNDER, RICHARD (1998). 'Viennese Wind-Instrument Makers, 1700–1800', *GSJ* 52: 170–91.

MEDFORTH, MARTIN (1981). 'The Valentines of Leicester: A Reappraisal of an 18th-Century Musical Family', *Musical Times*, 1666 (122), no. 12: 812–18.

MENDEL, ARTHUR (1978). 'Pitch in Western Music since 1500: A Re-examination', *Acta musicologica*, 50: 1–93.

MENESTRIER, CLAUDE-FRANÇOIS (1669). 'De l'harmonie', in *Traité des tournois, joustes, carrousels et autres spectacles publics*. Lyon.

—— (1682). *Des ballets anciens et modernes*. Paris. Repr. 1972.

MENKE, W. (1982). *Thematisches Verzeichnis der Vokalwerke von Georg Philipp Telemann*, i: *Cantaten zum Gottesdienstlichen Gebrauch*. Orig. typescript at D-F contains details of separate arias. Frankfurt am Main.

MENNICKE, C. (1906). *Hasse und die Brüder Graun als Symphoniker*. Leipzig.

MERSENNE, MARIN (1635). *Harmonicorum libri*. Paris. Repr. 1972.

—— (1636–7). *Harmonie universelle*, 3 vols. Paris. Facs. edn. 1963 pub. by CNRS, Paris.

MEUDE-MONPAS, J. J. O. DE (1787). *Dictionnaire de musique*. Paris.

MEUSEL, J. G. (1778–9). *Teutsches Künstlerlexikon*, 2 vols. 2nd edn. 1808–14. Lemgo.

MEYER, CLEMENS (1913). *Geschichte der Mecklenburg-Schweringer Hofkapelle*. Schwerin.

MEYER, EVE (1973). 'The Oboe Quartets of Florian Leopold Gassmann', *Music Review*, 34: 179–88.

MICHEL, WINFRIED, and TESKE, HERMIEN (1978). Introduction to Quantz (1729–41).

MIEHLING, KLAUS (1993). *Das Tempo in der Musik von Barock und Vorklassik*. Wilhelmshaven.

MILHOUS, JUDITH, and ROBERT D. HUME (1982). *Vice Chamberlain Coke's Theatrical Papers 1706–1715*. Carbondale, Ill.

—— —— (1983). 'New Light on Handel and the Royal Academy of Music in 1720', *Theatre Journal*, 35: 149–67.

MILLER, EDWARD (*c*.1799). *The New Flute Instructor*. London.

MIRIMONDE, A. P. DE (1974). *Sainte Cécile: metamorphoses d'un thème musical*. Geneva.

—— (1975). *L'Iconographie musicale sous les rois Bourbons*, 2 vols. (La Vie musicale en France sous les rois Bourbons). Paris.

MITFORD, NANCY (1970). *Frederick the Great*. London. Repr. 1984.

MOENS-HAENEN, GRETA (1984). 'Holzbläservibrato im Barock', *Brussels Museum of Musical Instruments Bulletin*, 14/1: 1–59.

—— (1988). *Das Vibrato in der Musik des Barock*. Graz.

MOLDENIT, JOACHIM VON (1753). *Sei sonate da flauto traverso e basso continuo con un discorso sopra la maniera di sonar il flauto traverso*. Hamburg.

MÖLLER, DIRK (1993). 'Die Holzblasinstrumente in den Opern Georg Friedrich Händels', *Concerto*, 89: 14–22.

MONTÉCLAIR, MICHEL PIGNOLET DE (1724/5). *Concerts*. Paris.

—— (1736). *Principes de musique*. Paris. Repr. 1972.

MOORE, A. L. (1981). 'Two Anonymous Eighteenth-Century Manuscripts for Trumpet with Oboe Ensemble from the Lilien Part-books (Sonsfeld Collection)' (DMA diss., North Texas State University).

MORBY, JOHN E. (1971). 'Musicians at the Royal Chapel of Versailles, 1683–1792' (Ph.D. diss., University of California at Berkeley).

MORRIS, CLAVER (1934). *The Diary of a West-Country Physician (1684–1726)*, ed. E. Hobhouse. London.

MORTIMER (1949). 'Lists from London Universal Directory, 1763', *GSJ* 2: 27–31.

MOSER, H. J. (1935). *Tönende Volksaltertümer*. Berlin.

MOUCHEREL, CHRISTOPHE (1734). 'Mémoire instructif pour faire les Devis, Desseins, Plans, Marchez et Reception des orgues', repr. in *Textes sur les instruments de musique au XVIIIᵉ siècle* (Geneva, 1972) and also N. Dufourcq, *Le Livre de l'orgue français* (Paris, 1971), i. 609–45.

MOZART, LEOPOLD (1756). *Versuch einer gründlichen Violinschule*. Augsburg. Repr. 1976. 3rd edn. 1787, repr. 1956.

—— (1778). Letter to his wife and son, 28 May 1778, in Anderson (1938), 798, 1350.

MUFFAT, GEORG (1701). *Auserlesene Instrumental-Music* (Passau, 1701). Printed in Kolneder (1970), 102–29.

MÜNSTER, ROBERT (1993). 'Courts and Monasteries in Bavaria', in Buelow (1993), 296–323.

MUSIC, DAVID W. (1983). 'The Recorder in Early America', *American Recorder*, 23: 102–3.

MYERS, HERBERT W. (1981). 'The Practical Acoustics of Early Woodwinds' (DMA diss., Stanford University).

—— (1989). 'Pitch and Transposition in the Renaissance and Early Baroque', in J. Kite-Powell (ed.), *A Practical Guide to Historical Performance: The Renaissance*, 248–56. New York.

—— (1997a). 'Praetorius's Pitch: Some Revelations of the *Theatrum Instrumentorum*', in *Perspectives in Early Brass Scholarship: Proceedings of the 1995 International Historic Brass Symposium, Amherst, Mass.*, 29–45. New York.

—— (1997b). 'Woodwinds', in Stewart Carter (ed.), *A Performer's Guide to Seventeenth-Century Music*, 69–97. New York.

NALIN, GIUSEPPE (1991). ' "Il vero indicio che una pivetta sii perfetta è . . ." ', *Aulos*, 4/2: 83–6.

NEEMAN, H. (1939). 'Die Lautenisten-Familie Weiss', *Archiv für Musikforschung*, 4: 157–89.

NEMEITZ, JOACHIM CHRISTOPH (1718). *Séjour de Paris, c'est-à-dire, instructions fidèles, pour les voyageurs de condition*. Frankfurt am Main.

NETTL, PAUL (1957). *Das Prager Quartierbuch des Personals der Krönungsoper 1723* (Mitteilungen der Kommission für Musikforschung, 8). Vienna.

NEUMANN, WERNER (1947). *Handbuch der Kantaten Johann Sebastian Bachs*. Wiesbaden. Repr. 1971.

NEUMANN, WERNER (1960). 'Das Bachische Collegium musicum', *Bach Jahrbuch*, 47: 5–27. Repr. in W. Blankenburg (ed.), *Johann Sebastian Bach* (Darmstadt, 1970).

NICHOLSON, CHARLES (*c*.1816). *Complete Preceptor for the German Flute*. London.

—— (1821). *Preceptive Lessons, for the Flute*. London.

NICKEL, E. (1971). *Der Holzblasinstrumentenbau in der Freien Reichstadt Nürnberg*. Munich.

NIEDT, FRIEDRICH ERHARD (1700–21). *Musicalische Handleitung*, 3 vols. Hamburg.

NOACK, ELISABETH (1967). *Musikgeschichte Darmstadts vom Mittelalter bis zur Goethezeit* (Beiträge zur Mittelrheinischen Musikgeschichte, 8). Mainz.

—— (1980). 'Erbach, Friedrich Karl', *New Grove* vi. 224.

NOACK, FRIEDRICH (1995). 'Darmstadt', *MGG²* ii. 1087–94.

NÖSSELT, HANS-JOACHIM (1980). *Ein ältest Orchester 1530–1980: 450 Jahre Bayerisches Hof- und Staatsorchester*. Munich.

NORTH, ROGER (*c*.1710–28). Theory of Sounds; Musical Grammarian (MSS); included in *Roger North on Music*, ed. John Wilson (London, 1959).

OEFNER, CLAUS (1995). 'Eisenach', *MGG²* ii. 1701–7.

OLDHAM, GUY (1961). 'Two Pieces for 5-Part Shawm Band by Louis Couperin', in *Music, Libraries and Instruments*, ed. V. Sherrington and G. Oldham, 11: 233–8. London.

OLESKIEWICZ, MARY A. (1998). 'Quantz and the Flute at Dresden: His Instruments, his Repertory and their Significance for the "Versuch" and the Bach Circle' (Ph.D. diss., Duke University).

OTTENBOURGS, STEFAAN (1988 and 1989). 'De Familie Rottenburgh', *Musica antiqua*, 5/4: 152–8; 6/1: 9–16.

OTTO, CRAIG A. (1977). *Seventeenth-Century Music from Kroměříž, Czechoslovakia: A Catalog of the Liechtenstein Music Collection on Microfilm at Syracuse University*. Syracuse, NY.

OWENS, SAMANTHA (1995). 'The Württemberg Hof-Musicorum c.1680–1721' (Ph.D. thesis, Victoria University of Wellington).

OZI, ÉTIENNE (1787). *Méthode nouvelle et raisonnée pour le basson*. Paris.

—— (1803). *Nouvelle Méthode de basson*. Paris.

I.P. (5 Apr. 1830). 'On the Oboe and Bassoon', *Harmonicon*, 1: 192–3.

PAGE, JANET K. (1988). 'The Hautboy in London's Musical Life, 1730–1770', *EM* 16: 348–71.

—— (1993). '"To soften the sound of the hoboy": The Muted Oboe in the 18th and Early 19th Centuries', *EM* 21: 65–80.

PANOFF, PETER (1938). *Militärmusik in Geschichte und Gegenwart*. Berlin.

PARKE, WILLIAM THOMAS (1830). *Musical Memoirs*. London.

PECKHAM, MARY ADELAIDE (1969). 'The Operas of Georg Philipp Telemann' (Ph.D. diss., Columbia University).

PERDUE, R. E. (1958). 'Arundo donax', *Economic Botany*, 12: 368–404.

PETIT, J. C. (*c*.1740). *Apologie de l'exellence* [sic] *de la musique*. London.

PETRI, JOHANN SAMUEL (1782). *Anleitung zur practischen Musik*. Lauban. First. edn. Leipzig, 1767.

PETZOLDT, RICHARD (1974). *Georg Philipp Telemann*, trans. H. Fitzpatrick. London. Orig. published Leipzig, 1967.

—— (1983), 'The Economic Conditions of the 18th-Century Musician' in Salmen (1983), 159–88; orig. 'Zur sozialen Lage des Musikers im 18. Jahrhundert', in Salmen (1971), 64–82.

PHILIDOR, PIERRE (1717–18). *Suittes*, Opp. 1–3. Paris.

PHILIP, ROBERT (1992). *Early Recordings and Musical Style*. Cambridge.

PIERRE, CONSTANT (1893). *Les Facteurs d'instruments de musique, les luthiers et la facture instru- mentale*. Paris.

—— (1899). *Notes inédites sur la musique de la Chapelle Royale (1532–1790)*. Paris.

—— (1975). *Histoire du Concert Spirituel 1725–1790*. Originally written in 1900. Paris.

PIGUET, MICHEL (1988). 'Die Oboe im 18. Jahrhundert', *Basler Jahrbuch für historische Musikpraxis*, 12: 81–107 (plus *Beiheft*).

—— (1997). 'Historical Oboes: Sound and Fingering', in *Utrecht 1994*, 3–7.

POTTIER, LAURENCE (1995). 'The Iconography of the Recorder in France During the Second Half of the Seventeenth Century', in *Utrecht 1993*, 127–44.

POWELL, ARDAL (1993). 'Die Eichentopf-Flöte: Die älteste erhaltene vierteilige Travers- flöte?' in *Tibia*, 1/95: 343–50.

—— (1996). 'The Hotteterre Flute: Six Replicas in Search of a Myth', *JAMS* 49: 225–63.

—— (1997). 'A Fake Grenser Flute by J. G. Otto, Dated 1798', *Traverso*, 9/1: 1–3.

—— with LASOCKI, DAVID (1995). 'Bach and the Flute: The Players, the Instruments, the Music', *EM* 23: 9–29.

PRAETORIUS, MICHAEL (1618a, 1620). Part 2, 'De Organographia' (1618, rev. 1619) and Part 4, 'Theatrum Instrumentorum seu Sciagraphia', (1620) in *Syntagma musicum*. Facs. edn., Kassel, 1958. Eng. trans. David Z. Crookes, *Michael Praetorius: Symtagma musicum II, de organographia, Parts I and II* (Oxford, 1986).

—— (1618b). *Syntagmatis musici tomus tertius*. Wolfenbüttel.

[PRELLEUR, PETER] (1730). *The Modern Musick-Master*. London. Facs. edn., Kassel, 1965.

PRICE, CURTIS A. (n.d.). 'Extracts from Restoration plays which refer to the oboe' (unpub- lished draft).

PRINTZ, WOLFGANG CASPAR [? Johann Kuhnau] (1690). *Musicus vexatus*. Freiberg.

PRINZ, ULRICH (1979). *Studien zum Instrumentarium Johann Sebastian Bachs mit Besonder Berücksichtigung der Kantaten* (Diss., Universität Tubingen).

—— (1985). 'Anmerkungen zum Instrumentarium in den Werken Johann Sebastian Bachs', in *300 Jahre Johann Sebastian Bach*, ed. U. Prinz (Tutzing), 89–98.

PRUNIÈRES, HENRY (1931). 'Les Ballets', Tome I, in J.-B. Lully, *Œuvres complètes*. Paris.

PURE, Abbé MICHEL DE (1668). *Idées des spéctâcles anciens et nouveaux*. Paris.

QUANTZ, JOHANN JOACHIM (1729–41). Solfeggi pour la Flute Traversiere avec l'enseigne- ment. MS copied between 1775 and 1782 by a Quantz student. Printed Winterthur, 1978.

—— (1752). *Essai d'une méthode pour apprendre à jouer de la Flûte Traversière* [in French and German]. Berlin. Eng. trans. Reilly (1966, 2nd edn. 1987).

—— (1755). 'Herrn Johann Joachim Quantzens Lebenslauf, von ihm selbst entworfen', in F. W. Marpurg (ed.), *Historisch-kritische Beyträge zur Aufnahme der Musik*, i, pt. 5, 197– 250. Berlin. Repr. Cologne, 1948 and Amsterdam, 1972. Eng. trans. in P. Nettl, *Forgotten Musicians* (New York, 1951), 280–319.

QUANTZ, JOHANN JOACHIM (1759). 'Vorbericht', *Sei duetti*, Opus 2. Berlin.

RACHOR, DAVID (1998). '*Werkstätt* [sic] *der heutigen Künste* of J. S. Halle: Implications on the Historical Bassoon Reed Gouge', *FoMRHIQ* 93: 15–17.

RACKWITZ, WERNER (1981). *Georg Phillip Telemann: Singen ist das Fundament zur Music in allen Dingen, eine Dokumentensammlung*. Leipzig.

RAGUENET, FRANÇOIS (1702). *Paralèle des italiens et des françois, en ce qui regarde la musique et les opéra*. Paris. Eng. trans. *A Comparison between the French and Italian Musick and Opera's* (London, 1709); repr. 1968 in *Musical Quarterly*, 32 (1946), 411–36 and Oliver Strunk, *Source Readings in Music History* (New York, 1950), 473–88.

RANUM, PATRICIA M. (1992). 'A Fresh Look at French Wind Articulations', *American Recorder*, 33/4: 9–16, 39. Further discussion, ibid. 34/1: 30–4 and 34/2: 34–9.

—— (1995). 'Tu-Ru-Tu and Tu-Ru-Tu-Tu: Toward an Understanding of Hotteterre's Tonguing Syllables', in *Utrecht 1993*, 217–54.

RASCH, RUDOLF (1993). 'The Dutch Republic', in Buelow (1993), 393–410.

RATNER, LEONARD G. (1991). 'Topical Content in Mozart's Keyboard Sonatas', *EM* 19: 615–19.

RAYNOR, HENRY (1972). *A Social History of Music*. London.

—— (1980). 'London: VI §4: Concert life', *New Grove* xi. 188–208.

RECORD, SAMUEL J., and GARRATT, GEORGE A. (1925). *Boxwoods* (Yale University School of Forestry Bulletin No. 14).

REES, ABRAHAM (1802–20). *The Cyclopaedia or Universal Dictionary of the Arts; New Cyclopaedia*. London.

REILLY, EDWARD R. (1966). *On Playing the Flute* (Eng. trans. of J. J. Quantz's *Essai*, 1752). London.

RENDALL, F. G. (1971). *The Clarinet: Some Notes on its History and Construction*, 3rd edn., rev. with some additional material by Philip Bate. London.

RIBOCK, JUSTUS JOHANNES HEINRICH (1782). *Bemerkungen über die Flöte, und Versuch einer kurzen Anleitung zur bessern Einrichtung und Behandlung derselben*. Stendal.

RIFKIN, JOSHUA (1978). 'Ein langsamer Konzertsatz Johann Sebastian Bachs', *Bach Jahrbuch*, 140–7.

—— (1999). 'Verlorene Quellen, verlorene Werke: Miszellen zu Bachs Instrumental-komposition', in Martin Geck (ed.), *Dortmunder Bach-Forschungen*, ii.

RIMBACH, E. L. (1966). 'The Church Cantatas of Johann Kuhnau' (Ph.D. diss., University of Rochester).

ROBIN, VINCENT (1995). 'Contrebasse de hautbois, ou cromorne? Eléments de recherche pour l'identification du cromorne français aux XVIIᵉ et XVIIIᵉ siècles', Mémoire de diplôme, Conservatoire Supérieur de Paris.

Roger North on Music, ed. John Wilson (London, 1959).

ROGNONI, FRANCESCO (1620). *Selva de varii passaggi, Parte seconda*. Milan.

ROSOW, LOIS (1989). 'How Eighteenth-Century Parisians Heard Lully's Operas: The Case of *Armide*'s Fourth Act', in Heyer (1989), 213–37.

ROTHWELL, EVELYN (1953). *Oboe Technique*. 2nd edn. 1971. London.

ROUSSEAU, JEAN (1687). *Traité de la viole*. Paris.

ROUSSEAU, JEAN-JACQUES (1768). *Dictionnaire de musique*. Paris. Eng. trans. by William Waring, *A Dictionary of Music* (London, 1771).

ROUVEL, DIETHER (1962). *Zur Geschichte der Musik am Fürstlich Waldeckschen Hofe zu Arolsen* (Kölner Beiträge zur Musikforschung, 22.) Regensburg.

RUBARDT, PAUL (1966). 'Johann Heinrich und Andreas Eichentopf, zwei bedeutende Musikinstrumentenmacher der Bachzeit', *Wissenschaftliche Zeitschrift der Humboldt-Universität*, 15/3: 411–13.

RUHNKE, MARTIN (1980). 'Telemann, Georg Philipp', *New Grove* xviii. 647–59.

RUSSELL, CRAIG H. (1989). 'Spain in the Enlightenment', in Zaslaw (1989), 350–67.

SACHS, CURT (1908). *Die Musikgeschichte der Stadt Berlin*. Berlin.

—— (1910). *Musik und Oper am Kurbrandenburgischen Hof*. Berlin.

SADIE, JULIE ANNE (1993). 'Paris and Versailles', in Buelow (1993), 129–89.

SADIE, STANLEY (1956). 'The Wind Music of J. C. Bach', *ML* 37: 107–17.

SALMEN, WALTER (1963). *Geschichte der Musik in Westfalen bis 1800*. Kassel.

—— (ed.) (1971). *Der Sozialstatus des Berufsmusikers vom 17. bis 19. Jahrhundert*. Kassel.

—— (1983). *The Social Status of the Professional Musician from the Middle Ages to the 19th Century*. New York.

SALTER, HUMPHREY (1683). *The Genteel Companion*. London.

SANDMAN, SUSAN (1974). 'Wind Band Music under Louis XIV: The Philidor Collection, Music for the Military and the Court' (Ph.D. diss., Stanford University).

SAUVEUR, JOSEPH (1700–13). *Collected Writings on Musical Acoustics*, ed. R. Rasch. Utrecht, 1984.

SCHAAL, R. (1948). *Johann Stephan und Johann Wolfgang Kleinknecht: Selbstbiographie, Biographie und Anhang: 'Über die Ansbacher Musik'*. Kassel.

SCHEIBE, JOHANN ADOLPH (1745). *Der critische Musicus* (periodical). Hamburg. Repr. 1970.

SCHERING, ARNOLD (1921). 'Die Leipziger Ratsmusik von 1650–1775', *AfMw* 3: 17–53.

—— (1926). *Musikgeschichte Leipzigs*, ii: *Von 1650 bis 1723*. Leipzig.

SCHICKHARDT, JOHANN CHRISTIAN (*c.*1710–12). *Principes de la flûte*. Amsterdam.

SCHLICHTE, JOACHIM (1979). *Thematischer Katalog der kirchlichen Musikhandschriften des 17. und 18. Jahrhunderts in der Stadt- und Universitätsbibliothek Frankfurt am Main*. Frankfurt am Main.

SCHMID, MANFRED HERMANN (1986). 'Die Blockflöten des Musikinstrumentenmuseums München', in *Bericht über das VI. Symposium zu Fragen des Musikinstrumentenbaus—Holzblasinstrumente des 17. und 18. Jahrhunderts*, 18–39. Michaelstein.

—— (1994). 'Kontrabaß-Oboe und Großbaß-Pommer: Zu Traditionsüberlagerungen im 18. Jahrhundert', in *Musik in Baden-Württemberg, Jahrbuch 1994*, ed. H. Völkl, i. 95–121. Stuttgart and Weimar.

SCHMIDT, GÜNTHER (1956). *Die Musik am Hofe der Markgrafen von Brandenburg-Ansbach*. Kassel and Basle.

SCHNEIDER, CHRISTIAN (1980). 'Ein Oboisten-Portrait von 1767', *Tibia*, 3/80: 205–7.

—— (1985). 'Zur Frage des "Stimmlochpflockes"', *Tibia*, 2/85: 366–8.

SCHNEIDER, C. A. (1936). *J. Fr. Fasch als Sonatenkomponist: Ein Beitrag zur Geschichte der Sonatenform* (Diss. Münster).

SCHNEIDER, HERBERT (1989). 'The Amsterdam Editions of Lully's Orchestral Suites', in Heyer (1989), 113–30.

—— (1995). 'IV. 17. und 18. Jahrhundert', in 'Frankreich', *MGG*² iii. 711–54.

SCHNEIDER, L. (1852). *Geschichte der Oper und des kgl. Opernhauses in Berlin*. Berlin.

SCHNOEBELEN, ANNE (1969). 'Performance Practices at San Petronio in the Baroque', *Acta musicologica*, 41: 37–55.

SCHOLES, PERCY A. (1969). *The Puritans and Music*. Oxford.

SCHRAMMEK, WINFRIED (1985). 'Orgel, Positiv, Clavicymbel und Glocken der Schloßkirche zu Weimar 1658 bis 1774', in *Bericht über die Wissenschaftliche Konferenz zum V. Internationalen Bachfest der DDR . . . , Leipzig . . . 1985*, 99–111.

SCHUBART, CHRISTIAN FRIEDRICH DANIEL (1806). *Ideen zu einer Ästhetik der Tonkunst*. Vienna. Repr. Hildesheim, 1969. Written mostly in the 1780s.

SCHULZE, HANS-JOACHIM (1981). 'Johann Sebastian Bachs Konzerte—Fragen der überlieferung und Chronologie', *Bach Studien*, 6: 9–26.

—— and WOLFF, CHRISTOPH (1986–). *Bach Compendium: analytisch-bibliographisches Repertorium der Werke Johann Sebastian Bachs*, 5 vols. (*BC*).

SEIFERT, HERBERT (1987). 'Die Bläser der kaiserlichen Hofkapelle zur Zeit von J. J. Fux', in *Johann Joseph Fux und die barocke Bläsertradition. Kongressbericht Graz 1985* (Alta Musica, 9), 9–23. Tutzing.

SELFRIDGE-FIELD, ELEANOR (1975). *Venetian Instrumental Music from Gabrieli to Vivaldi*. Oxford.

—— (1986). 'Music at the Pietà before Vivaldi', *EM* 14: 373–86.

—— (1987). 'The Viennese Court Orchestra in the Time of Caldara', in Brian W. Pritchard (ed.), *Antonio Caldara, Essays on his Life and Times*, 115–51. Aldershot and Brookfield, Vt.

—— (1988). 'Italian Oratorio and the Baroque Orchestra', *EM* 16: 506–13.

—— and ZASLAW, NEAL (1980). Table 1 in 'Orchestra', *New Grove* xiii. 690.

SELHOF, NICOLAS (1759). Catalogue . . . d'une partie très considerable de livres de musique . . . ainsi qu'une collection de toutes sortes d'instruments [Catalogue of the music library, instruments and other property of Nicolas Selhof]. Repr. Amsterdam, 1973.

SELLNER, JOSEPH (1825). *Theoretisch praktische Oboe Schule*. Vienna.

SEMMENS, RICHARD T. (1975). 'Woodwind Treatment in the Early Ballets of Jean-Baptiste Lully' (Master's thesis, University of British Columbia).

SERAUKY, WALTER (1939). *Musikgeschichte der Stadt Halle*, ii. Halle and Berlin.

SHAW, WATKINS (1994). 'Handel: Some Contemporary Performance Parts Considered', in *Eighteenth-Century Music in Theory and Practice: Essays in Honor of Alfred Mann*, ed. Mary Ann Parker, 59–76. Stuyvesant, NY.

SHELDON, DAVID A. (1968). 'The Chamber Music of Johann F. Fasch' (Ph.D. diss., Indiana University).

SIEGELE, ULRICH (1975). *Kompositionsweise und Bearbeitungstechnik in der Instrumentalmusik Johann Sebastian Bachs*. Neuhausen-Stuttgart.

SIEVERS, HEINRICH (1941). *250 Jahre Braunschweiges Staatstheater 1690–1940*. Braunschweig.

—— (1961). *Die Musik in Hannover*. Hannover.

SILVA, PINTO DA (1773 and 1776). Letters to Piaggio (Genova), in McClymonds (1978), 42.

SITTARD, J. (1890a). *Zur Geschichte der Musik und des Theaters am Württemburgischen Hofe*, ii. Stuttgart.

—— (1890b). *Geschichte der Musik- und Concertwesens in Hamburg*. Altona and Leipzig.

SMITH, DAVID HOGAN (1992). *Reed Design for Early Woodwinds*. Bloomington, Ind.

SMITH, ROBERT (1749). *Harmonics, or the Philosophy of Musical Sounds*. Cambridge. Repr. 1966. 2nd edn. 1759.

SMITH, W. C., and HUMPHRIES, CHARLES (1968). *A Bibliography of the Musical Works Published by the Firm of John Walsh During the Years 1721–1766*. London.

SMITHERS, DON L. (1973). *The Music and History of the Baroque Trumpet before 1721*. London.

—— (1990). 'Bach, Reiche and the Leipzig Collegia Musica', *HBSJ* 2: 1–50.

SNYDER, KERALA J. (1987). *Dietrich Buxtehude: Organist in Lübeck*. New York.

SORGE, GEORG ANDREAS (1748). *Gespräch zwischen einem Musico theoretico und einem Studioso musices*. Lobenstein.

—— (1758). 'Anmerkung über Herrn Quantzens . . . dis und es-Klappe auf der Querflöte', in Marpurg, *Historisch-kritische Beyträge*, iv. 1–7. Repr. 1970.

SPEER, DANIEL (1687). *Grund-richtiger . . . Unterricht der musicalischen Kunst*. Ulm.

—— (1697). *Grund-richtiger, kurtz- leicht- und möthiger jetzt wol- vermehrter Unterricht der musicalischen Kunst*. Ulm. A thorough revision of Speer (1687).

SPITZER, JOHN (1988). 'Improvised Ornamentation in a Handel Aria with Obbligato Wind Accompaniment', *EM* 16: 514–22.

STAEHELIN, MARTIN (1970). 'Der sogenannte Musettenbass', *Jahrbuch des Bernischen Historischen Museums*, 49–50: 93–121.

STAUFFER, GEORGE B. (1993). 'Leipzig: A Cosmopolitan Trade Centre', in Buelow (1993), 254–95.

STEIN, LOUISE K. (1993). 'The Iberian Peninsula', in Buelow (1993), 411–34.

STEUDE, WOLFRAM, LANDMANN, ORTRUN, *et al.* (1995). 'Dresden', *MGG²* ii. 1522–61.

STÖSSEL, J. C. and J. D. (1737). *Kurzgefasstes musicalisches Lexicon*. Chemnitz. 2nd edn. 1749, repr. 1975.

SWACK, JEANNE ROBERTA (1988). 'The Solo Sonatas of Georg Philipp Telemann: A Study of the Sources and Musical Style' (Ph.D. diss., Yale University).

TALBOT, JAMES (*c*.1692–5). 'Musica' [often called 'The Talbot Manuscript'; Oxford, Christ Church, Music MS 1187]. Transcribed in *GSJ* 1 (1948) by A. Baines.

TALBOT, MICHAEL (1973). 'Albinoni's Oboe Concertos', *Consort*, 29: 14–22.

—— (1990). *Tomaso Albinoni: The Venetian Composer and his World*. Oxford.

TANK, ULRICH (1980). 'Die Dokumente der Esterhazy-Archive zur fürstlichen Hofkapelle in der Zeit von 1761 bis 1770', *Haydn-Studien*, 4: 129–346.

TARUSKIN, RICHARD (1989). 'The Pastness of the Present and the Presence of the Past', in N. Kenyon (ed.), *Authenticity and Early Music*, 137–207. Oxford.

TECHRITZ, HERMANN (1932). *Sächsische Stadtpfeiffer* (Diss., Leipzig).

TECHRITZ, JOHANNES (1905). 'Die Dresdner Stadtmusici von 1572 bis 1872', *Dresdner Anzeiger*, Sonntagsbeilage no. 39.

TELEMANN, GEORG PHILIPP (24 Sept. 1716). Introduction and dedication, *Die kleine Kammermusik*. Frankfurt am Main. Included in Rackwitz (1981).

—— (1718). 'Lebens-Lauff', in J. Mattheson's *Grosse Generalbassschule* (Hamburg, 1731). Repr. in Rackwitz (1981).

—— (1725–6). Vorbericht, *Der Harmonische Gottesdienst* (Part 1). Hamburg.

—— (1740). 'Selbstbiographie (1739)', in J. Mattheson's *Grundlage einer Ehrenpforte*. Hamburg.

—— (1744). 'Neues musikalisches System', in L. C. Mitzler, *Musikalische Bibliothek*, 3/4: 713–19 (plus table). Leipzig.

—— (1767). 'Letzte Beschäftigung G. Ph. Telemanns im 86. Lebensjahre, bestehend in einer musikalischen Klang- und Intervallentafel', in Rackwitz (1981), 266–73.

TERRY, C. S. (1932). *Bach's Orchestra*. London.

THOINAN, ERNEST (1867–8). 'Les Philidor', *La France musicale*, 1867/51: 397–9, 52: 405–7; 1868/1: 1–3, 2: 9–11, 3: 17–18, 5: 29–31, 6: 37–8, 7: 45–6.

—— and MAUGER, N. (1894; suppl. 1912). *Les Hotteterres et les Chédevilles*. Paris.

THOMPSON, SUSAN E. (1999). 'Deutsche Schalmei: A Question of Terminology', *JAMIS* 25: 31–60.

THOURET, GEORG (1898). *Friedrich der Grosse als Musikfreund und Musiker*. Leipzig.

TILMOUTH, MICHAEL (1959). 'Chamber Music in England, 1675–1720' (Ph.D. diss., Cambridge University).

—— (1961–2). 'A Calendar of References to Music in Newspapers Published in London and the Provinces (1660–1719)', *RMA Research Chronicle*, 1 and 2. Second part indexes first.

—— (1973). 'York Minster Ms. M.16(s) and Captain Prendcourt', *ML* 54: 302–7.

—— (1980). 'String Quartet', *New Grove* xviii. 276–87.

TOSI, PIER FRANCESCO (1723). *Opinioni de' cantori antichi e moderni*. Bologna. Repr. 1968. *Observations on the Florid Song*, trans. J. E. Galliard (London, 1742); 2nd edn. 1743, repr. 1969.

TRICHET, PIERRE [MS *c*.1630–44]. *Traité des instruments de musique*, ed. F. Lesure in *Annales musicologiques*, 3 (1955), 283–387 and 4 (1956), 175–248.

TROMLITZ, JOHANN GEORG (1791). *Ausführlicher und gründlicher Unterricht die Flöte zu spielen*. Leipzig. Repr. 1985. Eng. trans. Ardal Powell (Cambridge, 1991).

TÜRK, DANIEL GOTTLOB (1789). *Klavierschule*. Leipzig and Halle. Repr. 1962.

UNVERRICHT, HUBERT (1980). 'Feldmusik', *New Grove* vi. 456.

UNWIN, ROBERT (1987). '"An English writer on music": James Talbot 1664–1708', *GSJ* 40: 53–72.

VANDENBROEK, OTHON JOSEPH (1793). *Traité général de tous les instrumens à vent*. Paris. Repr. 1973.

VANDERHAGEN, AMAND (*c*.1790). *Méthode nouvelle et raisonnée pour le hautbois*. Paris. 2nd edn. *c*.1798, repr. Geneva, 1971.

VÉNY, LOUIS-AUGUSTE (1828). *Méthode abrégée pour le hautbois*. 2nd edn. 1844–55: *Méthode complète . . .* Paris.

VERSCHUERE-REYNVAAN, JOOS (1795). *Muzikaal kunst Wordenboek*. Amsterdam. 1st edn. *Muzijkaal Kunst-Woordenboek* (Middelburg, 1789).

VESTER, FRANS (1985). *Flute Music of the 18th Century: An Annotated Bibliography*. Monteux.

VINQUIST, MARY (1974). 'Recorder Tutors of the Seventeenth and Eighteenth Centuries: Technique and Performance Practice' (Ph.D. diss., University of North Carolina).

VIRGILIANO, AURELIO (*c*.1600). *Il dolcimelo* (I-Bc, MS C. 33). Facs. edn., Florence, 1979.

VOGT, GUSTAVE (1816–25). *Méthode de hautbois* [MS, F-Pc]. Original text and English translation published in Burgess (forthcoming).

WADE, RACHEL W. (1981). *The Catalog of Carl Philipp Emanuel Bach's Estate: A Facsimile of the Edition by Schniebes, Hamburg*. New York.

WALTHER, JOHANN GOTTFRIED (1732). *Musikalisches Lexicon*. Leipzig. Repr. Kassel, 1953.

—— (1960). *Praecepta der musicalischen Composition*. Leipzig. (1708 in MS).

WARNER, THOMAS E. (1964). 'Indications of Performance Practice in Woodwind Instruction Books of the 17th and 18th Centuries' (Ph.D. diss., New York University).

—— (1967). *An Annotated Bibliography of Woodwind Instruction Books, 1600–1830*. Detroit.

WATERHOUSE, WILLIAM (1993). *The New Langwill Index*. London.

WEBER, WILLIAM (1989). 'London: A City of Unrivalled Riches', in Zaslaw (1989), 293–326.

WEIGEL, CHRISTOPH (1698). *Abbildung der gemein-nützlichen Haupt-Stände*. Regensburg. Repr. 1891, 1936.

WEIGEL, JOHANN CHRISTOPH (*c*.1722). *Musicalisches Theatrum*. Nuremberg. Repr. 1961.

WELLESZ, EGON (1919). 'Die Opern und Oratorien in Wien von 1660–1708', *Studien zur Musikwissenschaft*, 6: 5–138.

WERNER, ARNO (1911). *Städtische und fürstliche Musikpflege in Weissenfels*. Leipzig.

—— (1922). *Städtische und fürstliche Musikpflege zu Zeitz*. Bückeburg and Leipzig.

WHITE, PAUL J. (1993). 'The Early Bassoon Reed in Relation to the Development of the Bassoon from 1636' (D.Phil. diss., Oxford University).

WHITELY, WILLIAM (1816). *The Instrumental Preceptor*. Utica, NY.

WILHELMINE, FRÉDÉRIQUE SOPHIE, Margravine of Bayreuth (1750). Letter to Frederick, 21 March 1750, in *MGG* ix. 1805.

WILLIAMS, PETER (ed.) (1985). *Bach, Handel Scarlatti: Tercentenary Essays*. Cambridge.

WIND, THIEMO (1982). 'Alessandro Besozzi di Torino (1702–1793), een terreinverkennend onderzoek' (Kandidaatsscriptie, Universiteit Utrecht).

WOLFF, CHRISTOPH (1992). 'The Identity of the "Fratro Dilettisimo" in the Capriccio in B-flat Major and Other Problems of Bach's Early Harpsichord Works', in *The Harpsichord and its Repertoire* (Proceedings of the International Harpsichord Symposium, Utrecht 1990, ed. P. Dirksen), 145–56.

WÖRTHMÜLLER, WILLI (1954–5). 'Die Nürnberger Trompeten- und Posaunenmacher des 17. und 18. Jahrhunderts', in *Mitteilungen des Vereins für Geschichte der Stadt Nürnberg*, 45/46.

WOLF, EUGENE K. (1989). 'The Mannheim Court', in Zaslaw (1989), 213–39.

WOLFF, CHRISTOPH (1978). 'Bachs Leipziger Kantoratsprobe und die Aufführungsgeschichte der Kantate "Du wahrer Gott und Davids Sohn" BWV 23', *Bach Jahrbuch*, 78–94.

WOLFF, HELMUTH CHRISTIAN (1937). *Die Venezianische Oper in der zweiten Hälfte des 17. Jahrhunderts*. Berlin.

WOLLENBERG, SUSAN (1993). 'Vienna under Joseph I and Charles VI', in Buelow (1993), 324–54.

WOOD, BRUCE, and PINNOCK, ANDREW (1993). 'The Fairy Queen: A Fresh Look at the Issues', *EM* 21: 45–62.

WOOD, JULIA K. (1995). '"A flowing harmony": Music on the Thames in Restoration London', *EM* 23: 553–81.

WRAGG, J. (1792). *The Oboe Preceptor or the Art of Playing the Oboe*. London.

YOUNG, PHILLIP T. (1982). *Twenty-five Hundred Historical Woodwind Instruments*. New York.

—— (1988). *University of Victoria: Loan Exhibition of Historic Double Reed Instruments*. Victoria, BC.

—— (1993). *4900 Historical Woodwind Instruments*. London.

ZASLAW, NEAL (1979). 'The Compleat Orchestral Musician', *EM* 7: 46–57.

—— (1990). 'Lully's Orchestra', in *Jean-Baptiste Lully: Actes du colloque Saint-Germain-en-Laye, Heidelberg 1987*, ed. J. de La Gorce and H. Schneider, 539–53. Laaber.

—— (1993). 'The Origins of the Classical Orchestra', *Basler Jahrbuch für historische Musikpraxis*, 17: 9–40.

—— (ed.) (1989). *The Classical Era*. Englewood Cliffs, NJ.

ZEDLER, JOHANN HEINRICH (ed.) (1732–54). *Grosses vollständiges Universal-Lexikon aller Wissenschaften und Künste*, 68 vols. Halle and Leipzig.

ZOHN, STEVEN (1995). 'The Ensemble Sonatas of Georg Philipp Telemann: Studies in Style, Genre, and Chronology' (Ph.D. diss., Cornell University).

INDEX